Lecture Notes in Computer Science 13085

Formal Methods

Subline of Lectures Notes in Computer Science

More information about this subseries at https://link.springer.com/bookseries/7407

Radu Calinescu · Corina S. Păsăreanu (Eds.)

Software Engineering and Formal Methods

19th International Conference, SEFM 2021
Virtual Event, December 6–10, 2021
Proceedings

 Springer

Editors
Radu Calinescu 🆔
University of York
York, UK

Corina S. Păsăreanu
Carnegie Mellon University
Moffett Field, CA, USA

ISSN 0302-9743 ISSN 1611-3349 (electronic)
Lecture Notes in Computer Science
ISBN 978-3-030-92123-1 ISBN 978-3-030-92124-8 (eBook)
https://doi.org/10.1007/978-3-030-92124-8

LNCS Sublibrary: SL1 – Theoretical Computer Science and General Issues

This Springer imprint is published by the registered company Springer Nature Switzerland AG
The registered company address is: Gewerbestrasse 11, 6330 Cham, Switzerland

Preface

This volume contains the proceedings of SEFM 2021, the 19th International Conference on Software Engineering and Formal Methods, which was held as a virtual event during December 6–10, 2021. The conference brought together leading researchers and practitioners from academia, industry, and government to advance the state of the art in formal methods, to facilitate their uptake in the software industry, and to encourage their integration within practical software engineering methods and tools.

SEFM 2021 received 86 full-paper submissions and six tool-paper submissions, of which 22 submissions were accepted as full papers (an acceptance rate of 25.58%) and four submissions were accepted as tool papers. The papers were reviewed for quality, correctness, originality, and relevance. Each submission was reviewed by three Program Committee members, and an online post-reviewing discussion open to the entire Program Committee was held to make the final decisions. This volume contains the revised versions of the accepted papers, which cover a wide variety of topics, including run-time analysis and testing, security and privacy, parallel composition/CSP and probabilistic reasoning, verification and synthesis, reasoning about machine learning and cyber-physical systems, and formal methods for emerging areas within software engineering.

The conference program also featured three keynote talks by Ana Cavalcanti (University of York, UK), Marsha Chechik (University of Toronto, Canada), and Sebastian Uchitel (University of Buenos Aires, Argentina, and Imperial College London, UK). We are grateful to the three invited speakers for accepting our invitations to give keynote talks at the conference.

We would like to thank the authors who submitted their work to SEFM 2021. We are grateful to the members of the Program Committee and the additional reviewers for providing timely and insightful reviews, as well as for their participation in the post-reviewing discussions. We would also like to thank the SEFM Steeering Committee for their advice and support, and Antonio Cerone for overseeing the organization of the SEFM 2021 symposia and workshops as Workshop Chair. We thank the Publicity Chairs, Mario Gleirscher and Laura Nenzi, the Organizing Committee members Antonio Cerone and Jennifer Dick, and the webmaster, Ioannis Stefanakos, for all their help with planning, publicizing, and organizing the conference.

We gratefully acknowledge the convenience of the EasyChair system for handling the submission and review processes, and for preparing these proceedings. Finally, we also acknowledge the sponsorship and support from the Assuring Autonomy International Programme, Carnegie Mellon University (USA), Nazarbayev University (Kazakhstan), the University of York (UK), and the UKRI Trustworthy Autonomous Systems Node in Resilience.

October 2021

Radu Calinescu
Corina S. Păsăreanu

Organization

Program Chairs

Radu Calinescu   University of York, UK
Corina S. Păsăreanu   Carnegie Mellon University, Silicon Valley, USA

Program Committee

Erika Abraham	RWTH Aachen University, Germany
Jiri Barnat	Masaryk University, Czech Republic
Amel Bennaceur	The Open University, UK
Dirk Beyer	LMU Munich, Germany
Frank de Boer	Centrum Wiskunde & Informatica, The Netherlands
Ana Cavalcanti	University of York, UK
Alessandro Cimatti	Fondazione Bruno Kessler, Italy
Gabriel Ciobanu	Romanian Academy, Institute of Computer Science, Romania
Corina Cirstea	University of Southampton, UK
Rocco De Nicola	IMT School for Advanced Studies Lucca, Italy
Louise Dennis	University of Manchester, UK
Antonio Filieri	Imperial College London, UK
Mario Gleirscher	University of Bremen, Germany
Marieke Huisman	University of Twente, The Netherlands
Marie-Christine Jakobs	Technical University of Darmstadt, Germany
Raluca Lefticaru	University of Bradford, UK
Antónia Lopes	Universidade de Lisboa, Portugal
Tiziana Margaria	Lero, Ireland
Paolo Masci	National Institute of Aerospace, USA
Claudio Menghi	University of Luxembourg, Luxembourg
Laura Nenzi	University of Trieste, Italy
Hans de Nivelle	Nazarbayev University, Kazakhstan
Peter Ölveczky	University of Oslo, Norway
Gordon Pace	University of Malta, Malta
Catuscia Palamidessi	Inria, France
Colin Paterson	University of York, UK
M. Emilia Cambronero	University of Castilla-La Mancha, Spain
Violet Ka I. Pun	Western Norway University of Applied Sciences, Norway
Gwen Salaün	University of Grenoble Alpes, France
Augusto Sampaio	Federal University of Pernambuco, Brazil
Ina Schaefer	Technische Universität Braunschweig, Germany

Gerardo Schneider	Chalmers University of Technology and University of Gothenburg, Sweden
Marjan Sirjani	Mälardalen University, Sweden
Graeme Smith	University of Queensland, Australia
Youcheng Sun	Queen's University Belfast, UK
Silvia Lizeth Tapia Tarifa	University of Oslo, Norway
Elena Troubitsyna	KTH Royal Institute of Technology, Sweden
Marina Waldén	Abo Akademi University, Finland
Heike Wehrheim	University of Paderborn, Germany
Gianluigi Zavattaro	University of Bologna, Italy

Steering Committee

Frank de Boer	Centrum Wiskunde & Informatica, The Netherlands
Radu Calinescu	University of York, UK
Antonio Cerone (Chair)	Nazarbayev University, Kazakhstan
Rocco De Nicola	IMT School for Advanced Studies Lucca, Italy
Gwen Salaün	University of Grenoble Alpes, France
Marjan Sirjani	Mälardalen University, Sweden
Gianluigi Zavattaro	University of Bologna, Italy

Additional Reviewers

Abbaspour Asadollah, Sara
Alves, Vander
Aman, Bogdan
Attala, Ziggy
Azzopardi, Shaun
Baramashetru, Chinmayi Prabhu
Bargmann, Lara
Bartocci, Ezio
Baxter, James
Birkemeyer, Lukas
Cerna, Ivana
Costa, Gabriele
Damasceno, Carlos Diego
De Gouw, Stijn
Din, Crystal Chang
Edixhoven, Luc
Evans, Neil
Fava, Daniel
Foster, Simon
Galletta, Letterio
Giallorenzo, Saverio
Gorla, Daniele
Haltermann, Jan

Hentze, Marc
Hiep, Hans-Dieter
Hoang, Thai Son
Hughes, William
Inverso, Omar
Irfan, Ahmed
Jongmans, Sung-Shik
Kanav, Sudeep
Knüppel, Alexander
Krishna, Ajay
Kristensen, Lars
König, Jürgen
Lang, Frédéric
Lemberger, Thomas
Lenglet, Sergueï
Leuschel, Michael
Mercanti, Ivan
Moradi, Fereidoun
Pang, Jun
Pauck, Felix
Peters, Kirstin
Rehak, Vojtech
Requeno, Jose Ignacio

Richter, Cedric
Rubbens, Robert
Runge, Tobias
Salimi, Maghsood
Schlatte, Rudolf
Schupp, Stefan
Serwe, Wendelin
Sharifi, Zeinab
Sharma, Arnab
Shokri-Manninen, Fatima
Soderi, Simone

Steffen, Martin
Štill, Vladimír
Tokas, Shukun
Turin, Gianluca
Tyler, Benjamin
van den Bos, Petra
van Glabbeek, Rob
Visconti, Ennio
Weise, Nico
Windsor, Matt

Controller Synthesis for Adaptive Mobile Robots. Abstractions, All Change!? (Keynote Abstract)

Sebastian Uchitel

Universidad de Buenos Aires, Argentina and Imperial College London, UK

Abstract. Discrete event controller synthesis promises correct-by-construction strategies for controlling reactive systems to ensure user specified goals. Runtime synthesis takes this one step further, enabling correct runtime adaptation when a reactive system's goals, capabilities, or environment change. The need for synthesis in mobile robotic systems is particularly telling. Despite the wide availability of general purpose mobile robots (particularly Unmanned Aerial Vehicles – UAVs), the ability of end-users (individuals and organisations) to exploit them to their full potential is limited. Either complex and error prone programming is required or graphical mission planning interfaces are used to model simple, non-reactive missions. The use of synthesis and runtime synthesis for mobile robots has many challenges ahead. In this talk I will discuss how we addressed some of them by revisiting both (1) the abstractions used to specify and synthesise discrete event controllers and (2) the architectural abstractions needed to successfully deploy synthesis technology on both fixed wing and multi-rotor systems.

Contents

Machine Learning and Cyber-Physical Systems

Invited Papers

RoboWorld: Where Can My Robot Work?

Ana Cavalcanti[1(✉)], James Baxter[1], and Gustavo Carvalho[2]

[1] Department of Computer Science, University of York, York, UK
Ana.Cavalcanti@york.ac.uk
[2] Centro de Informática, Universidade Federal de Pernambuco, Recife, Brazil

Abstract. The behaviour of a robot affects and is affected by its environment. So, many of the expected and desirable properties of a robotic system depend on properties of its environment. While a complete model of that environment is very difficult, if not impossible, to construct, we can realistically capture assumptions about it. In this paper, we present RoboWorld, a controlled natural language with a process algebraic semantics that can be used to define (a) the operational requirements of a robot, and (b) how the robot interacts with its environment. RoboWorld is part of the RoboStar framework of domain-specific languages that support proof, simulation, and testing of robotic systems. RoboWorld plays a central role in all these forms of verification.

1 Introduction

The RoboStar framework[1] supports model-based engineering of robotic control software, covering design, simulation, and deployment. A number of RoboStar domain-specific languages facilitate the definition of models for which a semantics can be (automatically) provided using a state-rich hybrid version of a process algebra for refinement [10], which is cast in Hoare and He's Unifying Theories of Programming (UTP) [13] and formalised in Isabelle [9]. Here, we give an overall description of RoboWorld, the language for documenting operational requirements of a robotic system for use in simulation, test generation, and proof.

Figure 1 shows the various modelling and derived artefacts used in the RoboStar framework. Platform-independent design models of control software are written using a diagrammatic domain-specific language: RoboChart [20]. At the simulation level, the notation is called RoboSim [5]. RoboChart is event-based, while RoboSim, as expected of a simulation language, is cycle-based.

RoboWorld can be used to complement a RoboChart model by describing operational requirements in the form of assumptions about the environment. The RoboWorld requirements cover aspects of the arena in which the robot is expected to work and of the robotic platform. RoboWorld is a controlled natural language with a semantics compatible with that of RoboChart and RoboSim.

---

[1] www.cs.york.ac.uk/robostar/.

© Springer Nature Switzerland AG 2021
R. Calinescu and C. S. Păsăreanu (Eds.): SEFM 2021, LNCS 13085, pp. 3–22, 2021.
https://doi.org/10.1007/978-3-030-92124-8_1

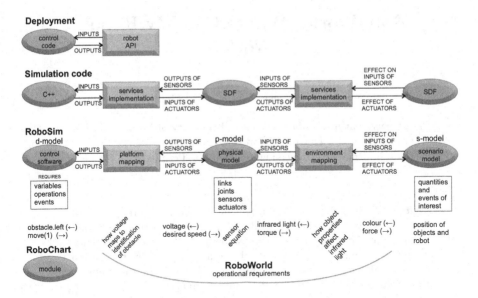

Fig. 1. RoboStar modelling and derived artefacts

As indicated in Fig. 1, RoboSim includes a notation to describe control software (d-models) as well as notations (under development) to describe physical models (p-models) [19] of robotic platforms (their links, joints, sensors, and actuators) and simulation scenarios (s-models). RoboSim p-models and s-models describe specific platforms and specific scenarios for use in a simulation. In contrast, a RoboWorld document describes assumptions that can be satisfied by any number of platforms and scenarios. So, RoboWorld documents specify properties that must be satisfied by RoboSim p-models and s-models.

Ongoing work enables the generation of a RoboSim d-model by transformation of a RoboChart model. The transformation ensures correctness of the RoboSim model with respect to the RoboChart model, in the context of assumptions that capture the cyclic nature of the simulation paradigm.

In contrast, since a RoboWorld document does not define a model, but assumptions about the robot and its environment, it cannot be used to generate p-models and s-models. This is, however, in line with current practice, where the starting point to identify operational requirements is the development of a simulation (if not of the actual program). Once the requirements are identified in a RoboWorld document, we can then verify whether a p-model or an s-model, or their combination, satisfies the assumptions documented using RoboWorld.

As shown in Fig. 1, to connect a d-model and a p-model, we use a platform mapping. This model defines how the sensors and actuators of the p-model are used to realise the services (variables, events, and operations) required by the d-model. Similarly, a RoboWorld document describes, besides assumptions about the robot and its arena, a mapping, which identifies how elements of the world are related to, or used to realise, the services required by a RoboChart model.

Another aspect of the RoboStar framework highlighted in Fig. 1 is that the modularity afforded by RoboSim d-models, p-models, and s-models, defined separately and connected by mappings, is carried over to simulation code. From RoboSim models, code can be obtained that uses C++ for the simulation of the software, and SDF (an XML-based notation used by robotics simulators[2], similar to URDF) to implement a simulation of the platform and the arena. The code is structured to match the model components. So, besides the usual benefits of modularity, we have a way to tackle the reality gap, which occurs when behaviour observed in simulation is not reproduced at deployment.

For example, it is not unusual to assume under simulation that the robot has perfect information about the position of obstacles in the arena. In RoboSim, this can be specified by a sensor in the physical model whose input and output are both the distance to an obstacle in the scenario and whose behaviour is defined just by the identity function. In this case, the platform mapping just uses that distance to define whether there is an obstacle in range.

Tackling the reality gap involves identifying assumptions like these that may have a significant impact on the behaviour of the robot. For that, with no models or modularity, roboticists are left with the difficult task of changing the simulation or deployed code and embark on a trial and error campaign.

By using the RoboStar framework, we can instead change the models and evaluate the impact of the changed assumptions in a systematic way at a lower cost. First, changes to the relevant RoboSim model and mapping are localised, with effect on other models contained. In our example, to obtain a more realistic simulation, we just need to change the p-model and the platform mapping. Second, RoboWorld provides an accessible way to check and record any impact on operational requirements. For example, we can check whether the changed RoboSim model satisfies existing RoboWorld assumptions and make any adjustments. In the example, we may need to add assumptions about the range or accuracy of sensors. The RoboWorld mapping avoids propagation of changes to the RoboChart model. Finally, if needed, we can regenerate code.

Going further, as indicated in Fig. 1, the RoboSim modularity matches the deployment perfectly. In the real world, the control software, the robotic platform, and the environment are separate entities. So, results of tests involving the deployed system can also be traced back to RoboChart and RoboWorld descriptions in the way described above for simulations.

Finally, testing, either using a simulation or the deployed systems, is in itself a challenging task. RoboChart models can be used to generate automatically tests that can be used in the setting above to evaluate the design and the impact of assumptions [3]. These tests define scenarios for exercising the control software. Without information about the valid scenarios, however, infeasible or useless tests can be generated. The formal semantics of a RoboWorld document can be used to eliminate such tests automatically.

---

[2] http://sdformat.org.

To summarise, RoboWorld documents are relevant to several aspects of the design and verification of a robotic system. First, they can document operational requirements that are often left as implicit assumptions. Second, they can be used to document and check the validity of simulation models, and of code automatically generated from such models. Third, they play a role in improving the quality of tests suites automatically generated from models.

Tool support for RoboWorld is provided by RoboTool[3]. It includes also facilities for (graphical) modelling, validation, and automatic generation of mathematical models for RoboChart and RoboSim.

In this paper, we provide an overview of the RoboWorld syntax, semantics, and tool support. Section 2 describes the structure of RoboWorld documents, and Sect. 3 gives an overview of the semantic models of RoboWorld documents. RoboTool support for RoboWorld is the object of Sect. 4. Application of RoboWorld in automatic test generation from RoboChart is discussed in Sect. 5. We conclude in Sect. 6, where we also discuss related and future work.

2   RoboWorld Syntax

The grammar of RoboWorld is defined using the Grammatical Framework (GF), a special-purpose functional programming language for developing controlled natural languages [25]. It provides native support for inflection paradigms (for example, singular and plural forms), as well as agreement between elements of a sentence (for instance, the verb must have the same number as the subject).

RoboChart and RoboSim both use state machines to specify software, akin to notations already in widespread use in the robotics literature [2,8,23,29], but enriched with facilities to specify timing. They can capture time budgets, timeouts, and deadlines. Both RoboChart models and RoboSim d-models describe a robotic platform in terms of the services it is required to provide. These services are characterised by variables, events, and operations: abstractions of sensors, actuators, and embedded software. Equally, RoboWorld documents can specify time assumptions, and RoboWorld mappings define variables, events, and operations in terms of elements of the environment described in the assumptions.

In this section, we use two examples to provide a description of RoboWorld documents. As a first example we present a ranger robot, whose RoboChart model is shown in Fig. 2. A RoboChart model defines a module that describes a robotic control software: in the example, the module is defined by the block called Ranger. A module contains a robotic platform, represented by the block named RangerRP in our example, and one or more controllers. In the example, we have just a reference to one controller called Movement.

The robotic platform records variables, events, and operations offered by the robot hardware and firmware for use by the robot control software. In our

---

[3] robostar.cs.york.ac.uk/robotool/.

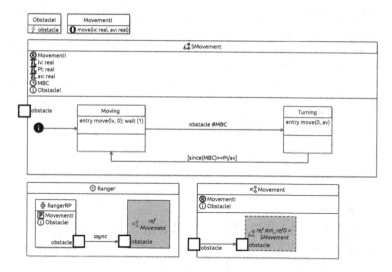

Fig. 2. Ranger RoboChart model

example, RangerRP declares two interfaces: MovementI, defining that RangerRP provides an operation move(lv, av) that causes the robot to move with linear velocity lv and angular velocity av, and ObstacleI, declaring that RangerRP defines an event obstacle that signals when the robot has detected an obstacle.

The behaviour of a controller can be defined by one or more state machines. The controller Movement contains a reference to a single state machine, SMovement, that describes the behaviour of the ranger robot. Both Movement and SMovement require the move() operation from MovementI and define the obstacle event from ObstacleI, which is connected as an input from the platform.

Within SMovement, execution begins in the Moving state, which calls the move() operation with a constant linear velocity lv and then waits for one time unit before offering a transition out of the state when an obstacle event occurs. When that transition is taken, a clock MBC is reset, and the machine enters a state Turning in which move() is called with a constant angular velocity av. The machine then waits until at least Pl/av time units have passed before returning to the Moving state. The behaviour of the robot is thus to stop and turn through π radians before resuming movement whenever an obstacle is detected.

The RoboWorld assumptions corresponding to this model are shown in Fig. 3. They are divided into sections to distinguish assumptions about the arena, assumptions about the robot, and assumptions about (other) elements of the arena, and mappings of robotic platform components onto the world. The first section, ARENA ASSUMPTIONS, captures assumptions over the arena as a whole. In particular, in this example, the assumptions state that the arena is two-dimensional and flat. It also declares elements of the arena that may be present, such as special regions of the arena or entities that the robot may interact with. In this case, it declares a type of entity called obstacle.

```
## ARENA ASSUMPTIONS ##

The arena is two-dimensional.

The gradient of the ground is 0.

There are entities called obstacle.

## ROBOT ASSUMPTIONS ##

The robot is a point mass.

## ELEMENT ASSUMPTIONS ##

One quarter of the arena contains obstacles.

The obstacles are point masses.

## MAPPING OF OUTPUT EVENTS ##

## MAPPING OF INPUT EVENTS ##

The event obstacle occurs when the distance from the robot to an obstacle is less than 0.5 m.

## MAPPING OF OPERATIONS ##

When the operation move(lv, av) is called, the velocity of the robot is set to lv m/s in the direction of
    the orientation of the robot and the angular velocity of the robot is set to av rad/s.

## MAPPING OF VARIABLES ##
```

Fig. 3. Ranger RoboWorld assumptions

The second section, ROBOT ASSUMPTIONS, contains assumptions about the shape and pose of the robot, and any capabilities it has in relation to other elements of the environment (carry or pick elements, for example). The ability to move is assumed to be a feature of every robot. In the case of the ranger, the shape of the robot is not important as far as the assumptions we make about its interactions with the world are concerned, so it is treated as a point mass.

The third section, ELEMENT ASSUMPTIONS, contains any assumptions about elements of the arena declared in the arena assumptions. These can be regions or entities in the arena. In the ranger model, there is only one element, obstacles, stated to occupy a quarter of the arena. The precise locations occupied by the obstacles are not defined, so the robot should handle obstacles in any location.

The final four sections contain mapping definitions (for OUTPUT and INPUT EVENTS, OPERATIONS, and VARIABLES) describing the relationship between the robotic platform services with the world. The first of these contains mappings of output events; it is empty in the case of the ranger, since it does not have any output events. The second section contains mappings of input events. The only input event for the ranger is obstacle, which is stated to occur whenever the robot is within 0.5 m of an obstacle. We can use any of the SI units.

The third mapping section is for operations of the platform, which in our example is just the move() operation. The move() operation is defined to set the velocity of the robot, in the direction it is currently pointing, to the provided parameter lv, and to set the angular velocity of the robot to the provided av.

The final section contains mappings of variables of the robotic platform. It is empty for the ranger, since there are no robotic platform variables in its model.

As a second example of the use of RoboWorld, we consider a rescue drone, which is tasked with flying out relief to a particular target, such as a person or vehicle. A RoboChart module Rescue for this example is shown in Fig. 4. It

contains a single controller Finder, which has a reference to a single state machine
FinderM. We omit the details of the state machine here, to focus on the robotic
platform used in the mapping definitions in RoboWorld. A full presentation of
the RoboChart model for the rescue drone can be found in [3].

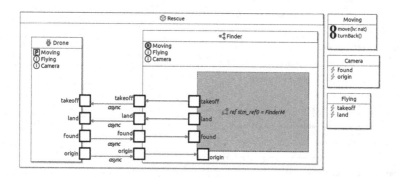

Fig. 4. Rescue RoboChart module

The robotic platform for the example in Fig. 4, called Drone, declares three
interfaces. The first, Moving, declares two operations related to the horizontal movement of the robot: move(lv), which causes the robot to move forward
with a velocity of lv, and turnBack(), which causes the robot to turn back to
face its starting location. The second interface, Flying, defines output events
related to the robot's vertical movement: takeoff, which signals the robot to
move upward, and land, which signals the robot to move downward to land. The
third interface, Camera, defines input events from a camera detecting targets on
the ground: found indicates that the target for the delivery has been identified,
and origin indicates the detection of the robot's starting location.

RoboWorld assumptions for the rescue drone are shown in Fig. 5. The arena
assumptions begin with an assumption that the arena is three-dimensional,
rather than two-dimensional as with the ranger model. After that, there are
two assumptions defining regions of the arena, one called origin and one called
target, which represent the areas detected by the events origin and found.

The first of the robot assumptions defines the initial location of the robot
to be at the origin. If there are no assumptions about the initial location of the
robot, it may be placed in any location that is not otherwise blocked by some
other object. The initial orientation of the robot is defined to be towards the
target. As with the ranger model, the robot is assumed to be a point mass.

The element assumptions restrict the two regions origin and target. The
origin is assumed to be one metre by one metre, and the ground under the
origin is assumed to have gradient zero. Unlike the ranger model, where the
entire arena is assumed to be flat, the rescue drone is intended to operate in
rough and inaccessible terrain such as mountains, so only the points where the
drone lands need to be flat. The origin is also assumed to be on the ground,

```
## ARENA ASSUMPTIONS ##

The arena is three-dimensional.

The arena has an origin.

The arena has a target.

## ROBOT ASSUMPTIONS ##

The initial location of the robot is at the origin.

The initial orientation of the robot is towards the target.

The robot is a point mass.

## ELEMENT ASSUMPTIONS ##

The origin has an x-width of 1 m and a y-width of 1 m.

The gradient of the ground under the origin is 0.

The origin is on the ground.

The target has an x-width of 1 m and a y-width of 1 m.

The gradient of the ground under the target is 0.

The target is on the ground.

The distance from the target to the origin is greater than 1 m.

## MAPPING OF OUTPUT EVENTS ##

When the event takeoff occurs, the velocity of the robot is set to 1 m/s upward.

When the event land occurs, the velocity of the robot is set to 1 m/s downward.

## MAPPING OF INPUT EVENTS ##

The event found occurs when the x-position of the robot is equal to the x-position of a location in the
     target, and the y-position of the robot is equal to the y-position of a location in the target.

The event origin occurs when the x-position of the robot is equal to the x-position of a location in the
     origin, and the y-position of the robot is equal to the y-position of a location in the origin.

## MAPPING OF OPERATIONS ##

When the operation move(lv) is called, the velocity of the robot is set to lv m/s towards the orientation of
     the robot.

The operation turnBack() is defined by a diagram where one time unit is 1 s.

## MAPPING OF VARIABLES ##
```

Fig. 5. Rescue drone RoboWorld assumptions

since it is intended to be a location where the robot lands, and we do not need the robot to begin in mid-air. The next three element assumptions state similar constraints on the target region. Finally, it is assumed that the target is at least one metre from the origin, so that the target and the origin cannot be in the same place and have some separation between them.

The output events of the RoboChart model are takeoff and land. The mapping definition for takeoff states that it has the effect of setting the robot's velocity to 1 m per second upward. Similarly, land sets the robot's velocity to 1 m per second downward. Thus, these events, when raised by the control software, begin the processes of taking off and landing. The two input events in RoboChart are: found and origin. They are triggered in similar situations: found when the robot is over the target region, and origin when the robot is over the origin. That is specified by stating that the event occurs when the x and y position of the robot is within the relevant region. The z-axis is ignored so that the robot can detect those regions when it is flying above them.

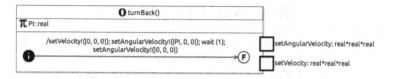

Fig. 6. Diagram for the turnBack() operation

While typically the RoboChart and RoboSim d-models are at comparable levels of abstraction, a RoboWorld document is typically a significant abstraction of a p-model or s-model, where, for example, the robot is regarded as a point. To allow for model reuse and various levels of abstraction already at the design level, however, RoboWorld documents can include a p-model or an s-model.

The operations defined for the rescue drone model are move(lv) and turn-Back(). The move(lv) operation is defined similarly to the move(lv,av) operation in the ranger model, with the robot's velocity set to lv metres per second in the direction of the robot's orientation. For turnBack(), the assumption in RoboWorld states that it is defined by a RoboChart diagram, with the size of the time unit used in the diagram set to one second in this case. This bridges a gap between a RoboChart model, which defines time in terms of units left unspecified, and the real world, by defining the value of a time unit.

The diagram itself is shown in Fig. 6. It consists of a simple state machine with one transition, a constant, PI, which represents the mathematical constant π, and two events setAngularVelocity and setVelocity, which take a triple of real numbers as their parameters, and represent facilities in the world to set the robot's angular and linear velocities. The action of the transition specifies the main behaviour of turnBack(). It first zeroes the velocity of the robot, so that it stops moving, then sets the angular velocity to PI radians per time unit about the vertical axis. The three components of the angle are yaw, pitch and roll, so rotation about the vertical axis is specified by the first component of angular velocity. The action then specifies a wait of one time unit, during which the robot rotates through π radians, then zeroes the angular velocity, leaving the robot hovering to wait for further commands from the software.

As in the ranger model, there are no platform variables in the rescue drone model, so the section for variable mappings is empty.

In summary, RoboWorld is a controlled, but very flexible language. It allows, for example, the introduction of new vocabulary (elements, for instance), in the document. It also respects the English grammar, allowing for the variations required for agreement with the gender and plurality of related words. In spite of that, it has a clear semantics that allows us to generate mathematical models. For example, the concepts of arena and entities have a clear semantics. In addition, the definition of the mappings give suitable semantics to sentences such as "The event ... occurs when ...", or "When the operation ... is called, ...". This includes binding parameters of operations, for example, for later use in the sentence. In the next section, we describe the formal semantics of RoboWorld.

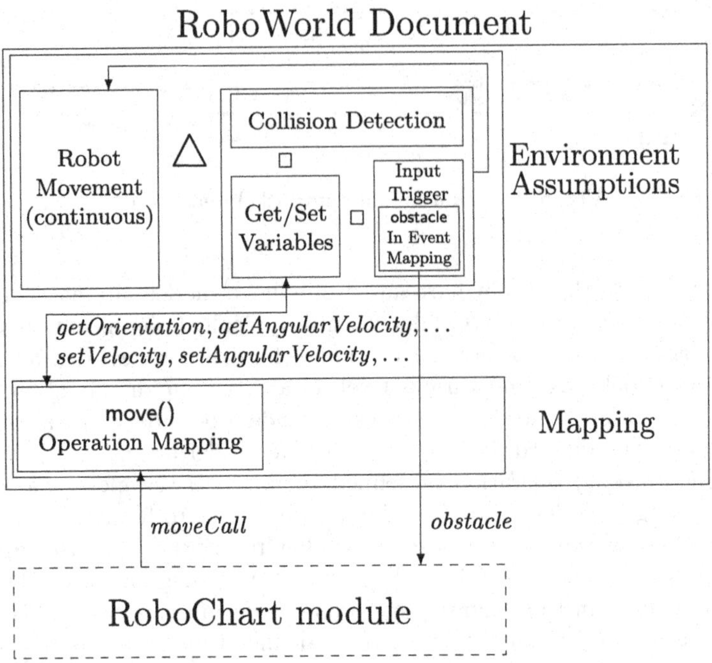

RoboWorld Document

Fig. 7. Structure of RoboWorld semantics: the Ranger example

3   RoboWorld Semantics

The semantics of the RoboStar notations use process algebras for refinement based on CSP [27]. For RoboWorld, due to the continuous nature of the arena and movement, we need to account for both discrete and continuous behaviour. So, we use a hybrid process algebra, called *CyPhyCircus* [21], which is based on the works presented in [14,16], but deals with variables and has support for automated proof. It is an extension of *Circus* [6], a process algebra that combines CSP with Z [30] for modelling abstract data types and operations.

In *CyPhyCircus*, *Circus*, and CSP, systems and components are specified by processes. They communicate with each other and their environment via channels; a communication is atomic and instantaneous. Figure 7 gives an overview of the structure of the *CyPhyCircus* process that describes the semantics of a RoboWorld document. The box at the bottom represents a *Circus* process that defines the semantics of a RoboChart module: Ranger or Rescue, in our examples. RoboTool generates automatically a CSP encoding of such a process.

As shown in Fig. 7, the process that defines the semantics of a RoboWorld document is defined by a parallel composition ([⟦ . . . ⟧]) of a process that captures the meaning of the environment assumptions and a process that captures the mapping definitions. The formal definition is as follows.

process *RoboWorldDocument* $\widehat{=}$
    (*EnvironmentAssumptions* $[\![$ *MappingInfoChannels* $]\!]$ *Mapping*)
    $\backslash$ *MappingInfoChannels*

These two processes interact via channels that get and set quantities of the environment to model movement, and potentially additional channels as required and defined by the mapping definitions. These channels are collected in a set called *MappingInfoChannels* and hidden ($\backslash$) in their composition.

For the Ranger example, the get and set channels deal with movement. We have get and set channels for the linear and angular velocities and accelerations of the robot. We also get its position and orientation, but there are no matching set channels for *getPosition* and *getOrientation*, since a model is not able to change the pose of the robot directly, without changing its velocity or acceleration.

The visible channels are those representing the services of the robotic platform in the RoboChart model. They are inputs and outputs of the RoboChart control software model. So, they are connected to the process that defines the RoboWorld document. In our example, we have channels *obstacle* and *moveCall*.

$InOut ::= in \mid out$

channel *obstacle* : *InOut*
channel *moveCall* : $\mathbb{R} \times \mathbb{R}$

Of course, *obstacle* corresponds to the event of the same name of the RangerRP platform. In the semantics, *obstacle* events communicate a value *in* of the enumeration type *InOut* defined above to indicate that they are inputs of the software. The channel *moveCall* represents calls to the operation move of RangerRP, and communicates the parameters of the call: two real numbers.

For a two-dimensional arena, the semantics defines the following constants to represent its bounds. Their specific values are left undefined (unless determined by the assumptions in the RoboWorld document).

$arenaNorthBound, arenaSouthBound : \mathbb{R}$
$arenaEastBound, arenaWestBound : \mathbb{R}$

The arena itself is represented by a set *arenaPositions* defined below containing pairs (x, y) of coordinates in the range defined by the bound constants.

$arenaPositions : \mathbb{P}(\mathbb{R} \times \mathbb{R})$

$arenaPositions = \{$
    $x : (arenaEastBound .. arenaWestBound);$
    $y : (arenaNorthBound .. arenaSouthBound)$
$\}$

Every entity has a position. In our example, the positions of the entities called obstacle are captured by the constant *obstaclePositions*: a set of arena coordinates. The assumption regarding the distribution of obstacles is captured in the predicate that constrains the values of *obstaclePositions*.

$$obstaclePositions : \mathbb{P}\ arenaPositions$$
$$\# obstaclePositions = (1/4) * \# arenaPositions$$

All these global constants are in scope for the definition of the processes used to define *RoboWorldDocument*, namely, *EnvironmentAssumptions* and *Mapping*.

First, we present the *EnvironmentAssumptions* process. The definition of the behaviour of a process can be given in terms of that of other processes, like the definition of *RoboWorldDocument*. Alternatively, it can be given by defining its (normally private) state, and actions over that state. An action differs from a process in that an action does not encapsulate a state. This is the approach we use to specify *EnvironmentAssumptions* and *Mapping*.

process *EnvironmentAssumptions* $\widehat{=}$ **begin**

Its state, defined below by a Z schema *EnvironmentState*, is characterised by components that record the position *pos* and orientation *ori* (pose), and the velocities and accelerations (linear and angular) of the robot.

$$\begin{array}{l} \_EnvironmentState \_\_\_\_ \\ \textbf{visible}\ pos : \mathbb{R} \times \mathbb{R} \\ \textbf{visible}\ ori : \mathbb{R} \\ \textbf{visible}\ vel : \mathbb{R} \times \mathbb{R} \\ \textbf{visible}\ acc : \mathbb{R} \times \mathbb{R} \\ \textbf{visible}\ angVel : \mathbb{R} \\ \textbf{visible}\ angAcc : \mathbb{R} \end{array}$$

state *EnvironmentState*

Since there are no other mobile entities in the document, there are no additional state components. The robot is assumed to be mobile.

The state components that are visible are, implicitly, functions over time, and their evolution is observed [21]. In our example, there are no encapsulated state components (declared without the **visible** modifier).

Below, we define the *CyPhyCircus* main action that describes the behaviour of *EnvironmentAssumptions*. After the components are all initialised to 0, the behaviour is that defined by another action *EnvironmentLoop*.

. . .

- $pos, vel, acc := (0,0), (0,0), (0,0)$; $ori, angVel, angAcc := 0, 0, 0$;
  $EnvironmentLoop$

end

$EnvironmentLoop$ is defined in the body of $EnvironmentAssumptions$. It is omitted above, but is presented below. Its structure is as illustrated in Fig. 7.

$EnvironmentLoop \cong$

$$RobotMovement \triangle \left(\left(\begin{array}{c} CollisionDetection \\ \Box \\ GetSetVariables \\ \Box \\ InputTrigger \end{array} \right) ; EnvironmentLoop \right)$$

$RobotMovement$ specifies the continuous evolution of all the state components in accordance with the law of movement. That evolution can be interrupted ($\triangle$) by one of the actions $CollisionDetection$, $GetSetVariables$, and $InputTrigger$, which are combined in an external choice ($\Box$). The channel communications triggered in these actions either output data from the state components for use in the $Mapping$ process, or input data to change their values.

The action $RobotMovement$ is defined below using a Z-like schema action to specify the continuous evolution of the state components. This is indicated by the symbol Λ in the state declaration $\Lambda EnvironmentState$.

$RobotMovement$ _____

$\Lambda EnvironmentState$

_____

$\frac{dpos}{dt} = vel$

$\frac{dvel}{dt} = acc$

$\frac{dori}{dt} = angVel$

$\frac{dangVel}{dt} = angAcc$

In the predicate of $RobotMovement$, we have standard equations of movement.

$CollisionDetection$ models the physical restriction that arises when the robot position pos reaches that of an obstacle obs in the set $obstaclePositions$ or reaches an arena bound. In all cases, the $velocity$ and $acceleration$ of the robot have their components set to 0. The several cases are characterised by a choice of guarded ($\&$) actions, whose behaviour is available only when the guard is true.

The assignments to *vel* and *acc* interrupt the evolution of *RobotMovement*.

$CollisionDetection \,\widehat{=}$
$$\left(\exists\, obs : obstaclePositions \bullet pos = obs\right) \,\&\, vel, acc := (0,0),(0,0)$$
$\square$
$$\left(pos.1 \geq arenaEastBound\right) \,\&\, vel, acc := (0,0),(0,0)$$
$\square$
$$\left(pos.1 \leq arenaWestBound\right) \,\&\, vel, acc := (0,0),(0,0)$$
$\square$
$$\left(pos.2 \geq arenaNorthBound\right) \,\&\, vel, acc := (0,0),(0,0)$$
$\square$
$$\left(pos.2 \leq arenaSouthBound\right) \,\&\, vel, acc := (0,0),(0,0)$$

The guards are properties of the variables whose evolution is defined by the action *RobotMovement* above. We omit the simple definition of the *GetSetVariables* action, which is also a choice, now based on channel communications. It is these communications that can interrupt *RobotMovement*.

The definition of *InputTrigger* is normally a choice of actions that capture the mapping definitions for the input events. In our example, there is just one input event obstacle. So, *InputTrigger* is defined just by the action *Obstacle_InEventMapping* that captures the RoboWorld definition for obstacle.

$InputTrigger \,\widehat{=}\, Obstacle\_InEventMapping$
$Obstacle\_InEventMapping \,\widehat{=}$
$$\left(\exists\, obs : obstaclePositions \bullet norm2\left(pos - obs\right) < 0.5\right) \,\&$$
$$obstacle.in \longrightarrow \textbf{Skip}$$

As described in RoboWorld, when the distance, defined as $norm2\left(pos - obs\right)$, between the robot and an *obstacle* in *obstaclePositions* is less than 0.5, the event *obstacle.in*, used in the process for the RoboChart module, is raised.

The mapping of output events and operations is defined by the process *Mapping*. It is normally a choice between processes that capture each of the RoboWorld mapping definitions. In our example, we have just the operation move, and so just one mapping captured by the process *Move_OperationMapping*.

process $Mapping \,\widehat{=}\, Move\_OperationMapping$

Move_OperationMapping is a standard *Circus* process, with no continuous variables or behaviour. It also has no state, and uses communications via the channels *getOrientation*, *setVelocity* and *setAngularVelocity* to read and update the state of *EnvironmentAssumptions*. The main action of *Move_OperationMapping* is *MoveCall*. It responds to an operation call, signalled by a communication on *moveCall* triggered by the process for the RoboChart module.

$MoveCall \,\widehat{=}$
$$moveCall?ls?as \longrightarrow getOrientation?yaw$$
$$\longrightarrow setVelocity!(ls * (sin\ yaw), ls * (cos\ yaw))$$
$$\longrightarrow setAngularVelocity!as \longrightarrow MoveCall$$

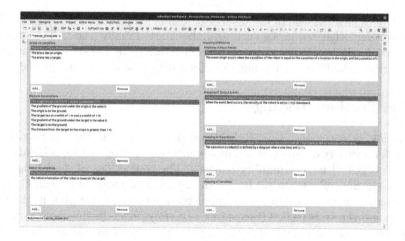

Fig. 8. The RoboWorld editor, with part of the Rescue assumptions open

Using the arguments *ls* and *as* of the operation call, passed in via the channel *moveCall*, and the *yaw* obtained using *getOrientation*, the values of the velocities are set according to the definition of the mapping in the RoboWorld document.

The processes above can be generated automatically from the RoboWorld document. The tool is under development and described next.

4 Tool

We have created an Eclipse plugin as part of the RoboTool suite of plugins to facilitate the writing of RoboWorld specifications. The plugin includes an editor for RoboWorld documents, which is shown in Fig. 8. It is divided into seven parts, corresponding to the seven sections of the RoboWorld assumptions and mapping definitions. Each part has buttons to add and remove sentences (assumptions or definitions). A sentence can be clicked on to allow it to be edited.

The sentences are parsed individually using GF, with a separate grammar for the assumptions and definitions in each section. The sentences are checked when they are first added, and after changes are made to them. A RoboWorld document is automatically constructed from the sentences in each part. The sentences are inserted under the correct section of the RoboWorld document as they are added, with the ordering of the sentences preserved.

The RoboWorld document can be viewed by selecting its tab at the bottom of the editor. This provides the ability to edit the document in another form and to add comments. These are lines that begin with "- -" and are ignored by RoboTool as part of a preprocessing. The RoboWorld document is kept consistent with the sectioned editor, and comments are preserved.

Having the RoboWorld editor as an Eclipse plugin allows for integration with the other RoboTool plugins. The editing of any diagrams takes advantage of the RoboChart editor. Generation of the semantics for a RoboWorld document is provided as a menu option in the RoboTool menu alongside semantics generation operations for other notations such as RoboChart. Finally, the CSP semantics generation for RoboChart can be used for generating the RoboWorld semantics of operations. Facilities for testing, described next, can also be integrated.

5   Verification: Testing

The *CyPhyCircus* semantics for RoboWorld documents described in Sect. 3 can be used for a variety of purposes as already mentioned. Ongoing work is encoding it in SpaceEx [11] for reachability analysis. The restrictions of model checking and bugs in SpaceEx when dealing with networks of automata mean that, at the moment, theorem proving is an appealing alternative. Our plan in the long run is to use the Isabelle/UTP encoding of *CyPhyCircus*. In the short term, we are exploring the possibility of flattening the network of hybrid automata that can be derived to match the process structure of the *CyPhyCircus* semantics. The loss of traceability, however, is likely to be a concern.

We report here preliminary work in which the semantics is discretised and encoded in FDR [12]. Here, the limitations are very severe, since FDR is not a tool to deal with hybrid models. We have, managed, however to illustrate the use of RoboWorld in testing and obtain some early validation of its semantics.

RoboTool has a plugin for automatic generation of tests using RoboChart models and mutation testing [3]. For the Rescue module (Fig. 4), we can generate the pairs of traces and forbidden continuations below. That work is based on the testing theory for *Circus* [4]; traces and their forbidden continuations is the information that we need to develop a test for traces refinement.

$(\langle takeoff.out, tock, moveCall.1 \rangle, takeoff.out)$
$(\langle takeoff.out, tock, moveCall.1, found.in, tock, tock \rangle, takeoff.out)$

The test execution for the first pair above is successful if we observe the output takeoff (represented by the event *takeoff.out*), the passage of one time unit (represented by the event *tock*), the call move(1) (represented by the event *moveCall.1*), and then takeoff does not occur.

The second pair above specifies a test in a similar way, but has a problem. The trace specifies that, after move(1), we have an input found immediately. This is not a feasible behaviour, since, as a result of a take off, the robot moves upwards, and cannot immediately find the origin, unless the target is at the origin. Without information about the environment, however, tests such as this are included in the test suite that is automatically generated by RoboTool.

In our approach, we can use the semantics for the RoboWorld document in Fig. 5 that captures the assumptions about the Rescue drone to eliminate such tests. For each test, we combine in parallel a discretised version of the process that captures the semantics of the RoboWorld document, as described in Sect. 3, with the simple process that describes the test. We can then use deadlock checking to determine whether the test is feasible. Below, we show the test process that we use for the second trace above.

$takeoff.out \longrightarrow tock \longrightarrow moveCall.1 \longrightarrow$
$found.in \longrightarrow tock \longrightarrow tock \longrightarrow$ **Stop**

This process accepts each of the events of the trace, in order, and then behaves like the process **Stop**. This is a timed deadlock, which performs no event other than *tock*, which marks the passage of time. A deadlock check in FDR does not identify the timed deadlock **Stop** as a deadlock.

The parallelism between the test process and the process that captures the RoboWorld semantics requires synchronisation on all events for the services of the platform (besides *tock*). In our example, these are *takeoff*, *moveCall*, and so on. So, the behaviour of the parallel process captures the effect of the test on the environment. Afterwards, we hide the platform events. This captures the fact that in a robotic system, we do not observe the behaviour of the software directly, but just via its effect on the environment.

Our checks eliminate the test above, and others with the same sort of problem. Deadlock freedom ensures that the test is compatible with the assumptions on the environment recorded using RoboWorld.

6   Conclusion

RoboWorld is a controlled natural language, part of the RoboStar framework, for documenting operational requirements of robotic systems. A sentence in RoboWorld adheres to an underlying grammar, which is defined using the Grammatical Framework. This framework provides native support for inflection paradigms and agreement between elements of a sentence. Despite the control imposed by its grammar, RoboWorld is a very flexible language, with an open vocabulary to define, for example, elements of the environment, with a precise semantics in *CyPhyCircus*. The well-behaved structure of sentences enables automatic generation of the semantics for a RoboWorld document.

In this paper, the syntax and semantics of RoboWorld documents are illustrated considering two examples: a ranger robot and a rescue drone. Tool support for RoboWorld, as part of the RoboTool suite of plugins, is under development.

The adoption of RoboWorld is relevant to several aspects of the design and verification of robotic systems. First, implicit assumptions about the environment are made explicit. Second, RoboWorld sentences can be used to check the validity of different models and generated code. Third, this documentation can be used to prevent the generation of infeasible or useless test cases.

Related Work. Formal modelling of the environment has already been addressed by other studies. In [15], a timed input/output conformance relation (s rtioco$_e$ t) is proposed to relate correct implementations s of specification t, under the environmental constraints expressed by e. The models of s, t, and e are given as timed automata. In [22], the system behaviour and the test environment are both modelled as state machines. Similarly to RoboWorld, in [28], environment restrictions are specified according to a controlled natural language. None of these works, however, is tailored for robotic systems, like RoboWorld. With the specialisation, RoboWorld includes domain concepts such as a mobile robotic platform, including its services and their definitions, and arenas.

When modelling the behaviour of robotic systems, some studies consider the environment to avoid unrealistic designs. For instance, in [7,24], implicit assumptions of the environment are to some extent captured by 3D and 2D grid maps, which describe a specific scenario where the designed robots are assumed to work. In [1], a UML profile is used for designing human-robot collaborative systems. This profile has specific stereotypes to model entities from a scenario that interact with the robot in class and component diagrams. The RoboWorld notion of arena corresponds to that of a layout in [1], but layouts are discrete spaces divided in sections that can be obstructed. In a component diagram, each section is a component, with connections representing adjacency. The component diagram is, therefore, a sort of map. Mathematical models for verification automatically generated use a temporal logic with a notion of discrete time. Differently, in the RoboStar framework, with the aid of RoboWorld, general assumptions of the environment are explicitly specified and can be used later to verify whether a specific scenario satisfies these assumptions.

In [17], the MontiArcAutomaton language [26] is used for modelling the components of robotic systems. In this approach, environment assumptions are specified as LTL properties, using AspectLTL [18], a language whose syntax is similar to the one considered by the SMV model checker. In RoboWorld, at the user discretion, properties of the environment are described in a more natural way, considering a controlled natural language, or referring to diagrams. Therefore, RoboWorld distinguishes itself by its flexibility on specifying general assumptions of the environments where my robot can work.

Future Work. As future work, we envisage pushing the limits of RoboWorld by considering other and more challenging case studies. Its syntax and semantics need to evolve to cope with situations and assumptions that have not been considered so far. Additionally, we also plan to improve the tool support for creating RoboWorld documents by, for instance, providing on-the-fly writing guidance. Scalability of verification and test generation is also a challenge to pursue, due to the need for dealing with both discrete and continuous behaviour.

Acknowledgements. The work reported here is funded by the Royal Academy of Engineering grant CiET1718/45, UK EPSRC grants EP/M025756/1 and EP/R025479/1, and UKRI TAS Verifiability Node EP/V026801/1. We are grateful to RoboStar for various discussions on RoboWorld.

References

1. Askarpour, M., Lestingi, L., Longoni, S., Iannacci, N., Rossi, M., Vicentini, F.: Formally-based model-driven development of collaborative robotic applications. J. Intell. Rob. Syst. **102**(3), 59 (2021)

2. Brunner, S.G., Steinmetz, F., Belder, R., Domel, A.: RAFCON: a graphical tool for engineering complex, robotic tasks. In: IEEE/RSJ International Conference on Intelligent Robots and Systems, pp. 3283–3290 (2016)
3. Cavalcanti, A., Baxter, J., Hierons, R.M., Lefticaru, R.: Testing robots using CSP. In: Beyer, D., Keller, C. (eds.) TAP 2019. LNCS, vol. 11823, pp. 21–38. Springer, Cham (2019). https://doi.org/10.1007/978-3-030-31157-5_2
4. Cavalcanti, A.L.C., Gaudel, M.-C.: Testing for refinement in Circus. Acta Informatica **48**(2), 97–147 (2011)
5. Cavalcanti, A.L.C.: Verified simulation for robotics. Sci. Comput. Program. **174**, 1–37 (2019)
6. Cavalcanti, A.L.C., Sampaio, A.C.A., Woodcock, J.C.P.: A refinement strategy for Circus. Formal Aspects Comput. **15**(2–3), 146–181 (2003)
7. Desai, A., Saha, I., Yang, J., Qadeer, S., Seshia, S.: DRONA: a framework for safe distributed mobile robotics. In: 2017 ACM/IEEE 8th International Conference on Cyber-Physical Systems (ICCPS), pp. 239–248 (2017)
8. Dhouib, S., Kchir, S., Stinckwich, S., Ziadi, T., Ziane, M.: RobotML, a domain-specific language to design, simulate and deploy robotic applications. In: Noda, I., Ando, N., Brugali, D., Kuffner, J.J. (eds.) SIMPAR 2012. LNCS (LNAI), vol. 7628, pp. 149–160. Springer, Heidelberg (2012). https://doi.org/10.1007/978-3-642-34327-8_16
9. Foster, S., Baxter, J., Cavalcanti, A., Miyazawa, A., Woodcock, J.: Automating verification of state machines with reactive designs and Isabelle/UTP. In: Bae, K., Ölveczky, P.C. (eds.) FACS 2018. LNCS, vol. 11222, pp. 137–155. Springer, Cham (2018). https://doi.org/10.1007/978-3-030-02146-7_7
10. Foster, S., Cavalcanti, A.L.C., Canham, S., Woodcock, J.C.P., Zeyda, F.: Unifying theories of reactive design contracts. Theoret. Comput. Sci. **802**, 105–140 (2020)
11. Frehse, G., et al.: SpaceEx: scalable verification of hybrid systems. In: Gopalakrishnan, G., Qadeer, S. (eds.) CAV 2011. LNCS, vol. 6806, pp. 379–395. Springer, Heidelberg (2011). https://doi.org/10.1007/978-3-642-22110-1_30
12. Gibson-Robinson, T., Armstrong, P., Boulgakov, A., Roscoe, A.W.: FDR3 — a modern refinement checker for CSP. In: Ábrahám, E., Havelund, K. (eds.) TACAS 2014. LNCS, vol. 8413, pp. 187–201. Springer, Heidelberg (2014). https://doi.org/10.1007/978-3-642-54862-8_13
13. Hoare, C.A.R., He, J.: Unifying Theories of Programming. Prentice-Hall (1998)
14. He, J.: From CSP to hybrid systems. In: A Classical Mind, pp. 171–189. Prentice-Hall (1994)
15. Larsen, K.G., Mikucionis, M., Nielsen, B.: Online testing of real-time systems using UPPAAL. In: Grabowski, J., Nielsen, B. (eds.) FATES 2004. LNCS, vol. 3395, pp. 79–94. Springer, Heidelberg (2005). https://doi.org/10.1007/978-3-540-31848-4_6
16. Liu, J., et al.: A calculus for hybrid CSP. In: Ueda, K. (ed.) APLAS 2010. LNCS, vol. 6461, pp. 1–15. Springer, Heidelberg (2010). https://doi.org/10.1007/978-3-642-17164-2_1
17. Maoz, S., Ringert, J.: Synthesizing a lego forklift controller in GR(1): a case study. In: Cerný, P., Kuncak, V., Madhusudan, P. (eds.) Proceedings Fourth Workshop on Synthesis, SYNT 2015, San Francisco, CA, USA, 18th July 2015, vol. 202. EPTCS, pp. 58–72 (2015)
18. Maoz, S., Sa'ar, Y.: AspectLTL: an aspect language for LTL specifications. In: Proceedings of the Tenth International Conference on Aspect-Oriented Software Development, AOSD 2011, pp. 19–30. Association for Computing Machinery, New York (2011)

19. Miyazawa, A., Cavalcanti, A.L.C., Ahmadi, S., Post, M., Timmis, J.: RoboSim physical modelling: diagrammatic physical robot models. Technical report, University of York, Department of Computer Science, York, UK (2020). robostar.cs.york.ac.uk/notations/

20. Miyazawa, A., Ribeiro, P., Li, W., Cavalcanti, A.L.C., Timmis, J., Woodcock, J.C.P.: RoboChart: modelling and verification of the functional behaviour of robotic applications. Softw. Syst. Model. **18**(5), 3097–3149 (2019)

21. Foster, S., Huerta y Munive, J.J., Struth, G.: Differential Hoare logics and refinement calculi for hybrid systems with Isabelle/HOL. In: Fahrenberg, U., Jipsen, P., Winter, M. (eds.) RAMiCS 2020. LNCS, vol. 12062, pp. 169–186. Springer, Cham (2020). https://doi.org/10.1007/978-3-030-43520-2_11

22. Peleska, J., Vorobev, E., Lapschies, F., Zahlten, C.: Automated model-based testing with RT-tester. Technical report, Universität Bremen (2011)

23. Pembeci, I., Nilsson, H., Hager, G.: Functional reactive robotics: an exercise in principled integration of domain-specific languages. In: 4th ACM SIGPLAN International Conference on Principles and Practice of Declarative Programming, pp. 168–179. ACM (2002)

24. Quottrup, M., Bak, T., Izadi-Zamanabadi, R.: Multi-robot planning: a timed automata approach. In: IEEE International Conference on Robotics and Automation, Proceedings, ICRA 2004, vol. 5, pp. 4417–4422 (2004)

25. Ranta, A.: Grammatical Framework: Programming with Multilingual Grammars. CSLI Publications (2011)

26. Ringert, J., Rumpe, B., Wortmann, A.: Architecture and Behavior Modeling of Cyber-Physical Systems with MontiArcAutomaton. CoRR, abs/1509.04505 (2015)

27. Roscoe, A.W.: Understanding Concurrent Systems. Texts in Computer Science. Springer, London (2011). https://doi.org/10.1007/978-1-84882-258-0

28. Santos, T., Carvalho, G., Sampaio, A.: Formal modelling of environment restrictions from natural-language requirements. In: Massoni, T., Mousavi, M.R. (eds.) SBMF 2018. LNCS, vol. 11254, pp. 252–270. Springer, Cham (2018). https://doi.org/10.1007/978-3-030-03044-5_16

29. Wachter, M., Ottenhaus, S., Krohnert, M., Vahrenkamp, N., Asfour, T.: The ArmarX Statechart concept: graphical programing of robot behavior. Frontiers Rob. AI **3**, 33 (2016)

30. Woodcock, J.C.P., Davies, J.: Using Z - Specification, Refinement, and Proof. Prentice-Hall (1996)

Validating Safety Arguments with Lean

Logan Murphy, Torin Viger, Alessio Di Sandro, Ramy Shahin,
and Marsha Chechik$^{(\boxtimes)}$

Department of Computer Science, University of Toronto, Toronto, Canada
{lmurphy,torinviger,adisandro,rshahin,chechik}@cs.toronto.edu

Abstract. Safety Assurance Cases (ACs) are structured arguments which demonstrate that a system fulfills its safety requirements. However, the reasoning used in ACs is often presented informally and thus difficult to rigorously evaluate. To protect against the acceptance of ACs based on fallacious reasoning, our previous work has proposed a framework for formalizing fragments of ACs and verifying their reasoning using the Lean Theorem Prover. This work expands on the use of Lean to automatically validate fragments of ACs, identifies challenges faced by AC developers who wish the leverage theorem proving software, and demonstrates our approach to mitigating these challenges.

Keywords: Assurance · Safety cases · Strategies · Theorem proving · Lean

1 Introduction

Cyber-physical systems have become ubiquitous in our lives, and are relied on in many domains that are safety-critical (e.g., medical devices, power plants, aerospace and automotive systems). Ensuring safety of these types of systems has always been a challenge, especially as they are expected to meet more requirements, and subsequently become more complex. Different safety procedures and guidelines have been adopted by the safety engineering communities in an attempt to address this problem. Those guidelines are often centered around developing a safety argument for the system, usually represented as a *Safety Assurance Case (AC)* [21].

An AC is a structured argument intended to show that a system is safe with respect to a set of hazards that have been identified as a part of a hazard analysis process. High-level safety claims in an AC are step-wise decomposed into more refined subclaims using *decomposition strategies*. Refinement of safety claims is recursively applied to subclaims until each leaf claim is directly associated with a piece of *evidence*. Different standardized graphical notations (e.g., *Goal Structured Notation (GSN)* [9], *Claims-Argument-Evidence (CAE)* [1]) are usually used to represent these hierarchical safety arguments.

AC notations make it easier to represent and communicate safety arguments. However, because safety claims and their decompositions are often expressed informally, the burden of validating the logical soundness of the overall safety

© Springer Nature Switzerland AG 2021
R. Calinescu and C. S. Păsăreanu (Eds.): SEFM 2021, LNCS 13085, pp. 23–43, 2021.
https://doi.org/10.1007/978-3-030-92124-8_2

24   L. Murphy et al.

argument typically falls on safety engineers. Manual inspection, especially of complex ACs, is not always a reliable way to find inconsistencies or omissions in the safety argument [8].

To illustrate the difficulty of manually validating informal ACs, consider developing an AC for a simple Floor-Cleaning System (FCS) – an automated system designed to vacuum floor tiles containing objects and clean grimy tiles without becoming damaged, modeled by the Labeled Transition System (LTS) [11] depicted in Fig. 1. A safety engineer may begin with a top-level claim C_1 asserting that the system never reaches a Damaged state, and decompose this claim into subclaims C_2 asserting that the system does not start in a Damaged state, and C_3 asserting that the system never becomes damaged when it is vacuuming, as done by strategy InvStr ("invalid strategy") shown in Fig. 2. They may further justify their belief that this decomposition is valid by appealing (erroneously) to induction, i.e., that the system cannot become damaged if it never begins in or transitions into a damaged state.

This argument is flawed because the FCS can perform actions other than vacuuming (e.g., cleaning, as shown in Fig. 1), and C_3 does not assert that these actions do no lead to a damaged state. Thus an inductive claim needs to be stronger than C_3. As stated, C_1 may not hold even if both C_2 and C_3 are true. While this example is intentionally chosen to be simple and the error can be identified by manually checking C_3 against the system's underlying model, such manual arguments become increasingly challenging and error-prone as the size of the AC and the complexity of system models increase. Flawed arguments can result in the deployment of systems with unsafe behaviors, potentially leading to drastic consequences (e.g., the British Royal Air Force Nimrod aircraft crash in 2006 [10]), emphasizing the need for more rigorous approaches to constructing and validating ACs.

One method of mitigating such reasoning errors in ACs is to formalize the AC's strategies so that they can be validated by a theorem prover [19]. To this end, our previous work [20] formalized a basic structure for AC claims and categorized AC strategies into different classes based on how the form of their parent claim relates to their decomposed claims. We identified the conditions under which each of these strategies is *deductive* (i.e., logically valid), and generated provably valid strategy templates to assist safety engineers in creating rigorous arguments. The first contribution of this paper is a detailed presentation of the theorem-proving approach behind the work reported in [19].

Yet using theorem provers to validate instances of these strategies introduces a number of challenges related to the argument's expressibility and interpretability. First, the engineer must be able to formulate these claims as formal logical statements. Next, they must be able to articulate these logical statements and encode relevant system models in the appropriate theorem proving language, and integrate these formal statements into the AC itself. Finally, they must be able to understand the theorem prover's output and debug their strategy if necessary. In addition, reviewers must be able to interpret the resultant formalized AC. Safety engineers are unlikely to have a technical skill set to be able to engage

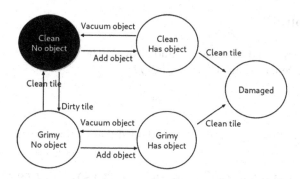

Fig. 1. A simplified FCS. Adapted from [20].

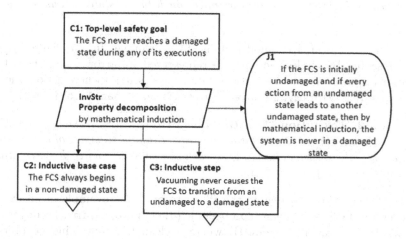

Fig. 2. A GSN AC fragment showing an invalid strategy `InvStr` for the FCS.

in the above activities. The second contribution of this paper is demonstration of the framework described in [19] as a method for bridging the gap between white-box and black-box theorem prover usage in the AC development, enabling non-expert users to access theorem-prover supported AC validation.

The rest of this paper is organized as follows: we describe the necessary background on models, properties and assurance case formalization in Sect. 2. Section 3 describes an automated strategy validation workflow: a method for using the Lean theorem prover to encode and reason about validity of AC strategies. This section also demonstrates the workflow on the FCS and identifies a set of challenges that a non-expert user would face when applying this method. Section 4 describes a tool-supported template-based approach to mitigate the challenges for non-expert users, and showcases the tooling using the FCS. We compare our approach with related work in Sect. 5 and conclude in Sect. 6 with a summary of the work and suggestions for future research directions.

2   Background

In this section, we fix the notation and provide the necessary background on models, assurance cases and their validation.

2.1   Models

We begin by recalling the definitions of labelled transition systems [11] and their executions.

Definition 1 (Labelled Transition System (LTS)). *An LTS $M = (S, A, \Delta)$ is a set of states S, a set of actions A, and a set of transitions $\Delta \in (S \times A \times S)$ where each $(s, a, s') \in \Delta$ denotes a transition between states s and s' via an action a.*

Figure 1 represents an LTS model of the FCS example. In this figure, states are represented by circles, actions are represented by arrows, and the set of transitions is given by all state-action-state tuples (s, a, s') where action a leads from s to s' (e.g., ((Grimy, No_object), cleanTile, (Clean, No_object))).

Definition 2 (Execution [20]). *Given an LTS $M = (S, A, \Delta)$, an execution $\{s_0, (a_1, s_1), (a_2, s_2) \ldots\}$ is an initial state $s_0 \in S$ and a sequence of action-state pairs (a_i, s_i), where each action $a_i \in A$, each state $s_i \in S$, and each state-action-state transition $(s_{i-1}, a_i, s_i) \in \Delta$.*

We use the notation $x[i]$ denote the ith state of x. An example of an execution over the FCS is {(Clean, No_object), (dirtyTile, (Grimy, No_object)), (cleanTile, (Clean, No_object))}, where a clean tile containing no objects becomes dirty, and is then cleaned. We can make assertions about an execution behaviour using properties:

Definition 3 (Property). *Given a type τ, a property of τ is a predicate $\mathbb{P} : \tau \to \{\text{True, False}\}$ which can be evaluated for any term x of type τ.*

An example property over an execution $x = \{s_0, (a_1, s_1) \ldots\}$ (i.e., a property where the type τ is executions) is $\mathbb{P} : (s_0 \neq (\text{Damaged}))$, which asserts that the execution does not begin in a damaged state.

2.2   Assurance Case Strategy Formalization

Assurance cases (ACs) are arguments designed to show that a system is acceptably safe. *Goal Structured Notation* (GSN) [9] is a notation for graphically representing ACs using a tree-like structure, consisting of the elements illustrated in Fig. 2. GSN ACs begin with a top-level root *claim* representing a high-level safety goal, which is then decomposed by *strategies* into more refined *subclaims* that can be directly supported by evidence. In Fig. 2, the top-level claim C_1 is decomposed by strategy InvStr into two subclaims C_2 and C_3. The justification

J_1 provides the developer's reasoning for why they believe it is appropriate to use InvStr in this context, and claims and strategies can also optionally be supported by *contexts* or *assumptions* to give further context to the argument. The triangular elements beneath C_2 and C_3 indicate that these sub-claims may be further decomposed (i.e., that this figure only represents a fragment of the complete AC). GSN will be used to denote ACs throughout this paper.

Our work in [20] formalizes the GSN notions of claims and strategies. A generalized version of this formalization is used by our framework for integrating theorem proving into the AC development process. The subsequent definitions follow the presentation in [19].

Definition 4 (Claim). *Given a type τ, let X denote a set of terms of type τ, and let $\mathbb{P}$ be a property of τ. The claim $C(\mathbb{P}, X)$ is assigned the meaning $\forall x \in X$, $\mathbb{P}(x)$, i.e., "Property $\mathbb{P}$ holds for every $x \in X$".*

Let $ex(M)$ denote the set of all possible executions of an LTS M. A property over the executions of M is defined as a predicate $\mathbb{P} : ex(M) \to \{True, False\}$ (Definition 3). A claim over some subset $X \subseteq ex(M)$ of executions of M is given by $C(\mathbb{P}, X)$. As an example, consider the property of FCS executions $\mathbb{P}_0$: "The execution never reaches the state (Damaged)". For each execution $x_0 = \{s_0, (a_1, s_1), (a_2, s_2), \ldots\}$, $\mathbb{P}_0$ is satisfied iff $s_i \neq$ (Damaged) for each state s_i in x_0. If we let X_0 denote all possible executions of the FCS, then $C(\mathbb{P}_0, X_0)$ asserts that all executions of the system never reach the state (Damaged).

A *strategy* is any method for decomposing a claim into a set of subclaims [9]. Following [20], we consider a strategy to be *valid* when the satisfaction of all supporting subclaims guarantees the satisfaction of the parent claim. This is formalized as follows:

Definition 5 (Valid Strategy [20]). *Suppose a strategy Str decomposes a claim C into subclaims C_1, ..., C_n. Str is valid iff $(C_1 \wedge \ldots \wedge C_n) \Rightarrow C$.*

In [20], we categorize strategies into classes based on the form of their parent and child claims, and prove the conditions under which each strategy class valid. The two main strategy classes we identify are *domain decompositions*, which decompose a claim $C(\mathbb{P}, X)$ into subclaims asserting that $\mathbb{P}$ holds over different subsets of X, and *property decompositions*, which decompose $C(\mathbb{P}, X)$ into subclaims asserting that different properties $\mathbb{P}_1 \ldots \mathbb{P}_n$ hold over X. We recall property decompositions below.

Definition 6 (Property decomposition). *Given a set of properties $\{\mathbb{P}_1, ..\mathbb{P}_n\}$, a property decomposition strategy decomposes a parent claim $C(\mathbb{P}, X)$ into n subclaims of the form $C(\mathbb{P}_1, X)$, ..., $C(\mathbb{P}_n, X)$.*

Property decompositions can be classified into further subtypes based on the form of the properties in each subclaim. Examples include decompositions by contrapositive, by cases, and by induction. The broader class of decompositions by induction is defined formally as follows:

Definition 7 (Property Decomposition by Induction). *Given a set of executions X of an LTS $M = (S, A, \Delta)$, let $\mathbb{P}_{state}$ be a property that can be evaluated over individual states (i.e., $\mathbb{P}_{state}\colon S \to \{True, False\}$). For any $x = \{s_0, (a_1, s_1) \dots\} \in X$, define the following properties:*

$\mathbb{P}_{init}(x) = \mathbb{P}_{state}(s_0)$

$\mathbb{P}_{ind}(x) = \forall i \in \mathbb{N}, \mathbb{P}_{state}(s_{i-1}) \implies \mathbb{P}_{state}(s_i)$

$\mathbb{P}(x) = \forall i \in \mathbb{N}, \mathbb{P}_{state}(s_i)$

A decomposition by induction decomposes a claim $C(\mathbb{P}, X)$ into two subclaims of the form $C(\mathbb{P}_{init}, X)$ and $C(\mathbb{P}_{ind}, X)$.

For example, the decomposition strategy in Fig. 2 could be correctly formalized using Definition 7 and the above template as follows: let $\mathbb{P}_{state}(s) = s \neq$ Damaged.

$\mathbb{P}_{init}(x) = x[0] \neq$ Damaged

$\mathbb{P}_{ind}(x) = \forall i \in \mathbb{N}, x[i] \neq$ Damaged $\implies x[i+1] \neq$ Damaged

$\mathbb{P}(x) = \forall i \in \mathbb{N}, x[i] \neq$ Damaged

A property decomposition strategy constructed using this template is always valid, as proved in [20]. We thus refer to the decomposition strategy by induction we have just defined as ValStr ("valid strategy"). The remaining strategy decomposition templates are also formalized, illustrated and proven valid in [20].

3   Lean-Validated Strategies

In this section, we demonstrate how the Lean Theorem Prover can be used to formally validate decomposition strategies. Lean [14] is an open source interactive theorem prover (ITP) and dependently-typed functional programming language. Given a term t and a type τ, we use t : τ to denote that t is of type τ. Logical propositions are defined in Lean as terms of type Prop. Given a term P of type Prop, a proof of the proposition P is a term whose type is P. Such an object may be referred to as a *proof-term*. Lean supports both declarative proofs, where proof terms are explicitly constructed, as well as *tactic proofs*, where a series of instructions (tactics) are used to indicate how Lean can construct a proof-term.

In what follows, we describe an automated strategy validation workflow which allows users to provide a Lean encoding of a decomposition strategy, and obtain either a proof of its validity or information about how the strategy could be altered (Sect. 3.1). We then demonstrate how the inputs to the workflow can be constructed by a Lean programmer, using the FCS and the strategies ValStr (a valid strategy defined at the end of Sect. 2.2) and InvStr (an invalid strategy shown in Fig. 2) as a running example (Sect. 3.2 and Sect. 3.3). We discuss our use of Lean's metaprogramming framework for proof automation (Sect. 3.4 and Sect. 3.5) and demonstrate the output of the validation workflow over both ValStr and InvStr. Finally, we identify some challenges which can be faced by safety engineers who wish to use this workflow to validate their strategies (Sect. 3.6).

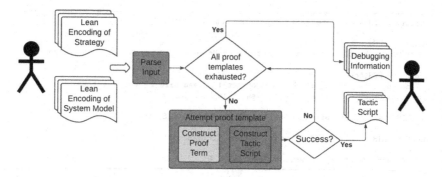

Fig. 3. The Lean workflow for validating an AC strategy. The blue substate indicates the part of the workflow which is certified by Lean's kernel.

3.1   A Strategy Validation Workflow

Figure 3 provides a high-level illustration of the automated strategy validation workflow we have implemented in Lean. First, Lean parses the user's input, ensuring that it correctly encodes a strategy specification over a system model, which must also be defined in Lean. Next, it begins iterating through a set of *proof templates* – a collection of proof strategies we have implemented for this specific context. For example, one proof template corresponds to searching through a library of lemmas, applying one whose conclusion matches the parent claim and whose premises match to the subclaims of the decomposition strategy. For each proof template, Lean attempts to construct a proof-term. When progress is made towards the proof, we log a corresponding tactic, providing a record of how to re-create each stage of the proof. If the proof term is completed, the validation process terminates, and a tactic script is stored in a separate file. If a given proof template cannot be completed, a new strategy is chosen. If all proof templates are exhausted without a complete proof being constructed, the program terminates, and any debugging information gathered during the workflow will be provided to the user.

3.2   Formalizing Models

We begin with creating a Lean encoding of the particular model over which the claims in the strategy are articulated. This requires (1) formalizing the *type* of system over which the strategy is defined, and (2) encoding a particular system as an instance of this type.

Listing 3.1 shows how this is achieved for the FCS. Line 1 formalizes Definition 1, allowing any types S and A to be used as the type of states and actions of an LTS. The Lean encoding of Definition 2 (executions) is omitted. Lines 3–12 illustrate the definition of the FCS as a specific object of type LTS. In particular, we define the types FCS_State and FCS_Action, as well as the set FCS_transitions, by explicitly enumerating them; the enumeration of the transitions is omitted. Line 12 combines these definitions in the forming of an LTS

```
1   structure LTS:= (S : Type) (Act : Type) (TR : set (S × Act × S))
2
3   inductive FCS_State
4     | Clean_No_object | Clean_Has_object | Grimy_No_object | Grimy_Has_object | Damaged
5
6   inductive FCS_Action
7     | Add_object_1 | Dirty_tile | Vacuum_object_1 | Clean_tile_1 | Add_object_2
8     | Vacuum_object_2 | Clean_tile_2 | Clean_tile_3
9
10  def FCS_transitions : set (FCS_State × FCS_Action × FCS_State) := { ... }
11
12  def FCS : LTS := LTS.mk FCS_State FCS_Action FCS_transitions
13
14  def Property (τ : Type) : Type := τ → Prop
```

Listing 3.1. Encoding LTSs and properties in Lean.

```
1   structure Claim (τ : Type) := make :: (X : set τ) (P : Property τ)
2
3   def meaning (C : Claim τ) : Prop := ∀ x ∈ C.X, C.P x
4   notation ⟦C⟧ := meaning C
5
6   structure Strategy (τ : Type) :=
7   (parent : Claim τ) (decomp : Claim τ → list (Claim τ))
8
9   def valid (S : Strategy τ) : Prop :=
10  let subclaims := (S.decomp) S.parent in
11  (∀ clm ∈ subclaims, ⟦clm⟧) → ⟦S.parent⟧
```

Listing 3.2. Core definitions used for strategy validation in Lean.

called FCS. Finally, line 14 encodes Definition 3: given a type τ, Property τ is the type of functions from τ to Prop.

3.3   Formalizing Strategies

The core Lean definitions, encoding those in Sect. 2.2, are shown in Listing 3.2. We sometimes use list instead of set, for simplicity. Corresponding to Definition 4, line 1 defines the record type Claim as having two fields: a set of τ and a property P over τ. This definition also introduces the explicit constructor Claim.make. Lean's syntax is extensible: line 4 defines a function meaning which takes a claim C to its associated first-order proposition in accordance with Definition 4, and line 5 introduces the notation ⟦C⟧ to denote this proposition.

Lines 7–12 formalize Definition 5 as follows. First, we define Strategy τ as a structure consisting of a parent claim and a function mapping any claim to a list of claims (the subclaims). Given S : Strategy, we define valid S to be a proposition stating that logical conjunction of the strategy's subclaims implies the strategy's parent claim. Since valid S is of type Prop, a term which is of type valid S is a Lean proof that this strategy is valid.

For each class of decomposition strategies we implement a data structure, referred to as *strategy specification*, encoding the information required to perform the decomposition. We then define a mapping toStrategy which takes each strategy specifications to a Strategy (as defined in Listing 3.2). To validate a decomposition strategy, Lean can simply be provided the strategy specification, and compute the induced **Strategy** using this mapping.

```
1   namespace property
2
3   structure strategySpec := (Clm : Claim τ) (Props : list (Property τ))
4
5   def toStrategy (S : strategySpec τ) : Strategy τ :=
6   { parent := S.Clm,
7     decomp := λ C, list.map (Claim.make C.X) S.Props }
8
9   end property
10
11  def ValStr_spec : property.StrategySpec (execution FCS) := {
12      Clm := { X := set.univ
13              P := λ x, ∀ i : ℕ, x[i] ≠ Damaged, },
14      Props := [ λ x, x[0] ≠ Damaged,
15               λ x, ∀ i : ℕ, x[i] ≠ Damaged  → x[i+1] ≠ Damaged ] }
```

Listing 3.3. Specification of a property decomposition for the FCS.

For example, a property decomposition is completely specified by its parent claim and by the set of properties used in the decomposition. We therefore define in Lean the type **property.strategySpec** with these fields, as shown in line 3 of Listing 3.3. We then define a mapping from **property.strategySpec** to **Strategy**, by mapping the **Claim** constructor to the list of properties in the specification. As in Definition 6, the set of executions is the same between the parent claim and the subclaims, so we apply this argument to **Claim.make** before performing the mapping.

Lines 11–15 of Listing 3.3 show the Lean specification of the the strategy **ValStr**, following the structure of a property decomposition by induction (Definition 7). Lines 12–13 encode the parent claim. We index the states of execution by natural numbers, and so the property in line 13 asserts, for some execution x, that none of the states of x are the **Damaged** state. The first and second properties encode $\mathbb{P}_{init}$ and $\mathbb{P}_{ind}$, respectively; the property on line 14 asserts that x does not begin in the **Damaged** state, while the property on line 15 asserts that x does not transition into the **Damaged** state.

3.4   Proof Automation

Lean is an *interactive* proof assistant, and it can require effort on the part of the user to complete a proof. *Metaprograms* [7], including proof tactics, can provide varying degrees of automation, allowing Lean to perform a significant amount of boilerplate or repetitive tasks. We have implemented metaprograms which can automatically validate certain classes of strategies defined in this framework, as well as tactics which help reduce the complexity of the resulting proof scripts.

Our implementation defined a data structure **proofData** which stores a variety of information about the proof search which can be relevant to the user, such as the set of properties successfully used to advance the proof, or a list of tactics which can be used to re-create the proof. Listing 3.4 contains a metaprogram contributing to a proof by induction over the set of natural numbers ℕ. In particular, this program attempts to map one of the decomposition properties (i.e., one of the subclaims) to the inductive case of the proof.

```
1    meta def solve_inductive_case (Γ : proofData τ) :
2      list expr → tactic (proofData τ)
3    | [ ]    := return Γ
4    | (h ::t) := do
5        τ ← infer_type h,
6        match τ with
7        | '(∀ i : ℕ, %%body) := do
8            index_expr ← local_context >>= get_index_expr,
9            let e := expr.mk_app h [index_expr],
10           tactic.apply e,
11           subclaim ← stringOfExpr h,
12           Γ ← Γ.try_match_IH subclaim,
13           return Γ
14         < | > solve_inductive_case t
15       | _ := solve_inductive_case t
16     end
```

Listing 3.4. A metaprogram to resolve inductive step of a proof by induction over $\mathbb{N}$.

Arguments to **solve_inductive_case** are a **proofData** object (Γ) and a list of Lean expressions (of type **expr**). This particular **list expr** forms the local proof *context*, including the decomposition properties used in the strategy and any other local variables or constants that may have been accumulated over the course of the proof. The metaprogram returns a new **proofData** within the **tactic** monad. Since we are at the inductive step of the proof, the local context contains an induction variable $k : \mathbb{N}$ and an inductive hypothesis of the form $P(k)$. The goal of the proof is of the form $P(k + 1)$. If the decomposition strategy supports a valid proof by induction, one of the premises will be a term whose type is of the form $\forall i : \mathbb{N}, P(i) \implies P(i + 1)$; the task of **solve_inductive_case** is to find this premise, instantiate the quantified premise with k, use this instantiation to resolve the goal, and to update Γ to reflect this usage.

The function is defined recursively on the proof context; if it is empty, Γ is returned. Otherwise, line 5 stores the type of the element h in a variable τ. We then perform pattern matching on τ: if it is not of the form $\forall i : \mathbb{N}, P$, we continue to the tail of the list (line 14). If the type is a match, line 8 extracts the induction variable from the proof context, and line 9 forms a new $e : \textbf{expr}$ by instantiating h with the induction variable. Line 10 uses the **apply** tactic with the newly formed expression, attempting to unify the type of the proof goal with the conclusion of e, i.e., the instantiated inductive subclaim. If the **apply** tactic succeeds, we invoke the metaprogram **try_match_IH** which tries to match the premise(s) of e with the inductive hypothesis (line 12). If this succeeds, we add the interactive tactic **inductive_case** and the identifier of h to Γ. If the matching of the premises to the IH fails, we record a Lean-provided error message in Γ.

If there is a failure at any point in the program (for instance, if h was a universally quantified premise not related to the inductive case), the program iterates to the next element of the proof context (line 14).

3.5   Application to the FCS

We now apply the strategy validation workflow to reasoning about the FCS, showing both a valid and an invalid decomposition strategy.

```
1  def ValStr : Strategy (execution FCS) := property.toStrategy ValStr_spec
2
3  theorem example_proof : valid S1 :=
4  by { by_induction_over_nat, base_case P1, inductive_case P2 }
```

Listing 3.5. Results of a successful validation.

A Successful Validation. Listing 3.5 illustrates the input and output of the strategy validation workflow on the strategy `ValStr`. Line 1 defines a property decomposition strategy over the type `execution FCS`, specifically by applying the mapping `property.toStrategy` to the specification of the property decomposition. Since Lean is able to prove the validity of this strategy, the workflow returns a tactic script which can be used to re-create a proof of its validity. In addition to serving as a witness to the theorem, this tactic script can provide insight into *why* the strategy is provably valid.

The tactic script in line 4 contains three tactics created specifically for property decompositions justified by induction over $\mathbb{N}$. The first, `by_induc-tion_over_nat`, translates the strategy specification into a more useful format; specifically, it takes each of the properties in the list `Props` as a premise in the proof context, and assigns each an identifier `P1,...Pn`, corresponding to their ordering in the list. The remaining tactics cover each case in the inductive proof, and indicate which property was used for the associated case. Recalling the definition of `FCS_strategySpec` from Listing 3.3, line 4 indicates that the property $x[0] \neq$ `Damaged` can be used to resolve the base case, while $\forall\ i : \mathbb{N}, x[i] \neq$ `Damaged` $\rightarrow x[i+1] \neq$ `Damaged` can be used to resolve the inductive case.

An Unsuccessful Validation. Listing 3.6 illustrates the results of applying the workflow to the invalid strategy `InvStr`. Lines 1–6 show an encoding of `InvStr` as a strategy specification. Since the sub-property corresponding to the base case of the proof is the same, we obtain a partial proof script indicating that the first element of `Props` can still be used to resolve this case of the proof. However, the proof script is incomplete, indicating that Lean was unable to validate the strategy. Furthermore, the procedure recorded the particular error message thrown by Lean which resulted in the failure of the inductive case of the proof (lines 15–18). If we analyze the error message in the context of the metaprogram `solve_inductive_case` we can infer that the validation failed because Lean could not unify $x[i] \neq$ `Damaged` with `x.action i` $\in$ `vacuum.actions`.

3.6   Theorem Proving for AC Validation: Challenges

A Lean programmer can use the strategy validation workflow to specify and validate a decomposition strategy. However, it is unrealistic to expect that all safety engineers responsible for AC development will have the necessary background in theorem proving to effectively use such a framework. In this section, we identify

```
1    def InvStr : Strategy (execution FCS) := property.toStrategy {
2      Clm := {  X := set.univ,
3                 P := λ x, ∀ i : ℕ, x[i] ≠ Damaged },
4      Props := [ λ x, x[0] ≠ Damaged,
5                 λ x, ∀ i : ℕ, ((x.action i) ∈ vacuum_actions) → (π.state i) ≠ Damaged]
6      }
7
8    theorem incomplete_proof : valid S1 :=
9    begin
10     by_induction,
11     base_case P1,
12   end
13
14   /-
15   invalid type ascription, term has type
16       x[i] ≠ Damaged
17   but is expected to have type
18       x.action i ∈ vacuum_actions
19   -/
```

Listing 3.6. Partial proof script and debugging information.

some of the challenges facing safety engineers without formal theorem proving experience who wish to validate their decomposition strategies using the Lean framework. In particular, we discuss *formalization* challenges (abbrev. **FC**), and *interpretation* challenges (abbrev. **IC**).

FC1: Formalizing Models. As shown in Sect. 3.2, the strategy validation workflow requires a Lean encoding of both the type of system model over which the claims are articulated, as well as a particular system as an instance of that type. Manually producing these encodings can only be done by safety engineers who are proficient in Lean.

FC2: Formalization of Decomposition Strategies. We also require the decomposition strategy itself be encoded in Lean. Whereas the semantics of a system model (e.g., LTS) may be unambiguous, a strategy expressed in natural language will generally require a very careful analysis to determine its precise meaning. Even if the semantics is fully understood, manually encoding a property decomposition in Lean can be complex, and safety engineers may erroneously define formal properties that do not accurately encode the original strategy.

IC1: Understanding a Successful Validation. When Lean is able to successfully validate a decomposition strategy, the results need to be incorporated into the AC. Furthermore, the AC in its entirety needs to be communicated to, and understood by, a wide variety of stakeholders, the majority of whom will likely be unfamiliar with theorem proving. A significant amount of effort is required to ensure that the results of validation can be leveraged in the AC without compromising its comprehensibility.

IC2: Debugging a Failed Validation. In the event Lean is unable to prove validity of a strategy, its feedback can take a variety of forms: a list of unresolved goals in the proof environment, a list of premises/subclaims which were not able to be used in the proof, etc. In particular, this data can consist mostly of Lean expressions, possibly containing "holes" or meta-variables. Interpreting the information returned by the workflow and determining how the input to the workflow should be altered can be a challenge even for a Lean expert, and hence it is very challenging for a user unfamiliar with Lean.

```
/**
 * Gets a set of predefined property templates that are available for the input model,
 * to be used in a property decomposition, grouped by categories.
 * @param model The model for which property templates are applicable.
 * @return A map of categories to lists of property templates.
 * @throws MMINTException If there is no encoder available for the input model.
 */
Map<String, List<PropertyTemplate>> getPropertyTemplates(Model model) throws MMINTException;

/**
 * Validates the correctness of a GSN property decomposition.
 * @param strategy The GSN property decomposition strategy.
 * @throws Exception If the validation fails.
 */
void validatePropertyDecomposition(PropertyDecompositionStrategy strategy) throws Exception;
```

Fig. 4. A fragment of the Java API for the formal validation of GSN strategies.

4 Towards a Black-Box Usage of Lean in AC Validation

In this section, we describe how to address the challenges (see Sect. 3.6) that a safety engineer would face trying to using Lean to reason about validity of GSN strategy decompositions by showing how to integrate Lean into the *MMINT-A* model management framework. *MMINT-A*[1] [4] is an Eclipse-based tool written in Java that provides an interactive workbench for managing the lifecycle of safety models – starting from the creation of GSN ACs and providing a number of features to support their evolution, such as querying and change impact analysis. We finally illustrate our approach using the FCS and the strategies ValStr (a valid strategy defined at the end of Sect. 2.2) and InvStr (an invalid strategy shown in Fig. 2).

4.1 Integrating Lean with *MMINT-A*

We extend *MMINT-A* by adding a generic programming interface to support the formal validation of GSN decomposition strategies (see Fig. 4), with the goals of extensibility and modularity. This way we decouple the use of a specific theorem prover from the GSN validation workflow, treating it as a black box. We then create a default Lean implementation, following the formalization described in Sect. 3. We wrap the Lean workflow from Fig. 3, provide the appropriate inputs,

---

[1] Available at http://github.com/adisandro/MMINT.

and process the outputs in the context of a safety AC within *MMINT-A*. In Fig. 5, we show how a safety engineer interacts with *MMINT-A* to validate a GSN property decomposition without requiring formal knowledge of Lean.

Model Encoder and Property Templates. As mentioned in Sect. 3.6, encoding the inputs to the Lean validation workflow presents a significant challenge for a safety engineer. To bridge this gap, we developed a *model encoder* to translate LTS models into their Lean representation, and a library of *property templates* to help translate natural language claims into formal Lean properties. Encoder and templates are pluggable modules that are provided by Lean experts. They are tied to a specific type of model, e.g. LTS, but are reusable across multiple model instances, e.g. the FCS. The engineer starts the decomposition workflow by selecting a claim in the GSN graphical editor. In Step 2, *MMINT-A* retrieves the related system model by following existing traceability links, together with its Lean encoder and property templates. The encoder is used in Step 3 to convert the system model into a Lean textual representation of it, addressing challenge **FC1**. For example, Listing 3.1 shows the resulting Lean encoding for the FCS. The API `getTemplateProperties` from Fig. 4 is invoked at the same time to retrieve a categorized list of property templates, given the related model as input.

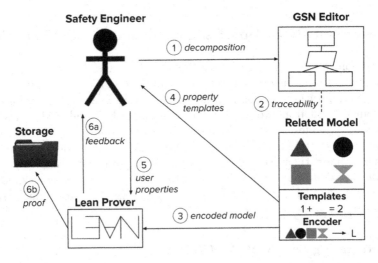

Fig. 5. The *MMINT-A* workflow for validating an AC strategy [19].

A *property template* is a logical property expressed both in natural language and in Lean, e.g., the pair "Damaged is not reached" and "$\lambda x, \forall \ i : \mathbb{N}, x[i] \neq$ Damaged". Templates contain variables that the user instantiates by providing elements from the system models over which the pra variable X can be replaced by the state Damaged. A safety expert can thus choose their decomposition properties using natural language from a set of predefined templates, which are replaced behind the scenes by their corresponding encoding in Lean. This (partly) addresses challenge **FC2**. In particular, we defined a set of property templates corresponding to LTL formulae, and described their semantics with respect to the executions of LTSs. We chose the majority of our templates from [6], with a few custom templates specifically designed for proofs by induction; for more information on our use of property templates, refer to [19]. As an example, Listing 4.1 shows an encoding of the strategy `ValStr` using LTL property templates instead of doing so manually. For example, "`absent.globally Damaged`" gets translated into to "$\lambda x, \forall\, i : \mathbb{N}, x[i] \neq \text{Damaged}$".

The safety engineer selects the decomposition properties in natural language from the set of templates in Step 4. They also choose the appropriate system model elements they want to use to replace the template variables. The resulting Lean-encoded properties are sent to the Lean prover (Step 5) using the API `validatePropertyDecomposition` from Fig. 4. Together with the encoder data from Step 3, this corresponds to the inputs of Fig. 3 (*Lean Encoding of Strategy* and *Lean Encoding of System Model*), saving the user from manually formalizing them and addressing challenges **FC1** and **FC2**.

```
1   def FCS_strategySpec)template : property.StrategySpec (execution FCS) := {
2       Clm := { X := set.univ
3                P := λ x, x ⊨ absent.globally Damaged},
4       Props := [ λ x, x ⊨ not_init Damaged,
5                  λ x, x ⊨ transitions_safe Damaged] }
```

Listing 4.1. Property decomposition by induction using property templates.

Feedback Loop and Proof Storage. Lean then returns the results of the validation and a proof for it, i.e., the *Debugging Information* and *Tactic Script* outputs from Fig. 3. The validation may fail in Step 6a, in which case *MMINT-A* parses the debugging information and gives feedback to the engineer about which of the chosen properties are failing. They can change their decomposition strategy and submit a new validation request to Lean, repeating Step 5. When the validation returns a positive result, we follow Step 6b and store the resulting proof as evidence for the AC, populating it with GSN elements that reflect the formalized strategy decomposition. Steps 6b and 6a address challenges **IC1** and **IC2**, respectively.

Note that any theorem prover can be easily plugged into *MMINT-A*, replacing Lean, by adding: (a) the code to programmatically invoke the theorem prover; (b) appropriate encoders to convert models into the language used by the theorem prover; (c) property templates to bridge the gap between natural language and theorem prover syntax; (d) a parser for the theorem prover output.

4.2 FCS Strategy Decomposition Example

We again illustrate the validation of the strategy `ValStr` over the FCS. This time, we demonstrate how our tool allows users to do formal reasoning without having any Lean experience. The goal of the safety engineer is to enforce a safety

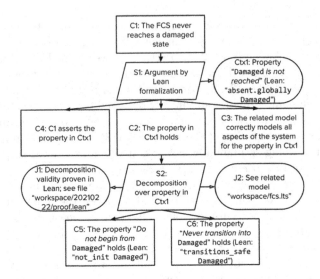

Fig. 6. The FCS AC property decomposition in *MMINT-A* [19].

claim stating (in natural language) that the FCS does not reach the `Damaged` state, i.e. the claim C_1 in Fig. 6. They reason that this can be achieved by not starting from the `Damaged` state, and by not transitioning into the `Damaged` state. To validate their reasoning, they aim to a) create the top-level formal claim C_2; b) decompose it into two sub-claims, C_5 and C_6; and c) check the correctness of the decomposition with justification J_1.

The decomposition workflow starts in *MMINT-A* by right-clicking on the claim C_1 and selecting *Property Decomposition*, i.e., Step 1 of Fig. 5. The tool proceeds by executing Steps 2 and 3: the FCS model is fetched through the trace link and transformed into its equivalent Lean encoding as shown in Listing 3.1, addressing challenge **FC1**. The tool also retrieves the property templates that are associated with LTS models, i.e., the 29 temporal properties described in [19], and presents them to the user at Step 4.

Figure 7 shows the dialogue where the user can select a property template and the model elements for variable replacement. In our example, the user first selects the template "X *is not reached*", and then chooses the `Damaged` state to replace the placeholder variable X. The resulting instantiated property template is "`Damaged` *is not reached*", which corresponds to the Lean property "`absent.globally Damaged`". The Lean translation is done by the tool transparently to the user, addressing challenge **FC2**, and it is stored together with the natural language representation. After specifying the parent claim, *MMINT-A* asks for the number of children claims in the GSN decomposition, and repeats the previous activity for each of them. The user adds two subclaims: claim C_5 using property template "*Do not begin from* X", substituting `Damaged` for variable X, creating the Lean property "`not_init Damaged`"; claim C_6 using property

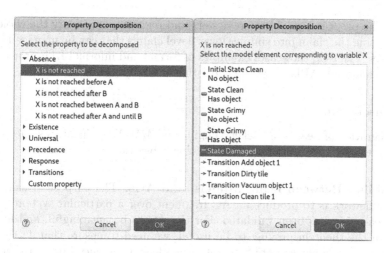

Fig. 7. The interface dialogs to select a property template in *MMINT-A* [19].

template "*Never transition into* X", substituting `Damaged` for variable X, creating the Lean property "`transitions_safe Damaged`".

MMINT-A bundles the three properties in Step 5 and sends them to the Lean validation workflow, together with the FCS encoding from Step 3, asking to check the validity of the decomposition. Lean replies positively and the proof is stored in Step 6b. The GSN editor in Fig. 6 is populated with a number of new AC elements to represent the successful decomposition. Strategy S_1, context `Ctx1` and claims C_2, C_3, C_4 represent the first layer of the formal decomposition, i.e. the translation of the top-level claim from natural language to Lean (similarly to the approach of the tool AdvoCATE [3]). C_3 and C_4 are the assumptions made during the conversion of C_1 into C_2. The real decomposition is represented by the second layer, with strategy S_2, claims C_5, C_6, and justification J_1 pointing to the Lean correctness proof. Incorporating the results of a successful Lean validation into the AC addresses challenge **IC1**.

To help mitigate **IC2**, we have modified the strategy workflow to leverage property templates for debugging strategies. For example, suppose the user requested that a specification encoding `InvStr` be sent for validation. As shown in Listing 3.6, we partially complete a proof by induction, and Lean is able to infer the form of the subclaim it requires to apply the inductive hypothesis and complete the proof. By matching this information against the property templates we have designed for property decomposition by induction, we can effectively determine the inductive property which would allow the strategy to be validated. Accordingly, when the user sends `InvStr` for validation, the interface stores a log and asks the user whether they want to replace the inductive sub-property with the one chosen by Lean. This approach offers a partial mitigation of **IC2**.

This example demonstrates how no Lean knowledge is necessary to formally prove and decompose an intuitive safety claim (staying away from the `Damaged` state). The proof is available to reviewers and regulators to justify the choice of decomposing the claim into simpler lower-level claims that can be managed independently. The FCS showcases examples of formal and informal LTL properties, but the validation APIs allows for any other kind of logic to be added.

4.3 Discussion

The integration of Lean as a backend engine and *MMINT-A* involves some design considerations that we briefly discuss in this subsection.

Traceability Between Lean, Models, and ACs. The purpose of using the Lean framework is to produce an AC fragment over a particular system model whose reasoning has been validated. For the AC to be meaningful, and for the results of the theorem proving to be useful, we need to ensure that 1) the AC correctly refers to elements of the system model, 2) the encoding of the model in Lean can be directly traced to the actual system model, and 3) the results of the theorem proving are correctly incorporated into the AC. Each of these relations between the AC, the model, and the theorem prover is a potential point of failure which must be manually inspected. *MMINT-A* is capable of managing *megamodels* [17], where a megamodel is composed of multiple models of the same system, each covering a different aspect of it. Traceability between the individual models (including the AC [4]) is managed within *MMINT-A*. With Lean integrated into the framework, it is essential to invalidate any AC elements impacted by any modifications to the system model(s) or the theorems imported from Lean. *MMINT-A* already supports change impact assessment of models connected by traceability links. Adding similar support to the integration links with Lean proofs is one of our future directions.

Improving Automation and Reasoning Capabilities. As the needs of the safety engineers change, the capabilities of the theorem proving layer may need to be extended or altered. For instance, a new set of system models or system properties would require a new set of definitions and data structures in Lean, and could require new metaprograms to effectively validate strategies concerning these models and properties. Furthermore, the level of debugging feedback provided by the theorem prover to safety engineers may be configurable. Effective round-trip engineering between the theorem proving layer and the modeling layer would involve allowing flexibility and configurability of the different components, and at the same time the ability to use formal proofs as black boxes when needed. Configurability and extensibility of how Lean proofs are used within *MMINT-A* are among of future research directions.

5 Related Work

The use of formal reasoning techniques (e.g., theorem proving, model checking) to automatically validate assurance cases, as opposed to manual inspection, has been suggested by Rushby [16]. Rushby adds that a prerequisite for AC structural reasoning is that each decomposition step has to be *deductively sound*. Deductively sound decomposition strategy templates were introduced in [20]. In this paper, we show how interactive theorem provers can be used to validate the correctness of deductive AC decomposition strategies.

Formal reasoning tools has also been used in safety assurance in several projects. The *Evidential Tool Bus (ETB)* [2] constructs an assurance case bottom-up starting from pieces of evidence generated by external tools. Evidence and argument composition rules are written by safety engineers in a Datalog extension. Another rule-based approach is *Model-Transformation Based Assurance (MTBA)* [5]. MTBA uses user-provided inference rules, verified computations, and links between pieces of evidence and subgoals to construct assurance cases via graph transformations. The *AdvoCATE* [3] *suite of tools* is used to validate some semantic correctness properties of assurance cases. Syntactic well-formedness constraints are provided by the users of AdvoCATE, and the assurance case is checked against those constraints. The *Structured Assurance Case Metamodel (SACM)* was formalized using the Isabelle theorem proving framework, and was embedded in Isabelle as an ontology for assurance cases [15]. We do not attempt to verify an end-to-end assurance case, but rather we focus on proving that claim decomposition strategies are deductively sound. The way we integrate the theorems and proofs written in Lean on one side, and the *MMINT-A* model management framework on the other, allows safety engineers (at least in some use-cases) to use formalized decomposition strategies without having to prove the correctness theorems themselves.

The use of interactive theorem provers to reason about software systems and prove correctness claims has been gaining traction. Examples include the use of the Coq theorem prover to certify the correctness of the CompCert C-language compiler [13], and using Isabelle/HOL to prove the correctness of the seL4 microkernel [12]. In the safety domain, Lean was used to prove the correctness of a change impact assessment algorithm applied to assurance cases of software product lines [18]. In this paper, on the other hand, we focus on the validity of the AC argument, and we assume the AC refers to a single product.

6   Conclusion

In this paper, we described how our formal approach to AC reasoning from [19] enables users to formally validate AC arguments without requiring theorem proving expertise, and expanded on the underlying framework for integrating theorem proving with safety assurance. We showed how theorem proving can be used directly by experts to validate ACs, identified challenges in extending theorem-proving AC support to non-experts, and showed how our approach addresses these challenges in transitioning from the white-box to the black-box usage of the theorem provers. The result is an approach that facilitates the development of ACs with provably valid strategies and mitigates reasoning errors that can false assurance of unsafe systems.

As future work, we plan to empirically measure the benefits of our approach in terms of mitigating formalization and analysis challenges through larger case studies. We also aim to increase the scope of representable properties, model types and proof tactics under our framework, and look to extend the debugging support provided to users when a decomposition cannot be validated. Lastly, we intend to explore other means of augmenting the AC development process via theorem proving, such as refactoring ACs into logically equivalent forms with more desirable quality attributes (e.g., fewer total claims or strategies).

References

1. Boomfield, R., Bishop, P.: Safety and assurance cases: past, present and possible future - an Adelard perspective. In: Proceedings of of SSS 2010. Springer, London (2010). https://doi.org/10.1007/978-1-84996-086-1_4
2. Cruanes, S., Hamon, G., Owre, S., Shankar, N.: Tool integration with the evidential tool bus. In: Giacobazzi, R., Berdine, J., Mastroeni, I. (eds.) VMCAI 2013. LNCS, vol. 7737, pp. 275–294. Springer, Heidelberg (2013). https://doi.org/10.1007/978-3-642-35873-9_18
3. Denney, E., Pai, G.: Tool support for assurance case development. J. Autom. Softw. Eng. **25**(3), 435–499 (2018)
4. Di Sandro, A., Selim, G.M.K., Salay, R., Viger, T., Chechik, M., Kokaly, S.: MMINT-A 2.0: tool support for the lifecycle of model-based safety artifacts. In: Proceedings of MODELS'20 Companion, pp. 15:1–15:5. ACM (2020)
5. Diskin, Z., Maibaum, T., Wassyng, A., Wynn-Williams, S., Lawford, M.: Assurance via model transformations and their hierarchical refinement. In: Proceedings of of MODELS 2018, pp. 426–436 (2018)
6. Dwyer, M., Avrunin, G., Corbett, J.: Property specification patterns for finite-state verification. In: Proceedings of the Second Workshop on Formal Methods in Software Practice (1998)
7. Ebner, G., Ullrich, S., Roesch, J., Avigad, J., de Moura, L.: A metaprogramming framework for formal verification. In: Proceedings of ICFP 2017, pp. 1–29. ACM (2017)
8. Greenwell, W.S., Knight, J.C., Holloway, C.M., Pease, J.J.: A taxonomy of fallacies in system safety arguments. In: Proceedings of ISSC 2006 (2006)
9. GSN Working Group: GSN Community Standard Version 2 (2011). http://www.goalstructuringnotation.info/
10. Haddon-Cave, C.: The Nimrod review: an independent review into the broader issues surrounding the loss of the RAF Nimrod MR2 Aircraft XV230 (2009)
11. Keller, R.M.: Formal verification of parallel programs. Commun. ACM **19**(7), 371–384 (1976)
12. Klein, G., et al.: seL4: formal verification of an OS Kernel. In: Proceedings of SOSP 2009, pp. 207–220 (2009)
13. Leroy, X.: A formally verified compiler back-end. J. Autom. Reason. **43**(4), 363–446 (2009)
14. de Moura, L., Kong, S., Avigad, J., van Doorn, F., von Raumer, J.: The lean theorem prover (system description). In: Felty, A.P., Middeldorp, A. (eds.) CADE 2015. LNCS (LNAI), vol. 9195, pp. 378–388. Springer, Cham (2015). https://doi.org/10.1007/978-3-319-21401-6_26

15. Nemouchi, Y., Foster, S., Gleirscher, M., Kelly, T.: Isabelle/SACM: computer-assisted assurance cases with integrated formal methods. In: Ahrendt, W., Tapia Tarifa, S.L. (eds.) IFM 2019. LNCS, vol. 11918, pp. 379–398. Springer, Cham (2019). https://doi.org/10.1007/978-3-030-34968-4_21
16. Rushby, J.: Mechanized support for assurance case argumentation. In: Nakano, Y., Satoh, K., Bekki, D. (eds.) JSAI-isAI 2013. LNCS (LNAI), vol. 8417, pp. 304–318. Springer, Cham (2014). https://doi.org/10.1007/978-3-319-10061-6_20
17. Salay, R., Kokaly, S., Di Sandro, A., Fung, N.L.S., Chechik, M.: Heterogeneous megamodel management using collection operators. Softw. Syst. Model. **19**(1), 231–260 (2019). https://doi.org/10.1007/s10270-019-00738-9
18. Shahin, R., Kokaly, S., Chechik, M.: Towards certified analysis of software product line safety cases. In: Habli, I., Sujan, M., Bitsch, F. (eds.) SAFECOMP 2021. LNCS, vol. 12852, pp. 130–145. Springer, Cham (2021). https://doi.org/10.1007/978-3-030-83903-1_9
19. Viger, T., Murphy, L., Di Sandro, A., Shahin, R., Chechik, M.: A lean approach to building valid model-based safety arguments. In: Proceedings of MODELS 2021 (2021)
20. Viger, T., Salay, R., Selim, G., Chechik, M.: Just enough formality in assurance argument structures. In: Casimiro, A., Ortmeier, F., Bitsch, F., Ferreira, P. (eds.) SAFECOMP 2020. LNCS, vol. 12234, pp. 34–49. Springer, Cham (2020). https://doi.org/10.1007/978-3-030-54549-9_3
21. Wilson, S.P., Kelly, T.P., McDermid, J.A.: Safety case development: current practice, future prospects. In: Proceedings of SAFECOMP 1997, pp. 135–156. Springer, London (1997). https://doi.org/10.1007/978-1-4471-0921-1_6

Run-time Analysis and Testing

Runtime Enforcement with Reordering, Healing, and Suppression

Yliès Falcone[(✉)] and Gwen Salaün[(✉)]

Univ. Grenoble Alpes, CNRS, Inria, Grenoble INP, LIG, 38000 Grenoble, France
{ylies.falcone,gwen.salaun}@univ-grenoble-alpes.fr

Abstract. Runtime enforcement analyses an execution trace, detects when this execution deviates from its expected behaviour with respect to a given property, and corrects the trace to make it satisfy the property. In this paper, we present new enforcement techniques that reorder actions when necessary, inject actions to the application to ensure progress of the property, and discard actions to avoid storing too many unnecessary actions. At any step of the enforcement, we provide a verdict, called enforcement trend in this work, which takes its value in a 4-valued truth domain. Our approach has been implemented in a tool and validated on several application examples. Experimental results show that our techniques better preserve the application actions, hence ensuring better service continuity.

1 Introduction

Runtime verification [1,10,18,22,25] is an alternative to traditional formal verification techniques, such as model checking, and avoids their complexity by analysing execution traces. Therefore, runtime verification has the advantage of scaling up very well without requiring a comprehensive model of the application, but at the expense of lower coverage. Runtime verification aims at verifying whether an execution trace satisfies a given correctness property. Runtime enforcement [13,20,21,24] goes beyond classic runtime verification by correcting the execution that deviates from its expected behaviour to ensure the satisfaction of a given property. To do so, a so-called *enforcement monitor* (or *enforcer* in short) accepts as input a sequence of actions and generates as output a sequence of actions respecting the property.

Existing enforcement techniques suffer from several issues. First, messages or actions involved in an execution trace may arrive to the enforcer in a different order, thus violating the property. This can occur in untimed distributed systems for instance, where it is impossible to guarantee the exact order of issued actions. Most enforcement techniques do not provide reordering strategy and discard many input actions in order to preserve the property validity. Second, the progress of the property might be prevented by the absence in the input execution trace of some specific action. A solution to ensure the property progress is to inject some expected actions to the application. Third, there is also a need

© Springer Nature Switzerland AG 2021
R. Calinescu and C. S. Păsăreanu (Eds.): SEFM 2021, LNCS 13085, pp. 47–65, 2021.
https://doi.org/10.1007/978-3-030-92124-8_3

of some removal strategies in order to decide when some actions need to be stored because they are useful in the future or deleted to avoid storing too many (unnecessary) actions.

In this paper, we present new enforcement techniques that combine reordering, healing, and suppression. Such combination presents several advantages. The enforcer first avoids any sequence of output actions that invalidates the property. It also outputs as many actions received as input as possible, and ensures progress in the property thanks to healing techniques. Finally, suppression techniques avoid to store unnecessary actions.

More precisely, the enforcement techniques take as input a sequence of actions and a property in an automata-based or logic-based formalism, and ensure that the property will not be violated. Reordering is ensured by using a bag to store the actions that do not arrive in the correct order. Healing techniques allow the addition of actions and thus ensure progress of the application and of the property. Suppression mechanisms are used in two different situations: (i) to systematically remove actions that can cause the violation of the property, and (ii) to avoid the storage of too many actions in the bag used for reordering purposes. At any moment, we provide a verdict, called enforcement trend in this work, taken from a 4-valued truth domain (forever positive, currently positive, possibly positive, possibly negative). The enforcement trend becomes possibly negative if we have to make intensive use of reordering and healing techniques for avoiding property violation. Note that forever false is always avoided by our enforcement techniques. Our approach has been implemented in a tool and validated on several examples of applications and properties. Our enforcement techniques take several parameters as input that govern the triggering of healing and suppression techniques, which can be used to tune its behaviour.

Let us illustrate on a real-world example. Imagine a dispatcher receives parcels and can move them to three conveyor belts. The initial behaviour is random or arbitrary in the sense that the dispatcher moves the parcel to any belt. However, we want the dispatcher to be fairer by moving a parcel to belts one after the other in a specific order. Reordering is helpful because it can be used to store temporarily a parcel when it is not respecting the ordering strategy of the new scheduler. However, reordering is not enough, because in some cases one may wait for a parcel aimed to a given belt for too long. In that situation, healing techniques are interesting to decide to move a parcel to a specific belt even if it was not originally planned for that one. Last but not least, suppose that the original dispatcher moves parcels to a specific belt more often than to the other belts, say the first one for instance. In that case, many actions to move parcels to that line will be issued by the dispatcher and stored in the buffer. To avoid filling the buffer with these unnecessary actions we can decide to remove some of them from the buffer.

The paper is organised as follows. Section 2 defines execution traces and the formalism used in this work for specifying properties. Section 3 presents the enforcement techniques including the possible enforcement trends and the characteristics of the enforcer. Section 4 illustrates the approach on a case study.

Section 5 introduces the tool support and different experiments we carried out to validate our solution. Section 6 discusses related work. Section 7 concludes.

2   Models

We introduce the required notions of execution traces, properties, and bags.

Execution Traces. We consider a finite set of actions A corresponding to the operations that can be executed by a program or application. An execution trace t is a sequence of actions over A. The concatenation of two actions α_1 and α_2 is denoted by $\alpha_1.\alpha_2$. The empty sequence is denoted by ϵ. Concatenation is extended to traces in the usual way. A trace σ is a *prefix* of a trace σ', noted $\sigma \preceq \sigma'$, if there exists a trace σ'' such that $\sigma' = \sigma.\sigma''$.

Properties. A property denotes a subset of (valid) execution traces in A^*. Considering a finite execution trace t and a property P, when $t \in P$, we say that t satisfies P. We model and define properties using finite-state automata.

Definition 1 (Property automaton). *A property automaton PA is a tuple* (S, s^0, Σ, T, va) *where:*

- *S is a (finite) set of* states *and $s^0 \in S$ is the* initial state*;*
- *$\Sigma \subseteq A$ is a finite set of actions called* alphabet*;*
- *$T : S \times \Sigma \to S$ is the total* transition function*;*
- *$va : S \to \{green, violet, red\}$ is the* verdict function*.*

Moreover, the verdict function is defined such that:

- *$va(s^0) \neq red$,*
- *$\forall (s, \alpha, s') \in T : va(s) = green \implies va(s') = green,$*
- *$\forall (s, \alpha, s') \in T : va(s) = red \implies va(s') = red.$*

A transition $(s_1, \alpha, s_2) \in T$ (also noted $s_1 \xrightarrow{\alpha}_T s_2$) indicates that the automaton can move from state s_1 to state s_2 by performing action α. States are associated with colors that are used to specify the satisfaction of the property: green states mean acceptance, violet states mean undetermined, and red states mean violation. We assume that the color of the initial state is not red. Property automata can be automatically generated from LTL properties according to existing monitor-synthesis techniques providing a finite-trace semantics to LTL. For instance, following [4,8], the property automaton is in a green (red, resp.) state whenever the current trace satisfies (does not satisfy, resp.) the property and all possible extensions do (do not, resp.) satisfy the property. Colors can also be assigned by the user. In such a case, we require that the marking of states is consistent with the 3-valued semantics defined in [4]. In particular, there is no transition from red states to green nor violet states, nor from green states to violet nor red states. Moreover, a property automaton is *deterministic* and *complete*. For $s \in S$, $Reach(s)$ is the set of states reachable from s with sequences over Σ, that is, the states related to s through the transitive closure of T. Moreover, for $s \in S$ and $\sigma \in \Sigma^*$, $Reach(s, \sigma)$ is the state reached from s following the transition function while reading σ. We associate action sequences with verdicts given by a property automaton: a sequence of actions $\sigma \in \Sigma^*$ is associated with the verdict of the state reached by reading σ on the property automaton: $[PA](\sigma) = va(Reach(s^0, \sigma))$.

Bags. The notion of *bag* is used by the runtime enforcer for storing actions. A bag is used to store possibly multiple occurrences of actions from a certain alphabet Σ without any order. We note $\mathbb{B}_\Sigma$ the set of bags over Σ. Function $add : \Sigma \times \mathbb{B}_\Sigma \to \mathbb{B}_\Sigma$ adds an action to a bag. Function $remove : \Sigma \times \mathbb{B}_\Sigma \to \mathbb{B}_\Sigma$ removes an instance of an action from a bag. Function $remove : 2^\Sigma \times \mathbb{B}_\Sigma \to \mathbb{B}_\Sigma$ is overloaded to define the removal of a set of actions from a buffer. Function $count : \mathbb{B}_\Sigma \to \mathbb{N}$ returns the number of actions in a bag. Function $actions : \mathbb{B}_\Sigma \to 2^\Sigma$ returns the actions stored in a bag, that is, the domain of the input bag. Predicate *empty* indicates whether a bag is empty.

3   Enforcement Techniques

In this section, we present successively the main ideas behind the enforcement techniques proposed in this paper, the details of how the enforcer works, and the formal characteristics ensured by the enforcer.

3.1   Overview

An enforcer takes as input an execution trace generated by a program or application in the form of a sequence of actions, as well as a temporal property described as a property automaton. The enforcer produces as output a sequence of actions that satisfies the property by avoiding red states, as is the case with standard enforcers as in e.g., [12,23,26]. In addition, the enforcer re-uses (previous) input actions as much as possible independently from their reception order. Any input action that is not part of the property alphabet is immediately returned as output. If the input action is part of the property alphabet: (i) if it makes the property automaton progress (there is one transition from the current state holding that action as label), the action is immediately returned as output, (ii) otherwise, the monitor needs to modify the input sequence of actions by using buffering or healing techniques. To do so, the enforcement techniques rely on three bags used by the monitor:

- a *buffer* is used to store temporarily actions that are not immediately required for making the property automaton progress;
- a *healer* stores actions that are injected to the output execution trace to ensure progress of the property automaton;
- a *well* is used to store and keep track of input actions that can only lead the property automaton to red states, and thus invalidate the property.

Moreover, the monitor takes three parameters as input. The first one (k_{heal}) corresponds to the number of actions stored in the buffer from which healing techniques are triggered. Basically, the underlying idea is to first determine whether we can make progress in the property automaton by reordering actions (and thus temporarily storing them in the buffer). However, if the buffer grows too much, we start healing by adding new actions to the system. Note that this parameter is not a bound of the buffer size. Indeed, healing ensures progress of the property automaton, but it does not ensure consumption of the actions stored in the buffer. Said differently, this parameter can be seen as a way to minimise the deviation with respect to the expected trace specified by the property. If this parameter is small, healing techniques will be triggered earlier, but at the price of injecting possibly more new actions as output.

The second parameter (k_{purge}) is optional and triggers the removal of actions in the buffer. It is a natural number corresponding to the number of action occurrences in the buffer from which we start suppressing part of them (half by default). For instance, if this parameter is fixed to 20, and at some point, 20 occurrences of some action are present in the buffer, we remove 10 of them. This parameter is useful to avoid storing too many actions in the buffer which may not be consumed.

The third parameter (k_{verd}) is related to the computation of verdicts that are called in this work *enforcement trends* since these are not definitive verdicts. At any moment of the monitoring, a truth value can be returned according to the current trace generated as output and to the current states of the different bags. We rely on a 4-valued truth domain in this work: forever positive, currently positive, possibly positive, and possibly negative. The property is forever true if a green state has been reached. The property is currently positive if the current state of the property automaton is violet, and the enforcer has not made use (yet) of reordering or healing techniques. The enforcement trend is possibly positive if the current state of the property automaton is violet, and the number of actions in the buffer and healer is below a threshold, which is the third parameter. The enforcement trend is possibly negative if the current state of the property automaton is violet, and the number of actions in the buffer and healer goes beyond the threshold.

To sum up, these three parameters are used by the enforcement mechanisms for different purposes:

- k_{heal} ($k_{heal} \geq 0$) corresponds to the number of actions stored in the buffer from which healing techniques are triggered. If $k_{heal} = 0$, healing techniques are activated from the beginning;
- k_{purge} ($k_{purge} \geq 0$) is the number of a certain occurrence of an action appearing in the buffer from which purging techniques are triggered. If $k_{purge} = 0$, purging techniques are not used at all;
- k_{verd} ($k_{verd} > 0$) is the number of actions stored in both the buffer and healer, which makes the enforcement trend go from possibly positive to possibly negative. If $k_{verd} = 1$, the enforcement trend becomes possibly negative as soon as we have one action in the buffer or in the healer.

In this work, k_{heal} and k_{verd} are computed automatically, by using the size of the property automaton alphabet or by statically analysing the property automaton. More precisely, we use for k_{heal} the length of the longest sequence or the length of the longest cycle (one iteration) in the property automaton. If there are more than k_{heal} actions in the buffer, it means we need to supplement buffering. As for k_{verd}, we choose a multiple of the size of the alphabet. For instance, if there are twice the number of elements of the alphabet in the buffer and healer, we consider we had to change quite significantly the input trace, and the enforcement trend changes from possibly positive to possibly negative. Another solution is to rely on machine learning techniques for computing these bounds by using the history of the execution trace and the decisions of the enforcer.

3.2   Enforcement Monitor

We detail how the enforcement techniques proposed in this paper work. The behaviour of the enforcer is described by a *transition system*, and requires as input three parameters k_{heal}, k_{purge} and k_{verd} as well as a property automaton $PA = (S, s^0, \Sigma, T, va)$. Let us start by defining the configurations of the enforcement monitor.

Definition 2 (Enforcement monitor configurations). *The set of configurations of the enforcement monitor is defined as $Conf = S \times \mathbb{B}_\Sigma \times \mathbb{B}_\Sigma \times \mathbb{B}_\Sigma$. A configuration of the enforcement monitor is a tuple (s, b, h, w) where s is a state of PA, and b (buffer), h (healer), and w (well) are three bags to store elements of Σ.*

The enforcement monitor takes one action from the execution trace as input, and generates none, one or several actions (at the same time) as output. More precisely, the monitor can react to an input action in different ways (see Definition 3 for a formal definition):

- *stop* if the monitor has reached a green state;
- *execute* the action as output if the action does not belong to Σ, or if the action belongs to Σ, the property automaton can execute this action in its current state, and there is no such action in the healer bag;
- *add to buffer* if the action belongs to Σ, leads to a red state, but can be used later in the property automaton (without going to a red state);
- *heal* by generating as output an action that can be executed from the current state in the property automaton. Healing techniques are triggered when adding a new action to the buffer, which makes k_{heal} to be reached;
- *remove from healer bag* if the action belongs to Σ, and there is such an action in the healer bag;
- *add to well* if the action belongs to Σ, leads to a red state, but cannot be used elsewhere in the property automaton;
- *purge buffer* when one specific action makes the buffer reach the k_{purge} bound. The monitor removes from the buffer a certain number of these actions (half by default).

Table 1. Transition rules of the enforcement monitor given an input action α.

$$\frac{\alpha \notin \Sigma}{(s, b, h, w) \overset{\alpha/\alpha}{\leadsto} (s, b, h, w)} \text{ (execute1)}$$

$$\frac{\alpha \in \Sigma \setminus h \quad s \overset{\alpha}{\to}_T s' \quad va(s') \neq red}{(s, b, h, w) \overset{\alpha/\alpha}{\leadsto} (s', b, h, w)} \text{ (execute2)}$$

$$\frac{\begin{array}{c} \alpha \in \Sigma \quad s \overset{\alpha}{\to}_T s' \quad\quad\quad\quad va(s') = red \\ \exists s'', s''' \in Q : s'' \in Reach(s) \wedge\ va(s''') \neq red \wedge\ s'' \overset{\alpha}{\to}_T s''' \end{array}}{(s, b, h, w) \overset{\alpha/\epsilon}{\leadsto} (s, add(\alpha, b), h, w)} \text{ (addtobuffer)}$$

$$\frac{\alpha \in \Sigma \cap h}{(s, b, h, w) \overset{\alpha/\epsilon}{\leadsto} (s, b, remove(\alpha, h), w)} \text{ (removefromhealer)}$$

$$\frac{\alpha \in \Sigma \quad \forall s' \in Reach(s) : s' \overset{\alpha}{\to}_T s'' \implies va(s'') = red}{(s, b, h, w) \overset{\alpha/\epsilon}{\leadsto} (s, b, h, add(\alpha, w))} \text{ (addtowell)}$$

In the following definition, we formally define the different sorts of transitions of the monitor. Note that for any input action, we apply only one of the following behaviours: stop, execute, add to buffer and eventually heal, remove from healer bag, or add to well. Correct termination is not present in this definition, because it makes the whole monitor stops in a green state. Healing techniques and buffer purge are presented aside because they do not need any input action to be executed. Triggering these two rules is possible every time an action is added to the buffer with the rule (addtobuffer). As far as healing techniques are concerned, they generate a single action as output, but this is systematically followed by a check to see whether actions from the buffer can be consumed and thus added to the output execution trace. If there are several actions that can be taken out from the buffer, the monitor always maximises this number, by executing the longest sequence of actions (random if there are several longest ones). Note that we could decide to apply several times the healing rule for ensuring a progress of several actions as output. However, we do not want to inject more actions as output than those executed by the system as input.

Definition 3 (Enforcement monitor). *The set of transitions of the enforcement monitor is the smallest subset of $Conf \times \Sigma \times \Sigma^* \times Conf$ abiding to the rules described in Tables 1 and 2. A transition $(s, b, h, w) \overset{\alpha/o}{\leadsto} (s', b', h', w')$ indicates a move from configuration (s, b, h, w) to configuration (s', b', h', w') while inputting $\alpha \in \Sigma$ and outputting $o \in \Sigma^*$.*

Table 2. Transition rules of the enforcement monitor after adding to buffer.

$$
\dfrac{
\begin{array}{c}
\forall i : \alpha_i \in b \qquad \beta = gen(s, PA) \\[4pt]
count(b) > k_{\text{heal}} \\[4pt]
Reach(s, \beta.\alpha_1 \ldots \alpha_n) = s'
\end{array}
}{
(s, b, h, w) \xrightsquigarrow{\epsilon/\beta.\alpha_1 \ldots \alpha_n} (s', remove(\{\alpha_1, \ldots, \alpha_n\}, b), add(\beta, h), w)
} \text{ (heal)}
$$

$$
\dfrac{
b(\alpha) > k_{\text{purge}}
}{
(s, b, h, w) \xrightsquigarrow{\epsilon/\epsilon} (s, b, h, purge(\alpha, w))
} \text{ (purgebuffer)}
$$

Rules in Table 1 apply when a new action is received as input. Rules in Table 2 apply when an action has been added to the buffer.

Function gen, used in the former definition (Table 2), generates an action that makes the property automaton progress, and thus possibly leads to the execution of additional actions as output (by taking them from the buffer). The healer never adds an action leading to a red state because our enforcement techniques systematically avoid red states. The healer does not add an action leading to a green state either, because we want the property to become true thanks to an input action. Therefore, the healer can output an action leading to a violet state or does not output anything (this is the case when outgoing transitions can lead to red and green states only).

Definition 4 (Healing). *Given a (current) state s of PA, the healer returns an action or the empty word as follows:*

$$
gen(s, PA) = \begin{cases} \alpha \text{ if } s \xrightarrow{\alpha}_T s' \text{ and } va(s') = violet; \\ \epsilon \text{ otherwise.} \end{cases}
$$

3.3   Enforcement Trend

An *enforcement trend* can be associated with the current configuration of the enforcement monitor. An enforcement trend has four possible values: forever positive, currently positive, possibly positive, and possibly negative. Recall that the enforcement monitor avoids that the output sequence makes the input property automaton reach red states.

Definition 5 (Enforcement trend). *The enforcement trend associated with a configuration (s, b, h, w) of the enforcement monitor is defined as:*

- *forever positive if $va(s) = green$;*
- *currently positive if $va(s) = violet$, empty(b) and empty(h);*
- *possibly positive if $va(s) = violet$ and $count(b) + count(h) < k_{verd}$;*
- *possibly negative if $va(s) = violet$ and $count(b) + count(h) \geq k_{verd}$.*

Note that parameter k_{verd} can be fixed in different ways: arbitrarily, using the size of the alphabet (e.g., twice or thrice the size of the alphabet) or by analysing statically the structure of the property automaton (e.g., length of the longest path to green states or length of the longest cycle if there is no green states).

3.4   Characteristics

The enforcement techniques proposed in this paper are online, untimed, and operational. Online means that the monitor takes as input a trace built from the running monitored system (as opposed to an offline postmortem trace). Untimed means that the enforcement monitor does not account from the physical time that elapses between these actions. Operational means that the provided definition describes *how* the enforcement monitor executes and can thus directly be used as a guide for the implementation.

In the rest of this section, we focus more particularly on the non-functional properties of enforcement monitors with healing. We revisit the classical characteristics of soundness, monotonicity, and transparency, taking into account the healer and the well. Moreover, we introduce two properties that stem from the addition of a healer to enforcement monitors, namely *progress* and *healing as a last resort*.

For this, we see and reason on an enforcement monitor as an enforcement function $E^{PA} : \Sigma^* \to \Sigma^* \times \mathbb{B}_\Sigma \times \mathbb{B}_\Sigma \times \mathbb{B}_\Sigma$, dedicated to a property automaton PA. The enforcement function describes the enforcement monitor as a relation between the input and the corresponding output, content of the buffer, content of the healer and content of the well. When $E^{PA}(in) = (o, b, h, w)$, it means that when the enforcement monitor inputs in (one action after the other), the overall produced output is o and the contents of the buffer, the healer, and the well are respectively b, h, and w.

In the following, we shall use the dot notation to refer to the elements in a configuration of the enforcement monitor and for $E^{PA}(in) = (o, b, h, w)$, we note $E^{PA}(in).\text{out} = o$, $E^{PA}(in).\text{buff} = b$, $E^{PA}(in).\text{heal} = h$, and $E^{PA}(in).\text{well} = w$.

An enforcement monitor is *sound*, meaning that for any input sequence, the property is not violated by the output sequence produced by the enforcement monitor.

Proposition 1 (Soundness). $\forall in \in \Sigma^* : [PA](E^{PA}(in).\text{out}) \neq red$

Proof (Sketch). Soundness holds because the enforcement monitor never produces an action as output if it leads to a red state starting from the state stored in its configuration. Moreover, the state stored in its configuration is the state reached by executing the output in the property automaton.

An enforcement monitor is *monotone*, meaning that it respects the following physical constraints: the produced output cannot be undone and the actions discarded in the well are definitely lost.

Proposition 2 states that the output (sequence) of the enforcer is a growing function of the input sequence.

Proposition 2 (Monotonicity when outputting actions).
$\forall in, in' \in \Sigma^* : in \preceq in' \implies E^{PA}(in).\text{out} \preceq E^{PA}(in').\text{out}$

Proof (Sketch). Monotonicity of the output is a straightforward consequence of the fact that the output sequence of the enforcement monitor is formed by concatenating the output actions produced while reading the input sequence.

Proposition 3 similarly states that the well of the enforcer is a set where one can only add new elements.

Proposition 3 (Monotonicity when discarding actions).
$\forall in, in' \in \Sigma^* : in \preceq in' \implies E^{PA}(in).\text{well} \subseteq E^{PA}(in').\text{well}$

Proof (Sketch). Monotonicity when discarding actions is a direct consequence of the fact that actions are only discarded with rule (addtowell), which accumulates actions in the well.

An enforcement monitor is *transparent*, meaning that (i) it intervenes (by making the output sequence differ from the input) only when the input sequence violates the property, and (ii) the input actions are found either in output, in the buffer or in the well, and only the healer can generate additional actions.

Proposition 4 (Transparency).

$- \forall in \in \Sigma^* : [PA](in) \neq red \implies E(in).\text{out} = in$
$- \forall in \in \Sigma^* :$
$\quad \text{actions}(E^{PA}(in).\text{out}) \cup \text{actions}(E^{PA}(in).\text{buff}) \cup \text{actions}(E^{PA}(in).\text{well})$
$\quad \backslash \text{actions}(E^{PA}(in).\text{heal}) = \text{actions}(in).$

Proof (Sketch). The first part of transparency holds because if the input sequence does not violate the property, then it means that it leads to a violet or a green state in the underlying property automaton. Henceforth, only rules (execute1) and (execute2) have been applied when inputting *in*.

The second part of transparency holds because input actions either go to output, to the buffer or to the well. Additional actions are exactly those in the healer part of the configurations. Actions created by the healer are later removed whenever they appear as input.

An enforcement monitor ensures progress, meaning that the produced output sequence keeps growing when the healer can ($|E(in).\text{buff}| \geq k_{\text{heal}}$) and should ($[PA](E(in).\alpha) = red$) intervene.

Proposition 5 (Progress).
$\forall in \in \Sigma^*, \forall \alpha \in \Sigma :$
$\quad |E^{PA}(in).\text{buff}| \geq k_{\text{heal}} \wedge [PA]\left((E^{PA}(in).\text{out}).\alpha\right) = red$
$\quad\quad \implies |E^{PA}(in.\alpha)| > |E^{PA}(in)|$

Proof (Sketch). Progress holds because when the buffer contains more than k_{heal} actions and $[PA]\left((E^{PA}(in).\text{out}).\alpha\right)$, only rule (heal) can apply. Function *gen* returns some action that lead to a violet state from the state reached in the property automaton after outputting $[PA](E^{PA}(in)).\text{out}$. Such a state is necessarily violet and the action thus necessarily exists because of the constraints on state colors.

An enforcement monitor *heals as a last resort*, meaning that whenever the healer intervenes (which is witnessed by its bag being non-empty), it means that the new input action cannot be produced as output and that the healing threshold has been reached for the buffer size.

Proposition 6 (Healing as last resort).
$\forall in \in \Sigma^*, \forall \alpha \in \Sigma :$
$$E^{PA}(in).\text{heal} = \epsilon \wedge E^{PA}(in \cdot \alpha).\text{heal} \neq \epsilon$$
$$\implies [PA](E^{PA}(in).\alpha) = red \wedge |E^{PA}(in).\text{buff}| \geq k_{\text{heal}}$$

Proof (Sketch). Healing as a last resort holds because healing can (only) happen by applying rule (heal), which requires that the buffer contains more than k_{heal} actions. Moreover, the input action causing healing to happen must have been put into the buffer by previously applying rule (addtobuffer) and this led to the buffer size to exceed k_{heal}.

4   Case Study

We illustrate our approach with the example mentioned in the introduction. Suppose that a delivery company uses a dispatcher, which receives parcels from an input conveyor belt and moves them to three output conveyor belts (we could extend this example to as many belts as required). The initial behaviour of the dispatcher is to move a parcel to any belt. Assume now we want the dispatcher to be fairer by moving a parcel to the belts one after the other in a specific order. To do so, we first need to model this specification using the property automaton given in Fig. 1, where we define the repetition of a fair repartition among three conveyor belts. When these actions arrive in a different order, this corresponds to an incorrect behaviour (red state). The automaton also exhibits a case of correct termination with the STOP transition going to a green state. The alphabet of the property is {BELT1, BELT2, BELT3, STOP} and the overall alphabet also consists of two other actions: PARCEL (arrival of a parcel) and PAUSE (pause of the input belt for five seconds for instance). We decide to start healing techniques when there are three actions in the buffer ($k_{\text{heal}} = 3$), which corresponds to the length of the longest sequence of actions in the automaton (without passing twice through the same state). We choose $k_{\text{verd}} = 8$, which is twice the number of elements in the alphabet of the property automaton.

Let us illustrate how our approach works in practice by using an excerpt of the application of the enforcement techniques on this example (Fig. 2), where we replace BELT1, BELT2 and BELT3 with B1, B2 and B3, respectively, for the

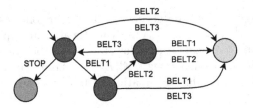

Fig. 1. Parcel dispatcher property automaton

sake of readability. Each row in the result shows an input action, the resulting output action(s), the states of buffer, healer, well if not empty, and finally the enforcement trend. At the beginning of this trace, all bags are empty and the trend is (currently) positive. The last output action was BELT2 (l.85), so we expect BELT3 to be the next action of the property automaton. However, the enforcer receives BELT1 (l.88) and BELT2 twice (l.92 and l.95), so it moves these three actions to the buffer. Then it receives BELT3 (l.99) and it can output BELT3, BELT1 and BELT2. This illustrates the use of reordering techniques.

We now look at an example of healing. At l.109, the buffer contains three actions (BELT2, BELT2, BELT3). The last output action was BELT3 (l.104), so BELT1 is required now. However, this is BELT2 that is received as input (l.110), which is a fourth action to add to the buffer, thus triggering healing techniques. The enforcement monitor decides to move a parcel to BELT1. This action is added to the healer and appears as output. This step forward in the property automaton also allows the consumption from the buffer of actions BELT2 and BELT3, explaining why we have three actions appearing as output on l.110.

Last but not least, looking at l.124 for instance, we see that there are two BELT1 in the healer, and the input action is BELT1 as well. In that situation, since the enforcer owes somehow two BELT1 actions to the application, it does not generate anything as output but just removes one BELT1 from the healer.

5   Tool Support and Experiments

In this section, we first present the implementation of the enforcement techniques. Second, we introduce different experiments carried out to evaluate our approach in terms of configuration size and enforcement trend. Finally, we compare our solution with another approach based only on reordering.

5.1   Tool Support

The enforcement techniques presented in this paper have been implemented in a prototype tool written in Python. Note that an option of the tool allows the user to make use of reordering techniques only or reordering and healing techniques together. The tool mainly consists of three modules: one for representing and manipulating property automata, one implementing several strategies for generating input actions, and one implementing the enforcement techniques.

85 - B3 → B3 B1 B2 - trend: currently positive
86 - PARCEL → PARCEL - trend: currently positive
87 - PAUSE → PAUSE - trend: currently positive
88 - B1 → - buffer: ['B1'] - trend: possibly positive
89 - PARCEL → PARCEL - buffer: ['B1'] - trend: possibly positive
90 - PAUSE → PAUSE - buffer: ['B1'] - trend: possibly positive
91 - PARCEL → PARCEL - buffer: ['B1'] - trend: possibly positive
92 - B2 → - buffer: ['B1', 'B2'] - trend: possibly positive
93 - PARCEL → PARCEL - buffer: ['B1', 'B2'] - trend: possibly positive
94 - PAUSE → PAUSE - buffer: ['B1', 'B2'] - trend: possibly positive
95 - B2 → - buffer: ['B1', 'B2', 'B2'] - trend: possibly positive
96 - PARCEL → PARCEL - buffer: ['B1', 'B2', 'B2'] - trend: possibly positive
97 - PARCEL → PARCEL - buffer: ['B1', 'B2', 'B2'] - trend: possibly positive
98 - PARCEL → PARCEL - buffer: ['B1', 'B2', 'B2'] - trend: possibly positive
99 - B3 → B3 B1 B2 - buffer: ['B2'] - trend: possibly positive
100 - PARCEL → PARCEL - buffer: ['B2'] - trend: possibly positive
101 - B2 → - buffer: ['B2', 'B2'] - trend: possibly positive
102 - PARCEL → PARCEL - buffer: ['B2', 'B2'] - trend: possibly positive
103 - PARCEL → PARCEL - buffer: ['B2', 'B2'] - trend: possibly positive
104 - B3 → B3 - buffer: ['B2', 'B2'] - trend: possibly positive
105 - PARCEL → PARCEL - buffer: ['B2', 'B2'] - trend: possibly positive
106 - PAUSE → PAUSE - buffer: ['B2', 'B2'] - trend: possibly positive
107 - PARCEL → PARCEL - buffer: ['B2', 'B2'] - trend: possibly positive
108 - B3 → - buffer: ['B2', 'B2', 'B3'] - trend: possibly positive
109 - PARCEL → PARCEL - buffer: ['B2', 'B2', 'B3'] - trend: possibly positive
110 - B2 → B1 B2 B3 - buffer: ['B2', 'B2'] - healer: ['B1'] - trend: possibly positive
111 - PARCEL → PARCEL - buffer: ['B2', 'B2'] - healer: ['B1'] - trend: possibly positive
112 - B3 → - buffer: ['B2', 'B2', 'B3'] - healer: ['B1'] - trend: possibly positive
113 - PAUSE → PAUSE - buffer: ['B2', 'B2', 'B3'] - healer: ['B1'] - trend: possibly positive
114 - B2 → B1 B2 B3 - buffer: ['B2', 'B2'] - healer: ['B1', 'B1'] - trend: possibly positive
115 - PARCEL → PARCEL - buffer: ['B2', 'B2'] - healer: ['B1', 'B1'] - trend: possibly positive
116 - PARCEL → PARCEL - buffer: ['B2', 'B2'] - healer: ['B1', 'B1'] - trend: possibly positive
117 - B3 → - buffer: ['B2', 'B2', 'B3'] - healer: ['B1', 'B1'] - trend: possibly positive
118 - PARCEL → PARCEL - buffer: ['B2', 'B2', 'B3'] - healer: ['B1', 'B1'] - trend: possibly positive
119 - PARCEL → PARCEL - buffer: ['B2', 'B2', 'B3'] - healer: ['B1', 'B1'] - trend: possibly positive
120 - B3 → B1 B2 B3 - buffer: ['B2', 'B3'] - healer: ['B1', 'B1', 'B1'] - trend: possibly positive
121 - PARCEL → PARCEL - buffer: ['B2', 'B3'] - healer: ['B1', 'B1', 'B1'] - trend: possibly positive
122 - PAUSE → PAUSE - buffer: ['B2', 'B3'] - healer: ['B1', 'B1', 'B1'] - trend: possibly positive
123 - PAUSE → PAUSE - buffer: ['B2', 'B3'] - healer: ['B1', 'B1', 'B1'] - trend: possibly positive
124 - B1 → - buffer: ['B2', 'B3'] - healer: ['B1', 'B1'] - trend: possibly positive
125 - PARCEL → PARCEL - buffer: ['B2', 'B3'] - healer: ['B1', 'B1'] - trend: possibly positive
126 - B1 → - buffer: ['B2', 'B3'] - healer: ['B1'] - trend: possibly positive
127 - PARCEL → PARCEL - buffer: ['B2', 'B3'] - healer: ['B1'] - trend: possibly positive
128 - B2 → - buffer: ['B2', 'B3', 'B2'] - healer: ['B1'] - trend: possibly positive
129 - PARCEL → PARCEL - buffer: ['B2', 'B3', 'B2'] - healer: ['B1'] - trend: possibly positive
130 - PAUSE → PAUSE - buffer: ['B2', 'B3', 'B2'] - healer: ['B1'] - trend: possibly positive
131 - B1 → - buffer: ['B2', 'B3', 'B2'] - trend: possibly positive
132 - PARCEL → PARCEL - buffer: ['B2', 'B3', 'B2'] - trend: possibly positive
133 - PARCEL → PARCEL - buffer: ['B2', 'B3', 'B2'] - trend: possibly positive
134 - B2 → B1 B2 B3 - buffer: ['B2', 'B2'] - healer: ['B1'] - trend: possibly positive
135 - PARCEL → PARCEL - buffer: ['B2', 'B2'] - healer: ['B1'] - trend: possibly positive
136 - PARCEL → PARCEL - buffer: ['B2', 'B2'] - healer: ['B1'] - trend: possibly positive
137 - B1 → - buffer: ['B2', 'B2'] - trend: possibly positive
138 - PAUSE → PAUSE - buffer: ['B2', 'B2'] - trend: possibly positive
139 - PARCEL → PARCEL - buffer: ['B2', 'B2'] - trend: possibly positive
140 - PARCEL → PARCEL - buffer: ['B2', 'B2'] - trend: possibly positive
141 - B3 → - buffer: ['B2', 'B2', 'B3'] - trend: possibly positive
142 - PARCEL → PARCEL - buffer: ['B2', 'B2', 'B3'] - trend: possibly positive
143 - PARCEL → PARCEL - buffer: ['B2', 'B2', 'B3'] - trend: possibly positive
144 - B1 → B1 B2 B3 - buffer: ['B2'] - trend: possibly positive
145 - PARCEL → PARCEL - buffer: ['B2'] - trend: possibly positive
146 - PARCEL → PARCEL - buffer: ['B2'] - trend: possibly positive
147 - B1 → B1 B2 - trend: currently positive
148 - PAUSE → PAUSE - trend: currently positive
149 - PARCEL → PARCEL - trend: currently positive

Fig. 2. Illustration of the enforcement techniques on the parcel dispatcher

5.2 Experiments

In our experiments, we applied our approach to several examples, from short
execution traces (hundreds of actions as input) to very long traces consisting
of hundreds of thousands of actions as input. The goal of these experiments is
to show the configuration size and the final enforcement trend, which is maintained as much as possible in the possibly positive value. Table 3 presents the

results of some representative experiments. The first five columns describe the example with a short textual description, the property automaton, the length of the simulation in terms of input actions, and the k_{heal} and k_{verd} parameters. In these experiments, k_{heal} is equal to twice the longest sequence in the property automaton and k_{verd} is equal to three times the size of the property automaton alphabet. The last four columns present the result by giving the average size of the three bags (buffer, healer, well) as well as the enforcement trend as a percentage. This trend shows for how many actions as input, the enforcement trend was currently or possibly positive. As an example, if the execution run consists of 1000 actions, and the enforcement trend is currently or possibly positive for 800 of these actions, the result is 80%. During these experiments, we chose to not purge the buffer, which corresponds to a value of 0 for k_{purge}. Each line of the table was computed by repeating 100 times the simulation. Since input traces are always different, this repetition allows us to compute more accurate output values. Note that we do not use property automata with green states, because green states make our simulation stop, and we prefer to run it for a specific length here (third column).

First of all, we can see in the table that the enforcement trend is mostly currently or possibly positive. We will show in the next subsection how our approach compares in that aspect with similar approaches. The variability of the enforcement trend in the table (70%, 80% or 90%) is due to the variability of the actions used as input. Similarly to the enforcement trend, we can see that the average number of actions in the buffer or generated by the healer remain rather stable when the length of the trace increases. This shows that, for these examples, the approach succeeds in maintaining a positive trend without making intensive use of reordering and healing, even when the size of the execution trace increases. Note also that the number of actions in the buffer remains on average below the k_{heal} parameter, even though the buffer contents can go above k_{heal}, which is not a bound of the buffer. This happens because we never prevent adding values to the buffer, even when healing is triggered. The final row of the table (no untimely reboot) shows an example where the well is used to store reboot actions that can only lead to red states.

5.3 Comparison

In the final part of this section, we compare the results obtained with our enforcement techniques with respect to an existing enforcement approach based on action reordering and suppression [9]. We chose that work because it provides solutions similar to those proposed in this paper. More precisely, we compare three techniques: (i) our approach where reordering is used but not healing, (ii) our approach where we use both reordering and healing, and (iii) the approach presented in [9]. In a first set of experiments, we chose the two first examples in Table 3 and we apply the three techniques to these two examples. Table 4 shows the results where we fixed the simulation length at 1,000 actions. The two last columns of this table show the two main differences between these

Table 3. Experimental results

Example	PA	|Simul.|	k_h	k_v	|B|	|H|	|W|	Positive?
Alternating in/out		1,000			2.07	1.04	0	85.82%
		5,000			2.37	1.66	0	78.57%
		10,000	4	6	2.51	2.07	0	74.67%
		50,000			2.48	1.96	0	75.29%
		100,000			2.52	1.99	0	75.20%
		500,000			2.52	2.08	0	75.09%
Belts dispatcher		1,000			4.05	0.85	0	90.75%
		5,000			5.34	1.55	0	76.93%
		10,000	6	9	5.65	1.73	0	73.84%
		50,000			5.85	1.78	0	71.88%
		100,000			5.82	1.76	0	72.36%
No 3 req. without store		1,000			1.56	0.03	0	95.06%
		5,000			1.88	0.16	0	91.74%
		10,000	8	6	1.95	0.13	0	91.67%
		50,000			2.01	0.21	0	90.45%
		100,000			1.96	0.18	0	91.20%
No untimely reboot		1,000			2.12	0.92	25.29	94.28%
		5,000			2.43	1.94	128.12	87.13%
		10,000	4	9	2.40	1.36	257.40	91.51%
		50,000			2.55	2.24	1281.91	84.91%
		100,000			2.47	1.84	2562.46	87.77%

approaches, namely the number of actions appearing as output and the enforcement trend. In our approach, we do not discard any action as input (we do not reach 1,000 because there are a few actions remaining in the buffer when we stop the simulation) and use all of them while trying to maintain a positive verdict for the property automaton. In contrast, [9] favors the preservation of a correct verdict by discarding valid input actions, those that do arrive in the right order and make the verdict become false (about 10% of input actions in Table 4).

In a second set of experiments carried out on the example presented in Sect. 4 (belts dispatcher), we compare our two approaches (reordering only vs. reordering + healing) using execution runs of different lengths (500, 1,000, and then every 1,000 up to 10,000). For each length, we repeated the simulation 100 times to have accurate results (one simulation instance means that we use the same trace as input for both approaches). As a result, we computed for how many actions as input, the enforcement trend was currently or possibly positive. Figure 3 shows the resulting curves for these two techniques with percentage of truth value over execution run (vertical axis) and execution run length (horizontal axis). We can see that reordering combined with healing techniques obtain

Table 4. Comparison with [9]

Approach	PA	|Simul.|	k_h	k_v	|Out. act.|	Positive?
Reordering					996.1	77.06%
Reordering + healing	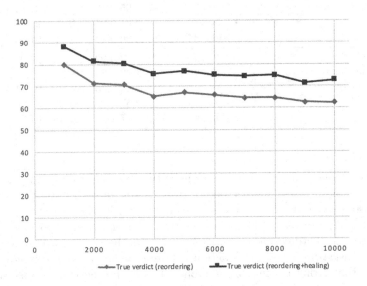	1,000	4	6	998.3	85.82%
Pinisetty *et al.* [9]					910.4	100%
Reordering					994.2	80.12%
Reordering + healing		1,000	6	9	996.7	90.75%
Pinisetty *et al.* [9]					902.8	100%

the best results by maintaining a positive enforcement trend for a larger number of inputs (about 70–90%), whereas results for reordering only provide lower positive results (about 60–80%).

Fig. 3. Reordering techniques only vs. Reordering + Healing Techniques (percentage of truth value on the vertical axis and execution run length on the horizontal axis)

6   Related Work

Several enforcement techniques have been proposed in the literature considering different kinds of inputs, architectures, or models. In this section, we compare our approach with closest related work. The interested reader can find comprehensive overviews of the related techniques in [11,15].

The approach in [5] monitors distributed systems with respect to LTL properties using an alternative to the orchestration and migration approaches. Their solution relies on a choreography-based architecture where monitors are organised as a tree across the distributed system. The choreography-based decentralised monitoring is formalised and shows how to synthesise a network from an LTL formula, resulting in an algorithm working on top of an LTL network.

Regarding runtime enforcement of untimed properties, several models and frameworks have been proposed. We can mention security automata [26]; which can stop the underlying system upon property violation, edit-automata [23] and generic enforcement monitors [12] which can insert or suppress actions. Regarding runtime enforcement of timed properties, [13] provides a recent overview of related work. As an example, [9] considers runtime enforcement for timed specifications modelled as timed automata. These enforcement mechanisms work by delaying actions to match timing constraints, and suppressing actions when no delaying is appropriate, thus possibly allowing for longer executions. Enforcement mechanisms are formalised at several levels of abstraction (enforcement function, monitor, and algorithms), which facilitates the design and implementation of these mechanisms.

The approach in [2] verifies distributed systems at runtime where components communicate with monitors over unreliable channels, meaning that messages can be delayed, reordered, or even lost. The authors propose an extension of the real-time logic MTL, which provides a new three-valued semantics that is well suited for runtime verification as it accounts for partial knowledge about a system's behaviour. They also present online algorithms that reason soundly and completely about streams where actions can occur out of order.

As proposed in some existing works, e.g. [2], we tackle the reordering problem by storing and delaying messages when necessary. In addition, we complement reordering with healing that injects some new actions to ensure progress of the application while satisfying the property being analysed. Removing actions is also supported in our solution as it is in some other work, e.g., [9]. The novelty of our work resides in the combination of these three techniques (reordering, healing, suppression).

7   Concluding Remarks

We have presented new enforcement techniques, which accept as input a sequence of actions and a property automaton, and generate as output a sequence of actions that satisfies the given property. These techniques rely on three mechanisms that reorder input actions when necessary, inject new actions to the application for ensuring property progress (healing), and remove actions if they are not required or if they risk to congest the buffering system. The enforcement techniques were implemented and validated on several examples.

A first perspective of this work is to support *distributed enforcement*. This entails considering actions from several components and several input execution traces. For this, we can take inspiration from the distributed and decentralized runtime verification approaches [3,7,15]. Distributed mechanisms would require to rely on synchronization mechanisms, similar to those used in choreography-based development [16,17], to take consistent distributed decisions. Another perspective is to compute automatically system-specific or domain-specific values for the parameters k_{heal} and k_{verd} by relying on the trace history and by using machine learning techniques. Finally, we plan to apply our enforcement approach to concrete application areas. One idea in that direction is to enforce properties during the execution of BPMN processes [19], particularly for optimization purposes [6,14].

Acknowledgements. The authors would like to thank the anonymous reviewers for their useful comments. This work was supported by the Région Auvergne-Rhône-Alpes within the *"Pack Ambition Recherche"* programme, the H2020-ECSEL-2018-IA call – Grant Agreement number 826276 (CPS4EU), the French ANR project ANR-20-CE39-0009 (SEVERITAS), and the LabEx PERSYVAL-Lab (ANR-11-LABX-0025-01) funded by the French program Investissement d'avenir.

References

1. Bartocci, E., Falcone, Y., Francalanza, A., Reger, G.: Introduction to runtime verification. In: Bartocci, E., Falcone, Y. (eds.) Lectures on Runtime Verification. LNCS, vol. 10457, pp. 1–33. Springer, Cham (2018). https://doi.org/10.1007/978-3-319-75632-5_1
2. Basin, D.A., Klaedtke, F., Zalinescu, E.: Runtime verification over out-of-order streams. ACM Trans. Comput. Log. **21**(1), 5:1–5:43 (2020)
3. Bauer, A., Falcone, Y.: Decentralised LTL monitoring. Formal Methods Syst. Des. **48**(1–2), 46–93 (2016)
4. Bauer, A., Leucker, M., Schallhart, C.: Runtime verification for LTL and TLTL. ACM Trans. Softw. Eng. Methodol. **20**(4), 14:1–14:64 (2011)
5. Colombo, C., Falcone, Y.: Organising LTL monitors over distributed systems with a global clock. Formal Methods Syst. Des. **49**(1–2), 109–158 (2016)
6. Durán, F., Rocha, C., Salaün, G.: Analysis of the runtime resource provisioning of BPMN processes using Maude. In: Escobar, S., Martí-Oliet, N. (eds.) WRLA 2020. LNCS, vol. 12328, pp. 38–56. Springer, Cham (2020). https://doi.org/10.1007/978-3-030-63595-4_3
7. El-Hokayem, A., Falcone, Y.: On the monitoring of decentralized specifications: semantics, properties, analysis, and simulation. ACM Trans. Softw. Eng. Methodol. **29**(1), 1:1–1:57 (2020)
8. Falcone, Y., Fernandez, J., Mounier, L.: What can you verify and enforce at runtime? Int. J. Softw. Tools Technol. Transf. **14**(3), 349–382 (2012)
9. Falcone, Y., Jéron, T., Marchand, H., Pinisetty, S.: Runtime enforcement of regular timed properties by suppressing and delaying events. Sci. Comput. Program. **123**, 2–41 (2016)
10. Falcone, Y., Krstic, S., Reger, G., Traytel, D.: A taxonomy for classifying runtime verification tools. Int. J. Softw. Tools Technol. Transf. **23**(2), 255–284 (2021)
11. Falcone, Y., Mariani, L., Rollet, A., Saha, S.: Runtime failure prevention and reaction. In: Bartocci, E., Falcone, Y. (eds.) Lectures on Runtime Verification. LNCS, vol. 10457, pp. 103–134. Springer, Cham (2018). https://doi.org/10.1007/978-3-319-75632-5_4

12. Falcone, Y., Mounier, L., Fernandez, J.-C., Richier, J.-L.: Runtime enforcement monitors: composition, synthesis, and enforcement abilities. Formal Methods Syst. Des. **38**(3), 223–262 (2011)

13. Falcone, Y., Pinisetty, S.: On the runtime enforcement of timed properties. In: Finkbeiner, B., Mariani, L. (eds.) RV 2019. LNCS, vol. 11757, pp. 48–69. Springer, Cham (2019). https://doi.org/10.1007/978-3-030-32079-9_4

14. Falcone, Y., Salaün, G., Zuo, A.: Semi-automated modelling of optimized BPMN processes. In: Proceedings of SCC 2021. IEEE (2021)

15. Francalanza, A., Pérez, J.A., Sánchez, C.: Runtime verification for decentralised and distributed systems. In: Bartocci, E., Falcone, Y. (eds.) Lectures on Runtime Verification. LNCS, vol. 10457, pp. 176–210. Springer, Cham (2018). https://doi.org/10.1007/978-3-319-75632-5_6

16. Güdemann, M., Poizat, P., Salaün, G., Ye, L.: VerChor: a framework for the design and verification of choreographies. IEEE Trans. Serv. Comput. **9**(4), 647–660 (2016)

17. Güdemann, M., Salaün, G., Ouederni, M.: Counterexample guided synthesis of monitors for realizability enforcement. In: Chakraborty, S., Mukund, M. (eds.) ATVA 2012. LNCS, pp. 238–253. Springer, Heidelberg (2012). https://doi.org/10.1007/978-3-642-33386-6_20

18. Havelund, K., Goldberg, A.: Verify your runs. In: Meyer, B., Woodcock, J. (eds.) VSTTE 2005. LNCS, vol. 4171, pp. 374–383. Springer, Heidelberg (2008). https://doi.org/10.1007/978-3-540-69149-5_40

19. ISO/IEC. International Standard 19510, Information technology - Business Process Model and Notation (2013)

20. Khoury, R., Hallé, S.: Runtime enforcement with partial control. In: Garcia-Alfaro, J., Kranakis, E., Bonfante, G. (eds.) FPS 2015. LNCS, vol. 9482, pp. 102–116. Springer, Cham (2016). https://doi.org/10.1007/978-3-319-30303-1_7

21. Khoury, R., Tawbi, N.: Which security policies are enforceable by runtime monitors? A survey. Comput. Sci. Rev. **6**(1), 27–45 (2012)

22. Leucker, M., Schallhart, C.: A brief account of runtime verification. J. Log. Algebraic Methods Program. **78**(5), 293–303 (2009)

23. Ligatti, J., Bauer, L., Walker, D.: Edit automata: enforcement mechanisms for run-time security policies. Int. J. Inf. Secur. **4**(1), 2–16 (2005)

24. Ligatti, J., Reddy, S.: A theory of runtime enforcement, with results. In: Gritzalis, D., Preneel, B., Theoharidou, M. (eds.) ESORICS 2010. LNCS, vol. 6345, pp. 87–100. Springer, Heidelberg (2010). https://doi.org/10.1007/978-3-642-15497-3_6

25. Sánchez, C., et al.: A survey of challenges for runtime verification from advanced application domains (beyond software). Formal Methods Syst. Des. **54**(3), 279–335 (2019)

26. Schneider, F.B.: Enforceable security policies. ACM Trans. Inf. Syst. Secur. **3**(1), 30–50 (2000)

Monitoring First-Order Interval Logic

Klaus Havelund[1(✉)], Moran Omer[2], and Doron Peled[2]

[1] Jet Propulsion Laboratory, California Institute of Technology, Pasadena, USA
[2] Department of Computer Science, Bar Ilan University, Ramat Gan, Israel

Abstract. Runtime verification is used for monitoring the execution of systems, e.g. checking sequences of reported events against formal specifications. Typically the specification refers to the individual monitored events. In this work we perceive the events as defining intervals, each defined by a *begin* and a subsequent *end* event. Allen's logic allows assertions about the relationship between such named intervals. We suggest a formalism that extends Allen's logic into a first-order logic that allows quantification over intervals; in addition, intervals can carry data. We provide a monitoring algorithm and describe an implementation and experiments performed with it. We furthermore describe an alternative method for monitoring properties in this logic, by translating them into first-order past-time temporal logic, monitored with the tool DejaVu.

1 Introduction

Runtime verification allows monitoring of system executions, represented as execution traces, against a specification, either online as traces are generated, or offline after their generation. The monitored trace consists typically of events that can also carry data. The specification is often given using a temporal logic or as a state machine. The runtime algorithm checks for compatibility with the execution in an incremental way, where some summary of the reported execution prefix is updated upon the arrival of each newly occurring event. This practice is aimed at both providing an early verdict, and at managing the incremental computational effort between consecutive events. Keeping pace with the speed of the reported events is a challenge to online monitoring.

While runtime verification, as described above, is concerned with monitoring specifications that refer to single observed *events*, we study here monitoring specifications that refer to observed *intervals*. We consider an interval as being generated from a pair of observed *begin* and *end* events, with appropriate parameters. The focus on intervals is motivated by our experience [14], that engineers, as a way of comprehending complexity, tend to perceive large traces as being partitioned into overlapping sections (intervals), each concerned with a particular task. Temporal logic does not capture this sectional view well, since the formulas get overly complex.

The research performed by the first author was carried out at Jet Propulsion Laboratory, California Institute of Technology, under a contract with the National Aeronautics and Space Administration. The research performed by the second and third authors was partially funded by Israeli Science Foundation grant 1464/18: "Efficient Runtime Verification for Systems with Lots of Data and its Applications".

R. Calinescu and C. S. Păsăreanu (Eds.): SEFM 2021, LNCS 13085, pp. 66–83, 2021.
https://doi.org/10.1007/978-3-030-92124-8_4

Allen's (temporal) logic [1], also referred to as *Allen's interval algebra*, is a popular formalism for reasoning about the relation between intervals that occur on a timeline. It is often used for planning in AI. Allen's logic deals with a finite set of named intervals, referring directly to the interval names, e.g., $A < B$ means that the interval A must end before the interval B begins. This can be quite restrictive for describing the behavior of systems, where many intervals with the same characteristics can occur, and where distinguishing specific intervals directly by name in the specification is inconvenient or even impossible.

We look at the more general problem of monitoring properties where we can *quantify over intervals*, as e.g., in the formula $\exists A \exists B \ (A < B)$, stating that there exist (at least) two intervals A and B such that A ends before B begins. We also consider the problem where intervals may contain data. Consequently, the logic allows expressing cases that involve relations between intervals that are embedded in the trace with many, sometimes irrelevant, intervals in between. The runtime verification allows "pattern matching" against these cases in a monitored trace.

We present a matching runtime verification algorithm. The algorithm decides whether any prefix of the execution (the currently observed trace) satisfies the specification. The runtime verification is based on updating a summary of the observed prefixes upon the arrival of each new interval *begin* and *end* event. The trick we employ is to maintain several sets of interval identifiers, and tuples of such, corresponding to the different Allen operators. These variables record those intervals and relations that have begun and not completed yet, as well as those intervals and relations that have been completed. For example, a *begin* event for one interval A followed by a *begin* event for another interval B, is stored (in some variable containing a set of such pairs) as a potential for an A interval, as well as (in a different variable) a potential for an A interval overlapping with a B interval, where A starts, then B starts, then A ends and then B ends. An occurrence of an *end* event for A and then an *end* event for B will complete the picture to decide that A overlapped with B, as well as, of course, having seen completed A and B intervals.

Our logic and runtime verification algorithm is implemented in the tool MonAmi[1]. The implementation encodes interval identifiers and data as bit vectors, which are then represented as BDDs. The bit vectors are obtained by a simple enumeration scheme. Such BDDs are useful for compacting interval identifiers and data when storing them in sets, and also makes negation (set complement) non-problematic. We provide an alternative monitoring algorithm by translating the specification into past first-order temporal logic and using the tool DejaVu. We experiment and compare the two methods.

Related Work. The use of BDDs in runtime verification has been explored in [12] for the first-order past time temporal logic DejaVu, which is an event logic, in contrast to the interval logic explored here. However, the enumeration scheme for creating bit vectors from data and then converting them to BDDs is similar. Numerous event logics have been developed during the past two decades, including [3–5,9,10,12,15,18,23,29], to mention just a few.

---

[1] **Moni**toring Allen logic modal intervals.

Monitoring of Allen logic is explored in [24]. In that logic, however, intervals are referred to by explicit names, such as $A < B$. This means that one can only specify static patterns, one instance of a particular pattern: that there is one A and one B, such that $A < B$. This is in contrast to MonAmi, where we can quantify over such intervals. Specifically this means that we can specify repeated patterns in the trace e.g., that every interval A with some specific data d is always followed by some other interval B with some data d'.

The most closely related monitoring system is nfer [14,21,22], also influenced by Allen's logic. Its specification formalism consists of Prolog-like interval-generating rules (see, e.g., Fig. 1). The objective of nfer is to *generate* intervals from a trace of events, as an abstraction of the trace, to e.g. support trace comprehension by humans. Generated intervals can, for example, be visualized. In contrast, the objective of Mon-Ami is to *verify* intervals, provided as input. nfer only allows a limited form of negation, referred to as *exclusive rules* in [21], making property specification harder, and it is unknown what the limitations are w.r.t. expressiveness. Our logic allows free negation, and consequently implication. nfer supports Boolean conditions over data as well as computations on data, resulting in new data being stored in the generated intervals. In order to reduce computational complexity, nfer operates in its default mode with a min-imality principle, where the before-operator (MonAmi's $<$ operator) only matches the smallest intervals, whereas MonAmi matches all candidate intervals. Section 6 compares MonAmi with nfer further.

A different kind of extension to Allen's logic, where the various relations between operators are promoted into modalities was suggested by Halpern and Shoham [11].

2 Preliminaries

To motivate the study of interval-based specification, we first present the original *Allen Temporal Logic* (ATL).

Syntax. In its basic form, ATL has the following syntax:

$$\varphi ::= (\varphi \wedge \varphi) \mid \neg\varphi \mid A < B \mid A\,m\,B \mid A\,o\,B \mid A\,s\,B \mid A\,d\,B \mid A\,f\,B \mid A = B$$

where A and B are *intervals* from a finite set of intervals $\mathfrak{I}$, m stands for *meets*, o for *overlaps*, s for *starts*, d for *during*, and f for *finishes*. The original definition of the logic also includes the symmetric versions of these operators, e.g., an operator for $A\,mi\,B$ for $B\,m\,A$, etc., which does not add to the expressive power.

Semantics. A *model* $M = \langle E, \prec, \asymp \rangle$ for Allen's logic, consists of a finite set of events $E = \{begin(A) \mid A \in \mathfrak{I}\} \cup \{end(A) \mid A \in \mathfrak{I}\}$, a linear order $\prec \subseteq E \times E$, and an equivalence relation $\asymp \subseteq E \times E$, where $\preceq = (\prec \cup \asymp)^*$ (the transitive closure of the union of the two relations), such that:

- For each $A \in \mathfrak{I}$, $begin(A) \prec end(A)$.
- $\asymp$ is a partition of the set E into equivalence classes.
- $(\prec \cap \asymp) = \emptyset$.
- For every $a, b \in E$, either $a \preceq b$ or $b \preceq a$.

Thus, M is a linear order between equivalence classes. We call the relation $\prec$ *before*, and $\asymp$ *coincides*. The semantics is given as follows.

- $M \models (\varphi \wedge \psi)$ if $M \models \varphi$ and $M \models \psi$.
- $M \models \neg\varphi$ if $M \not\models \varphi$.
- $M \models A < B$ if $end(A) \prec begin(B)$.
- $M \models A\,m\,B$ if $end(A) \asymp begin(B)$.
- $M \models A\,o\,B$ if $begin(A) \prec begin(B) \prec end(A) \prec end(B)$.
- $M \models A\,s\,B$ if $begin(A) \asymp begin(B)$ and $end(A) \prec end(B)$.
- $M \models A\,d\,B$ if $begin(B) \prec begin(A)$ and $end(A) \prec end(B)$.
- $M \models A\,f\,B$ if $begin(B) \prec begin(A)$ and $end(A) \asymp end(B)$.
- $M \models A = B$ if $begin(A) \asymp begin(B)$ and $end(A) \asymp end(B)$

As usual, we can define additional operators, in particular, $(\varphi \vee \psi) = \neg(\neg\varphi \wedge \neg\psi)$ and $(\varphi \rightarrow \psi) = (\neg\varphi \vee \psi)$. As an example, consider then the ATL formula:

$$((B_1\,d\,L \wedge B_2\,d\,L) \wedge B_1 < B_2) \tag{1}$$

It asserts about three intervals B_1, B_2 and L, that B_1 appears before B_2 and both are embedded within L. Monitoring Allen's logic is described in [24].

3   A First-Order Interval Logic

We will explore now the monitoring of a first-order logic variant of Allen's temporal logic, which we term FoATL. While the original logic refers to a fixed set of intervals, our variant allows quantification over the intervals that occur in the trace, which can optionally carry data. The logic also allows to relate different intervals with respect to their data values. The formalism supports monitoring of behaviors consisting of a large, perhaps unbounded, number of intervals, where patterns of behavior that consist of intervals are related in ways expressed using the specification. For example, a relationship such as in formula (1) can refer to any embedding within a sequence of intervals, matching this pattern, rather than referring to three particular intervals that appear in the input.

The Setting. We monitor a sequence of events of the form $begin(z)$ and $end(z)$, where z is a sequence of parameters. The first parameter is an *interval enumeration*, also referred to as interval *id*, used to identify matching *begin* and *end* events; the rest of the parameters, which can be of different types, is optional. An additional parameter can be e.g., a label representing the kind of interval, where a label *Boot* represents that it is a *boot* interval. For example, consider the sequence of events:

$$begin(1, Load), begin(2, Boot), end(2), begin(3, Boot), end(3), end(1)$$

These events form three intervals corresponding to the intervals L, B_1, and B_2 appearing in ATL formula (1). Our logic alters Allen's logic by adding quantification over the intervals. Hence, instead of fixed intervals, which can be referred to in a formula by their explicit name as constants, we allow interval *variables* $A, B, \dots$ that can be instantiated to any of the intervals that appear in the model (the observed trace). Moreover, the intervals can carry data, and we write in the logic $A(d)$ to denote that the data of the interval assigned to the variable A has the constant value d. We can also verify whether two intervals A and B carry the same value using $same(A, B)$.

We make a few simplifying assumptions in order to concentrate on the main challenges of runtime verification of a first-order interval logic. However, the presented approach is extensible and the restrictions can be easily removed:

- We assume a matching unique integer value per interval, an *enumeration*, though it does not have to appear in consecutive order, is given for each related pair of events, e.g., $begin(5)$ and $end(5)$.
- Events can contain additional parameters besides the enumeration. For simplicity, we assume that there is at most a *single* data value parameter, e.g., an integer or a string, and that it appears within the interval starting event, e.g., $begin(5, abc)$. In a more general setting, different numbers of parameters can appear for different intervals, and the parameters may appear only at the beginning, at the end or in both events defining the interval.
- The monitored events appear one at a time. As there is no co-incidence of events, the relations are restricted to $A < B$ (before), $A \circ B$ (overlaps) and $A i B$ (for *includes*, which is the symmetric operator of Allen's *d during*). Hence, there is a total order between the events. It reflects the implementation where observed events occur one at a time. It furthermore simplifies the presentation and *incurs no real restriction on the theory involved*.
- Quantification is applied to the (completed) intervals that have occurred. Thus, as in Allen's logic, the specification does not refer to intervals that were opened with $begin(A)$ and were not closed yet with $end(A)$. The logic can of course be extended to deal with unfinished intervals.
- We assume that as part of the monitoring, the restrictions on well formedness of the enumerations are checked. Multiple $begin(A)$ or $end(A)$ events cannot occur for the same interval A, and an $end(A)$ event cannot precede a $begin(A)$ event.
- We allow referring to the data elements in intervals, and also compare them. We offer in the syntax (and our implementation) the predicate *same* that relates intervals with the same data value. This can be extended to other relations that compare values.

Syntax of FoATL. The syntax is as follows.

$$\varphi ::= (\varphi \wedge \varphi) \mid \neg \varphi \mid A(d) \mid (A < B) \mid (A \circ B) \mid (A i B) \mid \exists A \varphi \mid same(A, B)$$

where A and B are variables (representing intervals) from a set of *interval* variables $\mathfrak{I}$, and d is a value from some fixed domain D of data values. Parentheses can be removed when clear from the context. A specification does not include free variables. Consider for example the following formula:

$$\exists A \exists B \exists C (A(Load) \wedge B(Boot) \wedge C(Boot) \wedge A i B \wedge A i C \wedge B < C).$$

This specification describes the existence of three intervals with the same relations between them as the intervals L, B_1, and B_2 appearing in the ATL formula (1).

Semantics of FoATL. Let $\mathfrak{J}$ be the finite set of *interval* variables over the enumerations in the observed execution prefix. We assume the following semantic components:

- $\sigma = e(1)e(2)\ldots e(n)$ is a sequence of events of the form $begin(i)$ or $begin(i,d)$, and $end(i)$ as described above.
- $\rho : \mathfrak{J} \mapsto \mathcal{U}$ is a mapping from the interval variables $\mathfrak{J}$ to a domain $\mathcal{U}$, which can be, e.g., the natural numbers, representing interval enumerations. We denote by $\rho[A \mapsto j]$ the mapping that is identical to ρ but returns the value j for the variable A.
- $data(j)$ is the data value associated with the interval whose enumeration is j.
- $start(j)$ is the number (position in the trace) of the event that starts the interval with enumeration j, i.e., the event $begin(j)$ (with an optional additional data value d).
- $finish(j)$ is the number (position in the trace) of the event that ends the interval with enumeration j, i.e., the event $end(j)$.

We can now define the semantics of the logic inductively on the structure of the formula.

- $(\rho,\sigma) \models (\varphi \wedge \psi)$ if $(\rho,\sigma) \models \varphi$ and $(\rho,\sigma) \models \psi$.
- $(\rho,\sigma) \models \neg\varphi$ if $(\rho,\sigma) \not\models \varphi$.
- $(\rho,\sigma) \models A(d)$ if $\rho(A) = j$ and $data(j) = d$.
- $(\rho,\sigma) \models (A < B)$ if $\rho(A) = j$ and $\rho(B) = k$ and $finish(j) < start(k)$.
- $(\rho,\sigma) \models (A \circ B)$ if $\rho(A) = j$ and $\rho(B) = k$ and $start(j) < start(k) < finish(j) < finish(k)$.
- $(\rho,\sigma) \models (A \mathbin{i} B)$ if $\rho(A) = j$ and $\rho(B) = k$ and $start(j) < start(k) < finish(k) < finish(j)$.
- $(\rho,\sigma) \models \exists A\varphi$ if there exist events $begin(j)$ (or $begin(j,d)$ for some d) and $end(j)$ in σ such that $\rho' = \rho[A \mapsto j]$ and $(\rho',\sigma) \models \varphi$.
- $(\rho,\sigma) \models same(A,B)$ if $\rho(A) = j$ and $\rho(B) = k$ and $data(j) = data(k)$.

Example Properties

1. $\neg\exists A\exists B\,(A < B \wedge same(A,B))$.
   Disjoint intervals cannot have the same data value.
2. $\neg\exists A\exists B\exists C\,((A \mathbin{i} B \wedge B \mathbin{i} C))$.
   No double nesting of intervals.
3. $\forall A\forall B\,((A < B \wedge (\neg\exists C(A < C \wedge C < B))) \rightarrow \neg(A(2) \wedge B(2)))$.
   No two adjacent intervals (one completely after the other without any interval in between) can have both the same value 2.
4. $\forall A\forall B\forall C\,(((A \circ B) \wedge (B \circ C)) \rightarrow \neg(A \circ C))$.
   At no point there is an overlapping of three intervals.

Interpretation. One can interpret the semantics of a formula over finite or infinite sequences. As the logic is tailored with an application of runtime verification in mind, one typical use is to require that for a given trace, all prefixes will satisfy a given FoATL specification. This is similar to the common use of temporal specifications of the form $\Box\varphi$, where φ is restricted to past modalities, i.e., to *safety properties* [2], typically seen in runtime verification, see, e.g., [12, 13]. Nevertheless, other uses are possible as well. Generally, our implementation returns a truth value for the inspected property for each prefix of the monitored trace. Note that satisfaction of a property over an infinite trace does not entail that it is satisfied by all finite prefixes, e.g., for $\varphi = \forall A \exists B\,(A < B)$, which asserts that there is no *rightmost* interval. Conversely, $\neg\varphi$ is satisfied by every finite trace that includes at least one interval, but will not hold for a trace with infinitely many linearly ordered intervals.

4   The Monitoring Algorithm

Calculating the Relations Between Intervals. Recall that in our setting, we are restricted to three possible relations between intervals: $<$, o, and i. Let X and Y be different intervals, defined by *begin* and *end* events, that appeared in the current observed monitored prefix. We distinguish the following three sets of pairs (X, Y) of enumerations of intervals.

- $X < Y$ (*before*). Events appear in the order $begin(X), end(X), begin(Y), end(Y)$.
- $X\,o\,Y$ (*overlaps*). Events appear in the order $begin(X), begin(Y), end(X), end(Y)$.
- $X\,i\,Y$ (*includes*). Events appear in the order $begin(X), begin(Y), end(Y), end(X)$.

We maintain for each prefix of an execution three sets of pairs of enumerations, $XXYY$ for $X < Y$, $XYXY$ for $X\,o\,Y$ and $XYYX$ for $X\,i\,Y$. Further sets of pairs (X, Y) correspond to possible prefixes of the four events $(begin(X), end(X), begin(Y)$, and $end(Y))$ in the above three cases, namely XY, XYY, XYX and XXY. The names of the sets reflect the order of appearance of interval events. For example, XXY represents pairs of intervals where some events of the type $begin(X), end(X), begin(Y)$ have already appeared in this order, but not yet $end(Y)$. When $end(Y)$ subsequently appears, this pair of intervals is removed from XXY and is added to $XXYY$.

We further define the set X of enumerations for events $begin(X)$ where an $end(X)$ has not yet appeared and XX as the set of enumerations, where both $begin(X)$ and $end(X)$ have occurred; this latter is the set of completed intervals. Together, this defines two sets of enumerations, and seven sets of pairs. Note that the names of these variables reflect *patterns* and are not to be taken literally. For example, the set denoted by XX will contain any interval Z where the begin and end events have been observed. It does not only contain intervals specifically named X.

We define these sets inductively on the length i of the trace: for $i = 0$, all the sets are empty; then the update of these sets after the ith event is defined according to Table 1. The rows correspond to the sets that are updated, and the columns to the ith event. The entries in the table detail how the set is updated after the ith event based on the values of the prior values of the sets. For example, for the set X (containing the open intervals), if the ith event is a $begin(Z)$ (or $begin(Z, d)$), then $X_i = X_{i-1} \cup \{Z\}$, and if the ith event is an $end(Z)$ (or $end(Z, d)$), then $X_i = X_{i-1} \setminus \{Z\}$. Our algorithm follows the updates in Table 1 upon arrival of any new event. We denote by $\mathcal{U}$ the universal set of enumerations. The empty set is denoted by $\emptyset$. We denote by $\overline{S}$ the complement of S, i.e., the set $\mathcal{U} \setminus S$. We will describe later how to implement these sets and operations using BDDs. Note that even through $\mathcal{U}$, the set of enumerations, can be infinite, at any point in time we have observed only a finite number of enumerations. Hence, both the current set of observed enumerations and its complement can be represented in a finitary way, as will be described later.

The following rules impose validity checks on the order of the $begin(Z,d)$ (d, the data value, is optional) and $end(Z,d)$ events, causing the system to halt when violated. Specifically, for any interval Z, we allow only one $begin(Z,d)$ respectively one $end(Z,d)$ to occur, and $begin(Z,d)$ must appear before $end(Z,d)$. That is, on observing:

- $begin(Z,d)$: If $\{Z\} \cap (X \cup XX) \neq \emptyset$ then output "multiple begin".
- $end(Z,d)$: If $\{Z\} \cap XX \neq \emptyset$ then output "multiple end".
  If $\{Z\} \cap X = \emptyset$ then output "intervals ends before it begins".

Table 1. The update table.

Set\Event	$begin(Z,d)$	$end(Z,d)$
X (opened)	$X \cup \{Z\}$	$X \cap \overline{\{Z\}}$
XX (closed)		$XX \cup \{Z\}$
XY	$XY \cup ((X \times \{Z\}))$	$XY \cap (\mathcal{U} \times \overline{\{Z\}}) \cap (\overline{\{Z\}} \times \mathcal{U})$
XYY		$(XYY \cap \overline{XYYX}) \cup (XY \cap (\mathcal{U} \times \{Z\}))$
$XYYX$ ($X\,iY$, includes)		$XYYX \cup (XYY \cap (\{Z\} \times \mathcal{U}))$
XYX		$(XYX \cap \overline{XYXY}) \cup (XY \cap (\{Z\} \times \mathcal{U})$
$XYXY$ ($X\,oY$, overlaps)		$XYXY \cup (XYX \cap (\mathcal{U} \times \{Z\}))$
XXY	$XXY \cup (XX \times \{Z\})$	$XXY \cap (\mathcal{U} \times \overline{\{Z\}})$
$XXYY$ ($X<Y$, before)		$XXYY \cup (XXY \cap (\mathcal{U} \times \{Z\}))$
XD (X has data d)		$XD \cup \{(Z,d)\}$

The order of updating the sets is important: a set that is a prefix of another set, e.g., XY is a prefix set of XYX, hence it is updated *after* the latter. Thus, upon arrival of a new event, the value of XYX is updated based on the *old value* of XY, *before* updating XY.

In order to handle intervals with data, we add another set, XD, of pairs of the form (Z,d), where Z is an interval enumeration and d is a data element. Then, upon the arrival of an event of the form $end(Z,d)$, we update $XD := XD \cup \{(Z,d)\}$. This construction can be easily extended to capture a different number of parameters n by keeping sets of $n+1$ tuples.

Using BDDs to Represent Relations. Our algorithm is based on representing relations between data elements using Ordered Binary Decision Diagrams (OBDD, although we write BDD) [6]. A BDD is a compact representation for a Boolean function (arguments as well as result are Booleans) as a directed acyclic graph (DAG).

A BDD is obtained from a binary tree that represents a Boolean formula with some Boolean variables $x_1 \ldots x_k$ by gluing together isomorphic subtrees. Each non-leaf node is labeled with one of the Boolean variables. A non-leaf node x_i is the source of two arrows leading to other nodes. A dotted arrow represents that x_i has the Boolean value *false* (i.e., 0), while a thick arrow represents that it has the value *true* (i.e., 1). The variables (nodes) in the DAG occur in the same order along all paths from the root (hence the letter 'O' in OBDD). Nodes may be absent along some paths, when the result of the Boolean function does not depend on the value of the corresponding Boolean variable. Each path leads to a leaf node that is marked by either *true* or *false*, corresponding to the Boolean value returned by the function for the Boolean values on the path.

A Boolean function, and consequently a BDD, can represent a set of integer values as follows. Each integer value is, in turn, represented using a bit vector: a vector of bits $x_1 \ldots x_k$ represents the integer value $x_1 \times 1 + x_2 \times 2 + \ldots x_k \times 2^k$, where the bit value of x_i is 1 for *true* and 0 for *false* and where x_1 is the *least* significant bit, and x_k is the *most* significant. For example, the integer 6 can be represented as the bit vector 110 (here, the most significant bit appears to the left) using the bits $x_1 = 0$, $x_2 = 1$ and $x_3 = 1$. To represent a *set* of integers, the BDD returns *true* for any combination of bits that represents and integer in the set. For example, to represent the set $\{4, 6\}$, we first convert 4 and 6 into the bit vectors 100 and 110, respectively. The Boolean function over x_1, x_2, x_3 is $(\neg x_1 \wedge x_3)$, which returns *true* exactly for these two bit vector combinations.

This representation can be extended to relations, or, equivalently, a set of tuples over integers. Here the Boolean variables are partitioned into n bitstrings $x^1 = x_1^1, \ldots, x_{k_1}^1, \ldots,$ $x^n = x_1^n, \ldots, x_{k_n}^n$, each representing an integer number, forming the bit string[2]:

$$x_1^1, \ldots, x_{k_1}^1, \ldots, x_1^n, \ldots, x_{k_n}^n.$$

Using BDDs Over Enumerations of Values. Representing data values such as strings and integers, which appear within the observed trace of events, may not lead to a good compact representation. Instead, based on the limited ability to compare data values allowed by FoATL, we represent in the BDD *enumerations* (natural numbers) for these values, rather than the values themselves. When a value (associated with a variable in the specification) appears for the first time in an observed event, we assign to it a new *enumeration*. Values can be assigned consecutive enumeration values[3]. We use a hash table to point from the value to its enumeration so that in subsequent appearances of this value the same enumeration will be used. For example, if the runtime verifier sees the input events $begin(1, a)$, $begin(2, b)$, $begin(3, c)$, it may encode the data a, b, and c as the bit vectors 000, 001, and 010, respectively. The approach results in several advantages:

1. It allows a shorter representation of very big values in the BDDs; the values are compacted into a smaller number of bits.
2. It contributes to the compactness of the BDDs because enumerations of values that are not far apart often share large bit patterns.
3. The monitoring algorithm is simple; the Boolean operators over summary elements: conjunction, disjunction, and negation, are replaced by the same operators over BDDs.

---

[2] In the implementation the same number of bits are used for all variables: $k_1 = k_2 = \ldots = k_n$.

[3] A refined algorithm can reuse enumerations that were used for values that can no longer affect the verdict of the RV process, see [12].

4. Given an efficient BDD package, the implementation can be very efficient. One can also migrate between BDD packages.
5. It allows full use of negation.

For implementing negation, we keep at least one enumeration value that represents all the enumerations that *did not* occur yet in *begin* and *end* events. For that matter, we can reserve the bitstring $11 \ldots 11$. When the number of values represented by the BDDs grows so that the BDD bits are insufficient, we dynamically add one more bit to the representation, doubling the available number of enumerations.

BDD Operators. We list now the operators on BDDs representing sets of value tuples, used in evaluating the verdict of the specification on the currently inspected prefix. A value tuple represents an interval and its data values, each being elements of the tuple. Recall, however, that we represent data by their enumerations (natural numbers), so we need to represent sets of tuples of enumerations. Recall furthermore that we can represent a tuple of data enumerations as a bit vector: $x_1^1, \ldots, x_{k_1}^1, \ldots, x_1^n, \ldots, x_{k_n}^n$, being the concatenation of the bit vectors for the individual enumerations. A set of such is naturally represented by the BDD that returns true (1) for all the bit-vectors in the set. Useful operators on such BDDs are:

$conj(\mathcal{B}, C)$ The conjunction (intersection) of the BDDs $\mathcal{B}$ and C.
$comp(\mathcal{B})$ The complement of the BDD $\mathcal{B}$.
$project(\mathcal{B}, X)$ Projects out the Boolean variables $x_1 \ldots x_n$ that correspond to the parameter X of $\mathcal{B}$, obtaining $\exists x_1 \ldots \exists x_n B$.
$restrict(z, \mathcal{B})$ Restricts a BDD $\mathcal{B}$ of the form XD relating intervals with their data i.e., with bits $x_1 \ldots x_n d_1 \ldots d_m$ to those sequences of bits where $x_1 \ldots x_n$ encodes the interval and $d_1 \ldots d_m$ encodes the data value z.
$rename(\mathcal{B}, X \leftarrow X', Y \leftarrow Y', \ldots)$ Replaces the bits $x_1 x_2 \ldots x_n$ with $x_1' \ldots x_n'$, the bits $y_1 \ldots y_n$ by $y_1' \ldots y_n'$, etc. in the BDD $\mathcal{B}$.

Other operators, such as, e.g., disjunction (union, or database co-join), can be defined in terms of the operators above in the standard way.

Completing the Algorithm. The algorithm for the complete logic starts with setting all the sets in Table 1 to BDDs representing the empty sets of elements/pairs, according to their types. Upon the arrival of each new event of the type $begin(z)$, (with or without an additional data parameter d) or $end(z)$, two steps are executed.

Step 1: The sets of values/pairs are updated according to Table 1.

Step 2: BDDs of the form B_φ for the subformulas φ of the monitored property are updated recursively as follows:

- $\mathcal{B}_{(\varphi \wedge \psi)} = conj(\mathcal{B}_\varphi, B_\psi)$.
- $\mathcal{B}_{\neg \varphi} = comp(\mathcal{B}_\varphi)$.
- $\mathcal{B}_{A(d)} = project(restrict(d, rename(XD, X \leftarrow A)), D)$.
- $\mathcal{B}_{A < B} = rename(XXYY, X \leftarrow A, Y \leftarrow B)$.

- $\mathcal{B}_{A \circ B} = rename(XYXY, X \leftarrow A, Y \leftarrow B)$.
- $\mathcal{B}_{A \mid B} = rename(XYYX, X \leftarrow A, Y \leftarrow B)$.
- $\mathcal{B}_{\exists A \varphi} = project(\mathcal{B}_\varphi, A)$.
- $\mathcal{B}_{same(A,B)} = project(conj(rename(XD, X \leftarrow A), rename(XD, X \leftarrow B)), D)$.

5   Alternative Algorithm Translating to Past First-Order LTL

Given a representation of intervals as pairs of events of the form $begin(Z, d)$ and $end(Z)$, we can perform monitoring by translating the specification into past first-order LTL, referred to as QTL, as used by the tool DejaVu [12, 20].

Syntax. The formulas of the core QTL logic are defined by the following grammar, where a is a constant representing a value in $domain(p)$. For simplicity of the presentation, we define here the logic with unary predicates, but this is not due to any principle limitation, and, in fact, DejaVu supports predicates with multiple arguments, including zero arguments, which correspond to propositions.

$$\varphi ::= true \mid false \mid p(a) \mid p(x) \mid (\varphi \lor \varphi) \mid (\varphi \land \varphi) \mid \neg\varphi \mid (\varphi \, S \, \varphi) \mid \ominus \varphi \mid \exists x \, \varphi \mid \forall x \, \varphi$$

The formulas have the following informal meaning. The formula $p(a)$ is true when the current (last observed) event is $p(a)$. The formula $p(x)$, for some variable $x \in V$, is true if x is bound to a constant a such that $p(a)$ appears as the current event. Variables get bound to constants with the quantifiers $\exists$ and $\forall$. The formula $(\varphi_1 \, S \, \varphi_2)$ (reads φ_1 *since* φ_2) means that φ_2 occurred in the past (including now) and since then (beyond that state) φ_1 has been true. This is the past dual of the common future time *until* modality. The property $\ominus \varphi$ means that φ is true in the previous step. This is the past dual of the common future time *next* modality. The formula $\exists x \, \varphi$ is true if there exists a constant a such that φ is true with x bound to a. The formula $\forall x \, \varphi$ is true if for all constants a, φ is true with x bound to a. We can also define the following additional temporal operators: $P \varphi = (true \, S \, \varphi)$ ("previously"), and $H\varphi = \neg P \neg \varphi$ ("always in the past" or "historically").

Semantics. Let σ be a sequence of events and i a natural number. Let γ be an assignment to the variables that appear free in a formula φ. Then $(\gamma, \sigma, i) \models \varphi$ if φ holds for the prefix $s_1 s_2 \ldots s_i$ of the trace σ with the assignment γ. This is a standard definition, agreeing, e.g., with [5]. Note that by using past operators, the semantics is not affected by states s_j for $j > i$. Let $free(\varphi)$ be the set of free (i.e., unquantified) variables of a subformula φ. We denote by $\gamma|_{free(\varphi)}$ the restriction (projection) of an assignment γ to the free variables appearing in φ. Let ε be an empty assignment. In any of the following cases, $(\gamma, \sigma, i) \models \varphi$ is defined when γ is an assignment over $free(\varphi)$, and $i \geq 1$.

- $(\varepsilon, \sigma, i) \models true$.
- $(\varepsilon, \sigma, i) \models p(a)$ if $p(a) \in \sigma[i]$.
- $([v \mapsto a], \sigma, i) \models p(v)$ if $p(a) \in \sigma[i]$.
- $(\gamma, \sigma, i) \models (\varphi \land \psi)$ if $(\gamma|_{free(\varphi)}, \sigma, i) \models \varphi$ and $(\gamma|_{free(\psi)}, \sigma, i) \models \psi$.
- $(\gamma, \sigma, i) \models \neg\varphi$ if not $(\gamma, \sigma, i) \models \varphi$.
- $(\gamma, \sigma, i) \models (\varphi \, S \, \psi)$ if for some $1 \leq j \leq i$, $(\gamma|_{free(\psi)}, \sigma, j) \models \psi$ and for all $j < k \leq i$, $(\gamma|_{free(\varphi)}, \sigma, k) \models \varphi$.

- $(\gamma, \sigma, i) \models \ominus \varphi$ if $i > 1$ and $(\gamma, \sigma, i - 1) \models \varphi$.
- $(\gamma, \sigma, i) \models \exists x \, \varphi$ if there exists $a \in domain(x)$ such that $(\gamma[x \mapsto a], \sigma, i) \models \varphi$.

The translation from FoATL to QTL is as follows:

- $\mathcal{T}(\varphi \wedge \psi) = \mathcal{T}(\varphi) \wedge \mathcal{T}(\psi)$.
- $\mathcal{T}(\neg \varphi) = \neg \mathcal{T}(\varphi)$.
- $\mathcal{T}(A(d)) = P(end(A) \wedge \ominus (P \, begin(A, d)))$.
- $\mathcal{T}(A < B) = P(end(B) \wedge \ominus P(begin(B, Bd) \wedge \ominus P(end(A) \wedge \ominus P \, begin(A, Ad))))$.
- $\mathcal{T}(A \circ B) = P(end(B) \wedge \ominus P(end(A) \wedge \ominus P(begin(B, Bd) \wedge \ominus P \, begin(A, Ad))))$.
- $\mathcal{T}(A \, i \, B) = P(end(A) \wedge \ominus P(end(B) \wedge \ominus P(begin(B, Bd) \wedge \ominus P \, begin(A, Ad))))$.
- $\mathcal{T}(\exists A \varphi) = \exists A \, \exists Ad \, \mathcal{T}(\varphi)$.
- $\mathcal{T}(same(A, B)) = \exists d(P(end(A) \wedge \ominus P \, begin(A, d)) \wedge P(end(B) \wedge \ominus P \, begin(B, d)))$.

It is interesting to note that the translation from FoATL to QTL does not make use of the operator $\mathcal{S}$, but only uses $\ominus$ and P. The translation has been implemented in MonAmi. We can now monitor a FoATL formula by translating it to QTL using the above translation scheme, and monitor the generated QTL property with DejaVu using the algorithm described in [12]. We later compare the results of monitoring using an optimization of this translation with monitoring using MonAmi.

6 Implementation

We implemented a prototype monitoring tool [19] for our logic FoATL, called MonAmi. It is a Python-based tool for monitoring intervals, formed by events, by checking them against a FoATL property. The tool works with Python 3.6 and above. It uses the 'dd' Python package [8] for generating and manipulating BDDs, which itself uses the CUDD BDD package [7] in C. MonAmi uses several input files that define the configuration of the initial parameters, the property file, and the trace file when monitoring in offline mode (log analysis). A trace $\mathcal{T}$ is a sequence of events $[begin, i, d]$ or $[end, i]$, where i is an interval enumeration, and d is the data. The tool can also be used for online monitoring, using the same algorithm, observing a trace dynamically generated by a program during its execution.

6.1 Experiments

To evaluate MonAmi, we performed a comparison with the interval-based nfer tool [14], mentioned in the related work section on page 3. We expressed four properties using the formalisms of these two tools, all related to receiving data from a *planetary rover*, and evaluated tool performances (time and memory) on traces of different sizes. The planetary rover scenario is inspired by realistic properties of the *Curiosity Mars rover* [17]. The rover's behavior is reported to ground via the following simplified intervals (amongst many): DL_IMAGE (downlink an image), DL_MOBPRM (downlink mobility parameter values), DL_ARMPRM (downlink robotic arm parameter values), DL_FAIL (downlink fails), INS_ON (instrument power turned on), INS_FAIL (instrument powering fails), INS_RECOVER (instrument recovers), GET_CAMDATA (reading camera data), STARVE (thread starves), and BOOT (re-boot rover, e.g. after a failure).

The four properties expressed in the formalisms of MonAmi and nfer are shown in Fig. 1. In nfer we state a property as a collection of Prolog-like interval-generating rules of the form id :− body, where the rule body contains Allen's operators applied to events and intervals generated by other rules. The result of a match of the body is a new interval with the name id, as specified by the rule head. Events and intervals can carry data, which can be used e.g. in **where**-conditions. The IVAL rule (used by all the four properties) generates intervals for all matching (same interval identifier) BEGIN and END events in the trace, and stores (**map**) their interval and data values in the generated IVAL event. The FOUND interval in each nfer property is generated when an error is detected. As mentioned previously, nfer allows negation, referred to as *exclusive rules* in [21]. The body of a rule can e.g. have the form 'A unless after B', meaning an A occurred and a B did not occur before. This form of negation has not been used in these properties.

```
1. !exist B1, B2, D .
      B1('BOOT') & B2('BOOT') & D('DL_IMAGE') &
      B1 < B2 &
      (B1 I D |
      B2 I D |
      (B1 < D & D < B2) |
      (B1 o D & !D I B2) |
      (D o B2 & !D I B1)
      )

2. !exist D, F .
      (D('DL_MOBPRM') | D('DL_ARMPRM')) &
      F('DL_FAIL') &
      D I F

3. !exist O, F, R .
      O('INS_ON') & F('INS_FAIL') & R('INS_RECOVER') &
      O < F & F < R &
      !exist X . (X('INS_ON') | X('INS_RECOVER')) & O < X & X < R

4. !exist D, G, S .
      D('DL_IMAGE') & G('GET_CAMDATA') & S('STARVE') &
      D I S & G I S
```

```
IVAL :− BEGIN before END
     where BEGIN.interval = END.interval
     map { interval → BEGIN.interval, data → BEGIN.data }

1. BOOT :− IVAL where IVAL.data = "BOOT"
   DL :− IVAL where IVAL.data = "DL_IMAGE"
   DBOOT :− BOOT before BOOT
   FOUND :− DL during DBOOT

2. DL :− IVAL where IVAL.data = "DL_MOBPRM" | IVAL.data = "DL_ARMPRM"
   FAIL :− IVAL where IVAL.data = "DL_FAIL"
   FOUND :− FAIL during DL

3. ON :− IVAL where IVAL.data = "INS_ON"
   FAIL :− IVAL where IVAL.data = "INS_FAIL"
   RECOVER :− IVAL where IVAL.data = "INS_RECOVER"
   EXEC :− ON before RECOVER
   FOUND :− FAIL during EXEC

4. DL :− IVAL where IVAL.data = "DL_IMAGE"
   GET :− IVAL where IVAL.data = "GET_CAMDATA"
   STARVE :− IVAL where IVAL.data = "STARVE"
   FOUND :− STARVE during (GET slice DL)
```

Fig. 1. Evaluated properties in MonAmi (left) and nfer (right).

The Properties. Property 1 states that there is no DL_IMAGE during two BOOT intervals (after the start of the first and before the end of the second). Property 2 states that there is no DL_FAIL during a DL_MOBPRM or DL_ARMPRM interval. Property 3 states that there is no INS_FAIL in between an INS_ON and a subsequent closest INS_RECOVER. Note how in the MonAmi specification we need to express the concept of *closest* as an additional constraint (that there is no INS_ON or INS_RECOVER in between). In nfer this is the default semantics, also referred to as the *minimality* principle, see discussion below. Property 4 states that there is no STARVE during a period where both an DL_IMAGE interval and a GET_CAMDATA interval are active. The nfer **slice** operator produces the intersection between two intervals. As mentioned, nfer's default execution mode uses a principle of *minimality*, where nfer's A **before** B operator (analog to MonAmi's A < B operator) searches the closest right-most B from a given A. The minimality principle, however, can be switched off; so it behaves like MonAmi.

Properties 1, 2, and 4 are in nfer evaluated with minimality switched off. nfer was origi-nally designed to run with minimality switched on. However, the C version of nfer offers the option of switching off minimality, while the Scala version was extended with this option in order to perform the experiment.

The Traces. We created 5 trace files for each property of different sizes, with 1000, 2000, 4000, 8000, and 16000 events. The traces were generated to evaluate the natural execution mode of MonAmi (stop on first violation) for these properties, by creating the traces to be violated only at the last event. These were generated with a trace generator, guided by one rule for each property. The maximal number of overlapping intervals was also controlled by a parameter (we chose a limit of 3). To ensure that violation will not occur in the middle of the trace we set the data to be different from the ones that appear in the property, except for the violating events. MonAmi is compared to two versions of nfer, a first prototype version in Scala [22], and a later developed version in C [21].

The Execution Modes. In addition, MonAmi is run in two different modes. Recall from the section *Completing the algorithm* on page 10 that the complete algorithm executes in two steps. In Step 1 the variables in Table 1 are updated. In Step 2, the formula is evaluated based on the value of these variables. When run in *small step* mode (S), both steps are executed for each new event. When run in *big step* mode (B), only Step 1 is executed for each new event, whereas Step 2 is only executed at the end of monitoring. It corresponds to only observing the formula's value after the final event, the semantics is unchanged. Small step mode will typically be used for online monitoring, whereas big step mode will typically be used for offline monitoring, e.g. analysis of log files. Obviously, only evaluating Step 2 once at the end provides an optimization. In our case, which is offline log analysis, we shall apply both modes for comparison. nfer evaluates its rules for each new event.

The Results. Table 2 shows the results of the evaluation. The experiments were carried out on a Dell Latitude 5401 laptop (Intel Core I7-9850H 9th Gen, 32GB RAM, 512GB SSD) with Ubuntu 20.04.2 LTS OS. W.r.t. memory, nfer/C overall performs the best and nfer/Scala the worst. MonAmi/B (big step) and MonAmi/S (small step) both perform very close to the good performance of nfer. W.r.t. time, again nfer/C has the best perfor-mance. MonAmi/B, however, performs as well as or close to nfer/C. MonAmi/S generally performs least well w.r.t. time, except for the second property where nfer/Scala performs worse for larger traces. The first property requires more time than the second property, especially for MonAmi/S. This can be contributed to the higher complexity of the first formula. The better performance of nfer/C in general can potentially be attributed to the fact that it is implemented in C, whereas MonAmi is implemented in a mix of Python and C.

Table 2. MonAmi's S and B modes versus nfer's Scala and C versions.

Property	Tool	1000	2000	4000	8000	16000
1	MonAmi/S	1.89 s	9.46 s	22.00 s	72.93 s	250.55 s
		51.86 MB	52.43 MB	54.19 MB	78.02 MB	90.50 MB
	MonAmi/B	0.31 s	0.60 s	1.25 s	3.82 s	6.82 s
		51.74 MB	52.48 MB	54.56 MB	58.94 MB	86.47 MB
	nfer/$Scala$	0.19 s	0.35 s	1.28 s	4.42 s	17.32 s
		140.41 MB	164.09 MB	395.83 MB	365.73 MB	385.23 MB
	nfer/C	0.03 s	0.05 s	0.15 s	0.52 s	1.96 s
		11.03 MB	11.48 MB	12.70 MB	15.15 MB	19.85 MB
2	MonAmi/S	0.37 s	0.83 s	2.88 s	7.98 s	10.65 s
		51.71 MB	52.65 MB	54.35 MB	57.30 MB	63.39 MB
	MonAmi/B	0.17 s	0.30 s	0.61 s	1.20 s	2.47 s 64.27
		51.67 MB	52.27 MB	54.34 MB	57.06 MB	MB
	nfer/$Scala$	0.25 s	0.41 s	1.19 s	4.32 s	18.73
		147.85 MB	196.26 MB	352.84 MB	392.45 MB	s 662.18 MB
	nfer/C	0.02 s	0.04 s	0.14 s	0.52 s	1.98 s
		11.00 MB	11.48 MB	12.75 MB	15.12 MB	19.89 MB
3	MonAmi/S	1.20 s	3.89 s	13.06 s	61.25 s	385.18 s
		51.69 MB	52.62 MB	54.30 MB	59.08 MB	86.24 MB
	MonAmi/B	0.19 s	0.36 s	0.82 s	1.69 s	3.58 s
		51.82 MB	52.48 MB	54.35 MB	57.09 MB	66.90 MB
	nfer/$Scala$	0.24 s	0.44 s	1.29 s	4.78 s	19.82 s
		142.16 MB	191.50 MB	332.99 MB	391.98 MB	562.61 MB
	nfer/C	0.02 s	0.05 s	0.15 s	0.54 s	2.12 s
		11.05 MB	11.49 MB	12.77 MB	15.18 MB	19.91 MB
4	MonAmi/S	0.51 s	1.49 s	4.74 s	17.31 s	54.80 s
		51.85 MB	52.55 MB	53.91 MB	57.21 MB	64.79 MB
	MonAmi/B	0.18 s	0.32 s	0.72 s	1.30 s	2.74 s
		51.70 MB	52.25 MB	53.88 MB	57.09 MB	65.87 MB
	nfer/$Scala$	0.20 s	0.39 s	1.23 s	4.86 s	18.29 s
		150.56 MB	199.01 MB	402.66 MB	361.00 MB	531.94 MB
	nfer/C	0.02 s	0.05 s	0.15 s	0.54 s	2.16 s
		11.10 MB	11.63 MB	13.01 MB	15.67 MB	21.08 MB

MonAmi and DejaVu. Table 3 shows the results of evaluating MonAmi against DejaVu. We evaluated the FoATL properties 1–4 on page 6, monitored by MonAmi, against their translations to QTL, monitored by DejaVu, using a manual translation inspired by the one presented in Sect. 5. The manual translation optimizes the resulting QTL formulas. In spite of this optimization, MonAmi clearly outperforms DejaVu on the translated formulas, both w.r.t. memory use and time. DejaVu's evaluation strategy corresponds to MonAmi's small step evaluation mode since the entire formula is evaluated in each step.

Table 3. MonAmi's S and B modes versus DejaVu(∞ means more than 1000 s)

Property	Tool	1000	2000	4000	8000	16000
1	MonAmi/S	0.81 s 211.21 MB	2.14 s 216.38 MB	4.72 s 226.11 MB	13.94 s 248.01 MB	25.14 s 268.81 MB
	MonAmi/B	0.28 s 214.49 MB	0.52 s 217.48 MB	0.98 s 226.99 MB	2.08 s 245.93 MB	4.27 s 275.67 MB
	DejaVu	0.24 s 2.61 GB	0.73 s 2.61 GB	3.94 s 2.63 GB	21.12 s 2.63 GB	136.56 s 4.34 GB
2	MonAmi/S	0.69 s 214.19 MB	1.68 s 217.72 MB	3.52 s 224.88 MB	9.22 s 244.99 MB	26.14 s 272.22 MB
	MonAmi/B	0.27 s 216.28 MB	0.49 s 220.33 MB	1.07 s 224.12 MB	2.19 s 239.32 MB	4.42 s 284.65 MB
	DejaVu	21.82 s 6.09 GB	454.51 s 6.08 GB	∞ N/A	∞ N/A	∞ N/A
3	MonAmi/S	1.33 s 212.67 MB	4.28 s 219.07 MB	12.71 s 231.48 MB	46.47 s 261.21 MB	82.86 s 304.59 MB
	MonAmi/B	0.28 s 217.32 MB	0.57 s 221.24 MB	1.47 s 230.17 MB	2.26 s 236.92 MB	5.13 s 264.54 MB
	DejaVu	0.40 s 6.15 GB	1.36 s 6.14 GB	5.59 s 6.14 GB	38.96 s 6.12 GB	∞ N/A
4	MonAmi/S	0.95 s 210.78 MB	2.36 s 216.76 MB	6.61 s 225.45 MB	23.26 s 240.86 MB	79.95 s 287.96 MB
	MonAmi/B	0.2918 s 217.39 MB	0.54 s 219.58 MB	1.11 s 226.81 MB	2.13 s 248.91 MB	4.78 s 284.80 MB
	DejaVu	2.01 s 6.08 GB	13.67 s 6.08 GB	92.59 s 6.09 GB	∞ N/A	∞ N/A

7 Conclusion

We described an extension to Allen's temporal logic, termed FoATL, that allows quantification over the intervals that occur in a monitored trace. We presented an efficient algorithm for runtime verification and implemented a prototype tool in Python. The implementation is based on representing sets of tuples of enumerations over the intervals and their data values as BDDs using the 'dd' package. We also presented a monitoring procedure that translates a FoATL formula into a first-order past-time temporal logic formula, monitored by the tool DejaVu. Experiments show that the direct implementation of our algorithm is far more efficient.

The closest tool related to MonAmi is nfer and we comment on the relation between these two tools and their capabilities. The FoATL logic allows for a very convenient form of quantification. nfer, in contrast, has the flavor of rule-based programming. FoATL allows free negation, and consequently implication, which is only allowed in a *limited sense* in the C version of nfer, and *not at all* in the Scala version. The limitation (if any) w.r.t. the expressiveness of nfer's notion of negation is unknown. MonAmi can be extended with time stamps, thereby allowing events to occur at the "same time", and therefore allowing the Allen operators *meets*, *starts*, *finishes*, and *equals*. nfer relies as default on the minimal interpretation of the before-operator, choosing the closest rightmost interval. MonAmi can be easily extended to also to allow this mode. Extending the logic to be first-order also w.r.t. data is considered for future work.

References

1. Allen, J.F.: Maintaining knowledge about temporal intervals. Commun. ACM **26**(11), 832–843 (1983)
2. Alpern, B., Schneider, F.B.: Recognizing safety and liveness. Distrib. Comput. **2**(3), 117–126 (1987)
3. D'Angelo, B., et al.: LOLA: runtime monitoring of synchronous systems. In: TIME 2005, pp. 166–174 (2005)
4. Barringer, H., Havelund, K.: TRACECONTRACT: a scala DSL for trace analysis. In: Butler, M., Schulte, W. (eds.) FM 2011. LNCS, vol. 6664, pp. 57–72. Springer, Heidelberg (2011). https://doi.org/10.1007/978-3-642-21437-0_7
5. Basin, D.A., Klaedtke, F., Müller, S., Zalinescu, E.: Monitoring metric first-order temporal properties. J. ACM **62**(2), 45 (2015)
6. Bryant, R.E.: Symbolic boolean manipulation with ordered binary-decision diagrams. ACM Comput. Surv. **24**(3), 293–318 (1992)
7. CUDD BDD package [https://davidkebo.com/cudd]
8. The 'dd' Python package for manipulating Binary decision diagrams (BDDs) and Multi-valued decision diagrams (MDDs) [https://github.com/tulip-control/dd]
9. Decker, N., Leucker, M., Thoma, D.: Monitoring modulo theories. J. Softw. Tools Technol. Transfer **18**(2), 205–225 (2016)
10. Hallé, S., Villemaire, R.: Runtime enforcement of web service message contracts with data. IEEE Trans. Serv. Comput. **5**(2), 192–206 (2012)
11. Halpern, J.Y., Shoham, Y.: A propositional modal logic of time intervals. J. ACM **38**(4), 935–962 (1991)
12. Havelund, K., Peled, D., Ulus, D.: First-order temporal logic monitoring with BDDs. In: FMCAD 2017, pp. 116–123 (2017)
13. Havelund, K., Roşu, G.: Synthesizing monitors for safety properties. In: Katoen, J.-P., Stevens, P. (eds.) TACAS 2002. LNCS, vol. 2280, pp. 342–356. Springer, Heidelberg (2002). https://doi.org/10.1007/3-540-46002-0_24
14. Kauffman, S., Havelund, K., Joshi, R., Fischmeister, S.: Inferring event stream abstractions. Formal Methods Syst. Des. **53**(1), 54–82 (2018)
15. Kim, M., Kannan, S., Lee, I., Sokolsky, O.: Java-MaC: a run-time assurance tool for Java. In: Proceedings of the 1st International Workshop on Runtime Verification (RV'01), Elsevier, ENTCS, vol. 55, no. 2 (2001)
16. Kupferman, O., Vardi, M.Y.: Model checking of safety properties. Formal Methods Syst. Des. **19**(3), 291–314 (2001)
17. Mars Curiosity Rover [https://mars.nasa.gov/msl]
18. Meredith, P.O., Jin, D., Griffith, D., Chen, F., Rosu, G.: An overview of the MOP runtime verification framework. J. Softw. Tools Technol. Transfer **14**, 249–289 (2011). https://doi.org/10.1007/s10009-011-0198-6
19. MonAmi tool source code [https://github.com/moraneus/MonAmI]
20. DejaVu tool source code [https://github.com/havelund/dejavu]
21. nfer in C [http://nfer.io]
22. nfer in Scala [https://github.com/rv-tools/nfer]

23. Reger, G., Cruz, H.C., Rydeheard, D.: MARQ: monitoring at runtime with QEA. In: Baier, C., Tinelli, C. (eds.) TACAS 2015. LNCS, vol. 9035, pp. 596–610. Springer, Heidelberg (2015). https://doi.org/10.1007/978-3-662-46681-0_55

24. Rosu, G., Bensalem, S.: Allen Linear (Interval) Temporal Logic - Translation to LTL and Monitor Synthesis. CAV 2006, pp. 263–277 (2006)

25. Sistla, A.P.: Theoretical Issues in the Design and Analysis of Distributed Systems, Ph.D Thesis, Harvard University (1983)

26. Sistla, A.P., Vardi, M.Y., Wolper, P.: The complementation problem for Büchi automata with applications to temporal logic. In: Brauer, W. (ed.) ICALP 1985. LNCS, vol. 194, pp. 465–474. Springer, Heidelberg (1985). https://doi.org/10.1007/BFb0015772

27. Stockmeyer, L.J., Meyer, A.R.: Word Problems Requiring Exponential Time: Preliminary Report, STOC, 1973, pp. 1–9 (1973)

28. Thomas, W.: Automata on infinite objects. In: Handbook of Theoretical Computer Science, Volume B: Formal Models and Sematics (B), pp. 133–191 (1990)

29. Ulus, D., Maler, O.: Specifying timed patterns using temporal logic. In: 21st International Conference on Hybrid Systems: Computation and Control, pp. 167–176. ACM (2018)

Exhaustive Property Oriented Model-Based Testing with Symbolic Finite State Machines

Niklas Krafczyk[ID] and Jan Peleska[✉][ID]

Department of Mathematics and Computer Science, University of Bremen,
Bremen, Germany
{niklas,peleska}@uni-bremen.de

Abstract. In this paper, we present new contributions to property oriented testing (POT) against Symbolic Finite State Machine (SFSM) models. While several POT approaches are known, none of these are exhaustive in the sense that every implementation violating the property is uncovered by a given test suite under certain hypotheses. On the other hand, numerous exhaustive theories for testing against models specified in various formalisms exist, but only for conformance testing. Since a hybrid approach using both models and properties seems to be preferred in industry, we present an approach to close this gap. For given properties that are at the same time represented in a reference model, we present a test suite derivation procedure and prove its exhaustiveness.

1 Introduction

Background: Property-Oriented Testing and Model-Based Testing. In the field of testing, two main directions have been investigated for quite a long time. In *property-oriented testing (POT)* [4,12], test data is created with the objective to check whether an implementation fulfils or violates a given property which may be specified by Boolean expressions (invariants, pre-/post-conditions) or more complex temporal formulae [12]. In *model-based testing (MBT)* [19], a reference model expressing the desired behaviour of an implementation is used for generating the test data and for checking the implementation behaviour observed during test executions. In the research community, the objective of MBT is usually to investigate whether an implementation conformed to the model according to some pre-defined equivalence or refinement relation.

In industry, however, testing of cyber-physical systems is usually performed by a hybrid approach, involving both properties and models. Requirements are specified as properties, and models are used as starting points of system and software design [13,14]. It is checked by review or by model checking that the models reflect the given properties in the correct way. Due to the complexity of large embedded systems like railway and avionic control systems, testing for

---

Funded by the Deutsche Forschungsgemeinschaft (DFG) – project number 407708394.

R. Calinescu and C. S. Păsăreanu (Eds.): SEFM 2021, LNCS 13085, pp. 84–102, 2021.
https://doi.org/10.1007/978-3-030-92124-8_5

model conformance only happens on sub-system or even module level, while testing on system integration level or system level is property-based, though models are available. In particular during regression testing, test cases are selected to check specific requirements, and hardly ever to establish full model conformance.

Problem Statement. The objective of this paper is to establish a sufficient black-box test condition for an implementation to satisfy an LTL safety property.[1] Reference models specifying the desired behaviour are represented as symbolic finite state machines (SFSMs) extending finite state machines (FSMs) in Mealy format by input and output variables, guard conditions, and output expressions. Recently, SFSMs have become quite popular in model-based testing (MBT) [16,18], because they can specify more complex data types than FSMs and can be regarded as a simplified variant of UML/SysML state machines. Also, they are easier to analyse than the more general Kripke structures which have been investigated in model checking [3], as well as in the context of MBT, for example in [7,8]. In contrast to Kripke structures, SFSMs only allow for a finite state space. This fact can be leveraged in test generation algorithms by enumerating all states and performing more efficient operations on this set of states instead of a potentially infinite one.

The existence of a model in addition to the property to be verified is exploited to guide the test case generation process. Moreover, the model is used as a test oracle which checks *more* than just the given property: if another violation of the expected implementation behaviour is detected while testing whether the property is fulfilled, this is a "welcome side effect". This approach deliberately deviates from the "standard approach" to check only for formula violations using, for example, the finite LTL encoding presented in [2] or observers based on some variant of automaton [5].

Main Contributions. The main contributions of this paper are as follows. (1) We present a test case generation procedure which inputs an LTL safety property to be checked and a reference model to guide the generation process and serve as a test oracle. (2) A theorem is presented and explained, stating that test suites generated by this procedure are exhaustive in the sense that every implementation violating the given property will fail at least one test case, provided that the true implementation behaviour is reflected by another SFSM contained in a well-defined fault-domain.[2] This hypothesis is necessary in black-box testing, because hidden internal states cannot be monitored [17,21].

---

[1] Safety properties are the only formulae to be investigated effectively by testing, since their violation by a system under test can be detected on a finite sequence of states or input/output traces, respectively [22].

[2] Due to the usual space limitations, the proof of the theorem is not presented here, but in technical report https://doi.org/10.5281/zenodo.5151777. It is interesting to note and explained in this report that the proof is a modified nondeterministic variant of a proof already published in [10, Theorem 2].

To the best of our knowledge, this mixed property-based and model-based approach to POT has not been investigated before outside the field of finite state machines. Only for the latter, strategies for testing simpler properties with additional FSM models have been treated by the authors in [9,10]. While the approach presented here is related to the one presented in [10], we will elaborate here how to derive test cases for properties on non-deterministic reference models. Furthermore, our approach is distinguished from [9,10] by operating on SFSMs and by using LTL formulae as the specification formalism for properties. SFSMs are considerably more expressive than FSMs for modelling complex reactive systems. Specifying properties in LTL is more general, intuitive, and elegant than the FSM-specific restricted specification style used in [9,10].

Overview. In Sect. 2, SFSMs are defined, and existing results about model simulations, equivalence classes, and abstractions to FSMs are reviewed and illustrated by examples. These (mostly well-known) facts are needed to prove the exhaustiveness of the test generation strategy described in Sect. 3. In Sect. 3, fault domains are introduced and a sufficient condition for exhaustive test suites for property verification is presented and proven. For implementing test suite generators, we can refer to algorithms already published elsewhere. Section 4 contains conclusions and sketches future work.

Throughout this paper, we refer to related work where appropriate.

2 Symbolic Finite State Machines, Simulations, Equivalence Classes, and FSM Abstractions

Definition of Symbolic Finite State Machines. A *Symbolic Finite State Machine (SFSM)* is a tuple $M = (S, s_0, R, V_I, V_O, D, \Sigma_I, \Sigma_O)$. Finite set S denotes the state space, and $s_0 \in S$ is the initial state. Finite set V_I contains input variable symbols, and finite set V_O output variable symbols. The sets V_I and V_O must be disjoint. We use V to abbreviate $V_I \cup V_O$. We assume that the variables are typed, and infinite domains like reals or unlimited integers are admissible. Set D denotes the union over all variable type domains. The *input alphabet* Σ_I consists of finitely many *guard conditions*, each guard being a quantifier-free first-order expression over input variables. The finite *output alphabet* Σ_O consists of *output expressions*; these are quantifier-free first-order expressions over (optional) input variables and at least one output variable. We admit constants, function symbols, and arithmetic expressions in these expressions but require that they can be solved based on some decision theory, for example, by an SMT solver. Set $R \subseteq S \times \Sigma_I \times \Sigma_O \times S$ denotes the *transition relation*.

This definition of SFSMs is consistent with the definition of 'symbolic input/output finite state machines (SIOFSM)' introduced in [16], but is slightly more general: SIOSFMs allow only assignments on output variables, while our definitions admits general quantifier-free first-order expressions. This is useful for specifying nondeterministic outputs and – of particular importance in this paper

– for performing data abstraction, as introduced below. Also, note that [16] only considers conformance testing, but not property-based testing.

Following [16], faulty behaviour of implementations is captured in a finite set of *mutant* SFSMs whose behaviour may deviate from that of the reference SFSM by (a) faulty or interchanged guard conditions, (b) faulty or interchanged output expressions, (c) transfer faults consisting of additional, lost, or misdirected transitions, and (d) added or lost states (always involving transfer faults as well). To handle mutants and reference model in the same context, we require that (a) the faulty guards are also contained in the input alphabet, and (b) the faulty output expressions are also contained in the output alphabet, (without occurring anywhere in the reference model).

A *valuation function* $\sigma : V \longrightarrow D$ associates each variable symbol $v \in V$ with a type-conforming value $\sigma(v)$. Given a first-order expression ϕ over variable symbols from V, we write $\sigma \models \phi$ and say that σ is a model for ϕ if, after replacing every variable symbol v in ϕ by its value $\sigma(v)$, the resulting Boolean expression evaluates to true. Only SFSMs that are *well-formed* are considered in this paper: this means that for every pair $(\phi, \psi) \in \Sigma_I \times \Sigma_O$ occurring in some transition $(s, \phi, \psi, s') \in R$, at least one model $\sigma \models \phi \wedge \psi$ exists for the conjunction $\phi \wedge \psi$ of guard and output expression. An SFSM with integer variables $x \in V_I$ and $y \in V_O$ and a transition $(s, x < 0, y^2 < x, s')$, for example, would not be well-formed.

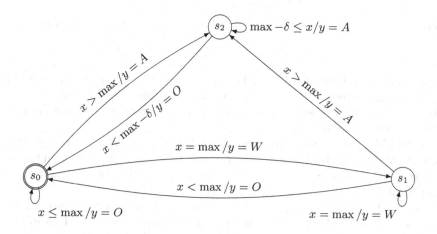

Fig. 1. Simple alarm system M (O = OK, W = warning, A = alarm, O < W < A).

Example 1. The SFSM in Fig. 1 describes a simple alarm indication system which inputs a sensor value $x : \mathbb{R}$ and raises an alarm ($y = A$) if x exceeds the threshold value max. After an alarm has been raised, the system remains in state s_2 until x drops below the value max $-\delta$, whereafter a transition to initial state s_0 is performed, accompanied by output $y = O$ ("value is OK"). If the threshold value max has been reached but not yet overstepped, a warning

$y = W$ may or may not be issued (nondeterministic decision). If the warning is given, the system transits to state s_1 and stays there until $x <$ max is fulfilled or an alarm needs to be raised because x exceeds the threshold. Output values O, W, A are typed by an enumeration.

Note that in this example, outputs could simply be specified by assignments, so the system could also be modelled as an SIOSFM. Example 4 below shows where the first-order representation is needed.

A *symbolic trace* of SFSM M is a finite sequence

$$\tau = (\phi_1/\psi_1)\dots(\phi_n/\psi_n) \in (\Sigma_I \times \Sigma_O)^*$$

satisfying (recall that s_0 is the initial state)

$$\exists s_1, \dots, s_n \in S : \forall i \in \{1, \dots, n\} : (s_{i-1}, \phi_i, \psi_i, s_i) \in R.$$

This means that there exists a state sequence starting from the initial state, such that each pair (s_{i-1}, s_i) of states is linked by a transition labelled with (ϕ_i, ψ_i). We use the intuitive notation (ϕ_i/ψ_i) inherited from Mealy machines for these predicate pairs, since ϕ_i specifies inputs and ψ_i outputs.

A *concrete trace* (also called *computation*) of M is a finite sequence of valuation functions

$$\kappa = \sigma_1 \dots \sigma_n \in (V \longrightarrow D)^*$$

such that a symbolic trace $\tau = (\phi_1/\psi_1)\dots(\phi_n/\psi_n)$ of M exists satisfying

$$(\sigma_1 \models \phi_1 \wedge \psi_1) \wedge \dots \wedge (\sigma_n \models \phi_n \wedge \psi_n).$$

If this condition is fulfilled, κ is called a *witness* of τ. This interpretation of SFSM computations corresponds to the synchronous interpretation of state machine inputs and outputs, as discussed in [20]: inputs and outputs occur simultaneously, that is, in the same computation step $\kappa(i)$.

An SFSM is *deterministic* if a sequence of input tuples already determines the sequence of associated outputs in a unique way. More formally, two computations $\kappa = \sigma_1 \dots \sigma_n$ and $\kappa' = \sigma_1' \dots \sigma_n'$ satisfying $\sigma_i|_{V_I} = \sigma_i'|_{V_I}$ for all $i = 1, \dots, n$ already fulfil $\kappa = \kappa'$.

As usual in the field of modelling formalisms for reactive systems, the *behaviour* of an SFSM is defined by the set of its computations. Two SFSMs are equivalent if and only if they have the same set of computations.

Example 2. The alarm system specified in Example 1 has a symbolic trace

$$\tau = (x \leq \text{max} /y = O).(x \leq \text{max} /y = O).$$
$$(x = \text{max} /y = W).(x > \text{max} /y = A).(x < \text{max} - \delta/y = O)$$

With constants max $= 100, \delta = 10$, the concrete trace

$$\kappa = \{x \mapsto 100, y \mapsto O\}.\{x \mapsto 50, y \mapsto O\}.$$
$$\{x \mapsto 100, y \mapsto W\}.\{x \mapsto 110, y \mapsto A\}.\{x \mapsto 89, y \mapsto O\}$$

is a witness of τ. The alarm system is nondeterministic, since it also has symbolic trace

$$\tau' = (x = \max /y = W).(x \leq \max /y = O).$$
$$(x = \max /y = W).(x > \max /y = A).(x < \max - \delta /y = O)$$

for which

$$\kappa' = \{x \mapsto 100, y \mapsto W\}.\{x \mapsto 50, y \mapsto O\}.$$
$$\{x \mapsto 100, y \mapsto W\}.\{x \mapsto 110, y \mapsto A\}.\{x \mapsto 89, y \mapsto O\}$$

is a witness. The input sequences of κ and κ' are identical, but the computations differ.

Testability Assumptions. To ensure testability, the following pragmatic assumptions and restrictions are made. (1) When testing nondeterministic implementations, it may be necessary to apply the input trace several times to reach a specific internal state, since the input trace may nondeterministically reach difference states. As is usual in nondeterministic systems testing, we adopt the *complete testing assumption*, that there is some known $k \in \mathbb{N}$ such that, if an input sequence is applied k times, then all possible responses are observed [6], and all states reachable by means of this sequence have been visited.
(2) Any two different states of the reference SFSM are *reliably distinguishable* [6]: if a computation κ could nondeterministically reach two different states s_1 or s_2 of M, then there exists an input sequence that, when applied to the unknown target state reached by κ, will lead to an output sequence allowing to determine whether the unknown state had been s_1 or s_2. Note that the alarm system modelled in Fig. 1 is reliably distinguishable for trivial reasons: the target state reached by a computation is already uniquely determined by the sequence of its input/output pairs.
(3) It is required that the output expressions in Σ_O are pairwise distinguishable by finitely many input values. This enables us to check the correctness of output expressions with finitely many test cases. Note that this is not a very hard restriction, since for many function classes with infinite domain and image, its members are uniquely determined by a finite number of arguments. For example, linear expressions $y = a \cdot x + b$ can be pairwise distinguished by two different values of x; and this fact can be generalised to polynomials of a fixed degree in several variables $x_1, \ldots, x_k$. Note that this restriction is vacuous for the alarm system modelled in Fig. 1, since its output expressions do not contain input x.

Property Specifications in LTL. To state behavioural properties of a given SFSM M, we use linear temporal logic LTL [3] with formulae over variable symbols from $V = V_I \cup V_O$. The syntax of LTL formulae φ used in this paper is given by grammar

$$\varphi ::= \phi \mid \neg\varphi \mid \varphi \wedge \varphi \mid \mathbf{X}\varphi \mid \varphi\mathbf{U}\varphi \mid \mathbf{F}\varphi \mid \mathbf{G}\varphi,$$

where ϕ denotes atomic propositions written as quantifier-free first-order expressions over symbols from V. The semantics of LTL formulae is defined over concrete traces κ of M by the following valuation rules.

$$
\begin{array}{llll}
\kappa^i \models \phi & \equiv & \kappa(i) \models \phi & \text{for quantifier-free first-} \\
& & & \text{order expressions } \phi \\
\kappa^i \models \neg\varphi & \equiv & \kappa^i \not\models \varphi & \text{for arbitrary LTL formulae } \varphi \\
\kappa^i \models \varphi \wedge \varphi' & \equiv & \kappa^i \models \varphi \text{ and } \kappa^i \models \varphi' & \text{for arbitrary LTL formulae } \varphi, \varphi' \\
\kappa^i \models \mathbf{X}\varphi & \equiv & i < \#\kappa - 1 \text{ and } \kappa^{i+1} \models \varphi & \text{for arbitrary LTL formulae } \varphi \\
\kappa^i \models \varphi\mathbf{U}\varphi' & \equiv & \exists i \leq j < \#\kappa : \kappa^j \models \varphi' \\
& \text{and} & \forall i \leq k < j : \kappa^k \models \varphi & \text{for arbitrary LTL formulae } \varphi, \varphi' \\
\kappa \models \varphi & \equiv & \kappa^0 \models \varphi & \text{for arbitrary LTL formulae } \varphi
\end{array}
$$

Here κ^i denotes the trace segment $\kappa(i).\kappa(i+1).\kappa(i+2)\dots$. The semantics of path operators $\mathbf{F}$ and $\mathbf{G}$ is defined via equivalences $\mathbf{F}\varphi \equiv (\text{true}\mathbf{U}\varphi)$ and $\mathbf{G}\varphi \equiv \neg\mathbf{F}\neg\varphi$.

Example 3. Consider the property **R1**. *If the value of x never exceeds threshold* max, *then an alarm will never be raised.* This is expressed by LTL formula (recall the ordering $O < W < A$ of output values)

$$\Phi_1 \equiv \mathbf{G}(x \leq \max) \implies \mathbf{G}(y < A)$$

Simulation Construction. Given an SFSM M, any set of atomic first-order expressions with free variables in V induces a *simulation* M^{sim}. Here, this well-known concept is only explained in an intuitive way, for a detailed introduction readers are referred to [3]. It will be shown below how abstracted SFSMs also facilitate property-oriented testing.

Any set of atomic first-order expressions over V can be separated into expressions $f_1, \dots, f_k$ containing free variables from V_I only and expressions $g_1, \dots, g_\ell$ each containing at least one free variable from V_O.

As a first step, this leads to a refinement M' of the model SFSM M by means of the following steps. (1) A transition (s, ϕ, ψ, s') is replaced by transitions $(s, \phi \wedge \alpha, \psi \wedge \beta, s')$, such that each α is conjunction of all $f_1, \dots, f_k$ in positive or negated form, and expression β is a conjunction of all $g_1, \dots, g_\ell$ in positive or negated form. (2) Only the transitions $(s, \phi \wedge \alpha, \psi \wedge \beta, s')$ possessing a model $\sigma : V \longrightarrow D$ for $\phi \wedge \alpha \wedge \psi \wedge \beta$ are added in this replacement.

Then a new SFSM M^{sim} is created as follows. (1) The states and the initial state of M^{sim} are those of M. (2) The transitions of M^{sim} are all $(s, \phi \wedge \alpha, \beta, s')$, where there exists an output expression ψ such that $(s, \phi \wedge \alpha, \psi \wedge \beta, s')$ is a transition of the refined SFSM M'.

An SFSM M^{sim} constructed according to this recipe is a *simulation* of M' in the following sense: For every computation $\kappa = \sigma_1 \dots \sigma_n$ of M', there exists a symbolic trace $\tau^{\text{sim}} = (\phi_1/\psi_1) \dots (\phi_n/\psi_n)$ of M^{sim}, such that (a) κ is witness of τ^{sim}, and (2) any conjunction of positive and negated $f_1, \dots, f_k$ and $g_1, \dots, g_\ell$ for which σ_i is a model is also an implication of $(\phi_i \wedge \psi_i)$.

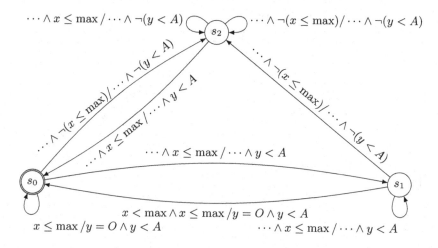

Fig. 2. Refinement M' of the simple alarm system from Fig. 1 with respect to atomic propositions $x \leq$ max and $y < A$. Here, the ellipses represent the original guard or output condition, respectively. The transition from $s1$ to $s0$ shows an actual example.

Example 4. From property $\Phi_1 \equiv \mathbf{G}(x \leq \text{max}) \implies \mathbf{G}(y < A)$ discussed in Example 3 the atomic propositions $f \equiv (x \leq \text{max})$ and $g \equiv (y < A)$ are extracted. The rules for creating a refined machine result in the machine shown in Fig. 2.

Applying the construction rules for the SFSM abstracted from the alarm system with respect to $f, g, \neg f, \neg g$ results in the machine shown in Fig. 3. As an example of a concrete trace of the alarm system, we take again

$$\kappa = \{x \mapsto 100, y \mapsto O\}.\{x \mapsto 50, y \mapsto O\}.$$
$$\{x \mapsto 100, y \mapsto W\}.\{x \mapsto 110, y \mapsto A\}.\{x \mapsto 89, y \mapsto O\}$$

This is a witness of the symbolic trace (we omit the other conjuncts besides $x \leq max$ and its negation)

$$\tau^{\text{sim}} = (\cdots \wedge x \leq \text{max} / y < A).(\cdots \wedge x \leq \text{max} / y < A).(\cdots \wedge x \leq \text{max} / y < A).$$
$$(\cdots \wedge \neg(x \leq \text{max})/\neg(y < A)).(\cdots \wedge x \leq \text{max} / y < A)$$

of the abstracted SFSM.

Input Equivalence Classes and FSM Abstraction. In [7,8] we have presented a testing theory allowing to abstract a variant of Kripke structures to FSMs by means of an input equivalence class construction. The SFSMs considered in this paper can be interpreted as Kripke structures of this variant. The main result of this theory is that test suites generated for the abstracted FSMs can be translated back to the concrete Kripke model level while preserving the

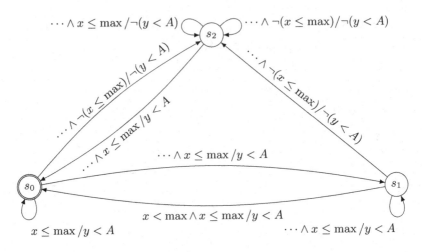

Fig. 3. Simulation M^{sim} of the simple alarm system from Fig. 1 with respect to atomic propositions $x \leq \max$ and $y < A$.

test strength of the original FSM-based suite. While the method proposed in this paper could also be formulated in this more general framework of Kripke structures being used as models and abstracted to FSMs, we decided to present it using SFSMs and abstract these to FSMs. This allows for a simpler description of the abstraction process and implies restrictions that would have to be mentioned explicitly and accounted for in the context of Kripke structures. These restrictions guarantee the existence of an FSM abstraction of the model.

We apply the test strength-preserving translation technique from FSM test cases to concrete Kripke test cases in Sect. 3 to prove that the test strategy introduced there is exhaustive in the sense that it will uncover every property violation of the SUT, provided that certain hypotheses are fulfilled. Therefore, the main facts of the testing theory elaborated in [7,8] are summarised in the following paragraphs.

The theory applies to systems with arbitrary (possibly infinite) input domains and finite domains for internal state variables and output variables. Since our SFSMs are allowed to work with infinite output domains, it is first necessary to create an abstraction with finite output domains.

Step 1. The refined reference model M' constructed above with the atomic propositions of the LTL formula under consideration is further refined by creating input equivalence classes. The classes are constructed by building all conjunctions of positive and negated guard conditions contained in the input alphabet. As before, expressions without a model are dropped. Recall that the input alphabet also contains the possible faulty guards. This further refinement of M' is denoted by M'_c.

The effect of this construction is as follows. A symbolic input sequence $\iota = \phi_1 \ldots \phi_k$ consisting of quantifier-free first-order input class expressions ϕ_i refining the original guards of M' determines finitely many possible symbolic traces in the reference model M'_c and in any possible SFSM over the same alphabet, specifying the true behaviour of a (correct or faulty) implementation. In the deterministic case, this symbolic trace is already uniquely determined by ι.

Step 2. From each refined input class, sufficiently many inputs are selected so that the output expressions that are expected when applying an input from this class in any state can be distinguished from any other output expression contained in Σ_O which would be faulty for inputs from this class.

Note that is some situations, an input class X is so small that the distinction between *all* output expressions is no longer possible. In this case, however, different output expressions would be admissible for the implementation, if their restrictions to X coincide. For example, if X only contains the input value $x = 0$, and $\Sigma_O = \{y = 3, y = 0, y = 3 \cdot x\}$, then output expressions $y = 0$ and $y = 3 \cdot x$ are indistinguishable on X. If output $y = 0$ is expected for input $x = 0$ in the given state, then both expressions would be acceptable in an implementation. The concrete input selections are represented again as valuation functions $s_x : V_I \longrightarrow D$.

The collected concrete inputs s_x selected from the input classes are used to define the (finite) input alphabet A_I of the FSM abstraction constructed by means of the recipe introduced here.

Step 3. Applying the finite number of inputs from each class to every possible output expression associated with this class yields a finite number of values from the possibly infinite output domain. These values are written as valuation functions $s_y : V_O \longrightarrow D$ and used as the output alphabet A_O of the FSM under construction.

Step 4. The state space and initial state of the FSM is identical to the states of M'.

Step 5. The transition relation of the FSM is defined by including (s, s_x, s_y, s') in the relation if and only if there exists a transition (s, ϕ, ψ, s') in M'_c such that $s_x \in A_I \wedge s_y \in A_O \wedge (s_x \cup s_y) \models \phi \wedge \psi$.

The observable, minimised FSM abstraction constructed in these 5 steps is denoted as $F(M'_c)$. The construction recipe above is illustrated in the following example.

Example 5. For the refined alarm system M' shown in Fig. 2, let us assume that the possibly faulty implementations may only mix up guard conditions, but do not mutate them. Then the input equivalence classes calculated according to the recipe described above are listed in the following table. Recall that the constants have been fixed as $\delta = 10$, max $= 100$.

Since the output expressions do not refer to input variable x, a single representative from each input class can be chosen to create the FSM abstraction: the output expressions of M'_c can always be distinguished by their concrete values.

Class	Specified by	Concrete input s_x for A_I
c_0	$x < \max -\delta$	$\{x \mapsto 50\}$
c_1	$\max -\delta \leq x < \max$	$\{x \mapsto 95\}$
c_2	$x = \max$	$\{x \mapsto 100\}$
c_3	$\max < x$	$\{x \mapsto 110\}$

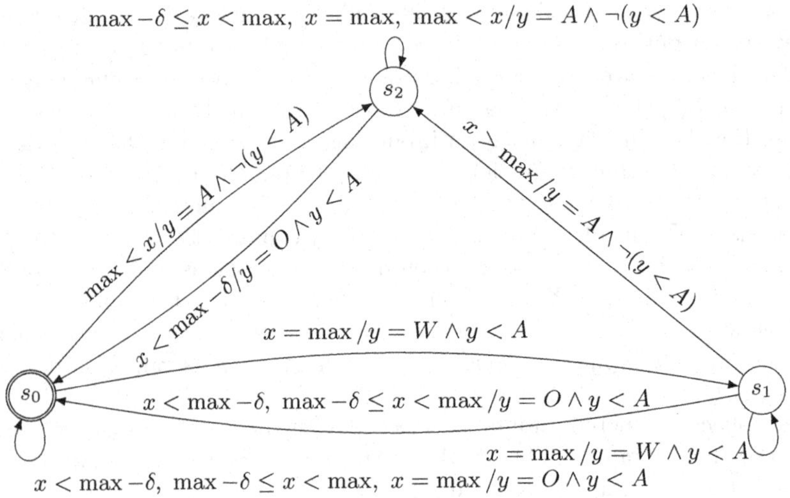

Fig. 4. Alarm system refinement M_c' resulting from application of input equivalence classes to M' from Fig. 2. For brevity, we have consolidated multiple transitions back into one for this figure, if the beginning and end states of these were the same as well as their output condition. This is signified by commas in their input condition, separating the input conditions of individual transitions.

The SFSM M_c' further refining M' by means of these input classes is shown in Fig. 4. We use a short-hand notation where one transition arrow can be labelled by several guards if the output expression is the same in each transition. The abstraction FSM $F(M_c')$ constructed according to the five steps described above is shown in Fig. 4.

The simulation M^{sim} of the alarm system is also refined by the same input equivalence classes. This results in the SFSM shown in Fig. 6. For this SFSM's abstracting FSM, we define output symbols

Symbol	Output expression
e_0	$y < A$
e_1	$\neg(y < A)$

Then we use the same concrete input alphabet as for $F(M_c')$. The resulting FSM is shown in Fig. 7.

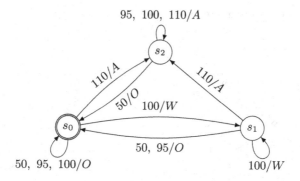

Fig. 5. Finite state machine $F(M'_c)$ abstracting the SFSM M'_c from Fig. 4. Input valuations $\{x \mapsto \text{value}\}$ are abbreviated by 'value', output valuations $\{y \mapsto \text{value}\}$ by 'value'.

After having made this FSM observable and minimal, the resulting prime machine $F(M_c^{\text{sim}})$ has the structure shown in Fig. 8.

Admissible Simulations. To specify precisely which types of simulations M_c^{sim} are admissible, we introduce the concept of *output abstractions* for FSMs. Let $\omega : A_O \longrightarrow A'_O$ be a function between output alphabets. Then any FSM $F = (S, s_0, T, A_I, A_O)$ with alphabet (A_I, A_O), state space S, initial state s_0, and transition relation $T \subseteq S \times A_I \times A_O \times S$ can be mapped to an FSM $\omega(F)$ which is constructed by creating FSM (S, s_0, T', A_I, A'_O) over alphabet (A_I, A'_O) and transition relation

$$T' = \{(s, a, \omega(b), s') \mid (s, a, b, s') \in T\},$$

and constructing the prime machine (i.e. the observable and reduced FSM) of (S, s_0, T', A_I, A'_O). The FSM F' is called the output abstraction of F with respect to ω. The mapping ω is called *state-preserving* for F, if $\omega(F)$ maps traces leading to the same state in F to traces leading to the same state in $\omega(F)$ as well.

It is easy to see that the prime machine $F(M_c^{\text{sim}})$ shown in Fig. 8 has been created from $F(M'_c)$ in Fig. 5 by means of the output abstraction $\omega = \{O \mapsto e_0, W \mapsto e_0, A \mapsto e_1\}$. Comparison of $F(M'_c)$ in Fig. 5 and Fig. 8 shows that this ω is state-preserving.

For deterministic FSMs, every output abstraction is state-preserving, but this is not always the case for nondeterministic FSMs. The exhaustive test suite generation procedure for property checking introduced in the next section requires that simulations are constructed by means of state-preserving output abstractions.

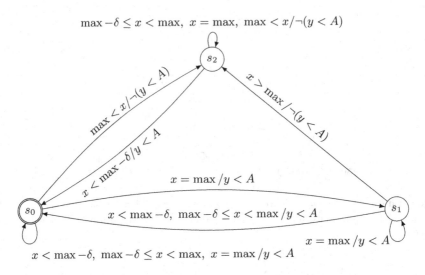

$$\mathrm{max} -\delta \leq x < \mathrm{max}, \; x = \mathrm{max}, \; \mathrm{max} < x/\neg(y < A)$$

$$x < \mathrm{max} -\delta, \; \mathrm{max} -\delta \leq x < \mathrm{max}, \; x = \mathrm{max}/y < A$$

Fig. 6. Alarm system simulation M_c^{sim} from Fig. 3 – further refined by input equivalence classes.

3   An Exhaustive Property-Based Testing Strategy

Prerequisites. Throughout this section, $M = (S, s_0, R, V_I, V_O, D, \Sigma_I, \Sigma_O)$ denotes an SFSM reference model specifying the required behaviour of some implementation whose true behaviour is represented by some (possibly non-equivalent) SFSM I, defined over the same alphabet, as explained in Sect. 2. Set P denotes a finite set of atomic quantifier-free first-order expressions with free variables in V. The properties to be tested are all contained in the set of LTL formulae over atomic expressions from P. As introduced in Sect. 2, the SFSM M_c' has been created from M by refining the guards and the output expressions according to the atomic expressions in P and the input equivalence classes induced by Σ_I. The FSM associated with M_c' is denoted by $F(M_c')$. It is assumed that $F(M_c')$ is a prime machine; this means that it is an observable and minimal FSM [15]. We assume that $F(M_c')$ has $n > 1$ states.[3] The simulation SFSM M_c^{sim} has the same input alphabet as M_c', but a (usually smaller) output alphabet containing output expressions of P only. The prime machine associated with M_c^{sim} is denoted by $F(M_c^{\mathrm{sim}})$. The input alphabet of $F(M_c')$ and $F(M_c^{\mathrm{sim}})$ (i.e. the concrete valuations selected from each input class) is denoted by A_I, the output alphabet of $F(M_c')$ by A_O, and that of $F(M_c^{\mathrm{sim}})$ by A_O^{sim}.

---

[3] If $F(M_c')$ had only one state, we would not have to consider SFSMs, since M could be represented by a stateless function.

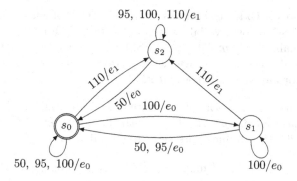

Fig. 7. Finite state machine abstracting the SFSM M_c^{sim} from Fig. 6.

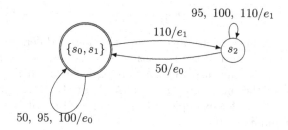

Fig. 8. Prime machine $F(M_c^{\mathrm{sim}})$ (observable, minimised FSM constructed from the FSM in Fig. 7).

Fault Domains. In black-box testing, fault domains[4] are introduced to constrain the possibilities of faulty behaviours of implementations. Without these constraints, it is impossible to guarantee exhaustiveness with *finite* test suites: the existence of hidden internal states leading to faulty behaviour after a trace that is longer than the ones considered in a finite test suite cannot be checked in black-box testing. In the context of this paper, a *fault domain* is a set of SFSMs, always containing the reference model (usually in refined form) representing the intended behaviour. It is assumed that the implementation's true behaviour is reflected by one of the SFSM models in the fault domain.

Now the fault domain $\mathcal{D}(M_c', m)$ contains all SFSMs possessing the same input alphabet and output alphabet as M_c', such that their abstractions to prime machines constructed in analogy to $F(M_c')$ do not have more than m states.

---

[4] The term 'fault domain' is slightly misleading, since its members do not all represent faulty behaviour. The term, however, is well-established [17], so we adopt it here as well.

Property-Related Exhaustiveness. Given the set P of quantifier-free atomic first-order expressions over variables from V, a test suite is *P-exhaustive* for a given fault domain $\mathcal{D}(M'_c, m)$, if every SFSM I representing an implementation behaviour fails at least one test whenever I contains a computation κ_I that is not a witness for any symbolic trace of M^{sim}_c.

Example 6. Consider again the alarm system M from Fig. 1 and the property $\Phi_1 \equiv \mathbf{G}(x \leq \max) \Longrightarrow \mathbf{G}(y < A)$. Then, with the guard refinements introduced for M'_c and M^{sim}_c, the atomic expressions to consider are

$$P = \{x < \max - \delta, \max - \delta \leq x < \max, x = \max, y < A\}.$$

Expressed in terms of P-elements, property Φ_1 can be equivalently expressed as

$$\Phi_1 \equiv \mathbf{G}(x < \max - \delta \vee \max - \delta \leq x < \max \vee x = \max) \Longrightarrow \mathbf{G}(y < A).$$

Now consider an implementation whose behaviour I differs from that of M only by the mutated guard in the transition from $s_0 \longrightarrow s_2$, where we assume that I's guard is $x \geq \max$ instead of $x > \max$, as specified in M. With this guard mutation as the only fault, I is in the fault domain $\mathcal{D}(M'_c, m)$ of the alarm system M. Then, for example, I has a computation (it is assumed again that $\max = 100$ and $\delta = 10$)

$$\kappa_I = \{x \mapsto 50, y \mapsto O\}.\{x \mapsto 100, y \mapsto A\}.$$

Abstracted to a symbolic trace over P, this results in

$$\tau_I = (x < \max - \delta / y < A).(x = \max / \neg(y < A)).$$

Obviously, this is not a symbolic trace of M^{sim}_c, as depicted in Fig. 6. Therefore, any P-exhaustive test suite should fail for I.

Test Suite Generation Procedure. In preparation of the test generation, SFSMs M'_c and M^{sim}_c are created for the given set of P of quantifier-free atomic first-order expressions over variables from V, as explained in Sect. 2. Then their FSM abstractions are constructed (also according to the recipe explained in Sect. 2), and their prime machines are constructed, as described in [15], resulting in FSMs $F(M'_c)$ and $F(M^{\text{sim}}_c)$, respectively. It is required that $F(M^{\text{sim}}_c)$ has been created from $F(M'_c)$ by means of a state-preserving output abstraction.

The rationale behind deriving these FSMs is as follows. FSM $F(M'_c)$ contains sufficiently detailed information to derive tests suitable for detecting any violation of observational equivalence. While the proof for this fact is quite technical, it is fairly intuitive to understand: By construction, $F(M'_c)$ uses concrete input values from every input equivalence class of any implementation whose true behaviour is reflected by an SFSM I in the fault domain $\mathcal{D}(M'_c, m)$. It is possible to derive a collection of input sequences from $F(M'_c)$, so that every input class of I is exercised from every state of I. To ensure this, the assumption that

I's FSM abstraction does not have more than m states is essential. Moreover, the input alphabet of $F(M'_c)$ has been constructed in such a way that sufficiently many values of each input class are exercised on the implementation, such that every output expression error will be revealed.

Next, we realise that testing for observational equivalence is actually more than we really need. So we wish to relax the test requirements in such a way that the test focus is to check whether the satisfaction for atomic properties from P along any computation of I conforms to that of M'_c. For this purpose, $F(M_c^{\mathrm{sim}})$ is needed. Typically, $F(M_c^{\mathrm{sim}})$ has fewer states than $F(M'_c)$ and I. Therefore, we cannot completely forget about $F(M'_c)$, because this machine influences the length of the traces used to test I. If tests were constructed from $F(M_c^{\mathrm{sim}})$, we would either use traces of insufficient length or use too many traces of adequate length, since $F(M_c^{\mathrm{sim}})$ does not provide any information about which traces of maximal length are relevant.

These intuitive considerations lead to the test suite generation procedure described next.

We create an FSM test suite H_P^{fsm} from $F(M'_c)$ and $F(M_c^{\mathrm{sim}})$ as follows. Let $V \subseteq \Sigma_I^*$ be a minimal *state cover* of $F(M'_c)$ containing the empty trace ε. A state cover is a set of input traces, such that for each state s of M'_c, there exists a trace from V reaching s. Define auxiliary sets (A_I^i denotes the set of FSM input traces of length i).

$$A = V \times V \qquad B = V \times \left(V.\bigcup_{i=1}^{m-n+1} A_I^i\right)$$

$$C = \{(\nu.\gamma', \nu.\gamma) \mid \nu \in V \land \gamma \in \left(\bigcup_{i=1}^{m-n+1} A_I^i\right) \land \gamma' \in \mathrm{Pref}(\gamma) - \{\varepsilon\}\}$$

Then define a set D of input trace pairs such that D contains (a) all trace pairs from A leading to different states in the FSM state space of $F(M'_c)$, (b) every trace pair of B and C leading to different states in $F(M_c^{\mathrm{sim}})$ (note that states distinguishable in $F(M'_c)$ may not be distinguishable anymore in $F(M_c^{\mathrm{sim}})$, but state pairs distinguishable in $F(M_c^{\mathrm{sim}})$ are always distinguishable in $F(M'_c)$).

Let function $\Delta : D \longrightarrow A_I^*$ map trace pairs (α, β) leading to distinguishable states (s_1, s_2) to input traces γ distinguishing (s_1, s_2). Now define test FSM test suite H_P^{fsm} by removing all true prefixes from the test case set

$$V.A_I^{m-n+1} \cup \{\alpha.\Delta(\alpha, \beta), \beta.\Delta(\alpha, \beta) \mid (\alpha, \beta) \in D\}.$$

Since the input traces in H_P^{fsm} are already sequences of concrete values (recall that the input alphabet of $F(M'_c)$ consists of concrete values taken from input equivalence classes), we can use them directly as test cases, to be executed against the system under test.

Proving P-Exhaustiveness. The following Lemma shows that M_c^{sim} is crucial for deciding whether an implementation satisfies an LTL formula over atomic expressions from P. It follows directly from the construction rules for M_c^{sim} in Sect. 2.

Lemma 1. *Suppose that the true behaviour of an implementation is given by SFSM $I \in \mathcal{D}(M_c', m)$. Suppose further that every computation of I is also a witness of a symbolic trace in M_c^{sim}. Then I satisfies every LTL formula over positive and negated atomic first-order expressions from P which is satisfied by the reference SFSM M.*

The following main theorem states the exhaustiveness of the test suite generation procedure described above.

Theorem 1. *The test suite H_P constructed above is P-exhaustive for all implementations whose true behaviour is specified by one of the SFSMs contained in the fault domain $\mathcal{D}(M_c', m)$ specified above.*

The proof of the theorem is performed along the following lines.[5] In a first step, the exhaustiveness of the FSM test suite which is created as part of the generation procedure is proven. This is quite similar to the proof presented in [10, Theorem 2], but operates here with a different FSM abstraction $F(M_c^{\text{sim}})$ that may also be nondeterministic. It is essential for this proof that simulations have been generated by means of state-preserving output abstractions.

A second step shows that the selection of concrete input values from input equivalence classes described in the previous section is adequate to uncover every deviation of the implementation behaviour from the specified behaviour. For the proof of this theorem, it is essential that all possible guard mutations and output expression mutations are already contained in the input and output alphabets, respectively. Moreover, it is exploited that sufficiently many concrete values have been selected from the input classes to distinguish faulty output expressions from correct ones.

In practice, it often cannot be decided whether an implementation regarded as a black-box is represented by an SFSM I inside $\mathcal{D}(M_c', m)$ or not. For guaranteed exhaustiveness, a grey-box approach performing preliminary static analyses on the implementation code would be required in order to *prove* that I is inside the fault domain. If this cannot be achieved, it is reassuring to know that test suites constructed according to the generation procedure above have significantly higher test strength than naive random testing, even if I lies outside the fault domain. This has been evaluated in [11].

4   Conclusion

In this paper, an exhaustive test suite for testing LTL properties has been presented. It is based on both a symbolic finite state machine model describing the

---

[5] Details are contained in the technical report https://doi.org/10.5281/zenodo.5151777.

expected behaviour and the formula. By using simulation and abstraction techniques, a test suite generation procedure has been presented which guarantees to uncover every property violation, while possibly finding additional violations of observational equivalence, provided that the implementation's true behaviour is captured by an element of the fault domain. The simulations and abstractions used frequently allow for test suites that are significantly smaller than those testing for equivalence between model and implementation. For a specific variant of properties which is less expressive than LTL, this has already been shown in [10]. We expect similar reductions for the full LTL property checking described here. This will be investigated in the near future, where we will implement the method proposed here as well as improvements upon it in the libfsmtest [1] software library.

Acknowledgements. The authors would like to thank Wen-ling Huang for her valuable inputs concerning the main theorem of this paper.

References

1. Bergenthal, M., Krafczyk, N., Peleska, J., Sachtleben, R.: libfsmtest - An Open Source Library for FSM-based Testing. In: Cavalli, A., Menéndez, H.D. (eds.) Testing Software and Systems - Proceedings of the IFIP-ICTSS 2021. Lecture Notes in Computer Science. Springer, Cham (2021, to appear)
2. Biere, A., Heljanko, K., Junttila, T., Latvala, T., Schuppan, V.: Linear encodings of bounded LTL model checking. Logical Methods Comput. Sci. **2**(5) (2006). https://doi.org/10.2168/LMCS-2(5:5)2006. http://arxiv.org/abs/cs/0611029. arXiv: cs/0611029
3. Clarke, E.M., Grumberg, O., Peled, D.A.: Model Checking. The MIT Press, Cambridge (1999)
4. Fernandez, J.-C., Mounier, L., Pachon, C.: Property oriented test case generation. In: Petrenko, A., Ulrich, A. (eds.) FATES 2003. LNCS, vol. 2931, pp. 147–163. Springer, Heidelberg (2004). https://doi.org/10.1007/978-3-540-24617-6_11
5. Giannakopoulou, D., Havelund, K.: Automata-based verification of temporal properties on running programs. In: Proceedings 16th Annual International Conference on Automated Software Engineering (ASE 2001), pp. 412–416. IEEE Computer Society, San Diego (2001). https://doi.org/10.1109/ASE.2001.989841. http://ieeexplore.ieee.org/document/989841/
6. Hierons, R.M.: Testing from a nondeterministic finite state machine using adaptive state counting. IEEE Trans. Comput. **53**(10), 1330–1342 (2004). https://doi.org/10.1109/TC.2004.85
7. Huang, W., Peleska, J.: Complete model-based equivalence class testing. Softw. Tools Technol. Transfer **18**(3), 265–283 (2016)
8. Huang, W.L., Peleska, J.: Complete model-based equivalence class testing for nondeterministic systems. Formal Aspects Comput. **29**(2), 335–364 (2017). https://doi.org/10.1007/s00165-016-0402-2. https://link.springer.com/article/10.1007/s00165-016-0402-2
9. Huang, W., Peleska, J.: Complete requirements-based testing with finite state machines. CoRR abs/2105.11786 (2021). https://arxiv.org/abs/2105.11786

10. Huang, W.l., Özoguz, S., Peleska, J.: Safety-complete test suites. Softw. Qual. J. (2018). https://doi.org/10.1007/s11219-018-9421-y
11. Hübner, F., Huang, W.L., Peleska, J.: Experimental evaluation of a novel equivalence class partition testing strategy. Softw. Syst. Model., 1–21 (2017). https://doi.org/10.1007/s10270-017-0595-8. https://link.springer.com/article/10.1007/s10270-017-0595-8
12. Machado, P.D.L., Silva, D.A., Mota, A.C.: Towards property oriented testing. Electron. Notes Theor. Comput. Sci. **184**(Supplement C), 3–19 (2007). https://doi.org/10.1016/j.entcs.2007.06.001. http://www.sciencedirect.com/science/article/pii/S157106610700432X
13. Peleska, J.: Model-based avionic systems testing for the airbus family. In: 23rd IEEE European Test Symposium, ETS 2018, Bremen, Germany, 28 May–1 June 2018, pp. 1–10. IEEE (2018). https://doi.org/10.1109/ETS.2018.8400703
14. Peleska, J., Brauer, J., Huang, W.: Model-based testing for avionic systems proven benefits and further challenges. In: Margaria, T., Steffen, B. (eds.) ISoLA 2018. LNCS, vol. 11247, pp. 82–103. Springer, Cham (2018). https://doi.org/10.1007/978-3-030-03427-6_11
15. Peleska, J., Huang, W.: Test automation - foundations and applications of model-based testing. University of Bremen, January 2017. http://www.informatik.uni-bremen.de/agbs/jp/papers/test-automation-huang-peleska.pdf
16. Petrenko, A.: Checking experiments for symbolic input/output finite state machines. In: 2016 IEEE Ninth International Conference on Software Testing, Verification and Validation Workshops (ICSTW), pp. 229–237, April 2016. https://doi.org/10.1109/ICSTW.2016.9
17. Petrenko, A., Yevtushenko, N., Bochmann, G.V.: Fault models for testing in context. In: Gotzhein, R., Bredereke, J. (eds.) Formal Description Techniques IX - Theory, Application and Tools, pp. 163–177. Chapman&Hall (1996)
18. Petrenko, A.: Toward testing from finite state machines with symbolic inputs and outputs. Softw. Syst. Model. **18**(2), 825–835 (2019)
19. Petrenko, A., Simao, A., Maldonado, J.C.: Model-based testing of software and systems: recent advances and challenges. Int. J. Softw. Tools Technol. Transf. **14**(4), 383–386 (2012)
20. van de Pol, J., Meijer, J.: Synchronous or alternating? In: Margaria, T., Graf, S., Larsen, K.G. (eds.) Models, Mindsets, Meta: The What, the How, and the Why Not? LNCS, vol. 11200, pp. 417–430. Springer, Cham (2019). https://doi.org/10.1007/978-3-030-22348-9_24
21. Pretschner, A.: Defect-based testing. In: Irlbeck, M., Peled, D.A., Pretschner, A. (eds.) Dependable Software Systems Engineering, NATO Science for Peace and Security Series, D: Information and Communication Security, vol. 40, pp. 224–245. IOS Press (2015). https://doi.org/10.3233/978-1-61499-495-4-224
22. Sistla, A.P.: Safety, liveness and fairness in temporal logic. Formal Aspects Comput. **6**(5), 495–511 (1994)

nfer – A Tool for Event Stream Abstraction

Sean Kauffman[✉]

Aalborg University, Aalborg, Denmark
seank@cs.aau.dk

Abstract. This work describes `nfer`, an open-source tool for event-stream abstraction and processing. `Nfer` implements the Runtime Verification logic of the same name, providing programming interfaces in C, R, and Python. Rules that dictate `nfer`'s behavior can be written in an external Domain-Specific Language (DSL), mined from historical traces, or given using an internal DSL in Python. The tool is designed for efficient online monitoring of event streams and can also operate as an offline tool to process completed logs.

1 Introduction

The exponential increase in the size and complexity of embedded software over time has led to a similar explosion in traces produced by that software [8]. Comprehending and verifying those traces at runtime requires tools with diverse interfaces that can handle large datasets and integrate with existing code.

`Nfer` is a formalism for abstracting and monitoring event streams [13–15] with an open-source implementation well-suited for a variety of tasks. The `nfer` language is based on Allen's Temporal Logic (ATL) [2] and is designed for expressing relationships between concurrent executions [12]. The implementation is available at http://nfer.io under the GPLv3 license and includes a command-line interpreter, the ability to learn rules from historical traces [11], an embedded monitor compiler, and language integrations with both R and Python.

`Nfer` combines elements of Complex Event Processing (CEP) systems [4,16,17], stream-processing frameworks [5,7], and rule-based logics [3,9]. Like many of these tools, `nfer` applies rules to event streams to generate new facts either online or offline. However, `nfer` treats time as a first-class citizen and produces temporal intervals carrying data using a rule syntax designed to describe context.

This paper describes the open-source implementation of `nfer`. Section 2 contains a programming guide for the `nfer` language, including a running example. Section 3 describes the `nfer` architecture. Section 4 compares `nfer` to TeSSLa, a popular stream processing tool. The paper concludes in Sect. 5.

2 Writing Nfer Rules

`Nfer`'s external domain-specific language (DSL) is a declarative, rule-based logic for inferring a hierarchy of intervals from an event stream. Rules specify how

© Springer Nature Switzerland AG 2021
R. Calinescu and C. S. Păsăreanu (Eds.): SEFM 2021, LNCS 13085, pp. 103–109, 2021.
https://doi.org/10.1007/978-3-030-92124-8_6

new intervals are created from old ones as well as from events. This section uses a running example to illustrate how **nfer** rules are formulated.

Inputs and outputs in **nfer** are temporal intervals of the type $\mathcal{I} \times \mathbb{N} \times \mathbb{N} \times \mathbb{M}$, where $\mathcal{I}$ is the finite set of identifiers (or names), $\mathbb{N}$ is the natural numbers representing begin and end timestamps, and $\mathbb{M}$ is the type of maps from strings to literals. Inputs supplied as events (only one timestamp) are represented internally as *atomic* intervals where the begin and end times are equal. Intervals can have temporal and data relationships, and those relationships define new intervals.

Below is a sequence of six events representing two systems powering on, performing a test, and powering off. In the table on the left, each event is shown as a row in the table with its identifier (name), begin, and end timestamps, as well as two data items: the id of the system and if the test succeeded. On the right of the figure, the same trace is shown on a timeline, with system id:1 above the line and system id:2 below the line. The TEST event with success:false is distinguished by the small shaded flag, where the successful one has a white flag.

Name	Begin	End	id	success
ON	10	10	1	
TEST	20	20	1	true
ON	30	30	2	
TEST	40	40	2	false
OFF	50	50	1	
OFF	60	60	2	

We want to capture periods where system runs had test failures. We also know that when two tests occur during a run, one may report a benign failure that should be ignored. We want to flag test failures where no other successful test occurred during the failed test's run. We begin with a simple, flawed rule.

OPERATING :– ON **before** OFF

This rule says that when an ON interval is seen **before** an OFF interval, create an interval named OPERATING with a begin time equal to the begin time of ON and an end time equal to the end time of OFF. The words OPERATING, ON, and OFF and all arbitrary and could be the names of any intervals, while the word **before** is a keyword that specifies a temporal relationship.

Unfortunately, this rule does not produce what we intended because nfer, by default, only creates *minimal* intervals. A minimal interval is one where no interval with the same name occurs **during** that interval. Only the interval $[30, 50]$ will be reported by this rule, while three intervals will be omitted: $[10, 50]$, $[10, 60]$, and $[30, 60]$. Minimality checking can be disabled to obtain all four intervals.

To generate the two intervals we intend, however, we need to apply a **manual constraint**. The **where** keyword specifies a manual constraint that must be satisfied in addition to those of the temporal relation. The constraint is an expression that must evaluate to a Boolean value and may refer to the timestamps and data of the intervals specified in the temporal relation part of the rule.

Data and timestamps are specified by separating the interval name to reference and its datum name with a period. This rule will generate the desired intervals by specifying that the id of the ON and OFF intervals must be equal.

RUNNING :– ON **before** OFF **where** ON.id = OFF.id **map** { id –> ON.id }

Note that the rule also adds the id of the system to the generated RUNNING intervals. New intervals have empty data maps by default, but data may be specified using the **map** keyword. Map expects a list of keys and associated expressions listed inside curly braces. Map expressions may return any type.

Name	Begin	End	id
RUNNING	10	50	1
RUNNING	30	60	2

Note that the temporal operator (e.g., **before**) typically defines the timestamps of generated intervals. The **begin** and **end** keywords specify expressions that manually override the begin and end timestamps of intervals created by the rule. This allows a rule to specify precisely the interval of interest, for example specifying a period 30 s after an event occurs.

Next, we want to identify the system executions where the test succeeded or failed. We can do that with the following rules.

TESTING :– t:TEST **during** r:RUNNING **where** t.id = r.id **map** {s –> t.success}
FAILURE :– TESTING **where** !TESTING.s

The first rule produces a TESTING interval when a TEST occurs **during** a RUNNING. The rule uses a different temporal operator (**during**, not **before**). It also uses *labels*, prepended to interval names with colons, to provide shorter handles to reference events in expressions. Labels are required when the temporal operator refers to two intervals with the same name.

The second rule produces a FAILURE interval when a TESTING interval has its *s* datum set to false. We mapped the *s* datum of TESTING to the *success* datum of TEST in the previous rule. The FAILURE rule has no temporal operator and will match all TESTING intervals.

To complete the specification, we need a rule that identifies when a FAILURE occurs without another TEST succeeding during the same period. Nfer supports testing for the absence of intervals using the **unless** keyword.

HAZARD :– FAILURE unless contain TEST **where** TEST.success

This rule matches a FAILURE interval when no TEST succeeded in the same period. In our example, the successful test occurred before the FAILURE interval began, so a HAZARD is produced.

Name	Begin	End	id	s
RUNNING	10	50	1	
TESTING	10	50		true
RUNNING	30	60	2	
TESTING	30	60		false
FAILURE	30	60		
HAZARD	30	60		

Nfer also supports mining rules from historical traces [11]. These can be useful as either the basis of a new specification or to check the accuracy of human-written rules. Nfer's mining algorithm works best when traces are generated by highly periodic systems, such as an embedded system running a real-time scheduler. The mining algorithm generates only **before** relations from events and does not yet support learning a hierarchy of rules.

To mine rules from the example in this section, we must extract the events from only one of the systems. Passing such a trace to the nfer's mining algorithm yields the following learned rules that describe **before** relations that hold between the three input event names.

```
learned_0  :- ON before TEST
learned_1  :- ON before OFF
learned_2  :- TEST before OFF
```

3   Nfer's Architecture

Nfer is designed for low-latency operation with minimal memory use. Every interface to nfer uses the same core components, written in C, with minimal external dependencies. Each interface then combines the nfer core with capabilities specific to its intended use-cases.

The nfer architecture is shown in Fig. 1. In the figure, each interface is shown as a separate box, with its sub-components shown as internal labeled boxes. Every interface shares the nfer core, made up of the optimized data-structures and algorithms for executing the nfer monitoring algorithm.

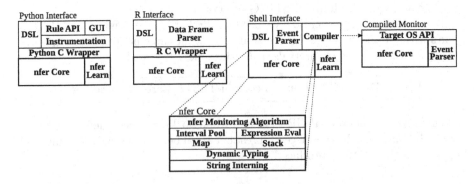

Fig. 1. nfer architecture, with labeled components for each interface

The `nfer` core consists of several custom data-structures designed to work together for efficiency. In `nfer`, all strings are interned and subsequently referenced by a zero-based integer identifier. This permits the map implementation to store values in an array indexed by string ids, making map lookups a simple memory offset calculation. Interning means string comparisons become integer comparisons and memory use for strings is reduced. Expression evaluation for `nfer`'s DSL is performed using a reverse-polish algorithm and a custom stack implementation. The `nfer` core excludes all recursion to facilitate embedded system operation including in expression evaluation, the interval pool's merge-sort implementation, and the `nfer` monitoring algorithm [14].

Nfer's language bindings in R and Python are implemented as native language wrappers around the compiled `nfer` core. The R library is designed for data processing and integrates closely with R's native data structures. In R, `nfer` rules may be loaded from file or mined and then applied to a data frame of events to produce a data frame of intervals. The Python module (available via PyPi as NferModule) includes instrumentation code for Python programs, a native Python rule DSL, and Graphical User Interface (GUI) for visualizing intervals at runtime. By using the compiled `nfer` core for interval processing, both tools are much faster than if the language was implemented natively.

An `nfer` specification may be compiled to a C program using the shell interface. Compiled monitors include the `nfer` core but use only static memory allocation, with the size of components set via compile-time configuration. Static memory allocation reduces the time needed to handle complex specifications but results in higher memory use, since sufficient space must be configured for any expected workloads. Nfer can suggest memory settings given a specification and trace. Compiled monitors are designed for embedded use and have been integrated with Linux and ERIKA Enterprise.

4   Comparison with TeSSLa

TeSSLa is a stream-processing language and tool designed for efficiently checking logical properties and computing temporal metrics from a trace [5]. Like `nfer`, TeSSLa can compute rich abstractions of a trace online using a formal language specification. Embedded TeSSLa [6], which runs on reconfigurable hardware, cannot use the dynamic data structures necessary to emulate `nfer`.

One important difference between `nfer` and TeSSLa is the simplicity of a specification to produce temporal intervals. As a general stream-programming framework, TeSSLa is capable of producing intervals but doing so requires more complex rules. For example, to implement the four rules from Sect. 2 in TeSSLa requires a specification of at least 34 lines.

We conducted an experiment using the example rules from Sect. 2. The specification is simple, but represents a typical use for `nfer` and is complex enough to demonstrate `nfer`'s speed. The TeSSLa specification we used and related documentation is available in the `doc/tessla` directory of `nfer`'s source code repository [1]. We ran two configurations of `nfer`, one interpreting the specification through the shell interface and one using a compiled monitor. We compared these with a compiled TeSSLa 1.2.2 monitor running on Oracle JRE 11.0.12. We generated system logs with varying numbers of operations where each operation resulted in three events. We ran each tool on each log ten times, allocating one core of an AMD EPYC 7642 running at 1.5 GHz.

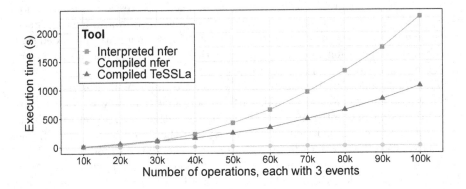

Fig. 2. Execution time used in the experiment

Figure 2 shows the result of the comparison, where lower execution times are better. In the figure, each mean execution time is shown as a point and the standard deviation is omitted as the error bars are too small to be visible. Although the interpreted version of nfer takes around twice the time of the compiled TeSSLa monitor, the compiled nfer monitor is much faster. We do not report on memory use since TeSSLa uses the Java Virtual Machine (JVM), making memory utilization difficult to separate from memory allocation.

There are other Runtime Verification (RV) tools that may be interesting to compare to nfer. In [10], we compared the latency of an nfer integration into a Python framework with the CEP system, Siddhi [17] and found nfer to be over 35 times faster. Some stream RV tools, such as RTLola [7], do not support dynamic data structures and, as such, cannot emulate the full nfer language.

5   Conclusion

The open-source implementation of the nfer logic described in this paper is distributed via the GPLv3 license. The tool is easy to install and use in the Unix command-line, R, and Python. It provides efficient online monitoring of event streams and offline analysis of timed data. Nfer may be used on embedded systems with no dynamic memory, and it can be used to visualize Python program execution in real-time.

The nfer project continues to evolve. Future work includes support for new data formats, MISRA-C compliance for compiled monitors, multi-threading support, and performance improvements. In-progress work will characterize the complexity of different nfer language subsets. Check http://nfer.io for updates.

References

1. Nfer web site. http://nfer.io/. Accessed 11 Oct 2021
2. Allen, J.F.: Maintaining knowledge about temporal intervals. Commun. ACM **26**(11), 832–843 (1983)
3. Barringer, H., Havelund, K.: TRACECONTRACT: a scala DSL for trace analysis. In: Butler, M., Schulte, W. (eds.) FM 2011. LNCS, vol. 6664, pp. 57–72. Springer, Heidelberg (2011). https://doi.org/10.1007/978-3-642-21437-0_7
4. Chen, J., DeWitt, D.J., Tian, F., Wang, Y.: NiagaraCQ: a scalable continuous query system for internet databases. In: International Conference on Management of Data (ACM SIGMOD 2000), pp. 379–390. ACM (2000)
5. Convent, L., Hungerecker, S., Leucker, M., Scheffel, T., Schmitz, M., Thoma, D.: TeSSLa: temporal stream-based specification language. In: Massoni, T., Mousavi, M.R. (eds.) SBMF 2018. LNCS, vol. 11254, pp. 144–162. Springer, Cham (2018). https://doi.org/10.1007/978-3-030-03044-5_10
6. Convent, L., Hungerecker, S., Scheffel, T., Schmitz, M., Thoma, D., Weiss, A.: Hardware-based runtime verification with embedded tracing units and stream processing. In: Colombo, C., Leucker, M. (eds.) RV 2018. LNCS, vol. 11237, pp. 43–63. Springer, Cham (2018). https://doi.org/10.1007/978-3-030-03769-7_5
7. Faymonville, P., Finkbeiner, B., Schwenger, M., Torfah, H.: Real-time stream-based monitoring (2019)
8. van Genuchten, M., Hatton, L.: Compound annual growth rate for software. IEEE Softw. **29**(4), 19–21 (2012)
9. Havelund, K.: Rule-based runtime verification revisited. Int. J. Softw. Tools Technol. Transfer **17**(2), 143–170 (2015)
10. Kauffman, S., Dunne, M., Gracioli, G., Khan, W., Benann, N., Fischmeister, S.: Palisade: a framework for anomaly detection in embedded systems. J. Syst. Archit. **113**, 101876 (2021)
11. Kauffman, S., Fischmeister, S.: Mining temporal intervals from real-time system traces. In: International Workshop on Software Mining (SoftwareMining 2017), pp. 1–8. IEEE (2017)
12. Kauffman, S., Fischmeister, S.: Event stream abstraction using Nfer: demo abstract. In: International Conference on Cyber-Physical Systems (ICCPS 2019), pp. 332–333. ACM Press (2019)
13. Kauffman, S., Havelund, K., Joshi, R.: nfer – a notation and system for inferring event stream abstractions. In: Falcone, Y., Sánchez, C. (eds.) RV 2016. LNCS, vol. 10012, pp. 235–250. Springer, Cham (2016). https://doi.org/10.1007/978-3-319-46982-9_15
14. Kauffman, S., Havelund, K., Joshi, R., Fischmeister, S.: Inferring event stream abstractions. Formal Methods Syst. Des. **53**(1), 54–82 (2018). https://doi.org/10.1007/s10703-018-0317-z
15. Kauffman, S., Joshi, R., Havelund, K.: Towards a logic for inferring properties of event streams. In: Margaria, T., Steffen, B. (eds.) ISoLA 2016. LNCS, vol. 9953, pp. 394–399. Springer, Cham (2016). https://doi.org/10.1007/978-3-319-47169-3_31
16. Bassiliades, N., Governatori, G., Paschke, A. (eds.): RuleML 2008. LNCS, vol. 5321. Springer, Heidelberg (2008). https://doi.org/10.1007/978-3-540-88808-6
17. Suhothayan, S., Gajasinghe, K., Loku Narangoda, I., Chaturanga, S., Perera, S., Nanayakkara, V.: Siddhi: a second look at complex event processing architectures. In: Workshop on Gateway Computing Environments (GCE 2011), pp. 43–50. ACM (2011)

Mining Shape Expressions with ShapeIt

Ezio Bartocci[1(✉)], Jyotirmoy Deshmukh[2(✉)], Cristinel Mateis[3(✉)],
Eleonora Nesterini[1,3(✉)], Dejan Ničković[3(✉)], and Xin Qin[2(✉)]

[1] TU Wien, Vienna, Austria
{ezio.bartocci,eleonora.nesterini}@tuwien.ac.at
[2] University of Southern California, Los Angeles, USA
{jdeshmuk,xinqin}@usc.edu
[3] AIT Austrian Institute of Technology, Vienna, Austria
{Cristinel.Mateis,Dejan.Nickovic}@ait.ac.at

Abstract. We present ShapeIt, a tool for mining specifications of cyber-physical systems (CPS) from their real-valued behaviors. The learned specifications are in the form of *linear shape expressions*, a declarative formal specification language suitable to express behavioral properties over real-valued signals. A linear shape expression is a regular expression composed of parameterized lines as atomic symbols with symbolic constraints on the line parameters. We present here the architecture of our tool along with the different steps of the specification mining algorithm. We also describe the usage of the tool demonstrating its applicability on several case studies from different application domains.

1 Introduction

Specification mining [1–3] is the process of inferring likely system properties from observing its execution and the behavior of its environment. This is an emerging research field that supports the engineering of cyber-physical systems (CPS) where computational units are tightly embedded with physical entities such as sensors and actuators controlling a physical process. CPS often operate (autonomously) in sophisticated and unpredictable environments.

In this context, mined properties can be used to complete existing incomplete or outdated specifications, to understand essential properties of black-box components (e.g., machine learning components) and to automate difficult tasks such as fault-localization [4,5], failure explanation [6] and falsification analysis [7]. The symbolic and declarative nature of formal specification languages provide an high-level and abstract framework that facilitates generalisation. Furthermore, mined specifications are re-usable, data-efficient, compositional and closer to human understanding.

This project has received funding from the European Union's Horizon 2020 research and innovation programme under grant agreement No 956123 and it is partially funded by the TU Wien-funded Doctoral College for SecInt: Secure and Intelligent Human-Centric Digital Technologies, and by the National Science Foundation under grant CCF-1837131.

R. Calinescu and C. S. Păsăreanu (Eds.): SEFM 2021, LNCS 13085, pp. 110–117, 2021.
https://doi.org/10.1007/978-3-030-92124-8_7

In this paper, we present SHAPEIT, a tool for automatic mining formal specifications from positive examples of time-series data encoding system behaviors or a discrete-time trace of the value of a particular system variable. SHAPEIT uses *Linear Shape Expressions* (LSEs) [8], a recent introduced declarative formalism suitable to express expected behaviors over noisy real-valued signals. A linear shape expression is a regular expression composed of parameterized lines as atomic symbols with symbolic constraints on the line parameters.

Given a set of time-series and a maximum error threshold, SHAPEIT implements the specification mining procedure [9] consisting of three steps: (1) **segmentation** of time-series into an optimal piecewise-linear approximation, (2) **abstraction** and **clustering** of linear segments into a finite set of symbols, where each symbol represent a set of similar lines, and (3) **learning** of linear shape expressions from the sequences of symbols generated in the previous step.

In the rest of the paper, we present the specification language and the architecture of the tool. We also show the usage of our tool, demonstrating the applicability to several different examples of time-series taken from the literature. The code of our tool is publicly available at: https://www.doi.org/10.5281/zenodo.5569447.

2 Shape Expressions

Linear shape expressions (LSE) [8] are regular expressions defined over parameterized *linear atomic shapes*, where a linear atomic shape is uniquely determined by three parameters: slope a, (relative) offset b and duration d. LSEs can have additional constraints over these parameters. We use the following syntax to define the fragment of LSEs supported by SHAPEIT.

$$\text{shape} := \text{line}(a, b, d) \mid \text{shape}_1 + \text{shape}_2 \mid \text{shape}_1 . \text{shape}_2 \mid (\text{shape})*$$
$$\text{cst} := x \text{ in } [\mathbf{c1}, \mathbf{c2}] \mid \text{cst}_1 \text{ and } \text{cst}_2$$
$$\text{SE} := \text{shape} : \text{cst}$$

where $\mathbf{c1}$ and $\mathbf{c2}$ are rational constants such that $\mathbf{c1} \leq \mathbf{c2}$.

A LSE SE consists of two main components, a regular expression shape that captures the qualitative aspect of the specification, and a constraint cst imposed on the LSE parameters. Shape expressions are evaluated against finite signals – sequences of (time, value) pairs. The semantics of LSE is defined in terms of a *noisy match* relation. We say that a signal is a ν-noisy match of a linear atomic shape, if there exists an ideal line segment with some slope a, relative offset b and duration d such that (1) a, b and d satisfy the constraint cst, and (2) the mean square error (MSE) between the signal segment and the ideal line segment is smaller than or equal to ν. This definition is inductively lifted to arbitrary LSEs. In essence, a signal is a ν-noisy match of an arbitrary LSE if there exists a sequence of linear atomic shapes with instantiated parameters such that: (1) the sequence is consistent with the qualitative (regular expression) part of the LSE, (2) the instantiated parameters satisfy the LSE constraint, and (3) the signal can be split into the sequence with the same number of segments, such that each signal segment is a ν-noisy match of its corresponding atomic shape. The formal syntax and semantics of shape expressions are presented in [9].

3   ShapeIt Architecture, Methods and Implementation

The architecture of SHAPEIT is depicted in Fig. 1. The tool consists of five components: (1) segmentation, (2) abstraction, (3) clustering, (4) automata learning and (5) translation from automata to regular expressions. SHAPEIT is implemented in Python 3 with the use of external Python and Java libraries.

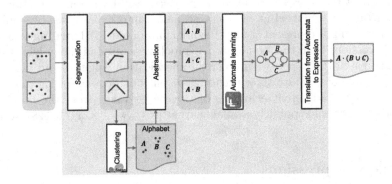

Fig. 1. Overview of SHAPEIT workflow.

Segmentation module implements the piecewise-linear approximation algorithm with quadratic complexity from [9] that given a time series and a mean square error (MSE) threshold computes the minimal sequence of segments such that for each segment of data, its linear regression MSE is below the threshold. The input of this module is a set of time-series and the output is a set of line segment sequences, where each line segment is characterized by slope, relative offset and duration parameters.

Abstraction and clustering module takes as input the set of line segments (computed by the segmentation module) and uses the k-Means clustering implementation from the scikit-learn library[1] to group lines with similar parameters. The user specifies a threshold on the derivative of the Within-Cluster-Sum-of-Squares (WCSS) error measure to determine the optimal number of clusters. The tool defines a finite alphabet in which each letter is associated to a different cluster. Each letter is also assigned the minimal bounding cube that contains all the points in its corresponding cluster. Each line segment is mapped to a letter in the alphabet, resulting in a set of finite words.

Automata learning module applies the Regular Positive and Negative Inference (RPNI) algorithm for passive learning from positive examples, implemented in the Java learnlib library[2], to infer a deterministic finite automaton (DFA) from

---

[1] https://scikit-learn.org/stable/.

[2] https://learnlib.de/.

a set of finite words. The integration of the Java library in our Python implementation is done using the JPype library.[3]

DFA to shape expressions module implements the algorithm for translating DFAs to regular expressions using the state elimination method. The NetworkX library[4] is used to represent and manipulate DFAs during the translation.

4 Evaluation

In the following, we evaluate the applicability of SHAPEIT[5] to find temporal patterns over different time-series datasets stored in the UCR Time Series Classification Archive [10]. Our experiments run on a Notebook Dell Latitude 5320, Intel Quad-Core i7-1185G7 (3,00 GHz/Turbo 4,80 GHz), RAM 32 GB. SHAPEIT software components run on Python version 3.8.8 and on Java version 16.0.2. For all the experiments we set to 10 the threshold on the derivative of the WCSS error discussed in Sect. 3.

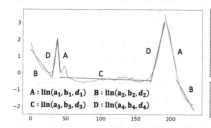

$a_1 \in [-0.5181, -0.1939]$ $b_1 \in [16.431, 44.369]$ $d_1 \in [4, 17]$

$a_2 \in [-0.0756, -0.0507]$ $b_2 \in [1.2833, 15.225]$ $d_2 \in [25, 31]$

$a_3 \in [-0.00159, -0.00089]$ $b_3 \in [-0.283, -0.205]$ $d_3 \in [128, 130]$

$a_4 \in [0.1679, 0.3339]$ $b_4 \in [-32.16, -8.74]$ $d_4 \in [7, 21]$

Constraints over line parameters slope (a_l), offset (b_l) and duration (d_l)

$$\varphi = (B \cdot D \cdot A \cdot C \cdot D \cdot A \cdot B)$$

Linear Shape Expression

Fig. 2. (Left) An example of piece-wise linear approximation of a trace in *Wine dataset* with $\varepsilon_{\max} = 0.05$ (Right) Generated Linear Shape Expression.

Wine dataset This dataset [10] consists of 111 traces, representing the food spectrograph of two kinds of wine. We consider only one class of wine data, containing 57 traces of length 234 samples (Fig. 2 shows one example).

By setting the maximum error threshold

# traces	$\|w\|$	$t_s(s)$	$t_c(s)$	$t_l(s)$	$t_{\text{total}}(s)$
1	10	$2.205 \cdot 10^{-4}$	$1.100 \cdot 10^{-6}$	$3.499 \cdot 10^{-4}$	$5.724 \cdot 10^{-4}$
1	100	$7.173 \cdot 10^{-2}$	$4.968 \cdot 10^{-3}$	$3.727 \cdot 10^{-4}$	$7.707 \cdot 10^{-2}$
1	234	$4.227 \cdot 10^{-1}$	$5.195 \cdot 10^{-3}$	$4.319 \cdot 10^{-4}$	$4.283 \cdot 10^{-1}$
10	10	$1.993 \cdot 10^{-3}$	$4.932 \cdot 10^{-3}$	$4.175 \cdot 10^{-4}$	$7.281 \cdot 10^{-3}$
10	100	$7.232 \cdot 10^{-1}$	$5.114 \cdot 10^{-3}$	$7.976 \cdot 10^{-4}$	$7.183 \cdot 10^{-1}$
10	234	4.353	$1.176 \cdot 10^{-2}$	$1.537 \cdot 10^{-3}$	4.366
57	10	$1.21 \cdot 10^{-2}$	$7.594 \cdot 10^{-3}$	$6.122 \cdot 10^{-4}$	$2.039 \cdot 10^{-2}$
57	100	4.110	$2.954 \cdot 10^{-2}$	$2.188 \cdot 10^{-2}$	4.161
57	234	$2.934 \cdot 10$	$2.983 \cdot 10^{-2}$	$4.201 \cdot 10^{-3}$	$2.937 \cdot 10$

Table 1. Computational cost of SHAPEIT.

---

[3] https://jpype.readthedocs.io/en/latest/.

[4] https://networkx.org/.

[5] commit in the repository used: d92341998d66615cf6a9c4f3bcc419df4cd988b6.

$\varepsilon_{\max}$ to 0.05 (a little insight into how the learned specification varies depending on this value can be found in Table 2), SHAPEIT obtains an alphabet of four letters, each one describing a set of segments characterized by the values of slope, relative offset and duration reported in Fig. 2.

The concatenation of letters D and A represents the peaks that appear in the shape (see Fig. 2), in which D describes the rising part (with positive slope) and A the decreasing one (with negative slope). Letter C represents the approximately constant part of the trace that separates the two peaks, while B describes the two extremes (they are both decreasing segments but less steep than the ones that come after the peaks' maxima).

In this particular application the values of slopes would be able to distinguish the different letters by their own: the intervals of slopes are indeed disjoint. The same happens for the relative offset but not for the duration.

SHAPEIT generates an LSE specification (see Fig. 2) that captures the two main peaks of the trace, but it is not able to recognize the little one that comes immediately after the first peak. The maximum error threshold $\varepsilon_{\max}$ should be reduced if one is interested in detecting also this little curve.

In Table 1, we report the time (expressed in seconds) required by the tool to complete the three different phases: segmentation (t_s), clustering (t_c) and automata learning (t_l). In the last column, t_{total} summarizes the total time needed. Varying the number of traces and their lengths, we can

$\varepsilon_{\max}$	φ	& clusters
0.05	$B \cdot\ D \cdot A \cdot C \cdot D \cdot A \cdot B$	4
0.1	$F \cdot\ E \cdot G \cdot I \cdot H \cdot F$	5
0.5	$K \cdot (L + M)$	3

Table 2. Sensitivity w.r.t. $\varepsilon_{\max}$

observe that almost always the segmentation represents the most expensive part of the computation, while the clustering and the automata learning can be both considered negligible in terms of computation time. The only exceptions are the two cases in which the total number of traces is 1 or 10 with traces long only 10: the values of t_s, t_c and t_l are comparable since the segmentation is very fast due to the low number of samples to approximate.

In Table 2, we compare the specifications learned varying the maximum error threshold $\varepsilon_{\max}$ from 0.05 to 0.5. The number of clusters does not decrease monotonically when increasing the maximum error allowed in the segmentation, while the specifications become shorter and therefore have less explanatory power.

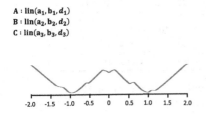

$A : \mathrm{lin}(a_1, b_1, d_1)$
$B : \mathrm{lin}(a_2, b_2, d_2)$
$C : \mathrm{lin}(a_3, b_3, d_3)$

$a_1 \in [0.02305, 0.03601]$ $b_1 \in [-14.509, -4.105]$ $d_1 \in [86, 153]$
$a_2 \in [-0.03827, -0.0184]$ $b_2 \in [1.268\ 9.312]$ $d_2 \in [55, 139]$
$a_3 \in [-0.03105, -0.027366]$ $b_3 \in [-10.396, 1.943]$ $d_3 \in [12, 68]$

Constraints over line parameters slope (a_i), offset (b_i) and duration (d_i)

$$\varphi = (B\ *) \cdot \left(A + (C \cdot A)\right) \cdot B \cdot \left((B + C)\ *\right) \cdot A$$

Linear Shape Expression

Fig. 3. (Left) Example of time series generated from the fish contour (see Fig. 20 of [11] for more details). (Right) Generated Linear Shape Expression.

Fish Data Set. This data set [10] is composed by 350 time series representing the shape of seven different species of fishes (chinook salmon, winter coho, brown trout, Bonneville cutthroat, Colorado River cutthroat trout, Yellowstone cutthroat and mountain whitefish). Starting from 50 images for each class, Lee *et al.* in [12] generated the data set leveraging a novel technique that transforms the contour of the fish into a time series (see Fig. 3 on the left) using a turn-angle function as illustrated in [11]. Setting to 0.05 the maximum threshold error, with SHAPEIT we are able to learn a specification (Fig. 3 on the right) from 26 shapes of the same species of fish, each one containing 463 samples.

The concatenation of letters B and A represents the predominant shape in the traces: the triangular repeating behavior where, in particular, A describes the rising part and B the descending one (see Fig. 3). Letter C is instead used to symbolize the noisy parts, both with positive and negative slope, that eventually separates these longer segments. The choice operator $(+)$ represents the possibility to have multiple symbols or expressions in different time series. Finally, the Kleene star $(*)$ is used to indicate that a symbol or an expression can appear zero or more times.

The learned specification provides insights about the relevant shapes in the time series data, displaying them in an human understandable language and therefore offering interpretability to the user. In this example, referring to the fish image in Fig. 3 on the left, we can associate the concatenation of letters B and A in the specification to the upper contour of the fish silhouette that is starting from the head and is ending with the tail. Since the same concatenation is then repeated in the specification, we can infer that the contour of the lower part of the fish is not significantly different from the upper one. Finally, letter C can be interpreted as the presence of a big fin that interrupts the predominant lines described by letters A and B.

5   Conclusion and Future Work

In this paper, we presented SHAPEIT, a tool for mining specifications that describe the behaviors of CPS. The tool requires a set of real-valued signals generated by the system under study as input and it returns as output the specification that better summarize the properties of the traces in the form of linear shape expression. SHAPEIT is structured in three phases: segmentation (approximating the traces with segments), abstraction and clustering (grouping lines with similar parameters) and automata learning (learning a DFA from words). Two additional values are needed as inputs to regulate the first two processes: a threshold expressing the maximum error allowed by the approximation and a threshold for the WCSS error to find an optimal number of clusters. We demonstrated the applicability of our tool over two different case studies (*Wine* and *Fish*) but other datasets are present in our repository. These data can be used as well to do experiments and gain confidence with SHAPEIT.

As possible future works, we are interested in exploring and learning more general Shape Expressions (not necessarily linear ones), probably gaining explanatory power at the cost of an increasing computation time. We will also study how to automatize the tuning of the two thresholds required by the tool for the segmentation and the clustering phases. In this paper, the segmentation tool finds automatically the optimal number of segments to be used for the approximation, given a maximum error allowed. However it has already been developed to work in the other way round: receiving the number of required segments as input and then finding the approximation that provides the minimum error. It will be therefore interesting to exploit this feature to embed some domain knowledge (in the form of number of segments) in the specification mining process. A step forward will be adding the possibility to set constraints to the parameters of the lines. Finally, an other direction of work could be trying to generalize the tool in order to make it able to handle online processes instead of only offline ones.

References

1. Nenzi, L., Silvetti, S., Bartocci, E., Bortolussi, L.: A robust genetic algorithm for learning temporal specifications from data. In: McIver, A., Horvath, A. (eds.) QEST 2018. LNCS, vol. 11024, pp. 323–338. Springer, Cham (2018). https://doi.org/10.1007/978-3-319-99154-2_20
2. Bartocci, E., Bortolussi, L., Sanguinetti, G.: Data-driven statistical learning of temporal logic properties. In: Proceedings of FORMATS, pp. 23–37 (2014)
3. Wang, F., Cao, Z., Tan, L., Zong, H.: Survey on learning-based formal methods: taxonomy, applications and possible future directions. IEEE Access 8, 108561–108578 (2020)
4. Bartocci, E., Ferrère, T., Manjunath, N., Nickovic, D.: Localizing faults in Simulink/state flow models with STL. In: HSCC, pp. 197–206, ACM (2018)
5. Jin, X., Donzé, A., Deshmukh, J.V., Seshia, S.A.: Mining requirements from closed-loop control models. IEEE TCAD 34(11), 1704–1717 (2015)
6. Bartocci, E., Manjunath, N., Mariani, L., Mateis, C., Ničković, D.: Automatic failure explanation in CPS models. In: Ölveczky, P.C., Salaün, G. (eds.) SEFM 2019. LNCS, vol. 11724, pp. 69–86. Springer, Cham (2019). https://doi.org/10.1007/978-3-030-30446-1_4
7. Bartocci, E., et al.: Specification-based monitoring of cyber-physical systems: a survey on theory, tools and applications. In: Bartocci, E., Falcone, Y. (eds.) Lectures on Runtime Verification. LNCS, vol. 10457, pp. 135–175. Springer, Cham (2018). https://doi.org/10.1007/978-3-319-75632-5_5
8. Ničković, D., Qin, X., Ferrère, T., Mateis, C., Deshmukh, J.: Shape. In: Finkbeiner, B., Mariani, L. (eds.) RV 2019. LNCS, vol. 11757, pp. 292–309. Springer, Cham (2019). https://doi.org/10.1007/978-3-030-32079-9_17
9. Bartocci, E., Deshmukh, J., Gigler, F., Mateis, C., Nickovic, D., Qin, X.: Mining shape expressions from positive examples. IEEE Trans. Comput. Aided Des. Integr. Circuits Syst. 39(11), 3809–3820 (2020)
10. Chen, Y., et al.: The UCR time series classification archive. July 2015. www.cs.ucr.edu/~eamonn/time_series_data/

11. Ueno, K., Xi, X., Keogh, E., Lee, D.-J.: Anytime classification using the nearest neighbor algorithm with applications to stream mining. In: Sixth International Conference on Data Mining (ICDM 2006), pp. 623–632 (2006)

12. Lee, D.J., Archibald, J.K., Schoenberger, R.B., Dennis, A.W., Shiozawa, D.K.: Contour matching for fish species recognition and migration monitoring. In: Smolinski, T.G., Milanova, M.G., Hassanien, A.E. (eds.) Applications of Computational Intelligence in Biology. Studies in Computational Intelligence, vol. 122, pp 183-207. Springer, Heidelberg (2008). https://doi.org/10.1007/978-3-540-78534-7_8

Security and Privacy

Refining Privacy-Aware Data Flow Diagrams

Hanaa Alshareef[1]([✉])(ID), Sandro Stucki[1](ID), and Gerardo Schneider[2](ID)

[1] Chalmers University of Technology, Gothenburg, Sweden
{hanaa,sandros}@chalmers.se
[2] University of Gothenburg, Gothenburg, Sweden
gersch@chalmers.se

Abstract. Privacy, like security, is a non-functional property, yet most software design tools are focused on functional aspects, using for instance Data Flow Diagrams (DFDs). In previous work, a conceptual model was introduced where DFDs were extended into so-called Privacy-Aware Data Flow Diagrams (PA-DFDs) with the aim of adding specific privacy checks to existing DFDs. An implementation to add such automatic checks has also been developed. In this paper, we define the notion of refinement for both DFDs and PA-DFDs as a special type of structure-preserving map (or graph homomorphism). We also provide three algorithms to find, check and transform refinements, and we show that the standard diagram "transform→refine/refine→transform" commutes. We have implemented our algorithms in a proof-of-concept tool called *DFD Refinery*, and have applied it to realistic scenarios.

Keywords: Privacy by design · DFDs · GDPR · Refinement

1 Introduction

Privacy compliance has become a primary concern for most companies since the enactment of strong and demanding regulations on personal data protection, such as the *European General Data Protection Regulation* (GDPR) introduced few years ago [16]. Enforcing privacy compliance, however, is not easy. Indeed, *privacy* refers to a whole family of properties, including confidentiality, secrecy, data minimization (DM), privacy impact assessment (PIA), user consent, the right to be forgotten, purpose limitation, and more. Furthermore, even for specific properties, privacy compliance is in general undecidable [28,30].

A good practice to handle the "privacy problem" is to follow the *Privacy by Design* (PbD) principle [11], where privacy is taken into account from the very beginning of the software development process. This approach has been shown to make the problem of privacy compliance more tractable [13].

This research has been partially supported by the Cultural Office of the Saudi Embassy in Berlin, Germany and by the Swedish Research Council (Vetenskapsrådet) under Grant 2018-04230 "Perspex".

R. Calinescu and C. S. Păsăreanu (Eds.): SEFM 2021, LNCS 13085, pp. 121–140, 2021.
https://doi.org/10.1007/978-3-030-92124-8_8

One such PbD approach was introduced by Antignac et al. [6,7], who proposed a technique based on model transformation for automatically adding privacy checks to *Data Flow Diagrams* (DFDs). They considered an extension of DFDs called *Business-oriented Data Flow Diagrams* (B-DFDs) and further extended them with checks for specific privacy concepts, namely retention time and purpose limitation. These checks are automatically added for each operation on sensitive (personal) data (storage, forwarding, and processing of data). The enhanced diagram is called a *Privacy-Aware Data Flow Diagram* (PA-DFD). In that proposal, the software engineer designs a B-DFD, pushes a button to obtain a PA-DFD, inspects it manually, with the aim to generate a program template from the PA-DFD to guide the programmer in the concrete implementation of the privacy checks. Antignac et al. outlined their transformation from B-DFDs to PA-DFDs through set of high-level graphical "rules". A full algorithm and reference implementation were later provided by Alshareef et al. [5].

B-DFDs have been shown to be useful for software engineers when designing functional properties, and the privacy-enhanced PA-DFDs are a step towards adding specific non-functional aspects to such designs.

One issue with B-DFDs (and PA-DFDs) is that they may become big when modeling real-life systems. The traditional solution to pragmatically circumvent this problem is to either compose smaller processes, following a bottom-up approach, or to start from a high-level design consisting of composite processes that are later refined into more detailed processes, following a top-down approach. In both cases, there is a need to relate different levels of abstraction. To do so we should have a precise definition of refinement, and a rigorous methodology to check and obtain suitable refinements preserving relevant properties.

In this paper, we are concerned with the formal refinement of both B-DFDs and PA-DFDs. Concretely, we make the following contributions:

1. We propose a notion of refinement for both B-DFDs and PA-DFDs, formalizing the comparison of different levels of abstractions of such diagrams. Our notion of refinement is declarative and applies both to top-down and bottom-up refinement; for PA-DFDs, it preserves privacy and types. Furthermore, our notion of refinement has the property that it commutes with transformation (from B-DFDs to PA-DFDs). Although many informal rules and conditions for DFD refinement have been proposed and discussed in the software engineering literature, ours is, to the best of our knowledge, the first formal definition of DFD refinement. Though we are primarily interested in its applications to B-DFDs and PA-DFDs, we think that it is flexible enough to be extended to many other flavors of DFDs. (Sect. 3.)
2. We provide three algorithms:
   (a) *Refinement Checking.* Given abstract and concrete B-DFDs, and a candidate mapping, our refinement checking algorithm assesses whether the mapping is a refinement according to our formal definition. (Sect. 3.2.)
   (b) *Refinement Search.* This algorithm takes partial (incomplete) mappings and proposes possible extensions to produce a complete refinement. When starting from an empty mapping, it produces all possible refinements between the abstract and concrete B-DFDs. (Sect. 3.2.)

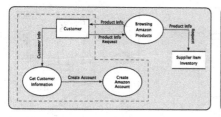 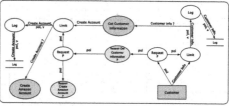

(a) Original B-DFD.   (b) Part of the resulting PA-DFD.

Fig. 1. Excerpts from DFDs modeling an e-store ordering system.

(c) *Refinement Transformation.* It is essential that privacy checks are preserved by refinements of PA-DFDs. Our third algorithm takes a (correct) mapping between abstract and concrete B-DFDs, and transforms it into a refinement between the corresponding PA-DFDs obtained by transforming the abstract and concrete B-DFDs. The resulting refinement ensures that all privacy checks between the abstract and concrete PA-DFDs are preserved. (Sect. 3.3.)

3. We have implemented the above algorithms in Python as part of a proof-of-concept tool called *DFD Refinery* (Sect. 4), and have applied it to a case study on an automated payment system (Sect. 5.)

2   Preliminaries

GDPR. The European *General Data Protection Regulation* (GDPR) contains 99 articles regulating *personal data* processing. It is organized around a number of key concepts, most notably its seven *principles* relating to personal data processing, the *rights* of data subjects and six *lawful grounds* for data processing operations. Relevant to this paper are the principles of *purpose limitation* (data may only be used for purposes to which the data subject consented) and *accountability*, as well as the *right to be forgotten* and the lawful ground of *consent*. See [16] and [23] for more details on the GDPR.

Data Flow Diagrams (DFDs). A *data flow diagram* (DFD) is a graphical representation of how data flows among software components. As shown in Fig. 1, DFDs are composed of *activators* and *flows*. Activators can be *external entities* (rectangles), *processes* (ellipses) and *data stores* (double horizontal lines). Processes may represent detailed low-level operations or complex high-level functionality that could be refined into sub-processes (the latter are drawn as double-lined ellipses). Data *flow* is represented by arrows.

Antignac et al. [6,7] extended DFDs with a *data deletion* type of flow and a data structure to specify personal data: (i) the *owner* of personal data, (ii) the *purpose* for which the data can be used as consented by the data subject, and (iii) the *retention* time for the data. This extension is referred to as *Business-oriented DFD* (B-DFD). Note that the data structure associated with B-DFDs is not relevant here.

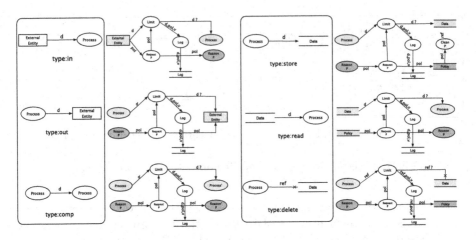

Fig. 2. Selection of B-DFD flow types and corresponding transformation rules [5].

Adding Privacy Checks to DFDs. Antignac et al. [6,7] further extended B-DFDs with privacy checks for purpose limitation and retention time, as well as privacy mechanisms to ensure accountability and policy management. The resulting diagrams are called *Privacy-Aware Data Flow Diagrams* (PA-DFDs). Building on that work, we defined and implemented an algorithm for transforming B-DFDs into PA-DFDs [5]. The transformation is rule-based, with one rule for every type of B-DFD flow.

Figure 2 shows a subset of basic B-DFD flow types and the corresponding transformation rules. (The remaining rules, which cover composite activators, are given in Appendix A.) The right-hand side of each rule shows the PA-DFD corresponding to the original B-DFD flow; it extends the original flow with new activators and flows implementing the necessary privacy mechanisms.

To represent these mechanisms, the set of activator types in PA-DFDs is augmented with five novel "Process" subtypes: "Limit", "Reason", "Request", "Log" and "Clean". "Limit" activators implement the principle of purpose limitation: they inspect whether the consent given by the data subject is compatible with the action of a downstream process and discard data values for which this is not the case. The corresponding policy is supplied by a "Request" activator. "Log" activators store the decisions of "Limit" activators (and the associated data) in a dedicated data store, ensuring the principle of accountability. The "Reason" activator is used to get an updated policy "pol" corresponding to a newly computed data value. Finally, "Clean" ensures that personal data is eliminated from the data store upon expiry, guaranteeing data retention policy.

To illustrate our transformation, consider the B-DFD shown in Fig. 1a and (part of) its corresponding PA-DFD in Fig. 1b. The two rules for the flow types in and comp have been applied to a subset of the B-DFD in Fig. 1a (the part inside the dashed line). Consider the in flow labeled "Customer Information", and the corresponding PA-DFD elements shown in the right half of Fig. 1b. In

addition to the original "Customer Info" data, the external entity "Customer" in
the PA-DFD now also provides an associated privacy policy information "pol".
The data flows to the "Limit" process which verifies that the data subject has
consented to the use of "Customer Info" for downstream processing. The consent
is specified in the policy "pol", received via the "Request" process. The data
value, its policy and the verdict ("v") of the "Limit" process are all logged by the
"Log" process in the "Log" store. If the verdict is positive, the data and policy
are forwarded to the process "Get Customer Information" and its associated
"Reason" process, respectively. The latter computes the updated privacy policy
information associated with the output flow "Create Account".

For details about PA-DFDs and our transformation, see Alshareef et al. [5].

Hierarchical Modeling (Refinement of DFDs). Refinement is a method
used to relate the abstract model of a software system to another more concrete
model while maintaining the abstract model's properties [1]. It is applicable to
system artifacts ranging from modeling and design levels to implementation and
programming levels. It is typical to specify invariants that define the properties
of the system being modeled at the most abstract level. These invariants must
be preserved by all the refined versions of the model.

Concerning refinement in DFDs, several works discuss *leveling* (hierarchical
modeling) and informal *consistency rules* [14,29,33]. The highest level of DFD
shows all external entities and the primary data flows between the external
entities and a system, represented as one composite process. This level is called
Context Diagram. It is typically decomposed into a lower-level diagram, called
the *Level 0* DFD, which can be further decomposed into a *Level 1* DFD, and so
on. There are two standard rules for ensuring consistency. First, every process,
data store and external entity on an abstract level is shown on a refined level
(*balancing rule*). Second, the input and output data flows specified in an abstract
level must hold on its refined version (*preservation of connectivity*). We formalize
these rules (and others) in the next section.

3 Refining B-DFDs and PA-DFDs

3.1 Refinement of Attributed Multigraphs

Following our previous work on PA-DFDs [5], we formally represent DFDs as
attributed multigraphs with activators as nodes and flows as edges.

Definition 1. *An* attributed multigraph *(or simply* graph*) G is a tuple $G = (\mathcal{N}, \mathcal{F}, \mathcal{A}, \mathcal{V}, s, t, \ell_{\mathcal{N}}, \ell_{\mathcal{F}})$ where $\mathcal{N}$, $\mathcal{F}$, $\mathcal{A}$ and $\mathcal{V}$ are sets of nodes, edges, attributes and attribute values, respectively; $s, t : \mathcal{F} \to \mathcal{N}$ are the source and target maps; $\ell_{\mathcal{N}} : \mathcal{N} \to (\mathcal{A} \to \mathcal{V})$ and $\ell_{\mathcal{F}} : \mathcal{F} \to (\mathcal{A} \to \mathcal{V})$ are attribute maps that assign values for the different attributes to nodes and flows, respectively.*

Examples of attributed multigraphs are shown in Fig. 3. The graph G_1 has nodes
$\mathcal{N} = \{E1, E2, CP1\}$ and edges $\mathcal{F} = \{d.1, \ldots, d.4\}$. G_1 is a multigraph since both
edges d.1 and d.2 connect the same source and target nodes: $s(d.1) = s(d.2) = E1$

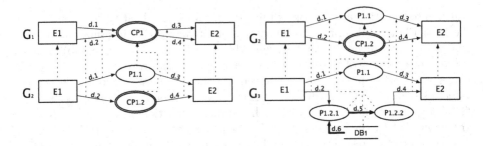

Fig. 3. Example of B-DFDs levels

and $t(\text{d.1}) = t(\text{d.2}) = \text{CP1}$. Attributes allow us to specify properties of activators and flows, such as their type or associated privacy information. For example, the graph G_1 has two kinds of nodes, external entities and composite processes. We formalize this by defining its attribute and value sets as $\mathcal{A} = \{\text{type}\}$ and $\mathcal{V} = \{\text{ext}, \text{cproc}\}$, and its node attribute map as $\ell_{\mathcal{N}}(\text{E1})(\text{type}) = \ell_{\mathcal{N}}(\text{E2})(\text{type}) = \text{ext}$ and $\ell_{\mathcal{N}}(\text{CP1})(\text{type}) = \text{cproc}$. Note that the attribute maps are partial, i.e., nodes and edges may lack values for certain attributes. If we extend the value set $\mathcal{V}$ with types for processes (proc) and data stores (db), we can encode the graphs G_2 and G_3 shown in Fig. 3 similarly.

Henceforth, we use the letters n, m to denote nodes and e, f to denote edges. We write $e \colon n \rightsquigarrow m$ to indicate that e has source $s(e) = n$ and target $t(e) = m$. For example, we have d.1: E1 $\rightsquigarrow$ CP1 in G_1. We use "." to select attributes, writing $n.a$ for $\ell_{\mathcal{N}}(n)(a)$ and $f.a$ for $\ell_{\mathcal{F}}(f)(a)$. For example, E1.type = ext in G_1. The set $S(G) \subseteq \mathcal{N}$ of *source nodes* in G is defined as $S(G) = \{n \mid \exists e.s(e) = n\}$; similarly, $T(G)$ denotes the set of *target nodes* in G.

The characteristic property of a refinement is that it preserves the essential structure of some abstract object in a more concrete (or refined) object. Since we model DFDs as graphs, it is therefore natural to represent refinements of DFDs as structure preserving maps, so-called *graph homomorphism*, between concrete and abstract graphs.

Definition 2. *Let G and H be attributed multigraphs with the same sets of attributes $\mathcal{A}_G = \mathcal{A}_H$ and values $\mathcal{V}_G = \mathcal{V}_H$. A homomorphism $h \colon G \to H$ from G to H is a pair of maps $h_{\mathcal{N}} \colon \mathcal{N}_G \to \mathcal{N}_H$ and $h_{\mathcal{F}} \colon \mathcal{F}_G \to \mathcal{F}_H$, such that, for all nodes n, edges e and attributes a,*

$$h_{\mathcal{N}}(s_G(e)) = s_H(h_{\mathcal{F}}(e)) \qquad\qquad h_{\mathcal{N}}(t_G(e)) = t_H(h_{\mathcal{F}}(e)) \qquad (1)$$
$$n.a = h_{\mathcal{N}}(n).a \qquad\qquad e.a = h_{\mathcal{F}}(e).a \qquad (2)$$

Condition (1) says that h preserves the connective structure of G in H; condition (2) says that h preserves attributes.

Conditions (1) and (2) are a bit too restrictive to represent DFD refinements. To see this, consider again the graphs G_1, G_2 and G_3 shown in Fig. 3. Intuitively, G_2 refines G_1 and G_3 refines G_2, so we would like to show that there are homomorphisms $g \colon G_3 \to G_2$ and $h \colon G_2 \to G_1$. But this is not the case. There are

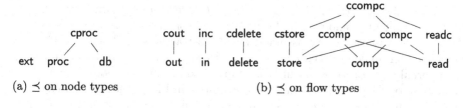

(a) $\preceq$ on node types   (b) $\preceq$ on flow types

Fig. 4. The subtyping preorder $\preceq$

obvious candidate maps $h_{\mathcal{N}}$ and $h_{\mathcal{F}}$, represented using dotted arrows in Fig. 3, but the map $h_{\mathcal{N}}$ violates condition (2) because it does not *strictly* preserve the type of P1.1. Concretely, we have CP1.type $=$ cproc $\neq$ proc $= h_{\mathcal{N}}$(P1.1.type). There is a similar problem if we try to map the lower processes and data store in G_3 to the composite process in G_2 as shown in the figure. In addition, there is no way to map the bold flows (d.5 and d.6) in G_3 to flows in G_2 without violating condition (1). It may be tempting to define $g_{\mathcal{N}}$(P1.2.1) $= g_{\mathcal{N}}$(P1.2.2) $=$ CP1.2, as shown via the dotted arrows, but by (1) this would require $h_{\mathcal{F}}$(d.5): CP1.2 $\rightsquigarrow$ CP1.2, which is impossible since the node CP1.2 has no *loops*, i.e., edges connecting CP1.2 to itself. (Indeed loops are forbidden in DFDs).

We address these two issues separately. First, we relax condition (2). We want to allow refinements to *weakly* preserve attributes (such as types). Concretely, we wish to treat processes and databases as *subtypes* of composite processes. To this end, we define a preorder $\preceq \subseteq \mathcal{V} \times \mathcal{V}$ on the set of types, according to the Hasse diagram shown in Fig. 4a, and weaken condition (2) in Definition 2 to

$$n.a \preceq h_{\mathcal{N}}(n).a \qquad\qquad e.a \preceq h_{\mathcal{F}}(e).a \qquad\qquad (3)$$

for all nodes n, edges e and attributes a. Note that this condition extends to attributes other than types, provided the preorder $\preceq$ is extended appropriately. A homomorphism $h\colon G \to H$ is called *lax* if it fulfills (3) and *strong* if it fulfills (2). Clearly, every (strong) homomorphism is also a lax homomorphism.

To allow "internal" edges like d.5 and d.6 in refinements without adding explicit loops in DFDs, we further adjust the definition of homomorphisms by introducing *implicit loops*.

Definition 3. *Let G and H be attributed multigraphs with the same sets of attributes $\mathcal{A}_G = \mathcal{A}_H$ and values $\mathcal{V}_G = \mathcal{V}_H$, and let $\preceq \subseteq \mathcal{V}_G \times \mathcal{V}_G$ be a preorder on values. An* abstraction $\alpha\colon G \to H$ *from G to H consists of a total map $\alpha_{\mathcal{N}}\colon \mathcal{N}_G \to \mathcal{N}_H$ and a partial map $\alpha_{\mathcal{F}}\colon \mathcal{F}_G \rightharpoonup \mathcal{F}_H$, such that, for all n, e and a,*

$$\alpha_{\mathcal{N}}(s_G(e)) = s_H(\alpha_{\mathcal{F}}(e)) \ \text{ and } \ \alpha_{\mathcal{N}}(t_G(e)) = t_H(\alpha_{\mathcal{F}}(e)) \qquad \text{if } e \in \mathrm{dom}(\alpha_{\mathcal{F}}),$$
$$\alpha_{\mathcal{N}}(s_G(e)) = \alpha_{\mathcal{N}}(t_G(e)) \qquad \text{otherwise.} \qquad (4)$$

$$n.a \preceq \alpha_{\mathcal{N}}(n).a \qquad and \qquad e.a \preceq \alpha_{\mathcal{F}}(e).a \qquad \text{if } e \in \mathrm{dom}(\alpha_{\mathcal{F}}). \qquad (5)$$

An abstraction is balanced *if $\alpha_{\mathcal{N}}$ and $\alpha_{\mathcal{F}}$ are surjective.*

Given an abstraction $\alpha\colon G \to H$, we call G the *concrete* graph and H the *abstract* graph of α, and we say that G *refines* H or that G is a *refinement* of H. Unless otherwise noted, we assume that all abstractions are balanced. If $\alpha_{\mathcal{F}}$ is undefined for an edge e, i.e., $e \notin \mathrm{dom}(\alpha_{\mathcal{F}})$, we say that e is *internal*. Intuitively, an internal edge $e\colon n_1 \rightsquigarrow n_2$ in G is mapped to an abstract edge "inside" the node $m = \alpha_{\mathcal{N}}(n_1) = \alpha_{\mathcal{N}}(n_2)$ in H. For example, in Fig. 3, the internal edge d.5 in G_3 is mapped to an abstract edge hidden inside the composite process CP1.2.

It is easy to verify that every graph G refines itself via the identity abstraction $\mathrm{id}_G = (\mathrm{id}_{\mathcal{N}_G}, \mathrm{id}_{\mathcal{F}_G})$, and that the composition of the maps underlying two abstractions $\alpha\colon G \to H$ and $\beta\colon H \to I$ induces an abstraction $(\beta \circ \alpha)\colon G \to I$.

A Note on Terminology. We deliberately chose the term *abstraction* rather than *refinement* for $\alpha\colon G \to H$ to avoid confusion. Although every abstraction corresponds to a refinement, some readers may find it more intuitive to think of a "refinement from G to H" as a process that takes an abstract G and produces a concrete refinement H of G with a corresponding abstraction $\alpha\colon H \to G$. In other words, abstractions go in the opposite direction of refinements. We continue to use the term "refinement" informally when there is no risk of confusion (e.g., to say that G is a refinement of H) but avoid its use in formal statements.

3.2   B-DFD Refinement

A B-DFD is an attributed multigraph with a fixed choice of attributes $\mathcal{A} = \{\mathsf{type}\}$ and values $\mathcal{V} = \mathcal{T}_{\mathsf{dn}} \uplus \mathcal{T}_{\mathsf{df}}$. The set of *data node types* $\mathcal{T}_{\mathsf{dn}}$, the set of *data flow types* $\mathcal{T}_{\mathsf{df}}$ and the associated *subtyping* order $\preceq$ are shown in Fig. 4. Since the type attribute plays an important role in B-DFDs (and PA-DFDs), we introduce shorthands for typing activators and flows. We write $n\colon t$ to abbreviate $n.\mathsf{type} = t$, and $f\colon n \rightsquigarrow_t m$ to indicate that $f\colon n \rightsquigarrow m$ and $f.\mathsf{type} = t$.

We require that B-DFDs be *well-formed*. First, the type t of a flow $f\colon n \rightsquigarrow_t m$ determines the types $n.\mathsf{type}$ and $m.\mathsf{type}$ of its source and target activators. The valid combinations of source, target and flow types are shown on the left-hand side of Figs. 2, 8 and 9. In addition to these flow typing constraints, we adopt the standard rules from the DFD literature for well-formed B-DFDs: diagrams should not contain loops (flows with identical source and target activators), activators cannot be isolated (disconnected from all other activators), and processes must have at least one incoming and outgoing flow (see e.g., [15,18]).

Definition 4. *A well-formed B-DFD is an attributed multigraph G, where $\mathcal{A}_G = \{\mathsf{type}\}$ and $\mathcal{V}_G = \mathcal{T}_{\mathsf{dn}} \uplus \mathcal{T}_{\mathsf{df}}$. In addition, for all flows f and activators n, m,*

- $n.\mathsf{type} \in \mathcal{T}_{\mathsf{dn}}$ *and* $f.\mathsf{type} \in \mathcal{T}_{\mathsf{df}}$;
- *if* $f\colon n \rightsquigarrow_{\mathsf{in}} m$ *then* $n\colon \mathsf{ext}$ *and* $m\colon \mathsf{proc}$;
- *if* $f\colon n \rightsquigarrow_{\mathsf{out}} m$ *then* $n\colon \mathsf{proc}$ *and* $m\colon \mathsf{ext}$;
- ⋮ *(12 more flow typing conditions, as shown in the LHS of Figs. 2, 8 and 9)*
- *if* $f\colon n \rightsquigarrow_{\mathsf{comp}} m$ *or* $f\colon n \rightsquigarrow_{\mathsf{ccompc}} m$ *then* $n \neq m$;
- *if* $n\colon \mathsf{cproc}$ *or* $n\colon \mathsf{proc}$ *then* $n \in S(G)$ *and* $n \in T(G)$
- *if* $n\colon \mathsf{ext}$ *or* $n\colon \mathsf{db}$ *then* $n \in S(G)$ *or* $n \in T(G)$

An abstraction $\alpha: G \to H$ between B-DFDs G and H is just an abstraction of the underlying attributed multigraphs with the additional condition that the source (and target) of internal edges need to be composite processes,

$$\alpha_{\mathcal{N}}(s(f)).\text{type} = \text{cproc} \quad \text{and} \quad \alpha_{\mathcal{N}}(t(f)).\text{type} = \text{cproc} \qquad \text{if } f \notin \text{dom}(\alpha_{\mathcal{F}}).$$

In earlier work, we described a *Type-inference* algorithm for checking the well-formedness of B-DFDs [5]. Here we introduce algorithms for checking the validity of a given abstraction map between abstract and concrete B-DFDs and for finding all possible abstraction maps between a pair of B-DFDs.

Checking Refinements. Assume we are given a pair of well-formed B-DFDs G and H, and we wish to establish that G refines H. How might we proceed? We may start by defining a pair $\alpha_{\mathcal{N}}, \alpha_{\mathcal{F}}$ of maps relating the concrete B-DFD G to the abstract B-DFD H. To guarantee the preservation of the connective structure and types, we need to check that the given maps form an abstraction. This is the purpose of the *Refinement Checking* algorithm (Algorithm 1).

Our tool detects and reports any violations of the abstraction conditions (4) and (5). In addition, *DFD Refinery* can suggest corrections for broken abstraction maps based on the given abstract and concrete B-DFDs.

Finding Refinements. The *Refinement Checking* algorithm works when abstraction maps are already available. However, defining such maps manually is a tedious and error-prone task, especially for large systems. Hence, rather than leaving it to software designers, we automate it. In general, there are several ways to relate an abstract model to a concrete model while maintaining the abstract model's properties. An refinement search algorithm should thus report all possible refinements and allow the designer to select the right one.

Algorithm 1: Refinement Checking

input : B-DFDs G, H and maps $\alpha_{\mathcal{N}}: \mathcal{N}_G \to \mathcal{N}_H$, $\alpha_{\mathcal{F}}: \mathcal{F}_G \rightharpoonup \mathcal{F}_H$.
output : An error message in case of failure.

1 **foreach** $f: m \rightsquigarrow n \in \mathcal{F}_G$ **do**
2 $\quad m' \leftarrow \alpha_{\mathcal{N}}(m); n' \leftarrow \alpha_{\mathcal{N}}(n)$;
3 $\quad$ **if** $f \notin \text{dom}(\alpha_{\mathcal{F}})$ **then**
4   $\quad\quad$ **if** $n' \neq m' \vee n'.\text{type} \neq \text{cproc}$ **then**
5    $\quad\quad\quad$ *Error*: "mapping of internal f is not internal";
6 $\quad$ **else**
7   $\quad\quad f' \leftarrow \alpha_{\mathcal{F}}(f)$;
8   $\quad\quad$ **if** $s_H(f') \neq m' \vee t_H(f') \neq n'$ **then**
9    $\quad\quad\quad$ *Error*: "mapping f to $\alpha_{\mathcal{F}}(f)$ does not preserve connections";
10   $\quad\quad$ **else if** $f.\text{type} \not\preceq f'.\text{type} \vee m.\text{type} \not\preceq m'.\text{type} \vee n.\text{type} \not\preceq n'.\text{type}$ **then**
11    $\quad\quad\quad$ *Error*: "mapping f to $\alpha_{\mathcal{F}}(f)$ does not preserve types";

Function ExtendPartial($G, H, \alpha_\mathcal{N}, \alpha_\mathcal{F}, U$) – extend partial abstractions.

---

input : B-DFDs G and H, partial maps $\alpha_\mathcal{N} \colon \mathcal{N}_G \rightharpoonup \mathcal{N}_H$, $\alpha_\mathcal{F} \colon \mathcal{F}_G \rightharpoonup \mathcal{F}_H$, and a set of unmapped flows $U \subseteq \mathcal{F}_G$.

output : A set of abstractions from G to H.

1 **if** $U = \emptyset$ **then**   — *have all flows been mapped?*
2 $\quad$ **return** $\{(\alpha_\mathcal{N}, \alpha_\mathcal{F})\}$

3 **else**
4 $\quad$ $f \colon m \rightsquigarrow n \leftarrow$ an arbitrary flow in U;
5 $\quad$ $U' \leftarrow U \setminus \{f\}$;
6 $\quad$ $L \leftarrow \emptyset$;   — *initialize result set*
7 $\quad$ **foreach** $m' \in \mathcal{N}_H$ **do**   — *find extension where f is internal*
   $\quad\quad$ — *check if the candidate conflicts with existing mappings of m and n*
8 $\quad\quad$ **if** $(m \in \mathrm{dom}(\alpha_\mathcal{N}) \wedge \alpha_\mathcal{N}(m) \neq m') \vee (n \in \mathrm{dom}(\alpha_\mathcal{N}) \wedge \alpha_\mathcal{N}(n) \neq m')$ **then**
9 $\quad\quad\quad$ **continue**;

   $\quad\quad$ — *check types*
10 $\quad\quad$ **if** $m'.\mathsf{type} \neq \mathsf{cproc} \vee m.\mathsf{type} \not\preceq \mathsf{cproc} \vee n.\mathsf{type} \not\preceq \mathsf{cproc}$ **then**
11 $\quad\quad\quad$ **continue**;
12 $\quad\quad$ $\alpha'_\mathcal{N} \leftarrow \alpha_\mathcal{N} \cup \{m \mapsto m', n \mapsto m'\}$;   — *compute updated node map*
13 $\quad\quad$ $L' \leftarrow$ ExtendPartial($G, H, \alpha'_\mathcal{N}, \alpha_\mathcal{F}, U'$);   — *extend the new mapping*
14 $\quad\quad$ $L \leftarrow L \cup L'$;

15 $\quad$ **foreach** $f' \colon m' \rightsquigarrow n' \in \mathcal{F}_H$ **do**   — *find candidates in H for mapping f*
   $\quad\quad$ — *check if the candidate conflicts with existing mappings of m and n*
16 $\quad\quad$ **if** $(m \in \mathrm{dom}(\alpha_\mathcal{N}) \wedge \alpha_\mathcal{N}(m) \neq m') \vee (n \in \mathrm{dom}(\alpha_\mathcal{N}) \wedge \alpha_\mathcal{N}(n) \neq n')$ **then**
17 $\quad\quad\quad$ **continue**;

   $\quad\quad$ — *check types*
18 $\quad\quad$ **if** $f.\mathsf{type} \not\preceq f'.\mathsf{type} \vee m.\mathsf{type} \not\preceq m'.\mathsf{type} \vee n.\mathsf{type} \not\preceq n'.\mathsf{type}$ **then**
19 $\quad\quad\quad$ **continue**;
20 $\quad\quad$ $\alpha'_\mathcal{N} \leftarrow \alpha_\mathcal{N} \cup \{m \mapsto m', n \mapsto n'\}$;   — *compute updated maps*
21 $\quad\quad$ $\alpha'_\mathcal{F} \leftarrow \alpha_\mathcal{F} \cup \{f \mapsto f'\}$;
22 $\quad\quad$ $L' \leftarrow$ ExtendPartial($G, H, \alpha'_\mathcal{N}, \alpha'_\mathcal{F}, U'$);   — *extend the new mapping*
23 $\quad\quad$ $L \leftarrow L \cup L'$;

24 $\quad$ **return** L;

The *Refinement Search* algorithm takes a pair of abstract and concrete B-DFDs and computes the full set of abstractions between them. We first define a helper function (ExtendPartial) to extend *partial* abstractions. The function takes a pair of B-DFDs G, H, a pair of partial abstraction maps $\alpha_\mathcal{N}$, $\alpha_\mathcal{F}$ and a set $U \subseteq \mathcal{F}_G$ of unmapped flows, i.e., those flows for which we wish to find candidate mappings. The function returns the set of all possible abstractions from G to H that extend $(\alpha_\mathcal{N}, \alpha_\mathcal{F})$. It does so using a naive, depth-first branch-and-bound strategy: it picks an unmapped flow $f \in U$, finds all candidate mappings for f, adds them to $\alpha_\mathcal{N}$, $\alpha_\mathcal{F}$, and recursively extends them. The *Refinement Search* algorithm then consists of a single call to ExtendPartial($G, H, \emptyset, \emptyset, \mathcal{F}_G$),

Note that the ExtendPartial function does not check whether the resulting abstractions are balanced (i.e., that all the maps involved are surjective). Hence, there is no guarantee that all nodes and flows in the abstract B-DFD actually have a refinement in the concrete B-DFD – the concrete diagram could just be a refinement of a subset of the abstract diagram. However, a balance check can easily be added via a post-processing phase that removes non-balanced abstractions (and we have implemented such a check in *DFD Refinery*).

3.3   PA-DFD Refinement

The primary difference between B-DFDs and PA-DFDs is that the latter contain additional activators and flows that implement privacy checks. We distinguish between three kinds of PA-DFD activators and flows: those that were already present in B-DFDs, called *data* flows and nodes (e.g., processes and data stores); those that handle and carry policy information, called *policy* flows and nodes (e.g., limit and reason processes); and those that track and manage system events, called *admin* flows and nodes (e.g., log processes and data stores). Some types of activators play multiple roles, e.g., a limit process is both a data and a policy node since it handles both data and policy information.

As with B-DFDs, we use attributed graphs to represent PA-DFDs formally.

Definition 5. *Define the set* $\mathcal{T}_{pn} = \{\text{limit, request, reason, policy-db}\}$ *of* policy node types *and the set* $\mathcal{T}_{an} = \{\text{log, log-db, clean}\}$ *of* admin node types. *A PA-DFD is an attributed graph* G, *where* $\mathcal{A} = \{\text{type, partner}\}$ *and* $\mathcal{V} = \mathcal{T}_{dn} \uplus \mathcal{T}_{pn} \uplus \mathcal{T}_{an} \uplus \{\text{pf, df}\} \uplus \mathcal{N}$. *In addition, the following must hold:*

- n.type $\in \mathcal{T}_{dn} \uplus \mathcal{T}_{pn} \uplus \mathcal{T}_{an}$ *and* f.type $\in \{\text{pf, df}\}$;
- *if* n.partner *is defined, then* n.partner $\in \mathcal{N}$.

The partner attribute is used by the transformation algorithm and can be ignored for the purposes of this paper (cf. [5]). In principle, the flows of PA-DFDs ought to be subject to similar typing conditions as those for well-formed B-DFDs. Following the principle used for well-formed B-DFDs, we could type each flow based on the types of its source and target. For example, the flows connecting request to limit activators could be given type reqlim. This would result in twenty-two new flow types. To simplify presentation, we instead use just two flow types for PA-DFDs: *plain* flows (pf) and *deletion* flows (df).

All the new node types are special kinds of processes or data stores and, as such, are considered subtypes of composite processes. To reflect this, we extend the subtyping relation as follows:

$$n \preceq n \qquad\qquad n \preceq \text{cproc} \qquad\qquad \text{for all } n \in \mathcal{T}_{pn} \uplus \mathcal{T}_{an}.$$

An abstraction $\alpha \colon G \to H$ between PA-DFDs G and H is just an abstraction on the underlying attributed multigraphs with the extra condition that, if $f \colon m \rightsquigarrow n$ in G is internal, then $\alpha_{\mathcal{N}}(m) = \alpha_{\mathcal{N}}(n) \colon \text{cproc}$.

Transforming Refinements. Having defined algorithms to check and find refinements between B-DFDs in the previous section, we could now do the same for refinements of PA-DFDs. However, the changes to the algorithms would be minimal and largely uninteresting. After all, PA-DFDs are still just a special type of attributed graph, and the definition of abstractions is robust against changes in the choice of attributes and values. Furthermore, we neither expect nor intend software engineers to manipulate PA-DFDs manually: they should be automatically generated from B-DFDs. The same principle should apply to refinements of PA-DFDs: rather than manually refining an automatically generated PA-DFD, we expect software engineers to refine an abstract B-DFD H into a concrete B-DFD G and then automatically transform the latter into a (concrete) PA-DFD G'. For this process to make sense, we require that the resulting PA-DFD G' be a refinement of the PA-DFD H' obtained by transforming the original abstract B-DFD H. Diagrammatically,

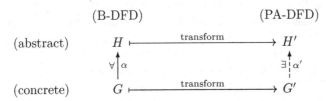

In fact, the process of finding a PA-DFD abstraction $\alpha'\colon G' \to H'$ corresponding to a B-DFD abstraction $\alpha\colon G \to H$ is itself a transformation (of abstractions) that can be automated. We have defined and implemented an algorithm for this transformation. Space constraints prevent us from reproducing the full algorithm here, so we give instead a high-level outline and illustrate the main ideas.

To track the relationship between the nodes and flows of the original B-DFDs G, H and the resulting PA-DFDs G', H', the refinement transformation takes, as additional inputs, four maps:

$$o_{\mathcal{N}_G} \colon \mathcal{N}_{G'} \to \mathcal{N}_G, \qquad\qquad o_{\mathcal{F}_G} \colon \mathcal{N}_{G'} \uplus \mathcal{F}_{G'} \to \mathcal{F}_G,$$
$$o_{\mathcal{N}_H} \colon \mathcal{N}_{H'} \to \mathcal{N}_H, \qquad\qquad o_{\mathcal{F}_H} \colon \mathcal{N}_{H'} \uplus \mathcal{F}_{H'} \to \mathcal{F}_H.$$

The maps keep track of which B-DFD nodes and flows resulted in the creation of a given PA-DFD node or flow. For instance, $o_{\mathcal{N}_G}$ maps every proc or reason node n in the concrete PA-DFD G' to the corresponding original proc node $o_{\mathcal{N}_G}(n)$ in the concrete B-DFD G. Conversely, the inverse image $o_{\mathcal{N}_G}^{-1}(m)$ of a node $m\colon$ proc in G is a set $\{m_1, m_2\}$ containing the pair of nodes $m_1\colon$ proc and $m_2\colon$ reason created during the transformation of n. The four maps can easily be generated as an output of the DFD transformation algorithm.

In much the same way that the transformation algorithm on DFDs first transforms nodes and then flows, the refinement transformation first transforms node mappings $(n \mapsto m) \in \alpha_{\mathcal{N}}$ and then the flow mappings $(e \mapsto f) \in \alpha_{\mathcal{F}}$.

1. The transformation of the node mappings proceeds by case analysis on the types $n.\mathsf{type}$ and $m.\mathsf{type}$. Only a few combinations are valid. For example, if

n: proc then either m: proc or m: cproc. If m: proc, we must have $o_{\mathcal{N}_G}^{-1}(n) = \{n_1: \text{proc}, n_2: \text{reason}\}$ and $o_{\mathcal{N}_H}^{-1}(m) = \{m_1: \text{proc}, m_2: \text{reason}\}$. This results in two new PA-DFD node mappings $n_1 \mapsto m_1$ and $n_2 \mapsto m_2$. If m: cproc instead, then $o_{\mathcal{N}_H}^{-1}(m) = \{m': \text{cproc}\}$, resulting in the two new mappings $n_1 \mapsto m'$ and $n_2 \mapsto m'$. The other cases are similar.

2. In a second step, we transform all the flow mappings. Because the number of (combinations of) flow types is larger, the process is more tedious but equally straightforward. We iterate over all $e: n_1 \rightsquigarrow n_2 \in \mathcal{F}_G$ and check whether e is internal. If so, e has no counterpart in the abstract B-DFD H and hence there is no edge there to transform. Intuitively, the edge is "hidden" inside a composite process in the abstract B-DFD H, and all the new edges and privacy checks from the concrete PA-DFD G' will also be "hidden" inside a new composite process in the abstract PA-DFD H'. Concretely, we know that there is a node $m = \alpha_{\mathcal{N}}(n_1) = \alpha_{\mathcal{N}}(n_2)$ with m: cproc in G. Hence, $o_{\mathcal{N}_H}^{-1}(m) = \{m': \text{cproc}\}$ in H, and we add mappings $n' \mapsto m'$ for all nodes $n' \in o_{\mathcal{F}_H}^{-1}(e)$ while leaving all edges $e' \in o_{\mathcal{F}_H}^{-1}(e)$ unmapped (they are internal). If e is not internal, the transformation of the associated edge mapping $e \mapsto f$ resembles that for a node mapping. By case analysis on the types e.type and f.type, we determine how the edges e and f were transformed. For example, if e.type = store then we must have f.type $\in \{\text{store}, \text{compc}, \text{cstore}, \text{ccompc}\}$. In each sub-case, $o_{\mathcal{F}_G}^{-1}(e)$ is the set of nodes and flows produced by the store transformation rule, while $o_{\mathcal{F}_H}^{-1}(f)$ is a similar set of nodes and flows associated with the transformation rule for the type f.type. In each case, there is a straightforward mapping between the corresponding nodes and flows, based on their type.

Our tool *DFD Refinery* implements the above algorithms.[1]

4 DFD Refinery

We have proposed a refinement framework comprising three algorithms, implemented in our *DFD Refinery* tool: *Refinement Checking*, *Refinement Search* and *Refinement Transformation*. *DFD Refinery* also includes an updated version of our previous tool for transforming B-DFDs into PA-DFDs [4,5].

DFD Refinery uses `draw.io`, a user-friendly, easy-to-use, cross-platform and open source third-party application for drawing DFDs. We use Henriksen's open source library [22] to provide additional support for manipulating DFDs. Since it is easy to import and export diagrams from/to XML format in `draw.io`, our tool processes DFD diagrams represented in an XML format and generates PA-DFD diagrams in the same format.

The abstraction maps for B-DFDs and PA-DFD produce CSV/Text files. Our tool is implemented in Python and has been tested on a MacBook Pro (See footnote 1).

---

[1] Source code available at https://github.com/alshareef-hanaa/Refining_PA-DFD.

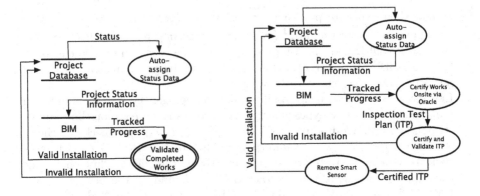

Fig. 5. Part of an automated payment system DFD: Level 0 (left) and Level 1 (right).

5   Case Study

To validate our algorithms, we have applied *DFD Refinery* to a realistic application: an automated payment system. The DFD (context diagram, Level 0 and Level 1) for this system is due to Chong and Diamantopoulos [12]; it has been reviewed by domain experts and models a system for making automatic payments to subcontractors in a construction project. Here we consider Levels 0 and 1 of the DFD.

We start our evaluation by applying the *Type-inference* and *Transformation* algorithms from our previous work [5] to check that the input B-DFD is well-formed and to obtain the corresponding PA-DFD. Had the designers of the Automated Payment System provided CSV files specifying abstractions for the three B-DFDs, we could have directly applied our *Refinement Checking* algorithm to verify their correctness. In the absence of such files, we instead apply our *Refinement Search* algorithm to the B-DFDs for Levels 0 and 1 (see Fig. 5).

The algorithm returns only one (balanced) abstraction since there is only one proper way to map the activators and flows of Level 1 to cover those on Level 0 according to our refinement framework. The resulting abstraction maps the processes ("Certify Works Onsite via Oracle", "Certify and Validate ITP", "Remove Smart Sensor") on Level 1 to the composite process "Validate Completed Works" on Level 1. Then, we apply our Transformation algorithm to each level of B-DFDs to obtain the corresponding PA-DFDs (see Figs. 6 and 7). During the transformation, we (automatically) create auxiliary maps to track the relationship between B-DFDs' activators and flows and the resulting PA-DFDs. For instance, the process "Auto-assign Status Data" is transformed into a process and its partner, "Reason Auto-assign Status Data". Likewise, the flows in the B-DFDs have their targets in the corresponding PA-DFDs. For example, "Tracked progress flow", which is typed as read, has seven target flows (e.g., "Tracked progress ?" and "Tracked progress,pol,v") and four activators (e.g., "Limit2", "Request2"). These tracking maps and the abstraction between the

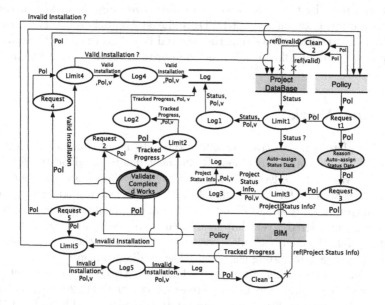

Fig. 6. Part of automated payment system PA-DFD level 0

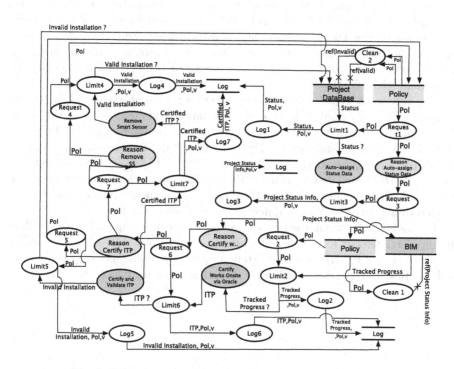

Fig. 7. Part of automated payment system PA-DFD level 1

B-DFDs are used by the *Refinement Transformation* algorithm to construct a valid abstraction between the PA-DFDs at Level 1 and Level 0. For instance, the B-DFD abstraction shows that the internal flow "Certified ITP" on Level 1 is mapped to (a hidden flow inside) the composite process "Validate Completed Works".

6 Related Work

The notion of refining abstract specifications into more concrete models, and even to executable code, is not new. Refinement has been advocated for the B method and variants like Event-B [1–3], for the Z method (e.g., [32]) and VDM (e.g., [25]), as well as for many other formal specification languages. In many such languages, notably B and Z and the refinement calculus [8], the support for refinement is considered a very important feature of the language and its design methodology. Refinement has also been introduced for other "diagrammatic" modeling languages, including class and use-case diagrams in UML [17].

There have been earlier attempts to formalize DFDs to reduce ambiguity and detect inconsistency and incompleteness (e.g., [9,19–21,26,27]), and some works provide formal techniques to support the definition of hierarchical DFDs (e.g., [10,24,27,31]). Representing DFDs in different levels of abstraction does not automatically guarantee consistency between the different abstract models. Lee and Tan [27] model DFDs using Petri Nets, and thus are able to check consistency of the DFDs by enforcing constraints on their Petri Net model. Though theoretically interesting, we believe the approach is not of practical use for software engineers as Petri Nets are more complicated to handle and understand than DFDs.

The only work we are aware of that defines a notion of refinement for DFDs is that by Ibrahim et al. [24]. Indeed, they have formalized some of the standard structured DFD rules to check the consistency of different models but only between the context and Level 0 DFDs. Our refining framework has a simple set of rules, including all the standard structured DFD rules, for checking if a concrete B-DFD is consistent with its abstraction. Ours is a rule-based approach built on the rigorous mathematical theory of graph homomorphisms, and can be applied to any two B-DFDs at different levels of abstraction.

To the best of our knowledge, no previous work has provided a formal definition of refinement for DFDs for arbitrary number of levels. Also, the notion of refinement for PA-DFDs is completely original, preserving not only structural and functional properties but also the underlying privacy concepts.

7   Conclusions

We have introduced *abstractions* as a new, formal notion of refinement for both DFDs and PA-DFDs and showed that the standard diagram relating transformations and refinements commute. We have provided three different algorithms for checking, finding and transforming refinements.

The *Refinement Checking* algorithm evaluates whether a pair of maps between an abstract and concrete B-DFD form an abstraction. The second algorithm takes a partial (or empty) abstraction between two B-DFDs and produces all possible extensions that form valid abstractions. Finally, the *Refinement Transformation* algorithm takes an abstraction witnessing that a concrete B-DFD refines an abstract one as its input and transforms it into an abstraction between the corresponding PA-DFDs obtained by transforming the abstract and concrete B-DFDs. The resulting PA-DFD abstraction witnesses that all privacy checks between the abstract and concrete PA-DFDs are preserved.

We have implemented the refinement algorithms and evaluated them on a case study. As future work, we intend to further extend our transformation (and refinement) so that it also covers accountability and policy management.

A   Additional Transformation Rules

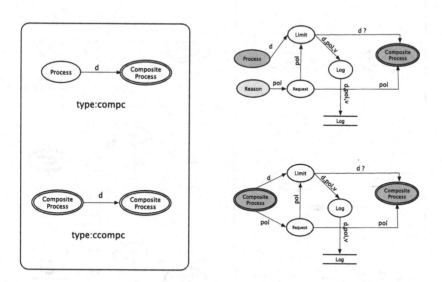

Fig. 8. B-DFD flow types and corresponding transformation rules – Part 2.

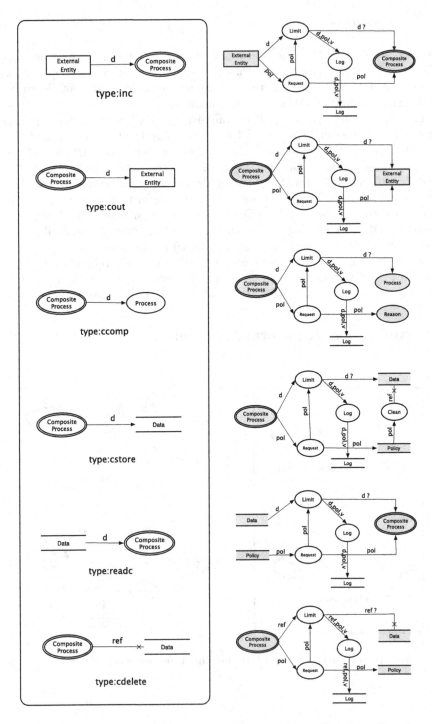

Fig. 9. B-DFD flow types and corresponding transformation rules – Part 3.

References

1. Abrial, J.R.: The B tool (Abstract). In: Bloomfield, R.E., Marshall, L.S., Jones, R.B. (eds.) VDM 1988. LNCS, vol. 328, pp. 86–87. Springer, Heidelberg (1988). https://doi.org/10.1007/3-540-50214-9_8
2. Abrial, J.R., Abrial, J.R.: The B-book: Assigning Programs to Meanings. Cambridge University Press, Cambridge (2005)
3. Abrial, J.R., Hallerstede, S.: Refinement, decomposition, and instantiation of discrete models: application to event-b. Fundamenta Informaticae **77**(1), 1–28 (2007)
4. Alshareef, H., Stucki, S., Schneider, G.: Transforming data flow diagrams for privacy compliance (long version). CoRR abs/2011.12028 (2020)
5. Alshareef, H., Stucki, S., Schneider, G.: Transforming data flow diagrams for privacy compliance. In: MODELSWARD 2021, pp. 207–215. SCITEPRESS (2021)
6. Antignac, T., Scandariato, R., Schneider, G.: A privacy-aware conceptual model for handling personal data. In: ISoLA 2016, pp. 942–957 (2016)
7. Antignac, T., Scandariato, R., Schneider, G.: Privacy compliance via model transformations. In: IWPE 2018, pp. 120–126. IEEE (2018)
8. Back, R.J.R., von Wright, J.: Refinement calculus, part I: sequential nondeterministic programs. In: de Bakker, J.W., de Roever, W.-P., Rozenberg, G. (eds.) REX 1989. LNCS, vol. 430, pp. 42–66. Springer, Heidelberg (1990). https://doi.org/10.1007/3-540-52559-9_60
9. Bruza, P.D., Van der Weide, T.: The semantics of data flow diagrams. University of Nijmegen, Department of Informatics (1989)
10. Butler, G., Grogono, P., Shinghal, R., Tjandra, I.: Analyzing the logical structure of data flow diagrams in software documents. In: Proceedings of the 3rd International Conference on Document Analysis and Recognition, vol. 2, pp. 575–578. IEEE (1995)
11. Cavoukian, A.: Privacy by design: origins, meaning, and prospects for assuring privacy and trust in the information era. In: Privacy Protection Measures and Technologies in Business Organisations, pp. 170–208. IGI Global (2012)
12. Chong, H.Y., Diamantopoulos, A.: Integrating advanced technologies to uphold security of payment: data flow diagram. Autom. Construct. **114**, 103–158 (2020)
13. Danezis, G., et al.: Privacy and data protection by design. ENISA Report (2015)
14. DeMarco, T.: Structure analysis and system specification. In: Broy, M., Denert, E. (eds.) Pioneers and Their Contributions to Software Engineering, pp. 255–288. Springer, Heidelberg (1979). https://doi.org/10.1007/978-3-642-48354-7_9
15. Dennis, A., Wixom, B.H., Roth, R.M.: Systems Analysis and Design. Wiley, New York (2018)
16. European Commission: General data protection regulation (GDPR). Regulation 2016/679, European Commission (2016)
17. Faitelson, D., Tyszberowicz, S.: UML diagram refinement (focusing on class-and use case diagrams). In: ICSE 2017, pp. 735–745. IEEE/ACM (2017)
18. Falkenberg, E., Pols, R.V.D., Weide, T.V.D.: Understanding process structure diagrams. Inf. Syst. **16**(4), 417–428 (1991)
19. France, R.B.: Semantically extended data flow diagrams: a formal specification tool. IEEE Trans. Softw. Eng. **18**(4), 329 (1992)
20. Fraser, M.D., Kumar, K., Vaishnavi, V.K.: Informal and formal requirements specification languages: bridging the gap. IEEE Trans. Softw. Eng. **17**(5), 454–466 (1991)

21. Gao, X.L., Miao, H.K., Liu, L.: Functionality semantics of predicate data flow diagram. J. Shanghai Univ. (English Ed.) **8**(3), 309–316 (2004)
22. Henriksen, M.: Draw.io libraries for threat modeling diagrams (2018). https:// github.com/michenriksen/drawio-threatmodeling
23. Hert, P.D., Papakonstantinou, V.: The new general data protection regulation: still a sound system for the protection of individuals? Comput. Law Secur. Rev. **32**(2), 179–194 (2016)
24. Ibrahim, R., et al.: Formalization of the data flow diagram rules for consistency check. arXiv preprint arXiv:1011.0278 (2010)
25. Jones, C.B.: Systematic Software Development Using VDM. Prentice Hall International Series in Computer Science (1990)
26. de Lara, J., Vangheluwe, H.: Using AToM^3 as a meta-CASE tool. In: Proceedings of the 4st International Conference on Enterprise Information Systems (ICEIS 2002), pp. 642–649 (2002)
27. Lee, P.T., Tan, K.: Modelling of visualised data-flow diagrams using petri net model. Softw. Eng. J. **7**(1), 4–12 (1992)
28. Schneider, G.: Is privacy by construction possible? In: Margaria, T., Steffen, B. (eds.) ISoLA 2018. LNCS, vol. 11244, pp. 471–485. Springer, Cham (2018). https:// doi.org/10.1007/978-3-030-03418-4_28
29. Tao, Y., Kung, C.: Formal definition and verification of data flow diagrams. J. Syst. Softw. **16**(1), 29–36 (1991)
30. Tsormpatzoudi, P., Berendt, B., Coudert, F.: Privacy by design: from research and policy to practice – the challenge of multi-disciplinarity. In: Berendt, B., Engel, T., Ikonomou, D., Le Métayer, D., Schiffner, S. (eds.) APF 2015. LNCS, vol. 9484, pp. 199–212. Springer, Cham (2016). https://doi.org/10.1007/978-3-319-31456-3_12
31. Wing, J.M., Zaremski, A.M.: Unintrusive ways to integrate formal specifications in practice. In: Prehn, S., Toetenel, W.J. (eds.) VDM 1991. LNCS, vol. 551, pp. 545–569. Springer, Heidelberg (1991). https://doi.org/10.1007/3-540-54834-3_32
32. Woodcock, J., Davies, J.: Using Z: Specification, Refinement, and Proof. Prentice Hall, Upper Saddle River (1996)
33. Woodman, M.: Yourdon dataflow diagrams: a tool for disciplined requirements analysis. Inf. Softw. Technol. **30**(9), 515–533 (1988)

Hybrid Information Flow Control
for Low-Level Code

Eduardo Geraldo[1]([✉]), José Fragoso Santos[2], and João Costa Seco[1]

[1] NOVA LINCS - NOVA University Lisbon, Costa da Caparica, Portugal
e.geraldo@campus.fct.unl.pt
[2] Instituto Superior Técnico and INESC-ID, Lisbon, Portugal

Abstract. Failure to ensure data confidentiality can have a significant financial and reputational impact on companies. To aggravate the
issue, frequently used methods like testing are insufficient when proving data confidentiality in software systems. Existing information flow
based approaches require heavy implementation and specification efforts
or lack the expressiveness programmers desire. To tackle the issues, we
propose a novel hybrid system for information flow control in low-level
languages. By combining an information flow monitor with a type system that instruments programs with runtime security checks, we support
value-dependent security types in a low-level setting. We formalise our
type system and monitor using a TAL-like calculus and prove that they
guarantee termination-insensitive non-interference. We present the first
hybrid type system for information flow control with support for value-
dependent types. We also introduce the first value-dependent hybrid
mechanism for a low-level intermediate representation.

1 Introduction

The increasing access to internet-based services and the information they store
leads to growing concerns over topics like data confidentiality. Users and regulatory entities expect companies to safeguard the data their systems store and
process; failure to do so can have severe financial and reputational consequences
such as fines a the loss of users.

Unfortunately, data protection is no easy task, with systems often exhibiting
logic flaws or programming mistakes resulting in information leaks. To ensure
systems' correctness, developers usually rely on testing, which requires complex test scenarios and careful I/O monitoring; hence test-based information
leak detection is an intricate, error-prone process. Heavily tested systems like
Github [9], Instagram [39], Facebook [32], and Twitter [1] registered incidents
where they wrote unciphered user passwords to system logs.

Information flow control [11,26,34,38] (IFC) is the best-suited technique for
information leak detection. The key idea behind it is to tag information and
its receptacles (e.g., variables or I/O channels) with security labels arranged in
a security lattice. Then, we track all data-processing operations and compute
the security level of each datum, stopping information of a given security level

© Springer Nature Switzerland AG 2021
R. Calinescu and C. S. Păsăreanu (Eds.): SEFM 2021, LNCS 13085, pp. 141–159, 2021.
https://doi.org/10.1007/978-3-030-92124-8_9

from flowing to receptacles of a lower security level. IFC aims to ensure the non-interference property [34], stating that secret inputs should not cause visible changes to public outputs; a sufficient condition to guarantee the absence of information leaks.

Mechanisms for IFC may enforce flow policies statically or dynamically. Static mechanisms [7,26,31], type systems for information flow control, detect leaks at compile-time with no impact on the runtime. However, they may reject correct programs, e.g. programs with leaks in unreachable code. Contrarily, dynamic mechanisms [4], based on reference monitors, are less prone to reject correct programs but introduce overhead at runtime; monitors have to oversee the execution of every instruction. Plus, they need a high testing coverage to be useful.

Hybrid approaches [38], combine a reference monitor for enacting flow policies at runtime and a type system for static IFC. The type system does most of the analysis, while the monitor only performs checks where necessary, i.e., code that is not possible to statically prove correct nor incorrect. This methodology avoids false positives while keeping the impact of the monitor to a minimum, meaning less overhead and fewer tests required to certify dynamically verified code.

In this paper, we present a formal system for hybrid value-dependent information flow control in SNITCH IR, a small imperative low-level language inspired by TAL [29]. The language relates to low-level languages like JVM bytecode [25], the Common Intermediate Language [13], or the LLVM's intermediate language [23]. Value-dependent security labels [26] allow for more expressive security policies.

We introduce a static semantics that verifies and rewrites programs, embedding them with a flow monitor to overview, when necessary, data transfer operations. As an approach to hybrid IFC, it eases specification efforts as it supports incomplete specifications; defers decisions on unknown labels to runtime. We are working on a prototype tool, SNITCH, to detect leaks through the hybrid analysis of JVM bytecode (currently capable of fully dynamic IFC).

We start this paper with the related work in Sect. 2 and some key concepts in Sect. 3. Then, we present a sound dynamic semantics that preserves termination insensitive non-interference in Sect. 4. Next, in Sect. 5, we introduce type system for hybrid value-dependent information flow control. Lastly, we end with some final comments and future directions for this work in Sect. 6.

2   Related Work

There is a vast body of works on the application of information flow research to real-world programming languages, ranging from type systems for strongly typed languages such as OCaml [37], and Java [8], to dynamic analysis for scripting languages, such as JavaScript [21] and Python [19]. For a more thorough overview, we refer the reader to [34] and [22]. Here, we focus on IFC for low-level languages, hybrid analysis for IFC, and expressive information flow types.

Hybrid Information Flow Control. Hybrid systems for IFC combine static analyses with different flavours of runtime monitoring. Most hybrid IFC analyses are based on gradual typing [36]. In fact, gradual information-flow type systems exist for lambda calculus [12,15] and a lightweight Java-like language [16]. These type systems allow for polymorphic security labels, providing annotations for denoting statically unknown labels. The programmer must add runtime casts in code points where values of a pre-determined security type are expected. While the static type system guarantees adherence to the specified policy on the static side of a cast, the runtime analysis checks the policy on the dynamic side.

Amongst the existing hybrid IFC approaches, the most closely related to ours is [18], which introduces a hybrid system for IFC in a fragment of JavaScript. It combines a type system with a no-sensitive-upgrade monitor to instrument programs so that the monitor only performs the necessary checks. Our work, however, faces specific challenges related to the low-level nature of SNITCH IR; most notably, the precise tracking of implicit flows in unstructured control flows.

Information Flow Control for Low Level Languages. There is a number of works on static and dynamic information flow analyses for low-level languages. Barth et al. [7]. were the first to design a type system for IFC in Java bytecode; later proved sound using the Coq proof assistant [6]. Their intermediate representation is similar to ours and make use of the concept of *control dependence regions*.

Aldous et al. [2] designed a static analysis for proving non-interference in a Dalvik-like language. They implemented the analysis and proved it sound. The analysis enriches the control flow graph of target programs with information computed by an abstract interpreter. The authors show that resulting graphs, called *execution point graphs*, can improve the precision of the analysis. They further showed [3] how to derive a sound IF monitor from their original analysis. We believe that we could use execution point graphs to improve the precision of the static component of our system; this is, however, left as future work.

Recently, Balliu et al. [5] showed how to leverage SMT solvers to prove the non-interference of ARMv7 binaries. They demonstrate the applicability of their approach by using it to verify a sophisticated kernel system call handler, combining handwritten assembly code with complex compiler-generated code.

Expressive Security Types. Multiple techniques to enhance the expressiveness of security policies have been proposed. For instance, the more flexible decentralised label model by Meyers and Liskov [30] replaces the security lattice with an ownership-based model. An entity can own an information receptacle, and only the entity or those authorized by the entity via read and write sets can read or write to the receptacle. The owner can delegate the control over the read and write sets to other entities through the "acts for" relation, another feature of the decentralised label model. This model is used with dynamic labels in JIF [31].

Also, value dependent approaches to hybrid systems include the runtime use of static analysis, invoked by the reference monitor [20], thus achieving a permissive IFC verification. This approach suits a purely dynamic setting as Javascript, but not low-level languages. We take the traditional approach instead, of having a static analysis establishing the border between guarded and unguarded code.

Purely static verification of flexible policies relies on dependent information security levels in type based information flow control systems [17, 26, 27]. The encoding of dependent security types is present in liquid information flow control [33], which also includes the ability to repair detected errors. Value-dependent IFC builds on top of the traditional approach by enhancing lattices with security labels parameterised with runtime values. These labels allow for dynamic security lattices capable of expressing many real-world situations.

We take inspiration in these approaches and propose a hybrid approach, applied to low-level languages, thus making the verification more expressive and applicable in real situations, requiring less annotation work from the developer.

3   Overview

To fend off bug-induced confidentiality breaches that pester information systems, we present a solution based on value-dependent hybrid IFC to detect and prevent information leaks. A system following such an approach exhibits the advantages of static and dynamic information flow control mechanisms while minimising their disadvantages and supports richer finer-grained information flow policies.

Our approach, as other hybrid approaches, relies on a type system and a reference monitor. The type system enforces flow policies and injects the monitor into target programs. Having the type system perform program rewriting bypasses a standalone instrumentation phase and allows for a seamless integration of the monitor based on the static analysis of each instruction.

We base our approach on a small low-level imperative language, depicted in Fig. 1 and inspired by work on typed assembly languages [29] and type-based program rewriting [35]. Our language easily relates to existing low-level languages such as the Java bytecode [25], LLVM's intermediate representation [23], and the Common Language Infrastructure (.NET) instructions [13]. Low-level representations have many advantages. For instance, many high-level languages compile to a single low-level one, e.g., Java, Scala, Groovy, Kotlin, and Clojure, all compile to JVM's bytecode; targeting a low-level language allows for tools to support multiple high-level ones. Furthermore, support for low-level languages brings support for compiled programs as long as it is possible to write specifications for them.

Reference monitors require program instrumentation [14] or an execution environment capable of monitoring executions. The latter results in deep cumbersome changes to third-party virtual machines; hard to automate and maintain. Thus, we instrument target programs, depending only on the higher stability of low-level languages.

Our hybrid approach starts with the static verification of the code, whose purpose is two-fold. As previously mentioned, the static analysis performs the static information flow verification, thus rejecting provably wrong programs, and instruments code that cannot be proved wrong. The combination results from the fact that the instrumentation is dependent on the results of the static analysis; statically correct code segments do not require runtime verifications.

Operands:

Registers $r ::= r_1 \mid r_2 \mid \; \dots \; \mid r_n$
Literals $c ::= c_1 \mid c_2 \mid \; \dots \; \mid c_n$
Operands $v ::= r \mid c$
Block Labels $\ell ::= \ell_1 \mid \ell_2 \mid \; \dots \; \mid \ell_n$

Annotations:

Security Label $k ::= k_1 \mid k_2 \mid \; \dots \; \mid k_n$
Label Interval $\widehat{k} ::= [k_l, k_u], \; k_l \sqsubseteq k_u$
Security Annotation $a ::= \widehat{k} \mid k$

Instructions:

Unguarded Instructions $i_u ::= r := v^a \mid r_d := r_s \oplus v^a$
Guarded Instructions $i_g ::= r := \overset{\circ}{=} v^k \mid r_d := \overset{\circ}{=} r_s \oplus v^k$
Instructions $i ::= i_u \mid i_g \mid \mathbf{pop} \; \ell$
Final Instructions $i_f ::= \mathbf{jump} \; \ell \mid \mathbf{if} \; r, \ell_t, \ell_f$
Sequences $I ::= i; I \mid i_f$

Fig. 1. SNITCH IR syntax.

Considering the hybrid nature of our approach, we foresee two types of security levels: concrete levels used at runtime and sets of symbolic levels employed in the static analysis. The latter, we abstract using security intervals. Considering SC the set of all security labels and $\rightarrow$ the partial order relation, we define comparisons and the least upper bound between labels as follows: equality ($=$) and its negation ($\neq$) have the usual semantics. Comparison between labels depends exclusively on the flow relation ($\sqsubseteq = \rightarrow$), $\forall a, b. \; a \sqsubseteq b \Leftrightarrow a \rightarrow b$. $\#$ reflects label divergence, $\forall a \in SC. \; \forall b \in SC. \; a \# b \Leftrightarrow a \not\sqsubseteq b \wedge b \not\sqsubseteq a$. $\sqcup$ yields the least upper bound of both arguments. The security classes (SC) together with the partial ordering ($\rightarrow$) and the least upper bound ($\sqcup$) forms the security lattice. We define a security interval A as $[a_L, a_U]$, where $a_L \sqsubseteq a_U$; a more compact notation for defining sets, $[a_L, a_U] = \{k \mid \forall k \in SC. \; a_L \sqsubseteq k \sqsubseteq a_U\}$. We define set divergence, the least upper bound between sets, and set comparison as follows: $A \# B = \forall k_a \in A. \; \forall k_b \in B. \; k_a \# k_b$ $A \sqcup B = \{k \mid \forall k_a \in A. \; \forall k_b \in B. \; k = k_a \sqcup k_b\}$, and

$$A \preccurlyeq B = \begin{cases} true & \forall k_a \in A. \; \forall k_b \in B. \; k_a \sqsubseteq k_b \\ false & \forall k_a \in A. \; \forall k_b \in B. \; k_b \sqsubseteq k_a \vee A \# B \\ \downarrow & otherwise \end{cases}$$

SNITCH IR foresees guarded and unguarded instructions, each having a different runtime behaviour. Guarded instructions require extra checks that unguarded instructions do not. The need for both types of instructions stems from the hybrid nature of our approach. In a fully dynamic setting, we would consider only guarded instructions. However, taking into account the results of the static analysis, it is possible to replace statically correct guarded instructions with their unguarded counterpart. The instruction set of SNITCH IR also includes a pop instruction, a control instruction required for manipulating scope-related data structures as we will show when presenting the runtime semantics.

$[\text{D-SafeAssignment}]$

$$(\Delta, \gamma, (\ell, pc) :: \sigma, \ell_c : r := v^k; I) \longrightarrow (\Delta, \gamma[r : v^{pc \sqcup k}], (\ell, pc) :: \sigma, \ell_c : I)$$

$[\text{D-UnsafeAssignment}]$

$$\frac{pc \sqsubseteq k_d}{(\Delta, \gamma[r : v_d^{k_d}], (\ell, pc) :: \sigma, \ell_c : r :\overset{\circ}{=} v^k; I) \longrightarrow (\Delta, \gamma[r : v^{pc \sqcup k}], (\ell, pc) :: \sigma, \ell_c : I)}$$

Fig. 2. Dynamic semantics for assignments.

Value-Dependent Security Labels. Although we use plain security labels in the syntax depicted in Fig. 1, our work can also be combined with value-dependent security labels as our semantics and soundness proofs are independent of the underlying security labels. In order to extend our system with support for value-dependent labels, we would first need to change the definition of security labels to account for value-dependencies:

$$\text{Security Label} \quad k ::= S[\![x]\!] \mid \bot \mid \top$$
$$\text{Security Classes} \ S ::= S_1 \mid S_2 \mid \ldots \mid S_n$$

Where S denotes a security class ($S \in SC$). At the static level value-dependent security classes are parametrized with function parameters, while at the dynamic level they are parametrized with their corresponding runtime values. For instance, one could use the label $\text{Student}(id)$ to denote the security level of information that can only be read by the student with the specified identifier; at runtime, the id would be replaced with the corresponding value for the student identifier.

It is the role of the runtime semantics to bind the static parameters of value-dependent security classes to their corresponding values. More precisely, when interpreting a function call, the function's parameters may be associated with security labels that depend on their corresponding values or on the values of the other parameters. In such cases, the security monitor binds the values of the parameters to the security labels that dependent on them.

4   Dynamic Semantics

We now define the semantics of the information flow monitor for SNITCH IR. The monitor handles guarded and unguarded instructions. The former entail runtime checks to avoid information leakage, while the latter only require label propagation. Our monitor ensures non-interference on the guarded fragment but has some runtime overhead, and requires significant testing to achieve high reliability. Thus, we present a type system, in Sect. 5, to perform program rewriting, adding guards only where necessary; the reference monitor does not verify at runtime statically correct operations.

$[\textsc{BranchT-Push}]$

$$\frac{\ell_{pd} = postDom(\ell_c) \quad \ell \neq \ell_{pd} \quad \sigma' = (\ell_{pd}, k \sqcup pc) :: (\ell, pc) :: \sigma}{(\Delta, \gamma[r:true^k], (\ell, pc) :: \sigma, \ell_c : \texttt{if } r\ ,\ell_t\ ,\ell_f) \longrightarrow (\Delta, \gamma[r:true^k], \sigma', \ell_t : \texttt{pop } \ell_t; \Delta(\ell_t))}$$

$[\textsc{BranchF-Push}]$

$$\frac{\ell_{pd} = postDom(\ell_c) \quad \ell \neq \ell_{pd} \quad \sigma' = (\ell_{pd}, k \sqcup pc) :: (\ell, pc) :: \sigma}{(\Delta, \gamma[r:false^k], (\ell, pc) :: \sigma, \ell_c : \texttt{if } r\ ,\ell_t\ ,\ell_f) \longrightarrow (\Delta, \gamma[r:false^k], \sigma', \ell_f : \texttt{pop } \ell_f; \Delta(\ell_f))}$$

$[\textsc{BranchT-NoPush}]$

$$\frac{\ell = postDom(\ell_c) \quad \sigma' = (\ell, k \sqcup pc) :: \sigma}{(\Delta, \gamma[r:true^k], (\ell, pc) :: \sigma, \ell_c : \texttt{if } r\ ,\ell_t\ ,\ell_f) \longrightarrow (\Delta, \gamma[r:true^k], \sigma', \ell_t : \texttt{pop } \ell_t; \Delta(\ell_t))}$$

$[\textsc{BranchF-NoPush}]$

$$\frac{\ell = postDom(\ell_c) \quad \sigma' = (\ell, k \sqcup pc) :: \sigma}{(\Delta, \gamma[r:false^k], (\ell, pc) :: \sigma, \ell_c : \texttt{if } r\ ,\ell_t\ ,\ell_f) \longrightarrow (\Delta, \gamma[r:false^k], \sigma', \ell_f : \texttt{pop } \ell_f; \Delta(\ell_f))}$$

$[\textsc{D-Jump}]$

$$\frac{}{(\Delta, \gamma, \sigma, \ell_c : \texttt{jump } \ell) \longrightarrow (\Delta, \gamma, \sigma, \ell : \texttt{pop } \ell; \Delta(\ell))}$$

$[\textsc{D-Pop}]$

$$\frac{}{(\Delta, \gamma, (\ell, -) :: \sigma, \ell_c : \texttt{pop } \ell; I) \longrightarrow (\Delta, \gamma, \sigma, \ell_c : I)}$$

$[\textsc{D-NoPop}]$

$$\frac{\ell \neq \ell'}{(\Delta, \gamma, (\ell, -) :: \sigma, \ell_c : \texttt{pop } \ell'; I) \longrightarrow (\Delta, \gamma, (\ell, -) :: \sigma, \ell_c : I)}$$

Fig. 3. Dynamic semantics for control instructions.

We define the operational semantics of the monitor by means of a transition system, with the reduction rules of Fig. 2 and Fig. 3 and using runtime configurations of the form $(\Delta, \gamma, \sigma, \ell_c : I)$. In a configuration, the code heap Δ maps code labels to instruction sequences, the store for register labels γ maps register names to pairs of values and their respective security levels. Finally, the stack σ tracks the current security level of the computation (pc), maintaining the nesting information needed to implement program scopes, relevant for IFC. We define a stack σ as a list of pairs of the form (ℓ, k), such that ℓ is the first post-dominant (function $postDom$, as used in Fig. 3) of the branching instruction adding the entry, and k the security level of the new scope. To denote the security level of the current scope we use pc. Finally, $\ell_c : I$ denotes the current basic block: ℓ_c represents the label of the block, and I the instructions comprising the block.

Assignments. The semantics for assignments, depicted in Fig. 2, emphasizes the hybrid nature of the information flow monitor, distinguishing guarded ($\overset{\circ}{=}$) from unguarded ($=$) instructions. The axiom $[\textsc{D-SafeAssignment}]$ defines the behaviour of unguarded assignments. It updates register r with the value v and security level k. Rule $[\textsc{D-UnsafeAssignment}]$, for guarded assignments, follows $[\textsc{D-SafeAssignment}]$ but includes a runtime check; the context's security

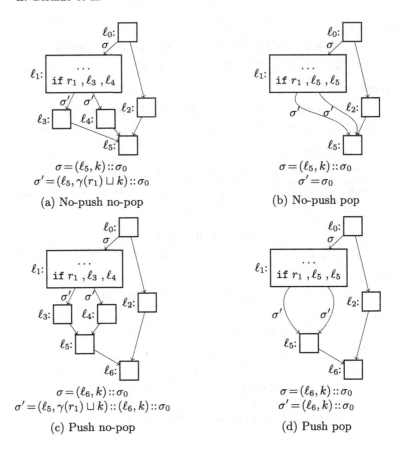

Fig. 4. Conditional jump influence on σ based on the control flow graph.

level (pc) must be smaller than or equal to the security level of the assigned register ($pc \sqsubseteq k_d$). This check is necessary to avoid implicit informations leaks, that is, leaks arising from the control structure of programs. It must not be possible to write to registers visible at a level lower than the context's level, nor should it be possible to write a value with a label lower than the context's label; visible registers remain visible and secret registers remain secret. SNITCH IR foresees binary operations ($r_d := r_s \oplus v^a$ and $r_d :\stackrel{\circ}{=} r_s \oplus v^k$) not semantically covered here. However, they follow [D-SAFEASSIGNMENT] and [D-UNSAFEASSIGNMENT], and the target register's label depends on the labels of all operands (r_s and v), plus the context's label (pc).

Control Flow Dependencies. SNITCH IR does not address the structure of a program, namely the scoping of conditions' security levels. So, we resort to an auxiliary data structure, a stack, to track such scopes. The security level of a new scope depends on the levels of outer scopes and the security level of the condition starting the scope. To overcome the lack of a well defined structure, we rely on post-dominance analyses [24] of the control flow graph (CFG) to determine the code contained in each scope.

In graph theory, a node a **post-dominates** a node b if every path from b to the exit node must go through a. Considering the graph in Fig. 4c, both ℓ_5 and ℓ_6 are **post-dominators** of ℓ_1, but ℓ_3 and ℓ_4 are not, due to the flow divergence in ℓ_1. Moreover, we say that ℓ_5 is the **first post-dominator** of ℓ_1, since it is the post-dominator closest to ℓ_1, i.e. the node where the flows that diverges at ℓ_1 merge.

Instructions starting a new scope (conditional jumps) push onto the stack a new security level and the label where the scope ends, the first node post-dominating the current instruction. When performing unconditional jumps (and degenerate conditional jumps), we need to check if the scope has ended and recover the previous context security level.

The stack invariant defines that the topmost entry always contains the label where the current context ends, and security levels do not decrease (see [BRANCHT-PUSH] and [BRANCHF-PUSH]). However, if a scope terminates in the same place as its parent, a new entry is not necessary. Instead, we update the topmost entry's security level to consider the new scope's security level and maintain the structure of σ. This is explicit in rules [BRANCHT-NoPUSH] and [BRANCHF-NoPUSH]. At runtime, we add pop in all rules for conditional branches. The runtime instruction pop is never present in the original source code. The reduction of unconditional jumps ([D-JUMP]) leaves σ unchanged but adds a pop to the next block; pop will always be the first instruction to execute after a jump. Rules [D-POP] and [D-NoPOP] define the behaviour of pop as it may or may not change σ. We must check if pop's label matches the label of σ's topmost entry. If it does, the scope ends and we pop σ ([D-POP]). Otherwise, σ remains unchanged ([D-NoPOP]).

The stack represents scope nesting in a program and identifies merging points where context security levels can decrease, i.e. scopes end. Figure 4 depicts four possible outcomes of the successive application of reduction rules pushing and popping entries in σ. Consider the conditional jump in block ℓ_1.

In Fig. 4a, [BRANCHT-NoPUSH] and [D-NoPOP] apply in sequence. The branch in ℓ_1 merges in the same place as the enclosing scope (ℓ_5), and the branches follow distinct paths ($\ell_3 \neq \ell_4$). The label at the top of σ (ℓ_5) stays the same, the security level accounts for the the condition's security level ($\gamma(r_1)$).

In Fig. 4b, rules [BRANCHT-NoPUSH] and [D-POP] apply in sequence. The branching ℓ_1 merges in the same place as the enclosing scope (ℓ_5), and both branches lead directly to it. Therefore, the scope closes, and the stack pops.

In Fig. 4c, [BRANCHT-PUSH] and [D-NoPOP] apply in sequence. The branching in ℓ_1 merges in a location (ℓ_5) other than the enclosing scope's end (ℓ_6), and the branches follow distinct paths ($\ell_3 \neq \ell_4$). We push a new pair to σ, with the scope's ending location and the appropriate security level.

Finally, in Fig. 4d, [BRANCHT-PUSH] and [D-POP] apply in sequence. The branching in ℓ_1 merges immediately after the jump in a location (ℓ_5) other than the end of the enclosing scope (ℓ_6); the scope is empty, σ remains unchanged.

The degenerate cases of Fig. 4b and d can result from a translation of structured programs and from compilers' optimizations.

4.1   Monitor Non-interference

Our monitor enforces non-interference for programs containing only guarded instructions ($[\![$D-UNSAFEASSIGNMENT$]\!]$). In this section, we sketch the non-interference proof, and later, we show that it also holds for well-formed rewritten programs with unguarded instructions. The proof consists in showing that two configurations of the same program are indistinguishable at an observation level g, if their initial states (σ and γ) are indistinguishable at g.

It is first convenient to define store (γ) and stack (σ) indistinguishability.

Definition 1 (Store Projection). *We define the projection of σ with relation to a security level g, $\gamma \lfloor_g$, as follows:*

$$\gamma \lfloor_g \triangleq \{r_1 : v_1^{k_1}, ..., r_n : v_n^{k_n}\}, \ \forall r_i \in dom(\gamma).\ \gamma(r_i) = v_i^{k_i} \ \wedge \ k_i \sqsubseteq g$$

Definition 2 (Store Indistinguishability). *We define the indistiguishability relation on stores γ, γ', written $\gamma \sim_g \gamma'$, as follows:*

$$\gamma \sim_g \gamma' \triangleq \gamma \lfloor_g = \gamma' \lfloor_g$$

Definition 3 (Stack Projection). *We define the projection of a stack σ at observation level g, written $\sigma \lfloor_g$, as follows:*

$$nil \lfloor_g \triangleq nil$$
$$((\ell, a) :: \sigma) \lfloor_g \triangleq (\ell, a) :: \sigma \lfloor_g \ If \ a \sqsubseteq g$$
$$((\ell, a) :: \sigma) \lfloor_g \triangleq \sigma \lfloor_g \qquad If \ a \not\sqsubseteq g$$

Definition 4 (Stack Indistinguishability). *We define the indistinguishability relation between two stacks, σ and σ', as follows:*

$$\sigma \sim_g \sigma' \triangleq \sigma \lfloor_g = \sigma' \lfloor_g$$

As an aid for the non-interference proof, resorting to Ω and Ω' as two configurations, we make a distinction between distinguish between computations observable at distinct security levels.

Definition 5 (High Transition). *A transition is high, written $\Omega \stackrel{\nearrow}{}_g \Omega'$, if the context security level (pc) is not lower than the observation level (g):*

$$\frac{(\Delta, \gamma, (\ell, pc) :: \sigma, \ell_c : I) \longrightarrow (\Delta, \gamma', \sigma', \ell_c' : I') \qquad pc \not\sqsubseteq g}{(\Delta, \gamma, (\ell, pc) :: \sigma, \ell_c : I) \stackrel{\nearrow}{}_g (\Delta, \gamma', \sigma', \ell_c' : I')}$$

Definition 6 (Low Transition). *A transition low, written $\Omega \stackrel{\searrow}{}_g \Omega'$, if the context security level (pc) is lower than the observation level (g):*

$$\frac{(\Delta, \gamma, (\ell, pc) :: \sigma, \ell_c : I) \longrightarrow (\Delta, \gamma', \sigma', \ell_c' : I') \qquad pc \sqsubseteq g}{(\Delta, \gamma, (\ell, pc) :: \sigma, \ell_c : I) \stackrel{\searrow}{}_g (\Delta, \gamma', \sigma', \ell_c' : I')}$$

Definition 7 (Mixed Transitions). *We define a mixed sequence of transitions, written $\Omega \xrightarrow{(L,H)}_g \Omega'$, as a combination of low (L) and high (H) transitions:*

$$\frac{(\Delta, \gamma, (\ell, pc) :: \sigma, \ell : I) \xrightarrow{l}_g (\Delta, \gamma_l, \sigma_l, \ell_l : I_l) \quad (\Delta, \gamma_l, \sigma_l, \ell_l : I_l) \xrightarrow{h}_g (\Delta, \gamma_h, \sigma_h, \ell_h : I_h) \quad (\Delta, \gamma_h, \sigma_h, \ell_h : I_h) \xrightarrow{(L-l, H-h)}_g (\Delta, \gamma', \sigma', \ell' : I')}{(\Delta, \gamma, (\ell, pc) :: \sigma, \ell : I) \xrightarrow{(L,H)}_g (\Delta, \gamma', \sigma', \ell' : I')}$$

If we reach a configuration Ω through a mixed sequence of L low transitions and H high transitions, then we there is Ω' such that we reach Ω' in l low transitions and h high transitions, and from Ω' we reach Ω through $L - l$ low transitions and $H - h$ high transitions. Take note that this also applies to programs starting in high transitions ($l = 0$).

The non-interference proof follows from verifying that both high and low transition sequences, when executed separately, preserve σ and γ indistinguishability.

We first prove the confinement of high transitions, expressed in the lemma below. Instructions executed at a security level not lower than g do not visibly change γ and σ. The proof follows from case analysis of the reduction relation.

Lemma 1 (Confinement)

> If $(\Delta, \gamma, \sigma, \ell_c : i; I) \rightarrow_g (\Delta, \gamma', \sigma', \ell'_c : I')$ then $\gamma \sim_g \gamma' \wedge \sigma \sim_g \sigma'$.

Store indistinguishability ($\gamma \sim_g \gamma'$) comes from two key aspects of rule [D-UNSAFEASSIGNMENT]: (i) guarded assignments do not write to registers whose security level is lower than the context security level; public information remains public; (ii) when writing to a register, the monitor computes the resulting security level using the computation's security label; secret information remains secret. Finally, control instructions do not modify γ, making them irrelevant in this proof.

We prove stack indistinguishability focusing on the rules for control instructions. [D-POP] removes the topmost entry from σ. In a high transition, where the topmost entry is secret, its removal does not change the visible part of stack σ. Rule [BRANCHT-PUSH] (and [BRANCHF-PUSH]) adds a new (ℓ, k) pair to σ with a higher security level ($PC(\sigma) \sqsubseteq k$). Thus, it does not introduce visible changes in the stack. Rule [BRANCHT-NOPUSH] updates the topmost entry of σ to a higher security level, and no changes to the stack are visible.

We now prove one-step non-interference for low transitions.

Lemma 2 (Low One-Step Non-interference)

> If $(\Delta, \gamma, \sigma, \ell_c : i; I) \rightarrow_g (\Delta, \gamma_f, \sigma_f, \ell_{cf} : I_f)$ and
>
> $(\Delta, \gamma', \sigma', \ell_c : i; I) \rightarrow_g (\Delta, \gamma'_f, \sigma'_f, \ell'_{cf} : I'_f)$ with $\gamma \sim_g \gamma' \wedge \sigma \sim_g \sigma'$
>
> then $\gamma_f \sim_g \gamma'_f$, $\sigma_f \sim_g \sigma'_f$, $\sigma_f = (\ell, pc) :: \sigma$, and $pc \sqsubseteq g \implies I_f = I'_f$.

This proof follows by inspecting the reduction rules; the same instruction on both configurations will produce identical effects on γ and σ and evolve equally. The only exception where $I_f \neq I'_f$ holds is when entering a sequence of high transitions. For $I_f \neq I'_f$ to hold the branch condition must evaluate to different values, which is only possible if the register in the condition is secret.

Considering programs as sequences of low and high transitions, we can prove non-interference by induction on the number of transitions.

Theorem 1 (Non-interference)

$\quad$ If $(\Delta, \gamma, \sigma, \ell_c : I) \xrightarrow{(x,y)}_g (\Delta, \gamma_f, \sigma_f, \ell_{cf} : I_f)$ and
$(\Delta, \gamma', \sigma', \ell_c : I) \xrightarrow{(x,z)}_g (\Delta, \gamma'_f, \sigma'_f, \ell'_{cf} : I'_f)$ with $\gamma \sim_g \gamma'$ and $\sigma \sim_g \sigma'$
$\quad$ then $\gamma_f \sim_g \gamma'_f$ and $\sigma_f \sim_g \sigma'_f$.

Two indistinguishable executions at the same point, by the transitive closure of Lemma 2, will remain indistinguishable until they start high transitions:

$$(\Delta, \gamma_a, \sigma_a, \ell_{ca} : I_a) \xrightarrow{i}_g (\Delta, \gamma_b, \sigma_b, \ell_{cb} : I_b)$$
$$(\Delta, \gamma_x, \sigma_x, \ell_{cx} : I_x) \xrightarrow{i}_g (\Delta, \gamma_y, \sigma_y, \ell_{cy} : I_y)$$

where $\gamma_a \sim_g \gamma_x$, $\sigma_a \sim_g \sigma_x$, $\ell_{ca} = \ell_{cx}$, $I_a = I_x$, $\gamma_b \sim_g \gamma_y$, $\sigma_b \sim_g \sigma_y$, $\ell_{cb} \neq \ell_{cy}$, $I_b \neq I_y$.
For high transitions, we apply the transitive closure of Lemma 1, concluding

$$(\Delta, \gamma_b, \sigma_b, \ell_{cb} : I_b) \xrightarrow{j}_g (\Delta, \gamma_c, \sigma_c, \ell_{cc} : I_c)$$
$$(\Delta, \gamma_y, \sigma_y, \ell_{cy} : I_y) \xrightarrow{k}_g (\Delta, \gamma_z, \sigma_z, \ell_{cz} : I_z)$$

This ensures that $\gamma_b \sim_g \gamma_c$, $\sigma_b \sim_g \sigma_c$, $\gamma_y \sim_g \gamma_z$, and $\sigma_y \sim_g \sigma_z$. By transitivity we have that $\gamma_c \sim_g \gamma_z$, $\sigma_c \sim_g \sigma_z$. For the hypothesis to apply, $I_c = I_z$ needs to hold. This condition is given by the properties of the control flow graph; if two executions diverge at the same point of the CFG then they will converge at the same point. With all conditions met, the proof follows by induction.

5   Static Semantics

We now present the procedure for rewriting unguarded SNITCH IR programs to their hybrid counterpart. Our relation approximates IFC, rejecting only programs proven incorrect, and producing an equivalent program with less (or equal number of) guarded instructions. We assume that source programs do not contain guarded assignments nor pop instructions. Only the type system introduces guarded assignments, and only the monitor adds pop instructions at runtime.

We define a rewriting system recursively in the structure of each basic block, iterating each via the rules in Fig. 5 and Fig. 6. The rewriting relation

$$\Delta, \widehat{\Gamma}, \widehat{\Sigma} \vdash \overline{\ell \mapsto I} \Downarrow \overline{\ell \mapsto I'}$$

takes three environments: the code repository Δ, storing each basic block's instructions; the environment $\widehat{\Gamma}$, tracking the security levels of all registers on

[FORALL]

$$\frac{\Delta, \widehat{\Gamma}, \widehat{\Sigma}, \widehat{\Gamma}(\ell_i) \vdash \ell_i : I_i \Downarrow I_i' \quad \forall (\ell_i, I_i) \in \overline{\ell \mapsto I}}{\Delta, \widehat{\Gamma}, \widehat{\Sigma} \vdash \overline{\ell \mapsto I} \Downarrow \overline{\ell \mapsto I'}}$$

[S-SAFEASSIGNMENT]

$$\frac{\Delta, \widehat{\Gamma}, \widehat{\Sigma}, \widehat{\gamma}[r : PC(\widehat{\Sigma}(\ell_c)) \sqcup k] \vdash \ell_c : I \Downarrow I' \quad PC(\widehat{\Sigma}(\ell_c)) \preccurlyeq \widehat{\gamma}(r)}{\Delta, \widehat{\Gamma}, \widehat{\Sigma}, \widehat{\gamma} \vdash \ell_c : r := v^k; I \Downarrow r := v^k; I'}$$

[S-UNSAFEASSIGNMENT]

$$\frac{\Delta, \widehat{\Gamma}, \widehat{\Sigma}, \widehat{\gamma}[r : PC(\widehat{\Sigma}(\ell_c)) \sqcup k] \vdash \ell_c : I \Downarrow I' \quad PC(\widehat{\Sigma}(\ell_c)) \preccurlyeq \widehat{\gamma}(r) = \downarrow}{\Delta, \widehat{\Gamma}, \widehat{\Sigma}, \widehat{\gamma} \vdash \ell_c : r := v^k; I \Downarrow r :\overset{\circ}{=} v^k; I'}$$

Fig. 5. Static semantics for assignments

entry for each basic block; and the map of stacks $\widehat{\Sigma}$, capturing the control flow structure and corresponding nesting of security levels in all blocks. Rule [FORALL] defines the rewriting of all blocks in a program $(\overline{\ell \mapsto I})$ to produce the final program $(\overline{\ell \mapsto I'})$. For each block, the rewriting procedure relies on the relation

$$\Delta, \widehat{\Gamma}, \widehat{\Sigma}, \widehat{\gamma} \vdash \ell_c : I \Downarrow I'$$

where the fourth environment, $\widehat{\gamma}$, initialized out of environment $\widehat{\Gamma}$, maps registers of the present basic-block to security levels (intervals). This judgment relates a valid unguarded set of instructions I, part of basic block ℓ_c, to a set of valid guarded and unguarded instructions I'. All unguarded instructions are guaranteed to preserve data confidentiality (non-interference). We present the soundness results of the checking/rewriting system in Sect. 5.1.

We define the semantics in a syntax-directed way, with non-terminating instructions depicted in Fig. 5, and block terminating instructions depicted in Fig. 6. Rule [S-SAFEASSIGNMENT] shows that the instruction is not modified since the safety conditions statically hold, i.e. the current security level $PC(\widehat{\Sigma}(\ell_c))$ is lower than the register's security level $\widehat{\gamma}(r)$. The changed register's security level now accounts for the level of the context, the level of the assigned value, in the rewriting of the subsequent instructions $(\widehat{\gamma}[r : \widehat{\Sigma}(\ell_c) \sqcup k])$.

If we know statically that the context's security level is lower than the security level of the register, rule [S-SAFEASSIGNMENT], the assignment is secure and is not trapped at runtime. If the comparison is undefined, i.e. security intervals intersect $(PC(\widehat{\Sigma}(\ell_c)) \preccurlyeq \widehat{\gamma}(r) = \downarrow)$, rule [S-UNSAFEASSIGNMENT], we rewrite it as a guarded assignment, so that the monitor prevents any leaks. Finally, if the context's level is higher or unrelated, no rule applies, the program gets rejected.

The rules included in Fig. 6 define the static semantics for jump and conditional jump instructions, comparing and validating the nesting structure of stacks and the compatibility between registers in the departing and landing blocks. Notice that these rules only check the structure of the control flow graph, and they do not introduce or rewrite the existing code as the previous set of rules.

⟦S-Branch-NoPush-NoPop⟧

$$\frac{\widehat{\gamma} \preccurlyeq \widehat{\Gamma}(\ell_i) \quad \widehat{\Sigma}(\ell_c) = (\ell, \widehat{pc}) :: \widehat{\sigma} \quad (\ell, \widehat{pc} \sqcup \widehat{\gamma}(r)) :: \widehat{\sigma} \preccurlyeq \widehat{\Sigma}(\ell_i) \\ postDom(\ell_c) = \ell \quad \ell_i \neq \ell \quad \ell_i \in \{\ell_t, \ell_f\}}{\Delta, \widehat{\Gamma}, \widehat{\Sigma}, \widehat{\gamma}[r:\widehat{k}] \vdash \ell_c : \texttt{if } r, \ell_t, \ell_f \Downarrow \texttt{if } r, \ell_t, \ell_f}$$

⟦S-Branch-NoPush-Pop⟧

$$\frac{\widehat{\gamma} \preccurlyeq \widehat{\Gamma}(\ell_i) \quad \widehat{\Sigma}(\ell_c) = (\ell, \widehat{pc}) :: \widehat{\sigma} \quad \widehat{\sigma} \preccurlyeq \widehat{\Sigma}(\ell_i) \\ postDom(\ell_c) = \ell = \ell_i \quad \ell_i \in \{\ell_t, \ell_f\}}{\Delta, \widehat{\Gamma}, \widehat{\Sigma}, \widehat{\gamma}[r:\widehat{k}] \vdash \ell_c : \texttt{if } r, \ell_t, \ell_f \Downarrow \texttt{if } r, \ell_t, \ell_f}$$

⟦S-Branch-Push-NoPop⟧

$$\frac{\widehat{\gamma} \preccurlyeq \widehat{\Gamma}(\ell) \quad \widehat{\Sigma}(\ell_c) = (\ell, \widehat{pc}) :: \widehat{\sigma} \quad (\ell', \widehat{pc} \sqcup \widehat{\gamma}(r)) :: \widehat{\Sigma}(\ell_c) \preccurlyeq \widehat{\Sigma}(\ell_i) \\ postDom(\ell_c) = \ell' \quad \ell' \neq \ell \quad \ell' \neq \ell_i \quad \ell_i \in \{\ell_t, \ell_f\}}{\Delta, \widehat{\Gamma}, \widehat{\Sigma}, \widehat{\gamma}[r:\widehat{k}] \vdash \ell_c : \texttt{if } r, \ell_t, \ell_f \Downarrow \texttt{if } r, \ell_t, \ell_f}$$

⟦S-Branch-Push-Pop⟧

$$\frac{\widehat{\gamma} \preccurlyeq \widehat{\Gamma}(\ell) \quad \widehat{\Sigma}(\ell_c) = (\ell, \widehat{pc}) :: \widehat{\sigma} \quad \widehat{\Sigma}(\ell_c) \preccurlyeq \widehat{\Sigma}(\ell) \\ postDom(\ell_c) = \ell_i \quad \ell_i \neq \ell \quad \ell_i \in \{\ell_t, \ell_f\}}{\Delta, \widehat{\Gamma}, \widehat{\Sigma}, \widehat{\gamma}[r:\widehat{k}] \vdash \ell_c : \texttt{if } r, \ell_t, \ell_f \Downarrow \texttt{if } r, \ell_t, \ell_f}$$

⟦S-Jump-NoPop⟧

$$\frac{\widehat{\gamma} \preccurlyeq \widehat{\Gamma}(\ell) \quad \widehat{\Sigma}(\ell_c) = (\ell', \widehat{pc}) :: \widehat{\sigma} \quad \ell \neq \ell' \quad \widehat{\Sigma}(\ell_c) \preccurlyeq \widehat{\Sigma}(\ell)}{\Delta, \widehat{\Gamma}, \widehat{\Sigma}, \widehat{\gamma} \vdash \ell_c : \texttt{jump } \ell \Downarrow \texttt{jump } \ell}$$

⟦S-Jump-Pop⟧

$$\frac{\widehat{\gamma} \preccurlyeq \widehat{\Gamma}(\ell) \quad \widehat{\Sigma}(\ell_c) = (\ell, \widehat{k}) :: \widehat{\sigma} \quad \widehat{\sigma} \preccurlyeq \widehat{\Sigma}(\ell)}{\Delta, \widehat{\Gamma}, \widehat{\Sigma}, \widehat{\gamma} \vdash \ell_c : \texttt{jump } \ell \Downarrow \texttt{jump } \ell}$$

Fig. 6. Static semantics for control instructions

The security level stack assigned to each block $(\widehat{\Sigma}(\ell_c))$ stores the nesting hierarchy ruling the block, containing information about where each scope ends. The stacks associated with basic blocks work in a similar fashion to the stack used in the monitor. They store pairs with a security level and the corresponding target label in an increasing sequence, depicting how deep the block is in the control flow graph. The security level stored at the top of the stack is the current scope's security level, and the label specifies the scope's closing point in the CFG.

Conditional jump instructions capture branching in the control flow graph and there are four rules to consider, each matching one of the cases depicted in Fig. 4. In Fig. 4(a), rule ⟦S-Branch-NoPush-NoPop⟧ captures the case where a new scope ends at the same node as its parent, and the next node is not the post-dominant node. In this case, the rule checks that the security level in both target blocks matches the current stack updated with the combination of the current level with the condition's security level $((\ell, \widehat{pc} \sqcup \widehat{\gamma}(r)) :: \widehat{\sigma} \preccurlyeq \widehat{\Sigma}(\ell_i))$. We also check that the registers in the next blocks match $(\widehat{\gamma} \preccurlyeq \widehat{\Gamma}(\ell))$. In Fig. 4(b), rule ⟦S-BRANCH-NoPUSH-POP⟧ captures the degenerated case where we start a new scope terminating in the same node as the parent, and we reach said node in one step; both branches jump to the same block. In this case, we need to check that the registers in the following blocks match and that the stack is one element shorter to close the current (and parent) scope(s) ($\widehat{\sigma} \preccurlyeq \widehat{\Sigma}(\ell_i)$) where $\widehat{\sigma}$ is the stack after the pop). In Fig. 4(c), rule ⟦S-BRANCH-PUSH-NoPOP⟧ reflects the case where we start a scope whose post-dominant differs from the parent scope's, and we jump to a node other than the post-dominant node of the current block. Here, we check that the registers match and that the target blocks expect a stack with a new entry, $((\ell', \widehat{pc} \sqcup \widehat{\gamma}(r)) :: \widehat{\Sigma}(\ell_c) \preccurlyeq \widehat{\Sigma}(\ell_i))$. Rule ⟦S-BRANCH-PUSH-POP⟧ captures the degenerated case where we start and terminate a new scope whose post-dominant is different from the parent's scope. We check the compatibility between the source and target registers ($\widehat{\gamma} \preccurlyeq \widehat{\Gamma}(\ell)$) and stack ($\widehat{\Sigma}(\ell_c) \preccurlyeq \widehat{\Sigma}(\ell)$).

Unconditional jump instructions, together with the degenerated cases from conditional jumps above (⟦S-BRANCH-NoPUSH-POP⟧ and ⟦S-BRANCH-PUSH-POP⟧), represent path convergence in the CFG. We cover two outcomes of the jump instruction. Rule ⟦S-JUMP-NoPOP⟧ checks if the registers match and if the stack is compatible with the target block's stack. Rule ⟦S-JUMP-POP⟧ checks if the registers match and if the stack, except for the topmost entry, is compatible with the target block's stack. We pop the topmost entry from $\widehat{\sigma}$ since we are jumping to the current scope's (and, potentially, parent scopes) end.

In summary, the static semantics checks that all basic blocks match a given specification for $\widehat{\sigma}$ and $\widehat{\gamma}$ and all jumps abide by the same nesting discipline, matching the security levels specified in the $\widehat{\sigma}$. Algorithmically, the checking and rewriting procedure takes as input Δ and the program $(\overline{\ell \mapsto I})$. It is necessary to synthesize the environments $\widehat{\Gamma}$ and $\widehat{\Sigma}$, and the output program $\overline{\ell \mapsto I'}$ from constraints collected when constructing the proof of rewriting, in the style of Hindley Milner type systems [10,28]. We next prove the soundness of the static checking procedure with relation to the dynamic semantics presented in Sect. 4, showing that no untrapped errors occur in the unguarded part of the program and that the reference monitor captures all remaining errors.

5.1   Soundness

The soundness result of our approach guarantees that only guarded instructions raise errors at runtime and are, therefore, rightfully trapped. Thus, we prove that all omitted verifications are unnecessary, as unguarded instructions will not cause any illegal flows.

The semantics in Sect. 4 only verifies guarded instructions, as unguarded instructions just require label propagation. Consider the extended semantics including the rules present in Fig. 5, Fig. 6, and Fig. 7. The latter contains new rules for unguarded assignments and error trapping for all instructions. We introduce two kinds of error, one that the monitor traps (⚡) and other that the monitor does not trap (☠). We want to prove that for well typed programs the latter never occurs. To relate the static and the dynamic semantics, we define an interpretation for static stores and stacks:

⟦D-SafeAssignment-Bad⟧

$$\frac{\gamma(r) = u^{k'} \quad PC(\sigma) \not\sqsubseteq k'}{(\Delta, \gamma, \sigma, \ell_c : r := v^k; I) \longrightarrow \text{☠}}$$

⟦D-UnsafeAssignment-Trapped⟧

$$\frac{\gamma(r) = u^{k'} \quad PC(\sigma) \not\sqsubseteq k'}{(\Delta, \gamma, \sigma, \ell_c : r \overset{\circ}{:=} v^k; I) \longrightarrow \text{☇}}$$

Fig. 7. Error aware dynamic rules

Definition 8 (Static Store Interpretation) *We define the interpretation of* $\widehat{\gamma}$, *written,* $⟦\widehat{\gamma}⟧$, *as follows:*

$$⟦\widehat{\gamma}⟧ \triangleq \{\gamma \mid \forall r \in dom(\gamma). \; r \in dom(\widehat{\gamma}) \wedge \gamma(r) = v^k \wedge k \in \widehat{\gamma}(r)\}$$

Definition 9 (Static Stack Interpretation) *We define the interpretation of* $\widehat{\sigma}$, *written,* $⟦\widehat{\sigma}⟧$, *as follows:*

$$⟦\widehat{\sigma}⟧ \triangleq \{\sigma \mid (\widehat{\sigma} = nil \wedge \sigma = nil)$$
$$\vee \; (\sigma = (\ell, k) :: \sigma' \wedge \widehat{\sigma} = (\ell, \widehat{k}) :: \widehat{\sigma}' \wedge k \in \widehat{k} \wedge \sigma' \in ⟦\widehat{\sigma}'⟧)\}$$

The soundness lemma for our type system with relation to the operational semantics is as follows.

Theorem 2 (Static Soundness)
  If $\Delta, \widehat{\Gamma}, \widehat{\Sigma}, \widehat{\gamma} \vdash \ell_c : I \Downarrow I'$ *and* $(\Delta, \gamma, \sigma, \ell_c : I') \overset{n}{\longrightarrow} \Omega'$ *with*
$\gamma \in ⟦\widehat{\gamma}⟧$ *and* $\sigma \in ⟦\widehat{\Sigma}(\ell_c)⟧$ *then* $\Omega' \neq \text{☠}$.

The structure of the proof resembles that of a proof of progress and follows by induction on the number of reduction steps. It follows that all well-formed rewriting judgments match the premises of the initial semantics (including the error ☇), and untrapped errors ☠ never occur. For the proof, we consider as base case, the scenario where we reach the final configuration trough zero transitions, i.e., we start in the final configuration. For the induction step, we prove that the monitor only transits to states other than ☠, otherwise we have that all other cases do not apply by contradiction.

Considering an assignment, according to rule ⟦D-SafeAssignment⟧, the system will not reduce to ☠. Moreover, due to ⟦S-SafeAssignment⟧, Definition 8, and Definition 9, the conditions for the induction hypothesis hold. When analysing a transition through ⟦D-SafeAssignment-Bad⟧, we reach a contradiction. According to this rule, we have that $PC(\sigma) \not\sqsubseteq k$ but by ⟦S-SafeAssignment⟧, Definition 8, and Definition 9, we have $PC(\sigma) \sqsubseteq k$. Rule ⟦D-UnsafeAssignment⟧ follows rule ⟦D-SafeAssignment⟧. When considering rule ⟦D-UnsafeAssignment-Trapped⟧, the system evolves to ☇ which, by definition, is different from ☠.

Binary operations (not covered in the semantics) are similar regular assignments, and the proof for binary operations follows the proofs for assignments. The remaining instructions never transit to ☠ , hence, it is only necessary to prove that they preserve the condition required for the induction hypothesis.

6   Conclusions

We presented SNITCH IR, a low-level language with a hybrid IFC mechanism with dependent security levels. The core of our approach is a rewriting procedure that checks the validity of unstructured programs and injecting guard into programs. Guarded instructions will check dynamically situations that do not fail in the permissive check of the type system. We prove that our monitor preserves termination insensitive non-interference in SNITCH IR, and we prove that the hybrid monitor is sound in that it satisfies the non-interference property while minimizing the runtime checks needed.

We identify as future research directions the formal support for an interprocedural analysis, and the extension of the language with function calls. Also, we envision the further integration of function parameters in the security lattice in the formal presentation.

Our current implementation supports fully dynamic analysis of JVM bytecode, and we aim to support the hybrid IFC analysis, a work in progress. Furthermore, we wish to extend the prototype to support other mainstream low-level languages. The particular aspects of dynamically allocated memory (records, arrays, and objects) are also interesting as future work.

Acknowledgements. This work is supported by FCT/MCTES SFRH/BD/149043/ 2019, FCT/MCTES Grant NOVA LINCS - UIDB/04516/2020 and GOLEM Lisboa-01-0247-Feder-045917, INESC-ID multi-annual funding (UIDB/50021/2020) and INFO-COS (PTDC/CCI-COM/32378/2017).

References

1. Agrawal, P.: Keeping your account secure. https://blog.twitter.com/official/en_us/topics/company/2018/keeping-your-account-secure.html. Accessed 15 Oct 2021
2. Aldous, P., Might, M.: Static analysis of non-interference in expressive low-level languages. In: Blazy, S., Jensen, T. (eds.) SAS 2015. LNCS, vol. 9291, pp. 1–17. Springer, Heidelberg (2015). https://doi.org/10.1007/978-3-662-48288-9_1
3. Aldous, P., Might, M.: A posteriori taint-tracking for demonstrating non-interference in expressive low-level languages. In: IEEE Security and Privacy Workshops, pp. 179–184 (2016)
4. Austin, T.H., Flanagan, C.: Efficient purely-dynamic information flow analysis. In: ACM SIGPLAN Workshop on Programming Languages and Analysis for Security (2009)
5. Balliu, M., Dam, M., Guanciale, R.: Automating information flow analysis of low level code. In: ACM SIGSAC Conference on Computer and Communications Security, pp. 1080–1091 (2014)

6. Barthe, G., Pichardie, D., Rezk, T.: certified lightweight non-interference java byte-code verifier. In: De Nicola, R. (ed.) ESOP 2007. LNCS, vol. 4421, pp. 125–140. Springer, Heidelberg (2007). https://doi.org/10.1007/978-3-540-71316-6_10

7. Barthe, G., Rezk, T.: Non-interference for a JVM-like language. In: TLDI 2005, pp. 103–112. (2005)

8. Barthe, G., Rezk, T., Naumann, D.: Deriving an information flow checker and certifying compiler for java. In: IEEE Symposium on Security and Privacy, pp. 230–242 (2006)

9. Cimpanu, C.: Github accidentally recorded some plaintext passwords in its internal logs (May 2018), https://www.bleepingcomputer.com/news/security/github-accidentally-recorded-some-plaintext-passwords-in-its-internal-logs/. Accessed 15 Oct 2021

10. Damas, L., Milner, R.: Principal type-schemes for functional programs. In: ACM SIGPLAN-SIGACT Symposium on Principles of Programming Languages, pp. 207–212 (1982)

11. Denning, D.E.: A lattice model of secure information flow. Commun. ACM 236–243 (1976)

12. Disney, T., Flanagan, C.: Gradual information flow typing. In: STOP 2011 (2011)

13. ECMA International: Standard ECMA-335 - Common Language Infrastructure (CLI), December 2010

14. Erlingsson, U., Schneider, F.B.: Sasi enforcement of security policies: a retrospective. In: Workshop on New Security Paradigms, pp. 87–95 (1999)

15. Fennell, L., Thiemann, P.: Gradual security typing with references. In: IEEE Computer Security Foundations Symposium, pp. 224–239 (2013)

16. Fennell, L., Thiemann, P.: LJGS: gradual security types for object-oriented languages. In: European Conference on Object-Oriented Programming, pp. 9:1–9:26 (2016)

17. Ferreira, P.J.A.D.: M.sc. dissertation. information flow analysis using data-dependent logical propositions, faculdade de Ciências e Tecnologia, Universidade Nova de Lisboa (2012)

18. Fragoso Santos, J., Jensen, T., Rezk, T., Schmitt, A.: Hybrid typing of secure information flow in a Javascript-like language. In: Ganty, P., Loreti, M. (eds.) TGC 2015. LNCS, vol. 9533, pp. 63–78. Springer, Cham (2016). https://doi.org/10.1007/978-3-319-28766-9_5

19. Ghosal, S., Shyamasundar, R.K.: Pifthon: A compile-time information flow analyzer for an imperative language. CoRR (2021)

20. Hedin, D., Bello, L., Sabelfeld, A.: Value-sensitive hybrid information flow control for a javascript-like language. In: IEEE Computer Security Foundations Symposium, p. 351–365 (2015)

21. Hedin, D., Sabelfeld, A.: Information-flow security for a core of Javascript. In: 2012 IEEE 25th Computer Security Foundations Symposium, pp. 3–18 (2012)

22. Hedin, D., Sabelfeld, A.: A perspective on information-flow control. In: Software Safety and Security - Tools for Analysis and Verification, pp. 319–347 (2012)

23. Lattner, C., Adve, V.: LLVM: a compilation framework for lifelong program analysis and transformation. In: International Symposium on Code Generation and Optimization, March 2004

24. Lengauer, T., Tarjan, R.E.: A fast algorithm for finding dominators in a flowgraph. ACM Trans. Program. Lang. Syst. 121–141 (1979)

25. Lindholm, T., Yellin, F., Bracha, G., Buckley, A.: The Java Virtual Machine Specification, Java SE 8 Edition (2014)

26. Lourenço, L., Caires, L.: Dependent information flow types. In: SIGPLAN Not, pp. 317–328, January 2015
27. Lourenço, L., Caires, L.: Information flow analysis for valued-indexed data security compartments. In: Abadi, M., Lluch Lafuente, A. (eds.) TGC 2013. LNCS, vol. 8358, pp. 180–198. Springer, Cham (2014). https://doi.org/10.1007/978-3-319-05119-2_11
28. Milner, R.: A theory of type polymorphism in programming. J. Comput. Syst. Sci. 348–375 (1978)
29. Morrisett, G., Walker, D., Crary, K., Glew, N.: From system f to typed assembly language. ACM Trans. Program. Lang. Syst. **21**, 527–568 (1999)
30. Myers, A.C., Liskov, B.: Protecting privacy using the decentralized label model. ACM Trans. Softw. Eng. Methodol. **9**, 410–442 (2000)
31. Myers, A.C., Zheng, L., Zdancewic, S., Chong, S., Nystrom, N.: Jif 3.0: Java information flow (2006). Accessed 15 Oct 2021
32. O'Flaherty, K.: Facebook exposed up to 600 million passwords - here's what to do, March 2019. https://www.forbes.com/sites/kateoflahertyuk/2019/03/21/facebook-has-exposed-up-to-600-million-passwords-heres-what-to-do/#6f301fe4bc90. Accessed on 15 Oct 2021
33. Polikarpova, N., Stefan, D., Yang, J., Itzhaky, S., Hance, T., Solar-Lezama, A.: Liquid information flow control. Lang, Proc. ACM Program (2020)
34. Sabelfeld, A., Myers, A.: Language-based information-flow security. IEEE J. Sel. Areas Commun. **21**(1), 5–19 (2003)
35. Schneider, F.B., Morrisett, G., Harper, R.: A language-based approach to security. In: Wilhelm, R. (ed.) Informatics. LNCS, vol. 2000, pp. 86–101. Springer, Heidelberg (2001). https://doi.org/10.1007/3-540-44577-3_6
36. Siek, J., Taha, W.: Gradual typing for objects. In: Ernst, E. (ed.) ECOOP 2007. LNCS, vol. 4609, pp. 2–27. Springer, Heidelberg (2007). https://doi.org/10.1007/978-3-540-73589-2_2
37. Simonet, V., Rocquencourt, I.: Flow caml in a nutshell. In: First APPSEM-II Workshop, April 2003
38. Toro, M., Garcia, R., Tanter, E.: Type-driven gradual security with references. ACM Trans. Program. Lang. Syst. **40**, 1–55 (2018)
39. Winder, D.: Facebook quietly confirms millions of unencrypted Instagram passwords exposed - change yours now, April 2019. https://www.forbes.com/sites/daveywinder/2019/04/19/facebook-quietly-confirms-millions-of-unencrypted-instagram-passwords-exposed-change-yours-now/#22e5d5844537. Accessed 15 Oct 2021

Upper Bound Computation of Information Leakages for Unbounded Recursion

Johannes Bechberger[1]([✉])(ⓘ) and Alexander Weigl[2](ⓘ)

[1] Institute for Program Structures and Data Organization, Karlsruhe, Germany
[2] Institute of Information Security and Dependability (KASTEL),
Karlsruhe Institute of Technology, Karlsruhe, Germany

Abstract. Confidentiality is an important security goal that is ensured by the absence of information flow between secrets and observable outputs. Quantitative information flow (QIF) analyses quantify the amount of knowledge an attacker can gain on the secrets by observing the outputs. This paper presents a novel approach for calculating an upper bound for the leakage of confidential information in a program regarding min-entropy. The approach uses a data flow analysis that represents dependencies between program variables as a bit dependency graph. The bit dependency graph is interpreted as a flow network and used to compute an upper bound for the leakage using a maximum flow computation. We introduce two novelties to improve the precision and soundness: We strengthen the precision of the data flow representation by using the path conditions. We add sound support of unbounded loops and recursion by using summary graphs, an extension of a common technique from compiler engineering. Our approach computes a valid upper bound of the leakage for all programs regardless of the number of loop iterations and recursion depth. We evaluate our tool against a state-of-the-art analysis on 13 example programs.

Keywords: Security analysis · Quantitative information flow · Bit dependency graphs

1 Introduction

Information Flow. The analysis of secure information flow (IF) tries to find the information flow of confidential secret information to output variables that can be observed by unclassified personnel or attackers. It is an important analysis to ensure the confidentiality of programs. Traditionally, the result of an IF analysis is a qualitative answer: either there is an influence of confidential information on attacker-observable outputs (we say the program leaks information) or not. Qualitative Information Flow is an established area of research that produced tools that scale to large programs and support a variety of language features.

R. Calinescu and C. S. Păsăreanu (Eds.): SEFM 2021, LNCS 13085, pp. 160–177, 2021.
https://doi.org/10.1007/978-3-030-92124-8_10

```
input int h;
output int o := h % 2
```

Fig. 1. Program that leaks only one bit of information from the secret input *h* to the public output *o*.

The problem is that small leaks may often be acceptable and sometimes necessary; it is necessary to know the amount of leaked information. Secure Qualitative Information Flow cannot distinguish between a program that leaks only a single bit, like the program given in Fig. 1, and a program that leaks the whole secret, as the information flow is not quantified. The urge to distinguish between such cases leads to the need of quantifying the leakage.

Quantitative Information Flow (QIF) aims to calculate the leakage, the amount of secret information which is gained by an attacker, by executing a program. Applications range from ensuring the security of distributed applications to formally certifying data storage systems [19]. Typically, an attacker has access to the program code and can only see low outputs *o* after program termination. The quantified leakage of the program from Fig. 1 is clearly lower than the leakage of the program that leaks the whole secret. In the following, we call a QIF analysis *sound* if and only if the analysis computes an upper bound.

```
input int h;
int z := 0;
while (z ≠ h) {
      z := z + 1;
}
output int o := z
```

Fig. 2. *Laundering Attack* which leaks the secret input over all iterations of the loop.

Motivating Example. We consider now the program in Fig. 2 with signed fixed-width integers. This program demonstrates the *Laundering Attack*, and leaks the whole secret into the public output. This leakage occurs indirectly due to control statements. Each iteration of the loop itself only leaks the information whether $z = h$ for a specific z, but all iterations together leak the whole secret. Figure 2 is an example of how a small leak can be extended into a leak of the secret. A related real-world example is the brute-force attack on passwords, checking all possible passwords to find the correct one, with each call to the password check routine leaking only a small amount of information.

Many static QIF analyses based on abstract interpretation, model counting, or program algebras were proposed in recent years. They have in common that they only investigate programs up to a prior set upper bound on execution paths. If the upper bound is too small, the estimated leakage might be too low. This can be observed in our evaluation in Sect. 7. The usage of a prior set upper bound means that current analyses can only consider a limited number of loop iterations. There are multiple static analyses that support both loops and functions, but in practice, only a limited recursion depth and a limited number of loop iterations can be soundly analyzed due to resource limitations. As a result, these analyses cannot give, in practice, an upper bound for the leakage of all analyzed programs, an example for such a program is the Laundering Attack in Fig. 2.

Contribution. We present *Nildumu*[1], a novel over-approximative static QIF analysis for a while-language with recursion and fixed-length arrays with copy semantics. It supports both unbounded loops and recursion, contrary to the current state of the art. The analysis does this by considering a limited number of execution paths, like previous approaches, over-approximating the effects of the remaining iterations and recursive calls. The basis of the analysis is a bit dependency graph, which records the dependencies between the values in a program on the bit-level. During the construction of the graph, path conditions are taken into account. The bit dependency graph is extended using the novel summary graphs, which are used to improve the precision of the over-approximation. The evaluation shows that the analysis is approximately as precise as current analyses based on model counting while being sound for every number of considered execution paths.

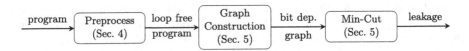

Fig. 3. Structure of our analysis.

Overview. We first describe the related static analyses in Sect. 2 and the theoretical foundations in Sect. 3. We then describe our analysis itself. The analysis is structured into different parts, as seen in Fig. 3: The program is first transformed into an equivalent loop-free program with recursion, lowering arrays to int variables. This loop-free program is then transformed into a simplified form so that variables are only assigned once. These transformations are given in Sect. 4. Then the summary graphs are computed for every function, and with them, the bit dependency graph is created, presented in section Sect. 5. The actual computation of the leakage is then based on the bit dependency graph, using a maximum flow computation. We then give an improvement of the precision of the analysis harnessing the knowledge gathered from path conditions in Sect. 6. We follow this by an evaluation in Sect. 7 comparing the analysis with a state-of-the-art model counting analysis and end with the conclusion and future work in Sect. 8.

2   Related Work

There are multiple static QIF analyses based on abstract interpretation, as presented by Smith in [27], like *jpf-qif* developed by Phan et al. [26]. Recent advances in the field of approximative model counting resulted in the development of analyses that can process code written in C and C++, like *ApproxFlow* [4]. In contrast to the SAT-based model counting, *Moped-QLeak* [9] uses binary decision

---

[1] Nildumu is Lojban for "is a quantity".

diagrams (BDD) for computing a summary of a program and using this summary to compute its leakage. Model-counting and BDD-based analyses rely on inlining and unwinding and are prone to under-approximations, as mentioned in the introduction.

Furthermore, there are two static analyses by Mu [23] and Clark et al. [12] that use a Program Dependence Graph (PDG) to track the dependencies between variables in a graph representation of the program. This differs from our approach, which tracks the dependencies between individual bits instead of variables. These analyses compute the value probability distributions for each program variable. Both analyses are based on the notions given in [18], describing an algebra for an imperative language. The analyses using these techniques can soundly analyze programs of a while-language using a probabilistic denotational semantic. But these analyses do not support recursion and are limited to small programs. Newer approaches [1] improve on these analyses based on newer work on the formalization of hyperproperties, but they are not yet implemented in tools. The advantage of these approaches is that they support multiple leakage measures.

Finally, although there is no other bit dependency graph based analysis, there is one dynamic analysis using byte dependency graphs: The dynamic analysis by McCamant and Ernst [21] uses dynamic tainting instead of statically tracking the flow of information through the program with a byte level granularity. Other dynamic analyses exist, but they are usually based on black box approaches [10,11] that do not consider the program code at all.

As stated previously, none of these tools support the static analysis of programs with both arbitrary numbers of loop iterations and recursion depth.

3   Foundations

We use the information-theoretical notion of QIF as presented by Smith [28]. The entropy $H(X)$ describes the amount of information of a random variable X. It gives the minimal number of bits that are required to encode the information of X (Shannon Entropy).

In the following, we consider only sequential programs, similar to [28], where the attacker only observes the output O after the execution of the program finishes and has no information on the secret input H. In QIF, we are interested in the information shared between H and O. This information is called *mutual information*. It is denoted as $H(\text{H}; \text{O})$ and expresses the information gained on H by observing O. The actual leakage $I(\text{H}; \text{O})$ is then defined as the reduction of the uncertainty by observing O: $I(\text{H}; \text{O}) = H(\text{H}) - H(\text{H}; \text{O})$.

In the following, we use the min-entropy H_∞, which is based on the concept of vulnerability [28] and quantifies the probability that the secret is guessed by the attacker in one try. Formally, the vulnerability $V(\text{H})$ is defined as $V(\text{H}) = \max_{h \in \mathcal{H}} P[\text{H} = h]$ with the resulting entropy being $H_\infty(\text{H}) = \log \frac{1}{V(\text{H})}$ [17]. In particular, $V(\text{X})$ is the worst-case probability that X's value can be guessed correctly in one try.

Assuming we have a deterministic program with a uniformly distributed secret, the min-entropy leakage I_∞ is calculated by counting the different possible outputs of a program [28]. Formally, let O be the set of possible outputs of the program, then the leakage is

$$I_\infty(\mathtt{H}; \mathtt{O}) = \log_2 |O|.$$

This leakage is an upper bound of the leakage over all distributions of $\mathtt{H}$.

Soundness. To work with estimations of static QIF analyses that are not exact, we define *soundness* as follows: An analysis is *sound* if and only if the calculated leakage for all programs p with the secret input $\mathtt{H}$ and public output $\mathtt{O}$, $\hat{I}^p(\mathtt{H}; \mathtt{O})$, is an upper bound of the actual leakage $I^p(\mathtt{H}; \mathtt{O})$, i.e., $I^p(\mathtt{H}; \mathtt{O}) \leq \hat{I}^p(\mathtt{H}; \mathtt{O})$.

Program Dependency Graph (PDG). A PDG is a data dependence graph with added control flow edges [15]. Such a graph consists of nodes that represent variables and operations. There is an edge from a node a to a node b present in this graph if the value of b directly depends on the value of a (data dependence) or if the value of a directly affects whether or not b is executed (control dependence). Our analysis uses a PDG as its underlying representation of the program structure.

Constant Bit Analysis. For our QIF analysis, we exploit a static intra-procedural constant bit analysis on a PDG. A constant bit analysis aims to find bits that are statically known. We base our analysis on the analysis described by Budiu et al. [7] which uses a *bit lattice* ($\mathbb{B}$). This lattice contains the possible statically known information on a bit. A bit is a constant (0 or 1), might be both ($\top_\mathbb{B}$), or is never evaluated ($\bot_\mathbb{B}$).

A constant bit analysis associates each node in the PDG with a tuple of elements from the bit lattice representing the knowledge that we have of each bit of the value of each node.

4 Preprocessing

Shape of Programs. In this paper, we consider programs of a while-language containing the typical imperative statements: assignments, if-statements and while-loops (cf. Fig. 4). Moreover, the programming language contains functions that might be directly or mutually recursive. Also, functions can have multiple return values, an assignment of the form $(v_1, \ldots, v_k) := f()$ allows to assign the return values of the function call $f()$ to multiple variables v_1 to v_n. Additionally, the dot denotes bit-access operator, i.e., $e.n$ denotes the nth bit of the expression e. To identify the secret and public information, variables declaration can contain the modifier *input* (secret) and *output* (public). All variables without such a modifier are considered as hidden and non-confidential.

The only supported data types are signed fixed-sized integers and fixed-length arrays. Integers are represented in two's complement with an arbitrary but fixed bit-width called W in the following. Boolean values are represented by the integers 0 and 1.

Preprocessing. We start the analysis by preprocessing programs into an array- and loop-free form to simplify the QIF analysis. Arrays have a fixed-length, and therefore can be split into single variables that represent its entries. This technique is known as *scalar replacement of aggregates* [24]. Every access of an array element with a constant index can directly be mapped onto the corresponding variable. All other accesses are replaced with if-else-cascades to determine the correct variable.

Loops are transformed into recursive functions. The transformation rule is given in Fig. 5 which requires multiple return values. The application of this rule for the example in Fig. 2 is in Fig. 6. This transformation is followed by the inlining of all functions on their call-sites with argument passing and return statements replaced by variable assignments. Recursive functions are only inlined up to a user-specified bound. This is a common technique that is used in model checking and program analyses to support functions [3,24]. Note that the function calls are preserved when the inlining bound is hit. Thus, the resulting program is not free of function calls, which are handled later in our QIF analysis by over-approximating the behavior of the remaining (recursive) function calls. The inlining increases the precision of the analysis as every inlined function call is not over-approximated and increases its run-time.

After the inlining, we translate the program into Static Single Assignment form (SSA). We introduce fresh variables, such that every variable is only assigned once. Moreover, we ensure that the right-hand side of each assignment is an atomic expression. An atomic expression is either a function call or a binary operator with variables (v) or constants (n) as operands. The final result is a program that only consists of if- and function call statements, as well as assignments $v = e$ and return statements **return** e where e is an atomic expression.

5   Bit Dependency Graph

This section covers the novel generation of the bit dependency graph for a program with arbitrary recursive functions (Sect. 5.1, Sect. 5.3) but without loops and arrays. The construction is based on the constant bit analysis and results in

---

$$
\begin{aligned}
&\textit{Var. def} \quad V ::= (\textbf{input} \mid \textbf{output})^? \; t \; v \\
&\textit{Func. call} \quad C ::= f(E_1, \ldots, E_m) \\
&\textit{Expression } E ::= v \mid n \mid E \odot E \mid E.n \\
&\textit{Statements } S ::= V \mid v := E \mid (v_1, \ldots, v_k) := C \mid v[E] := E \mid \\
&\qquad\qquad\qquad\qquad S; \; S \mid \textbf{while } (E) \; \{ \; S \; \} \mid \textbf{if } (E) \; \{ \; S \; \} \; (\textbf{else } \{ \; S \; \})^? \\
&\textit{Func. def} \quad F ::= t_1 \; \ldots \; t_k \; f(t_{p1} \; v_1, \; \ldots, \; t_{pm} \; v_m) \; \{ \; S; \; \textbf{return } E_1, \ldots, E_k \; \} \\
&\textit{Program} \quad P ::= F^* \; S
\end{aligned}
$$

Fig. 4. The grammar of the considered while-language. Placeholder v denotes a variable name, t a type name, n an integer constant and $\odot$ a typical binary operator like addition, multiplication, or exclusive-or on integers.

166   J. Bechberger and A. Weigl

$$t_{w_1} \ldots t_{w_n} \; f_l \; (t_{w_1} \; w_1, \; \ldots, \; t_{w_n} \; w_n, \; t_{r_1} \; r_1, \; \ldots, \; t_{r_m} \; r_m) \; \{$$

$$\mathbf{while} \; (E) \; \{ \quad \Rightarrow \quad \begin{array}{l} \mathbf{if} \; (E) \; \{ \\ \quad S; \; (w_1, \ldots, w_n) := f_l(w_1, \ldots, w_n, r_1, \ldots, r_m) \; \} \\ \quad \mathbf{return} \; w_1, \ldots, w_n \\ \} \end{array}$$

$$(w_1, \ldots, w_n) := f_l(w_1, \ldots, w_n, r_1, \ldots, r_m)$$

Fig. 5. Translation of a loop into a semantically equivalent function, with $w_1, \ldots, w_n$ being the variables written in the loop and $r_1, \ldots, r_m$ being other variables that are accessed in the loop.

$$\mathbf{while} \; (z \neq h) \; \{ \quad \Rightarrow \quad \begin{array}{l} \mathbf{int} \; f_l(\mathbf{int} \; z, \; \mathbf{int} \; h) \; \{ \\ \quad \mathbf{if} \; (z \neq h) \; \{ \\ \quad\quad z := z + 1; \; z := f_l \; (z, \; h) \; \} \\ \quad \mathbf{return} \; z \\ \} \end{array}$$

$$z := f_l(z, \; h)$$

Fig. 6. Translation of the loop from Fig. 2 using the schema from Fig. 5.

a graph that expresses the dependencies between single bits. We use this graph to approximate the leakage of a program (Sect. 5.2).

Definition 1 (Bit Dependency Graph). *A bit dependency graph $G = (V, E)$ is a directed graph of nodes where each node represents a bit that belongs to the value of a node in the underlying PDG. This graph contains an edge from v_1 to v_2 if v_2 data or control depends on v_1.*

Each bit node in the graph represents a single bit of the information on a variable at a specific program location, due to the SSA form. Thus, a bit dependency graph represents the dependencies between variables at the bit-level. A peculiarity in this definition is that an edge between two nodes (bits) expresses the possibility of a dependency. To achieve a sound analysis, the set of distinct paths between nodes must always be a superset of the actual bit dependencies defined by the program.

In the following, we call nodes that are reachable from a node $v \in V$ the *transitive successors* of v and nodes $v_i \in V$ for which an edge $(v, v_i) \in E$ exists *successors* of v.

Construction. We construct a bit dependency graph from a PDG during the constant bit analysis by collecting the dependencies between the individual bits associated with the PDG nodes.

Let $G = (V, E)$ be the bit dependency graph for a given preprocessed program. The preprocessed program only consists of control statements, function calls, atomic assignments and return statements, as described before. The set of vertices of the graph is $V := \{x.i \mid 1 \leq i \leq W, x \text{ is a PDG node}\}$ that contains a node for each bit of every PDG node and thereby every variable in the program. The set of edges E is formed by using specific function handlers. A function handler, defined in Sect. 5.1, models a bit dependency graph from the arguments to the return value. We treat every operator in the following as an implicitly defined function, e.g. $a + b$ is treated as $f_+(a, b)$. Let us consider the case of two arguments in function calls (or binary operators), $x := f(y, z)$ (or $x := y \odot z$): We add edges between the bit nodes of y, z and x if there is a data or control dependency between them. We can trivially extend this to functions with higher arity.

Due to the preprocessing, we only need to consider assignments with function calls and single operator expressions. Each specific function or operator requires a function handler.

Example 1. The bit dependency graph for the program x := y | z with two bit integers is given in Fig. 7. The nodes y_i and z_i are connected to x_i since each bit of the result depends on the corresponding bits of the operands.

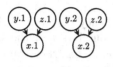

Fig. 7. Graph for x := y | z

In the remaining, we define the concept of function handlers (Definition 2) and discuss different handlers (Sect. 5.1 and Sect. 5.3). We afterwards state the relationship between the bit dependency graph and the leakage computation Sect. 5.2.

5.1   Handling Functions

We formally introduce the concept of a function handler h_c, which models the bit dependencies from the arguments $a_1, \ldots, a_n$ to the return value x. A function handler returns a specific bit dependency graph for a specific function call $x := f(a_1, \ldots, a_n)$. Therefore, the handler can react to specific arguments, e.g. an optimization for neutral elements of operators are possible $(a + 0 = a)$.

In the best case, this function handler represents the bit dependencies precisely. In the worst case, if no such function handler exists, we add an approximative sub-graph. Such an approximative sub-graph leads to a sound analysis if it is an over-approximation, i.e., it adds at least as many distinct paths between every parameter node and every return node as the precise sub-graph.

Definition 2 (Function Handler). *A function handler for a specific function call c, $x := f(a_1, \ldots, a_n)$, with the tuple of bit nodes $A_c = (a_1.1, \ldots, a_1.W, \ldots, a_n.1, \ldots, a_n.W)$ related to the arguments $a_1, \ldots, a_n$, is formally defined as a function $h_c : A_c \mapsto (V_c, E_c)$ with $A_c \subseteq V_c$.*

The resulting graph $G_c = (V_c, E_c)$ is an over-approximation of the application of f and the return value nodes R_c are used as the nodes of x.

We distinguish two kinds of handlers: the *built-in* and the *summary* handlers. We describe in the following the built-in handlers and detail the *summary* handlers in Sect. 5.3.

Built-In Handler. For operators and built-in functions, we define handlers that model their effect: We interpret non-bitwise operators as their equivalent combination of bit-wise operators and over-approximate more complex operators like multiplication. This allows the analysis to only implement the bit-wise operators directly. The built-in handlers are more precise than the summary handlers but have to be implemented directly in the core analysis.

5.2 From Bit Dependency Graph to Leakage

We can compute an approximation of the leakage by using network flow algorithms. Commonly, a directed node-weighted flow network $N_G = (G = (V, E), \gamma, v_{source} \in V, v_{sink} \in V)$ consists of a directed graph G, a node capacity $\gamma \colon V \to \{1, \infty\}$ and a source and a sink node for the flow. A comparable idea based on an edge-weighted flow network has first been used by McCamant and Ernst [21].

Construction of the Flow Network. Given a bit dependency graph $G = (V, E)$ with the nodes $V_{input} \subseteq V$ representing the secret input bits and the nodes $V_{output} \subseteq V$ representing the public output bits, we can construct the corresponding node-weighted flow network N_G as follows: We introduce a new source node v_{source} which has as successors all input nodes V_{input} and a new sink node v_{sink} which is a successor of all output nodes V_{output}:

$$N_G = (G' = (V', E'), \gamma, v_{source}, v_{sink}) \qquad V' = V \cup \{v_{source}, v_{sink}\}$$
$$E' = E \cup \{(v_{source}, v) \mid v \in V_{input}\} \cup \{(v, v_{sink}) \mid v \in V_{output}\}$$
$$\gamma(v) \mapsto \begin{cases} \infty & : v \in \{v_{source}, v_{sink}\} \\ 1 & : otherwise \end{cases}$$

Theorem 1 (Leakage Computation using Minimum Cuts). *The size of the minimum node cut of the network N_G is an upper bound of the leakage of a program with the bit dependency graph G.*

Proof Sketch. First two observations: A single bit can only be statically unknown if it is either a secret input bit or it transitively depends on at least one secret input bit. Consider now the bits $b_1, \ldots, b_n$ that form the bit vector b which are statically unknown. b can than have at most 2^n different values at runtime.

If we can find the bits $b'_1, \ldots, b'_m$ so that all paths from v_{source} to $b_1, \ldots, b_n$ contain these bits, then b can have at most 2^m values: The vector b' can have at most 2^m values and every value of b' leads to one value of b at runtime.

The minimum cut M is the b' with the minimal combined weight if we consider b to be the vector of public output bits. $2^{|M|}$ is therefore an upper bound on the number of different output values at runtime and as a result M is an upper bound for the min-entropy of the underlying program (see Sect. 3).

Computation. We can compute the minimum node cut by transforming the node-weighted network into an edge-weighted network [14, Algorithm 9] on which we compute the minimum edge cut. The minimum edge cut can be computed by using maximum flow algorithms as a result of the max-flow min-cut theorem [6]. Another possibility is to use a Partial MaxSAT solver as presented in Sect. 6.

5.3 Summary Function Handler

By treating bit dependency graphs as node-weighted network flow graphs, we can reconsider function handlers and define *summary* handlers. We first define the concept of summary graphs, their construction, and at last their application in form of a function handler.

Definition 3 (Summary Graphs). *A summary graph G_s for a bit dependency graph G of a function f consists of the parameter nodes P, the return nodes R and the intermediary nodes Γ. The edges of G_s and Γ, satisfy the following constraint: The information flow between P and R is the same in G_s as in G.*

Summary graphs are modeled after the transitive dependence graphs for functions introduced by Horwitz et al. [16]. These dependence graphs consist of summary edges and are commonly used in compiler engineering for program slicing. A summary edge connects a parameter node with a return node if and only if there is a transitive dependency between them. A summary graph is a transitive dependence graph on bit-level that includes the nodes from the minimum-node-cut as intermediary nodes Γ to improve the precision.

Construction. Minimal summary graphs for each function are constructed iteratively using a fixed-point iteration over the call-graph. It uses a graph without any edges as a starting point for every function. The fixed-point iteration computes the summary graph for a given function f in each iteration using the following steps:

1. Construct the bit dependency graph G for f with parameters as secret inputs and return values as public outputs, using the current iteration's summary graphs whenever a function is called.
2. Reduce the graph G with parameter nodes P and return nodes R: Construct the flow network N_G and compute the minimum node cut Γ. Reduce the graph to a graph $G' = (V', E')$ that consists of $V' = P \cup R \cup \Gamma$ and transitive edges between P and $R \cup \Gamma$, and Γ and R.
3. Set $G = G'$ for the next iteration of the summary graph for f.

Using this construction, the summary graphs for all functions in the program can be pre-computed. Every iteration of the fixed-point iteration in the construction adds at least one new distinct path between the parameter and return nodes of at least one function. The fixed-point iteration terminates, as the number of distinct paths is bounded. Therefore, the construction itself terminates.

Example 2. We consider the function f given in Fig. 8a with three bit integers. Figure 8b shows the graph $\mathcal{G}(f)$ for the function and the resulting summary graph in Fig. 8c. This shows how the size of the summary graph is reduced.

170   J. Bechberger and A. Weigl

```
int f(int x){
    int r := 0;
    if (x * 3 = 1){
        r := 0b111
    }
    return r
}
```

(a) Example program

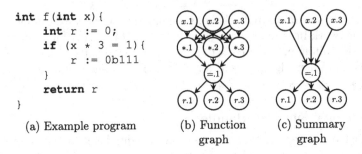

(b) Function graph

(c) Summary graph

Fig. 8. Example function with its graphs, omitting constant nodes.

Summary Handler. The summary handler is a function handler which uses a copy of the precomputed summary graph G_s^f for a function f on its call-site c.

$$h_c^{summary} : A_c \mapsto \text{copy}(G_s^f)[P \mapsto A_c]$$

Summary function handlers summarize the effect of a function on the leakage computation. They are still an over-approximation as they cannot use the information the constant bit propagation has on the arguments at any given call-site.

Soundness. We follow with Menger's Theorem for directed graphs [6] that the minimum node cut is equivalent to the number of internally node disjoint paths, as all nodes have weight 1. By the construction of the reduced graph G', the disjointedness of paths is preserved by the graph reduction, thus the set of disjoint paths is a superset of the disjoint paths of G. The summary handler is therefore sound.

6 Increasing the Precision

```
if (x & 1 = (y >> 1) & 1){
    z := x
}
```

Fig. 9. Example for path conditions

Knowledge from path conditions is not used in the construction of the bit dependency graph as described in Sect. 5. We extend the previous graph construction to take this knowledge into account, which increases the precision of our analysis. We annotate each bit node b with a function $repl_b : \mathbb{B} \to 2^{2^{Bit}}$ which returns the sets of bits that can be considered equal under the assumption that b has a given value. We use these functions to compute the equal bits for every path condition. In particular $repl_{cond}(1)$ returns the bits that are considered equal in the current context under the assumption that *cond* evaluates to true.

For example, we know that x & 1 = (y >> 1) & 1 evaluated to **true** in the then branch of the if-statement in Fig. 9, therefore we can infer that the first bit of x is equivalent to the second bit of y, $\{x.1, y.2\} \in repl_{x\&1=(y>>1)\&1}(1)$. The propagation of knowledge is based on the notion of propagated predicates, first formalized by Wegbreit [29]. Every path condition leads to new knowledge on bits.

This knowledge leads us to a set of bit dependency graphs, as we know in each context-specific bits that can be replaced by other bits, e.g. the bits belonging to x.1 with the bits belonging to y.2 in the example above. Inserting an edge from either bit in the specific context leads to a sound over-approximation. Therefore every of the possible graphs leads to an over-approximated leakage. In our example, we can replace the edge $(v_{x.1}, v_{z.1})$ with the edge $(v_{y.2}, v_{z.1})$ leading us to a set of graphs. We can either use simple heuristics to choose a specific graph or use a Partial MaxSAT (PMSAT) solver for leakage computation to optimize the chosen edges (Sect. 6) to minimize the calculated leakage.

Heuristic-Based Graph Selection. We select the graph, which promises the smallest leakage, by applying a simple greedy edge selection heuristic: In principle, we prefer edges that start in constant bits. The idea is that it improves the constant propagation and the precision of the analysis, as constant bits do not depend on the secret input. The advantage of this heuristic is its computational simplicity. Its main disadvantage is that it does depend on one of the possible edges starting in a constant bit, arbitrarily choosing an edge otherwise, not guaranteeing an optimal result. A preliminary evaluation showed that this did not affect the precision of the analysis for the programs in the evaluation. This heuristic is therefore used in the evaluation.

PMSAT-Based Leakage Computation. In general, an instance of PMSAT consists of formulas in conjunctive normal form (CNF) that consist of soft and hard clauses conjunctively combined with disjunctively connected (negated) propositional variables. A PMSAT solver, like Open-WBO [20], tries to find a satisfying variable assignment such that the variable assignment meets all given hard clauses, and the most possible soft clauses [8]. Finding such a solution is NP-complete but its usage removes the need for heuristics for incorporating the knowledge on replacement edges.

In the following, we give the encoding of the node-weighted flow network $N = (G' = (V', E'), \gamma, v_{source}, v_{sink})$ into hard and soft constraints: For each vertex v, we introduce the propositional variables c_v and r_v, which represents the participation of the vertex in the minimum cut: If c_v holds, add vertex v to the minimum cut, or if r_v holds, cut the graph after the successors v_s of vertex v (c_{v_s}) or their successor transitively. The hard constraints $\Gamma(v)$ for every node v are therefore defined as:

$$\Gamma(v) := \underbrace{d_v \rightarrow (c_v \vee r_v)}_{(1)} \wedge \underbrace{r_v \rightarrow \bigwedge_{s \in successors(v)} (d_s \vee \bigvee_{i=1}^{n} d_{s_i})}_{(2)}$$

We create the helper variable d_v in (1) that states that we cut the graph either at the vertex or after the vertex. (2) states that if we consider cutting the graph after v then we have to either cut the graph after every successor s. If there are any replacements (v, s_i) for the edge (v, s), we can cut at or after any of the s_i instead. If v does not have any successors, $\Gamma(v)$ degenerates to $d_v \rightarrow c_v$.

We add the hard constraints $\neg c_{v_{source}}$ and $\neg c_{v_{sink}}$ as the source and the sink cannot, by definition, be part of the minimum cut. We add $r_{v_{source}}$ as the minimum cut consists of transitive successors of v_{source} and $\neg r_{v_{sink}}$ as we cannot cut after the sink. We finally add the soft constraint $\neg c_v$ for every node v, leading us to the final formula:

$$\underbrace{\bigwedge_{v \in V'} \Gamma(v) \wedge \neg c_{v_{source}} \wedge \neg c_{v_{sink}} \wedge r_{v_{source}} \wedge \neg r_{v_{sink}}}_{\text{hard}} \quad \wedge \quad \underbrace{\bigwedge_{v \in V'} \neg c_v}_{\text{soft}}$$

A PMSAT solver tries to maximize the number of fulfillable $\neg c_v$ clauses and thereby minimize the number of nodes participating in the minimum cut, leading us to a leakage computation.

7   Evaluation

We compare *Nildumu*[2] with *ApproxFlow*[3]. As stated before, we found no other tool that supports both unbounded loops and unbounded recursion and use ApproxFlow as a state-of-the-art analysis. ApproxFlow is based on model counting. It works by first creating a SAT formula representing a program using CBMC [13] and then counting the number of different assignments for the output variables using an approximate model counter. Although we do compare the runtimes of both tools, the value of the comparison is limited, as both tools are based on different libraries using different language runtimes.

Tool Configuration. The tools are evaluated with different levels of inlining and unwinding to show the effect of this parameter on the approximated leakage. We consider 2, 8, and 32 as both unrolling and inlining levels. A level of 32 is the default for ApproxFlow. ApproxFlow is by default configured so that its results differ by at most 0.8 bits from the real leakage with a probability of 80%, as ApproxFlow uses an approximate model counter. We use the same inlining levels in combination with the summary handler for Nildumu. For the sake of completeness, we also present the datapoints for Nildumu without path conditions support (32^w).

---

[2] Nildumu is available as open-source with a GUI at https://github.com/ parttimenerd/nildumu with the full evaluation reproducible using the docker image `parttimenerd/nildumu`. The evaluation used version `49ebe88948874`.

[3] We used a modified version of ApproxFlow [4] with an update to ApproxMC4, publicly available at https://github.com/parttimenerd/approxflow.

Table 1. The computed leakage for all benchmarked programs with different unrolling levels k. The timeout was 2 h, timeouts are marked with a dash ("-"). Under-approximations of programs are marked as bold and underlined and over-approximations larger than one bit are marked as overlined, as a deviation of 0.8 bits is accepted for ApproxFlow with the default configuration. The second column I gives the actual leakages of the programs with $\sim$ marking the estimate by ApproxFlow as explained before and the third column I_{max} gives the maximum possible leakage, considering only the number of input and output bits.

Program	I [bit]	I_{max} [bit]	ApproxFlow			Nildumu			
			k=2	8	32	2	8	32	32^w
Laundering Attack	32.0	32.0	**<u>1.6</u>**	**<u>3.2</u>**	**<u>5.0</u>**	32.0	32.0	32.0	32.0
Binary Search (N=16)	16.0	32.0	**<u>2.0</u>**	**<u>8.0</u>**	16.0	$\overline{32.0}$	$\overline{32.0}$	16.0	$\overline{32.0}$
Binary Search (N=32)	32.0	32.0	**<u>2.0</u>**	**<u>8.0</u>**	32.0	32.0	32.0	32.0	32.0
Electronic Purse	2.0	32.0	**<u>1.6</u>**	2.0	2.0	$\overline{5.0}$	$\overline{5.0}$	$\overline{5.0}$	$\overline{32.0}$
Illustrative Example	4.1	32.0	4.1	4.1	4.1	5.0	5.0	5.0	$\overline{24.0}$
Implicit Flow	2.8	32.0	2.8	2.8	2.8	3.0	3.0	3.0	3.0
Masked Copy	16.0	32.0	16.0	16.0	16.0	16.0	16.0	16.0	16.0
Mix and Duplicate	16.0	32.0	16.0	16.0	16.0	16.0	16.0	16.0	16.0
Population Count	5.0	32.0	5.0	5.0	5.0	$\overline{10.0}$	$\overline{10.0}$	$\overline{10.0}$	$\overline{10.0}$
Sanity Check	4.0	32.0	$\overline{31.0}$	$\overline{31.0}$	$\overline{31.0}$	$\overline{32.0}$	$\overline{32.0}$	$\overline{32.0}$	$\overline{32.0}$
Sum	32.0	32.0	32.0	32.0	32.0	32.0	32.0	32.0	32.0
Smart Grid	$\sim$ 7.0	32.0	**<u>1.6</u>**	**<u>3.1</u>**	**<u>5.5</u>**	$\overline{32.0}$	$\overline{32.0}$	$\overline{32.0}$	$\overline{32.0}$
Preference Ranking (N=5)	$\sim$ 132.2	160.0	$\overline{160.0}$	132.1	132.1	$\overline{160.0}$	$\overline{135.0}$	$\overline{135.0}$	$\overline{135.0}$
Preference Ranking (N=10)	$\sim$ 294.4	320.0	$\overline{320.0}$	$\overline{320.0}$	-	$\overline{320.0}$	$\overline{320.0}$	$\overline{301.0}$	$\overline{301.0}$
Single Preference (N=5)	$\sim$ 8.0	160.0	$\overline{98.6}$	8.0	8.0	$\overline{160.0}$	$\overline{25.0}$	$\overline{25.0}$	$\overline{25.0}$
Single Preference (N=10)	$\sim$ 7.9	320.0	$\overline{258.6}$	$\overline{77.7}$	$\overline{17.7}$	$\overline{320}$	$\overline{320.0}$	$\overline{100.0}$	$\overline{100.0}$

Table 2. The mean execution time for all benchmarked programs in seconds. The timeout was 2 h and the standard deviation was at maximum 10%.

Program	ApproxFlow			Nildumu			
	k=2	8	32	2	8	32	32^w
Laundering Attack	0.1	0.1	0.2	1.4	1.4	2.0	1.4
Binary Search (N=16)	0.1	0.2	0.3	3.6	3.6	6.5	3.4
Binary Search (N=32)	0.1	0.2	0.6	3.6	3.6	7.2	3.5
Electronic Purse	0.2	0.3	3.8	1.3	1.5	1.2	2.0
Illustrative Example	0.1	0.1	0.1	0.6	0.6	0.7	0.6
Implicit Flow	0.1	0.1	0.1	0.7	0.7	0.9	0.7
Masked Copy	0.2	0.2	0.2	0.5	0.5	0.8	0.4
Mix and Duplicate	0.2	0.2	0.2	0.5	0.5	0.8	0.5
Population Count	0.1	0.1	0.1	0.7	0.6	0.9	0.6
Sanity Check	0.3	0.3	0.3	0.6	0.6	0.9	0.6
Sum	0.3	0.3	0.3	0.6	0.5	0.7	0.5
Smart Grid	0.2	0.3	0.3	53.1	101.9	248.9	36.6
Preference Ranking (N=5)	11.8	154.	422.7	144.4	149.4	148.4	274.3
Preference Ranking (N=10)	377.6	4061.7	-	402.7	442.0	819.8	2442.9
Single Preference (N=5)	6.0	1.2	1.2	43.7	43.8	44.1	293.0
Single Preference (N=10)	16.6	197.8	3520.7	162.5	163.9	163.8	3373.4

Benchmark Process. Both tools are run 5 times for every combination of program and unrolling level to account for randomness in the underlying system and in ApproxFlow. The benchmarking took place on an Intel Xeon Gold 6230 CPU with 512 GiB of RAM, running a Linux 5.4.0 kernel with OpenJDK 1.8.0 and CBMC 5.21.0. Both tools are restricted to two cores.

Benchmark Programs. We use the Laundering Attack from Fig. 2 and the commonly used benchmarks described in [2,9,22,25]. These benchmarks from literature can be categorized into programs that are focused on the handling of loops (Binary Search [22] and Electronic Purse [9]), the handling of conditions (Illustrative Example [22] and Implicit Flow [22]), the handling of bit operations (Mix and Duplicate [25] and Population Count [25]), and the handling of arithmetic or comparison operations (Sanity Check [25] and Sum [2]). We omit programs that use features not supported by the compared analyses.

We additionally use the Smart Grid and E-Voting examples from [5]. We use two versions of the E-Voting example as used by [4]: Ranking and single preference-based voting. There are no exact leakages known for these larger programs a priori, as the leakage depends on multiple configuration parameters. To estimate the exact leakage for the Smart Grid and E-Voting examples, we used ApproxFlow with the unrolling level being the respective loop bound, and set the allowed deviation to 0.1 bits and a correctness probability of 0.95. Both the lower allowed deviation and the higher correctness probability increase the run-time and the precision and result in different values than the default configuration for the same unrolling levels.

Results. The computed leakages are given in Table 1 and show that Nildumu over-approximates the leakage for every program and every level of inlining, in contrast to ApproxFlow which under-approximates the leakage if the unrolling and inlining level is lower than required by each program. Table 1 also shows that Nildumu has worse precision for most test cases involving arithmetic and comparison operators. Furthermore, Table 2 gives the execution time for all programs and shows that Nildumu is slower than ApproxFlow. Additional benchmarks showed that Nildumu does not produce better results, performance and leakage-wise, when using the PMSAT based leakage computation with Open-WBO.

Discussion. ApproxFlow is by design more precise for programs where it can fully unroll all loops and inline all functions, as it models operators directly as a SAT formula. Nildumu only uses simple dependencies between bits and not complex, SAT-based dependencies as ApproxFlow and has, therefore, worse precision, especially for arithmetic operators. Nonetheless, Nildumu analyses the presented benchmark programs with comparable precision and gives an over-approximation for every benchmark and unrolling limit. The results also show that using Nildumu without support for path conditions leads to worse precision with performance gains for only part of the benchmarks.

The run-time of Nildumu is worse than the run-time of ApproxFlow. This is partly due to its implementation in Java, compared to ApproxFlow which is a small Python wrapper combining two tools written in C++, and due to the additional computation of summary graphs which is especially expensive as this computation over-approximates the effect of all remaining recursion.

8 Conclusion and Future Work

In this paper, we presented a QIF analysis exploiting bit dependency graphs that supports a while-language with loops, recursive functions, fixed-width integers, and fixed-size arrays. To our knowledge, this is the first analysis that supports recursion (and loops) without a limit on the recursion depth using summary graphs as an adaptation of the well-known concept of summary edges. This reduces the set of assumptions on the processed programs. The analysis computes an upper bound of the information leakage using min-entropy regardless of the level of inlining.

The evaluation results presented in Sect. 7 show that the analysis produces comparably good results for typical examples, but also that the arithmetic and comparison expressions are conservatively approximated, and that the performance and precision could be improved. Especially the construction of summary graphs and the handling of arrays should be improved to reduce the execution time of the analysis. The analysis could therein profit from parallelization.

Furthermore, the used summary graphs are currently limited as their construction ignores the specific call-sites and their context. This problem should be addressed in future extensions of this approach, for example by the techniques already developed for data flow analyses in compilers. There is ongoing work to support a broader range of language features (like input and output streams) as well as using CBMC as a front-end to improve the real-world applicability of Nildumu. The precision could be improved by using interval-based lattices or incorporating more operator semantics using techniques from the field of bounded model checking. Furthermore, the analysis could be extended into a component-based analysis which analyzes program components and the flows between them.

Acknowledgements. This work was supported by the German Research Foundation (DFG) as part of the Transregional Collaborative Research Centre "Invasive Computing" (SFB/TR 89), and by the German Federal Ministry of Education and Research within the framework of the project KASTEL SVI in the Competence Center for Applied Security Technology (KASTEL).

References

1. Assaf, M., Signoles, J., Totel, E., Tronel, F.: The cardinal abstraction for quantitative information flow. In: Workshop on Foundations of Computer Security 2016 (FCS 2016), Lisbon, Portugal (June 2016). https://hal.inria.fr/hal-01334604
2. Backes, M., Köpf, B., Rybalchenko, A.: Automatic discovery and quantification of information leaks. In: 2009 30th IEEE Symposium on Security and Privacy, SP 2009, pp. 141–153. IEEE, Washington, DC (May 2009). https://doi.org/10.1109/SP.2009.18

3. Beyer, D., Gulwani, S., Schmidt, D.A.: Combining model checking and data-flow analysis. In: Handbook of Model Checking, pp. 493–540. Springer, Cham (2018). https://doi.org/10.1007/978-3-319-10575-8_16

4. Biondi, F., Enescu, M.A., Heuser, A., Legay, A., Meel, K.S., Quilbeuf, J.: Scalable approximation of quantitative information flow in programs. In: VMCAI 2018. LNCS, vol. 10747, pp. 71–93. Springer, Cham (2018). https://doi.org/10.1007/978-3-319-73721-8_4

5. Biondi, F., Legay, A., Quilbeuf, J.: Comparative analysis of leakage tools on scalable case studies. In: Fischer, B., Geldenhuys, J. (eds.) SPIN 2015. LNCS, vol. 9232, pp. 263–281. Springer, Cham (2015). https://doi.org/10.1007/978-3-319-23404-5_17

6. Bondy, J.A., Murty, U.S.R.: Graph Theory. Graduate Texts in Mathematics, Springer, Heidelberg (2008). https://doi.org/10.1007/978-1-84628-970-5

7. Budiu, M., Sakr, M., Walker, K., Goldstein, S.C.: BitValue inference: detecting and exploiting narrow bitwidth computations. In: Bode, A., Ludwig, T., Karl, W., Wismüller, R. (eds.) Euro-Par 2000. LNCS, vol. 1900, pp. 969–979. Springer, Heidelberg (2000). https://doi.org/10.1007/3-540-44520-X_137

8. Cha, B., Iwama, K., Kambayashi, Y., Miyazaki, S.: Local search algorithms for partial maxsat. In: Proceedings of the Fourteenth National Conference on Artificial Intelligence and Ninth Conference on Innovative Applications of Artificial Intelligence, AAAI 1997/IAAI 1997, pp. 263–268. AAAI Press (1997)

9. Chadha, R., Mathur, U., Schwoon, S.: Computing information flow using symbolic model-checking. In: Leibniz International Proceedings in Informatics, LIPIcs, vol. 29, pp. 505–516 (2014). https://doi.org/10.4230/LIPIcs.FSTTCS.2014.505

10. Cherubin, G., Chatzikokolakis, K., Palamidessi, C.: F-BLEAU: fast black-box leakage estimation. In: Proceedings - IEEE Symposium on Security and Privacy 2019, pp. 835–852 (May 2019). https://doi.org/10.1109/SP.2019.00073

11. Chothia, T., Kawamoto, Y., Novakovic, C.: LeakWatch: estimating information leakage from java programs. In: Kutyłowski, M., Vaidya, J. (eds.) ESORICS 2014, Part II. LNCS, vol. 8713, pp. 219–236. Springer, Cham (2014). https://doi.org/10.1007/978-3-319-11212-1_13

12. Clark, D., Hunt, S., Malacaria, P.: A static analysis for quantifying information flow in a simple imperative language. J. Comput. Secur. **15**(3), 321–371 (2007). https://doi.org/10.3233/JCS-2007-15302

13. Clarke, E., Kroening, D., Lerda, F.: A tool for checking ANSI-C programs. In: Jensen, K., Podelski, A. (eds.) TACAS 2004. LNCS, vol. 2988, pp. 168–176. Springer, Heidelberg (2004). https://doi.org/10.1007/978-3-540-24730-2_15

14. Esfahanian, A.H.: Connectivity algorithms (2013)

15. Ferrante, J., Ottenstein, K.J., Warren, J.D.: The program dependence graph and its use in optimization. In: Paul, M., Robinet, B. (eds.) Programming 1984. LNCS, vol. 167, pp. 125–132. Springer, Heidelberg (1984). https://doi.org/10.1007/3-540-12925-1_33

16. Horwitz, S., Reps, T., Binkley, D.: Interprocedural slicing using dependence graphs. ACM Trans. Program. Lang. Syst. (TOPLAS) **12**(1), 26–60 (1990). https://doi.org/10.1145/989393.989419

17. Klebanov, V.: Precise quantitative information flow analysis - a symbolic approach. Theor. Comput. Sci. **538**, 124–139 (2014). https://doi.org/10.1016/j.tcs.2014.04.022

18. Malacaria, P.: Assessing security threats of looping constructs. In: Conference Record of the Annual ACM Symposium on Principles of Programming Languages, pp. 225–235 (2007). https://doi.org/10.1145/1190216.1190251

19. Mantel, H.: Information flow control and applications—bridging a gap—. In: Oliveira, J.N., Zave, P. (eds.) FME 2001. LNCS, vol. 2021, pp. 153–172. Springer, Heidelberg (2001). https://doi.org/10.1007/3-540-45251-6_9

20. Martins, R., Manquinho, V., Lynce, I.: Open-WBO: a modular MaxSAT solver. In: Sinz, C., Egly, U. (eds.) SAT 2014. LNCS, vol. 8561, pp. 438–445. Springer, Cham (2014). https://doi.org/10.1007/978-3-319-09284-3_33

21. McCamant, S., Ernst, M.D.: Quantitative information flow as network flow capacity. In: Proceedings of the ACM SIGPLAN Conference on Programming Language Design and Implementation (PLDI), vol. 43 (2008)

22. Meng, Z., Smith, G.: Calculating bounds on information leakage using two-bit patterns. In: Proceedings of the ACM SIGPLAN 6th Workshop on Programming Languages and Analysis for Security, PLAS 2011, pp. 1:1–1:12. ACM, New York (2011). https://doi.org/10.1145/2166956.2166957

23. Mu, C.: Computational program dependence graph and its application to information flow security. Newcastle University, Computing Science (2011)

24. Muchnick, S.: Advanced Compiler Design Implementation. Morgan Kaufmann, Burlington (1997)

25. Newsome, J., McCamant, S., Song, D.: Measuring channel capacity to distinguish undue influence. In: Proceedings of the ACM SIGPLAN Fourth Workshop on Programming Languages and Analysis for Security, PLAS 2009, pp. 73–85. ACM, New York (2009). https://doi.org/10.1145/1554339.1554349

26. Phan, Q.S., Malacaria, P., Tkachuk, O., Păsăreanu, C.S.: Symbolic quantitative information flow. SIGSOFT Softw. Eng. Notes 37(6), 1–5 (2012). https://doi.org/10.1145/2382756.2382791

27. Smith, G.: Recent developments in quantitative information flow (invited tutorial). In: 2015 30th Annual ACM/IEEE Symposium on Logic in Computer Science, pp. 23–31 (July 2015). https://doi.org/10.1109/LICS.2015.13

28. Smith, G.: On the foundations of quantitative information flow. In: de Alfaro, L. (ed.) 12th International Conference on Foundations of Software Science and Computational Structures (FOSSACS 2009), vol. 5504, pp. 288–302. Springer, Heidelberg (2009). https://doi.org/10.1007/978-3-642-00596-1

29. Wegbreit, B.: Property extraction in well-founded property sets. IEEE Trans. Softw. Eng. SE 1(3), 270–285 (1975). https://doi.org/10.1109/TSE.1975.6312852

On the Security and Safety of
AbU Systems

Michele Pasqua$^{(\boxtimes)}$ and Marino Miculan

Department of Mathematics, Computer Science and Physics, University of Udine,
Udine, Italy
{michele.pasqua,marino.miculan}@uniud.it

Abstract. *Attribute-based memory updates* (AbU in short) is an interaction mechanism recently introduced for adapting the Event-Condition-
Action (ECA) programming paradigm to distributed systems, particularly suited for the IoT. It can be seen as a memory-based counterpart
of *attribute-based communication*, keeping the simplicity of ECA rules.

In this paper, we introduce *behavioral equivalences* for AbU, with the
aim of formally defining *security and safety requirements* for AbU systems. As a consequence, the proposed requirements can help in assuring
the security and safety of IoT devices, which are more and more perva-
sive in our daily life. Finally, we propose (syntactic) sufficient conditions
to *statically verify* the introduced requirements.

Keywords: ECA rules · Bisimulations · Formal methods · Autonomic
computing · Verification

1 Introduction

In the Event-Condition-Action (ECA) programming paradigm, the behaviour of
a system is defined by a set of rules of the form "**on** *Event* **if** *Condition* **do** *Action*"
which means: when *Event* occurs, if *Condition* is verified then execute *Action*. Due
to its reactive nature, this paradigm is well-suited for programming "smart" systems, such as in IoT scenarios [7,14]: ECA systems react to inputs (as events) from
the environment performing *internal* actions (updating the node local memory)
and *external* actions, which influence the environment itself. Indeed, all main platforms in the field of Home/Automotive IoT (e.g., IFTTT, Samsung SmartThings,
Microsoft PowerAutomate, etc.) adopt this programming style.

Despite the simplicity of usage, actual ECA platforms suffer from scalability
problems due to the strongly centralized underlying infrastructure: IoT devices
are managed by a central coordinator node (often deployed on the cloud) and
they cannot communicate directly with each other. This also opens up to availability (what happens when the central node is not reachable?) and privacy
(users' data are continuously sent to remote, unknown, locations) problems.

To mitigate these issues, the ECA paradigm has been recently extended
with *attribute-based memory updates* (AbU) [33], a communication mechanism

Work supported by the Italian MIUR project PRIN 2017FTXR7S *IT MATTERS
(Methods and Tools for Trustworthy Smart Systems)*.

R. Calinescu and C. S. Păsăreanu (Eds.): SEFM 2021, LNCS 13085, pp. 178–198, 2021.
https://doi.org/10.1007/978-3-030-92124-8_11

designed for reactive *and* distributed programming. In this model, nodes (e.g., IoT devices) can directly communicate (without a central node) and are self-coordinating, in a truly decentralized setting. In this respect, computation moves from the *cloud* to the *edge* (akin *fog computing*), since ECA rules are deployed directly on the nodes. In particular, in AbU an event on a node can cause the update of the states of (possibly many) *remote* nodes, selected "on the fly" by means of the rule condition. For instance, a rule like

$$login > @(\overline{role} = \text{'logger'}) : \overline{log} \leftarrow \overline{log} \cdot time$$

means "when the (local) variable *login* changes, on every node whose *role* is 'logger' append my current (local) *time* to the (remote) variable *log*". Therefore, AbU allows us to propagate effects to collections of nodes at once, abstracting from their identities (or even their existence). Attribute-based communication (that can be encoded in AbU [33]) subsumes several interaction paradigms used in smart systems, e.g., channels, agents, pub/sub, broadcast/multicast [1,2]. Hence, AbU combines the best of the two worlds: the flexibility of a decentralized interaction mechanism (AbC) with the simplicity of ECA rules.

The simplicity and expressiveness of the AbU programming model comes to a price: the combination of rules may yield unexpected interactions, especially when a new component is added to an existing system. As an example, adding rules publishing content on social networks from a folder on a file server could inadvertently disclose sensitive pictures, e.g., taken from a security camera, if these are saved on the same folder. Therefore, an important problem of AbU systems is how to prevent these unwanted interactions between rules.

In this paper, we focus on two important security and safety requirements. The first is a form of *noninterference* [21]: given a *security policy* defining the allowed information flows between resources, we aim at assessing if an AbU system is *secure*, i.e., if it does not exhibit forbidden information flows. The second is a form of *non-interaction*: we aim at assessing whether different nodes will not interact by acting on common resources in unexpected ways. This is a *safety* requirement, as the unintended nodes interaction will not happen.

To formally model the requirements we introduce suitable *behavioral equivalences* between AbU systems, following the approach of [7]. These equivalences are (weak) bisimulations hiding the observations that are not related to the requirements check (and that would trivially break the equivalence). However, we need to generalize the definitions of [7] in order to deal with specific aspects of AbU. Indeed, an AbU rule may update at once resources at different levels of security; hence, we have to generalize the notion of *hiding bisimilarity* of [7], in order to compare observations involving different security levels at once. Leveraging this equivalence, we propose syntactic sufficient conditions and an algorithm to *statically* check noninterference and non-interaction of AbU systems.

Another aspect typical of IoT scenarios, concerns the interaction with the physical environment. This can introduce *implicit information flows* between resources which appear unrelated from the programmer's point of view; e.g., a flow from the resource controlling a lamp to the resource reading the state of a light sensor. To deal with this issue, we extend our framework with a notion of *semantic dependency*, representing the implicit flows given by the environment.

Synopsis. After a summary of related work in Sect. 2, in Sect. 3 we provide a short introduction to AbU, an ECA-inspired calculus extended with attribute-based memory updates. Then, in Sect. 4 we define some behavioral equivalences for AbU systems, to model two requirements which are crucial when designing secure and safe AbU systems. In Sect. 5 we propose two verification mechanisms to statically check the previously defined requirements, while in Sect. 6 we deal with the problem of implicit resources interactions. Finally, in Sect. 7 we have conclusions and directions for future work. Full proofs of the results can be found in the companion technical report [36].

2   Related Work

AbU [33] is a recently introduced calculus that aims at adapting the ECA programming paradigm to distributed computing. It is inspired by the AbC calculus [2,3], from which takes the idea of attribute-based communication. AbC is a core calculus of SCEL [23], a language introduced to model Collective Adaptive Systems (CAS) [4] and particularly suited for autonomic computing. Attribute-based communication has been adapted to fit the ECA programming style, in a way transparent to the user, making AbU very suitable for application scenarios like the IoT. We refer to [33] for the comparison of AbU with related approaches.

Security and safety of IoT devices is a critical problem; among many works, we refer to recent surveys [5,18] which overview these risks in the IoT from a general point of view. Here, we recall the closely related work about security and safety of platforms based on ECA rules and about information-flow control for the IoT. For an overview on information-flow control in process algebra, we refer the reader to Focardi and Gorrieri [27].

Security and Safety of ECA Platforms. The ECA paradigm is the standard for programming IoT devices, adopted by all major IoT platforms (like IFTTT, Samsung SmartThings, Microsoft PowerAutomate, etc.). In this context, IoT devices are managed by means of *apps* that users can downloaded (and customize) from the platform store. Recent studies point out the security and safety risks regarding this kind of apps, based of ECA rules. Surbatovich et al. [37] analyzed a dataset of 20K IFTTT apps, providing an empirical evaluation of potential secrecy and integrity violations, including violations due to cross-app interactions. Celik et al. [16,17] proposed some mechanisms to enforce (statically and dynamically) cross-app interaction vulnerabilities. Chi et al. [19] proposed a systematic categorization of threats arising from unintentional or malicious interactions of apps in IoT platforms. To detect cross-app interactions, they use symbolic execution techniques to analyze the apps code. Ding et al. [24] proposed a framework combining device physical channel analysis and static analysis to generate all potential interaction chains among IoT apps. They leverage Natural Language Processing to identify similarities between services, and proposed a risk-based approach to classify the actual risks of the discovered interaction chains. Nguyen et al. [35] designed IoTSan, a verification mechanism based on model-checking to reveal cross-app interaction flows. Similarly, SafeChain by Hsu et al. [28] leveraged model checking techniques to identify cross-app vulnerabilities in IFTTT apps.

Another line of work focuses on enforcement mechanisms for checking security and safety of a *single* app, rather than an ensemble of apps. Fernandes et al. [25] presented FlowFence, an approach for building secure apps via information-flow tracking and controlled declassification. Celik et al. [15] leveraged static taint tracking to identify sensitive data leaks in an IoT app. Bastys et al. [9,10] identified new attack vectors in IFTTT apps and showed that 30% of apps from their dataset can be subject to such attacks. As a countermeasure, they investigated static and dynamic information-flow tracking via security types. Fernandes et al. [26] proposed the use of decentralization and fine-grained authentication tokens to limit privileges and prevent unauthorized actions inside an app.

Even if grounded by the same programming paradigm, i.e., based on ECA rules, all the above-mentioned work focuses on specific platforms, restricting the applicability to specific use cases. Instead, the requirements we propose in this work are built on top of AbU, thus providing a general setting in which security and safety can be verified interdependently from the application scenario.

Concerning more general ECA programming, [38,39] presented verification mechanisms to check properties (such as termination, confluence, redundant or contradicting rules) on IRON [22], a language based on ECA rules for the IoT domain. Other works proposed approaches to verify ECA programs by using Petri Nets [30] and BDD [11]. In [13,14], the authors presented a tool-supported method for verifying and controlling the correct interactions of ECA rules. All these works, differently from AbU, are not designed for distributed systems.

Information-Flow Control for the IoT. Several works proposed information-flow control for enforcing confidentiality and integrity policies in the IoT domain. Newcomb et al. [34] proposed IOTA, a calculus for home automation. Based on the core formalism of IOTA, the authors developed an analysis for detecting whenever an event can trigger two conflicting actions, and an analysis for determining the action(s) that may influence a given event. Bodei et al. [12] proposed a calculus, IoT-LySa, supporting an information-flow analysis that safely approximates the abstract behavior of IoT systems. The calculus adopts asynchronous multi-party communication among nodes taking care of node proximity. Again, all the above-mentioned work focuses on specific platforms, while our approach based on AbU can be easily adapted to multiple application scenarios.

In their seminal work, Volpano and Smith [40] presented a *flow-insensitive* type system for imperative languages. Flow-insensitive type systems result very often too restrictive, rejecting lots of (practically) secure programs. To gain more permissiveness, Hunt and Sands [29] proposed a type system for an imperative language which is *flow-sensitive*. The latter has been further extended by Balliu et al. [6,7] in order to fit the IoT setting (in particular, apps based on ECA rules). The proposed type system verifies a notion of non-interference based on a suitable *hiding bisimulation* (a particularly designed weak bisimulation). We take inspiration from [7] to define the notion of security and safety requirements of this paper, generalizing the definition of hiding bisimulation.

3   Attribute-Based Memory Updates in Short

In this section we recall AbU [33], a calculus for ECA programming with
attribute-based memory updates. The latter is a communication mechanism allowing a node to update at once the memories of many nodes, which are selected
by means of their attributes. These features are introduced without sacrificing
coding simplicity: ECA rules are still used to program the devices. Thus, AbU
merges the simplicity of ECA programming with a powerful distributed communication mechanism; as such, it turns out to be particularly suited for smart
devices, which can now interact and self-coordinating directly without any central controlling node. This results particularly useful in IoT scenarios, as we can
see from the example that we sketch at the end of this section.

3.1   AbU Syntax and Semantics

An AbU *node* $R\langle \Sigma, \Theta \rangle$ consists of a *state* $\Sigma \in \mathbb{X} \to \mathbb{V}$, mapping resources to
values, and an *execution pool* $\Theta \subseteq \bigcup_{n \in \mathbb{N}} \mathbb{U}^n$, which is a set of *updates*, namely
finite lists of pairs $(x, v) \in \mathbb{U}$, meaning that the resource x will take the value v
after the execution of the update. Each node is equipped with a finite list R of
ECA rules, generated by the following grammar.

rule ::= evt ⊳ act, task	cnd ::= φ | @φ
evt ::= x | evt evt	φ ::= $\bot$ | $\top$ | $\neg\varphi$ | $\varphi \wedge \varphi$ | $\varphi \vee \varphi$ | $\varepsilon \bowtie \varepsilon$
act ::= ϵ | $x \leftarrow \varepsilon$ act | $\overline{x} \leftarrow \varepsilon$ act	ε ::= v | x | $\overline{x}$ | $\varepsilon \otimes \varepsilon$
task ::= cnd : act	$x \in \mathbb{X}$ $v \in \mathbb{V}$

Finally, an AbU system S is either a *node* or a parallel composition $S_1 \parallel S_2$
of systems. An ECA rule evt ⊳ act, task has a listening *event* evt (a finite list
of resources): when one of the resources in evt is modified, the rule is fired,
namely the *default* action act and task are evaluated. Evaluation does not change
the resources state immediately; instead, it yields update operations which are
added to the execution pools, and applied later on. An action is a finite list
of assignments of value expressions to *local* x or *remote* $\overline{x}$ resources. A task
consists in a condition cnd and an action act. A *condition* is a boolean expression,
optionally prefixed with the modifier @: when @ is not present, the task is *local*;
otherwise (@ is present) the task is *remote*. In local tasks, the condition is checked
in the local node and, if it holds, the action is evaluated. For remote tasks, on
every node where the condition holds, the action is evaluated. The evaluation of
an action yields an update, which is added to the current node pool in the case
of default actions and local tasks; and added to remote nodes pools in the case
of remote tasks. In the following, in order to simplify the notation, when a rule
has an empty default action we write evt ⊳ task in place of evt ⊳ ϵ, task.

The (small-step) semantics of AbU is modeled as a labeled transition system
$S_1 \xrightarrow{\alpha} S_2$ whose labels are given by $\alpha ::= T$ \| upd ⊳ T \| upd ▶ T. Here, T is a
finite list of tasks and upd is an update. We have slightly modified the labels

$$\text{(Exec)}\ \frac{\begin{array}{c} \mathsf{upd} \in \Theta \quad \mathsf{upd} = (x_1, v_1) \dots (x_k, v_k) \quad \Sigma' = \Sigma[v_1/x_1 \dots v_k/x_k] \\ \Theta'' = \Theta \setminus \{\mathsf{upd}\} \quad X = \{x_i \mid i \in [1..k] \wedge \Sigma(x_i) \neq \Sigma'(x)\} \\ \Theta' = \Theta'' \cup \mathsf{DefUpds}(R, X, \Sigma) \cup \mathsf{LocalUpds}(R, X, \Sigma) \quad T = \mathsf{ExtTasks}(R, X, \Sigma) \end{array}}{R\langle \Sigma, \Theta \rangle \xrightarrow{\ \mathsf{upd} \rhd T\ } R\langle \Sigma', \Theta' \rangle}$$

$$\text{(Input)}\ \frac{\begin{array}{c} v_1, \dots, v_k \in \mathbb{V} \quad \Sigma' = \Sigma[v_1/x_1 \dots v_k/x_k] \quad X = \{x_1, \dots, x_k\} \\ \Theta' = \Theta \cup \mathsf{DefUpds}(R, X, \Sigma) \cup \mathsf{LocalUpds}(R, X, \Sigma) \quad T = \mathsf{ExtTasks}(R, X, \Sigma) \end{array}}{R\langle \Sigma, \Theta \rangle \xrightarrow{\ (x_1, v_1) \dots (x_k, v_k) \blacktriangleright T\ } R\langle \Sigma', \Theta' \rangle}$$

$$\text{(Disc)}\ \frac{\Theta'' = \{[\![\mathsf{act}]\!]\Sigma \mid \exists i \in [1..n] \,.\, \mathsf{task}_i = @\varphi : \mathsf{act} \wedge \Sigma \models \varphi\} \quad \Theta' = \Theta \cup \Theta''}{R\langle \Sigma, \Theta \rangle \xrightarrow{\ \mathsf{task}_1 \dots \mathsf{task}_n\ } R\langle \Sigma, \Theta' \rangle}$$

$$\text{(Step)}\ \frac{S_1 \xrightarrow{\alpha} S_1' \quad S_2 \xrightarrow{T} S_2'}{S_1 \parallel S_2 \xrightarrow{\alpha} S_1' \parallel S_2'}\ \alpha \in \{\mathsf{upd} \rhd T, \mathsf{upd} \blacktriangleright T\}$$

Fig. 1. AbU semantics for nodes and systems.

w.r.t. [33] since, in order to define the security and safety requirements, we need to *observe* which resources are updated. A transition can modify the state and the execution pool of the nodes but, at the same time, each node does not have a global knowledge about the system. The semantic rules are in Fig. 1. Rule (EXEC) executes an update picked from the pool; rule (INPUT) models an external modification of some resources. The execution of an update, or the change of resources, may trigger some rules of the nodes. Hence, after updating a node state, the node launches a *discovery phase*, for finding new updates to add to the local pool (or some pools of remote nodes), given by the activation of some rules. The discovery phase is composed by two parts, the local and the external one. A node $R\langle \Sigma, \Theta \rangle$ performs a local discovery by means of the functions DefUpds and LocalUpds, that add to the local pool Θ all updates originated by the activation of some rules in R. Then, by means of the function ExtTasks, the node computes a list of tasks that may update external nodes and sends it to all nodes in the system[1]. This is modeled with the labels $\mathsf{upd} \rhd T$, produced by the rule (EXEC), and $\mathsf{upd} \blacktriangleright T$, produced by the rule (INPUT). On the other side, when a node receives a list of tasks (executing the rule (DISC) with a label T) it evaluates them and adds to its pool the actions generated by the tasks whose condition is satisfied. Finally, rule (STEP) completes and synchronizes (on all nodes in the system) a discovery phase originated by a state change of a node in the system.

3.2   AbU in Action: an IoT Example

Consider a scenario where a swarm of drones is in charge of taking specific measurements, randomly picked in a large uninhabited area. Each drone is equipped with a battery that periodically needs to be recharged by returning to a docking

---

[1] See [33] for the definition of the functions DefUpds, LocalUpds and ExtTasks.

station. It may happen that a drone runs out of energy before returning to the charging spot. In this case, the low-battery drone asks for help from its neighbors. If a drone has some energy to share and it is close enough to the requester, it will enter the "rescue mode". A drone in "rescue mode" will reach the drone that needs help, sharing with it some energy. This phase is not modeled in the example for space reasons. We can model this scenario in AbU as follows.

Suppose we have four drones. For each drone we have an AbU node with a resource *battery*, indicating the battery level of the drone; a resource *position*, indicating where is located the drone; a resource *mode*, indicating in which operative state is the drone; and a resource *helpPos*, indicating the position of a drone that needs help. Formally, the AbU system modeling the drones-swarm scenario is $R\langle \Sigma_1, \varnothing \rangle \parallel R\langle \Sigma_2, \varnothing \rangle \parallel R\langle \Sigma_3, \varnothing \rangle \parallel R\langle \Sigma_4, \varnothing \rangle$, where R contains, among the others, the following two AbU rules:

$$battery \gg @(battery < 5 \wedge \overline{battery} > 80) : \overline{helpPos} \leftarrow position \qquad (1)$$

$$helpPos \gg (|position - helpPos| < 7.0) : mode \leftarrow \text{'rescue'} \qquad (2)$$

Now suppose that the execution states of the drones are the following:

$$\Sigma_1 = [battery \mapsto 4 \quad position \mapsto 2.0 \quad mode \mapsto \text{'measure'} \quad helpPos \mapsto 0.0]$$
$$\Sigma_2 = [battery \mapsto 81 \quad position \mapsto 15.0 \quad mode \mapsto \text{'measure'} \quad helpPos \mapsto 0.0]$$
$$\Sigma_3 = [battery \mapsto 97 \quad position \mapsto 6.0 \quad mode \mapsto \text{'measure'} \quad helpPos \mapsto 0.0]$$
$$\Sigma_4 = [battery \mapsto 65 \quad position \mapsto 8.0 \quad mode \mapsto \text{'measure'} \quad helpPos \mapsto 0.0]$$

The rule (1) says that when the current drone battery level is low (*battery* < 5), then the current drone have to send to all (@) neighbors with some energy to share ($\overline{battery} > 80$) its position, performing a remote update ($\overline{helpPos} \leftarrow position$). In the example, the first node can fire the rule (1), since its battery level is low. Then, it pre-evaluates the task condition, yielding $4 < 5 \wedge battery > 80$, which is sent to the other nodes, together with the pre-evaluation of the task action, i.e., $helpPos \leftarrow 2.0$. Among all receivers, only the second and the third nodes are interested in the communication, since they are the only with battery level greater than 80. So they both add to their pool the update $(helpPos, 2.0)$. This ends the discovery phase originated by the first node.

The rule (2), instead, is fired when a drone receives a help request (i.e., when its resource *helpPos* changes) and basically checks if the current drone position is close to the requester position ($|position - helpPos| < 7.0$). If it is the case, the current drone enters the rescue mode performing a local update ($mode \leftarrow \text{'rescue'}$). In the example, when the second and the third nodes execute the update $(helpPos, 2.0)$, the task of the rule (2) may be executed. For the second node this does not happen, since $|15.0 - 2.0| < 7.0$ is not true (the node is too far from the first node). Instead, $|6.0 - 2.0| < 7.0$ and the third node can execute the rule task, adding to its pool the update $(mode, \text{'rescue'})$.

4 Behavioral Equivalences for AbU Systems

In this section, we provide a semantic characterization of security and safety requirements for AbU systems, based on the notion of bisimulation. The security requirement we aim to assess is a form of *noninterference* [21], adapted to AbU systems. In particular, given a security policy defining the allowed information flow between resources, we aim at assessing whether an AbU system is *secure*, namely if it does not exhibit forbidden information flows (for instance, a flow from a confidential resource to a public one). Concerning the safety requirement, we consider the following scenario, quite common in the IoT world. We have some nodes, equipped with some ECA rules, whose behavior is known and safe for the user, and we have another node, also safe for the user. Is the ensemble of all such nodes still *safe*? This is a sort of *non-interaction* check, namely, we check whether different nodes interact with each other by acting on common resources in a way not intended by the user (leading to possibly inconsistent states).

We define these requirements by means of suitable *behavioral equivalences* between AbU systems, following (and generalizing) the approach of [7]. Intuitively, we aim at defining two bisimulations that capture, semantically, the security and safety requirements. To do so, we need a particular (weak) bisimuation hiding the system labels that are not related to the requirements check, and that would trivially break the bisimulation.

In particular, a *hiding bisimulation*, parametric on a function h, makes non-observable (i.e., hides) all labels α such that $h(\alpha) = \diamond$, that are dubbed *hidden labels*. Differently from [7], where in the hiding bisimulation we can only have non-observable or *fully* observable labels, using the function h we can also specify labels that are *partially* observable. Here partially means that we can fix an abstraction on what we can observe about not hidden labels. In other words, partially observable labels can be mimicked in the bisimulation game by other labels which are observationally equivalent, fixed a given labels abstraction. Formally, let $\mathcal{L}$ be the set of all AbU system labels and $h \in \mathcal{L} \to \mathcal{L} \cup \{\diamond\}$ be a function. We denote with $\twoheadrightarrow_h$ the relation involving any possible hidden label, i.e., $\twoheadrightarrow_h \triangleq \bigcup \{\xrightarrow{\alpha} \mid h(\alpha) = \diamond\}$, and with $\Rightarrow_h$ its transitive closure, i.e., $\Rightarrow_h \triangleq \twoheadrightarrow_h^*$. Then, $\xRightarrow{\alpha}_h \triangleq \Rightarrow_h \xrightarrow{\alpha} \Rightarrow_h$ means that we can perform an arbitrary, possibly empty, sequence of hidden labels, but at least one α label must be present.

Definition 4.1 (Hiding bisimulation). *Let $h \in \mathcal{L} \to \mathcal{L} \cup \{\diamond\}$ be a function. A symmetric relation $\mathcal{R}$ between AbU systems is a* hiding bisimulation, *parametric on h, if and only if whenever $S_1 \mathcal{R} S_2$ and $S_1 \xrightarrow{\alpha} S_1'$ we have the following.*

- *if $h(\alpha) = \diamond$ then $S_2 \Rightarrow_h S_2'$, for some S_2, with $S_1' \mathcal{R} S_2'$*
- *if $h(\alpha) \neq \diamond$ then $S_2 \xRightarrow{\beta}_h S_2'$, for some β and S_2, with $h(\alpha) = h(\beta)$ and $S_1' \mathcal{R} S_2'$*

We say that two AbU systems S_1 and S_2 are hiding bisimilar with respect to h, written $S_1 \approx_h S_2$, if $S_1 \mathcal{R} S_2$ for some hiding bisimulation $\mathcal{R}$, parametric on h.

4.1   A Bisimulation for Security

AbU resources (e.g., IoT components) may have different security clearance: a security camera should definitely not leak any information to a resource that publicly hosts pictures on Internet. In the following, we assume a *security policy* $\mathcal{P} \in \mathbb{X} \to \mathrm{SL}$, which associates a security level $\ell \in \mathrm{SL}$, taken from a complete lattice $\langle \mathrm{SL}, \sqsubseteq, \sqcup, \sqcap, \top, \bot \rangle$, with each resource used by an AbU system. The lattice consists of a set SL of security levels, an ordering relation $\sqsubseteq$, the join $\sqcup$ and meet $\sqcap$ operators, as well as a top security level $\top$ and a bottom security level $\bot$. For the sake of simplicity, in the following we consider the standard two-points security lattice $\{\mathsf{L}, \mathsf{H}\}$, where the bottom is L, representing *public* data, and the top is H, representing *confidential* data. The goal is to achieve classic *noninterference* [21] results stating that an AbU system is interference-free if its L-level resources are not affected by changes occurring at its H-level resources. So, information can securely flow from a resource x to a resource y if[2] $\mathcal{P}(x) \sqsubseteq \mathcal{P}(y)$.

A security policy $\mathcal{P}$ induces an equivalence relation between AbU nodes states. Given two states Σ_1 and Σ_2, we say that they are L-equivalent if they agree on the values associated to all resources with security level L.

Definition 4.2 (L-equivalence). *Let $\mathcal{P} \in \mathbb{X} \to \{\mathsf{L}, \mathsf{H}\}$ be a security policy. We say that the AbU nodes states Σ_1 and Σ_2 are L-equivalent, written $\Sigma_1 \equiv_\mathsf{L} \Sigma_2$, if for each resource $x \in \mathbb{X}$ we have that $\mathcal{P}(x) = \mathsf{L}$ entails $\Sigma_1(x) = \Sigma_2(x)$.*

We can extend this notion to arbitrary sets of states: $\overline{\Sigma} = \{\Sigma_1, \ldots, \Sigma_n\}$ is L-equivalent to $\overline{\Sigma}' = \{\Sigma_1, \ldots, \Sigma_m\}$ when $\forall \Sigma \in \overline{\Sigma} \, \forall \Sigma' \in \overline{\Sigma}' \,.\, \Sigma \equiv_\mathsf{L} \Sigma'$. In other words, two sets are L-equivalent when their elements are pair-wise L-equivalent. We abuse notation using symbol $\equiv_\mathsf{L}$ for L-equivalence of states and sets of states.

As discussed at the beginning of the section, the goal is to formalize a bisimulation-based notion of noninterference. Intuitively, the runtime behavior at the security level L of an interference-free AbU system does not change when we vary *only* resources with security clearance H. Similarly to what has been done in [7], a notion of hiding bisimilarity can be used to hide (but not to suppress) labels involving changes affecting H-level resources. In particular, updates involving H-level resources only must be *hidden*, updates involving L-level resources only must be *fully* observable, and updates with mixed resources must be *partially* observable (we need to make observable assignments to L-level resources only). We use the hiding bisimulation of Definition 4.1, with a specific function h, to define noninterference for AbU sets of rule lists and, in turn, for AbU systems.

Consider the function h_L hiding discovery labels and execution labels involving H-level resources only, i.e., $h_\mathsf{L}(T) \triangleq \diamond$ and $h_\mathsf{L}((x_1, v_1) \ldots (x_k, v_k) \rhd T) \triangleq \diamond$, given $\sqcap_{i \in [1..k]} \mathcal{P}(x_i) = \mathsf{H}$. Furthermore, input labels are fully observable, i.e., $h_\mathsf{L}(\mathsf{upd} \blacktriangleright T) \triangleq \mathsf{upd} \blacktriangleright T$. Finally, consider a projection function that given an update upd returns its projection $\mathsf{upd}|_\mathsf{L}$ on assignments to L-level resources only. We have that $h_\mathsf{L}((x_1, v_1) \ldots (x_k, v_k) \rhd T) \triangleq (x_1, v_1) \ldots (x_k, v_k)|_\mathsf{L}$, when $\sqcap_{i \in [1..k]} \mathcal{P}(x_i) = \mathsf{L}$. This means that we abstract an execution label into the

---

[2] The ordering $\sqsubseteq$ for the two-points lattice is trivially defined as: $\{(\mathsf{L}, \mathsf{L}), (\mathsf{L}, \mathsf{H}), (\mathsf{H}, \mathsf{H})\}$.

projection on L-level resources of its update. Note that, when an update upd involves L-level resources only, we have that $\text{upd}|_L = \text{upd}$, hence the label is fully observable (no abstraction). We call h_L the *hiding function for noninterference*.

In the following definition we make use of some auxiliary notions. Given a *rule list set* $\overline{R} = \{R_1, \ldots, R_n\}$, where each R_i is a list of AbU rules, we define $\text{comp}(\overline{R})$ as the set comprising all possible sets of states *compatible* with $\overline{R}$. Compatibility here means that states are defined for all and only the resources present in the rules. Formally, $\overline{\Sigma} = \{\Sigma_1, \ldots, \Sigma_n\}$ is compatible with $\overline{R}$ when there exists a bijection $f \in \overline{\Sigma} \to \overline{R}$ such that $\text{dom}(\Sigma_i) = \text{vars}(f(\Sigma_i))$, for all $i \in [1..n]$. We also need a system initialization function $\text{sys}(\overline{R}, \overline{\Sigma})$ that takes a set of states and a rule list set and returns an AbU system with all pools empty. Formally, given $\overline{R} = \{R_1, \ldots, R_n\}$ and $\overline{\Sigma} = \{\Sigma_1, \ldots, \Sigma_n\} \in \text{comp}(\overline{R})$, we define $\text{sys}(\overline{R}, \overline{\Sigma}) = R_1\langle\Sigma_1, \varnothing\rangle \parallel \ldots \parallel R_n\langle\Sigma_n, \varnothing\rangle$, where $f(\Sigma_i) = R_i$ for each $i \in [1..n]$.

Definition 4.3 (AbU noninterference). *Let $\mathcal{P} \in \mathbb{X} \to \{L, H\}$ be a security policy. We say that the rule list set $\overline{R} = \{R_1, \ldots, R_n\}$ is interference-free, written $\text{NI}(\overline{R})$, whenever:* $\forall \overline{\Sigma}, \overline{\Sigma}' \in \text{comp}(\overline{R}) . \overline{\Sigma} \equiv_L \overline{\Sigma}' \implies \text{sys}(\overline{R}, \overline{\Sigma}) \approx_{h_L} \text{sys}(\overline{R}, \overline{\Sigma}')$.

An IoT-Centric Version of Noninterference. The mere initialization of an H-level resource might activate a rule, thus leaking information about the *occurrence/presence* of an H-level event. The noninteference of Definition 4.3 ignores such presence leaks, as it is commonly done in language-based security. This design choice is usually justified by the fact that it increases the permissiveness of the enforcement mechanisms, but it is not a realistic assumption in the IoT context.

Example 4.1. Consider the AbU rule $motion \gg (00 : 00 < time \wedge time < 06 : 00) : light \leftarrow$ 'on', where *motion* is confidential while *time* and *light* public (i.e., $\mathcal{P}(motion) = H$ and $\mathcal{P}(time) = \mathcal{P}(light) = L$). Basically, the rule turns on the lights when, during the night, some movements in a room are detected. According to Definition 4.3 there is no harmful information flow. Nevertheless, observing the (public) resource *light* we can infer that the (confidential) resource *motion* has been changed (i.e., a robber may infer that someone is in the room).

Note that Definition 4.3 does not trivially ignores rule triggers, when checking noninterference. Indeed, it is able to capture harmful flows generated by rules acting on confidential triggers, as we can see in the following example.

Example 4.2. Consider the following AbU rules:

$$GPS \gg (GPS - center > 5.0) : area \leftarrow \text{'exit'} \tag{3}$$

$$area \gg (\top) : log \leftarrow log \cdot \text{'border crossed at:'} \cdot time \tag{4}$$

where *area*, *GPS* and *center* are confidential while *log* and *time* public (i.e., $\mathcal{P}(area) = \mathcal{P}(GPS) = \mathcal{P}(center) = H$ and $\mathcal{P}(log) = \mathcal{P}(time) = L$). Rule (3) checks when the node exits a specific area, while rule (4) logs when the area borders are crossed (exiting or entering the area). Here, we have an information flow from the (confidential) resource *GPS* to the (public) resource *log*, which is not allowed by the security requirement and, indeed, is captured by Definition 4.3.

What we want to remark with Example 4.2 is that Definition 4.3 is not able to capture presence leaks originated by external changes (i.e., inputs), but it is still able to capture presence leaks due to internal resources modifications (i.e., updates execution). In order to capture information flows due to generic resource presence leaks, we need a stronger (i.e., more restrictive) requirement.

Given an AbU rule list set $\overline{R} = \{R_1, \ldots, R_n\}$, we define the H-*level events set* evset($\overline{R}$) of $\overline{R}$ as all the H-level resources in the events of all rules in $\overline{R}$. Then, the L-*level twin* of $\overline{R}$ is the rule list set $\overline{R}_L$ where all resources in evset($\overline{R}$) are substituted in $\overline{R}$ with their primed version. As an example, the L-level twin of $\overline{R}$ given by rules (3) and (4) of Example 4.2 is $\overline{R}_L = \{area' \gg (\top) : log \leftarrow log \cdot$ 'border crossed at:'$\cdot time$ $GPS' \gg (GPS' - center > 5.0) : area' \leftarrow$ 'exit'$\}$. Note that, $center$ is not modified since it does not belong to evset($\overline{R}$) = $\{area, GPS\}$.

The L-level twin will be used in the following definition of noninterference. We have taken inspiration from self-composition verification mechanisms [8], where a k-hypersafety [20] verification problem for a program is reduced to a safety verification problem on its k-product program [8]. Indeed, noninterference is a 2-bounded subset-closed hyperproperty [32], so we can, in principle, verify it on two copies of the program, where variables are renamed. Consider the case where we rename the H-level resources that rules are listening on (i.e., H-level rules triggers), we take L-equivalent execution states (as for standard noninterference), and we run the two copies of the AbU system (which differ syntactically only on H-level triggers). It is easy to see that a change in the L-level behavior of the two systems can only be due to presence leaks originated from H-level triggers.

Definition 4.4 (AbU presence-sensitive noninterference). *Let* $\mathcal{P} \in \mathbb{X} \rightarrow \{L, H\}$ *be a security policy. We say that the rule list set* $\overline{R} = \{R_1, \ldots, R_n\}$ *is presence-sensitive interference-free, written* PNI($\overline{R}$) *whenever:*

$$\forall \overline{\Sigma} \in \text{comp}(\overline{R}) \, \forall \overline{\Sigma}' \in \text{comp}(\overline{R}_L) . \, \overline{\Sigma} \equiv_L \overline{\Sigma}' \implies \text{sys}(\overline{R}, \overline{\Sigma}) \approx_{h_L} \text{sys}(\overline{R}_L, \overline{\Sigma}')$$

Using the noninterference notion of Definition 4.4, the AbU rules of Example 4.1 are now considered not secure. Presence-sensitive noninterference is a stronger requirement than classic (presence-insensitive) noninterference. Indeed, Definition 4.3 is a particular case of Definition 4.4: if PNI($\overline{R}$) then we trivially have that NI($\overline{R}$).

4.2   A Bisimulation for Safety

We provide now a semantic characterization of *safe* interaction between AbU systems, where with safety we mean that two systems do not exhibit unintended behaviors when deployed together. For instance, consider a node equipped with a rule that opens the window when the room temperature exceeds a given threshold, and another node equipped with a rule that turns on the thermostat at home when the user leaves his work location. Both nodes can be considered safe, in isolation, but when deployed together they may interact with each other, causing an (unexpected) opening of the window when the user is not at home (clearing a way for burglary). Another unsafe scenario is when two nodes interact by updating some common resource (of remote nodes) in a inconsistent manner, e.g., a valve that is opened by a node and closed by the other at the same time.

Following [7], we would like to say that an AbU system S does not interact with, or is *transparent* for, another AbU system R if the behavior of R when running in parallel with S does not differ from its behavior when running in isolation. In particular, we would like to say that S is transparent for R if S $\parallel$ R $\approx_h$ R for some bisimilarity $\approx_h$ that hides the updates originated from S.

Let $\overline{R^S}$ and $\overline{R^R}$ be the rule list sets of S and R, respectively. We can use the hiding bisimulation of Definition 4.1 to formalize a semantic-based notion of rule list sets transparency (and, in turn, of the corresponding systems). Our intention is to hide only those updates originated from rules in $\overline{R^S}$. Consider the function h_S such that: $h_S(\alpha) \triangleq \diamond$ when $\alpha = T$ or $\alpha = \mathsf{upd} \triangleright T$, given $\mathsf{source}(\mathsf{upd}) = \overline{R^S}$; and $h_S(\alpha) \triangleq \alpha$ when $\alpha = \mathsf{upd} \blacktriangleright T$ or $\alpha = \mathsf{upd} \triangleright T$, given $\mathsf{source}(\mathsf{upd}) \neq \overline{R^S}$. Here, we assume to have a function source returning the set of rules that has generated a given update. A mechanism for retrieving such information can be easily obtained augmenting AbU nodes with unique identifiers and recording in the AbU system labels $\mathsf{upd} \triangleright T$ the node performing the update. For the sake of readability, we do not modify the syntax and the semantics of the calculus.

Definition 4.5 (AbU transparency). *Let $\overline{R^S}$ and $\overline{R^R}$ be two rule list sets. We say that $\overline{R^S}$ is* transparent *for $\overline{R^R}$, written $\overline{R^S} \nrightarrow \overline{R^R}$, if for each $\overline{\Sigma} \in \mathsf{comp}(\overline{R^S} \cup \overline{R^R})$ we have that $\mathsf{sys}(\overline{R^S} \cup \overline{R^R}, \overline{\Sigma}) \approx_{h_S} \mathsf{sys}(\overline{R^R}, \overline{\Sigma})$.*

When $\overline{R^S}$ is transparent for $\overline{R^R}$ and $\overline{R^R}$ is transparent for $\overline{R^S}$, the two rule list sets are said independent, *written $\overline{R^S} \leftrightarrow \overline{R^R}$.*

In other words, if $\overline{R^S}$ is transparent for $\overline{R^R}$ then a system with $\overline{R^S}$ as rule list set does not affect in any way the behavior of a system with $\overline{R^R}$ as rule list set.

Example 4.3. Consider an AbU node managing a security camera. It is equipped with an AbU rule $camera \triangleright (\top) : \overline{cloud.private} \leftarrow camera$ that basically uploads an image to the "private" folder of a given cloud service, when the camera detects some movements. Then, we can have another node managing the cloud service: when a new picture in the folder "public" is uploaded, the node will post it on Instagram. This can be modeled with the rule $cloud.public \triangleright (\top) : instagram.post \leftarrow cloud.public$, which is self-explanatory. Until now, everything is ok, the two nodes are safe, even if executed together. Indeed, Definition 4.5 is fulfilled: taking S as the system comprising the camera-node and R as the system comprising the cloud-node, we have that S and R are independent.

Things change if we consider a buggy version of the camera node $camera \triangleright (\top) : \overline{cloud.public} \leftarrow camera$. In this case, the node uploads the sensitive image to the "public" folder, instead to the "private" folder. Now, we have an unintended interaction chain: when the camera collects a sensitive image, the latter is automatically posted on Instagram. This interaction is capture by Definition 4.5, indeed the system S is now not transparent for the system R.

Algorithm IFRules($rule_1 \ldots rule_n$)

1 | $\quad$ **return** $\bigvee_{i \in [1..n]}$ IFSingleRule($rule_i$)

Procedure IFSingleRule($x_1 \ldots x_n \gg act_1, \varphi : act_2$)

2 | $\quad evtLevel := \bigsqcup_{i \in [1..n]} \mathcal{P}(x_i)$

3 | $\quad assigLevel := $ Assign(act_1) $\sqcap$ Assign(act_2)

4 | $\quad presLeaks := evtLevel \sqcap assignLevel \neq evtLevel$

5 | $\quad ctx := $ Const(φ)

6 | $\quad flows := $ IFAct(act_1, κ) $\vee$ IFAct(act_2, ctx)

7 | $\quad$ **return** $presLeaks \vee flows$

Procedure IFAct($x_1 \leftarrow \varepsilon_1 \ldots x_n \leftarrow \varepsilon_n, ctx$)

8 | $\quad flow := $ **false**

9 | $\quad$ **for** $i = 1$ **to** n **do**

10 | $\quad\quad isConst := $ Const(ε_i) $= \not{L} \vee ctx = \not{L}$

11 | $\quad\quad$ **if** $\mathcal{P}(x_i) = $ L $\wedge isConst$ **then**

12 | $\quad\quad\quad$ | $flow := $ **true**

$\quad\quad$ **end**

$\quad$ **end**

13 | $\quad$ **return** $flow$

Procedure Assign($x_1 \leftarrow \varepsilon_1 \ldots x_n \leftarrow \varepsilon_n$)

14 | $\quad$ **return** $\bigsqcap_{i \in [1..n]} \mathcal{P}(x_i)$

Algorithm 1. Information flows detection algorithm.

On the Compositionality of Requirements Checking. Independence is crucial when we aim at verifying *dynamically* a given requirement. In fact, suppose to have an AbU system R, that we know to satisfy a given requirement (e.g., termination [33], noninterference, etc.). If we combine (at runtime) R with another AbU system S satisfying the same requirement, and we known that the added system is independent from R, then we automatically have that S ∥ R is compliant with the requirement. In other words, with independent systems we can reason about the satisfaction of a given requirement in a compositional way.

Note that, for some kind of properties (e.g., termination [33]) independence is not strictly necessary: transparency is a sufficient condition for guaranteeing compositionality. Indeed, if we have that the systems S and R are loop-free (i.e., they satisfy the termination requirement), and S is transparent for R, then we can conclude that S ∥ R is loop-free as well.

5 Checking Security and Safety of AbU Systems

In this section, we provide verification mechanisms for checking the safety and security requirements introduced in Sect. 4. They are static, in the sense that they do not require the execution of the AbU systems under test: the check is purely based on the inspection of systems rules.

5.1 Verifying Security

In order to provide a syntactic sufficient condition for noninterference we define a verification method detecting potential harmful information flows, parametric in the security policy $\mathcal{P}$. The detection process for a list of AbU rules is depicted in Algorithm 1. The algorithm returns *true* when harmful information flows are detected in, at least, one rule (line **1**). In this case the whole list of rules does not satisfy noninterference. The procedure at lines **2..7** of Algorithm 1 looks for information flows inside single rules, and it works as follows.

First, it checks potential presence leaks. Line **2** computes the security level of the rule event: if at least one resource in the event is H-level then *evtLevel* is H (it is L when all resources are L-level). Line **3** checks if the default and the task actions contain assignments to L resources, by means of the procedure at line **14**. If at least one assignment in the actions has a L-level resource in the left-hand side then *assignLevel* is L. Then, in line **4**, we compute if there is a potential presence leak: $evtLevel \sqcap assignLevel \neq evtLevel$ means that the event contains a H-level resource and we have assignments to L-level resources in the actions.

Second, it checks potential harmful information flows in the default and the task actions. Line **5** computes a *constancy analysis* on the task condition[3], in order to capture *implicit* information flows. The function Const returns κ when all L-level resources are constants; $\not\kappa$ otherwise. Here, constancy means that no variety is conveyed from H-level resources (the only ones that may change in Definition 4.4) to L-level resources (assumed to be initially constant in Definition 4.4). It is defined inductively on the structure of φ: $\texttt{Const}(\bot) = \texttt{Const}(\top) \triangleq \kappa$; $\texttt{Const}(\neg\varphi) \triangleq \texttt{Const}(\varphi)$; $\texttt{Const}(\varphi_1 \wedge \varphi_2) \triangleq \texttt{Const}(\varphi_1) \uplus \texttt{Const}(\varphi_2)$; $\texttt{Const}(\varphi_1 \vee \varphi_2) \triangleq \texttt{Const}(\varphi_1) \uplus \texttt{Const}(\varphi_2)$; and $\texttt{Const}(\varepsilon_1 \bowtie \varepsilon_2) \triangleq \texttt{Const}(\varepsilon_1) \uplus \texttt{Const}(\varepsilon_2)$. Here, $\uplus$ is the join operator of the complete lattice $\{\kappa, \not\kappa\}$, with partial order $\Subset \triangleq \{(\kappa, \kappa), (\kappa, \not\kappa), (\not\kappa, \not\kappa)\}$. The constancy analysis for value expressions is defined inductively on the structure of ε: $\texttt{Const}(v) \triangleq \kappa$; $\texttt{Const}(x) = \texttt{Const}(\overline{x}) \triangleq \kappa$ if $\mathcal{P}(x) = \texttt{L}$; $\texttt{Const}(x) = \texttt{Const}(\overline{x}) \triangleq \not\kappa$ if $\mathcal{P}(x) = \texttt{H}$; and $\texttt{Const}(\varepsilon_1 \otimes \varepsilon_2) \triangleq \texttt{Const}(\varepsilon_1) \uplus \texttt{Const}(\varepsilon_2)$. Line **6** computes the information flows in the default and in the task actions. Implicit information flows can only happen in the task action, so for the default action we compute *explicit* information flows only, calling the IFAct function with κ as context. Instead, for the task action, IFAct is called with the context computed by the constancy analysis on the task condition, in order to track implicit flows. At line **7**, the procedure returns *true* when presence leaks are detected or when information flows are present in the rules actions.

Finally, the procedure at lines **8..13** computes the potential information flows of an action[4], parametric on a given context. It is a loop inspecting all assignments of the action. The condition at line **11** performs the check. Only two cases lead to harmful information flows: a L-level resource is assigned with a not constant expression (explicit flow); a L-level resource is assigned inside a not constant context (implicit flow). Recall that, not constancy means that variety is conveyed from H-level resources to L-level resources.

Algorithm 1 detects potentially harmful information flows when considering a single list of AbU rules, namely a single node. Nevertheless, it is easy to note that the algorithm does not take into account inter-nodes communication, hence the verification on a rule list set, i.e., a set of nodes, boils down to the verification on a single rules list comprising all rules in the set. Intuitively, if we have a forbidden information flow between two nodes, then that information flow must be present internally in one of the nodes as well.

---

[3] The modifier @ does not influence the analysis, we omit it in the algorithm.

[4] Remote updates $\overline{x} \leftarrow \varepsilon$ do not influence the analysis, we omit them in the algorithm.

Proposition 5.1. *Consider a rule list set* $\{R_1, \ldots, R_n\}$. *Let* R *be the list comprising all rules of all elements in* $\{R_1, \ldots, R_n\}$. *Then we have that:*

$$\bigvee\nolimits_{i \in [1..n]} \mathtt{IFRules}(R_i) = false \Longleftrightarrow \mathtt{IFRules}(R) = false$$

Theorem 5.1 (Soundness for Security). *Let* $\mathcal{P} \in \mathbb{X} \to \{\mathsf{L}, \mathsf{H}\}$ *be a security policy and* $\overline{R} = \{R_1, \ldots, R_n\}$ *be a rule list set. Let* R *be the list comprising all rules of all elements in* $\{R_1, \ldots, R_n\}$. *If* $\mathtt{IFRules}(R) = false$ *then* $\mathsf{PNI}(\overline{R})$.

Recall that presence-sensitive noninterference implies the classic presence-insensitive version of noninterference. Hence, we can extend the soundness result as follows: if $\mathtt{IFRules}(R) = false$ then $\mathsf{NI}(\overline{R})$.

Example 5.1. Take the AbU rule of Example 4.1. We have that Algorithm 1 will correctly mark it as not secure, capturing a presence leak. Indeed, the L-level resource *light* is assigned, when an H event is present, due to the H-level resource *motion* (the same applies for the AbU rules of Example 4.2). Now consider the AbU rule $access \gg (user.role = \text{`guest'}) : log \leftarrow user.name \cdot time$ that logs the access time of users that have role 'guest' only. Suppose that the user role is confidential, while all other resources are public (i.e., $\mathcal{P}(access) = \mathcal{P}(user.name) = \mathcal{P}(time) = \mathcal{P}(log) = \mathsf{L}$ and $\mathcal{P}(user.role) = \mathsf{H}$). We have an implicit information flow here, from *user.role* to *log*. Indeed, Algorithm 1 will correctly mark it as not secure: we assign a L-level resource (*log*) inside an action with a not constant context, given by $\mathtt{Const}(user.role = \text{`guest'}) = \not\!\!\!k$.

5.2 Verifying Safety

In order to provide a syntactic sufficient condition for transparency we have to specify what are the resources that a system may potentially update (*sinks*) and what are the resources that may influence a rule behavior (*sources*). The first are the left-hand sides of assignments in rules actions, while the latter are the rules events. In addition to the events, also resources involved in tasks condition and resources used in the actions should be considered sources. Indeed, take the AbU rules $x \gg (x < 3) : z \leftarrow 4$ and $x \gg (\top) : z \leftarrow w$. The resources y and w should be considered sources, since their modification by an external node influences the behavior of the rules (even if they are not rule events).

More formally, let $\mathsf{LHS}(x_1 \leftarrow \varepsilon_1 \ldots x_n \leftarrow \varepsilon_n) \triangleq \{x_1, \ldots, x_n\}$ and $\mathsf{RHS}(x_1 \leftarrow \varepsilon_1 \ldots x_n \leftarrow \varepsilon_n) \triangleq \bigcup_{i \in 1[..n]} \mathsf{Vars}(\varepsilon_i)$ (they are defined analogously when the action contains remote assignments $\overline{x} \leftarrow \varepsilon$). The sinks and sources of a rule are $\mathsf{snk}(\mathit{evt} \gg \mathtt{act}_1, \mathtt{cnd} : \mathtt{act}_2) \triangleq \mathsf{LHS}(\mathtt{act}_1) \cup \mathsf{LHS}(\mathtt{act}_2)$ and $\mathsf{src}(x_1 \ldots x_n \gg \mathtt{act}_1, \mathtt{cnd} : \mathtt{act}_2) \triangleq \{x_1, \ldots, x_n\} \cup \mathsf{RHS}(\mathtt{act}_1) \cup \mathsf{RHS}(\mathtt{act}_2) \cup \mathsf{Vars}(\mathtt{cnd})$, respectively. Given an AbU system, with rule list set $\overline{R} = \{R_1, \ldots, R_n\}$, its *sinks* $\mathsf{snk}(\overline{R})$ consists in all sinks of all rules in each R_i, with $i \in [1..n]$. Similarly, its *sources* $\mathsf{src}(\overline{R})$ consists in all sources of all rules in each R_i, with $i \in [1..n]$.

Now, everything is in place to provide a syntactic condition for transparency, where a system S is said syntactically transparent for (or, it does not interact with) a system R when the execution of S does not fires any rule of R.

Definition 5.1 (Syntactic Transparency). *Let $\overline{R^S}$ and $\overline{R^R}$ be two rule list sets. We say that $\overline{R^S}$ is* syntactically transparent *for $\overline{R^R}$, written $\overline{R^S} \not\mathrel{+\!\circ} \overline{R^R}$, when* $\mathsf{snk}(\overline{R^S}) \cap \mathsf{src}(\overline{R^R}) = \varnothing$. *When $\overline{R^S}$ and $\overline{R^R}$ are syntactically transparent with respect to each other, i.e., when $\mathsf{snk}(\overline{R^S}) \cap \mathsf{src}(\overline{R^R}) = \varnothing$ and $\mathsf{snk}(\overline{R^R}) \cap \mathsf{src}(\overline{R^S}) = \varnothing$, we say that $\overline{R^S}$ and $\overline{R^R}$ are* syntactically independent, *written $\overline{R^S} \mathrel{\circ\!+\!\circ} \overline{R^R}$.*

Thus, Definition 5.1 provides an easy-to-verify syntactic condition to check our semantic-based notion of safe interaction formalized in Definition 4.5.

Theorem 5.2 (Soundness for Safety). *Let $\overline{R^S}$ and $\overline{R^R}$ be two rule list sets. If $\overline{R^S} \not\mathrel{+\!\circ} \overline{R^R}$ then $\overline{R^S} \mathrel{+\!\circ} \overline{R^R}$.*

Example 5.2. Continuing Example 4.3, we have syntactic independence between (the first version of) the systems, since $\mathsf{snk}(\{camera > (\top) : \overline{cloud.private} \leftarrow camera\}) \cap \mathsf{src}(\{cloud.public > (\top) : instagram.post \leftarrow cloud.public\}) = \varnothing$ (and vice versa). Instead, for the buggy version of the rules we have that $\{camera > (\top) : \overline{cloud.public} \leftarrow camera\} \not\mathrel{+\!\circ} \{cloud.public > (\top) : instagram.post \leftarrow cloud.public\}$ does not hold. Indeed, the sets $\mathsf{snk}(\{camera > (\top) : \overline{cloud.public} \leftarrow camera\})$ and $\mathsf{src}(\{cloud.public > (\top) : instagram.post \leftarrow cloud.public\})$ have $\{cloud.public\}$ as intersection, capturing the unintended interaction.

5.3 On the Completeness of the Verification Mechanisms

The proposed verification mechanisms are sound, i.e., they do not expose false negatives, but they are *not complete*, i.e., they may expose false positives. Indeed, consider the two AbU rules: $l_1 > (h_1) : l_2 \leftarrow 3$ (5) and $l_1 > (\neg h_1) : l_2 \leftarrow 3$ (6), with $\mathcal{P}(l_1) = \mathcal{P}(l_2) = \mathsf{L}$ and $\mathcal{P}(h_1) = \mathsf{H}$. Algorithm 1 will flag as not secure an AbU system equipped with these rules, even if there is no interference (for both presence-sensitive and presence-insensitive versions). Another incompleteness witness consists in the following single AbU rule: $h_1 > (l_1 < 3) : l_2 \leftarrow l_2$ (7), which is rejected by our verification mechanism but it is, indeed, secure.

Similarly, also syntactic transparency rules out safe systems. For instance, consider a system with the rule list set $\{x > (\bot) : y \leftarrow 3\}$, which is transparent for a system with rule list set $\{y > (\top) : z \leftarrow 2\}$, i.e., $\{x > (\bot) : y \leftarrow 3\} \not\mathrel{+\!\circ} \{y > (\top) : z \leftarrow 2\}$. We have that $\mathsf{snk}(\{x > (\bot) : y \leftarrow 3\}) \cap \mathsf{src}(\{y > (\top) : z \leftarrow 2\}) = \{y\}$, hence $\{x > (\bot) : y \leftarrow 3\} \not\mathrel{+\!\circ} \{y > (\top) : z \leftarrow 2\}$ does not hold.

Every sound verification mechanism necessarily suffers from completeness issues, but we can always improve precision to mitigate the problem. For instance, refining the procedure IFAct of Algorithm 1, we can easily allow rule (7). Instead, for rules (5) and (6), we need an inter-procedural version of the constancy analysis.

6 Dealing with Implicit Interactions

We now study the challenge posed by *implicit interactions* that arises whenever two (physical) resources, e.g., temperature and thermostat, are semantically related, though they differ syntactically.

$$\text{(EXEC)} \dfrac{\begin{array}{c} \text{upd} \in \Theta \quad \text{upd} = (x_1, v_1) \dots (x_k, v_k) \quad \Sigma' = \Sigma[v_1/x_1 \dots v_k/x_k] \\ \Theta'' = \Theta \setminus \{\text{upd}\} \quad X = \text{clo}(\mathcal{K}, \{x_i \mid i \in [1..k] \land \Sigma(x_i) \neq \Sigma'(x)\}) \\ \Theta' = \Theta'' \cup \text{DefUpds}(R, X, \Sigma) \cup \text{LocalUpds}(R, X, \Sigma) \quad T = \text{ExtTasks}(R, X, \Sigma) \end{array}}{R\langle \Sigma, \Theta \rangle \xrightarrow{\text{upd} \rhd T}_{\mathcal{K}} R\langle \Sigma', \Theta' \rangle}$$

$$\text{(INPUT)} \dfrac{\begin{array}{c} v_1, \dots, v_k \in \mathbb{V} \quad \Sigma' = \Sigma[v_1/x_1 \dots v_k/x_k] \quad X = \text{clo}(\mathcal{K}, \{x_1, \dots, x_k\}) \\ \Theta' = \Theta \cup \text{DefUpds}(R, X, \Sigma) \cup \text{LocalUpds}(R, X, \Sigma) \quad T = \text{ExtTasks}(R, X, \Sigma) \end{array}}{R\langle \Sigma, \Theta \rangle \xrightarrow{(x_1, v_1) \dots (x_k, v_k) \blacktriangleright T}_{\mathcal{K}} R\langle \Sigma', \Theta' \rangle}$$

Fig. 2. Modified AbU semantics rules.

Example 6.1. Consider the rules $button \rhd (button = \text{'pressed'}) : \overline{robotCleaner} \leftarrow$ 'on' and $motion \rhd (motion = \top \land time < 12{:}00) : \overline{alarm} \leftarrow$ 'on', deployed on different nodes. The first activates a robot cleaner in the house when a button on the phone is pressed. The second rings an alarm when some movement in the house is detected, during the morning. Though there are no (syntactic) interactions between the two rules, we clearly know that when the robot cleaner starts moving, then the motion sensor is activated and consequently the alarm will ring. We cannot catch this interaction with the LTS of Fig. 1, namely we mark the nodes as independent.

We model these kind of *semantic dependencies* by means of a binary relation $\mathcal{K} \subseteq \mathbb{X} \times \mathbb{X}$ such that $(x, y) \in \mathcal{K}$ when the resource y may be affected by changes occurring at the resource x (which is analogous to the *dependency policy* of [7]). We write $\text{clo}(\mathcal{K}, x)$ to denote the reflexive and transitive closure of the semantic dependencies relation $\mathcal{K}$ with respect to the resource x only. More generally, given a set of resources $X \subseteq \mathbb{X}$ we define $\text{clo}(\mathcal{K}, X) \triangleq \bigcup_{x \in X} \text{clo}(\mathcal{K}, x)$. In Example 6.1 we would have that $\mathcal{K} \triangleq \{(robotCleaner, motion)\}$, allowing us to capture the semantic dependence between the robot cleaner and the motion sensor.

Note that, if $(x, y) \in \mathcal{K}$ we may assume that each time the resource x changes then the resource y can be somehow affected. We represent this abstract information extending the discovery phase in the AbU semantics to all the resources affected by x. In other words, when we perform an execution or an input step in the semantics, we discover the actually modified resources *and* all the related resources, given by $\mathcal{K}$. We can easily define a labeled transitions semantics $\rightarrow_{\mathcal{K}}$, parametric on given semantic dependencies. In particular, we just have to modify the rules (EXEC) and (INPUT) of the original AbU semantics as depicted in Fig. 2. Considering again Example 6.1, when the (EXEC) rule performs the update $(robotCleaner, \text{'on'})$ then $\text{clo}(\mathcal{K}, \{robotCleaner\}) = \{robotCleaner, motion\}$ and, hence, the rule concerning the motion sensor is selected by the discovery. Indeed, the nodes equipped with the rules in Example 6.1 now fail transparency, since in the bisimulation game the system without the cleaner-rule cannot perform the L-level update firing the alarm.

7   Conclusion

In this paper, we have studied security and safety requirements of AbU systems, a new model for distributed computation merging the simplicity of ECA programming with attribute-based communication. AbU is particularly suited to program IoT devices, in a decentralized setting. Hence, these requirements can be used to tackle security and safety issues in the IoT. The first is a form of *noninterference*: we can assess if an AbU system does not exhibit forbidden information flows between resources, according to a given security policy. The second is a form of *non-interaction*: we can assess whether different nodes will not interact by acting on shared resources in unexpected ways.

To formally capture these requirements we have introduced two suitable bisimulations, generalizing the notion of *hiding bisimilarity* of [7], in order to deal with specific aspects of AbU systems. Leveraging these definitions, we have then given two sound verification mechanisms to *statically* check noninterference and non-interaction of AbU systems.

Future Work. Semantic dependencies are an out-of-band information that must be externally provided. Indeed, is not part of the AbU language and comes from external environmental factors (e.g., temperature can be influenced by walls insulation). Nevertheless, we can leverage Natural Language Processing techniques or machine learning in order to compute (i.e., infer) this information, starting from AbU rules. We plan to enhance our verification mechanisms with *heuristics for implicit interactions* as a future work.

Another aspect to investigate is the intentional information release. In some practical scenarios, noninterference is a too restrictive requirement, and a controlled release of confidential information is desirable. To this end, we can add a *declassification mechanism* to downgrade the security level of expressions.

As already mentioned at the end of Sect. 5, we plan to improve the precision of the information flows detection algorithm. In particular, we aim to develop an inter-procedural constancy analysis, leveraging model-checking techniques.

Static analysis is sometimes too restrictive. So, we can move from static to *dynamic verification* (i.e., runtime monitoring), in order to detect violations at runtime of the security and safety requirements. This would enhance permissiveness at the expense of soundness. Then, the system developer would be in charge of choosing the strategy that best fits the particular application scenario.

Finally, we plan to develop other requirements, not strictly related to security and safety aspects. Indeed, *correctness requirements* are important as well, in general, and in the IoT context, in particular. An example is *rules confluence*: in some practical IoT scenarios it is important to ensure that rules execution order does not impact the overall system behavior. To this end, it can be useful to model AbU systems as (graph) rewriting systems, as it has been done for multi-agent systems in, e.g., [31].

References

1. Abd Alrahman, Y., De Nicola, R., Loreti, M.: On the power of attribute-based communication. In: Albert, E., Lanese, I. (eds.) FORTE 2016. LNCS, vol. 9688, pp. 1–18. Springer, Cham (2016). https://doi.org/10.1007/978-3-319-39570-8_1
2. Abd Alrahman, Y., De Nicola, R., Loreti, M.: Programming interactions in collective adaptive systems by relying on attribute-based communication. Sci. Comput. Program. **192**, 102428 (2020). https://doi.org/10.1016/j.scico.2020.102428
3. Abd Alrahman, Y., De Nicola, R., Loreti, M., Tiezzi, F., Vigo, R.: A calculus for attribute-based communication. In: 30th Symposium on Applied Computing, pp. 1840–1845. ACM (2015). https://doi.org/10.1145/2695664.2695668
4. Anderson, S., Bredeche, N., Eiben, A., Kampis, G., van Steen, M.: Adaptive collective systems: herding black sheep (2013)
5. Balliu, M., Bastys, I., Sabelfeld, A.: Securing IoT apps. IEEE Secur. Priv. **17**(5), 22–29 (2019). https://doi.org/10.1109/MSEC.2019.2914190
6. Balliu, M., Merro, M., Pasqua, M.: Securing cross-app interactions in IoT platforms. In: 32nd IEEE Computer Security Foundations Symposium, Hoboken, NJ, USA, pp. 319–334. IEEE (2019). https://doi.org/10.1109/CSF.2019.00029
7. Balliu, M., Merro, M., Pasqua, M., Shcherbakov, M.: Friendly fire: cross-app interactions in IoT platforms. ACM Trans. Priv. Secur. **24**(3), 16:1-16:40 (2021). https://doi.org/10.1145/3444963
8. Barthe, G., D'Argenio, P.R., Rezk, T.: Secure information flow by self-composition. In: Proceedings of CSF, pp. 100–114 (2004)
9. Bastys, I., Piessens, F., Sabelfeld, A.: Tracking information flow via delayed output. In: Gruschka, N. (ed.) NordSec 2018. LNCS, vol. 11252, pp. 19–37. Springer, Cham (2018). https://doi.org/10.1007/978-3-030-03638-6_2
10. Bastys, I., Balliu, M., Sabelfeld, A.: If this then what? Controlling flows in IoT apps. In: ACM CCS, pp. 1102–1119. ACM (2018)
11. Beyer, D., Stahlbauer, A.: BDD-based software verification. Int. J. Softw. Tools Technol. Transf. **16**(5), 507–518 (2014)
12. Bodei, C., Degano, P., Ferrari, G.L., Galletta, L.: Tracing where IoT data are collected and aggregated. Log. Methods Comput. Sci. **13**(3), 1–38 (2017). https://doi.org/10.23638/LMCS-13(3:5)2017
13. Cano, J., Delaval, G., Rutten, E.: Coordination of ECA rules by verification and control. In: Kühn, E., Pugliese, R. (eds.) COORDINATION 2014. LNCS, vol. 8459, pp. 33–48. Springer, Heidelberg (2014). https://doi.org/10.1007/978-3-662-43376-8_3
14. Cano, J., Rutten, E., Delaval, G., Benazzouz, Y., Gurgen, L.: ECA rules for IoT environment: a case study in safe design. In: 8th International Conference on Self-Adaptive and Self-Organizing Systems Workshops, USA, pp. 116–121. IEEE (2014). https://doi.org/10.1109/SASOW.2014.32
15. Celik, Z.B., et al.: Sensitive information tracking in commodity IoT. In: USENIX, pp. 1687–1704. USENIX Association (2018)
16. Celik, Z.B., McDaniel, P.D., Tan, G.: Soteria: automated IoT safety and security analysis. In: USENIX, Boston, MA, pp. 147–158. USENIX Association (2018). https://www.usenix.org/conference/atc18/presentation/celik
17. Celik, Z.B., Tan, G., McDaniel, P.D.: IoTGuard: dynamic enforcement of security and safety policy in commodity IoT. In: NDSS. The Internet Society (2019)
18. Celik, Z.B., Fernandes, E., Pauley, E., Tan, G., McDaniel, P.: Program analysis of commodity IoT applications for security and privacy: challenges and opportunities. ACM Comput. Surv. **52**(4), 1–30 (2019). https://doi.org/10.1145/3333501

19. Chi, H., Zeng, Q., Du, X., Yu, J.: Cross-app interference threats in smart homes: categorization, detection and handling. In: 50th International Conference on Dependable Systems and Networks, pp. 411–423 (2020). https://doi.org/10.1109/DSN48063.2020.00056

20. Clarkson, M.R., Schneider, F.B.: Hyperproperties. J. Comput. Secur. **18**(6), 1157–1210 (2010). http://dl.acm.org/citation.cfm?id=1891823.1891830

21. Cohen, E.: Information transmission in computational systems. Oper. Syst. Rev. **11**, 133–139 (1977)

22. Corradini, F., Culmone, R., Mostarda, L., Tesei, L., Raimondi, F.: A constrained ECA language supporting formal verification of WSNs. In: 2015 IEEE 29th International Conference on Advanced Information Networking and Applications Workshops, pp. 187–192 (2015). https://doi.org/10.1109/WAINA.2015.109

23. De Nicola, R., et al.: The SCEL language: design, implementation, verification. In: Wirsing, M., Hölzl, M., Koch, N., Mayer, P. (eds.) Software Engineering for Collective Autonomic Systems. LNCS, vol. 8998, pp. 3–71. Springer, Cham (2015). https://doi.org/10.1007/978-3-319-16310-9_1

24. Ding, W., Hu, H.: On the safety of IoT device physical interaction control. In: ACM CCS, CCS 2018, pp. 832–846. ACM (2018)

25. Fernandes, E., Paupore, J., Rahmati, A., Simionato, D., Conti, M., Prakash, A.: FlowFence: practical data protection for emerging IoT application frameworks. In: USENIX, pp. 531–548. USENIX Association (2016)

26. Fernandes, E., Rahmati, A., Jung, J., Prakash, A.: Decentralized action integrity for trigger-action IoT platforms. In: NDSS. The Internet Society (2018)

27. Focardi, R., Gorrieri, R.: Classification of security properties. In: Focardi, R., Gorrieri, R. (eds.) FOSAD 2000. LNCS, vol. 2171, pp. 331–396. Springer, Heidelberg (2001). https://doi.org/10.1007/3-540-45608-2_6

28. Hsu, K., Chiang, Y., Hsiao, H.: SafeChain: securing trigger-action programming from attack chains. IEEE Trans. Inf. Forensics Secur. **14**(10), 2607–2622 (2019)

29. Hunt, S., Sands, D.: On flow-sensitive security types. In: Conference Record of the 33rd Symposium on Principles of Programming Languages, POPL 2006, pp. 79–90. ACM, New York (2006). https://doi.org/10.1145/1111037.1111045

30. Jin, X., Lembachar, Y., Ciardo, G.: Symbolic verification of ECA rules. In: Moldt, D. (ed.) Joint Proceedings of PNSE 2013 and ModBE 2013, Milano, Italy, vol. 989, pp. 41–59. CEUR-WS.org (2013). http://ceur-ws.org/Vol-989/paper17.pdf

31. Mansutti, A., Miculan, M., Peressotti, M.: Multi-agent systems design and prototyping with bigraphical reactive systems. In: Magoutis, K., Pietzuch, P. (eds.) DAIS 2014. LNCS, vol. 8460, pp. 201–208. Springer, Heidelberg (2014). https://doi.org/10.1007/978-3-662-43352-2_16

32. Mastroeni, I., Pasqua, M.: Verifying bounded subset-closed hyperproperties. In: Podelski, A. (ed.) SAS 2018. LNCS, vol. 11002, pp. 263–283. Springer, Cham (2018). https://doi.org/10.1007/978-3-319-99725-4_17

33. Miculan, M., Pasqua, M.: A calculus for attribute-based memory updates. In: Cerone, A., Ölveczky, P.C. (eds.) ICTAC 2021. LNCS, vol. 12819, pp. 366–385. Springer, Cham (2021). https://doi.org/10.1007/978-3-030-85315-0_21

34. Newcomb, J.L., Chandra, S., Jeannin, J.B., Schlesinger, C., Sridharan, M.: IOTA: a calculus for internet of things automation. In: New Ideas, New Paradigms, and Reflections on Programming and Software, pp. 119–133. Onward! (2017)

35. Nguyen, D.T., Song, C., Qian, Z., Krishnamurthy, S.V., Colbert, E.J.M., McDaniel, P.: IoTSan: fortifying the safety of IoT systems. In: CoNEXT 2018, pp. 191–203. ACM (2018)

36. Pasqua, M., Miculan, M.: On the security and safety of AbU systems (supplementary material) (2021). https://doi.org/10.5281/zenodo.5570332
37. Surbatovich, M., Aljuraidan, J., Bauer, L., Das, A., Jia, L.: Some recipes can do more than spoil your appetite: analyzing the security and privacy risks of IFTTT recipes. In: WWW 2017, pp. 1501–1510. ACM (2017)
38. Vannucchi, C., et al.: vIRONy: a tool for analysis and verification of ECA rules in intelligent environments. In: International Conference on Intelligent Environments, pp. 92–99. IEEE (2017). https://doi.org/10.1109/IE.2017.32
39. Vannucchi, C., et al.: Symbolic verification of event-condition-action rules in intelligent environments. J. Reliab. Intell. Environ. 3(2), 117–130 (2017). https://doi. org/10.1007/s40860-017-0036-z
40. Volpano, D.M., Irvine, C.E., Smith, G.: A sound type system for secure flow analysis. J. Comput. Secur. 4(2/3), 167–188 (1996)

Parallel Composition/CSP
and Probabilistic Reasoning

Parallelized Sequential Composition and Hardware Weak Memory Models

Robert J. Colvin[1,2(✉)]

[1] Defence Science and Technology Group, Canberra, Australia
[2] University of Queensland, Brisbane, Australia
r.colvin@uq.edu.au

Abstract. Since the 1960s processors have, for efficiency, sometimes executed instructions out of program order, provided that the (sequential) semantics is preserved. On uniprocessor architectures this behaviour is not observable, however multicore architectures can expose instruction reorderings as unexpected, or "weak", behaviours, which are notoriously difficult to reason about. In this paper we introduce a novel program operator, *parallelized sequential composition*, where '$c_1 \overset{M}{;} c_2$' may execute instructions of c_2 before those of c_1, depending on M, which controls the reordering of atomic instructions. When appropriately instantiated the operator exhibits many of the weak behaviours of TSO, Release Consistency, Arm, and RISC-V, and generalises sequential and parallel composition. We show how the nondeterminism introduced by reordering can be reasoned about by reduction to sequential or parallel forms, from where established techniques (such as rely/guarantee or Owicki-Gries) can be applied. This gives a more direct, intuitive and compositional framework for reasoning about weak behaviours that arise from processor reordering than semantics that are based on complex data structures over properties of global traces. The semantics and theory is encoded and verified in Isabelle/HOL, and we use its implementation in the Maude rewriting engine to empirically show its behaviours agree with hardware.

1 Introduction

The 1960s saw significant improvements in processor efficiency, including allowing out-of-order instruction execution in cases where program semantics would not be lost [67] and maximising use of multiple computation units [68]. These advances meant that instructions could be distributed in parallel among several computational subunits, and streamlined interactions with main memory. These features did not visibly intrude on programmers: the conditions under which parallelization could take place ensured the *sequential semantics* of any computation was maintained.

In a concurrent system the effect of out-of-order execution may be exposed, and this has provided a challenge for developing efficient, correct and secure concurrent software for modern processors [3]. Order can be restored by injecting artificial dependencies, but the performance cost is significant. For instance,

© Springer Nature Switzerland AG 2021
R. Calinescu and C. S. Păsăreanu (Eds.): SEFM 2021, LNCS 13085, pp. 201–221, 2021.
https://doi.org/10.1007/978-3-030-92124-8_12

performance concerns hamper the mitigation of the Spectre class of security vulnerabilities [40] that arise in-part from out-of-order loads.

Current approaches to defining the semantics of, and reasoning about, weak memory models, are typically either low-level, in the sense of including processor-specific details, or involve specifications over global traces and data structures that maintain a partial order on events across threads. While this has been effective in elucidating behaviours, the reasoning frameworks induced from such semantics have tended to need new types of logic and suffer from a lack of compositionality. Our motivation in this paper is to lift reasoning to the program level, and to as much as possible admit the application of existing techniques for sequential programs. As such we introduce the novel *parallelized sequential composition* operator as a primitive of an imperative language. The program '$c_1 \overset{M}{;} c_2$', for some function on instructions M, may execute c_1 and c_2 in order, or it may interleave actions of c_2 with those of c_1 according to M. We give the weakest M such that $c_1 \overset{M}{;} c_2$ preserves program-order sequential semantics, and show how modern *hardware weak memory models* are strengthenings of this concept. The language, its semantics, and the properties in the paper are encoded and machine-checked in the Isabelle/HOL theorem prover [54]. We use the semantics as a basis for a model checker, encoded in Maude [20], which we use to empirically show conformance of our semantics to established models.

In Sect. 2 we provide a foundation for instruction reordering and give a range of theoretical memory models. In Sect. 3 we fully define the syntax and semantics of an imperative language, IMP+pseq, that includes conditionals, loops, and parallelized sequential composition, and show how to reason about programs using standard techniques. In Sect. 4 we define TSO [64], Release Consistency [31], Arm [58] and RISC-V [62] as instances of parallelized sequential composition. We discuss related work in Sect. 5.

2   Foundations of Instruction Reordering

In this section we provide a foundation for exploring theoretically significant memory models that underlie modern processors. We start with a basic imperative language containing just assignments and guards as atomic actions (type *Instr*) with parallelized sequential composition as combinator (we give a richer language in Sect. 3.1).

$$\alpha \ ::= \ x := e \ | \ (\!| e |\!) \qquad\qquad c \ ::= \ \mathbf{nil} \ | \ \alpha \ | \ c_1 \overset{M}{;} c_2 \qquad (1)$$

An action α may be an assignment $x := e$ (where e is an expression), the typical notion of an update encompassing stores and loads, or a guard action $(\!| e |\!)$, representing a test on the state (does e evaluate to *True*), which can be used to model conditionals/branches. A command c is either the terminated command **nil** (corresponding to a no-op), an action α, or the composition of two commands according to some memory model M.

The intention is that a simple command $\alpha \overset{M}{;} \beta$ is free to execute instruction β before instruction α (possibly with modifications due to forwarding, described later) provided the constraints of M are obeyed. Clearly this potential reordering of instructions may destroy the programmer's intention if unconstrained; however the reordering (or parallelization) of *independent* instructions can potentially be more efficient than the (possibly arbitrary) order specified by the programmer. For example, consider a load followed by an update $r := x \overset{\text{M}}{;} y := 1$. If x is held in main memory, retrieving its value may take many processor cycles. Rather than idle the independent instruction $y := 1$ can be immediately issued without compromising the programmer's intention *assuming a single-threaded context*.

A memory model M is formed from a *reordering relation* on instructions (Sect. 2.1) and a *forwarding* function (Sect. 2.2).

2.1 Reorderings

First consider the base of a memory model, the "reordering relation", which is a binary relation on instructions. We write $\alpha \overset{\text{M}}{\Leftarrow} \beta$ if β may be reordered before instruction α according to the reordering relation of M, and $\alpha \overset{\text{M}}{\nLeftarrow} \beta$ otherwise. The *sequentially consistent* memory model forbids any reordering.

Model 1 (SC). *For all* $\alpha, \beta \in \mathit{Instr}$, $\alpha \overset{\text{SC}}{\nLeftarrow} \beta$.

We may now explicitly state the notion of a *sequential* model [45], which is the minimal property that any practical memory model M should establish. Assume an 'effect' function eff that returns the relation between pre- and post-states for a given program executed in program order.

Definition 1. M *is* sequential *if* $\mathsf{eff}(c_1 \overset{\text{M}}{;} c_2) \subseteq \mathsf{eff}(c_1 \overset{\text{SC}}{;} c_2)$.

That is, M is *sequential* if the result of any reordering (on a single thread) is one that could have been achieved when executed in program order. The weakest sequential memory model, which we call EFF, allows reordering when sequential semantics is maintained.

Model 2 (EFF). $\alpha \overset{\text{EFF}}{\Leftarrow} \beta$ *iff* $\mathsf{eff}(\beta \overset{\text{SC}}{;} \alpha) \subseteq \mathsf{eff}(\alpha \overset{\text{SC}}{;} \beta)$

Theorem 1. EFF *is sequential.*

Proof. The property $\alpha \overset{\text{EFF}}{\Leftarrow} \beta$ lifts to commands. $\square$

EFF is impractical since processors cannot make semantic judgements dynamically; however we propose the following memory model as the weakest that is practical, in the sense it uses a simple syntactic test.[1]

Model 3 (G$_0$). $\alpha \overset{\text{G0}}{\Leftarrow} \beta$ *iff* $\mathsf{wv}(\alpha) \not\cap \mathsf{fv}(\beta)$ *and* $\mathsf{wv}(\beta) \not\cap \mathsf{fv}(\alpha)$

Model G$_0$ allows instructions to be reordered unless a variable that β references ($\mathsf{fv}(\beta)$) is modified by α, or vice versa, using the notation below.

$$\mathsf{fv}(.)/\mathsf{wv}(.)/\mathsf{rv}(.) \text{ Free/written/read vars} \quad (2) \qquad s_1 \not\cap s_2 \mathrel{\widehat=} s_1 \cap s_2 = \varnothing \quad (3)$$

---

[1] Essentially Hoare's "disjointness" [32] and separation logic's "non-interference" [19].

Reorderings eliminated by G_0 include $x := 1 \overset{G_0}{\nLeftarrow} x := 2$, $x := 1 \overset{G_0}{\nLeftarrow} r := x$ and $r := x \overset{G_0}{\nLeftarrow} x := 1$. If $\neg(\mathsf{wv}(\alpha) \mathbin{\unicode{0x2AFD}} \mathsf{rv}(\beta))$ then there is a *data dependency* between α and β, i.e., the value of a variable that β depends on is being computed by α. It is straightforward that $(\alpha \overset{G_0}{\Leftarrow} \beta) \Rightarrow (\alpha \overset{EFF}{\Leftarrow} \beta)$ i.e., G_0 is stronger than EFF. We can therefore infer that G_0 is *sequential* by the following theorem.

Theorem 2. *If* M *is stronger than* EFF *then* M *is* sequential.

Proof. A stronger model admits fewer behaviours (see later: (17)).   □

The memory model G_0 is lacking in the age of multicore processors because it does not require two consecutive loads of the same *shared* variable to be performed in order. For instance, consider the program $Ex \mathrel{\widehat{=}} (r_1 := x \overset{c_0}{\mathbin{;}} r_2 := x) \parallel (x := 1 \overset{c_0}{\mathbin{;}} x := 2)$. The two loads should read values of x in a globally "coherent" manner, that is, the value for x loaded into r_1 must occur no later than that loaded by r_2. Hence program Ex should not reach the final state $r_1 = 2 \wedge r_2 = 1$. However, although $x := 1 \overset{G_0}{\nLeftarrow} x := 2$, we have $r_1 := x \overset{G_0}{\Leftarrow} r_2 := x$ in the first thread.

To handle coherence we divide the set of variables, Var, into mutually exclusive and exhaustive sets Shared and Local, with specialised definitions.

$$\mathsf{sv}(.), \mathsf{rsv}(.), \mathsf{wsv}(.) \qquad \text{As (2), restricted to Shared} \qquad (4)$$

To maintain "coherence per location" we extend G_0 to G by adding a constraint on the loaded shared variables. Additionally, since we are now explicitly concerned with concurrent behaviour, we add the **"fence"** instruction type to restore order. We call this an "artificial" constraint, since it is not based on "natural" constraints arising from the preservation of sequential semantics.

Model 4 (G). $\alpha \overset{G}{\Leftarrow} \beta$ *iff* $(\alpha \overset{G_0}{\Leftarrow} \beta \wedge \mathsf{rsv}(\alpha) \mathbin{\unicode{0x2AFD}} \mathsf{rsv}(\beta))$, *except:* $\alpha \overset{G}{\nLeftarrow} \mathbf{fence} \overset{G}{\nLeftarrow} \alpha$.

When specifying a memory model we typically give the base relation first, and then list the "exceptions", which take precedence; we also let $\alpha \overset{M}{\Leftarrow} \beta \overset{M}{\Leftarrow} \gamma$ abbreviate $\alpha \overset{M}{\Leftarrow} \beta \wedge \beta \overset{M}{\Leftarrow} \gamma$, and similarly for $\overset{}{\nLeftarrow}$.

Model G strengthens the condition of G_0 to require loads from main memory to (appear to) be kept in program order per shared variable. In addition fences block reordering, reinstating program-order execution explicitly (at the cost of efficiency). We consider G to be the weakest model of practical consideration in a concurrent system as it is both *sequential* and maintains coherence-per-location.

Definition 2. *Model* M *is* coherent *if it is stronger than* G.

Most modern processors are coherent. A memory model that is not coherent is one that allows any instructions to be reordered under any circumstances, i.e., the complement of SC. If we disallow forwarding in this model (discussed in the next section), this weakest memory model corresponds to parallel composition.

Model 5 (PAR). $\alpha \overset{\text{PAR}}{\Longleftarrow} \beta$ *for all* $\alpha, \beta \in Instr$.

We may define $c \parallel d \triangleq c \overset{\text{PAR}}{\,;\,} d$, lifting instruction-level parallelism to thread-level parallelism.

The key point about the SC memory model is that reasoning is "straightforward", or classical, in that all the accepted techniques work. This is the property of *sequential consistency* [45], formalised below. We first introduce notation for constraining memory models within a program.

Definition 3. *Command* $c_{\langle M \rangle}$ *is structurally identical to* c *but every parallelized sequential composition, except for instances of* PAR, *is parameterized by* M.

The notation $c_{\langle M \rangle}$ lets us consider programs executed under some specific model M (parallel composition is left unchanged as we are typically only interested in thread-local effects).

Definition 4 (Sequentially consistent). *A memory model* M *is sequentially consistent if, for any programs* c *and* d, $c_{\langle M \rangle} \parallel d_{\langle M \rangle}$ *is equivalent to* $c_{\langle SC \rangle} \parallel d_{\langle SC \rangle}$.

By definition SC is sequentially consistent, however even sequentially consistent uniprocessors are not as strong as SC, for instance, some speculate loads and reissue them if a change is detected. Note the difference between *sequential* and *sequentially consistent*: a sequentially consistent memory model is sequential, but not vice versa. None of TSO, Arm or RISC-V are sequentially consistent in general, but are for programs where, for example, shared variables are accessed according to a lock-based programming discipline.

2.2   Forwarding

We now complicate matters significantly by considering *forwarding*, where the effect of an earlier operation can be taken into account when deciding if instructions can be reordered.[2] For instance, given a program $x := 1 \overset{c}{\,;\,} r := x$, we have $x := 1 \overset{c}{\not\Leftarrow} r := x$ because $\mathsf{wv}(x := 1) = \{x\} \subseteq \mathsf{fv}(r := x)$. In practice however it is possible to *forward* the new value of x to the later instruction – it is clear that the value assigned to r will be 1 if x is local, and in any case is a valid possible assignment to r even if x is shared. We define $\beta_{\ll\alpha}$, representing the effect of forwarding the (assignment) instruction α to β, where the expression $f_{[x \backslash e]}$ is f with references to x replaced by e.

Definition 5. $\beta_{\ll\alpha} = \beta$, *except:*

$$(i)\ (y := f)_{\ll x := e} = y := (f_{[x \backslash e]}) \qquad and \qquad (ii)\ (\!|f|\!)_{\ll x := e} = (\!|f_{[x \backslash e]}|\!)$$

Essentially, forwarding allows the text of the program to be used to evaluate an expression in an instruction that is being reordered. The forwarding function (type $Instr \rightarrow Instr \rightarrow Instr$) and a reordering relation $\overset{R}{\Leftarrow}$ (type $\mathbb{P}(Instr \times Instr)$)

---

[2] We use the term "forwarding" (from Arm) [9], also called "bypassing" in TSO [64].

combine to form a memory model (type $Instr \rightarrow \mathbb{P}(Instr \times Instr)$) as shown in (5) (we write $\overset{M}{\Leftarrow}$ to denote the relation $\overset{R}{\Leftarrow}$ that underpins M).

$$\text{M} \;\widehat{=}\; \lambda\alpha.\{(\beta_{\langle\!\langle\alpha}, \beta) \mid \alpha \overset{R}{\Leftarrow} \beta_{\langle\!\langle\alpha}\} \;\;(5) \quad \beta' \langle\!\langle \alpha \overset{M}{\langle\!\langle} \beta \;\widehat{=}\; (\beta', \beta) \in \text{M}(\alpha) \;\;(6)$$

Thus a memory model M for a given action α returns a set of pairs (β', β) where β reorders with α, after the effect of forwarding α to β (β') is taken into account. For convenience we sometimes use the notation $\beta' \langle\!\langle \alpha \overset{M}{\langle\!\langle} \beta$ (6), which notationally conveys the bringing forward of β with respect α. For example, since $(r := x)_{\langle\!\langle x := 1} = (r := (x_{[x \backslash 1]})) = r := 1$, the load $r := x$ "reorders" with $x := 1$, becoming $r := 1$, that is, $r := 1 \langle\!\langle x := 1 \overset{G_0}{\langle\!\langle} r := x$.

2.3 Strengthening Memory Models

We strengthen a memory model by strengthening the relation for each action.

Definition 6. $\text{M}_1 \subseteq \text{M}_2 \;\widehat{=}\; \forall \alpha \bullet \text{M}_1(\alpha) \subseteq \text{M}_2(\alpha)$

As we explore in the rest of the paper, the Total Store Order model strengthens G considerably (or alternatively, weakens SC for the particular case of stores and loads), while ARM strengthens G to prevent stores from coming before branches. ARM, RISC-V, and the release consistency models RC_{pc} and RC_{sc} are related as below, focusing on their common instruction types; since each introduces unique instruction types a direct comparison is not possible.

Theorem 3. $\text{SC} \subseteq \text{TSO} \subseteq \text{ARM} \subseteq \text{RC}_{sc} \subseteq \text{RISC-V} \subseteq \text{RC}_{pc} \subseteq \text{G} \subseteq \text{G}_0 \subseteq \text{EFF}$.

Proof. Straightforward from definitions above and in Sect. 4.   □

Well-Behaved Models. A memory model could theoretically allow arbitrary reorderings and effects of forwarding; however from a reasoning perspective we limit ourselves to *well-behaved* memory models.

Definition 7. *A memory model* M *is* well-behaved *if: i) the result of reordering is deterministic, that is, for any α, β there is at most one β' such that $\beta' \langle\!\langle \alpha \overset{M}{\langle\!\langle} \beta$, and furthermore, either $\beta' = \beta_{\langle\!\langle\alpha}$ or $\beta' = \beta$; and ii) if an action α allows reordering with any β then it must also allow reordering with internal ("silent") steps (defined in Sect. 3.2).*

Condition i) ensures determinacy and sequential semantics, while ii) simplifies reasoning. All models we consider, except PAR, are well-behaved.

3 An Imperative Language with Instruction Reordering

In this section we give the full syntax and semantics for an imperative programming language, "IMP+pseq", which uses parallelized sequential composition.

3.1 Syntax

As given in Fig. 1 an instruction α may be an update $x := e$, a guard $(\!|e|\!)$, or a barrier/fence $\textbf{barrier}(f)$.[3] A barrier instruction is parameterised by some f specifying the barrier type; we leave it underspecified at this point (since different models introduce their own barrier types) except that, since typically models have at least a "full" fence, we define $\textbf{fence} \mathrel{\hat{=}} \textbf{barrier}(\mathsf{full})$.

$$\alpha ::= x := e \ \mid \ (\!|e|\!) \ \mid \ \textbf{barrier}(f)$$

$$f ::= \ldots \ \mid \ \mathsf{full}$$

$$c ::= \textbf{nil} \ \mid \ \alpha \ \mid \ c_1 \overset{\text{M}}{;} c_2 \ \mid \ c_1 \sqcap c_2 \ \mid \ c_\text{M}^*$$

$$c_1 \cdot c_2 \mathrel{\hat{=}} c_1 \overset{\text{SC}}{;} c_2 \qquad c_1 \parallel c_2 \mathrel{\hat{=}} c_1 \overset{\text{PAR}}{;} c_2 \tag{7}$$

$$c_\text{M}^0 \mathrel{\hat{=}} \textbf{nil} \qquad c_\text{M}^{n+1} \mathrel{\hat{=}} c \overset{\text{M}}{;} c_\text{M}^n \tag{8}$$

$$(\textbf{if } b \textbf{ then } c_1 \textbf{ else } c_2)_\text{M} \mathrel{\hat{=}} (\!|b|\!) \overset{\text{M}}{;} c_1 \sqcap (\!|\neg b|\!) \overset{\text{M}}{;} c_2 \tag{9}$$

$$(\textbf{while } b \textbf{ do } c)_\text{M} \mathrel{\hat{=}} ((\!|b|\!) \overset{\text{M}}{;} c)_\text{M}^* \overset{\text{M}}{;} (\!|\neg b|\!) \tag{10}$$

$$\alpha \overset{\alpha}{\to} \textbf{nil} \quad (11) \qquad c_\text{M}^* \overset{\tau}{\to} c_\text{M}^n \quad (12) \qquad c \sqcap d \overset{\tau}{\to} c \quad (13) \qquad c \sqcap d \overset{\tau}{\to} d \quad (14)$$

$$\frac{c_1 \overset{\alpha}{\to} c_1'}{c_1 \overset{\text{M}}{;} c_2 \overset{\alpha}{\to} c_1' \overset{\text{M}}{;} c_2} \quad (15) \qquad \textbf{nil} \overset{\text{M}}{;} c_2 \overset{\tau}{\to} c_2 \quad (16) \qquad \frac{c_2 \overset{\beta}{\to} c_2' \quad \beta' \ll c_1 \ll \beta}{c_1 \overset{\text{M}}{;} c_2 \overset{\beta'}{\to} c_1 \overset{\text{M}}{;} c_2'} \quad (17)$$

Fig. 1. Syntax and semantics of IMP+pseq

A command c may be the terminated command $\textbf{nil}$, a single instruction α, the parallelized sequential composition of two commands $c_1 \overset{\text{M}}{;} c_2$ (where M is a memory model), a nondeterministic choice between two commands $c_1 \sqcap c_2$, or an iteration c_M^* (parameterised by M as it implicitly contains sequencing).

In (7) we use parallelized sequential composition to define '$\cdot$' as the usual notion of sequential composition (see Model 1), and '$\parallel$' as the usual interleaving notion of parallel composition (see Model 5). In (8) we define finite iteration of a command, c_M^n, as the n-fold parallelized sequential composition of c with reordering according to M. Conditionals are modelled using guards and choice (9). By allowing instructions in c_1 or c_2 to be reordered before the guards one can model *speculative execution*, i.e., early execution of instructions which occur after a branch point. We define a while loop using iteration (10).

3.2 Operational Semantics

The meaning of IMP+pseq is formalised using an operational semantics, which generates a sequence of actions (instructions) allowing syntactic analysis to decide on allowed reorderings.

---

[3] We give an atomic expression evaluation semantics for assignments and guards, which is typically reasonable for assembler-level instructions.

The operational semantics of an instruction is simply a step labelled by the instruction itself, after which it is terminated, i.e., becomes **nil** (11). The semantics of loops is given by unfolding a nondeterministically-chosen finite number of times (12).[4] The special instruction $\tau \mathrel{\widehat{=}} (\!|\mathit{True}|\!)$ is a *silent step* (defined below), having no effect on the state, possibly corresponding to some internal actions of a microprocessor or, as in this case, an abstract step of unrolling a loop that has no other visible consequence. A nondeterministic choice can choose either branch (13, 14). A parallelized sequential composition $c_1 \overset{\text{M}}{;} c_2$ can take a step if c_1 can take a step (15), and continues with c_2 when c_1 has terminated (16), as in standard sequential composition. Together these rules give a standard sequential semantics for imperative programs.

Rule (17), unique to IMP+pseq, states that given a program $c_1 \overset{\text{M}}{;} c_2$, an instruction β of c_2 can happen before c_1, provided that $\beta' \ll c_1 \overset{\text{M}}{\ll} \beta$, which is the straightforward lifting of M from instructions ((5) and (6)) to commands

Visible, Silent and Infeasible Actions. A visible action is any action with a visible effect, for instance, fences, assignments, and guards with free variables. Silent actions include any guard which is *True* in any state *and* contains no free variables; for instance, $(\!|0 = 0|\!)$ is silent while $(\!|x = x|\!)$ is not. A third category of actions, infeasible α, includes exactly those guards $(\!|b|\!)$ where b evaluates to *False* in every state, e.g., $(\!|\mathit{False}|\!)$ and $(\!|x \neq x|\!)$.

Trace Semantics. Given a program c the operational semantics generates a *trace*, that is, a finite sequence of steps $c_0 \xrightarrow{\alpha_1} c_1 \xrightarrow{\alpha_2} \ldots$ where the labels in the trace are actions. We write $c \overset{t}{\Rightarrow} c'$ to say that c executes the actions in trace t and evolves to c'. Traces of *visible* actions are accumulated into the trace, and *silent* actions (such as τ) are discarded, i.e., we have a "weak" notion of equivalence [52]. The meaning of a command c is its set of all terminating behaviours (with behaviours containing infeasible actions being excluded).

Refinement and Equivalence. We take the usual (reverse) subset inclusion definition of refinement, i.e., $c \sqsubseteq d$ if every behaviour of d is a behaviour of c; our notion of command *equivalence* is refinement in both direction.

Reduction Rules. From these definitions we can derive expected properties for the standard operators, which we have machine checked in Isabelle/HOL (details are in [21]). Below we give some reduction rules which can be used to simplify programs involving parallelized sequential composition (cf. [69]).

$$c_1 \overset{\text{M}}{;} c_2 \sqsubseteq c_1 \cdot c_2 \quad (18) \qquad \alpha \overset{\text{M}}{\not\Leftarrow} \beta_{\ll\alpha} \;\Rightarrow\; \alpha \overset{\text{M}}{;} \beta = \alpha \cdot \beta \quad (22)$$

$$c \sqcap d \sqsubseteq c \quad (19) \qquad \beta' \ll \alpha \overset{\text{M}}{\ll} \beta \;\Rightarrow\; \alpha \overset{\text{M}}{;} \beta \sqsubseteq \beta' \cdot \alpha \quad (23)$$

$$(c_1 \overset{\text{M}}{;} c_2) \overset{\text{M}}{;} c_3 = c_1 \overset{\text{M}}{;} (c_2 \overset{\text{M}}{;} c_3) \quad (20) \qquad \beta' \ll \alpha \overset{\text{M}}{\ll} \beta \;\Rightarrow\; \alpha \overset{\text{M}}{;} \beta = (\alpha \cdot \beta) \sqcap (\beta' \cdot \alpha) \quad (24)$$

$$c_1 \overset{\text{M}}{;} \textbf{fence} \overset{\text{M}}{;} c_2 = c_1 \cdot \textbf{fence} \cdot c_2 \quad (21) \qquad \beta \ll \alpha \overset{\text{M}}{\ll} \beta \;\Rightarrow\; \alpha \overset{\text{M}}{;} \beta = (\alpha \parallel \beta) \quad (25)$$

---

[4] We use finite loops only to avoid the usual complications infinite loops introduce, which are orthogonal to the effects of instruction reordering.

Sequential composition is always a refinement of parallelized sequential composition (18). A choice may be resolved to its left operand (19) (a symmetric law holds for the right operand). Parallelized sequential composition is associative (20), provided both instances are parameterised by the same model M. A full fence restores order and hence sequential reasoning (21). Now consider two instructions in sequence, $\alpha \overset{\text{M}}{;} \beta$. If β cannot be reordered according to M (after taking forwarding into account) then the actions must be executed sequentially (22), however if reordering is allowed then reverse-order is a possible behaviour (23). These two possibilities can be combined to reduce parallelized sequential composition to a choice over sequential compositions, eliminating the memory model (24). If there is no forwarding ($\beta_{\ll\alpha} = \beta$) and reordering is allowed the composition reduces to parallel (25).

Monotonicity. Monotonicity (congruence) holds for the standard operators of IMP+pseq, but monotonicity of parallelized sequential composition contains a subtlety in that the allowed traces of $c_1 \overset{\text{M}}{;} c_2$ are dependent on the reorderings allowed by c_1 with respect to M (Rule (17)). To handle this we need a stronger notion of refinement, written $c \overset{\text{M}}{\sqsubseteq} c'$, where traces are augmented to track the reorderings allowed (similarly to refusal sets in CSP's failures/divergences model), allowing strengthening only; see [21] for details.

$$c \overset{\text{M}}{\sqsubseteq} c' \wedge d \sqsubseteq d' \wedge \text{M}' \subseteq \text{M} \ \Rightarrow\ c \overset{\text{M}}{;} d \sqsubseteq c' \overset{\text{M}'}{;} d' \tag{26}$$

State-Based Semantics. The action-trace semantics can be converted into a typical pairs-of-states semantics straightforwardly, based on an "effect" function eff (of type $Instr \rightarrow \mathbb{P}(\Sigma \times \Sigma)$, where Σ is the set of total mappings from variables to values) that returns a relation on states given an instruction. The relationship with standard Plotkin style operational semantics [57] is straightforward, i.e.,

$$\text{if } c \overset{\alpha}{\longrightarrow} c' \text{ and } (\sigma, \sigma') \in \text{eff}(\alpha) \text{ then } \langle c, \sigma \rangle \longrightarrow \langle c', \sigma' \rangle$$

The advantage of our approach is that syntax of the action α can be used to reason about allowed reorderings using (17), whereas in general one cannot reconstruct or deduce an action from a pair of states.

Hoare Logic with IMP+pseq. Given a command c and predicate q, $wp(c)(q)$ returns the set of (pre) states σ where every post-state related to σ by eff(c) satisfies q.

Theorem 4. *For sequential* M, $wp(c_1 \overset{\text{M}}{;} c_2) = wp(c_1 \cdot c_2)$

Proof. By Definition 1 and Theorem 1.   □

We define Hoare logic judgements in the standard way using weakest preconditions, i.e., $\{p\}\, c\, \{q\} \ \hat{=}\ p \Rightarrow wp(c)(q)$.[5] Hence we can derive the standard

---

[5] We deal only with partial correctness as we consider only finite traces.

rules of weakest preconditions and Hoare logic for commands such as nonde-terministic choice and sequential composition, but, unsurprisingly, there are no general compositional rules for parallelized sequential composition. One notable derivable law is the following.

$$\{p\}\, c_1\, \{r\} \wedge \{r\}\, c_2\, \{q\} \;\Rightarrow\; \{p\}\, c_1\, \overset{\text{M}}{;}\, \textbf{fence}\, \overset{\text{M}}{;}\, c_2\, \{q\} \tag{27}$$

For any M with **fence** a full fence (as in Model 4), inserting a fence restores sequential reasoning (27), which follows from (21), and shows the advantage of our approach: fences do not need special treatment in the analysis, they simply remove nondeterminism introduced by reordering.

For the examples that follow we wish to show *reachability* of some postcondi-tion, as opposed to the all-possible-states formulation of standard Hoare triples. We therefore define $\langle\!\langle p \rangle\!\rangle\, c\, \langle\!\langle q \rangle\!\rangle \;\hat{=}\; \neg\{p\}\, c\, \{\neg q\}$, which says that it is *possible* for command c to reach a state q starting pre-state p (that is, it is *not* the case that $\neg q$ is always reached).[6] We use properties of Hoare logic to establish (or deny) properties of programs executing under weak memory models.

$$c = c'_{\langle\text{SC}\rangle} \;\Rightarrow\; \{p\}\, c\, \{q\} \Leftrightarrow \{p\}\, c'_{\langle\text{SC}\rangle}\, \{q\} \tag{28}$$
$$c \sqsubseteq c' \wedge \{p\}\, c'\, \{\neg q\} \;\Rightarrow\; \neg\{p\}\, c\, \{q\} \tag{29}$$
$$c \sqsubseteq c' \wedge \{p\}\, c'\, \{q\} \;\Rightarrow\; \langle\!\langle p \rangle\!\rangle\, c\, \langle\!\langle q \rangle\!\rangle \quad (\text{provided } \text{eff}((|p|) \cdot c) \neq \varnothing) \tag{30}$$

(28) is simply monotonicity of a Hoare triple, but we make the reduction of c to a sequential form $c'_{\langle\text{SC}\rangle}$ explicit (recall Definition 3); Hoare logic is used as the basis for reasoning about concurrent programs in the Owicki-Gries method [56], and so (28) enables the application of standard techniques for concurrent programs once the program in question has been reduced to a sequential form. (29) states that reducing c to a (sequential) form c' that establishes $\neg q$ confirms that c does not satisfy q (starting from p). On the other hand, (30) states that reducing c to a (sequential) form c' that establishes q confirms that c can potentially reach q (starting from p).[7] We use these formats to show how the nondeterminism inherent in weak memory models can change behaviours: some undesirable postcondition q can be ruled out in the sequential case (using (29)) but becomes possible under some weaker model (using (30)).

We now encode some well-known memory models in our framework and show how properties and behaviours can be derived from the base we have provided.

---

[6] This definition of reachability follows the conjugation pattern for allowed/reachable states, e.g., [33,53,72]; it is related to, but different from, O'Hearn's incorrectness logic [55] (which is stronger except in the special case when post-state q is *False*).

[7] The proviso on (30) rules out miraculous cases (if $(|p|) \cdot c$ is infeasible then $\{p\}\, c\, \{q\}$ trivially holds for all q, but q is not reachable in this case).

4 Hardware Weak Memory Models

4.1 Total Store Order (TSO)

The "total store order" memory model (used in Intel, AMD and SPARC processors; for a history see [64]) maintains program order on stores but is relaxed in the sense that it allows loads to come before stores. Assume $x \in$ Shared, $r \in$ Local.

Model 6 (TSO). $\alpha \overset{\text{TSO}}{\not\Longleftarrow} \beta$ *except:* $x := e \overset{\text{TSO}}{\Longleftarrow} r := f$ *if* $x \notin$ sv(f) *and* $r \notin$ fv(e).

TSO allows loads to come before independent stores, and, due to forwarding, for dependent loads to "bypass". That is, even though $x := 1 \overset{\text{TSO}}{\not\Longleftarrow} r := x$, due to forwarding we have $r := 1 \ll x := 1 \overset{\text{TSO}}{\ll} r := x$. Note that TSO allows independent register operations to also be reordered before stores.

We can show the defining behaviours of TSO (as opposed to SC) at the language level in this framework. For instance, for any values v and w,

i) $(x := v \overset{\text{TSO}}{;} y := w) = (x := v \cdot y := w)$ states that stores are kept in program order by TSO (an instance of (22));

ii) $(x := v \overset{\text{TSO}}{;} r := x) \sqsubseteq (r := v \cdot x := v)$ states that a load of x preceded by a store to x can use the stored value immediately (an instance of (23)); only later will the store become visible to the rest of the system – the classic *bypassing* behaviour;

iii) $(x := v \overset{\text{TSO}}{;} r := y) = (x := v \parallel r := y)$ states that a load of y preceded by a store of x, for distinct x and y, could be executed in either order.

Perhaps the simplest system which can observe this third behaviour is the "store buffer" test, $\text{SB} \mathrel{\hat{=}} x := 1 \cdot r_1 := y \parallel y := 1 \cdot r_2 := x$. In a sequentially consistent system at least one register must read the value 1, that is, $\{x = y = 0\}\, \text{SB}\, \{\neg(r_1 = r_2 = 0)\}$ (see [43]). However under TSO both registers may read 0.

Theorem 5. $\{x = y = 0\}\, \text{SB}_{\langle \text{TSO} \rangle}\, \{r_1 = r_2 = 0\}$

Proof. Recall from Definition 3 that $\text{SB}_{\langle \text{TSO} \rangle}$ is SB with both instances of $\overset{\text{SC}}{;}$ (written above as '.') replaced by $\overset{\text{TSO}}{;}$. The instructions in each process may be reordered, i.e., $r_1 := y \overset{\text{TSO}}{\Longleftarrow} x := 1$ and $r_2 := x \overset{\text{TSO}}{\Longleftarrow} y := 1$. Hence,

$\text{SB}_{\langle \text{TSO} \rangle} = (r_1 := y \overset{\text{TSO}}{;} x := 1) \parallel (r_2 := x \overset{\text{TSO}}{;} y := 1)$ by Definition 3, defn. SB.

$\quad = r_1 := y \parallel x := 1 \parallel r_2 := x \parallel y := 1$ by defn. TSO, (25)

$\quad \sqsubseteq r_1 := y \cdot r_2 := x \cdot x := 1 \cdot y := 1$ by interleaving

By Hoare logic, $\{x = y = 0\}\, r_1 := y \cdot r_2 := x \cdot x := 1 \cdot y := 1\, \{r_1 = r_2 = 0\}$. The proof is completed by (30). $\qquad\qquad\square$

Inserting fences into both branches reinstates sequential behaviour by (21).

Note that reasoning is relatively direct in this framework: we can use properties of the model and the structure of the program to reduce reasoning to sequential cases where established techniques can be applied, or a particular case that violates a desired property can be enumerated. Other reasoning frameworks typically monitor reorderings with respect to global abstract (graph) data structures, requiring custom assertion languages, even for simple cases.

4.2   Release Consistency

The *release consistency* memory model [31] has been highly influential, having guided the development of the C language memory model [16], with the concepts incorporated into Arm [58] and RISC-V [62]. The key concept revolves around *release writes* and *acquire loads*: a release write is stereotypically used to set a flag to indicate a block of computation has ended, and an acquire load is correspondingly used to observe a release write. Code before the release should happen before, and code after the acquire should happen after; conceptually these are weaker (one-way) fences. Release consistency's motivation was finding an easy-to-implement mechanism for interprocess communication that is feasible and inexpensive computationally, and relatively straightforward for programmers. We extend the action syntax of IMP+pseq to include *ordering constraints* (OC) as annotations to any action, with RL for release and AQ for acquire.

$$\text{OC} \quad ::= \quad \text{RL} \quad | \quad \text{AQ} \qquad\qquad \alpha \quad ::= \quad \dots \quad | \quad \alpha^{\text{OC}} \qquad\qquad (31)$$

Forwarding for the new annotated actions is defined inductively, i.e., $(\beta^{\text{OC}})_{\!\langle\!\langle \alpha} = (\beta_{\!\langle\!\langle \alpha})^{\text{OC}}$ and $\beta_{\!\langle\!\langle(\alpha^{\text{OC}})} = \beta_{\!\langle\!\langle \alpha}$, and we define $\text{eff}(\alpha^{\text{OC}}) = \text{eff}(\alpha)$.

Following [31] we give two variants, RC_{pc} ("processor consistency") and RC_{sc} ("sequential consistency"), the latter of which is a strengthening of the former. For simplicity we assume that G (Model 4) controls reordering outside of annotation considerations, although in the theory of [31] stronger constraints are possible.

Model 7 (RC_{pc}). $\alpha \overset{RC_{pc}}{\Longleftarrow} \beta$ *iff* $\alpha \overset{G}{\Longleftarrow} \beta$ *except:*

$(i)\alpha \overset{RC_{pc}}{\overset{/}{\Longleftarrow}} \beta^{\text{RL}} \overset{RC_{pc}}{\Longleftarrow} \gamma$ *iff* $\beta \overset{RC_{pc}}{\Longleftarrow} \gamma$, *and (ii)* $\alpha \overset{RC_{pc}}{\Longleftarrow} \beta^{\text{AQ}} \overset{RC_{pc}}{\overset{/}{\Longleftarrow}} \gamma$ *iff* $\alpha \overset{RC_{pc}}{\Longleftarrow} \beta$

Model 8 (RC_{sc}). $\alpha \overset{RC_{sc}}{\Longleftarrow} \beta$ *iff* $\alpha \overset{RC_{pc}}{\Longleftarrow} \beta$ *except:* $\alpha^{\text{RL}} \overset{RC_{sc}}{\overset{/}{\Longleftarrow}} \beta^{\text{AQ}}$.

RC_{pc} straightforwardly follows the intuition of [31], where a release action β^{RL} is always blocked from reordering and hence all earlier instructions must be complete before it can execute, but it does not block later instructions from happening early (provided β does not on its own block later instructions, calculated by recursively applying the reordering relation). An acquire action is the converse. RC_{sc} strengthens RC_{pc} by additionally requiring order between release and acquire actions in the one thread (the reverse direction is already implied).

Consider the program $\text{MP} \;\widehat{=}\; (x:=1 \overset{RC_{pc}}{;} (y:=1)^{\text{RL}}) \parallel ((r_1:=y)^{\text{AQ}} \overset{RC_{pc}}{;} r_2:=x)$ which is the classic "message passing" pattern, with release-acquire annotations.

Theorem 6. $\{x = y = 0\}\, \text{MP}\, \{r_1 = 1 \Rightarrow r_2 = 1\}$

Proof. The release annotation on the write to y means that $y:=1$ cannot come before $x:=1$, that is, although $x:=1 \overset{RC_{pc}}{\Longleftarrow} y:=1$, we have $x:=1 \overset{RC_{pc}}{\overset{/}{\Longleftarrow}} (y:=1)^{\text{RL}}$. Similarly the acquire tag in the other process prevents the loads of y and x from reordering. Hence, $\text{MP} \;=\; x:=1 \cdot (y:=1)^{\text{RL}} \parallel (r_1:=y)^{\text{AQ}} \cdot r_2:=x \;=\; \text{MP}_{(sc)}$ by (22) and Model 7. Having reduced to a sequential form we may apply (28), that is, we can employ standard techniques to complete the proof. This is straightforward using Owicki-Gries reasoning (checked in Isabelle/HOL [21]), noting that because the stores are executed in the order x, y, and read in reverse order, if the latter store is observed then the former must have taken effect.   □

Note that without the annotations the instructions in each process can be reordered, under which conditions it is straightforward to find a behaviour that contradicts $r_1 = 1 \Rightarrow r_2 = 1$.

4.3 Arm Version 8

In this section we consider the latest version of Arm v8, which is simpler than earlier versions due to it being "multicopy atomic" [10,58]. Arm's instruction set includes a "control fence" isb $\hat{=}$ **barrier**(ctrl), a write barrier dsb.st $\hat{=}$ **barrier**(ww), and a full fence dsb $\hat{=}$ **fence**. To specify the model we use abbreviations for defining store (str) and load (ld) instructions, which is based on their read/write shared variables, i.e., for guard or assignment α, str$(\alpha) \Leftrightarrow$ wsv$(\alpha) \neq \varnothing \wedge$ rsv$(\alpha) = \varnothing$, and ld$(\alpha) \Leftrightarrow$ wsv$(\alpha) = \varnothing \wedge$ rsv$(\alpha) \neq \varnothing$ (while str(**barrier**(f)) = ld(**barrier**(f)) = *False*).

Model 9 (ARM). $\alpha \overset{\text{ARM}}{\Longleftarrow} \beta$ *if* $\alpha \overset{\text{RC}_{sc}}{\Longleftarrow} \beta$ *except:*

(i) $\alpha \overset{\text{ARM}}{\Longleftarrow}$ dsb.st $\overset{\text{ARM}}{\Longleftarrow} \alpha$ *if* str(α), *(ii)* $(\!| b |\!) \overset{\text{ARM}}{\Longleftarrow}$ isb $\overset{\text{ARM}}{\Longleftarrow} \alpha$ *if* ld(α), *and*
(iii) $(\!| b |\!) \overset{\text{ARM}}{\Longleftarrow} \alpha$ *if* str(α)

Store fences maintain order between stores, while control fences are blocked by branches and correspondingly block loads; when taken in conjunction a control fence enforces order between loads within and before a branch, preventing the observable effects of speculative execution. Guards block stores, which is a practical consideration to do with speculating down branches: one cannot commit stores until it is known that the branch will be taken. Other than these exceptions, ARM behaves as RC$_{sc}$ for release/acquire annotations,[8] fundamentally behaving as G (Model 4).

As an example of the weak nature of Arm, i.e., issuing loads before the branch condition for the load is evaluated, consider the following behaviour of a variant of the reader process of MP where the second load is guarded. Define MP$_w \hat{=} x := 1 \cdot y := 1$ and MP$_r \hat{=} r_1 := y \overset{\text{ARM}}{;}$ (**if** $r_1 = 1$ **then** $r_2 := x)_{\text{ARM}}$. Note that in MP$_w$ we use strict sequential ordering to keep the stores in order.

Theorem 7. $\neg\{x = y = 0\}$ MP$_w \parallel$ MP$_r \{r_1 = 1 \Rightarrow r_2 = 1\}$

Proof. Consider the following behaviour of MP$_r$.

$\quad$ MP$_r \hat{=} r_1 := y \overset{\text{ARM}}{;}$ (**if** $r_1 = 1$ **then** $\underline{r_2 := x})_{\text{ARM}}$

$\quad \sqsubseteq r_1 := y \overset{\text{ARM}}{;} (\!| r_1 = 1 |\!) \overset{\text{ARM}}{;} r_2 := x$ $\qquad$ Definition (9), (19)

$\quad \sqsubseteq r_1 := y \overset{\text{ARM}}{;} r_2 := x \cdot (\!| r_1 = 1 |\!)$ $\qquad$ by (23) from G (Model 4)

$\quad \sqsubseteq r_2 := x \cdot r_1 := y \cdot (\!| r_1 = 1 |\!)$ $\qquad$ by (23) from G (Model 4)

---

[8] Arm's **LDAPR** explicitly weakens the ordering between release/acquire instructions, which can be handled by distinguishing annotations syntactically rather than within the memory model definition.

The load of x (underlined) may be reordered before the branch point, and subsequently before the load of y. Now, even with the stores to x and y being strictly ordered in MP_w, we can straightforwardly find an interleaving satisfying: $\{x = y = 0\}\, r_2 := x \cdot x := 1 \cdot y := 1 \cdot r_1 := y \cdot (\!| r_1 = 1 |\!) \, \{r_1 = 1 \wedge r_2 = 0\}$. This post-state implies $\neg(r_1 = 1 \Rightarrow r_2 = 1)$, and we complete the proof by (29).   □

Placing an isb instruction inside the branch, before the second load, however, prevents this (possibly unexpected) behaviour.

Conformance. We validate our model using litmus tests [8,51]. Arm has released an official axiomatic model using the herd tool [9] available online via the herd-tools7 application [25] (see [10], Sect. B2.3). Using the diy7 tool and the official model [4] we generated a set of 99,881 litmus tests covering forbidden behaviours of up to 4 processes using the instruction types covered in Model 9. In addition we used a further 5757 litmus tests covering allowed and forbidden behaviours using the tests for an earlier version of Arm [9] and a set covering more recent features [50]. We ran these tests using the model checking tool based on the semantics; in each case (approximately 105,000 tests) Model 9 agreed with the published model.

4.4 RISC-V

The RISC-V memory model [11,62] is influenced by Arm's weak ordering on loads and stores (corresponding to G), but has release consistency annotations using the weaker RC_{pc} (Model 7) rather than the stronger RC_{sc} (Model 8). It also defines six different types of artificial barriers (more are technically possible but their use is not recommended [11]): a full fence given by fence rw, rw $\hat{=}$ **fence**; a store fence given by fence w, w $\hat{=}$ **barrier**(ww) (identical to Arm's dsb.st); a corresponding load fence fence r, r; two new types fence rw, w and fence r, rw described below; and a barrier used to mimic TSO's in-built weakening where loads can come before stores, which we define as fence.tso $\hat{=}$ fence r, rw $\overset{\text{R-V}}{;}$ fence rw, w. Additionally RISC-V has a barrier fence.i which has a technical specification beyond what is considered here, and so it is defined as a no-op (τ).

Model 10 (RISC-V). $\alpha \overset{\text{R-V}}{\Longleftarrow} \beta$ *if* $\alpha \overset{\text{RC}_{pc}}{\Longleftarrow} \beta$, *except:*

(i) $\alpha \overset{\text{R-V}}{\nLeftarrow}$ fence r, r $\overset{\text{R-V}}{\nLeftarrow} \alpha$ *if* ld(α), *(ii)* $\alpha \overset{\text{R-V}}{\nLeftarrow}$ fence rw, w $\overset{\text{R-V}}{\Longleftarrow} \beta$ *if* ld(β), *(iii)* $\alpha \overset{\text{R-V}}{\Longleftarrow}$ fence r, rw $\overset{\text{R-V}}{\nLeftarrow} \beta$ *if* str(α), *and* *(iv)* $(\!| b |\!) \overset{\text{R-V}}{\nLeftarrow} \alpha$ *if* str(α).

RISC-V's load fence, fence r, r, restricts ordering with loads, and is the straightforward dual of Arm's store fence (dsb.st, Model 9). RISC-V's fence rw, w barrier is intended to maintain order between loads and stores and later stores only, allowing later loads to potentially come earlier; it therefore allows reordering of loads, but blocks everything else. Similarly the fence r, rw barrier ensures order between loads and later loads and stores, and hence can 'jump' over stores but is blocked by loads, which therefore are strictly ordered with later loads and stores. Like Arm, RISC-V prevents stores from taking effect before branches are resolved (see [62] [Rule 11, A.3.8]).

Conformance. We tested our model against the litmus tests outlined in the RISC-V manual [62] and made available online with expected results [29]. Restricting attention to those tests involving instructions we consider in Model 10 (and Model 7) our tests agree with the official model in all 3937 cases, covering the RC_{pc} behaviours and the six barrier types defined above, with G (Model 4) controlling interactions between stores and loads.

5   Related Work

There has been significant work in defining the semantics of processor-level instruction reordering since the 1980s [27,30,37,45,65] and more recently under the umbrella of weak memory models [14,15,17,18,24,26,35,36,39,42,61]. To the best of our knowledge we are the first to encode the basis for instruction reordering as a parameter to the language, rather than as a parameter to the semantics. The resulting framework has two main advantages over existing frameworks: i) by focussing on instruction reordering, which is based on the actual operation of processor pipelines, our *specifications* of hardware weak memory models are relatively simple (Sect. 4), with common aspects extracted (Sect. 2); and ii) we allow compositional reasoning, including structural reduction rules that admit existing techniques for analysing programs. In the literature weak memory model specifications are often described via properties of the global system, e.g., the axiomatic style [5,6,9,48,66,71] for which specifications are relatively straightforward for the cases considered in this paper ([21] includes a detailed comparison), but that style does not easily admit compositional reasoning/reduction techniques. Another common approach to formalisation is with a semantics that is closer to the behaviour of a real microarchitecture, e.g., [28,58,63] (a direct semantic comparison to the operational model of [64] is contained in [21]), but the specifications are therefore specific to a processor and implementation, and proving properties of the system is similarly less abstract (but clearly that style is suitable for model checking, e.g., [1,2,7,13,41]). The "PipeCheck" framework [47,49,70] is designed to validate that processors faithfully implement their intended memory model, using a detailed pipeline semantics based on an axiomatic specification; potentially our framework could be applicable as it mimics in-pipeline reordering (see [21]). The Promising semantics [38,46,59] is operational and can be instantiated with different memory models (including software memory models), where (as with the axiomatic approach) weak behaviours are captured via properties of global traces recorded in abstract global data structures. A proof system for that framework introduces custom assertion language for reasoning with those data structures [43].

This paper supersedes [22], which defines only a simple prefixing command for actions (a special case of parallelized sequential composition). That paper does not consider a general theory for memory models (Sect. 2), and does not address TSO, Release Consistency, or RISC-V (but does consider POWER), and showed conformance for Arm against an older version without release/acquire atomics, against a much smaller set of litmus tests (approximately 400 vs over 100,000 in this paper). That theory is not machine-checked, contains only a few simple refinement rules, and does not employ OG reasoning. The paper does, however, include a simple extension of the language to allow composite atomic actions (such as compare-and-swap), and gives a global data structure corresponding to POWER's cache coherence system to handle the lack of multicopy atomicity in that model; both extensions are compatible with the framework in this paper.

Our operational approach based on out-of-order instruction execution follows work such as Arvind et al. [12], and the development of the Release Consistency and related models [31]. Our parallelized sequential composition is operationally similar to "weak sequential composition" [60], developed for a different domain. The algebraic approach we adopt to reducing programs is similar in style to the Concurrent Kleene Algebra [34], where sequential and parallel composition contribute to the event ordering.

6   Conclusion

In this paper we have formalised instruction-level parallelism (ILP), a feature of processors since the 1960s, and a major factor in the weak behaviours associated with modern memory consistency models. We showed how modern memory models build on generic properties of instruction reordering (EFF, G_0, G) that preserve sequential semantics using simple syntactic tests. We defined a program operator (parallelized sequential composition) which supports compositional reasoning about behaviours over the structure of parallel processes, and generalises sequential (SC) and parallel (PAR) composition. We empirically validated the models for large sets of litmus tests for Arm and RISC-V, and showed how stereotypical results emerge across a range of models, for instance, the "store buffer" pattern of TSO where loads can come before stores, the "message passing" paradigm from release consistency using release/acquire flags to control interprocess communication, and load speculation from Arm. We developed a model checker based on the semantics in Maude [20] and machine-checked the theory in Isabelle [54].

The semantics of the IMP+pseq language is relatively straightforward, being a trace-based imperative semantics, extended by a single rule to allow reordering. This operational concept chimes with how reordering arises in real processors, i.e., out-of-order execution within the pipeline. Reordering is controlled via a pair-wise specification on atomic instructions, which is also relatively straightforward to specify, being based on concepts from sequential semantics with the addition of barriers, and some extra rules around branches to control speculative execution. In comparison, many existing formal frameworks for weak memory models have quite complex operational semantics which use global properties of traces or architecture-specific features to capture nondeterminism due to reorderings. This complexity carries over into the associated reasoning frameworks. Because we let the nondeterminism be represented in the program text itself, our framework admits the application of existing techniques for reasoning about programs. This is evident in the examples we give, which involve direct manipulation of the program to elucidate the absence of presence of reordering.

Of course reasoning about specific code may still be quite complex, but this will be due to the properties of code and model in question, not the underlying semantic framework.

As future work we intend to extend the semantics to cover other features of modern processors that contribute to their memory models, for instance, POWER's cache system that lacks multicopy atomicity, TSO's global locks, and Arm's global monitor for controlling load-linked/store-conditional instructions. As these features are global they cannot be captured directly as behaviours of per-processor pipelines [44]. Ongoing work includes extending the framework with microarchitectural features for reasoning about security vulnerabilities [23] and investigating the interaction of language-level weak memory models, such as those of C and Java, with underlying hardware weak memory models. Since the C11 model builds on the Release Consistency model (Sect. 4.2), has special barrier types, and atomic actions corresponding to stores and loads, we have a firm basis for reasoning about the behaviours of compiler translations and optimisations for specific hardware.

Acknowledgements. We thank Graeme Smith, Kirsten Winter, Nicholas Coughlin and Ian Hayes for feedback on this work, and anonymous reviewers of earlier versions. We also thank Luc Maranget, Jade Alglave, and Christopher Pulte for assistance with litmus test analysis.

References

1. Abd Alrahman, Y., Andric, M., Beggiato, A., Lafuente, A.L.: Can we efficiently check concurrent programs under relaxed memory models in Maude? In: Escobar, S. (ed.) WRLA 2014. LNCS, vol. 8663, pp. 21–41. Springer, Cham (2014). https://doi.org/10.1007/978-3-319-12904-4_2

2. Abdulla, P.A., Arora, J., Atig, M.F., Krishna, S.: Verification of programs under the release-acquire semantics. In: PLDI 2019, pp. 1117–1132. Association for Computing Machinery (2019)

3. Adve, S.V., Gharachorloo, K.: Shared memory consistency models: a tutorial. Computer **29**(12), 66–76 (1996)

4. Alglave, J.: How to generate litmus tests automatically with the diy7 tool, 2020. Accessed June 2020. https://community.arm.com/developer/ip-products/processors/b/processors-ip-blog/posts/generate-litmus-tests-automatically-diy7-tool

5. Alglave, J., Cousot, P., Maranget, L.: Syntax and semantics of the weak consistency model specification language cat. CoRR, abs/1608.07531 (2016)

6. Alglave, J., Deacon, W., Grisenthwaite, R., Hacquard, A., Maranget, L.: Armed cats: formal concurrency modelling at Arm. ACM Trans. Program. Lang. Syst. **43**(2), 1–54 (2021)

7. Alglave, J., Kroening, D., Nimal, V., Tautschnig, M.: Software verification for weak memory via program transformation. In: Felleisen, M., Gardner, P. (eds.) ESOP 2013. LNCS, vol. 7792, pp. 512–532. Springer, Heidelberg (2013). https://doi.org/10.1007/978-3-642-37036-6_28

8. Alglave, J., Maranget, L., Sarkar, S., Sewell, P.: Litmus: running tests against hardware. In: Abdulla, P.A., Leino, K.R.M. (eds.) TACAS 2011. LNCS, vol. 6605, pp. 41–44. Springer, Heidelberg (2011). https://doi.org/10.1007/978-3-642-19835-9_5
9. Alglave, J., Maranget, L., Tautschnig, M.: Herding cats: modelling, simulation, testing, and data mining for weak memory. ACM Trans. Program. Lang. Syst. 36(2), 7:1–7:74 (2014)
10. Arm Ltd.: Arm® Architecture Reference Manual, for the Armv8-A architecture profile (2020)
11. Armstrong, A., et al.: ISA semantics for ARMv8-a, RISC-V, and CHERI-MIPS. Proc. ACM Program. Lang. 3(POPL) (2019)
12. Arvind, A., Maessen, J.-W.: Memory model = instruction reordering + store atomicity. In: Proceedings of the 33rd Annual International Symposium on Computer Architecture, ISCA 2006, USA, pp. 29–40. IEEE Computer Society (2006)
13. Atig, M.F., Bouajjani, A., Burckhardt, S., Musuvathi, M.: On the verification problem for weak memory models. In: POPL 2010, pp. 7–18. ACM (2010)
14. Atig, M.F., Bouajjani, A., Burckhardt, S., Musuvathi, M.: What's decidable about weak memory models? In: Seidl, H. (ed.) ESOP 2012. LNCS, vol. 7211, pp. 26–46. Springer, Heidelberg (2012). https://doi.org/10.1007/978-3-642-28869-2_2
15. Batty, M., Memarian, K., Nienhuis, K., Pichon-Pharabod, J., Sewell, P.: The problem of programming language concurrency semantics. In: Vitek, J. (ed.) ESOP 2015. LNCS, vol. 9032, pp. 283–307. Springer, Heidelberg (2015). https://doi.org/10.1007/978-3-662-46669-8_12
16. Boehm, H.-J., Adve, S.V.: Foundations of the C++ concurrency memory model. In: PLDI 2008, pp. 68–78. ACM (2008)
17. Boudol, G., Petri, G.: Relaxed memory models: an operational approach. In: POPL 2009, pp. 392–403. Association for Computing Machinery (2009)
18. Boudol, G., Petri, G., Serpette, B.: Relaxed operational semantics of concurrent programming languages. EPTCS 89, 19–33 (2012)
19. Brookes, S.: A semantics for concurrent separation logic. Theoret. Comput. Sci. 375(1–3), 227–270 (2007)
20. Clavel, M., et al.: Maude: specification and programming in rewriting logic. Theoret. Comput. Sci. 285(2), 187–243 (2002)
21. Colvin, R.J.: Parallelized sequential composition, pipelines, and hardware weak memory models. CoRR, abs/2105.02444 (2021)
22. Colvin, R.J., Smith, G.: A wide-spectrum language for verification of programs on weak memory models. In: Havelund, K., Peleska, J., Roscoe, B., de Vink, E. (eds.) FM 2018. LNCS, vol. 10951, pp. 240–257. Springer, Cham (2018). https://doi.org/10.1007/978-3-319-95582-7_14
23. Colvin, R.J., Winter, K.: An abstract semantics of speculative execution for reasoning about security vulnerabilities. In: Sekerinski, E., et al. (eds.) FM 2019. LNCS, vol. 12233, pp. 323–341. Springer, Cham (2020). https://doi.org/10.1007/978-3-030-54997-8_21
24. Crary, K., Sullivan, M.J.: A calculus for relaxed memory. In: POPL 2015, pp. 623–636. ACM (2015)
25. Deacon, W., Alglave, J.: The herd ARMv8 model (2016). Accessed June 2020. https://github.com/herd/herdtools7/blob/master/herd/libdir/aarch64.cat
26. Doherty, S., Dongol, B., Wehrheim, H., Derrick, J.: Verifying C11 programs operationally. In: PPoPP 2019, pp. 355–365. ACM (2019)
27. Dubois, M., Scheurich, C., Briggs, F.: Memory access buffering in multiprocessors. In: Proceedings of the 13th Annual International Symposium on Computer Architecture, ISCA 1986, pp. 434–442. IEEE Computer Society Press (1986)

28. Flur, S., et al.: Modelling the ARMv8 architecture, operationally: concurrency and ISA. In: POPL 2016, pp. 608–621. ACM, New York (2016)
29. Flur, S., Maranget, L.: RISC-V architecture concurrency model litmus tests (2019). Accessed June 2020. https://github.com/litmus-tests/litmus-tests-riscv
30. Fox, A.C.J., Harman, N.A.: Algebraic models of correctness for microprocessors. Formal Aspects Comput. **12**(4), 298–312 (2000)
31. Gharachorloo, K., Lenoski, D., Laudon, J., Gibbons, P., Gupta, A., Hennessy, J.: Memory consistency and event ordering in scalable shared-memory multiprocessors. In: ISCA 1990, pp. 15–26. ACM (1990)
32. Hoare, C.A.R.: Towards a theory of parallel programming. In: Operating System Techniques, pp. 61–71. Academic Press (1972). Proceedings of Seminar at Queen's University, Belfast, Northern Ireland, August-September 1971
33. Hoare, C.A.R.: Some properties of predicate transformers. J. ACM **25**(3), 461–480 (1978)
34. Hoare, C.A.R.T., Möller, B., Struth, G., Wehrman, I.: Concurrent Kleene algebra. In: Bravetti, M., Zavattaro, G. (eds.) CONCUR 2009. LNCS, vol. 5710, pp. 399–414. Springer, Heidelberg (2009). https://doi.org/10.1007/978-3-642-04081-8_27
35. Hou, Z., Sanan, D., Tiu, A., Liu, Y., Hoa, K.C.: An executable formalisation of the SPARCv8 instruction set architecture: a case study for the LEON3 processor. In: Fitzgerald, J., Heitmeyer, C., Gnesi, S., Philippou, A. (eds.) FM 2016. LNCS, vol. 9995, pp. 388–405. Springer, Cham (2016). https://doi.org/10.1007/978-3-319-48989-6_24
36. Jagadeesan, R., Petri, G., Riely, J.: Brookes is relaxed, almost! In: Birkedal, L. (ed.) FoSSaCS 2012. LNCS, vol. 7213, pp. 180–194. Springer, Heidelberg (2012). https://doi.org/10.1007/978-3-642-28729-9_12
37. Jones, R.B., Skakkebæk, J.U., Dill, D.L.: Reducing manual abstraction in formal verification of out- of- order execution. In: Gopalakrishnan, G., Windley, P. (eds.) FMCAD 1998. LNCS, vol. 1522, pp. 2–17. Springer, Heidelberg (1998). https://doi.org/10.1007/3-540-49519-3_2
38. Kang, J., Hur, C.-K., Lahav, O., Vafeiadis, V., Dreyer, D.: A promising semantics for relaxed-memory concurrency. In: POPL 2017, pp. 175–189. ACM (2017)
39. Kavanagh, R., Brookes, S.: A denotational semantics for SPARC TSO. Electron. Notes Theor. Comput. Sci. **336**, 223–239 (2018)
40. Kocher, P., et al.: Spectre attacks: exploiting speculative execution. In: Security and Privacy, pp. 1–19. IEEE (2019)
41. Kokologiannakis, M., Vafeiadis, V.: HMC: model checking for hardware memory models. In: ASPLOS 2020, pp. 1157–1171. ACM (2020)
42. Lahav, O., Giannarakis, N., Vafeiadis, V.: Taming release-acquire consistency. In: POPL 2016, pp. 649–662. Association for Computing Machinery (2016)
43. Lahav, O., Vafeiadis, V.: Owicki-Gries reasoning for weak memory models. In: Halldórsson, M.M., Iwama, K., Kobayashi, N., Speckmann, B. (eds.) ICALP 2015. LNCS, vol. 9135, pp. 311–323. Springer, Heidelberg (2015). https://doi.org/10.1007/978-3-662-47666-6_25
44. Lahav, O., Vafeiadis, V.: Explaining relaxed memory models with program transformations. In: Fitzgerald, J., Heitmeyer, C., Gnesi, S., Philippou, A. (eds.) FM 2016. LNCS, vol. 9995, pp. 479–495. Springer, Cham (2016). https://doi.org/10.1007/978-3-319-48989-6_29
45. Lamport, L.: How to make a multiprocessor computer that correctly executes multiprocess programs. IEEE Trans. Comput. **28**(9), 690–691 (1979)
46. Lee, S.-H., et al.: Promising 2.0: global optimizations in relaxed memory concurrency. In: PLDI 2020, pp. 362–376. Association for Computing Machinery (2020)

47. Lustig, D., Pellauer, M., Martonosi, M.: PipeCheck: specifying and verifying microarchitectural enforcement of memory consistency models. In: 47th Annual IEEE/ACM International Symposium on Microarchitecture, pp. 635–646 (2014)

48. Mador-Haim, S., et al.: An axiomatic memory model for POWER multiprocessors. In: Madhusudan, P., Seshia, S.A. (eds.) CAV 2012. LNCS, vol. 7358, pp. 495–512. Springer, Heidelberg (2012). https://doi.org/10.1007/978-3-642-31424-7_36

49. Manerkar, Y.A., Lustig, D., Martonosi, M., Gupta, A.: PipeProof: automated memory consistency proofs for microarchitectural specifications. In: 51st Annual IEEE/ACM International Symposium on Microarchitecture, pp. 788–801 (2018)

50. Maranget, L.: AArch64 model vs. hardware. Accessed Jan 2020. http://moscova.inria.fr/~maranget/cats7/model-aarch64/

51. Maranget, L., Sarkar, S., Sewell, P.: A tutorial introduction to the ARM and POWER relaxed memory models (2012)

52. Milner, R.: A Calculus of Communicating Systems. Springer, Heidelberg (1982). https://doi.org/10.1007/3-540-10235-3

53. Morgan, C.: Of wp and CSP. In: Feijen, W.H.J., van Gasteren, A.J.M., Gries, D., Misra, J. (eds.) Beauty Is Our Business: A Birthday Salute to Edsger W. Dijkstra, pp. 319–326. Springer, New York (1990). https://doi.org/10.1007/978-1-4612-4476-9_37

54. Nipkow, T., Wenzel, M., Paulson, L.C. (eds.): Isabelle/HOL. LNCS, vol. 2283. Springer, Heidelberg (2002). https://doi.org/10.1007/3-540-45949-9

55. O'Hearn, P.W.: Incorrectness logic. Proc. ACM Program. Lang. 4(POPL) (2019)

56. Owicki, S., Gries, D.: An axiomatic proof technique for parallel programs I. Acta Inf. 6(4), 319–340 (1976)

57. Plotkin, G.D.: A structural approach to operational semantics. J. Log. Algebr. Program. 60–61, 17–139 (2004)

58. Pulte, C., Flur, S., Deacon, W., French, J., Sarkar, S., Sewell, P.: Simplifying ARM concurrency: multicopy-atomic axiomatic and operational models for ARMv8. Proc. ACM Program. Lang. 2(POPL) (2017)

59. Pulte, C., Pichon-Pharabod, J., Kang, J., Lee, S.-H., Hur, C.-K.: Promising-ARM/RISC-V: a simpler and faster operational concurrency model. In: PLDI 2019, pp. 1–15. ACM (2019)

60. Rensink, A., Wehrheim, H.: Weak sequential composition in process algebras. In: Jonsson, B., Parrow, J. (eds.) CONCUR 1994. LNCS, vol. 836, pp. 226–241. Springer, Heidelberg (1994). https://doi.org/10.1007/978-3-540-48654-1_20

61. Ridge, T.: A rely-guarantee proof system for x86-TSO. In: Leavens, G.T., O'Hearn, P., Rajamani, S.K. (eds.) VSTTE 2010. LNCS, vol. 6217, pp. 55–70. Springer, Heidelberg (2010). https://doi.org/10.1007/978-3-642-15057-9_4

62. RISC-V International. The RISC-V Instruction Set Manual. Volume I: User-Level ISA; Volume II: Privileged Architecture (2017)

63. Sarkar, S., Sewell, P., Alglave, J., Maranget, L., Williams, D.: Understanding POWER multiprocessors. SIGPLAN Not. 46(6), 175–186 (2011)

64. Sewell, P., Sarkar, S., Owens, S., Nardelli, F.Z., Myreen, M.O.: x86-TSO: a rigorous and usable programmer's model for x86 multiprocessors. Commun. ACM 53(7), 89–97 (2010)

65. Shasha, D., Snir, M.: Efficient and correct execution of parallel programs that share memory. ACM Trans. Program. Lang. Syst. 10(2), 282–312 (1988)

66. Steinke, R.C., Nutt, G.J.: A unified theory of shared memory consistency. J. ACM 51(5), 800–849 (2004)

67. Thornton, J.E.: Parallel operation in the control data 6600. In: Proceedings of the October 27–29, 1964, Fall Joint Computer Conference, Part II: Very High Speed Computer Systems, AFIPS 1964, pp. 33–40. ACM (1964)
68. Tomasulo, R.M.: An efficient algorithm for exploiting multiple arithmetic units. IBM J. Res. Dev. **11**(1), 25–33 (1967)
69. Travkin, O., Wehrheim, H.: Verification of concurrent programs on weak memory models. In: Sampaio, A., Wang, F. (eds.) ICTAC 2016. LNCS, vol. 9965, pp. 3–24. Springer, Cham (2016). https://doi.org/10.1007/978-3-319-46750-4_1
70. Trippel, C., Lustig, D., Martonosi, M.: Security verification via automatic hardware-aware exploit synthesis: the CheckMate approach. IEEE Micro **39**(3), 84–93 (2019)
71. Wickerson, J., Batty, M., Sorensen, T., Constantinides, G.A.: Automatically comparing memory consistency models. SIGPLAN Not. **52**(1), 190–204 (2017)
72. Winter, K., Zhang, C., Hayes, I.J., Keynes, N., Cifuentes, C., Li, L.: Path-sensitive data flow analysis simplified. In: Groves, L., Sun, J. (eds.) ICFEM 2013. LNCS, vol. 8144, pp. 415–430. Springer, Heidelberg (2013). https://doi.org/10.1007/978-3-642-41202-8_27

Checking Opacity and Durable Opacity with FDR

Brijesh Dongol[(✉)] and Jay Le-Papin

University of Surrey, Guildford, UK
{b.dongol,jay.le-papin}@surrey.ac.uk

Abstract. Software transactional memory (STMs) is a software-enabled form of transactional memory, typically implemented as a language library, that provides fine-grained concurrency control on behalf of a programmer. STM algorithms have been recently adapted to cope with non-volatile memory (NVM), aka persistent memory, which is a new paradigm for memory that preserves its contents even after power loss. This paper presents a model checking approach to validating correctness of STM algorithms using FDR (a model checker for CSP specifications). Our proofs are based on operational transactional memory specifications that allow proofs of (durable) opacity, the main safety property for STMs under volatile and persistent memory, to be verified by refinement. Since FDR enables automatic proofs of refinement, we obtain an automatic technique for checking both opacity and durable opacity of bounded models of STM algorithms.

1 Introduction

Transactional Memory (TM) [21] provides programmers with an easy-to-use synchronisation mechanism for concurrent access to shared data, whereby blocks of code may be treated as *transactions* that execute with an illusion of atomicity. A transaction may complete by *committing* (all of its operations appear to take place atomically) or *aborting* (none of its operations take effect).

Software Transactional Memory (STM) implements TM in software, allowing programmers to use TM without relying on dedicated hardware. STMs have been widely studied and a variety of implementations have been proposed for a variety of applications and workload scenarios [18,20]. STMs have also been adapted to a range of memory architectures. A recent iteration is the adaptation of STMs to *non-volatile memory* (NVM) (aka *persistent memory*) architectures [36,37]. Unlike conventional memory, the contents of NVMs are persistent across a system crash (e.g., a power failure), allowing the system state to be *recovered* from NVM instead of restarting from disk. However, due to differences in speed, NVMs are updated at a different rate, i.e., less frequently than volatile memory, and

---

Dongol is supported by VeTSS project "Persistent Safety and Security" and EPSRC grants EP/R019045/2, EP/R032556/1 and EP/V038915/1.

R. Calinescu and C. S. Păsăreanu (Eds.): SEFM 2021, LNCS 13085, pp. 222–242, 2021.
https://doi.org/10.1007/978-3-030-92124-8_13

hence implementations must carefully manage synchronisation between volatile and non-volatile memory.

A widely accepted correctness condition for TM is *opacity* [17,18], which requires all transactions, including aborting transactions, to agree on a single sequential global ordering of transactions. Moreover, no transactional read can return a value that is inconsistent with the global ordering of committed transactions. In the presence of NVM, transactions must additionally ensure consistency across crashes. TM here (aka durable TM) is designed to satisfy a recently defined correctness condition called *durable opacity* [6].

Algorithms implementing STMs are sophisticated—for efficiency they implement fine-grained concurrency control, local read/write sets, etc. Under NVM architectures, the algorithms additionally require redo/undo logs and explicit programmer-controlled FLUSH instructions that synchronise contents between volatile and persistent memory. Because STMs are typically used as a concurrency abstraction mechanism within programming language libraries [18,20,37], proving correctness of the underlying STM algorithms is an important problem.

A number of papers have addressed full verification of several STMs [1,2,9,11, 13,27,28,38] and durable STMs [5,6] by proving *refinement* between the implementation and a TM specification called TMS2 [14] (in settings without NVM) and DTMS2 [6] (in settings with NVM). Both TMS2 and DTMS2 are abstract operational specifications whose traces are guaranteed to be opaque [29] and durably opaque [14], respectively. Thus, any refinement of TMS2 and DTMS2 is also guaranteed to be opaque and durably opaque. The aforementioned verification methods have been shown to apply to a large number of sophisticated implementations and have been mechanised using a variety of theorem provers (Isabelle, PVS, KIV). These proofs are parametric, and hence, apply to an arbitrary number of transactions, performing an arbitrary number of operations over a arbitrary data values. Unfortunately, such proofs are also time consuming as they require a large amount of manual input, including the manual generation and verification of the necessary invariants and simulation relations.

FDR [16] is a model checker for CSP [23,35] and provides support for automatic refinement checking for bounded models. Recently, Lowe [32] has demonstrated the use of FDR to automatically check *linearizability* [22] of concurrent data structures. We adapt Lowe's approach and develop methods for proving (durable) opacity of STMs using FDR. This is done by encoding an abstract specification of an STM (such as TMS2) and an STM implementation (such as TML) as bounded models in FDR, then using FDR's automatic refinement checking to show that the model implementation is a refinement of the model specification. Although the models verified are bounded (w.r.t. number of threads, size of data structure, etc.), the fully automatic nature of the proofs means that the checks can be valuable in validating designs prior to performing a full proof of correctness.

The paper comprises the following contributions: **(1)** We demonstrate how the abstract TMS2 [14] and DTMS2 [6] specifications can be encoded in FDR. Since TMS2 and DTMS2 are abstractions of many different TM implementations, our encodings can be reused across proofs of other algorithms. (2) We show that it is feasible to check both opacity and durable opacity using FDR. Despite the many years of research into correctness of TM, there is surprisingly little work on actual results on model checking STMs. Ours is the first set of results on model checking durable opacity thereby extending model checking of STMs to NVM architectures. (3) We evaluate the effectiveness of FDR as a tool for refinement checking by providing benchmarks against durable and standard versions of known algorithms.

```
Init. glb = 0, log := ∅

TMBegin:
B1 do loc := glb
B2 until even(loc);
     return ok;

TMRead(addr):
R1 val := *addr;
R2 if (glb = loc) then
       return val;
     else return abort;

Recover:
C1 while ¬ log.isEmpty()
C2   SOME (addr, val).
       (addr, val) ∈ log;
C3   *addr := val ;
C4   FLUSH(addr) ;
C5   log.pdelete((addr, val));
C6 glb := 0
```

```
TMCommit:
E1 if odd(loc) then
E2   log.pempty();
E3   glb := loc + 1;
     return commit;

TMWrite(addr,val):
W1 if even(loc) then
W2   if ¬ cas(glb, loc, loc + 1) then
         return abort;
W3   else loc++;
W4 if ∀ v. (addr, v) ∉ log then
W5   log.pinsert((addr, *addr));
W6 *addr := val;
W7 FLUSH(addr);
     return ok;
```

Fig. 1. A transactional mutex lock (D)TML. Line numbers for **return** statements are omitted. Code in purple must be added to ensure durability. (Color figure online)

2   Example: (Durable) Transactional Mutex Lock

Figure 1 presents TML [7] and DTML [6], which are examples of an opaque and a durably opaque STM algorithm, respectively. TML is assumed to be executed in an architecture without crashes, whereas DTML is assumed to execute under NVM. Thus, DTML extends TML with additional instructions (shown in purple) designed to cope with crashes as well as a recovery operation.

TML. TML adopts a strict policy for transactional synchronisation: as soon as one transaction has successfully written to a variable, all other transactions running concurrently will be aborted when they invoke another read or write operation. To enforce this policy, TML uses a global counter glb (initially 0) and local variable loc, which is used to store a copy of glb. Variable glb records whether there is a *live writing transaction*, i.e., a transaction that has started, has not yet ended nor aborted, and has executed (or is executing) a write operation. More precisely, `glb` is odd if there is a live writing transaction, and even otherwise. Initially, we have no live writing transactions and thus `glb` is 0 (and hence even). The algorithm for TML is the algorithm in Fig. 1 with the code in purple removed.

Operation `TMBegin` copies the value of `glb` into its local variable `loc` and checks whether `glb` is even. If so, the transaction is started; otherwise, the process attempts to start again by rereading `glb`. A `TMRead` operation succeeds as long as `glb` equals `loc` (meaning no writes have occurred since the transaction began), otherwise it aborts the current transaction. The first execution of `TMWrite` attempts to increment `glb` using a `cas` (compare-and-swap), which atomically compares the first and second parameters, and sets the first parameter to the third if the comparison succeeds. If the `cas` attempt fails, a write by another transaction must have occured, and hence, the current transaction aborts. Otherwise `loc` is incremented (making its value odd) and the write is performed. Note that because `loc` becomes odd after the first successful write, all successive writes that are part of the same transaction will perform the write directly after testing `loc` at line W1. Further note that if the `cas` succeeds, `glb` becomes odd, which prevents other transactions from starting, and causes all concurrent live transactions still wanting to read or write to abort. Thus a writing transaction that successfully updates `glb` effectively locks shared memory. Operation `TMCommit` checks to see if a write has occurred by testing whether `loc` is odd. If the test succeeds, `glb` is set to `loc + 1`.

DTML. The algorithm for DTML is the algorithm in Fig. 1 including the code in purple, which has been introduced to manage synchronisation between volatile and persistent memory. DTML introduces `FLUSH` instructions (where `FLUSH x` copies the contents of `x` from volatile to persistent memory) and a persistent log, `log` (which we explain below). After a crash we assume that all contents of persistent memory are copied into volatile memory, and that the `Recover()` operation is executed immediately afterwards, prior to executing any new transactions.

A distinguishing feature of TML is that it performs writes in an *eager* manner, i.e., it updates shared memory during the write operation[1]. This is potentially problematic in an NVM context since writes that have completed may not be committed if a crash occurs prior to executing the commit operation. That is, writes of uncommitted transactions should not be seen by any transactions that start after a crash occurs. DTML makes use of an *undo log* mapping addresses to their persistent memory values prior to executing the first write operation for that address. Logged values are made persistent before the address is overwritten. Thus, if a crash occurs prior to a transaction committing, the transaction can be recovered to a safe state by undoing uncommitted transactional writes.

As discussed above, DTML uses a `log`, which we assume is *durably linearizable* [10, 25]. Each operation of a durably linearizable object is guaranteed to take

---

[1] This is in contrast to lazy implementations that defer transactional writes until the commit operation is executed (e.g., [8, 12]).

effect in persistent memory prior to the operation returning, and thus can be assumed to be an *atomic durable operation* from the perspective of a user. There are many examples of durably linearizable logs, e.g., [39], and we do not consider their implementation in detail in this paper. In Fig. 1, we use `pinsert()`, `pempty()` and `pdelete()` to stress that these operations are durably linearizable.

3 Opacity and Durable Opacity

The formal definition of opacity has been extensively covered in the literature [2,3,9,13,29,30], while the formal definition of durable opacity may be found in [5,6]. In this paper we eschew these formalities in favour of conceptual descriptions, focussing instead on the operational TMS2 and DTMS2 specifications (see Sect. 4), which approximate (durable) opacity.

Both opacity and durable opacity are defined in terms of *histories* of externally visible events, which are external calls (invocations) and returns (responses) of STM operations. For example, in (D)TML, we have a pair of events for each of the operations `TMBegin`, `TMRead`, `TMWrite` and `TMCommit`, noting that an operation call may return with an abort.

A *concurrent history* comprises an interleaving of (external) events from the different operations executed by different transactions. Each history is assumed to be *well formed*, i.e., the history, when restricted to a single transaction starts with a `TMBegin`, possibly followed by a number of `TMRead` and `TMWrite` operations, possibly followed by a `TMCommit` operation. A transaction is complete in a history if it has responded with `TMCommit(ok)` or an `abort` event, and once completed, the transaction must not execute any further operations. However, a transaction within a history may not be complete, i.e., may be a *live* transaction.

Opacity is defined over concurrent histories, and builds on the notion of strict serialisability for database transactions. Like strict serialisability, it requires that all non-aborted complete transactions be ordered to form a sequential history that is valid w.r.t. a standard memory semantics. The reordering must respect real-time order, i.e., if transaction T_1 completes before another transaction T_2 begins, then the reordering must respect this order. Concurrent (i.e., overlapping) transactions may, however, be serialised in any order. Opacity additionally requires that aborted transactions fit within a serialised order such that the aborted transaction is valid w.r.t. the memory semantics until the aborted operation is executed. Finally, opacity requires that a live transaction behaves like an aborted transaction. That is, (1) a committed transaction must not read from the writes of a live transaction, and (2) live transactions must also be consistent with the serialisation order of committed transactions.

A *durable concurrent history* is a concurrent history interleaved with `crash` events. A durable concurrent history is *well formed* iff the history with *crash* events removed is well formed and, moreover, no transaction that started before the crash continues executing after the crash.

Durable opacity, defined over durable concurrent histories, simply requires that the given history is opaque after all crash events are removed. Note that this means that any live transactions before a crash are aborted, and the writes of any committed transactions are persisted, i.e., are not lost after crash.

Example 1. An example of a durably opaque history is given below, where we elide the invocations and response events and the begin/commit operations, focussing instead on the allowable order of the transactions 1–9. We use $R_i\, x\, v$ to denote a completed read operation by transaction T_i on variable x returning value v. Similarly $W_i\, x\, v$. We use $R_i\, x\_$ to denote a read operation that has been invoked but not returned. All transactions except for transactions 4 and 5 are committed. Transaction 4 is a live transaction that is interrupted by a system crash, and transaction 5 is an aborted complete transaction.

Our task in showing that the history is durably opaque is to remove the crash events, and showing that the remaining history is opaque. Here, we must find a total order among *all* (including live and aborted) transactions so that the values returned by the reads are consistent with the memory semantics w.r.t. the committed transactions. This total order must respect the real-time order of transactions, e.g., T_1 and T_2 may not be reordered. Assuming all variables are initialised to 0, an ordering that satisfies these constraints is: $T_5\, T_1\, T_3\, T_2\, T_4\, T_6\, T_7\, T_8$. Other orders are possible, however, for example, T_1 cannot occur before T_5 even though T_5 aborts (if it did, $R_5\, y\, 0$ would be inconsistent with the memory semantics).

4   Proving Opacity and Durable Opacity

We use the operational specification described by TMS2 and DTMS2 to model opacity and durable opacity, respectively. TMS2 and DTMS2 have already been shown to be opaque [29] and durably opaque [6], respectively. Thus, any refinement of these specifications is guaranteed to also be (durably) opaque.

Input/Output Automata. We present our operational specifications using Input/Output Automata (IOA) [33].

Definition 1. *An* Input/Output Automaton (IOA) *is a labeled transition system A with a set of* states *$states(A)$, a set of* actions *$acts(A)$, a set of* start states *$start(A) \subseteq states(A)$, and a* transition relation *$trans(A) \subseteq states(A) \times acts(A) \times states(A)$ (so that the actions label the transitions).*

The set $acts(A)$ is partitioned into input $input(A)$, output $output(A)$ and internal actions $internal(A)$. The internal actions represent events of the system that are not visible to the external environment. The input and output actions are externally visible, representing the automaton's interactions with its environment. Thus, we define the set of *external actions*, $external(A) = input(A) \cup output(A)$.

An *execution* of an IOA A is a sequence $\sigma = s_0 a_0 s_1 a_1 s_2 \ldots s_n a_n s_{n+1}$ of alternating states and actions, such that $s_0 \in start(A)$ and for all states s_i, $(s_i, a_i, s_{i+1}) \in trans(A)$. A *trace* of A is any sequence of (external) actions obtained by projecting the external actions of any execution of A. The set of traces of A, denoted $traces(A)$, represents A's externally visible behaviour. For automata C and A, we say that C is a *refinement* of A iff $traces(C) \subseteq traces(A)$. Later, we will see that this notion of trace refinement coincides with FDR.

External actions (Invoke/ response actions of TMRead, TMWrite *and* TMCommit *operations are omitted for space reasons, but are similar to the invoke/response of* TMBegin*)*

inv_t(TMBegin)
Pre: $pc_t = $ notStarted
Eff: $pc_t := $ beginPending
       $beginIdx_t := len(mems) - 1$

$resp_t$(TMBegin)
Pre: $pc_t = $ beginPending
Eff: $pc_t := $ ready

$resp_t$(Abort)
Pre: $pc_t \notin \{$notStarted, ready,
       commitResp, committed, aborted$\}$
Eff: $pc_t := $ aborted

crash
Pre: *true*
Eff: $pc := \lambda t : T.$
       if $pc_t \notin \{$notStarted, committed$\}$
       then aborted
       else pc_t
       $mems = \langle last(mems) \rangle$

Internal actions

DoCommitReadOnly$_t(n)$
Pre: $pc_t = $ doCommit
       $dom(wrSet_t) = \varnothing$
       $validIdx(t, n)$
Eff: $pc_t := $ commitResp

DoCommitWriter$_t$
Pre: $pc_t = $ doCommit
       $rdSet_t \subseteq last(mems)$
Eff: $pc_t := $ commitResp
       $mems :=$
         $mems \frown (last(mems) \oplus wrSet_t)$

DoRead$_t(l, n)$
Pre: $pc_t = $ doRead(l)
       $l \in dom(wrSet_t) \vee validIdx(t, n)$
Eff: if $l \in dom(wrSet_t)$ then
         $pc_t := $ readResp$(wrSet_t(l))$
       else $v := mems(n)(l)$
         $pc_t := $ readResp(v)
         $rdSet_t := rdSet_t \oplus \{l \rightarrow v\}$

DoWrite$_t(l, v)$
Pre: $pc_t = $ doWrite(l, v)
Eff: $pc_t := $ writeResp
       $wrSet_t := wrSet_t \oplus \{l \rightarrow v\}$

where $validIdx(t, n) \;\hat{=}\; beginIdx_t \leq n < len(mems) \wedge rdSet_t \subseteq mems(n)$

Fig. 2. The transition relation of TMS2 and DTMS2, which extends TMS2 with a crash event. $f \oplus g = \lambda k.$ if $k \in dom(g)$ then $g(k)$ else $f(k)$ denotes *functional override* of function f by function g.

TMS2 *and* DTMS2. Formally, TMS2 and DTMS2 are specified by an IOA (partially shown in Fig. 2).[2] We assume a set, L, of *locations* and a set, V, of *values*, and a mapping, $L \rightarrow V$, representing the memory store. Both TMS2 and DTMS2 keep track of a *sequence, mems* $\in seq(L \rightarrow V)$, of memory stores,

---

[2] The full model is given in Appendix A.

one for each committed writing transaction. This makes it simpler to determine whether reads are consistent with previously committed write operations. Each committing transaction containing at least one write adds a new memory version to the end of the memory sequence.

For each transaction t there is a program counter variable pc_t, which ranges over a set of *program counter values*, which are used to ensure that each transaction is well-formed, and to ensure that each transactional operation takes effect between its invocation and response. There is also a *begin index* variable $beginIdx_t \in \mathbb{N}$, that is set to the index of the most recent memory version when the transaction begins. This variable is used to ensure the real-time ordering property between transactions. Finally, there is a *read set*, $rdSet_t \in L \twoheadrightarrow V$, and a *write set*, $wrSet_t \in L \twoheadrightarrow V$, which record the values that the transaction has read and written during its execution, respectively.

The read set is used to determine whether the values that have been read by the transaction are consistent with the same version of memory (using *validIdx*). The write set, on the other hand, is required because writes are modelled using *deferred update* semantics: writes are recorded in the transaction's write set, but are not published to any shared state until the transaction commits.

DTMS2 extends TMS2 with a *crash* action, which models both a crash and a recovery. It sets the program counter of every live transaction to *aborted*, which prevents these transactions from performing any further actions after the crash. Note that since transaction identifiers are not reused, the program counters of completed transactions need not be set to any special value (e.g., *crashed*). After restarting, it must not be possible for any new transaction to interact with memory states prior to the crash. We therefore reset the memory sequence to be a singleton sequence containing the last memory state prior to the crash.

In TMS2, we make no distinction between volatile and non-volatile memory. Interestingly, from the point-of-view of the specification, since durable opacity ensures that transactions are only externally visible when they have persisted, the volatile memory state need not be modelled at the level of DTMS2 [6].

The following ensures that TMS2 and DTMS2 can be used as intermediate specifications for the proofs of opacity and durable opacity.

Theorem 1. (Soundness [6, 29]). *Each trace of TMS2 is opaque and each trace of DTMS2 is durably opaque.*

Corollary 1. *For any IOA A, (1) if A refines TMS2, then A is opaque, and (2) if A refines DTMS2, then A is durably opaque.*

5 CSP and FDR Models

In this section, we review CSP (Sect. 5.1) and provide some details of our FDR encoding. We discuss the models for opacity in detail, but note that similar principles apply to persistent memory and durable opacity (see [15]). Section 5.2 provides details of the basic setup and FDR model of the TMS2 shared memory, and Sect. 5.3 describes part of the encoding of TMS2 itself. Finally, Sect. 5.4 describes our encoding of the implementations.

5.1   Overview of CSP

As discussed above, FDR is a model checker for CSP [23,35]. A challenge in modelling arises from the fact that STM algorithms are *shared-memory* algorithms whereas CSP is a process algebra that is designed to model and reason about *communicating systems*. As such CSP has no notion of shared state; this must be modelled by special *processes* that respond to *atomic events* over *shared channels*.

This section provides a brief overview of the fragment of CSP [35] that we use, closely following the description by Lowe [32]. The first key component is a *channel*, which is declared, possibly over some number of values, using the keyword **channel**. For example, assuming types X and Y, the declaration **channel** c:X.Y denotes a set of events of the form c.x.y, where x ∈ X and y ∈ Y. Channels may take an input denoted by ?, and produce an output denoted by !, e.g., c?x!y represents an event on channel c with an input x and output y. Inputs and outputs may be freely combined for each value accepted by the channel.

The second key component is that of a *process*, which includes primitive processes such as SKIP (representing successful termination) and STOP (representing deadlock). Events and processes can be combined using a *prefix* operator: for an event c and process P, the notation c → P represents a process that offers the event c, and if c occurs behaves like P. Processes can also be combined using operators such as *external choice*, denoted $P \square Q$, which behaves as either process P or process Q with the choice made by the environment, and *interleaving parallel composition* $P \;|||\; Q$. These operators can be indexed, e.g., $\square\, x : X \bullet P(x)$ represents indexed external choice. Notation $b\&P$ denotes the guarded process **if** b **then** P **else** STOP that behaves like P provided b holds, otherwise it behaves as STOP.

The behaviours of processes can also be dictated by a set of events. For a set of events A, $P\backslash A$ represents P with the events from A hidden, and $P \,[\!|\, A \,|\!]\, Q$ executes P and Q in parallel and synchronises on events in A. Notation $\|x : X \bullet [A(x)]P(x)$ denotes replicated alphabetised parallel composition where each process $P(x)$ is given the alphabet $A(x)$. Finally, the notation $[\!|\, A \,|\!]\, x : X \bullet P(x)$ represents replicated generalised parallel, comprising the parallel composition of processes $P(x)$ that synchronise on events from A.

FDR is a typed language and supports types such as $(|\, X \Rightarrow Y \,|)$ defining a map type from type X to Y, and $<X>$ defining a list over X and (X, Y) defining a pair over X and Y.

A *trace* of a process is a sequence of visible events, and we say that P *refines* Q iff each trace of P is a possible trace of Q. This treatment coincides with the IOA definitions, and hence CSP is suited to verifying IOA refinement. Moreover, since FDR enables automatic checking of refinement, it provides us with ability to check (durable) opacity automatically. The challenge is to develop efficient representations of the different models, which we discuss in more detail in the following sections.

```
datatype TID = T0 | T1
datatype AddrType = M0 | M1 | MNull
Addr = diff(AddrType, {MNull})
datatype ValueType = D0 | D1 | DNull
Value = diff(ValueType, {DNull})
datatype TMEvent = Begin | Read | Write | Commit | Abort
TMInv = diff(TMEvent, {Abort})
TMResp = TMEvent
channel inv: TID . TMInv . AddrType . ValueType
channel resp: TID . TMResp . AddrType . ValueType
channel lock, unlock
```

Fig. 3. Basic setup

5.2 Setup and TMS2 Shared Memory

The basic setup, common across all models is given in Fig. 3. The datatypes TID, AddrType and ValueType describe the thread identifiers, memory addresses controlled by the TM, and the allowable data values at each memory address, respectively. We define channels inv and resp to record traces of the different models, as well as channels lock and unlock to ensure atomicity of the DoRead and DoCommitReadOnly and DoCommitWriter operations, which contain several actions over shared memory (details below).

The processes used to model shared memory accesses in TMS2 and DTMS2 are given in Fig. 4. We keep track of the maximum memory index using the function MaxIdxHandler, which synchronises on events getMaxIdx!maxIdx (occurring when another process requests the current maximum) and finishNewMem (occurring when a new memory is installed). For the former event, the current maximum is unchanged, whereas for the latter, the current maximum is incremented.

Perhaps the most interesting aspect is the model of the sequence of memories. A naive encoding using a map of type $(|\text{Int} \Rightarrow (|\text{Addr} \Rightarrow \text{Value}|)|)$ is highly inefficient (see Sect. 6). Instead, we start with function MemoryN_TMS(n, a, v), defining a mapping from the memory index n, address a and value v to a process. This function synchronises with read requests from the do operations of TMS2 using readMem_TMS.n.a!v (see Fig. 5), and read requests from new memories using readMem_TMS'.n.a!v (see finishNewMem branch of setupMem, described below). The purpose of both channels readMem_TMS and readMem_TMS' is to return the value for the given memory index and address. We require two different channels because they have different synchronisation requirements: readMem_TMS synchronises with the operations of TMS2, whereas readMem_TMS' synchronises with other MemoryN_TMS processes at other memory indices.

The branch setupMem.n is used by a committing writer transaction to install a new memory, where n > 0 is the index of the new memory to be installed. Once

```
maxMemories = card(TID)
MemRange = {0..maxMemories}

channel getMaxIdx: MemRange
channel finishNewMem

MaxIdxHandler :: (Int) → Proc
MaxIdxHandler(maxIdx) =
    getMaxIdx!maxIdx →  MaxIdxHandler(maxIdx)
□ maxIdx ≤ maxMemories & finishNewMem → MaxIdxHandler(maxIdx+1)

channel readMem_TMS, readMem_TMS': MemRange . Addr . Value
channel setupMem: {1..maxMemories}
channel newMem: Addr . Value

MemoryN_TMS :: (Int, AddrType, ValueType) → Proc
MemoryN_TMS(n, a, v) =
    readMem_TMS.n.a!v → MemoryN_TMS(n, a, v)
□ readMem_TMS'.n.a!v → MemoryN_TMS(n, a, v)
□ (n > 0 & setupMem.n →
        (   newMem.a?v' → finishNewMem → MemoryN_TMS(n, a, v')
         □ finishNewMem → readMem_TMS'.(n-1).a?v' → MemoryN_TMS(n, a, v')))
□ (□ i : diff(MemRange, {n}) • readMem_TMS'.i.a?_ → MemoryN_TMS(n, a, v))

MemHandlerN(n) = [|{|setupMem, finishNewMem|}|] a:Addr • MemoryN_TMS(n, a, D0)
MemHandler_TMS = [|{|readMem_TMS'|}|] n : MemRange • MemHandlerN(n)
GlobalMem_TMS = MemHandler_TMS [|{finishNewMem}|] MaxIdxHandler(0)
```

Fig. 4. TMS2 memory setup

setupMem.n occurs, the process waits for either a newMem.a?v or finishNewMem
event to occur. Event newMem.a?v' is called by a committing writer writing v'
to address a. After all writes have been written back, the committing writer
calls finishNewMem, which synchronises with each MemoryN_TMS(n, a, v) process as well as MaxIdxHandler as described above. When this occurs, either
MemoryN_TMS(n, a, v) was updated by the writer (first branch in setupMem.n),
or it was not (second branch in setupMem.n), in which case it pulls the value v'
for a from the previous index by calling readMem_TMS'.(n-1).a?v'. The final
branch of MemoryN_TMS is required to allow MemoryN_TMS processes at memory
index i memory indices processes to "escape" a setupMem.n call if the index that
is being setup is different from n.

The global memory is constructed by first defining MemHandlerN(n), which
initialises memory index n for each address a with value D0 so that the processes
synchronise over event setupMem.n (for all n) and finishNewMem. Processes
MemHandlerN(n), for each n, are combined in MemHandler_TMS, where processes
at different levels (in particular n and n-1) synchronise over readMem_TMS'

```
TMCommit_TMS :: (TID, Int, (|AddrType ⇒ ValueType|),
                       (|AddrType ⇒ ValueType|)) → Proc
TMCommit_TMS(t, beginIdx, rdSet, wrSet) =
  inv!t.Commit.MNull.DNull → ( DoCommit_TMS(t, beginIdx, rdSet, wrSet)
                                □ Abort_TMS(t))
DoCommit_TMS :: (TID, Int, (|AddrType ⇒ ValueType|),
                       (|AddrType ⇒ ValueType|)) → Proc
DoCommit_TMS(t, beginIdx, rdSet, wrSet) =
  lock → getMaxIdx?maxIdx →
  maxIdx < maxMemories &
  if wrSet == emptyMap then      -- DoCommitReadOnly
    (□ n: {beginIdx..maxIdx} •
                   CoValidate(mapToList(rdSet), n, t, wrSet, RO))
      □ unlock → Abort_TMS(t)
  else CoValidate(mapToList(rdSet), maxIdx, t,  wrSet, WR)  -- DoCommitWriter
datatype CoSwitch = RO | WR
CoValidate :: (⟨(AddrType, ValueType)⟩, Int, TID,
                   (|AddrType ⇒ ValueType|), CoSwitch) → Proc
CoValidate(<>, n, t, wrSet, sw) =
  sw == RO & unlock → resp!t.Commit.MNull.DNull → SKIP
□ sw == WR & setupMem!(n + 1) → WriteBack_TMS(mapToList(wrSet), t)
CoValidate(rdList, n, t, wrSet, sw) =
  let (a, v) = head(rdList) within
    readMemory_TMS!n.a?val →
    (val == v & CoValidate(tail(rdList), n, t, wrSet, sw))
```

Fig. 5. FDR encoding of TMS2 operations (sample)

events. Finally, the global memory is defined by GlobalMem_TMS, which combines MemHandler_TMS and MaxIdxHandler(0), synchronising over finishNewMem.

5.3   TMS2 Model

As an example, we describe our model of the TMS2 commit operation in Fig. 5, demonstrating the use of invocation and response events (in blue) and the expected interaction between TMS2 operations and the memory from Sect. 5.2.

TMCommit is an operation over a transaction id (type TID), the local begin index beginIdx (type Int), and the local read and write sets (type (|AddrType ⇒ ValueType|)). The begin index, read set and write set are as described in Sect. 4. TMCommit invokes inv!t.Commit.MNull.DNull then either aborts or performs the operation DoCommit_TMS, which starts by taking the global lock ensuring the remainder of the operation is atomic. DoCommit_TMS first synchronises with the process MaxIdxHandler (see Fig. 4) to obtain the current value of maxIdx. Then, if the write set wrSet is empty it attempts to validate against one of the memories between beginIdx and wrSet and aborts if this fails. If wrSet is non-empty, it validates against the memory at index maxIdx then inserts a new memory starting with setupMem!(n+1) (recalling that n == maxIdx).

The function `CoValidate` (commit validate) is inductive over the first argument (which is a list of address-value pairs) representing the read set converted from a map to a list. It is used to validate the read set against the memory index n. Case "<>" defines the base case, where `CoValidate` performs a case switch on the value of `sw`, either behaving as a read only transaction (case `RO`), or a writing transaction (case `WR`) by additionally performs a write back (details omitted). In the inductive case "rdList", assuming `(a,v)` is the head of `rdList`, we check whether the value of the nth memory at address `a` has value `v`. If so, it continues processing, otherwise the process stops.

We omit the details of the other TMS2 operations, but their models are similarly derived from the IOA specification (Fig. 2). The full system is defined in Fig. 6. Process `Synchroniser` is used to ensure atomicity of the TMS2 "do" operations, and the transactions of TMS2 are modelled by `Transactions_TMS`, comprising an interleaving of transactions starting with `TMBegin_TMS(t)` synchronised by `Synchroniser`. The combined TM operations and the global memory is modelled by `SyncTransactions_TMS`, which synchronises `Transactions_TMS` and `GlobalMem_TMS` (see Fig. 4) on the events in `syncSet_TMS`. The full TMS2 model is given by `FinalTMS2`, which hides events on all channels except for `inv` and `resp`. Therefore, the traces of `FinalTMS2` coincide with histories as required by opacity (see Sect. 3).

```
Synchroniser = lock → unlock → Synchroniser
Transactions_TMS = (|||t : TID • TMBegin_TMS(t))[|{|lock, unlock|}|] Synchroniser
syncSet_TMS = {|newMem, readMem_TMS, getMaxIdx, finishNewMem, setupMem|}
SyncTransactions_TMS = Transactions_TMS [|syncSet_TMS|] GlobalMem_TMS
FinalTMS2 =
  SyncTransactions_TMS\union(syncSet_TMS,{|readMem_TMS', lock, unlock|})
```

Fig. 6. Integrated TMS2 model

5.4   Encoding STM Implementations

The final components to be encoded are the models of TML and DTML. Here, we start with functions modelling the shared memory state through dedicated channels for reading and writing to memory. We also introduce a process for handling modifications to `glb`, including a `CASGlb` channel, that performs an atomic compare and swap on `glb` [32]. These models are similar to the models of the shared state in Sect. 5.2 and hence the details deferred to our mechanisation [15].

With the models of the shared memory in place, the encoding of the algorithms is straightforward. As an example, we provide an encoding of the write operation of TML in Fig. 7. The transactions of all threads are defined using the interleaving operator to obtain `Transactions`, which is combined with the memory model to obtain, `SyncTransactions`[3]. Finally, we obtain `FinalTML` from `SyncTransactions` by hiding all channels except `inv` and `resp`.

---

[3] Details of `SyncTransactions` is not shown, since it is composed using synchronisation in a similar manner to `SyncTransactions_TMS` in TMS2 (see Sect. 5.3).

```
TMWrite :: (TID, Int, AddressType, ValueType) → Proc
TMWrite(t, loc, a, v) =
  inv!t.Write.a.v →
    if isEven(loc) then CASGlb!loc.(loc + 1)?result →
      if result then
        writeMem!a.v → resp!t.Write.MNull.DNull →
        Idle(t, loc + 1)
      else resp!t.Abort.MNull.DNull → SKIP
    else
      writeMem!a.v → resp!t.Write.MNull.DNull → Idle(t, loc)
Transactions = ||| t : TID • TMBegin(t)
  ...
FinalTML = SyncTransactions \ syncSetTrans
```

Fig. 7. FDR encoding of TML operations (sample)

With these models in place, we check opacity by checking refinement between TMS2 and TML, which is encoded in FDR as the assertion `FinalTMS2 [T= FinalTML`. As already mentioned, FDR is able check such refinements without any additional input from the user.

6 Evaluation and Experiments

In our abstract model of TMS2 (Sect. 5.2), we access the sequence of shared memories, *mems* in Fig. 2, using a channel with dedicated events for each shared memory index and address. This means that memory accesses take constant time for *any* memory index and *any* address. Hence, a read/commit operations are linear w.r.t. the size of the read/write sets. This compares favourably to a quasilinear complexity of a naive encoding, i.e., one in which the memory sequence *mems* is modelled using a map of type $(|\text{Int} \Rightarrow (|\text{Addr} \Rightarrow \text{Value}|)|)$. Here quasilinear complexity arises since map operations typically have $O(\log n)$ complexity [16].

In our experiments, the encoding described in Sect. 5.2 allowed us to reduce the time taken to check refinement of small models (two transactions, two memory locations and two data values) from approximately 10 s to less than 1 s by replacing the naive model of *mems* with the representation described in Sect. 5.2. The difference is even more dramatic in the context of larger models, where the naive representation times out when *any* of the parameters are increased.

In our experiments, we check correctness of durable and non-durable versions of two algorithms: TML and DTML (see Sect. 4) as well as NOREC [8] and its durable version DNOREC [5]. TML and NOREC (and consequently DTML and DNOREC) differ in their design. TML is an *eager* algorithm which performs writes in place (as the TMWrite operation is executed), whereas NOREC is a *lazy* algorithm that updates shared memory (non-atomically) as part of a the commit operation. FDR is able to check both types of algorithms automatically without any further user input.

Table 1. Timing results (seconds)

T, A, V	2, 2, 2	2, 2, 3	2, 2, 4	2, 2, 5	2, 2, 6	2, 2, 7	2, 3, 2	2, 4, 2	3, 2, 2	2, 3, 3
TML	1	3.2	8.9	21.5	46.6	103.9	44.4	TO	635.1	326.7
DTML	1.1	3.6	10.0	23.9	54.6	121.0	51.0	–	781.1	348.3
NOrec	1.2	4.5	13.5	38.2	94.9	235.9	51.6	–	633.8	515.2
DNOrec	1.5	5.3	14.8	40.8	100.7	264.0	55.2	–	798.2	567.8

As part of our experiments, we also tested faulty versions of the algorithms. FDR was able to find bugs in all cases in which code modifications led to violation of (durable) opacity. We also discovered benign changes, which have liveness implications, but do not impact the safety, i.e., (durable) opacity. For instance, in TML (see Fig. 1), switching the test at line B2 to odd(loc) is a benign safety bug since no transaction will be able to start, and indeed, FDR does not report any (durable) opacity violation. On the other hand, changing the test at line R2 to glb ≠ loc is a (durable) opacity bug, and this is also correctly reported by FDR. For the durable algorithms (DTML and DNOREC), we experimented with faults such as omission of flush instructions, incorrect log updates, and buggy recovery code. In all cases, FDR managed to report durable opacity violations. More interestingly, in all cases, violations were detected even when testing with bounded models comprising two threads, two addresses and two values.

For the correct versions of the algorithms, we have timed the performance of checking various size models (Table 1), where we altered the number of threads (T), addresses (A) and values (V). Each increment of T roughly doubles the time taken, an increment of A causes an approximately 50-fold increase, with a second increase timing out (TO). An increment of T causes upto a 700-fold increase in the time taken. The final column (2, 3, 3) times the impact of increasing both A and V. Interestingly, the timing differences between the different algorithms are marginal for small values of T, A, V, across both the durable and non-durable versions. For larger values, of V, we can see that (D)NOREC take significantly longer to check than (D)TML. It is also interesting that both durable models take longer than the non-durable models when increasing the number of threads (column (3, 2, 2)); this is potentially due to the increase in memory required to represent both volatile and non-volatile state.

7   Related Work

Despite the many years of research into transactional memory, including several papers dedicated to their verification, there is surprisingly little work on model checking approaches. The majority of works on verifying opacity of STMs have focussed on manual proofs of *simulation* [1,6,9,11,13,38] and specialised logics [31]. Automated approaches have used the PAT model checker [2] (which presents a semi-automated approach) and reductions to alternative criteria [19,26,30], e.g., *conflict freedom* [19] and *markability* [30], which in turn guarantee transactional correctness.

Baek et al. have built a model checker specifically for checking correctness of STMs [4]. However, they only check serializability (a weaker condition than opacity), and their approach is limited to two transactions executing three operations each, and two memory locations. On the other hand, their examples include the sophisticated TL2 algorithm [12], which implements fine-grained per-location locking. Our work, in contrast, does not bound the number of operations executed by each transaction, and our refinement-based approach is more flexible as it allows the specifications to be altered depending on the properties of interest.

8   Conclusions

We have demonstrated the feasibility of using FDR to validate correctness of TML and NOREC as well as their durable versions (DTML and DNOREC) by model checking refinement w.r.t. the abstract specifications TMS2 and DTMS2. The main challenge is the efficient encoding of the abstract specifications TMS2 and DTMS2. Our encodings are highly efficient as can be seen by the time taken to check small models (Table 1). Moreover, these encodings can be reused to check opacity of other algorithms. As seen in Sect. 7, FDR encodings of implementations are straightforward and translations from particular languages to FDR models could even be automated (we leave this as future work).

In future work, we intend to extend the approach to cope with (more realistic) memory models integrating weak memory and persistency [34]. Here, a recent attempt at model checking durable concurrent data structures reported significant difficulties, with even small models timing out [24].

A   Full (D)TMS2 Automata

State Variables:

$mems : seq(L \rightarrow V)$, initially satisfying $\mathrm{dom}(mems) = \{0\}$ and $initMem(mems(0))$

$pc_t : PCVal$, for each $t \in T$, initially $pc_t = \mathrm{notStarted}$ for all $t \in T$

$beginIdx_t : \mathbb{N}$ for each $t \in T$, unconstrained initially

$rdSet_t : L \nrightarrow V$, initially empty for all $t \in T$

$wrSet_t : L \nrightarrow V$, initially empty for all $t \in T$

Transition Relation:

External actions

$inv_t(\mathtt{TMBegin})$
Pre: $pc_t = \mathrm{notStarted}$
Eff: $pc_t := \mathrm{beginPending}$
    $beginIdx_t := len(mems) - 1$

$resp_t(\mathtt{TMBegin})$
Pre: $pc_t = \mathrm{beginPending}$
Eff: $pc_t := \mathrm{ready}$

$inv_t(\mathtt{TMRd}(l))$
Pre: $pc_t = \mathrm{ready}$
Eff: $pc_t := \mathrm{doRead}(l)$

$resp_t(\mathtt{TMRd}(v))$
Pre: $pc_t = \mathrm{readResp}(v)$
Eff: $pc_t := \mathrm{ready}$

$inv_t(\mathtt{TMWr}(l, v))$
Pre: $pc_t = \mathrm{ready}$
Eff: $pc_t := \mathrm{doWrite}(l, v)$

$resp_t(\mathtt{TMWr})$
Pre: $pc_t = \mathrm{writeResp}$
Eff: $pc_t := \mathrm{ready}$

$inv_t(\mathtt{TMCommit})$
Pre: $pc_t = \mathrm{ready}$
Eff: $pc_t := \mathrm{doCommit}$

$resp_t(\mathtt{TMCommit})$
Pre: $pc_t = \mathrm{commitResp}$
Eff: $pc_t := \mathrm{committed}$

$resp_t(\mathtt{Abort})$
Pre: $pc_t \notin \{\mathrm{notStarted, ready},$
    $\mathrm{commitResp, committed, aborted}\}$
Eff: $pc_t := \mathrm{aborted}$

crash
Pre: *true*
Eff: $pc := \lambda\, t : T.$
    if $pc_t \notin \{\mathrm{notStarted, committed}\}$
    then aborted
    else pc_t
    $mems = \langle last(mems) \rangle$

Internal actions

$\mathtt{DoCommitReadOnly}_t(n)$
Pre: $pc_t = \mathrm{doCommit}$
    $\mathrm{dom}(wrSet_t) = \varnothing$
    $validIdx(t, n)$
Eff: $pc_t := \mathrm{commitResp}$

$\mathtt{DoCommitWriter}_t$
Pre: $pc_t = \mathrm{doCommit}$
    $rdSet_t \subseteq last(mems)$
Eff: $pc_t := \mathrm{commitResp}$
    $mems :=$
        $mems \frown (last(mems) \oplus wrSet_t)$

$\mathtt{DoRead}_t(l, n)$
Pre: $pc_t = \mathrm{doRead}(l)$
    $l \in \mathrm{dom}(wrSet_t) \vee validIdx(t, n)$
Eff: **if** $l \in \mathrm{dom}(wrSet_t)$ **then**
    $pc_t := \mathrm{readResp}(wrSet_t(l))$
    else $v := mems(n)(l)$
        $pc_t := \mathrm{readResp}(v)$
        $rdSet_t := rdSet_t \oplus \{l \rightarrow v\}$

$\mathtt{DoWrite}_t(l, v)$
Pre: $pc_t = \mathrm{doWrite}(l, v)$
Eff: $pc_t := \mathrm{writeResp}$
    $wrSet_t := wrSet_t \oplus \{l \rightarrow v\}$

where $validIdx(t, n) \mathrel{\widehat{=}} beginIdx_t \leq n < len(mems) \wedge rdSet_t \subseteq mems(n)$

B   (D)NOREC

For reference, the code for NOREC [8] and DNOREC [5] is given below, with the recovery code used by DNOREC highlighted in purple.

```
Init:
I1 glb := 0

TMBegin:
B1 do loc := glb;
B2 until even(loc)
      return ok;

TMRead(addr):
R1 if addr ∈ dom(wrSet) then
      return wrSet(addr)
R2 v := *addr
R3 while loc ≠ glb
R4    loc := TMValidate
R5    v := *addr
R6 rdSet.insert(addr, v);
      return v

TMWrite(addr,val):
W1 wrSet.insert(addr,val)
      return ok;

Recovery:
C1 glb := 0
C2 for ∀ (addr,val) ∈ log
C3    *addr := val;
C4    flush(addr);
C5 log.pempty()
```

```
TMCommit:
E1  if wrSet.isEmpty()
       then return ok;
E2  while !cas(glb, loc, loc + 1)
E3     loc := TMValidate
E4  for ∀ (addr,val) ∈ wrSet
E5     oldv := *addr;
E6     log.pinsert((addr, oldv));
E7     *addr := val;
E8     flush(addr);
E9  log.pempty()
E10 glb := loc + 2;
       return ok;


TMValidate:
V1 while true
V2    time  := glb
V3    if odd(time) then goto V2
V4    for ∀(addr,val) ∈ rdSet do
V5       if *addr ≠ val
            then abort
V6    if time = glb
         then return time
```

References

1. Armstrong, A., Dongol, B.: Modularising opacity verification for hybrid transactional memory. In: Bouajjani, A., Silva, A. (eds.) FORTE 2017. LNCS, vol. 10321, pp. 33–49. Springer, Cham (2017). https://doi.org/10.1007/978-3-319-60225-7_3
2. Armstrong, A., Dongol, B., Doherty, S.: Proving opacity via linearizability: a sound and complete method. In: Bouajjani, A., Silva, A. (eds.) FORTE 2017. LNCS, vol. 10321, pp. 50–66. Springer, Cham (2017). https://doi.org/10.1007/978-3-319-60225-7_4

3. Attiya, H., Gotsman, A., Hans, S., Rinetzky, N.: A programming language perspective on transactional memory consistency. In: Fatourou, P., Taubenfeld, G. (eds.) PODC 2013, pp. 309–318. ACM (2013)

4. Baek, W., Bronson, N.G., Kozyrakis, C., Olukotun, K.: Implementing and evaluating a model checker for transactional memory systems. In: Calinescu, R., Paige, R.F., Kwiatkowska, M.Z. (eds.) ICECCS, pp. 117–126. IEEE Computer Society (2010)

5. Bila, E., Derrick, J., Doherty, S., Dongol, B., Schellhorn, G., Wehrheim, H.: Modularising verification of durable opacity. CoRR abs/2011.15013 (2020)

6. Bila, E., Doherty, S., Dongol, B., Derrick, J., Schellhorn, G., Wehrheim, H.: Defining and verifying durable opacity: correctness for persistent software transactional memory. In: Gotsman, A., Sokolova, A. (eds.) FORTE 2020. LNCS, vol. 12136, pp. 39–58. Springer, Cham (2020). https://doi.org/10.1007/978-3-030-50086-3_3

7. Dalessandro, L., Dice, D., Scott, M., Shavit, N., Spear, M.: Transactional mutex locks. In: D'Ambra, P., Guarracino, M., Talia, D. (eds.) Euro-Par 2010. LNCS, vol. 6272, pp. 2–13. Springer, Heidelberg (2010). https://doi.org/10.1007/978-3-642-15291-7_2

8. Dalessandro, L., Spear, M.F., Scott, M.L.: Norec: streamlining STM by abolishing ownership records. In: Govindarajan, R., Padua, D.A., Hall, M.W. (eds.) PPoPP, pp. 67–78. ACM (2010)

9. Derrick, J., Doherty, S., Dongol, B., Schellhorn, G., Travkin, O., Wehrheim, H.: Mechanized proofs of opacity: a comparison of two techniques. Formal Aspects Comput. 30(5), 597–625 (2017). https://doi.org/10.1007/s00165-017-0433-3

10. Derrick, J., Doherty, S., Dongol, B., Schellhorn, G., Wehrheim, H.: Verifying correctness of persistent concurrent data structures. In: ter Beek, M.H., McIver, A., Oliveira, J.N. (eds.) FM 2019. LNCS, vol. 11800, pp. 179–195. Springer, Cham (2019). https://doi.org/10.1007/978-3-030-30942-8_12

11. Derrick, J., Dongol, B., Schellhorn, G., Travkin, O., Wehrheim, H.: Verifying opacity of a transactional mutex lock. In: Bjørner, N., de Boer, F. (eds.) FM 2015. LNCS, vol. 9109, pp. 161–177. Springer, Cham (2015). https://doi.org/10.1007/978-3-319-19249-9_11

12. Dice, D., Shalev, O., Shavit, N.: Transactional locking II. In: Dolev, S. (ed.) DISC 2006. LNCS, vol. 4167, pp. 194–208. Springer, Heidelberg (2006). https://doi.org/10.1007/11864219_14

13. Doherty, S., Dongol, B., Derrick, J., Schellhorn, G., Wehrheim, H.: Proving opacity of a pessimistic STM. In: Fatourou, P., Jiménez, E., Pedone, F. (eds.) OPODIS. LIPIcs, vol. 70, pp. 35:1–35:17. Schloss Dagstuhl - Leibniz-Zentrum für Informatik (2016)

14. Doherty, S., Groves, L., Luchangco, V., Moir, M.: Towards formally specifying and verifying transactional memory. Formal Asp. Comput. 25(5), 769–799 (2013)

15. Dongol, B., Le-Papin, J.: FDR models for "Checking Opacity and Durable Opacity with FDR", October 2021. https://doi.org/10.6084/m9.figshare.16752550.v1

16. Gibson-Robinson, T., Armstrong, P., Boulgakov, A., Roscoe, A.W.: FDR3 — a modern refinement checker for CSP. In: Ábrahám, E., Havelund, K. (eds.) TACAS 2014. LNCS, vol. 8413, pp. 187–201. Springer, Heidelberg (2014). https://doi.org/10.1007/978-3-642-54862-8_13

17. Guerraoui, R., Kapalka, M.: On the correctness of transactional memory. In: Chatterjee, S., Scott, M.L. (eds.) PPOPP, pp. 175–184. ACM (2008)

18. Guerraoui, R., Kapalka, M.: Principles of Transactional Memory. Synthesis Lectures on Distributed Computing Theory. Morgan & Claypool Publishers, San Rafael (2010)

19. Guerraoui, R., Henzinger, T.A., Singh, V.: Model checking transactional memories. Distrib. Comput. **22**(3), 129–145 (2010)
20. Harris, T., Larus, J.R., Rajwar, R.: Transactional Memory. Synthesis Lectures on Computer Architecture, 2nd edn. Morgan & Claypool Publishers, San Rafael (2010)
21. Herlihy, M., Moss, J.E.B.: Transactional memory: architectural support for lock-free data structures. In: Smith, A.J. (ed.) ISCA, pp. 289–300. ACM (1993)
22. Herlihy, M., Wing, J.M.: Linearizability: a correctness condition for concurrent objects. ACM TOPLAS **12**(3), 463–492 (1990)
23. Hoare, C.A.R.: Communicating sequential processes. Commun. ACM **21**(8), 666–677 (1978)
24. Iiboshi, H., Ugawa, T.: Towards model checking library for persistent data structures. In: NVMSA, pp. 119–120. IEEE (2018)
25. Izraelevitz, J., Mendes, H., Scott, M.L.: Linearizability of persistent memory objects under a full-system-crash failure model. In: Gavoille, C., Ilcinkas, D. (eds.) DISC 2016. LNCS, vol. 9888, pp. 313–327. Springer, Heidelberg (2016). https://doi.org/10.1007/978-3-662-53426-7_23
26. Koskinen, E., Parkinson, M.J.: The push/pull model of transactions. In: Grove, D., Blackburn, S.M. (eds.) PLDI, pp. 186–195. ACM (2015)
27. Lesani, M.: On the Correctness of Transactional Memory Algorithms. Ph.D. thesis, UCLA (2014)
28. Lesani, M., Luchangco, V., Moir, M.: A framework for formally verifying software transactional memory algorithms. In: Koutny, M., Ulidowski, I. (eds.) CONCUR 2012. LNCS, vol. 7454, pp. 516–530. Springer, Heidelberg (2012). https://doi.org/10.1007/978-3-642-32940-1_36
29. Lesani, M., Luchangco, V., Moir, M.: Putting opacity in its place. In: Workshop on the Theory of Transactional Memory (2012)
30. Lesani, M., Palsberg, J.: Decomposing opacity. In: Kuhn, F. (ed.) DISC 2014. LNCS, vol. 8784, pp. 391–405. Springer, Heidelberg (2014). https://doi.org/10.1007/978-3-662-45174-8_27
31. Lesani, M.: Transaction protocol verification with labeled synchronization logic. In: Badger, J.M., Rozier, K.Y. (eds.) NFM 2019. LNCS, vol. 11460, pp. 280–297. Springer, Cham (2019). https://doi.org/10.1007/978-3-030-20652-9_19
32. Lowe, G.: Analysing lock-free linearizable datatypes using CSP. In: Gibson-Robinson, T., Hopcroft, P., Lazić, R. (eds.) Concurrency, Security, and Puzzles. LNCS, vol. 10160, pp. 162–184. Springer, Cham (2017). https://doi.org/10.1007/978-3-319-51046-0_9
33. Lynch, N.A., Tuttle, M.R.: Hierarchical correctness proofs for distributed algorithms. In: PODC, pp. 137–151. ACM, New York, NY, USA (1987)
34. Raad, A., Wickerson, J., Vafeiadis, V.: Weak persistency semantics from the ground up: formalising the persistency semantics of ARMV8 and transactional models. PACMPL **3**(OOPSLA), 135:1–135:27 (2019)
35. Roscoe, A.W.: Understanding Concurrent Systems. Texts in Computer Science. Springer, London (2010). https://doi.org/10.1007/978-1-84882-258-0
36. Rudoff, A.: Persistent memory programming. Login USENIX Mag. **42**(2), 34–40 (2017)

37. Scargall, S.: Programming Persistent Memory. Apress, Berkeley (2020). https://doi.org/10.1007/978-1-4842-4932-1
38. Schellhorn, G., Wedel, M., Travkin, O., König, J., Wehrheim, H.: FASTLANE Is Opaque – a case study in mechanized proofs of opacity. In: Johnsen, E.B., Schaefer, I. (eds.) SEFM 2018. LNCS, vol. 10886, pp. 105–120. Springer, Cham (2018). https://doi.org/10.1007/978-3-319-92970-5_7
39. Zuriel, Y., Friedman, M., Sheffi, G., Cohen, N., Petrank, E.: Efficient lock-free durable sets. PACMPL **3**(OOPSLA), 128:1–128:26 (2019)

Translation of CCS into CSP, Correct up to Strong Bisimulation

Gerard Ekembe Ngondi[1,2]([⊠]) [iD], Vasileios Koutavas[1,2]([⊠]) [iD],
and Andrew Butterfield[1,2]([⊠]) [iD]

[1] Trinity College Dublin, Dublin, Ireland
[2] Lero - The Irish Software Research Centre, Limerick, Ireland
{Gerard.Ekembe,Vasileios.Koutavas,Andrew.Butterfield}@tcd.ie

Abstract. We present a translation of CCS into CSP which is correct with respect to strong bisimulation. To our knowledge this is the first such translation to enjoy a correctness property. This contributes to the unification of the CCS and CSP families of concurrent calculi, in the spirit of Hoare and He's unification programme through Unifying Theories of Programming. To facilitate this translation, we define CCSTau, the extension of CCS with visible synchronisation actions and the hiding operator. This separation of concerns between synchronisation and hiding turns out be sufficient to obtain our correct translation. Our translation, implemented in a Haskell prototype, makes it possible to use CSP-based verifiers such as FDR to reason about trace and failure (hence may- and must-testing) preorders for CCS processes.

Keywords: Concurrency theory · Calculus of Communicating Systems (CCS) · Communicating Sequential Processes (CSP) · Correct translation

1 Introduction

The CCS/Pi-calculus [1,16,17] and CSP/CSPmob [4,14,22] families of calculi are established formalisms for analysing concurrent systems. Not long after their inception there have been efforts to relate the two calculi and bridge their differences [15]. This would have clear benefits for theoreticians as it would allow them a deeper understanding of the nature of concurrency and the ability to transition from one mathematical formulation to the other in a rigorous manner. It would also benefit practitioners working in Process Algebra as it would allow them to use verification technology from both worlds to address challenges in assuring system correctness modelled in either family of calculi. To achieve this, semantics preserving transformations between CCS and CSP are needed.

In previous work, Van Glabbeek [10] builds a general framework for comparing the expressiveness of process calculi, with an application proposing a translation from CSP to CCS that is correct up to trace equivalence. Hatzel et al. [12] propose an encoding from CSP into asynchronous CCS with two notable

R. Calinescu and C. S. Păsăreanu (Eds.): SEFM 2021, LNCS 13085, pp. 243–261, 2021.
https://doi.org/10.1007/978-3-030-92124-8_14

encodings of CSP multiway synchronisation into CCS binary synchronisation. Brookes [3] encodes CSP models as synchronisation trees showing that CSP failure equivalence is implied by CCS observational equivalence under certain restrictions. He and Hoare [13] build a retract between CCS and CSP semantics.

To our knowledge however, no translation from CCS into CSP exists to date. The present paper aims to fill this gap. In particular, we present a translation from finite state CCS into CSP that is correct up to strong bisimulation, i.e., the source and target terms are strongly bisimilar. This correctness criterion allows us to use a prototype implementation of our translation to leverage FDR [5] for reasoning about trace and failure refinements of CCS terms. The translation is efficient as it only polynomially increases the size of the term. In the worst case, the target term has $O(nm)$ additional communication prefixes, where n and m are the maximum number of prefixes with the same name and corresponding co-name, respectively, in the source term. For practical systems with a relatively small number of synchronising prefixes this translation is thus tractable.

One major challenge in achieving a correct translation from CCS to CSP has been the reconciliation of the different communication primitives in the two languages, and how these interact with other primitives in the language. To bridge the gap between binary CCS and multiway CSP synchronisations, our translation assigns a unique name a_{ij} to every pair of $a/\overline{a}$-prefixes that might synchronise, and carefully annotates the interfaces between parallel processes to enable these synchronisations, effectively implementing binary synchronisation in multiway CSP semantics. Moreover, a unique name a_i is assigned to every CCS prefix that may be interleaved. This separation of interleaving and synchronisation is key to obtaining our translation (see Example 8). Finally, the CCS mixed-choice operator is translated to CSP external choice with a special *tau*-event to enable internal choice resolution (see Example 9). We use CSP hiding to turn internal synchronisation events a_{ij} and *tau* events into proper CSP τ-events.

Our translation from CCS to CSP relies on a novel intermediate language called CCSTau. This is a CCS-like calculus with *observable* binary synchronisation and the CSP hiding operator. Our translation is then obtained by the composition of an initial translation from CCS into CCSTau, a number of transformations within the CCSTau language itself, and a final translation from CCSTau into CSP including hiding of internal transitions. This sequence of smaller translation steps simplifies the task at hand and allows us to obtain a correct, up to strong bisimulation, overall translation. The contributions of this work are summarised as follows.

- We provide the first translation from finite state CCS to CSP which is correct up to strong bisimulation. The translation is efficient and only polynomially increases the size of the term.
- We propose CCSTau, which adapts CCS by making synchronisation actions visible and introducing CSP-like hiding, as a middle-ground between CCS and CSP. This calculus is instrumental in disentangling complex CCS behaviour

Table 1. CCS transition semantics (omitting symmetric rules).

$$\text{Prefix}: \alpha.P \xrightarrow{\alpha} P \qquad \text{SumL}: \frac{P \xrightarrow{\alpha} P'}{P+Q \xrightarrow{\alpha} P'} \qquad \text{Rec}: \frac{P[\mu X.P/X] \xrightarrow{\alpha} P'}{\mu X.P \xrightarrow{\alpha} P'}$$

$$\text{ParL}: \frac{P \xrightarrow{\alpha} P'}{P|Q \xrightarrow{\alpha} P'|Q} \qquad \text{Com}: \frac{P \xrightarrow{\overline{a}} P' \quad Q \xrightarrow{a} Q'}{P|Q \xrightarrow{\tau} P'|Q'} \qquad \text{Res}: \frac{P \xrightarrow{\alpha} P' \quad \alpha \notin B \cup \overline{B}}{P \upharpoonright B \xrightarrow{\alpha} P' \upharpoonright B}$$

such as mixed choice and combined interleaving/synchronisation and encoding it into CSP.

– We provide a prototype implementation of our translation in Haskell [23] which enables the use of the FDR refinement tool [5] to reason about may- and must-testing refinement of CCS processes.

In the rest of the paper we briefly overview definitions for CCS and CSP (Sect. 2), and provide the high-level intuitions of our translation (Sect. 3). We then define CCSTau, the extension of CCS with visible synchronisation actions and the hiding operator (Sect. 4), before defining the actual translation (Sect. 5 and Sect. 6) and prove its correctness (Sect. 7). Section 8 discusses an alternative translation, correct up to failure equivalence. Section 9 evaluates our translation against Gorla's criteria [11] for valid translations. Finally, we present conclusions and discuss future work (Sect. 10).

2   CCS, CSP, Correct Translations: a Brief Overview

CCS (Calculus of Communicating Systems) [1,17] and CSP (Communicating Sequential Processes) [14,22] are process algebras that allow reasoning about concurrent systems. Here we overview the main definitions of the two calculi.

2.1   CCS

In CCS [17], we assume a set of countable names $\mathcal{N}$, ranged over by a, b, c, with a total bijective function $\bar{\ }$ with the property that $\overline{\overline{a}} = a$. This function identifies *co-names*, the names that can synchronise. The symbol τ denotes an unobservable internal move. We let α range over names and τ. The syntax of CCS processes is given by the grammar

$$P, Q, R ::= 0 \mid \alpha.P \mid P+Q \mid P|Q \mid P \upharpoonright B \mid \mu X.P \mid X$$

The set of names that a process can use, denoted by $\mathcal{A}(P)$ for a given CCS process P, is defined hereafter.

Definition 1 (Alphabet/Sort of CCS processes [17, Chap. 2, Def. 2]).

$$\mathcal{A}(0) \triangleq \{\} \qquad\qquad \mathcal{A}(P+Q) \triangleq \mathcal{A}(P) \cup \mathcal{A}(Q)$$
$$\mathcal{A}(\tau.P) \triangleq \mathcal{A}(P) \qquad\qquad \mathcal{A}(P\,|\,Q) \triangleq \mathcal{A}(P) \cup \mathcal{A}(Q)$$
$$\mathcal{A}(a.P) \triangleq \{a\} \cup \mathcal{A}(P) \qquad \mathcal{A}(P \upharpoonright B) \triangleq \mathcal{A}(P) \backslash (B \cup \overline{B})$$

The semantics of CCS is traditionally given as a Labelled Transition System (LTS), shown in Table 1. Term 0 (or NIL) is the process that performs no action, whereas $\alpha.P$ performs an action α, where α is either a name a or τ, and then behaves like P (Prefix rule). The choice term $P + Q$ behaves either like P or Q (SumL rule). The parallel $P|Q$ runs P and Q in parallel; P and Q may interleave (Par rule) or synchronise on co-actions, resulting in a silent τ action (Com rule). Restriction $P \upharpoonright B$ cannot engage in actions consisting of names in $B \cup \overline{B}$, where $\overline{B} = \{\bar{a}|a \in B\}$ (Res rule); however, names in $B \cup \overline{B}$ can be used for internal synchronisation in P. Term $\mu X.P$ encodes recursion, where variable X, appearing as a process in P, denotes a recursive unfolding (Rec rule). We only consider closed processes where X is under a corresponding μX operator. Moreover, as we are interested in finite state processes, we apply the sufficient requirement that no parallel operator appears under recursion.

Equivalence based on bisimulations is the preferred choice for distinguishing CCS processes (cf. [17,21]).

Definition 2 (Strong Bisimulation [21]). *A strong bisimulation is a symmetric binary relation $\mathcal{R}$ on processes satisfying the following: $P\mathcal{R}Q$ and*

- $P \xrightarrow{\alpha} P'$ *imply that* $\exists Q' : Q \xrightarrow{\alpha} Q' \wedge P'\mathcal{R}Q'$
- $Q \xrightarrow{\alpha} Q'$ *imply that* $\exists P' : P \xrightarrow{\alpha} P' \wedge P'\mathcal{R}Q'$

P *is* strong bisimilar *to* Q, *written* $P \sim Q$, *if $P\mathcal{R}Q$ for some strong bisimulation* $\mathcal{R}$.

Example 3. In CCS, internal and external choices can be combined thus yielding a *mixed* choice, e.g., $a.P + b.Q + \tau.R$. According to Table 1, this process enables external choice between a and b, meaning that the context of the process, through synchronisation on a or b, can force this process to become P or Q. Additionally, the process itself can non-deterministically decide to evolve to R, resolving the choice independently from external stimuli. As we show in Example 9, this mixed choice in CCS needs to be encoded specifically into CSP, where internal reductions do not resolve an external choice. □

2.2 CSP

In CSP, we assume again a countable set of names $\mathcal{N}$, called the set of observable events and ranged over by a, b, c, the special $\checkmark$ event denotes termination, and the τ event denotes an internal move. We let α range all events. The syntax of CSP processes we consider is given by the grammar:[1]

$$P, Q, R ::= \text{SKIP} \mid \text{STOP} \mid a \to P \mid P \sqcap Q \mid P \square Q \mid P \parallel_B Q \mid$$

$$P\backslash B \mid f(P) \mid \mu X.P \mid X$$

The alphabet of CSP processes is defined hereafter.

---

[1] In what follows, whether P, Q, R refer to CCS or CSP will be clear by the context.

Table 2. CSP transition semantics (omitting symmetric rules).

Term : $SKIP \xrightarrow{\checkmark} STOP$ Prefix : $(a \to P) \xrightarrow{a} P$ InChL : $P \sqcap Q \xrightarrow{\tau} P$

ExChL1 : $\dfrac{P \xrightarrow{a} P'}{P \,\square\, Q \xrightarrow{a} P'}$ ExChL2 : $\dfrac{P \xrightarrow{\tau} P'}{P \,\square\, Q \xrightarrow{\tau} P' \,\square\, Q}$ Rec : $\dfrac{P[\mu\, X.P/X] \xrightarrow{\alpha} P'}{\mu\, X.P \xrightarrow{\alpha} P'}$

Hide1 : $\dfrac{P \xrightarrow{a} P' \quad [a \notin B]}{P \backslash B \xrightarrow{a} P' \backslash B}$ Hide2 : $\dfrac{P \xrightarrow{a} P' \quad [a \in B]}{P \backslash B \xrightarrow{\tau} P' \backslash B}$ Ren : $\dfrac{P \xrightarrow{\alpha} P'}{f(P) \xrightarrow{f(\alpha)} f(P')}$

ParL : $\dfrac{P \xrightarrow{a} P' \quad [a \notin B^{\checkmark}]}{P \parallel_B Q \xrightarrow{a} P' \parallel_B Q}$ Sync : $\dfrac{P \xrightarrow{a} P' \quad Q \xrightarrow{a} Q' \quad [a \in B^{\checkmark}]}{P \parallel_B P \xrightarrow{a} P' \parallel_B Q'}$

Definition 4 (Alphabet of CSP processes [14]).

$$\mathcal{A}(STOP) \triangleq \{\}$$
$$\mathcal{A}(a \to P) \triangleq \{a\} \cup \mathcal{A}(P)$$
$$\mathcal{A}(P \sqcap Q) \triangleq \mathcal{A}(P) \cup \mathcal{A}(Q)$$
$$\mathcal{A}(P \,\square\, Q) \triangleq \mathcal{A}(P) \cup \mathcal{A}(Q)$$

$$\mathcal{A}(P \parallel_B Q) \triangleq \mathcal{A}(P) \cup \mathcal{A}(Q)$$
$$\mathcal{A}(P \backslash B) \triangleq \mathcal{A}(P) \backslash B$$
$$\mathcal{A}(f(P)) \triangleq \{f(a) \,|\, a \in \mathcal{A}(P)\}$$

We present the semantics of CSP as an LTS in Table 2, following Schneider [22]: Term $SKIP$ refuses to engage in any event, terminates immediately (Term rule), and does not diverge. Term $STOP$ is unable to interact with its environment. The prefix process $\alpha \to P$ first engages in event α then behaves like P (Prefix rule). Term $P \sqcap Q$ behaves like P or Q, with the choice decided internally (InChL), whereas $P \,\square\, Q$ behaves like P or Q, with the choice decided by the environment (ExtChL1,2 rules). Parallel $P \parallel_B Q$ runs processes P and Q in parallel, which must synchronise on the set of events in B and the $\checkmark$ event (ParL and Sync rules). The renaming term $f(P)$ engages in $f(a)$ whenever P engages in a (Ren rule). Hiding $P \backslash A$ engages in all events of P except those in A (Hide1, 2 rules), and $\mu\, X.P$ runs P recursively (Rec rule).

Equivalence based on (enriched versions of) traces is the preferred choice for distinguishing CSP processes (cf. [14,21,22]).

Definition 5 (Failure equivalence [21]). *A* failure *is a pair* (tr, A), *where tr is a finite sequence of actions (or* trace*) and* A *a set of actions. The failure* (tr, A) *belongs to process* P *if, for some* P': $P \xrightarrow{tr} P' \wedge \forall a \in A : \neg(P' \xrightarrow{a})$.

P is failure equivalent *to* Q, *written* $P =_{\mathcal{F}} Q$, *if they have the same sets of failures.*

2.3 Correct Translations

A correct translation of one language into another is a mapping from the valid expressions in the first language to those in the second, that preserves their meaning [10]. Below we recap the main two definitions of correctness.

Let $\mathcal{L} = (\mathbb{T}_{\mathcal{L}}, [\![\,]\!]_{\mathcal{L}})$ denote a language as a pair of a set $\mathbb{T}_{\mathcal{L}}$ of valid expressions in $\mathcal{L}$ and a surjective mapping $[\![\,]\!]_{\mathcal{L}} : \mathbb{T}_{\mathcal{L}} \to \mathcal{D}_{\mathcal{L}}$ from $\mathbb{T}_{\mathcal{L}}$ to some set of meanings $\mathcal{D}_{\mathcal{L}}$. Candidate instances of $[\![\,]\!]_{\mathcal{L}}$ are *traces* and *failures* (Definition 5).

Definition 6 (Correct Translation up to Semantic Equivalence [10]). *A translation* $\mathsf{T} : \mathbb{T}_{\mathcal{L}} \to \mathbb{T}_{\mathcal{L}'}$ *is* correct up to *a semantic equivalence* $\approx$ *on* $\mathcal{D}_{\mathcal{L}} \cup \mathcal{D}_{\mathcal{L}'}$ *when* $[\![\mathsf{T}(E)]\!]_{\mathcal{L}'} \approx [\![E]\!]_{\mathcal{L}}$ *for all* $E \in \mathbb{T}_{\mathcal{L}}$.

Operational correspondence allows matching the transitions of two processes, which can help determine the appropriate relation (semantic equivalence) between a term and its translation. Let the operational semantics of $\mathcal{L}$ be defined by the labelled transition system $(\mathbb{T}_{\mathcal{L}}, Act_{\mathcal{L}}, \to_{\mathcal{L}})$, where $Act_{\mathcal{L}}$ is the set of labels and $E \xrightarrow{\lambda}_{\mathcal{L}} E'$ defines transitions with $E, E' \in \mathbb{T}_{\mathcal{L}}$ and $\lambda \in Act_{\mathcal{L}}$.

Definition 7 (Labelled Operational Correspondence [8,20]). *Let* $\mathsf{T} : \mathbb{T}_{\mathcal{L}} \to \mathbb{T}_{\mathcal{L}'}$ *be a mapping from the expressions of a language* $\mathcal{L}$ *to those of a language* $\mathcal{L}'$, *and let* $\mathsf{f} : Act_{\mathcal{L}} \to Act_{\mathcal{L}'}$ *be a mapping from the labels of* $\mathcal{L}$ *to those of* $\mathcal{L}'$. *A translation* $\langle \mathsf{T}, \mathsf{f} \rangle$ *is* operationally corresponding *w.r.t. a semantic equivalence* $\approx$ *on* $\mathcal{D}_{\mathcal{L}} \cup \mathcal{D}_{\mathcal{L}'}$ *if it is:*

- *Sound:* $\forall E, E' : E \xrightarrow{\lambda}_{\mathcal{L}} E'$ *imply that* $\exists F : \mathsf{T}(E) \xrightarrow{\mathsf{f}(\lambda)}_{\mathcal{L}'} F$ *and* $F \approx \mathsf{T}(E')$
- *Complete:* $\forall E, F : \mathsf{T}(E) \xrightarrow{\lambda'}_{\mathcal{L}'} F$ *imply that* $\exists E' : E \xrightarrow{\lambda}_{\mathcal{L}} E'$ *and* $F \approx \mathsf{T}(E') \wedge \lambda' = \mathsf{f}(\lambda)$

3 Intuitions of the Translation

In this section, we illustrate some of the differences between CCS and CSP, and how we address them in the different stages of our translation shown in Fig. 1. We start with the challenges in translating CCS binary into CSP's multiway synchronisation in a term where both interleaving and synchronisation of prefixes is possible.

$$\boxed{CCS} \xrightarrow{c2ccs\tau} \boxed{CCSTau} \xrightarrow{ix, \ g^*} \xrightarrow{conm} \boxed{CCSTau} \xrightarrow{tl} \boxed{CSP} \xrightarrow{\backslash\{tau, a_{ij}\}, \ ai2a} \boxed{CSP}$$

Fig. 1. Translation workflow

Example 8. Consider the CCS process $(a.P \mid \bar{a}.Q) \mid \bar{a}.R$ composed of three parallel sub-processes $a.P$, $\bar{a}.Q$ and $\bar{a}.R$. According to CCS semantics, binary synchronisation can occur between $a.P$ and either $\bar{a}.Q$ or $\bar{a}.R$. Both synchronisations result to τ-transitions in the LTS (Sync in Table 1).

We initially translate this process into CCSTau through the $c2ccs\tau$ function (Definition 11), which gives us $((a.P' \mid \bar{a}.Q') \backslash \{\tau[a|\bar{a}]\} \mid \bar{a}.R') \backslash \{\tau[a|\bar{a}]\}$. As we will see in the following section, in CCSTau, $a.P'$ can perform an observable $\tau[a|\bar{a}]$ synchronisation with one of the other two parallel processes. This transition is turned into an internal τ-transition via the hiding operator $(-\backslash\{\tau[a|\bar{a}]\})$ borrowed from CSP. After this first translation, the source and target terms have the same transition system, i.e., they are strongly bisimilar (Theorem 12).

We then apply a sequence of three transformations within CCSTau. The first one, ix (Property 13), assigns a unique index to the names of every prefix, thus obtaining the process $a_1.P'' \mid \bar{a}_2.Q'' \mid \bar{a}_3.R''$. The ix-indexed process cannot perform any synchronisation and therefore hiding of synchronisation actions is removed. However, the next transformation, g^* (Definition 15), adds new prefixes, denoted with double indices, which re-introduces these synchronisations (though without hiding them):

$$(a_1 + a_{12} + a_{13}).P''' \mid ((\bar{a}_2 + \bar{a}_{12}).Q''') \mid (\bar{a}_3 + \bar{a}_{13}).R'''$$

where $(a + b).S$ is syntactic sugar for $a.S + b.S$. For simplicity in this example, we assume that a does not appear in P, Q and R.

At this stage in our translation, every prefix that may lead to an interleaved action is represented by an a_i prefix, while every possible synchronisation has its own unique name and co-name, $a_{ij}, \bar{a}_{ij}$. In this way, we separate synchronisation from interleaving, which is crucial for translating into CSP.

Note here that the introduction of the additional a_{ij} prefixes also introduces interleaved a_{ij} transitions. These will be removed by hiding at a following stage of the translation.

Transformation $conm$ (Definition 18) identifies co-names synchronisation events, and tl (Definition 20) maps CCS operators to corresponding CSP constructs while filling in the interface sets in every CSP parallel operator. We thus obtain:

$$((a_1 \,\square\, a_{12} \,\square\, a_{13}) \to P'''' \underset{\{a_{12}\}}{\|} (\bar{a}_2 \,\square\, a_{12}) \to Q'''') \underset{\{a_{13}\}}{\|} (\bar{a}_3 \,\square\, a_{13}) \to R''''$$

To obtain a CSP process with a transition system identical to the original CCS term, we need to apply the final two stages of the translation. These introduce a top-level hiding operator for tau events (not relevant in this example) and all a_{ij} synchronisation events, as well as a renaming operation $ai2a$ (Definition 25) which maps all a_i names to a. The final CSP term is thus:

$$\left(((a \,\square\, a_{12} \,\square\, a_{13}) \to P'''' \underset{\{a_{12}\}}{\|} (\bar{a} \,\square\, a_{12}) \to Q'''') \underset{\{a_{13}\}}{\|} (\bar{a} \,\square\, a_{13}) \to R''''\right) \backslash \{a_{12}, a_{13}\}$$

The original CCS and final CSP terms have indeed strongly bisimilar LTSs (Theorem 30). □

Example 9. Consider again the mixed choice $a.P + b.Q + \tau.R$ (Example 3). After applying the $c2ccs\tau$ translation and the ix, g^* and $conm$ transformations, we obtain the CCSTau term: $a_1.P' + b_2.Q' + \tau.R'$. We assume here that P, Q, R do not contain $\bar{a}$ and $\bar{b}$ prefixes and thus no hiding or additional n_{ij} prefixes are introduced. Translation tl is the most important for this example. It results in the CSP process $a_1 \to P'' \,\square\, b_2 \to Q'' \,\square\, tau \to R''$. Crucially, the last prefix involves the special name tau, which is different than τ and can indeed resolve the choice. In order to turn tau into a CSP τ move, the translation then hides this name and, with the application of the final renaming function $ai2a$, the CSP term we obtain is $(a \to P''' \,\square\, b \to Q''' \,\square\, tau \to R''') \setminus \{tau\}$ which indeed has an LTS which is strongly bisimilar to that of the original CCS term. □

4   From CCS to CCSTau

We define CCSTau to serve as a middle-ground calculus between CCS and CSP for our translation. CCSTau is obtained from CCS, as described in Sect. 2.1, by two modifications: making binary synchronisation observable, and introducing CSP-style hiding.

To make binary synchronisation observable we introduce an additional action which can appear on the transitions of our LTS: $\tau[a|\bar{a}]$. We let β range over CCS actions α and the new synchronisation actions $\tau[a|\bar{a}]$, and define the CCSTau LTS with rules of the form $P \xrightarrow{\beta} Q$. To make synchronisation observable we use the following Com rule, instead of that in Table 1.

$$\text{Com} : \frac{P \xrightarrow{\bar{a}} P' \quad Q \xrightarrow{a} Q'}{P|_T Q \xrightarrow{\tau[\bar{a}|a]} P'|_T Q'}$$

Note that we annotate the parallel operator with a T-subscript to make clear that it is the CCSTau parallel. Its alphabet contains visible synchronisations.

Definition 10. $\mathcal{A}(P|_T Q) \cong \mathcal{A}(P) \cup \mathcal{A}(Q) \cup \{\tau[a|\bar{a}] \mid a \in \mathcal{A}(P), \bar{a} \in \mathcal{A}(Q)\}$

To introduce hiding, we extend CCS syntax with the hiding construct: $P ::= \dots \mid P\backslash_T B$. The set B contains actions which are names a or $\tau[a|\bar{a}]$, with the closure condition that "if $a \in B$ then $\bar{a} \in B$ and $\tau[a|\bar{a}] \in B$." We introduce the following hiding rules in the LTS which are similar to the CSP rules (Table 2)

$$\text{Hide1} : \frac{P \xrightarrow{\beta} P' \quad \beta \notin B}{P\backslash_T B \xrightarrow{\beta} P'\backslash_T B} \qquad\qquad \text{Hide2} : \frac{P \xrightarrow{\beta} P' \quad \beta \in B}{P\backslash_T B \xrightarrow{\tau} P'\backslash_T B}$$

The remaining LTS rules consist of Prefix, SumL (and its symmetric), ParL, Res and Rec from Table 1, with the only change that we now use β instead of α for transition annotations. Note that CCSTau restriction cannot restrict $\tau[a|\bar{a}]$ actions as these are single-name actions only.

Encoding CCS into CCSTau. We describe here a translation of CCS processes into CCSTau. This encoding is concerned with hiding the now-observable synchronisation actions.

Definition 11 (c2ccsτ). *Translation function c2ccsτ, when applied to a CCS process, returns a CCSTau process.*

$$c2ccs\tau(0) \cong 0 \qquad\qquad c2ccs\tau(P \upharpoonright B) \cong c2ccs\tau(P) \upharpoonright B$$
$$c2ccs\tau(\alpha.P) \cong \alpha.c2ccs\tau(P) \qquad c2ccs\tau(\mu X.P) \cong \mu X.c2ccs\tau(P)$$
$$c2ccs\tau(P + Q) \cong c2ccs\tau(P) + c2ccs\tau(Q) \qquad c2ccs\tau(X) \cong X$$
$$c2ccs\tau(P|Q) \cong (c2ccs\tau(P)|_T c2ccs\tau(Q))\backslash_T \{\tau[a|\bar{a}] \mid a \in \mathcal{A}(P), \bar{a} \in \mathcal{A}(Q)\}$$

In the above definition the only interesting case is parallel which hides the CCStau synchronisation actions, leaving all other actions unaffected. The following theorem shows that the translated terms are strongly bisimilar to the original CCS terms, when there is no parallel under recursion.[2]

Theorem 12. *Let P be a CCS process. Then: $P \sim c2ccs\tau(P)$.*

Proof. By observing that $c2ccs\tau$ is the identity CCS-to-CCSTau translation on parallel-free processes, and then proving the conditions of bisimulation via rule induction on the LTS transitions.   □

5   CCSTau Transformations

We provide a translation of CCSTau into CSP in two parts. Here we describe the first part involving the CCSTau transformations, ix, g^*, $conm$, mentioned in Sect. 3.

Indexing (ix). The intention here is that an indexing function assigns unique indices to every prefix in a CCS process. There are many straightforward schemes to choose these indices from the set of natural numbers $\mathbb{N}$. Here, instead of defining a concrete scheme, we specify how it should distribute over CCSTau operators.

Property 13.

$$ix(\tau.P) = \tau.ix(P) \qquad\qquad ix(P \restriction \{a\}) = ix(P) \restriction \{a_i | a_i \in \mathcal{A}(ix(P))\}$$
$$ix(a.P) = a_i.ix_{-i}(P) \qquad ix(P_{\backslash_\tau}\{a\}) = ix(P)_{\backslash_\tau}\{a_i | a_i \in \mathcal{A}(ix(P))\}$$
$$ix(P + Q) = ix_1(P) + ix_2(Q) \quad ix(P_{\backslash_\tau}\{\tau[a|\bar{a}]\}) = ix(P)$$
$$ix(P|_\tau Q) = ix_1(P)|_\tau ix_2(Q) \qquad ix(\mu\, X.P) = \mu\, X.i\, x(P)$$

where ix_{-i} is some indexing scheme which does not assign the i-index, and ix_1, ix_2 are some indexing schemes that assign disjoint indices.

Since ix generates unique indexed names, $ix(P)$ cannot synchronise, whence hidden $\tau[a|\bar{a}]$ synchronisations are dropped out. They will be recovered later on.

In the following, we assume an indexing function ix which satisfies the above properties. Our Haskell implementation [23] indeed implements such an indexing function.

Explicit Binary Synchronisation (g^*). Given an indexed process $ix(P)$, function g^* generates, by over-approximation, a unique name a_{ij} for every possible synchronisation pair $(a_i, \bar{a}_j)$ from $ix(P)$.

Given a set S of names in the context, the next definition shows how g^* applies to a CCSTau action and set of actions. For technical convenience, the definition ensures that smaller indices always come first.

---

[2] Although more involved versions of $c2ccs\tau$ would lift the restriction on recursion here, the same restriction would be needed for the end-to-end translation into CSP.

Definition 14 $(g^*(S, a), g\pi_2(S, a))$.

$$g^*(S, \tau) \cong \{\tau\}$$
$$g^*(S, a_i) \cong \{a_i\} \cup g\pi_2(S, a_i) \qquad g\pi_2(S, a_i) \cong \{a_{ij} \mid \bar{a}_j \in S, i < j\}$$
$$g^*(S, B) \cong \bigcup_{a_i \in B} g^*(S - \{a_i\}, a_i) \qquad\qquad \cup \{a_{ji} \mid \bar{a}_j \in S, j < i\}$$

We can now define our transformation function g^* over CCSTau processes.

Definition 15 $(g^*(S, P))$. *Let* P, Q *be ix-indexed CCSTau processes and* S *a set of names such that* $S \cap \mathcal{A}(P) = S \cap \mathcal{A}(Q) = \{\}$.

$$g^*(S, 0) \cong 0 \qquad\qquad g^*(S, P \upharpoonright B) \cong g^*(S, P) \upharpoonright g^*(S, B)$$
$$g^*(S, \alpha.P) \cong \sum_{b \in g^*(S, \alpha)} b.g^*(S, P) \qquad g^*(S, P \backslash_\tau B) \cong g^*(S, P) \backslash_\tau g^*(S \cup B, B)$$
$$g^*(S, P + Q) \cong g^*(S, P) + g^*(S, Q) \qquad g^*(S, \mu X.P) \cong \mu X.g^*(S, P)$$
$$g^*(S, P \mid_\tau Q) \cong g^*(S \cup \mathcal{A}(Q), P) \mid_\tau g^*(S \cup \mathcal{A}(P), Q)$$

When P is the top context, we require $S = \{\}$. We define: $g^*(P) \cong g^*(\{\}, P)$.

Condition $S \cap \mathcal{A}P = \{\}$ allows us to separate P from its context, while the condition that the processes are ix-indexed excludes processes where indexing has not been applied consistently such as $g^*((a_1 + a_2) \upharpoonright \{a_2\})$.

For restriction, no $a_i \in B$ should be able to interact with the environment. Hence, (dummy) synchronisations between B and S, $\{a_{ij} \mid a_i \in B, \bar{a}_j \in S \mid i < j\} \cup \{a_{ji} \mid a_i \in B, \bar{a}_j \in S \mid j < i\}$, should also be restricted.

Example 16.

1. $g^*((a_1.0 \mid_\tau \bar{a}_2.0) \upharpoonright \{a_1, a_2\}) = ((a_1.0 + a_{12}.0) \mid_\tau (\bar{a}_2.0 + \bar{a}_{12}.0)) \upharpoonright \{a_1, a_2\}$
2. $g^*((a_1.0 \mid_\tau \bar{a}_2.0) \upharpoonright \{a_1, a_2\} \mid_\tau \bar{a}_3.0)$
   $= ((a_1.0 + a_{12}.0 + a_{13}.0) \mid_\tau (\bar{a}_2.0 + \bar{a}_{12}.0)) \upharpoonright \{a_1, a_2, a_{13}\}) \mid_\tau \bar{a}_3.0$

Proper synchronisations remain unrestricted as illustrated above with a_{12}. Since CCS restriction '$- \upharpoonright \{a_{ij}\}$' will be translated to CSP '$- \underset{a_{ij}}{\|} STOP$' (cf. Definition 19), restricting proper synchronisation names would lead to deadlock in CSP. Instead, they will be added into the CSP interface-parallel operator later on (cf. Definition 20).

For hiding, no $a_i \in B$ should be visible. Unlike restriction, we must hide both dummy and proper synchronisations involving hidden a_is.

Example 17.

1. $g^*((a_1.0 \mid_\tau \bar{a}_2.0) \backslash_\tau \{a_1, a_2\}) = ((a_1.0 + a_{12}.0) \mid_\tau (\bar{a}_2.0 + \bar{a}_{12}.0)) \backslash_\tau \{a_1, a_2, a_{12}\}$
2. $g^*((a_1.0 \mid_\tau \bar{a}_2.0) \backslash_\tau \{a_1, a_2\} \mid_\tau \bar{a}_3.0)$
   $= ((a_1.0 + a_{12}.0 + a_{13}.0) \mid_\tau (\bar{a}_2.0 + \bar{a}_{12}.0)) \backslash_\tau \{a_1, a_2, a_{12}, a_{13}\}) \mid_\tau \bar{a}_3.0$

Identifying Co-names (*conm*). Unlike CCSTau, synchronisation occurs in CSP between pairs of events that have the same name. That is, $(a \rightarrow P) \underset{\{a\}}{\|} \bar{a} \rightarrow Q$ would behave like $(a \rightarrow P) \underset{\{a\}}{\|} b \rightarrow Q$, *not* $(a \rightarrow P) \underset{\{a\}}{\|} a \rightarrow Q$. Before going into CSP, we need to ensure that a can synchronise with $\bar{a}$, more precisely, we only need a_{ij} to synchronise with $\bar{a}_{ij}$. This can be achieved through the following renaming function, *conm*, which transforms any $\bar{a}_{ij}$-name into an a_{ij}-name.

Definition 18 (*conm*). *Let a_i, a_{ij} range over g^*-indexed names. Then:*

$$conm \;\hat{=}\; \{\tau \mapsto \tau, a_i \mapsto a_i, \bar{a}_i \mapsto \bar{a}_i, a_{ij} \mapsto a_{ij}, \bar{a}_{ij} \mapsto a_{ij} \mid i < j\}$$

6   From CCSTau to CSP

Translation into CSP (*tl*). The translation of CCSTau processes into CSP requires us to translate CCSTau prefixes. To do this we use a fresh (not previously used) CSP event *tau*, which we will later hide, thus creating a true CSP internal transition. Moreover, we need to translate CCS restriction, which is part of the CCSTau language, into CSP. We do this by introducing a deadlock for the restricted names.

Definition 19. *Let P be a CSP process. Then:* $P \restriction_{csp} B \;\hat{=}\; P \underset{B\cup\bar{B}}{\|} STOP.$

We can now present the translation *tl* from CCSTau to CSP.

Definition 20. *Let P and Q be CCSTau processes; let tau be a fresh, non-synchronising, CSP event.*

$$tl(0) \;\hat{=}\; STOP \qquad\qquad tl(P|_{\tau}Q) \;\hat{=}\; tl(P) \underset{\{a|a\in\mathcal{A}(P)\cap\mathcal{A}(Q)\}}{\|} tl(Q)$$

$$tl(\tau.P) \;\hat{=}\; tau \rightarrow tl(P) \qquad tl(P \restriction B) \;\hat{=}\; tl(P) \restriction_{csp} B$$

$$tl(a.P) \;\hat{=}\; a \rightarrow tl(P) \qquad tl(P\backslash_{\tau}B) \;\hat{=}\; tl(P) \backslash_{csp} B$$

$$tl(P + Q) \;\hat{=}\; tl(P) \;\square\; tl(Q) \qquad tl(\mu X.P) \;\hat{=}\; \mu X.tl(P)$$

The following example illustrates the rationale for our encoding restriction into CSP.

Example 21. In CCSTau (as in CCS) restriction obeys the law: $(a.P) \restriction \{a\} \sim 0$. Definition 19 obeys the same law, viz., $(a \rightarrow t2csp(P)) \restriction_{csp} \{a\} = STOP$.

$$tl((a.P) \restriction \{a\}) = tl(a.P) \restriction_{csp} \{a\} = (a \rightarrow tl(P)) \underset{\{a\}}{\|} STOP$$

The last process behaves like $STOP$ which is the *tl*-translation of 0.   □

Hereafter, it will be convenient to refer to the composition of all CCSTau transformations and the *tl*-translation into CSP as a single function, which we call *t2csp*.

Definition 22 (*t2csp*). *Let P be a CCSTau process. Then:*

$$t2csp(P) \mathrel{\hat{=}} (tl \circ conm \circ g^* \circ ix(P)) \backslash_{csp} \{tau\}$$

Example 23. We illustrate the translation of CCSTau parallel operator, to be contrasted with the translation of CCS parallel operator (cf. Example 26).

$$
\begin{aligned}
&t2csp(a.0|_T \bar{a}.0)\\
&= tl\big(conm\big(g^*(\{\,\}, ix(a.0|_T\bar{a}.0))\big)\big)\backslash_{csp}\{tau\} &&\text{(t2csp-Def. 22)}\\
&= tl\big(conm\big(g^*(\{\,\}, (a_1.0|_T\bar{a}_2.0))\big)\big)\backslash_{csp}\{tau\} &&\text{(ix-Prop. 13)}\\
&= tl\big(conm\big((a_1.0 + a_{12}.0)|_T(\bar{a}_2.0 + \bar{a}_{12}.0)\big)\big)\backslash_{csp}\{tau\} &&\text{(gstar-Def. 15)}\\
&= tl\big((a_1.0 + a_{12}.0)|_T(\bar{a}_2.0 + a_{12}.0)\big)\backslash_{csp}\{tau\} &&\text{(conm-Def. 18)}\\
&= \big((a_1 \to STOP \,\square\, a_{12} \to STOP) \underset{\{a_{12}\}}{\|}\\
&\qquad (\bar{a}_2 \to STOP \,\square\, a_{12} \to STOP)\big)\backslash_{csp}\{tau\} &&\text{(tl-Def. 20)}
\end{aligned}
$$

Final CSP Transformations ($-\backslash_{csp}\{a_{ij}\}, ai2a$). The final stages of our translation consists of hiding every a_{ij} synchronisation name (thus effectively turning them into τ) and renaming of all a_i names to a.

Definition 24. *Let a_i range over g^*-indexed names; $ai2a \mathrel{\hat{=}} \{a_i \mapsto a, \bar{a}_i \mapsto \bar{a}\}$.*

The following definition gives the end-to-end translation from CCS to CSP, as described in Sect. 3.

Definition 25. *Let P be a CCS process. Then:*

$$ccs2csp(P) \mathrel{\hat{=}} ai2a \circ (t2csp \circ c2ccs\tau(P)) \backslash_{csp}\{a_{ij}|a_{ij} \in \mathcal{A}(t2csp(c2ccs\tau(P)))\}$$

Example 26. In Sect. 3, we discuss at length the translation of CCS binary synchronisation into CSP. This can be illustrated more succinctly as follows:

$$
\begin{aligned}
&ccs2csp(a.0|\bar{a}.0)\\
&= ai2a \circ t2csp\big(c2ccs\tau(a.0|\bar{a}.0)\big)\backslash_{csp}\{a_{ij}|..\} &&\text{(ccs2csp-Def. 25)}\\
&= ai2a \circ t2csp\big((a.0|_T\bar{a}.0)\backslash_T\{\tau[a|\bar{a}]\}\big)\backslash_{csp}\{a_{ij}|..\} &&\text{(c2ccs}\tau\text{-par-Def. 11)}\\
&= ai2a \circ tl \circ conm \circ g^*(\{\,\}, ix((a.0|_T\bar{a}.0)\backslash_T\{\tau[a|\bar{a}]\}))\backslash_{csp}\{tau\}\backslash_{csp}\{a_{ij}|..\}\\
&&&\text{(t2csp-Def. 22)}\\
&= ai2a \circ tl \circ conm \circ g^*\big((a_1.0|_T\bar{a}_2.0)\big)\backslash_{csp}\{tau\}\backslash_{csp}\{a_{ij}|..\} &&\text{(ix-Prop. 13)}\\
&= ai2a \circ tl \circ conm\big((a_1.0 + a_{12}.0)|_T(\bar{a}_2.0 + \bar{a}_{12}.0)\big)\backslash_{csp}\{tau\}\backslash_{csp}\{a_{12}\} &&\text{(gstar-Def. 15)}\\
&= ai2a \circ tl\big((a_1.0 + a_{12}.0)|_T(\bar{a}_2.0 + a_{12}.0)\big)\backslash_{csp}\{tau, a_{12}\} &&\text{(conm-Def. 18)}\\
&= ai2a \circ \big((a_1 \,\square\, a_{12} \to STOP) \underset{\{a_{12}\}}{\|} (\bar{a}_2 \,\square\, a_{12} \to STOP)\big)\backslash_{csp}\{tau, a_{12}\} &&\text{(tl-Def. 20)}\\
&= \big((a \,\square\, a_{12} \to STOP) \underset{\{a_{12}\}}{\|} (\bar{a} \,\square\, a_{12} \to STOP)\big)\backslash_{csp}\{tau, a_{12}\} &&\text{(ai2a-Def. 24)}
\end{aligned}
$$

7   Correctness of the Translation

Here we discuss the correctness up to a semantic equivalence (Definition 6) of functions g^*, $t2csp$, and $ccs2csp$ defined above. In each case, we use labelled operational correspondence to relate a source term to its translation. In the end, the labelled operational correspondence between a CCS term and its CSP translation is a strong bisimulation, hence, translation $ccs2csp$ is correct up to strong bisimulation.

First, we consider the correctness of g^*.

Theorem 27 (Operational Correspondence between P and $g^*(S, ix(P))$).
Let P be a CCSTau process. Let $c4star(S, P) \,\widehat{=}\, g^*(S, ix(P))$. Then:

1. $P \xrightarrow{\tau} P'$ *imply that* $\forall S | S \cap Aix(P) = \{\} : c4star(S, P) \xrightarrow{\tau} Q$ *and* $Q \equiv c4star(S, P')$
2. $\forall S | S \cap Aix(P) = \{\} : c4star(S, P) \xrightarrow{\tau} Q$ *imply that* $\exists! P' : P \xrightarrow{\tau} P'$ *and* $Q \equiv c4star(S, P')$
3. $P \xrightarrow{a} P'$ *imply that* $\forall S | S \cap Aix(P) = \{\} : c4star(S, P) \xrightarrow{a_i} Q$ *and* $Q \equiv c4star(S, P')$
4. $\forall S | S \cap Aix(P) = \{\} : c4star(S, P) \xrightarrow{a_i} Q$ *imply that* $\exists! P' : P \xrightarrow{a} P'$ *and* $Q \equiv c4star(S, P')$
5. $P \xrightarrow{a} P'$ *imply that* $\forall S | S \cap Aix(P) = \{\} : c4star(S, P) \xrightarrow{a_{ij}} Q$ *and* $Q \equiv c4star(S, P')$
6. $\forall S, \exists i, j | i \neq j \wedge a_i \in S \wedge \bar{a}_j \in Aix(P) : c4star(S, P) \xrightarrow{a_{ij}} Q$ *imply that* $\exists! P' : P \xrightarrow{a} P'$ *and* $Q \equiv c4star(S, P')$
7. $P \xrightarrow{\tau[a|\bar{a}]} P'$ *imply that* $\forall S | S \cap Aix(P) = \{\} : c4star(S, P) \xrightarrow{\tau[a_{ij}|\bar{a}_{ij}]} Q$ *and* $Q \equiv c4star(S, P')$
8. $\forall S | S \cap Aix(P) = \{\} : c4star(S, P) \xrightarrow{\tau[a_{ij}|\bar{a}_{ij}]} Q$ *imply that* $\exists! P' : P \xrightarrow{\tau[a|\bar{a}]} P'$ *and* $Q \equiv c4star(S, P')$

Proof. By co-induction on the transitions of P and $c4star(S, P)$ respectively. E.g., consider every rule yielding a τ transition, e.g., Prefix, Sum. Induction over each rule yields structural induction over P. Apply the definition of c4star, then $c4star(S, P)$ has a τ transition by successive application of the Sum rule then the Prefix rule. Conversely, given $c4star(S, P)$, induction over each rule yields structural induction over $c4star(S, P)$.

Since a_{ij}-names denote synchronisation, $\tau[a_{ij}|\bar{a}_{ij}]$-actions only should be visible/allowed, viz., a_{ij}-names must be restricted. Hence, $g^*(S, ix(P))$ is not correct. We obtain a correct translation by restricting all a_{ij} names.

Corollary 28 (Correctness up to Strong Bisimulation of $g^*(S, ix(P))$).
Let P be a CCSTau process. Then, $g^*(S, ix(P)) \upharpoonright \{g\pi_2(S, a_i) | a_i \in Aix(P)\}$ is correct up to strong bisimulation.

Proof. Apply the restriction operator, $\upharpoonright \{g\pi_2(S, a_i)|a_i \in Aix(P)\}$, *to every clause in Theorem 27. This eliminates clauses 5 and 6 since* a_{ij} *can no longer occur.*

Theorem 29 (Operational Correspondence of $t2csp$**).** *Let* P *be a CCSTau process. Then:*

1. $P \xrightarrow{\tau} P'$ *imply that* $\forall S | S \cap Aix(P) = \{\} : t2csp(S, P) \xrightarrow{\tau} t2csp(S, P')$
2. $\forall S | S \cap Aix(P) = \{\} : t2csp(S, P) \xrightarrow{\tau} Q$ *imply that* $\exists! P' : P \xrightarrow{\tau} P'$ *and* $Q = t2csp(S, P')$
3. $P \xrightarrow{a} P'$ *imply that* $\forall S | S \cap Aix(P) = \{\} : t2csp(S, P) \xrightarrow{a_i} t2csp(S, P')$
4. $\forall S | S \cap Aix(P) = \{\} : t2csp(S, P) \xrightarrow{a_i} Q$ *imply that* $\exists! P' : P \xrightarrow{a} P'$ *and* $Q = t2csp(S, P')$
5. $P \xrightarrow{\tau[a|\bar{a}]} P'$ *imply that* $\forall S | S \cap Aix(P) = \{\} : t2csp(S, P) \xrightarrow{a_{ij}} t2csp(S, P')$
6. $\forall S | S \cap Aix(P) = \{\} : t2csp(S, P) \xrightarrow{a_{ij}} Q$ *imply that* $\exists! P' : P \xrightarrow{\tau[a|\bar{a}]} P'$ *and* $Q = t2csp(S, P')$

Proof. By co-induction on the transitions of P *and* $t2csp(P)$ *respectively.*

Theorem 30 (Correctness of $ccs2csp$**).** *Let* P *be a CCS process. Then:*

1. $P \xrightarrow{\tau} P'$ *imply that* $\forall S | S \cap Aix(P) = \{\} : ccs2csp(S, P) \xrightarrow{\tau} ccs2csp(S, P')$
2. $\forall S | S \cap Aix(P) = \{\} : ccs2csp(S, P) \xrightarrow{\tau} Q$ *imply that* $\exists! P' : P \xrightarrow{\tau} P'$ *and* $Q = ccs2csp(S, P')$
3. $P \xrightarrow{a} P'$ *imply that* $\forall S | S \cap Aix(P) = \{\} : ccs2csp(S, P) \xrightarrow{a} ccs2csp(S, P')$
4. $\forall S | S \cap Aix(P) = \{\} : ccs2csp(S, P) \xrightarrow{a} Q$ *imply that* $\exists! P' : P \xrightarrow{a} P'$ *and* $Q = ccs2csp(S, P')$

We say that ccs2csp is correct up to strong bisimulation.

Proof. Apply c2ccsτ (Definition 11), this turns CCS process P *into CCSTau process* $ccs2\tau(P)$. *Apply* $-\backslash_{csp}\{a_{ij}\}$, *this hides every* a_{ij} *from* $t2csp(c2ccs\tau(P))$. *As a consequence, this eliminates clauses 5 and 6 from Theorem 29. Then apply ai2a, this renames every* a_i *into an* a. *Thus, every* a_i *from Theorem 29 becomes an* a.

The above theorems culminate to the following correctness result of our end-to-end translation.

Corollary 31 (Correctness of the Translation up to Strong Bisimulation). *Let* P *be a CCS process. Then:* $ccs2csp(P) \sim P$.

A trivial consequence of this corollary is that $P \sim Q \Leftrightarrow ccs2csp(P) \sim ccs2csp(Q)$. Since strong bisimulation is included in failure equivalence, we have $P \sim Q \Leftrightarrow ccs2csp(P) =_{\mathcal{F}} ccs2csp(Q)$. We illustrate this subsequently.

Example 32. In CCS, we have: $(a.0|\bar{a}.0) \upharpoonright \{a\} + b.0 \sim \tau.0 + b.0$. We check that:
$ccs2csp\big((a.0|\bar{a}.0) \upharpoonright \{a\} + b.0\big) =_{\mathcal{F}} ccs2csp(\tau.0 + b.0)$.
We have:

$$ccs2csp\big((a.0|\bar{a}.0) \upharpoonright \{a\} + b.0\big)$$

$$= ai2a \circ t2csp \circ c2ccs\tau\big((a.0|\bar{a}.0) \upharpoonright \{a\} + b.0\big) \qquad \text{(ccs2csp-Def. 25)}$$

$$= ai2a \circ t2csp\big((a.0|_T \bar{a}.0)\backslash_T \{\tau[a|\bar{a}]\} \upharpoonright \{a\} + b.0\big) \qquad \text{(c2ccs}\tau\text{-par-Def. 11)}$$

$$= ai2a \circ \big[\big((a_1 \;\square\; a_{12} \to STOP) \underset{\{a_{12}\}}{\parallel} (a_2 \;\square\; a_{12} \to STOP)\big)\upharpoonright_{csp}\{a_1, a_2\} \;\square$$

$$(b \to STOP)\big]\backslash_{csp}\{tau, a_{12}\} \qquad \text{(Ex. 23, t2csp-Def. 22)}$$

$$= \big[\big((a \;\square\; a_{12} \to STOP) \underset{\{a_{12}\}}{\parallel} (a \;\square\; a_{12} \to STOP)\big)\upharpoonright_{csp}\{a\} \;\square$$

$$b \to STOP\big]\backslash_{csp}\{tau, a_{12}\} \qquad \text{(ai2a-Def. 24)}$$

$$= \big[\big((a \;\square\; a_{12} \to STOP) \underset{\{a_{12}\}}{\parallel} (a \;\square\; a_{12} \to STOP) \underset{\{a\}}{\parallel} STOP\big) \;\square$$

$$(b \to STOP)\big]\backslash_{csp}\{tau, a_{12}\} \qquad \text{(res-Def. 19)}$$

$$= (a_{12} \to STOP \;\square\; b \to STOP)\backslash_{csp}\{a_{12}\} \qquad \text{(CSP)}$$

$$= (STOP \;\square\; b \to STOP) \sqcap STOP \qquad \text{(CSP[17, §3.5.1, L10])}$$

We also have:

$$ccs2csp(\tau.0 + b.0)$$

$$= ai2a \circ t2csp \circ c2ccs\tau(\tau.0 + b.0) \qquad \text{(ccs2csp-Def. 25)}$$

$$= ai2a \circ t2csp \circ (\tau.0 + b.0) \qquad \text{(ccs2csp-Def. 11)}$$

$$= ai2a \circ (tau \to STOP \;\square\; b \to STOP)\backslash_{csp}\{tau\} \qquad \text{(t2csp-Def. 22)}$$

$$= (tau \to STOP \;\square\; b \to STOP)\backslash_{csp}\{tau\} \qquad \text{(ai2a-Def. 24)}$$

$$= (STOP \;\square\; b \to STOP) \sqcap STOP \qquad \text{(CSP[17, §3.5.1, L10])}$$

8 Alternative Translation, Correct up to Failure Equivalence

De Nicola and Hennessy [18] define a version of CCS, called TCCS, which removes from CCS the summation operator and τ action, and adds external ($\square$) and internal ($\sqcap$) choice operators. They further provide a translation from CCS to TCCS that is correct up to *must equivalence* ([18, Thm. 4.4]). Reusing their translation ([18, Def. 4.1]), we arrive at the following CCS-to-CSP translation:

$$ccs2csp_2(P) \triangleq ai2a \circ (tl_2 \circ conm \circ g^* \circ ix(P)) \backslash_{csp} \{a_{ij}\} \qquad (ccs2csp_2\text{-def})$$

$$tl_2(\alpha.P) \triangleq \begin{cases} tl_2(P) & \text{if } \alpha = \tau \\ \alpha \rightarrow tl_2(P) \end{cases} \qquad (tl_2\text{-prefix})$$

$$tl_2(P+Q) \triangleq \begin{cases} tl_2(P) \ \square \ tl_2(Q) & \text{if } \forall P' : \neg(P \xrightarrow{\tau} P' \vee Q \xrightarrow{\tau} P') \\ \left(tl_2(P) \ \square \ tl_2(Q)\right) \sqcap \bigsqcap \{tl_2(P')|P \xrightarrow{\tau} P' \vee Q \xrightarrow{\tau} P'\} \end{cases}$$

$$(tl_2\text{-choice})$$

$$tl_2(P) \triangleq tl(P) \qquad \text{if } P \text{ is not prefix or choice}$$

Example 33. In particular, from the definition of $ccs2csp_2$, we derive:

$$ccs2csp_2(a.P + b.Q) = a \rightarrow ccs2csp_2(P) \ \square \ b \rightarrow ccs2csp_2(Q)$$
$$ccs2csp_2(\tau.P + b.Q) = (ccs2csp_2(P) \ \square \ b \rightarrow ccs2csp_2(Q)) \sqcap ccs2csp_2(P)$$
$$ccs2csp_2(\tau.P + \tau.Q) = (ccs2csp_2(P) \ \square \ ccs2csp_2(Q)) \sqcap ccs2csp_2(P) \sqcap ccs2csp_2(Q)$$

(tl_2-prefix) implies that τ prefixes are absent from the LTS of the CSP translation. As a consequence, P and $ccs2csp_2(P)$ *are not strong bisimilar*; however, they are failure equivalent: $P =_{\mathcal{F}} ccs2csp_2(P)$. Note that $ccs2csp$ (Definition 25) is failure equivalent to $ccs2csp_2$: $ccs2csp_2(P) =_{\mathcal{F}} ccs2csp(P)$.[3]

9   Structural Properties of the Translation

In the literature of evaluating the relative expressiveness of different calculi, different evaluation criteria for encodings have been proposed (e.g., [6,8,10,11, 19,20]). Gorla [11] notably proposes five requirements for a translation to be *valid*: on the structural end, it must enjoy the compositionality and name invariance properties; on the behavioural end, operational correspondence, divergence reflection, and success sensitiveness.

The translation from CCS to CSP we provide here (*ccs2csp*, Definition 25) is correct up to strong bisimulation (Corollary 31). This is a stronger result than operational correspondence, and by definition, implies both divergence reflection (viz., if a CSP translation diverges then its source CCS term does) and success sensitiveness (viz., a CCS term converges if, and only if, its CSP translation converges, and both converge to the same success final term). Correctness up to strong bisimulation also implies name invariance. E.g., let P be a CCS process, f a given renaming function; then $ccs2csp(f(P)) \sim f(ccs2csp(P))$.

---

[3] E.g., let $P = Q = 0$ in Example 33 then, compare the mixed choice case with Example 32.

Our translation is not compositional in the sense of Gorla [11], whereby a compositional translation $T : \mathcal{L}_1 \rightarrow \mathcal{L}_2$ is such that $T(op(S_1, ..., S_k)) = C_{op}^N(T(S_1), ..., T(S_k))$, where op is any operator of $\mathcal{L}_1$, C_{op}^N a context that coordinates translated subterms, and $N = fn(S_1, ..., S_k)$. However, Gorla acknowledges the existence of correct translations that are not compositional and further acknowledges that his proposal is not adequate to deal with encodings defined as a family of translations T_Σ, where Σ denotes auxiliary parameters of the translation (including sets of names) [11, Conclusion]. Our encoding from CCS to CSP, $ccs2csp$ (Definition 25), falls into the latter category.

10   Conclusion and Future Work

In this paper we have studied the relationship between CCS and CSP as part of a greater work that aims to link also Pi-calculus [16] with CSPmob [4]. Many extensions were necessary in order to define the links from CCS to CSP. We have not explored here links in the opposite direction, from CSP to CCS. We leave this to future work. For reference, van Glabbeek [10] proposes a link from CSP to CCS that is correct up to trace equivalence.

We have defined CCSTau, which extends CCS with visible synchronisations and the hiding operator. This allowed us to separate synchronisation from hiding in a CCS context. We notably show that CCS is a subset of CCSTau. We then defined the translation from CCSTau to CSP. In order to achieve this, we extended CSP with the restriction operator.

The most difficult feature to translate was the CCS synchronisation mechanism. In CCS, a single name is capable of both interleaving and synchronisation; and synchronisation (automatically) implies hiding. This is unlike CSP where all these issues are handled in separate operators. The constraint then was to preserve CCS binary synchronisation from capture by CSP multiway synchronisation. To resolve this, we have proposed the g^* renaming approach: if two CCS processes can synchronise on an action b, then a name unique to these two processes, say b_{ij}, is generated to substitute b. Hence, only two processes will ever be able to synchronise on b_{ij} after application of g^*. This guarantees that in CSP, there will never be more than two processes capable of synchronising on b_{ij}, thus avoiding capture by multiway synchronisation. We show that the g^*-based translation is correct. Another solution is possible: extend CSP with binary synchronisation, then translate CCS binary synchronisation into CSP binary synchronisation. We leave the presentation of this alternative to a future publication.

We have proposed here the translation from CCS to CSP only. The main reason for this is our interest in using CSP tools such as FDR for reasoning about CCS processes. With regard to this concern, the g^*-renaming approach is more readily implementable than the second approach. The latter would require extending FDR with semantics (viz. rules) for m-among-n synchronisation.

A natural extension of this paper is to translate Pi-calculus [16] into CSPmob [4]. Assuming that CCS is a subset of Pi-calculus and given that CSP is a subset of CSPmob, we will focus our attention on mobility constructs hence. Our final goal is to formalise our results in Unifying Theories of Programming (UTP) [13]. One advantage of the latter would be the extension of both CCS and CSP with a richer notion of state. For illustration, Garavel [9] deplores the limitations of the prefix operator in both CCS and CSP and shows that a richer form of sequential composition can be achieved based on a richer notion of state. Moving to UTP will also allow us to mechanise our results using ongoing mechanisation of UTP theories in Isabelle [7], and link up with Isabelle mechanisation of Psi-calculi [2] (a variant of Pi-calculus).

Acknowledgments. The authors are grateful to the anonymous reviewers for their suggestions on how to improve this paper. This work was funded in part by the Science Foundation Ireland grant 13/RC/2094 (LERO), and co-funded by the European Union's Horizon 2020 research and innovation programme under the Marie Skłodowska-Curie grant agreement No 754489. For the purpose of Open Access, the authors have applied a CC BY public copyright licence to any Author Accepted Manuscript version arising from this submission.

References

1. Aceto, L., Larsen, K.A., Ingolfsdottir, A.: An Introduction to Milner's CCS (2005). http://twiki.di.uniroma1.it/pub/MFS/WebHome/intro2ccs.pdf. Accessed 30 July 2021
2. Bengtson, J., Parrow, J., Weber, T.: Psi-calculi in Isabelle. J. Autom. Reason. **56**(1), 1–47 (2015). https://doi.org/10.1007/s10817-015-9336-2
3. Brookes, S.D.: On the relationship of CCS and CSP. In: Diaz, J. (ed.) ICALP 1983. LNCS, vol. 154, pp. 83–96. Springer, Heidelberg (1983). https://doi.org/10.1007/BFb0036899
4. Ngondi, G.E.: Denotational semantics of channel mobility in UTP-CSP. Formal Aspects Comput. **33**(1), 803–826 (2021). https://doi.org/10.1007/s00165-021-00546-3
5. FDR Documentation. https://cocotec.io/fdr/manual/. Accessed 30 July 2021
6. Felleisen, M.: On the expressive power of programming languages. Sci. Comput. Program. **17**, 35–75 (1991). https://doi.org/10.1016/0167-6423(91)90036-W
7. Foster, S., Zeyda, F., Woodcock, J.: Isabelle/UTP: a mechanised theory engineering framework. In: Naumann, D. (ed.) UTP 2014. LNCS, vol. 8963, pp. 21–41. Springer, Cham (2015). https://doi.org/10.1007/978-3-319-14806-9_2
8. Fu, Y., Lu, H.: On the expressiveness of interaction. TCS **411**, 1387–1451 (2010). https://doi.org/10.1016/j.tcs.2009.11.011
9. Garavel, H.: Revisiting sequential composition in process calculi. J. Log. Algebraic Methods Program **84**, 742–762 (2015). https://doi.org/10.1016/j.jlamp.2015.08.001
10. van Glabbeek, R.: Musings on encodings and expressiveness. In: EPTCS, vol. 89, pp. 81–98 (2012). https://doi.org/10.4204/EPTCS.89.7
11. Gorla, D.: Towards a unified approach to encodability and separation results for process calculi. In: van Breugel, F., Chechik, M. (eds.) CONCUR 2008. LNCS, vol. 5201, pp. 492–507. Springer, Heidelberg (2008). https://doi.org/10.1007/978-3-540-85361-9_38

12. Hatzel, M., Wagner, C., Peters, K., Nestmann, U.: Encoding CSP into CCS. In: EXPRESS/SOS Workshop. EPTCS, vol. 190, pp. 61–75 (2015). https://doi.org/10.4204/EPTCS.190.5
13. He, J., Hoare, C.A.R.: CSP is a retract of CCS. TCS **411**, 1311–1337 (2010). https://doi.org/10.1016/j.tcs.2009.12.012
14. Hoare, C.A.R.: Communicating Sequential Processes. Prentice-Hall, Hoboken (1985)
15. Hoare, C.A.R.: Why ever CSP. ENTCS **162**, 209–215 (2006). https://doi.org/10.1016/j.entcs.2006.01.031
16. Milner, R.: Communicating and Mobile Systems: The Pi-Calculus. Cambridge University Press, Cambridge (1999)
17. Milner, R.: Communication and Concurrency. Prentice-Hall, Hoboken (1989)
18. De Nicola, R., Hennessy, M.: CCS without τ's. In: Ehrig, H., Kowalski, R., Levi, G., Montanari, U. (eds.) CAAP 1987. LNCS, vol. 249, pp. 138–152. Springer, Heidelberg (1987). https://doi.org/10.1007/3-540-17660-8_53
19. Parrow, J.: Expressiveness of process algebras. ENTCS **209**, 173–186 (2008). https://doi.org/10.1016/j.entcs.2008.04.011
20. Peters, K.: Comparing process calculi using encodings. In: EXPRESS/SOS Workshop. EPTCS, vol. 300, pp. 19–38 (2019). https://doi.org/10.4204/EPTCS.300.2
21. Sangiorgi, D.: Introduction to Bisimulation and Coinduction. Cambridge University Press, Cambridge (2012)
22. Schneider, S.: Concurrent and Real-Time Systems - The CSP Approach. Wiley, Hoboken (2000)
23. Haskell Prototype Automation of CCS-to-CSP Translation: GitHub Repository. https://github.com/andrewbutterfield/ccs2csp. Accessed 30 July 2021

Probabilistic BDI Agents: Actions, Plans, and Intentions

Blair Archibald, Muffy Calder, Michele Sevegnani, and Mengwei Xu[✉]

University of Glasgow, Glasgow, UK
{blair.archibald,muffy.calder,michele.sevegnani,mengwei.xu}@glasgow.ac.uk

Abstract. The Belief-Desire-Intention (BDI) architecture is a popular framework for rational agents, yet most verification approaches are limited to analysing qualitative properties, for example whether an intention completes. BDI-based systems, however, operate in uncertain environments with dynamic behaviours: we may need quantitative analysis to establish properties such as the probability of eventually completing an intention. We define a probabilistic extension to the Conceptual Agent Notation (CAN) for BDI agents that supports probabilistic action outcomes, and probabilistic plan and intention selection. The semantics is executable via an encoding in Milner's bigraphs and the BigraphER tool. Quantitative analysis is conducted using PRISM. While the new semantics can be applied to any CAN program, we demonstrate the extension by comparing with standard plan and intention selection strategies (*e.g.* ordered or fixed schedules) and evaluating probabilistic action executions in a smart manufacturing scenario. The results show we can improve significantly the probability of intention completion, with appropriate probabilistic distribution. We also show the impact of probabilistic action outcomes can be marginal, even when the failure probabilities are large, due to the agent making smarter intention selection choices.

Keywords: BDI agents · Quantitative analysis · Bigraphs

1 Introduction

A well-studied and popular architecture for developing rational agents is the Belief-Desire-Intention (BDI) paradigm. BDI paradigm builds upon a sound theoretical foundation to model an agent where (B)eliefs represent what the agent knows, (D)esires what the agent wants to bring about, and (I)ntentions the desires the agent is currently acting upon. BDI agents have inspired many agent-oriented programming languages including AgentSpeak [1], CAN [2], and CANPLAN [3], 3APL [4], and 2APL [5] along with a collection of mature software toolkits and platforms including JACK [6], Jason [7], and Jadex [8]. BDI agents have been recognised for their efficiency and scalability in areas such as business [9], healthcare [10], and engineering [11].

In BDI languages, desires and intentions are often represented using a plan library. Each plan describes a course of actions which an agent can perform

© Springer Nature Switzerland AG 2021
R. Calinescu and C. S. Păsăreanu (Eds.): SEFM 2021, LNCS 13085, pp. 262–281, 2021.
https://doi.org/10.1007/978-3-030-92124-8_15

to address an event given some beliefs hold, while the set of intentions are the plans currently being executed. Typically BDI languages: (1) assume that action outcomes (*i.e.* the effects on *external* environment) are deterministic, (2) remain agnostic *internally* to the choice of an applicable plan to bring about its desires, (3) remain agnostic *internally* to the order that intentions are progressed. These assumptions facilitate the verification of agent behaviour through a non-deterministic underlying transition system (*e.g.* [12,13]), where plan and intention selection denotes branching choices and actions have a single outcome. Unfortunately, this often does not adequately represent behaviour in uncertain environments such as cyber-physical robotics systems (*e.g.* surveyed in [14]) with uncertain sensors, and actuators.

For example, the outcome of an action may be probabilistic due to sensor noise and imprecise actuation, and plans and intentions are not created equally and are likely to have different characteristics such as preference and urgency. As a result, there is a growing need for formal techniques that can handle quantitative properties of agent-based systems under uncertainty.

We employ the following robot packaging task for smart manufacturing as an example, giving detailed quantitative analysis in Sect. 4. The robot insulates products with suitable wrapping bags, to prevent temperature rise and consequent spoilage, and then transfers the wrapped products to a storage location. There are two types of wrapping bags: premium and standard. The standard wrapping is preferred as the cheaper option, however it may not be effective if the product temperature is already too high, and/or the packaging occasionally breaks, which results in damaged product (*i.e.* a negative action outcome). Before wrapping the products, the robot also has to decide which product to handle first (as there may be multiple products waiting), meaning handling a product before it spoils requires a notion of urgency. While it is important to prioritise the more urgent products, it is also sensible to progress less urgent ones from time-to-time, before they also become urgent. So we need to model and *quantify* agent behaviour when there is a range of choices, inherent uncertainty, and characteristics of preference and urgency. For example, we may wish to know the probability the robot can complete packaging under different schedules, negative outcomes, and decisions.

In the BDI community, probabilistic action outcomes are usually implicit—requiring the agent to *sense* failures and *revise* the beliefs (*i.e.* to enable new plans)—and are often disregarded when modelling. Although most agent language semantics specify non-deterministic *plan selection*, e.g. in [2], it is typical in practice for plans to be ordered—either statically [7] or at run-time [15]—to enforce deterministic branching. While desirable to exploit the highest ordered plan, it may be worthwhile exploring other non-highest order plans every now and then to avoid being stuck in a local maximum. Similarly, *intention selection* is also not implemented in a fully non-deterministic fashion either, but in a fixed schedule, *e.g.* round robin (executing a step of each intention in turn).

We argue that the highest ordering (*i.e.* local maximum) and fixed schedules (*e.g.* round robin) are not always the best approach to plan/intention selection and suggest agents should support probabilistic plan/intention selection along with the need to evaluate the undesired outcomes of actions. Therefore, we present a formal approach to specify, model, and quantitatively analyse BDI agents with probabilistic action outcomes and plan/intention selections drawn from a probability distribution. Quantitative verification, *e.g.* asking the probability some intention completes, aids the design of agents by enabling plan and intention selection functions to be explored, and mitigates the risk of operating in the uncertain environments by providing quantitative assurance.

We have extended the operational semantics of CAN language in [2] to a probabilistic setting. CAN is chosen as it features a high-level agent programming language that captures the essence of BDI concepts without describing implementation details such as data structures. As a superset of AgentSpeak [1], CAN includes advanced BDI agent behaviours such as reasoning with *declarative goals*, *concurrency*, and *failure recovery*, which are necessary for our smart manufacturing example modelled in Sect. 4. Importantly, although we focus on CAN, the language features are similar to those of other mainstream BDI languages and the same modelling techniques would apply to other BDI programming languages. We build on our previous work on an executable semantics of CAN [16], based on Milner's Bigraphs [17] and provide the resulting probabilistic *executable* semantics.

We use probabilistic bigraphs [18] that allow a (relative) weight to be assigned to bigraph reaction rules and we extend the rules in CAN specifying plan selection, intention selection, and probabilistic action outcomes (specified by the user). For automated verification, we export a Discrete Time Markov Chain (DTMC) from the bigraph model for analysis in probabilistic model checkers, *e.g.* PRISM [19]. We believe this is the first rigorous quantitative analysis through formal modelling applied to plan selection, intention selection, and action execution within mainstream BDI agents.

We make the following research contributions:

- a probabilistic extension of the semantics of CAN language;
- an executable semantics of CAN based on probabilistic bigraphs;
- an evaluation, in a smart manufacturing case, of probabilistic plan and intention selection under probabilistic action outcomes, against standard counterparts, *e.g.* ordered plan selection and round robin intention selection.

The paper is organised as follows. In Sect. 2 we provide a brief overview of BDI agents and Bigraphs. In Sect. 3 we propose the probabilistic extension of CAN semantics. In Sect. 4 we evaluate our approach on a smart manufacturing example. We discuss related work in Sect. 5 and conclude in Sect. 6.

2   Background

2.1   BDI Agents

A BDI agent has an explicit representation of beliefs, desires, and intentions. The beliefs correspond to what the agent believes about the environment, while the desires are a set of *external* events that the agent can respond to. To respond to those events, the agent selects a plan (given its beliefs) from the pre-defined plan library and commits to the selected plan by turning it into a new intention.

The CAN language formalises a classical BDI agent consisting of a belief base $\mathcal{B}$ and a plan library Π. The belief base $\mathcal{B}$ is a set of formulas encoding the current beliefs and has belief operators for entailment (*i.e.* $\mathcal{B} \models \varphi$), and belief atom addition (resp. deletion) $\mathcal{B} \cup \{b\}$ (resp. $\mathcal{B} \setminus \{b\}$)[1]. A plan library Π is a collection of plans of the form $e : \varphi \leftarrow P$ with e the triggering event, φ the context condition, and P the plan-body. The triggering event e specifies why the plan is triggered, while the context condition φ determines *when* the plan-body P is able to handle the event. Events can be either be external (*i.e.* from the environment in which the agent is operating) or internal (*i.e.* sub-goals that the agent itself tries to accomplish). The language used in the plan-body is defined by the following grammar:

$$P = nil \mid +b \mid -b \mid act \mid ?\varphi \mid e \mid P_1; P_2 \mid P_1 \triangleright P_2 \mid P_1 \parallel P_2 \mid$$
$$e : (|\varphi_1 : P_1, \cdots, \varphi_n : P_n|) \mid goal(\varphi_s, P, \varphi_f)$$

where nil is an empty program, $+b$ and $-b$ belief addition and deletion, act a primitive action, $?\varphi$ a test for φ in the belief base, and e is a sub-event (i.e. internal event). Actions act take the form $act = \varphi \leftarrow \langle \phi^+, \phi^- \rangle$, where φ is the pre-condition, and ϕ^+ and ϕ^- are the addition and deletion sets (resp.) of belief atoms, i.e. a belief base $\mathcal{B}$ is revised to be $(\mathcal{B} \setminus \phi^-) \cup \phi^+$ when the action executes. To execute a sub-event, a plan (corresponding to that event) is selected and the plan-body added in place of the event. In this way we allow plans to be nested (similar to sub-routine calls in other languages). In addition, there are composite programs $P_1; P_2$ for sequence, $P_1 \triangleright P_2$ that executes P_2 in the case that P_1 fails, and $P_1 \parallel P_2$ for interleaved concurrency. A set of relevant plans (those that respond to the same event) is denoted by $e : (|\psi_1 : P_1, \cdots, \psi_n : P_n|)$. Finally, a declarative goal program $goal(\varphi_s, P, \varphi_f)$ expresses that the declarative goal φ_s should be achieved through program P, failing if φ_f becomes true, and retrying as long as neither φ_s nor φ_f is true (see in [3] for details).

The operational semantics for CAN are defined over configurations $\mathcal{C}$ and transitions $\mathcal{C} \rightarrow \mathcal{C}'$. A transition $\mathcal{C} \rightarrow \mathcal{C}'$ denotes a single execution step between configuration $\mathcal{C}$ and $\mathcal{C}'$. We write $\mathcal{C} \rightarrow$ (resp. $\mathcal{C} \nrightarrow$) to state that there is (resp. is not) a $\mathcal{C}'$ such that $\mathcal{C} \rightarrow \mathcal{C}'$. A derivation rule consists of a (possibly empty) set of premises p_i ($i = 1, \ldots, n$) on $\mathcal{C}$, and a conclusion, denoted by

$$\frac{p_1 \quad p_2 \quad \cdots \quad p_n}{\mathcal{C} \rightarrow \mathcal{C}'} l$$

where l is a rule name. We write $\mathcal{C} \xrightarrow{l} \mathcal{C}'$ to denote $\mathcal{C}$ evolves to $\mathcal{C}'$ through the application of derivation rule l.

A basic configuration $\langle \mathcal{B}, P \rangle$, where P is the plan-body program being executed (*i.e.* the current intention), is used in rules that define the execution of

---

[1] Any logic is allowed providing entailment is supported. A propositional logic with natural number comparisons is used in our examples.

a single intention. The agent configuration is defined as $\langle E^e, \mathcal{B}, \Gamma \rangle$ where E^e stands for the a set of pending external events and Γ the current set of intentions (partially executed plan-body programs). The semantics of CAN language is specified by two types of transitions. The first transition type, denoted as $\rightarrow$, specifies *intention-level* evolution in terms of basic configuration $\langle \mathcal{B}, P \rangle$ and the second type, denoted as $\Rightarrow$, specifies *agent-level* evolution over the agent configuration $\langle E^e, \mathcal{B}, \Gamma \rangle$. For example, in the *intention-level* evolution, the transition for belief addition and a belief test can be given as follows:

$$\frac{}{\langle \mathcal{B}, +b \rangle \rightarrow \langle \mathcal{B} \cup \{b\}, nil \rangle} +b \qquad \frac{\mathcal{B} \models \varphi}{\langle \mathcal{B}, ?\varphi \rangle \rightarrow \langle \mathcal{B}, nil \rangle} \ ?$$

We refer the reader to [2,20] for a full overview of the semantics of CAN.

2.2   Bigraphs

Bigraphs are a graph-based universal modelling formalism, introduced by Milner [17], and extended to probabilistic systems [18]. As a graph-based rewriting formalism, over rules called reaction rules, bigraphs not only provide an intuitive diagrammatic representation, which is ideal for visualising the execution process of the systems, but also offer compositional reasoning via explicit abstractions (sites/regions/names), customised rewriting rules, and multiple ways to relate entities (placement and linking). They have been used both for modelling ubiquitous systems [21–23] and as a unifying theory of existing process calculi [24,25] and their semantics.

The evolution of bigraphs is described through over a rewriting system specified via reaction rule $l \longrightarrow r$ that replace a bigraph matching l with a bigraph matching r in some larger bigraph[2]. Given an initial bigraph and set of reaction rules we can derive a non-deterministic transition system capturing the behaviour of the system. We have used this to encode the existing CAN language semantics in order to symbolically analyse BDI agent behaviour [16]. The encoding defines a bigraph equivalent for any CAN agent, and defines reaction rules that faithfully model the operational semantics (essentially a tree exploration).

Probabilistic bigraphs [18] allow reaction rules to be weighted, *e.g.* $t_1 = l_1 \xrightarrow{2} r_1$ and $t_2 = l_2 \xrightarrow{1} r_2$, such that if both (and only) t_1 and t_2 are applicable then t_1 is twice as likely to apply as t_2. In this case the transition system generated is a DTMC that can be analysed by probabilistic model checker, *e.g.* PRISM [19].

To execute (probabilistic) bigraphical reactive systems, we employ BigraphER [26], an open-source language and toolkit for bigraphs. It also allows exporting transitions systems, *e.g.* DTMCs, for analysis in specialised model checking tools. To aid writing logical formulas over the transition systems, states may be labelled using bigraph patterns that assign a state *predicate* label if it contains (a match of) given bigraph patterns.

---

[2] Similar to term rewriting lifted to graph structures.

3   Probabilistic Extension of CAN Semantics

In this section we detail how action outcomes, plan selection, and intention selection from CAN can be extended to support probabilistic reasoning.

3.1   Probabilistic Action Outcomes

Agents execute actions that both interact with an external environment (*e.g.* pick up an object), and in-turn revise the internal belief base (*e.g.* the agent believes it holds the object). Action execution is specified in CAN as:

$$\frac{act : \varphi \leftarrow \langle \phi^-, \phi^+ \rangle \quad \mathcal{B} \vDash \varphi}{\langle \mathcal{B}, act \rangle \rightarrow \langle (\mathcal{B} \setminus \phi^- \cup \phi^+), nil \rangle} \ act$$

This states that an action applies only if the precondition φ holds, and the outcome is to update the belief base by adding and removing the atoms specified by ϕ^+ and ϕ^-, respectively. Other than beliefs, the agent has no notion of the environment and these are assumed to be side-effects.

In practice, we know the outcomes of an action are uncertain (*e.g.* due to actuator malfunctions). For example, an agent may execute an action to pick up an object but fail to do so because a robotic arm fails. In this case, updating the beliefs that an object is held leads to misalignment between the true environment and the agent's representation of it. This form of uncertainty has been considered extensively in the planning literature and has led to, *e.g.* probabilistic planning domain definition languages (PPDDL) [27], that consider multiple outcomes with associated probabilities (*e.g.* estimated from the historic data).

We follow a similar approach and sample action outcomes from a probability distribution $\mu = [(\phi_1^-, \phi_1^+) \mapsto p_1, \ldots, (\phi_n^-, \phi_n^+) \mapsto p_n]$ with $\sum_{i=1}^n p_i = 1$. That is, we use actions in the form $a : \varphi \leftarrow \mu$ where the original action form is the special case of μ being a delta distribution (single outcome with probability 1). Defined using probabilistic transitions $\mathcal{C} \rightarrow_p \mathcal{C}'$ (*i.e.* move from $\mathcal{C}$ to $\mathcal{C}'$ with probability p) [28], we introduce a probabilistic action execution as follows:

$$\frac{act : \varphi \leftarrow \mu \quad \mu(\phi^-, \phi^+) = p \quad \mathcal{B} \vDash \varphi}{\langle \mathcal{B}, act \rangle \rightarrow_p \langle (\mathcal{B} \setminus \phi^- \cup \phi^+), nil \rangle} \ act^p$$

Importantly we do not expect programming language *implementations* based on these semantics to draw action outcomes probabilistically. Instead it is used solely for modelling, allowing us to capture environmental effects in a semantics where they are usually ignored.

3.2   Plan Selection and Its Probabilistic Extension

BDI agents employ a user-provided plan library to respond to events. Each plan has i) a triggering event defining what event the plan can respond to, ii) a precondition defining what beliefs must hold for the plan to apply, and iii) a plan-body defining what steps should be taken to execute the plan. To address a pending event (*e.g.* from the external environment), the agent retrieves a set of *relevant* plans: those with a matching triggering event, captured as follows:

$$\frac{\Delta = \{\varphi : P \mid (e' = \varphi \leftarrow P) \in \Pi \wedge e' = e\}}{\langle \mathcal{B}, e \rangle \rightarrow \langle \mathcal{B}, e : (\mid \Delta \mid) \rangle} \; event$$

Given a set of relevant plans, the agent then selects an *applicable* plan (one where the precondition is true) as specified by rule *select*:

$$\frac{\varphi : P \in \Delta \quad \mathcal{B} \models \varphi}{\langle \mathcal{B}, e : (\mid \Delta \mid) \rangle \rightarrow \langle \mathcal{B}, P \triangleright e : (\mid \Delta \setminus \{\varphi : P\} \mid) \rangle} \; select$$

If there are no applicable plans a separate rule (unshown) propagates the failure.

Plan Selection Strategies

Notice that the preceding *select* rule does not specify which plan should be selected in case of multiple applicable plans, *i.e.* it is non-deterministic.

However, in practice, we often want more control over which plan is chosen, and different plans are likely to be more/less preferred based on domain-specific characteristics, *e.g.* costs. Therefore, in many implementations the choice is often made deterministically by a plan selection function of the following form:

$$\delta : 2^{\mathcal{B}} \times 2^{\Pi} \rightarrow \Pi \cup \{\bot\}$$

where $\mathcal{B}$ is the belief base and Π the plan library. Given a belief base and a set of (relevant) plans it returns an applicable plan or $\bot$, *i.e.* no applicable plan.

While a common heuristic is to select the plan with the highest order based on some characteristics (*e.g.* preference), it may not lead to globally optimal behaviours due to action side-effects. We argue that it should be possible to *prioritise* plan choice based on plan characteristics, but not assume a totally fixed ordering in order to allow exploration of non-highest order plans that might have better properties. This is akin to discrepancy search techniques [29] to go against the heuristic, and is particularly useful for declarative goals to avoid repeating the same plan obsessively.

To allow non-strict orderings we sample plans based on a probability distribution, *i.e.* with the following plan selection function:

$$\delta^p : 2^{\mathcal{B}} \times 2^{\Pi} \rightarrow Dist(\Pi) \cup \{\bot\}$$

where $Dist(\Pi)$ is the set of discrete probability distribution over the plan library and $\bot$ stands for no applicable plan available. Using δ^p we can define a probabilistic *select* rule as follows:

$$\frac{\varphi : P \in \Delta \quad \delta^p(\mathcal{B}, \Delta) = \mu \quad \mu \neq \bot \quad \mu(\varphi : P) = p}{\langle \mathcal{B}, e : (\mid \Delta \mid) \rangle \rightarrow_p \langle \mathcal{B}, P \triangleright e : (\mid \Delta \setminus \{\varphi : P\} \mid) \rangle} \; select^p$$

where μ is the probability distribution returned from δ^p such that any non-relevant and non-applicable plans are being assigned the probability 0.

Trialling different distributions is possible by changing δ^p which could, for example, be extracted from historic data through machine learning. With our approach, it allows quantifying *exact* probabilistic effects of different δ^p choices.

3.3   Intention Selection and Its Probabilistic Extension

BDI agents may pursue multiple intentions in parallel, allowing them to respond quickly to new events whilst continuing to handle existing events. As parallelism is interleaved (rather than simultaneous), at each step the agent must decide which intention to progress. Similarly to plan selection, the default CAN semantics specifies a non-deterministic choice for intention selection in following two cases:

$$\frac{P \in \Gamma \quad \langle \mathcal{B}, P \rangle \to \langle \mathcal{B}', P' \rangle}{\langle E^e, \mathcal{B}, \Gamma \rangle \Rightarrow \langle E^e, \mathcal{B}', (\Gamma \setminus \{P\}) \cup \{P'\} \rangle} A_{step}$$

$$\frac{P \in \Gamma \quad \langle \mathcal{B}, P \rangle \nrightarrow}{\langle E^e, \mathcal{B}, \Gamma \rangle \Rightarrow \langle E^e, \mathcal{B}, \Gamma \setminus \{P\} \rangle} A_{update}$$

That is, we can either select to progress *any* progressable intention (*i.e.* $\langle \mathcal{B}, P \rangle \to \langle \mathcal{B}', P' \rangle$) or drop *any* unprogressable intention (*i.e.* $\langle \mathcal{B}, P \rangle \nrightarrow$).

As expected, we also want more control over the order of intention execution in practice. This is critical as the wrong choice can cause failure to one or more events, for example, if deadlines are involved (real-time systems, *e.g.* in [30]).

Intention Selection Strategies

Many implementations provide a simple first-in-first-out strategy or round-robin scheduling (which ensures a notion of fairness between the intentions). Alternatively we may force a strict ordering on intentions based on the current situation, *e.g.* deadlines. Similar to plan selection we can express (deterministic) intention choice as a function which *chooses* the next intention to progress:

$$\eta = 2^{\mathcal{B}} \times 2^{\Gamma} \to \Gamma \cup \{\bot\}$$

where $\bot$ stands for no active intentions available for selection.

Again we argue that forcing a deterministic choice is not always appropriate and that you may require flexibility to choose from a distribution. We provide the following function to allow intention selection based on a distribution:

$$\eta^p = 2^{\mathcal{B}} \times 2^{\Gamma} \to Dist(\Gamma) \cup \{\bot\}$$

where $Dist(\Gamma)$ is the set of discrete probability distributions over Γ.

While the plan selection decides how to evolve a single intention (in terms of intention-level configuration $\langle \mathcal{B}, P \rangle$), the intention selection determines what it means to evolve an agent (in terms of agent-level configuration $\langle E^e, \mathcal{B}, \Gamma \rangle$). As such, agent-level transitions depend on the intention-level transitions and we need to account for this in the transition probabilities. To have a probabilistic agent step, we assume, for a chosen progressable intention $P \in \Gamma$, $\langle \mathcal{B}, P \rangle \to_{p'} \langle \mathcal{B}', P' \rangle$ holds, for example, if a plan selection for the given intention P is required based on $select^P$. For unprogressable intentions we have $\langle \mathcal{B}, P \rangle \nrightarrow_1$. We present the following probabilistic intention selection rules:

$$\frac{P \in \Gamma \quad \eta^p(\mathcal{B}, \Gamma) = \mu \quad \mu \neq \bot \quad \mu(P) = p \quad \langle \mathcal{B}, P \rangle \to_{p'} \langle \mathcal{B}', P' \rangle}{\langle E^e, \mathcal{B}, \Gamma \rangle \Rightarrow_{p \cdot p'} \langle E^e, \mathcal{B}', (\Gamma \setminus \{P\}) \cup \{P'\} \rangle} A^p_{step}$$

$$\frac{P \in \Gamma \quad \eta^p(\mathcal{B}, \Gamma) = \mu \quad \mu \neq \bot \quad \mu(P) = p'' \quad \langle \mathcal{B}, P \rangle \nrightarrow_1}{\langle E^e, \mathcal{B}, \Gamma \rangle \Rightarrow_{p''} \langle E^e, \mathcal{B}, \Gamma \setminus \{P\} \rangle} A^p_{update}$$

where $\sum_{p''} p'' + \sum_{p,p'} p \cdot p' = 1$ and $p, p', p'' \in [0, 1]$. Finally, other than the four new probabilistic rules (act^p, $select^p$, A^p_{step}, and A^p_{update}), the other CAN rules (unshown) all transition with uniform probability to future states.

3.4   Situation-Aware Distributions for Plan and Intention Selection

The plan and intention selection function δ^p and η^p are abstract and do not specify how to construct the resulting probability distributions in practice. In this section we give a declarative mechanism for calculating situation-aware distributions at *run-time*. In contrast, action outcomes are typically statically defined based on estimates of environmental effects at design time.

Our approach is to specify a situation value function for plans and intentions that assigns them a real-valued *weight* such that if $w_i < w_j$ then we should prefer the plan/intention with the weight w_j. Specific probabilities are then determined through normalisation. As intentions ultimately address external events, we measure the situation value of an intention by considering the characteristics of its related external event. As such, we adopt the notation of [15] and *extend* it to external events by annotating both plans and external events, namely $e : \varphi \leftarrow P[\theta]$ and $e'[\theta]$ where e is an event, φ the context condition, P the plan-body, $e' \in E^e$ an external event, and θ a situation value description. Importantly, each plan and external event can have a *different* situation value description. Same as in [15], we define θ to be $\langle d_0, \{(\varphi_1, d_1), \cdots, (\varphi_n, d_n)\}, f \rangle$ where d_0 is the default value and values d_i are aggregated using function f (*e.g.* to perform a sum) whenever $\mathcal{B} \models \varphi_i$ holds, $d_i \in \mathbb{R}_{\geq 0}$ ($1 \leq i \leq n$), and $0 \leq n$. Details of the value description such as its expressivity and supported functions can be found in [15].

4   Evaluation

We demonstrate, using a smart manufacturing example and existing probabilistic model checking tools, how to quantitatively model BDI agent programs. Specifically, we evaluate our probabilistic, situation-aware, plan/intention selection against common strategies such as always selecting the most preferred plan. The results are promising, with the intention completion probability using situation-aware distributions being 97% higher than some strictly ordered plan and intention selection strategies. The models are freely available in BigraphER format online[3]. For quantitative analysis we use PRISM by importing the DTMC produced by BigraphER. While we only give details of a single case study, users of the executable semantics can employ BigraphER to "run" models with different settings, *e.g.* external events, plan libraries, custom situation value descriptions.

---

[3] https://bitbucket.org/uog-bigraph/prob_bdi_models_sefm21/src/master/.

4.1 Smart Manufacturing Example

We consider a robotic packaging scenario, *extended* from [30], where a robot packs products and moves them to a storage area. Products have specific temperatures and must be packed in a suitable wrapping bag to prevent decay. If the product stays on the production line too long, the temperature increases and it is spoiled and lost. Given multiple waiting products the robot must *choose* which to handle first (intention selection). Once chosen, the robot must then decide which wrapping to use: either premium or standard (plan selection). Premium wrapping is expensive but always stops product decay and never breaks. On the other hand, standard wrapping is cheap, only works if the product temperature remains low, and has a risk of breaking (a negative action outcome).

Complexity arises from the following factors: (1) losses avoided depend on *when* a product is packed, (2) *when* a product is packed determines which wrappings are applicable – earlier packing means cheaper bags, (3) cheaper wrappings introduce uncertainty as they may break. A formal model of the agent system allows us to quantitatively reason about the robot's behaviours under this uncertainty and use these results as evidence, *e.g.* for regulatory certification, or to help improve the design of the robot, *e.g.* using a standard wrapping as often possible but within tolerable failure threshold.

4.2 Agent Design

We consider a simplified scenario with two products that are initially present on the production line, *i.e.* there are no dynamic events. Agent design is given in Fig. 1 and we assume propositional logic with numerical comparisons.

```
1  // Plans
2  e_product1 : true ← goal(success1,e_process_product1,failure1)
3  e_process_product1 : φ11 ← wrap_standard1; move_product_standard1 [θ11]
4  e_process_product1 : φ12 ← wrap_premium1; move_product_premium1 [θ12]
5  e_product2 : true ← goal(success2,e_process_product2,failure2)
6  e_process_product2 : φ21 ← wrap_standard2; move_product_standard2 [θ21]
7  e_process_product2 : φ22 ← wrap_premium2; move_product_premium2 [θ22]
8  // External events
9    e_product1 [θ13]
10   e_product2 [θ23]
```

Fig. 1. Agent design employing the syntax of Sect. 2.1 combined with the situation value descriptions given in Sect. 3.4.

Products awaiting processing are captured by external events shown in lines 9 and 10, *e.g.* e_product1 with its situation value description θ_{13} (explained below). The agent responds to the events using a declarative goal on line 2 that states it wants to achieve the state success1 (*i.e.* wrapped and moved) through addressing the (internal) event e_process_product1; failing if failure1 (*i.e.* dropped or decayed) ever becomes true. Two plans (in lines 3 and 4), which represent the different wrappings, can handle the event e_process_product1 each with different situation value descriptions. Event e_product2 is handled in a similar way (in line 5–7).

There is a probabilistic outcome for the move_product_standard1 action, such that it has a 10% chance of causing failure1 by dropping the product accidentally, else it succeeds (adding success1 to the beliefs), whereas move_product_premium1 action always succeeds. In Sect. 4.5 we will investigate the effect with varying probability. To allow situational awareness, we encode (discrete) temporal information, for progress and deadline, as agent belief atoms. Progress determines how far (in terms of agent steps) an agent is through an intention, while deadline determines how many steps we can make before the product spoils. Mirroring implementations, we update beliefs based on timings in the background, without executing an explicit action. In this case, the progress increases whenever a specific intention is stepped, whereas deadline decreases after a step of *any* intention.

Table 1 gives the specifications for quantitative reasoning. A short commentary is as follows. $deadline_1 = 8$ and $deadline_2 = 12$ are the initial deadlines of two external events, namely e_product1 and e_product2. The precondition $\varphi_{11} = deadline_1 \geq 3$ indicates that $deadline_1$ is greater than or equal to 3. The situation value description $\theta_{11} = \langle 1, \{\varphi_{11}, 1\}, sum \rangle$ indicates that if φ_{11} holds, then $\theta_{11}(\varphi_{11}) = 1 + 1 = 2$. The situation value description θ_{13} for the external event e_product1 is defined as a function $(deadline_1 + progress_1)^{-3}$. Intuitively, if $deadline_1 + progress_1$ is smaller relative to other products, then it has been progressed less and the deadline is approaching, so it is more urgent. Importantly, the choice of situation value descriptions are made by the agent designer, *i.e.* $(deadline_1 + progress_1)^{-3}$ was their choice. Our approach enables the analysis of alternative functions quantitatively, before deploying the agent.

Table 1. Quantitative specifications with $x \in \{1, 2\}$.

Initial deadlines	Preconditions	Situation value descriptions
$deadline_1 = 8$	$\varphi_{x1} = deadline_x \geq 3$	$\theta_{x1} = \{1, \{\varphi_{x1}, 1\}, sum\}$
$deadline_2 = 12$	$\varphi_{x2} = deadline_x \geq 0$	$\theta_{x2} = \{1, \{\varphi_{x3}, 1\}, sum\}$
	$\varphi_{x3} = 3 \geq deadline_x \geq 0$	$\theta_{x3} = (deadline_x + progress_x)^{-3}$

Table 2. Plan and intention selection strategies.

Plan selection strategies	Intention selection strategies
SMP: Select Most Preferred	**SMU**: Select Most Urgent
PSD: Preference Situational Distribution	**FIFO**: First-In-First-Out
	RR: Round Robin
	PUSD: Pure Urgency Situational Distribution
	LUSD: Layered Urgency Situational Distribution
	OLUSD: Optimised Layered Urgency Situational Distribution

4.3 Plan and Intention Selection Strategies

Table 2 lists the plan/intention selection strategies we analyse. We do not evaluate uniform random plans or intention selection strategies, as these do not capture any domain specific information (*e.g.* regarding preferences). Whereas **SMP** plan selection always selects the highest weighted plan, **PSD** selects a plan by sampling distribution based on preference. For intention selection, **SMU** always selects the intention closest to the deadline similar to **SMP**. **FIFO** and **RR** are fixed orders where the former always selects the intention which arrives first and the latter selects each intention in turn. **PUSD** selects an intention by sampling from distribution where situation value description is given by $(deadline + progress)^{-3}$. Unlike **PUSD**, **LUSD** only deems an intention urgent if the product is not packed or spoiled. As such, it will not select an intention in which the product is packed when there is another intention whose product is not packed. Finally, **OLUSD** selects an intention similarily to **LUSD** but the situation value description is revised to be $|deadline + progress - steps\_required|^{-3}$, which accounts for the steps remaining to pack a product (to avoid spoilage).

4.4 Plan and Intention Selection Analysis

To perform quantitative analysis, we use BigraphER to generate a DTMC— the underlying transition system of probabilistic bigraphs [18]—with bigraphs as states and probabilities as transitions. Each state is labelled by bigraph patterns [22]: if the pattern matches the current state then the predicate is true. In our example, we reason about the dynamic properties using Probabilistic Computation Tree Logic (PCTL) [31]. For example, the property $\mathcal{P}_{=?}\mathbf{F}[\phi]$ expresses the expected probability of ϕ holding *eventually* (in some state). We use S1, F1 (resp. S2, F2) to denote product 1 (resp. 2) successfully, or unsuccessfully being processed[4] by the robot. For model analysis we use these as state-labels[4] in the transition system for all states where a particular product succeeds/fails. Table 3 gives the probability of processing the products either successfully or with a failure, under the plan/intention selection strategies listed in Table 2. For example, $\mathcal{P}_{=?}\mathbf{F}[S1 \wedge S2]$ is the probability both products being processed successfully.

---

[4] Implemented using bigraph patterns, where a specific match is constructed that only holds when that specific product was processed/failed.

Table 3 shows the necessity for good plan/intention selection, with the first 3 combinations *never* successfully processing both products, *i.e.* (S1, S2), and **PUSD** having very limited success ($p = 0.03$). In particular, the intention strategy of **RR** (which selects each intention in turn) is the worst, failing both products in all cases. Using **PUSD** has an almost 50% chance of succeeding with product 1 or failing both. This indicates the weighting function is skewed toward product 1 at the detriment of product 2, leading to the improved **LUSD** strategy. This is a key advantage of our approach: discovering potential pitfalls and trialling new strategies without changing the underlying agent programs and semantics. Similar reasoning, that now product 2 was succeeding more often, led to another strategy **OLUSD** being trialled with extremely good success rates, *i.e.* $p = 0.98$. We should never expect the probability of (S1, S2) $= 1$ due to the action outcome uncertainty (*e.g.* the wrapping bag breaks).

Table 3. Probability of product 1, product 2 for the properties, *e.g.* (S1, S2) with different plan and intention selection strategies listed in Table 2.

Intention

Plan	prop	SMU		FIFO		RR	
		(S1,S2)	(S1,F2)	(S1,S2)	(S1,F2)	(S1,S2)	(S1,F2)
P l a n — S M P	S / M / P	0	0.9	0	0	0	0
		(F1,S2)	(F1, F2)	(F1,S2)	(F1,F2)	(F1,S2)	(F1,F2)
		0	0.1	0.9	0.1	0	1
		(S1,S2)	(S1,F2)	(S1,S2)	(S1,F2)	(S1,S2)	(S1,F2)
	P / S / D	0	0.93	0	0	0	0
		(F1,S2)	(F1,F2)	(F1,S2)	(F1,F2)	(F1,S2)	(F1,F2)
		0	0.07	0.93	0.07	0	1

Plan	prop	PUSD		LUSD		OLUSD	
		(S1,S2)	(S1,F2)	(S1,S2)	(S1,F2)	(S1,S2)	(S1,F2)
P l a n — S M P	S / M / P	0.03	0.48	0.510	0	0.97	0
		(F1,S2)	(F1,F2)	(F1,S2)	(F1,F2)	(F1,S2)	(F1,F2)
		0.08	0.41	0.482	0.008	0.037	0
		(S1,S2)	(S1,F2)	(S1,S2)	(S1,F2)	(S1,S2)	(S1,F2)
	P / S / D	0.03	0.49	0.513	0	0.98	0
		(F1,S2)	(F1,F2)	(F1,S2)	(F1,F2)	(F1,S2)	(F1,F2)
		0.08	0.4	0.481	0.05	0.02	0

In this example, we find that plan selection has limited effect compared to intention selection, which is key to this application. This itself is a valuable insight. In general, probabilistic sampling that improves success rates, even marginally, should be used as it can result in great savings—particularly in large scale processes, *e.g.* an expected two-product successful behaviour tending to occur 98% of the time instead of 97%. Given the complexity of agent behaviours, determining this expected probability precise, without such a model, would be difficult.

Table 4. DTMC generation: final size and timing.

Strategies	States	Transitions	Build time (s)	Rule applications
(SMP, SMU)	31	30	66.57	217
(SMP, FIFO)	31	30	65.85	211
(SMP, RR)	19	18	52.13	143
(PSD, SMU)	36	36	92.26	273
(PSD, FIFO)	36	36	92.25	268
(PSD, RR)	19	18	51.72	143
(SMP, PUSD)	572	845	2447.37	5300
(SMP, LUSD)	323	478	1518.36	3116
(SMP, OLUSD)	323	478	1481.07	3116
(PSD, PUSD)	697	1039	17435.90	6836
(PSD, LUSD)	417	614	2106.64	4157
(PSD, OLUSD)	417	614	2098.51	4157

Table 4 details the DTMC that was used in the evaluation of each property: the number of states and transitions, build time, and rule applications. The last is the number of applications of reaction rules, including instantaneous reaction rules—an advanced feature of BigraphER—that allows agents to progress an intention without showing all sub-steps. For example, this includes belief revision, where we see only final output of a step of executing an action. As the internal steps still have to be generated, much of the build time is spent doing that—accounting for the low number of states, but large build time. We also have to check all required rules and, as bigraphs do not natively support numerical types, this includes many *generated* rules for different parameter values.

The build times for non-interleaved intention selection strategies, *e.g.* (**SMP, SMU**) and (**PSD, RR**) is in the order of minutes whereas the build times for interleaved selection strategies, *e.g.* (**SMP, PUSD**) and (**PSD, PUSD**), is significantly higher (up to 5 h). This is expected due to the combinatorial nature of interleavings and the large number of rules that need to be checked for applicability in each state. Since our executable semantics is intended to be used at design time we do not believe this to be an issue in practice. Model optimisations may be possible, or statistical model checking used, for particularly large agent designs, and ultimately there may be a numerical plug-in for BigraphER.

4.5   Action Outcome Analysis

The effects of different action outcomes are shown in Fig. 2 where the probability of standard wrapping failing is increased from 10% to 90% for two strategy pairs: (**PSD, SMU**) and (**PSD, OLUSD**).

We can see that negative action outcomes have a much larger effect on strictly ordered intention selection (**SMU**), *e.g.* the probability of (S1,F2) decreases from over 90% to below 40%. Meanwhile, (**PSD, OLUSD**) is more robust to action outcome changes. For example, the probability of (S1, S2) in (**PSD, OLUSD**) has a minor decrease of no more than 20%. This is due to increased interleaving of these two intentions, rendering the standard wrapping inapplicable more often.

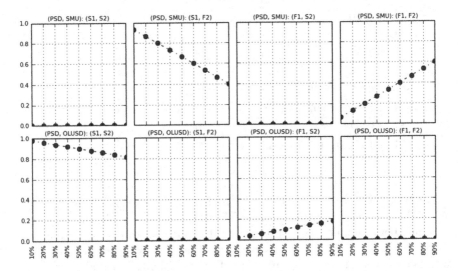

Fig. 2. Probability of reaching the end state (product 1, product 2) with increasing failure probability in (**PSD, SMU**) and (**PSD, OLUSD**).

When the cases become less complex, *e.g.* there is only one product with plenty time to process and all actions always succeed, the plan/intention choice of a BDI agent becomes trivial. In another words, our approach is particularly useful when situations are not straightforward and have complex domain information. Future work, however, is required to account for the *cost*, in terms of wrapping bags, of achieving different success rates and robustness to action outcomes while keeping the overall cost low, *i.e.* multi-objective optimisation.

5   Related Work

We are not the first to consider probabilistic verification of BDI agents. The work [32] uses a two-stage verification methods that first *generates* a model through program model checking (of a system implementation), and then converts this model to PRISM input format for analysis. However, unlike our focus on probabilistic extensions of the BDI semantics itself, the BDI agent used in [32] does not contain any probabilistic aspects. Instead, the *environment* where the agent executes enables the probabilistic reasoning. Similarly, the work of [33] facilitates probabilistic verification of BDI agents by encoding them in PRISM. In this case, instead of generating the model based on an implementation, they implement a significantly simplified version of AgentSpeak directly in PRISM. The simplifications deviate from realistic BDI agents, *e.g.* enabling truly-concurrent intentions (and no intention selection) and treating plan selection as non-deterministic. Our approach captures an extension of the *full* CAN semantics while still providing PRISM verification capabilities.

Works studying plan and intention selection strategies have also been conducted within the BDI community. For example, the work of [30] compiles agent programs to TÆMS (Task Analysis, Environment Modelling, and Simulation) framework to represent the coordination aspects of problems such as "enables" and "hinders" relations between tasks. A Design-To-Criteria scheduler is then used for intention selection to determine the full set of decisions that the agent needs to perform. An increasingly popular topic in the BDI community is intention progression [34], *e.g.* the contest[5]. The intention problem includes the means (i.e. plan) to achieve a given event and which of the currently adopted plans (i.e. intentions) to progress at the current moment, when handling multiple intentions in parallel. Unlike our focus on automated quantitative analysis of BDI agents, their goal (same as [30]) is to help the agent to make better decisions, by modifying or replacing the original BDI reasoning entirely, through other advanced decision-making techniques such as automated planning techniques [35]. For example, the work [36] showed that many of the intention progress issues can be modelled in planning domain definition language (PDDL) [37] (the de-facto standard planning language) and resolved through suitable planners. such as modern highly efficient (online) planner [38]. Finally, it is not a new idea to integrate advanced decision-making techniques into BDI agents to improve performance. There is a large amount of work (surveyed in [39]) to employ planning to dynamically synthesise new plans to achieve an event even when no pre-defined plan worked or exists. One work [40], for example, shows in detail how the integration of planning and BDI can be done at the semantic level.

Besides BDI agents, quantitative verification techniques have also applied to other types of agent systems. For example, the work of [41] considers uncertain communication channels between systems of interacting agents. For verification the multi-agent system is transformed to finite state Markov chains for establishing quantitative temporal properties of the system. Similar to our evaluation of plan/intention selection strategies, the work of [42] provides a quantitative assessment for a decentralised control policies in multi-vehicle scenarios. Specifically they study conflict resolution policies to ensure that a policy never causes

---

[5] https://sites.google.com/site/intentionprogression/home.

collisions under some mild assumptions on the initial conditions. For an overview of general agent-based verification we refer to [43] for the interested readers.

6   Conclusions

A quantitative evaluation and comparison framework can aid design-time specification, allowing us to reason about rational agents operating under uncertainty, for example due to uncertain environments or failure prone actuators, and inherently quantifiable agent characteristics such as plan preference.

We have extended the CAN language (which formalises the behaviour of a classical BDI agent) to a probabilistic setting, which allows both probabilistic action outcomes and probabilistic plan and intention selection. The extended semantics employs probabilistic bigraphs, which enable quantitative analysis with BigraphER and probabilistic model checking in PRISM. Importantly, our executable framework allows (non-expert) users to experiment with their own agent models without worrying about the underlying bigraph theory.

Through a smart manufacturing example we have shown that it is possible to reason about several plan and intention selection strategies, and that probabilistic plan and intention selection strategies can reduce the impact of undesirable outcomes, compared with ordered or fixed strategies. In this example, we found that plan selection has limited effect compared to intention selection, which is a valuable insight. In particular, due to the agent making smarter intention selection choices, the impact of action outcomes can be marginal—even when the failure probabilities are large.

Acknowledgements. This work is supported by the Engineering and Physical Sciences Research Council, under PETRAS SRF grant MAGIC (EP/S035362/1) and S4: Science of Sensor Systems Software. (EP/N007565/1).

References

1. Rao, A.S.: AgentSpeak(L): BDI agents speak out in a logical computable language. In: Van de Velde, W., Perram, J.W. (eds.) MAAMAW 1996. LNCS, vol. 1038, pp. 42–55. Springer, Heidelberg (1996). https://doi.org/10.1007/BFb0031845
2. Winikoff, M., Padgham, L., Harland, J., Thangarajah, J.: Declarative and procedural goals in intelligent agent systems. In: the 8th International Conference on Principles of Knowledge Representation and Reasoning. Morgan Kaufman (2002)
3. Sardina, S., Padgham, L.: A BDI agent programming language with failure handling, declarative goals, and planning. Auton. Agents Multi-agent Syst. **23**, 18–70 (2011). https://doi.org/10.1007/s10458-010-9130-9
4. Hindriks, K.V., Boer, F.S.D., Hoek, W.V.D., Meyer, J.J.C.: Agent programming in 3APL. Auton. Agents Multi-agent Syst. **2**(4), 357–401 (1999)
5. Dastani, M.: 2APL: a practical agent programming language. Auton. Agents Multi-agent Syst. **16**(3), 214–248 (2008). https://doi.org/10.1007/s10458-008-9036-y

6. Winikoff, M.: Jack intelligent agents: an industrial strength platform. In: Bordini, R.H., Dastani, M., Dix, J., El Fallah Seghrouchni, A. (eds.) Multi-Agent Programming. MSASSO, vol. 15, pp. 175–193. Springer, Boston (2005). https://doi.org/10.1007/0-387-26350-0_7
7. Bordini, R.H., HüJomi, J.F., Wooldridge, M.: Programming Multi-agent Systems in AgentSpeak Using Jason, vol. 8. Wiley, Hoboken (2007)
8. Pokahr, A., Braubach, L., Jander, K.: The Jadex project: programming model. In: Ganzha, M., Jain, L. (eds.) Multiagent Systems and Applications. Intelligent Systems Reference Library, vol. 45, pp. 21–53. Springer, Heidelberg (2013). https://doi.org/10.1007/978-3-642-33323-1_2
9. Benfield, S.S., Hendrickson, J., Galanti, D.: Making a strong business case for multiagent technology. In: the 5th International Joint Conference on Autonomous Agents and Multiagent systems, pp. 10–15 ACM (2006)
10. Braubach, L., Pokahr, A.: Negotiation-based patient scheduling in hospitals. In: Iantovics, B., Kountchev, R. (eds.) Advanced Intelligent Computational Technologies and Decision Support Systems. Studies in Computational Intelligence, vol. 486, pp. 107–121. Springer, Cham. (2014). https://doi.org/10.1007/978-3-319-00467-9_10
11. McArthur, S., et al.: Multi-agent systems for power engineering applications - part I: concepts, approaches, and technical challenges. IEEE Trans. Power Syst. **22**(4), 1743–1752 (2007)
12. Bordini, R.H., Fisher, M., Visser, W., Wooldridge, M.: Verifying multi-agent programs by model checking. Auton. Agents Multiagent Syst. **12**(2), 239–256 (2006). https://doi.org/10.1007/s10458-006-5955-7
13. Dennis, L.A., Fisher, M., Lincoln, N.K., Lisitsa, A., Veres, S.M.: Practical verification of decision-making in agent-based autonomous systems. Autom. Softw. Eng. **23**(3), 305–359 (2014). https://doi.org/10.1007/s10515-014-0168-9
14. Chen, H.: Applications of cyber-physical system: a literature review. J. Ind. Integr. Manage. **2**(03), 1750012 (2017)
15. Padgham, L., Singh, D.: Situational preferences for BDI plans. In: the 2013 International Conference on Autonomous Agents and Multi-agent Systems, pp. 1013–1020 (2013)
16. Archibald, B., Calder, M., Sevegnani, M., Xu, M.: Modelling and verifying BDI agents with bigraphs. arXiv preprint arXiv:2105.02578 (2021)
17. Milner, R.: The Space and Motion of Communicating Agents. Cambridge University Press, Cambridge (2009)
18. Archibald, B., Calder, M., Sevegnani, M.: Probablistic bigraphs. arXiv preprint arXiv:2105.02559 (2021)
19. Kwiatkowska, M., Norman, G., Parker, D.: PRISM 4.0: verification of probabilistic real-time systems. In: Gopalakrishnan, G., Qadeer, S. (eds.) CAV 2011. LNCS, vol. 6806, pp. 585–591. Springer, Heidelberg (2011). https://doi.org/10.1007/978-3-642-22110-1_47
20. Sardina, S., Padgham, L.: Goals in the context of BDI plan failure and planning. In: the 6th International Joint Conference on Autonomous Agents and Multiagent Systems, pp. 16–23 (2007)
21. Sevegnani, M., Kabác, M., Calder, M., McCann, J.A.: Modelling and verification of large-scale sensor network infrastructures. In: 23rd International Conference on Engineering of Complex Computer Systems, ICECCS, pp. 71–81 (2018)
22. Benford, S., Calder, M., Rodden, T., Sevegnani, M.: On lions, impala, and bigraphs: modelling interactions in physical/virtual spaces. ACM Trans. Comput.-Hum. Interact. (TOCHI) **23**(2), 1–56 (2016)

23. Tsigkanos, C., Li, N., Jin, Z., Hu, Z., Ghezzi, C.: Scalable multiple-view analysis of reactive systems via bidirectional model transformations. In: 35th IEEE/ACM International Conference on Automated Software Engineering, pp. 993–1003 (2020)
24. Bundgaard, M., Sassone, V.: Typed polyadic pi-calculus in bigraphs. In: ACM SIGPLAN International Conference on Principles and Practice of Declarative Programming, pp. 1–12 (2006)
25. Sevegnani, M., Pereira, E.: Towards a bigraphical encoding of actors. In: International Workshop on Meta Models for Process Languages (2014)
26. Sevegnani, M., Calder, M.: BigraphER: rewriting and analysis engine for bigraphs. In: Chaudhuri, S., Farzan, A. (eds.) CAV 2016, Part II. LNCS, vol. 9780, pp. 494–501. Springer, Cham (2016). https://doi.org/10.1007/978-3-319-41540-6_27
27. Younes, H.L., Littman, M.L.: PPDDL1.0: An extension to PDDL for expressing planning domains with probabilistic effects. Technical report CMU-CS-04-162 2, 99 (2004)
28. Di Pierro, A., Wiklicky, H.: An operational semantics for probabilistic concurrent constraint programming. In: the 1998 International Conference on Computer Languages, pp. 174–183. IEEE (1998)
29. Prosser, P., Unsworth, C.: Limited discrepancy search revisited. J. Exp. Algorithmics (JEA) **16**, 1–6 (2011)
30. Bordini, R.H., Bazzan, A.L.C., Jannone, R.D.O., Basso, D.M., Vicari, R.M., Lesser, V.R.: AgentSpeak (XL) efficient intention selection in BDI agents via decision-theoretic task scheduling. In: the First International Joint Conference on Autonomous Agents and Multiagent Systems: Part 3, pp. 1294–1302 (2002)
31. Hansson, H., Jonsson, B.: A logic for reasoning about time and reliability. Formal Aspects Comput. **6**(5), 512–535 (1994). https://doi.org/10.1007/BF01211866
32. Dennis, L.A., Fisher, M., Webster, M.: Two-stage agent program verification. J. Logic Comput. **28**(3), 499–523 (2018)
33. Izzo, P., Qu, H., Veres, S.M.: A stochastically verifiable autonomous control architecture with reasoning. In: IEEE Conference on Decision and Control, pp. 4985–4991 (2016)
34. Logan, B., Thangarajah, J., Yorke-Smith, N.: Progressing intention progression: a call for a goal-plan tree contest. In: AAMAS, pp. 768–772 (2017)
35. Geffner, H., Bonet, B.: A concise introduction to models and methods for automated planning. Synth. Lect. Artiif. Intell. Mach. Learn. **8**(1), 1–141 (2013)
36. Xu, M., McAreavey, K., Bauters, K., Liu, W.: Intention interleaving via classical replanning. In: 2019 IEEE 31st International Conference on Tools with Artificial Intelligence (ICTAI), pp. 85–92 IEEE (2019)
37. McDermott, D., et al.: PDDL-the planning domain definition language. Technical report (1998)
38. Keller, T., Eyerich, P.: Prost: probabilistic planning based on UCT. In: Twenty-Second International Conference on Automated Planning and Scheduling (2012)
39. Meneguzzi, F., Silva, L.: Planning in BDI agents: a survey of the integration of planning algorithms and agent reasoning. Knowl. Eng. Rev. **30**, 1–44 (2015)
40. Xu, M., Bauters, K., McAreavey, K., Liu, W.: A formal approach to embedding first-principles planning in BDI agent systems. In: Ciucci, D., Pasi, G., Vantaggi, B. (eds.) SUM 2018. LNCS (LNAI), vol. 11142, pp. 333–347. Springer, Cham (2018). https://doi.org/10.1007/978-3-030-00461-3_23
41. Dekhtyar, M.I., Dikovsky, A.J., Valiev, M.K.: Temporal verification of probabilistic multi-agent systems. In: Avron, A., Dershowitz, N., Rabinovich, A. (eds.) Pillars of Computer Science. LNCS, vol. 4800, pp. 256–265. Springer, Heidelberg (2008). https://doi.org/10.1007/978-3-540-78127-1_14

42. Pallottino, L., Scordio, V.G., Frazzoli, E., Bicchi, A.: Probabilistic verification of a decentralized policy for conflict resolution in multi-agent systems. In: IEEE International Conference on Robotics and Automation, pp. 2448–2453 (2006)
43. Bakar, N.A., Selamat, A.: Agent systems verification: systematic literature review and mapping. Appl. Intell. **48**(5), 1251–1274 (2018). https://doi.org/10.1007/s10489-017-1112-z

A Debugger for Probabilistic Programs

Alexander Hoppen and Thomas Noll[✉]

Software Modelling and Verification Group, RWTH Aachen University, 52056
Aachen, Germany
alexander.hoppen@rwth-aachen.de, noll@cs.rwth-aachen.de

Abstract. We provide a prototype implementation of a recording-based
debugger for imperative probabilistic programs supporting randomised
choice, conditioning, and loops. In order to handle different branches
of execution, we take a semantics-based approach that employs weakest
preexpectations and that introduces iteration limits for approximating
the behaviour of potentially non-terminating loops, while giving hard
bounds on the corresponding value without loop iteration limits.

Keywords: Probabilistic programs · Debugging · Semantics-based
methods · Weakest preexpectations

1 Introduction

Interactive debugging, which allows software to be inspected at the source code
level by stepping through statements, setting breakpoints, and examining and
changing variable values whenever execution is paused, plays an integral role
in modern software development workflows [11]. Many programming languages
and software development environments offer tool support to aid in this activity,
known as *debuggers* [1]. While traditional debuggers only allow forward execution
of a program, *recording-based* debuggers like Mozilla's `rr` debugger [2] also enable
the user to jump to previous execution states.

This is especially useful in situations where the program's semantics are
non-obvious at first glance, such as *probabilistic programs*, which implement a
programming paradigm in which probabilistic models are specified using a probabilistic programming language and inference for these models is performed automatically. It attempts to unify probabilistic modelling and traditional general-
purpose programming in order to make the former easier and more widely applicable [4].

We note that debuggers for probabilistic programming languages, both traditional and recording-based, are currently scarce. The only approach we are aware
of is the DePP tool [9], which employs a programming model that supports constructs for invoking inference in the language and that represents such inference

---

The work presented in this tool paper is based on the Master's thesis by Alexander
Hoppen [5].

R. Calinescu and C. S. Păsăreanu (Eds.): SEFM 2021, LNCS 13085, pp. 282–289, 2021.
https://doi.org/10.1007/978-3-030-92124-8_16

operations using an extended form of Bayesian networks. This allows to automatically identify programming errors such as the assumption of independence between variables that are actually correlated, or premature inference operations. However, in contrast to our approach, analysing the detailed behaviour of probabilistic program by interactive, step-wise execution is not supported.

2 Probabilistic Programs

To start, let us introduce the probabilistic programming language supported by our tool. Our language has a C-like syntax and supports the standard constructs of variable declaration, variable assignment, if and while.

```
1   bool aliceInfections = true
2   bool bobInfected = false
3   int infectDay = 0
4   while aliceInfections {
5     if bobInfected == false { infectDay = infectDay + 1 }
6     prob 0.1 { bobInfected = true }
7     prob 0.6 { aliceInfections = false }
8   }
9   observe bobInfected
```

Fig. 1. A structured probabilistic to compute the probability at which day Bob caught the virus, given that he caught the virus.

To highlight the additional probabilistic capabilities of our language, consider Fig. 1, which models a hypothetical transmission of the SARS-CoV2 virus in an intuitive, algorithmic way. Suppose there are two people, Alice and Bob, who meet every day, modelled by the while-loop. Alice is initially infected with the virus. While she is infectious, every time they meet there is a 10% chance that she infects Bob. This probabilistic transmission of the virus is modelled by a prob-statement. prob-statements behave similar to if-statements, but execute the if- and else-branch with a given probability. For example after the first loop iteration, bobInfected will be true with a probability of 10%. This also highlights the main characteristic of probabilistic programs. bobInfected is not *either* true *or* false (as it is the case in traditional programs), but carries a variable *distribution* over the possible values true and false. The next day Alice continues to be infectious with a likelihood of 40%, again modelled by a prob-statement. The probability that Bob also catches the virus is now described by the likelihood that bobInfected is true at the end of the while-loop, which can be computed to be 15.62% as shown in the following sections.

For further analysis of the virus's spread, we want to compute the probability that Bob catches the virus on day 1, 2, etc., given that he did catch the virus. As can be seen in Fig. 1 computing the day that he catches the virus can be done by a simple infectDay counter. The fact that we only want to consider such runs in which Bob catches the virus can be modelled by an observe-statement, which intuitively filters out all runs in which bobInfected is false.

3   Weakest Preexpectations

Our semantic interpretation of probabilistic programs is based on *weakest pre-expectations*, which constitute a quantitative generalisation of the classical concept of weakest preconditions as introduced by Dijkstra [3]. He employs so-called predicate transformers, which push a postcondition G backward through a program P and yield the weakest precondition F describing the largest set of states such that whenever P is started in a state satisfying F, P terminates in a state satisfying G.

Weakest preexpectations generalise this approach by employing expectation transformers which act on real-valued functions called *expectations*, mapping program states to non-negative reals. These transformers push a postexpectation g backward through a probabilistic program P and yield a preexpectation f, such that f represents the expected value of g after executing P. Here, the term expectation coined by [8] may appear somewhat misleading at first. One should think of an expectation as a random variable rather than an expected value.

Definition 1. *Given a set $\mathcal{V}$ of (declared) program variables, the set of* variable assignments *is defined by* $\mathbb{A} = \big(\mathcal{V} \rightharpoonup (\mathbb{B} \cup \mathbb{R})\big)$.

An expectation *is a function that maps variable assignments to probabilities. We define* $\mathbb{P} = \{\, p \in \mathbb{R} \mid 0 \le p \le 1\,\}$ *as the set of all probabilities and the set of all expectations as* $\mathbb{E} = (\mathbb{A} \to \mathbb{P})$. $\mathbb{E}$ *is ordered point-wise by* $\le$.

In the following, we restrict ourselves to such expectations that can be expressed as finite arithmetic expressions over $\mathcal{V}$. An expectation refers to both the function and the arithmetic expression that describes it. It will become clear from the context which representation is meant.

Definition 2 (wp). *For a program P and an expectation $f \in \mathbb{E}$, the* weakest preexpectation *$\mathsf{wp}(P, f) \in \mathbb{E}$ of f is defined according to Fig. 2. In the figure, $f[var := expr]$ denotes the expectation that results from replacing all occurrences of $var \in \mathcal{V}$ in the definition of f by the arithmetic expression $expr$ over $\mathcal{V}$, and $[\![expr]\!]$ the expectation that returns 1 or 0 depending on the validity of the Boolean argument $expr$. Moreover, the lfp operator yields the least fixpoint of a continuous function on the complete partial order of expectations.*

Definition 3 (wlp). *Similar to the weakest preexpectation, the* weakest liberal preexpectation *$\mathsf{wlp}(P, f) \in \mathbb{E}$ is defined like wp with the only difference that it uses the greatest fixed point operator gfp instead of lfp for loops.*

Definition 4 (woip). *Finally, we define the* weakest observe-ignoring preexpectation *$\mathsf{woip}(P, f) \in \mathbb{E}$ just like wp but ignore all observe-statements. That is, we have $\mathsf{wp}(\mathbf{observe}\ expr, f) = f$.*

P	$\mathsf{wp}(P, f)$
$P_1; P_2$	$\mathsf{wp}(P_1, \mathsf{wp}(P_2, f))$
$(\texttt{int} \mid \texttt{bool} \mid \varepsilon) \; var = expr$	$f[var := expr]$
$\texttt{observe } expr$	$[\![expr]\!] \cdot f$
$\texttt{if } expr \; \{ \; P_{\text{if}} \; \} \texttt{ else } \{ \; P_{\text{else}} \; \}$	$[\![expr]\!] \cdot \mathsf{wp}(P_{\text{if}}, f) + [\![\neg expr]\!] \cdot \mathsf{wp}(P_{\text{else}}, f)$
$\texttt{prob } expr \; \{ \; P_{\text{if}} \; \} \texttt{ else } \{ \; P_{\text{else}} \; \}$	$expr \cdot \mathsf{wp}(P_{\text{if}}, f) + (1 - expr) \cdot \mathsf{wp}(P_{\text{else}}, f)$
$\texttt{while } expr \; \{ \; P_{\text{body}} \; \}$	$\mathsf{lfp } X. ([\![expr]\!] \cdot \mathsf{wp}(P_{\text{body}}, X) + [\![\neg expr]\!] \cdot f)$

Fig. 2. Transformation functions of the wp operator.

As an intuitive application of weakest preexpectations, we want to note that for an expectation $f \in \mathbb{E}$, $\frac{\mathsf{wp}(P,f)}{\mathsf{wlp}(P,1)}$ computes the expected value of f after program execution, given that all $\texttt{observe}$-statements are satisfied. We refer to [7] for an in-depth explanation of this fact.

4 Loop Iteration Limits

While the definition of weakest preexpectations offers a well-founded basis for determining a probabilistic program's semantics, it does not directly provide algorithmic access because the least (resp. greatest) fixed point of a loop is not computable in general. To solve this problem, we introduce *loop iteration limits*. Intuitively, an iteration limit for a loop in a program P is a non-negative integer $b \in \mathbb{N}$. Whenever the execution of P would traverse the loop more than b times, we declare that execution branch as having diverged and stop its execution. We are able to do so because we do not need to compute values that are correct to the last decimal digit. For applications like debugging, it is usually sufficient to compute approximate values for variables together with an approximation error.

Observation 1. We can view the loop iteration limits as a syntactic transformation of the program. When imposing an iteration limit b on a loop, we are unrolling the loop to a series of b if-statements as follows:

```
1  if  expr  { P_body } // repeat if-statement b times
2  if  expr  { while true {} }
```

Definition 5 (wp_β, wlp_β, woip_β). *wp_β, wlp_β and woip_β are analogous to wp, wlp and woip resp. but take a set of loop iteration bounds β into account.*

Theorem 1. *When applying the above definition of loop unrolling, the value of interest $\frac{\mathsf{wp}(P,f)}{\mathsf{wlp}(P,1)}$ is restricted as follows. For the proof we refer to [6].*

$$\frac{\mathsf{wp}_\beta(P, f)}{\mathsf{wlp}_\beta(P, 1)} \leq \frac{\mathsf{wp}(P, f)}{\mathsf{wlp}(P, 1)} \leq \frac{\mathsf{wp}_\beta(P, f) + (1 - \mathsf{woip}_\beta(P, 1))}{\mathsf{wlp}_\beta(P, 1) - \mathsf{wlp}_\beta(P, 0)}$$

The above theorem yields hard bounds on the approximation error. Should the computed range not yield the desired accuracy, larger iteration limits can be chosen to improve accuracy.

5   Weakest Preexpectations at Intermediate Execution States

With the definition of computable weakest preexpectation operators at hand, let us turn towards the development of a debugger for probabilistic programs. For every execution state, deterministic programs have a unique successor state that is reached by executing the current statement. Deterministic debuggers allow software developers to reach that next execution state through step-wise execution, e.g. by a *Step Over* command.

In probabilistic programs, however, this is no longer the case. While non-branching statements like assignments still have a unique successor, the branching statements `if`, `prob` and `while` do not. For `if` *expr* { P_{if} } `else` { P_{else} } where *expr* is `true` with 60% and `false` with 40%, both branches are viable – it is up to the user to decide which branch he or she wants to jump into.[1] This gives us the following three debugger commands for probabilistic programs:

- **Step Over:** Execute the current statement and jump to the next statement.[2]
- **Step Into True:** If execution is currently at a branching statement, only focus on runs that satisfy the condition and jump to the first statement of the `true`-branch. For `if`- and `prob`-statements, this means jumping into the if-branch. For `while`-statements, this means jumping into the loop's body. If the current statement is not branching, the semantics is equivalent to *Step Over*.
- **Step Into False:** Analogous to *Step Into True*. For `if`- and `prob`-statements jump into the `else`-branch, for `while`-statements terminate the loop, for non-branching statements equivalent to *Step Over*.

So far we have talked vaguely about focussing on certain runs. Fortunately, there already exists a construct that performs exactly the operation we require, namely `observe`-statements. We can thus view a *Step Into True* command as executing a virtual `observe` (*expr* == `true`) statement right before the branching statement (which afterwards has a unique successor). The *Step Into False* command analogously executes a virtual `observe` (*expr* == `false`) statement.

5.1   Execution History of a Program

To compute variable values at the intermediate execution states, we describe an execution state by the debugger commands that were executed to reach it.

Definition 6 (Augmented execution history). *An augmented execution history* $h^P = \big((h_0, P_0), \dots, (h_n, P_n)\big)$ *with* $h_i \in \{\, \mathbf{so}, \mathbf{sit}, \mathbf{sif} \,\}$ *is the list of debugger*

---

[1] The same logic also applies to `prob`- and `while`-statements. For loops, the user can jump into the loop's body or exit the loop.

[2] Here, `if`-, `prob` and `while`-statements are viewed as single statements that include their bodies.

commands that have been executed since the start of the program together with the statements P_i they have been executed on. **so** *stands for* Step Over, **sit** *for* Step Into True *and* **sif** *for* Step Into False.

With execution histories being defined, we can also define WP-inference on them.

Definition 7 (wph). *The* wph *operator performs WP-inference of an augmented execution history h^P and a postexpectation $f \in \mathbb{E}$.*

$$
\text{wph}(h^P, f) = \begin{cases} f & \text{if } h^P = () \\ \text{see table below} & \text{if } h^P = ((h_0, P_0)) \\ \text{wph}\big((h_0^P, \ldots h_{n-1}^P), \text{wph}(h_n^P, f)\big) & \text{if } h^P = (h_0^P, \ldots, h_n^P), n \geq 1 \end{cases}
$$

P_0	$h_0 = $ **so**	$h_0 = $ **sif**	$h_0 = $ **sit**
`(int | bool | `ε`) var = expr`	$\text{wp}(P_0, f)$		
`observe` *expr*	$\text{wp}(P_0, f)$		
`if` *expr* `{ `P_{if}` } else { `P_{else}` }`	$\text{wp}(P_0, f)$	$[\![expr]\!] \cdot f$	$[\![\neg expr]\!] \cdot f$
`prob` *expr* `{ `P_{if}` } else { `P_{else}` }`	$\text{wp}(P_0, f)$	$expr \cdot f$	$(1 - expr) \cdot f$
`while` *expr* `{ `P_{body}` }`	$\text{wp}(P_0, f)$	$[\![expr]\!] \cdot f$	$[\![\neg expr]\!] \cdot f$

Definition 8 (wlph, woiph). *The* wlph *operator for execution histories is analogous to* wph *with the only difference that it delegates to* wlp *where* wph *delegates to* wp. *Similarly the* woiph *operator delegates to* woip *instead of* wp.

Definition 9 ($\text{wph}_\beta, \text{wlph}_\beta, \text{woiph}_\beta$). *The* wph_β, wlph_β *and* woiph_β *operators compute the weakest preexpectation of an execution history while taking loop iteration limits β into account. They are defined analogously to* wph, wlph *and* woiph *but delegate to* wp_β, wlp_β *and* woip_β *instead of* wp, wlp *and* woip.

Note that we need to define the wph_β family of operators with loop iteration limits in mind because a developer might jump over a loop using a *Step Over* command and is thereby not limiting the number of loop iterations through explicit debugger commands.

Just like we computed the expected value of $f \in \mathbb{E}$ after program execution using $\frac{\text{wp}(P,f)}{\text{wlp}(P,1)}$ to, we use $\frac{\text{wph}(h^P,f)}{\text{wlp}(h^P,1)}$ to compute the expected value of f after execution of the augmented execution history h^P.

Theorem 2. *Like in Theorem 1, we can bound the incomputable value of $\frac{\text{wph}(h^P,f)}{\text{wlp}(h^P,1)}$ by computable values that take loop iteration limits into account.*

$$
\frac{\text{wph}_\beta(h^P, f)}{\text{wlph}_\beta(h^P, 1)} \leq \frac{\text{wph}(h^P, f)}{\text{wlph}(h^P, 1)} \leq \frac{\text{wph}_\beta(h^P, f) + \big(1 - \text{woiph}_\beta(h^P, 1)\big)}{\text{wlph}_\beta(h^P, 1) - \text{wlph}_\beta(h^P, 0)}
$$

6   Implementation

Based on the ideas of the algorithms described in this paper, a recording-based debugger for probabilistic programs has been implemented. The debugger is available both as a graphical user interface, which runs on macOS, as well as a command line tool that runs on both macOS and Linux. The source code can be found at [10].

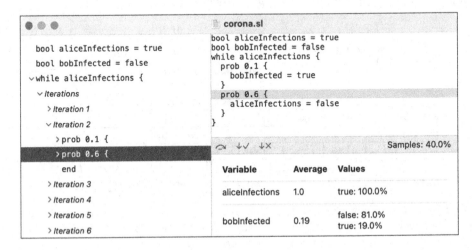

Fig. 3. Screenshot of the debugger's graphical user interface.

Figure 3 shows a screenshot of the debugger's graphical user interface. Its left-hand side displays a structured outline of the program's execution, that is being generated during a sample-based execution of the program. For each executed statement, a corresponding entry is being added to the execution outline. Clicking on one of the entries in the execution outline jumps to the corresponding execution state. The statement that will be executed next is highlighted in the source code on the top right and the current variable values, together with their approximation error if necessary, are displayed on the bottom right. The user can step through the program manually using the three debugger buttons *Step Over*, *Step Into True* and *Step Into False* on top of the variables view.

References

1. Aggarwal, S.K., Kumar, M.S.: Debuggers for programming languages. In: The Compiler Design Handbook, pp. 297–329. CRC Press (2002)
2. Corporation, M.: Mozilla RR debugger (2020). https://rr-project.org
3. Dijkstra, E.W.: A Discipline of Programming. Prentice-Hall, Hoboken (1976)
4. Gordon, A.D., Henzinger, T.A., Nori, A.V., Rajamani, S.K.: Probabilistic programming. In: Future of Software Engineering, pp. 167–181. ACM (2014)

5. Hoppen, A.: Design and implementation of an interactive exploration tool for probabilistic programs. Master's thesis, RWTH Aachen University, Germany (2020). https://publications.rwth-aachen.de/record/802809

6. Hoppen, A., Noll, T.: A debugger for probabilistic programs. Technical report, RWTH Aachen University (2020). https://moves.rwth-aachen.de/wp-content/uploads/probabilistic-debugger-report.pdf

7. Katoen, J.-P., Gretz, F., Jansen, N., Kaminski, B.L., Olmedo, F.: Understanding probabilistic programs. In: Meyer, R., Platzer, A., Wehrheim, H. (eds.) Correct System Design. LNCS, vol. 9360, pp. 15–32. Springer, Cham (2015). https://doi.org/10.1007/978-3-319-23506-6_4

8. McIver, A., Morgan, C., Morgan, C.C.: Abstraction, Refinement and Proof for Probabilistic Systems. Springer, New York (2005). https://doi.org/10.1007/b138392

9. Nandi, C., Grossman, D., Sampson, A., Mytkowicz, T., McKinley, K.S.: Debugging probabilistic programs. In: MAPL 2017, pp. 18–26. ACM (2017)

10. Noll, T.: A debugger for probabilistic programs, October 2021. https://git.rwth-aachen.de/moves/probabilistic-debugger

11. Telles, M., Hsieh, Y.: The Science of Debugging. Coriolis (2001)

Verification and Synthesis

Verification of Programs with Exceptions Through Operator Precedence Automata

Francesco Pontiggia[1](✉), Michele Chiari[1](✉) ⓘ, and Matteo Pradella[1,2](✉) ⓘ

[1] DEIB, Politecnico di Milano, Milan, Italy
francesco.pontiggia@mail.polimi.it,
{michele.chiari,matteo.pradella}@polimi.it
[2] IEIIT, Consiglio Nazionale delle Ricerche, Milan, Italy

Abstract. Operator Precedence Languages are one of the most expressive classes of context-free languages that enable Model Checking. Recently, the First-Order complete Precedence Oriented Temporal Logic (POTL) has been introduced for expressing properties on models defined through Operator Precedence Automata (OPA), a variant of Pushdown Automata for OPLs; moreover, an efficient tool called Precedence Oriented Model Checker (POMC) was devised for POTL. We propose here the core algorithms of POMC for on-the-fly depth-first exploration of the search space: for OPA, a *reachability* algorithm; for their ω-word variant, a *fair-cycle detection* algorithm. We have refined the tool with a user-friendly DSL called MiniProc for expressing procedural code with exceptions. We show how the expressiveness of POMC can be used to verify programs which make use of exceptions, thus overcoming the limits of LTL-based Model Checking. We demonstrate the effectiveness of POMC through a case study.

Keywords: Linear Temporal Logic · Operator Precedence Languages · Model Checking · Software verification · Exceptions

1 Introduction

In Model Checking, some of the most critical aspects are how to specify the model and the properties to be verified. Different formalisms have been proposed in the literature, and some have been successfully exploited due to their ease of development and nice performances when implemented in practice. Well-established tools (such as SPIN [19]) usually support the verification of properties expressed in Linear Temporal Logic (LTL) on models provided as Transition Systems or Finite State Automata (generally Büchi automata). Unfortunately, LTL can express only the First-Order definable fragment of regular languages. Transition Systems, although they can have an infinite set of states, thus being non-regular, are more suitable for hardware verification, since they do not have the concept of stack. Conversely, many relevant program behaviors regard execution traces composed of matching and nested (possibly even recursive) function

© Springer Nature Switzerland AG 2021
R. Calinescu and C. S. Păsăreanu (Eds.): SEFM 2021, LNCS 13085, pp. 293–311, 2021.
https://doi.org/10.1007/978-3-030-92124-8_17

calls and returns, hence they involve the manipulation of the stack. They are context-free, and cannot be modeled by regular formalisms; likewise, many useful properties cannot be specified on them with LTL. To mention one, the evolution of the call stack of active subroutines (to verify stack inspection properties at a certain point of the execution [13, 20]).

To fill this gap, attempts have been made by introducing logics based on languages which are context-free, but enjoy many nice properties of regular languages, and are regarded as being in the middle between context-free and regular languages. They are informally defined as Structured Context Free Languages [23], because the structure of the syntax tree of a sentence is built in the sentence itself, and in many cases immediately visible. Remarkable results have been obtained with Visibly Pushdown Languages (VPL) [7], and the derived logics CaRet [6] and Nested Word Temporal Logic (NWTL) (which is First-Order complete) [2]. In VPLs, sentences embed matches between characters: these matches are used to model function calls and returns. Consequently, with NWTL it is possible to define specifications on generic procedural programs [4]. Unfortunately, the matching relation is necessarily one-to-one. This property makes VPLs and NWTL not suitable to deal with behaviors in which a single event must be put in relation with multiple ones: for example, exception handling (e.g., to verify exception safety properties [1]), and context-switching policies in real time operating systems.

Regarding the modelling formalisms, *Extended Recursive State Machines* (ERSMs) and *Pushdown Systems* are equivalent abstractions [3] which have been proposed to model generic imperative programming languages. On the practical side, the former is supported by the tool VERA [5], which adopts an *on-the-fly* approach to perform reachability and fair-cycle detection analysis. Conversely, the latter is supported by the MOPED model checker [12, 14, 21], a BDD-based LTL model checker. However, none of them accepts CaRet or NWTL specifications. Both tools are able to deal with the family of *Boolean Programs* [8], which have a closer syntax to that of a program with assignments. They present procedures with call-by-value parameter passing and recursion, and a restricted form of recursion. With respect to ERSMs and Pushdown Systems, they do not allow array or bounded-integer variables. All the three formalisms do not present exceptions. Boolean programs are used in the SLAM verification toolkit [9]. SLAM provides a regression test suite made of 64 C programs, that are automatically abstracted and translated into Boolean Programs, and then verified through the ad-hoc BEBOP [8] model checker.

Operator Precedence Languages (OPLs) are a class of Context Free Languages introduced for efficient parsing [15]. Recently, their investigation has been resumed and applied to verification. OPLs allow to specify a many-to-one or one-to-many relation between sentence characters, and thus strictly include the class of VPLs [23]. Therefore, this class is a good fit for the verification of the mentioned exception handling behaviors or context-switching policies. A new logic based on OPLs, named Precedence Oriented Temporal Logic (POTL) [11], has been introduced, overcoming the previous, less expressive Operator Precedence Temporal Logic (OPTL) [10].

Alongside, a formal definition of the class of automata corresponding to OPLs has been given, with Operator Precedence Automata (OPA), and Operator Precedence Büchi Automata (OPBA) [22] which are OPA accepting infinite (or ω-) Operator Precedence words. The languages accepted by OPBA are called Operator Precedence ω-Languages (ω-OPLs). A first step towards the practical application of OP languages to the verification of real world programs has been taken in [11], which deals with some simple case studies regarding only hand-made OPA—hence, finite-word—models. In this paper we go a step further, and present the latest version of POMC,[1] the Precedence Oriented Model Checker. POMC has been completed with an implementation of the model checking algorithm for ω-languages, therefore the tool now fully supports OPBA models.

To this regard, we outline the implemented reachability (for OPA) and fair-cycle detection (for OPBA) algorithms. The models can be provided either as plain automata or through a domain-specific language (DSL) called *Mini-Proc*, internally converted into automata by POMC. Although not Turing complete, MiniProc resembles mainstream programming languages. Thanks to these advancements, we present a larger case study on the Quicksort algorithm. We study three different implementations of the recursive Quicksort algorithm by modeling them with MiniProc. In particular, the third one is equipped with exception handling constructs: we verify on it various relevant properties, ranging from exception safety to stack inspection.

The paper is organized as follows: Sects. 2 and 3 provide theoretical background and definitions; Sect. 4 describes the model-checking algorithms implemented in POMC; Sect. 5 describes the MiniProc DSL; Sect. 6 reports the Quick-Sort case study; Sect. 7 concludes with future work directions.

2   Background: Operator Precedence Languages

We assume some familiarity with classical formal language theory concepts such as context-free grammar, parsing, shift-reduce algorithm, syntax tree (ST) [17,18]. Operator Precedence Languages (OPLs) are usually defined through their generating grammars [15]; in this paper, however, we characterize them through their accepting automata [22] which are the natural way for stating equivalence properties with logic characterization, and for model checking. Readers not familiar with OPLs may refer to [23] for more explanations on the following basic concepts.

Let Σ be a finite alphabet, and ε the empty string. We use a special symbol $\# \notin \Sigma$ to mark the beginning and the end of any string. An *operator precedence matrix* (OPM) M over Σ is a partial function $(\Sigma \cup \{\#\})^2 \to \{\lessdot, \doteq, \gtrdot\}$, that, for each ordered pair (a, b), defines the *precedence relation* (PR) $M(a, b)$ holding between a and b. If the function is total we say that M is *complete*. We call the

---

[1] https://github.com/michiari/POMC.

pair (Σ, M) an *operator precedence alphabet*. Relations $<, \doteq, >$, are respectively named *yields precedence*, *equal in precedence*, and *takes precedence*. By convention, the initial # yields precedence, and other symbols take precedence on the ending #. If $M(a, b) = \pi$, where $\pi \in \{<, \doteq, >\}$, we write $a \pi b$. For $u, v \in \Sigma^+$ we write $u \pi v$ if $u = xa$ and $v = by$ with $a \pi b$. The role of PRs is to give structure to words: they can be seen as special and more concise parentheses, where e.g. one "closing" $>$ can match more than one "opening" $<$. Despite their graphical appearance, PRs are not ordering relations.

Definition 1. *An* operator precedence automaton (OPA) *is a tuple* $\mathcal{A} = (\Sigma, M, Q, I, F, \delta)$ *where:* (Σ, M) *is an operator precedence alphabet, Q is a finite set of states (disjoint from Σ), $I \subseteq Q$ is the set of initial states, $F \subseteq Q$ is the set of final states, $\delta \subseteq Q \times (\Sigma \cup Q) \times Q$ is the transition relation, which is the union of the three disjoint relations $\delta_{shift} \subseteq Q \times \Sigma \times Q$, $\delta_{push} \subseteq Q \times \Sigma \times Q$, and $\delta_{pop} \subseteq Q \times Q \times Q$. An OPA is deterministic iff I is a singleton, and all three components of δ are—possibly partial—functions.*

To define the semantics of OPA, we need some new notations. Letters $p, q, p_i, q_i, \ldots$ denote states in Q. We use $q_0 \xrightarrow{a} q_1$ for $(q_0, a, q_1) \in \delta_{push}$, $q_0 \dashrightarrow^{a} q_1$ for $(q_0, a, q_1) \in \delta_{shift}$, $q_0 \xRightarrow{q_2} q_1$ for $(q_0, q_2, q_1) \in \delta_{pop}$, and $q_0 \overset{w}{\rightsquigarrow} q_1$, if the automaton can read $w \in \Sigma^*$ going from q_0 to q_1. Let $\Gamma = \Sigma \times Q$ and $\Gamma' = \Gamma \cup \{\perp\}$ be the *stack alphabet*; we denote symbols in Γ' as $[a, q]$ or $\perp$. We set $smb([a, q]) = a$, $smb(\perp) = \#$, and $st([a, q]) = q$. For a stack content $\gamma = \gamma_n \ldots \gamma_1 \perp$, with $\gamma_i \in \Gamma$, $n \geq 0$, we set $smb(\gamma) = smb(\gamma_n)$ if $n \geq 1$, $smb(\gamma) = \#$ if $n = 0$.

A *configuration* of an OPA is a triple $c = \langle w, q, \gamma \rangle$, where $w \in \Sigma^*\#$, $q \in Q$, and $\gamma \in \Gamma^*\perp$. A *computation* or *run* is a finite sequence $c_0 \vdash c_1 \vdash \ldots \vdash c_n$ of *moves* or *transitions* $c_i \vdash c_{i+1}$. There are three kinds of moves, depending on the PR between the symbol on top of the stack and the next input symbol:

push move: if $smb(\gamma) < a$ then $\langle ax, p, \gamma \rangle \vdash \langle x, q, [a, p]\gamma \rangle$, with $(p, a, q) \in \delta_{push}$;

shift move: if $a \doteq b$ then $\langle bx, q, [a, p]\gamma \rangle \vdash \langle x, r, [b, p]\gamma \rangle$, with $(q, b, r) \in \delta_{shift}$;

pop move: if $a > b$ then $\langle bx, q, [a, p]\gamma \rangle \vdash \langle bx, r, \gamma \rangle$, with $(q, p, r) \in \delta_{pop}$.

Shift and pop moves are not performed when the stack contains only $\perp$. Push moves put a new element on top of the stack consisting of the input symbol together with the current state of the OPA. Shift moves update the top element of the stack by *changing its input symbol only*. Pop moves remove the element on top of the stack, and update the state of the OPA according to δ_{pop} on the basis of the current state of the OPA and the state of the removed stack symbol. They do not consume the input symbol, which is used only to establish the $>$ relation, remaining available for the next move. The OPA accepts the language $L(\mathcal{A}) = \{x \in \Sigma^* \mid \langle x\#, q_I, \perp \rangle \vdash^* \langle \#, q_F, \perp \rangle, q_I \in I, q_F \in F\}$.

We now introduce the concept of *chain*, which makes the connection between PRs and context-free structure explicit, through brackets.

Definition 2. *A* simple chain $^{c_0}[c_1 c_2 \ldots c_\ell]^{c_{\ell+1}}$ *is a string $c_0 c_1 c_2 \ldots c_\ell c_{\ell+1}$, such that: $c_0, c_{\ell+1} \in \Sigma \cup \{\#\}$, $c_i \in \Sigma$ for every $i = 1, 2, \ldots \ell$ $(\ell \geq 1)$, and $c_0 < c_1 \doteq$*

$c_2 \ldots c_{\ell-1} \doteq c_\ell \gtrdot c_{\ell+1}$. *A composed chain is a string* $c_0 s_0 c_1 s_1 c_2 \ldots c_\ell s_\ell c_{\ell+1}$, *where* ${}^{c_0}[c_1 c_2 \ldots c_\ell]^{c_{\ell+1}}$ *is a simple chain, and* $s_i \in \Sigma^*$ *is the empty string or is such that* ${}^{c_i}[s_i]^{c_{i+1}}$ *is a chain (simple or composed), for every* $i = 0, 1, \ldots, \ell$ ($\ell \geq 1$). *Such a composed chain will be written as* ${}^{c_0}[s_0 c_1 s_1 c_2 \ldots c_\ell s_\ell]^{c_{\ell+1}}$. c_0 *(resp.* $c_{\ell+1}$*) is called its* left *(resp.* right*) context; all symbols between them form its* body.

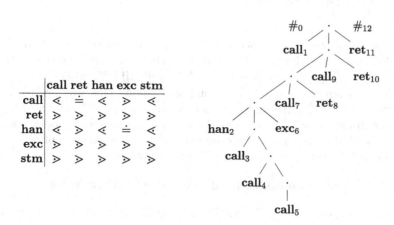

	call	ret	han	exc	stm
call	$\lessdot$	$\doteq$	$\lessdot$	$\gtrdot$	$\lessdot$
ret	$\gtrdot$	$\gtrdot$	$\gtrdot$	$\gtrdot$	$\gtrdot$
han	$\lessdot$	$\gtrdot$	$\lessdot$	$\doteq$	$\lessdot$
exc	$\gtrdot$	$\gtrdot$	$\gtrdot$	$\gtrdot$	$\gtrdot$
stm	$\gtrdot$	$\gtrdot$	$\gtrdot$	$\gtrdot$	$\gtrdot$

Fig. 1. OPM $M_{\mathbf{call}}$ (left) and the ST corresponding to word w'_{ex} (right). Dots are internal nodes.

A finite word w over Σ is *compatible* with an OPM M iff for each pair of letters c, d, consecutive in w, $M(c, d)$ is defined and, for each substring x of $\#w\#$ that is a chain of the form ${}^a[y]^b$, $M(a, b)$ is defined.

As an example, consider word $w_{ex} = \mathbf{call\ han\ call\ call\ exc\ call\ ret\ ret}$ on alphabet $\Sigma_{\mathbf{call}} = \{\mathbf{call, ret, exc, han, stm}\}$, which is compatible with $M_{\mathbf{call}}$ of Fig. 1. w_{ex} models the execution trace of a program: first, a function is called; it installs an exception handler **han**, and then two more function calls occur. The last one throws an exception **exc**, which is caught by the handler. Before returning, the first function calls another one, which returns immediately. w_{ex} has a clear structure: **calls** should match **rets** or **excs** that terminate them, and **hans** to **excs** they catch. Label **stm** represents a generic statement (e.g. an assignment), but we do not use it for now. Such structure is encoded by chains, which can be identified through the traditional operator precedence parsing algorithm. We apply it to w_{ex} (for a more complete treatment, cf. [17,23]).

First, write all precedence relations between consecutive characters, according to $M_{\mathbf{call}}$. Then, recognize all innermost patterns of the form $a \lessdot c \doteq \ldots \doteq c \gtrdot b$ as simple chains, and remove their bodies. Then, write the precedence relations between the left and right contexts of the removed body, a and b, and iterate this process until only ## remains. This procedure is applied to w_{ex} as follows:

$$1 \mid \text{\# < call < han < call < \underline{call} > exc > call} \doteq \text{ret > ret > \#}$$
$$2 \mid \text{\# < call < han < \underline{call} > exc > call} \doteq \text{ret > ret > \#}$$
$$3 \mid \text{\# < call < \underline{han} \doteq \underline{exc} > call} \doteq \text{ret > ret > \#}$$
$$4 \mid \text{\# < call < \underline{call} \doteq \underline{ret} > ret > \#}$$
$$5 \mid \text{\# < \underline{call} \doteq \underline{ret} > \#}$$
$$6 \mid \text{\# } \doteq \text{ \#}$$

The chain body removed in each step is underlined. In step 1, $^{\text{call}}[\text{call}]^{\text{exc}}$ is a simple chain, so its body **call** is removed. Then, in step 2 we recognize the simple chain $^{\text{han}}[\underline{\text{call}}]^{\text{exc}}$, which means $^{\text{han}}[\text{call}[\text{call}]]^{\text{exc}}$, where [call] is the chain body removed in step 1, is a composed chain. This way, we recognize, e.g., $^{\text{han}}[\text{call}]^{\text{exc}}$, $^{\text{call}}[\text{han exc}]^{\text{call}}$ as simple chains, and $^{\text{han}}[\text{call}[\text{call}]]^{\text{exc}}$ and $^{\text{call}}[\text{han}[\text{call}[\text{call}]]\text{exc}]^{\text{call}}$ as composed chains (with inner chain bodies enclosed in brackets). Below we show the structure of w'_{ex} a longer version of w_{ex}, which is an isomorphic representation of its ST as depicted in Fig. 1.

$$\text{\#[call[[[han[call[call[call]]]]exc]call ret]call ret]ret]\#}$$

Each chain corresponds to an internal node, and the fringe of the subtree rooted at it is the chain's body.

Let $\mathcal{A}$ be an OPA. We call a *support* for the simple chain $^{c_0}[c_1 c_2 \ldots c_\ell]^{c_{\ell+1}}$ any path in $\mathcal{A}$ of the form $q_0 \xrightarrow{c_1} q_1 \dashrightarrow \ldots \dashrightarrow q_{\ell-1} \xdashrightarrow{c_\ell} q_\ell \xRightarrow{q_0} q_{\ell+1}$. The label of the last (and only) pop is exactly q_0, i.e. the first state of the path; this pop is executed because of relation $c_\ell > c_{\ell+1}$. We call a *support for the composed chain* $^{c_0}[s_0 c_1 s_1 c_2 \ldots c_\ell s_\ell]^{c_{\ell+1}}$ any path in $\mathcal{A}$ of the form $q_0 \overset{s_0}{\rightsquigarrow} q'_0 \xrightarrow{c_1} q_1 \overset{s_1}{\rightsquigarrow} q'_1 \dashrightarrow$
$\ldots \dashrightarrow q_\ell \overset{s_\ell}{\rightsquigarrow} q'_\ell \xRightarrow{q'_0} q_{\ell+1}$ where, for every $i = 0, 1, \ldots, \ell$: if $s_i \neq \epsilon$, then $q_i \overset{s_i}{\rightsquigarrow} q'_i$ is a support for the chain $^{c_i}[s_i]^{c_{i+1}}$, else $q'_i = q_i$.

Chains fully determine the parsing structure of any OPA over (Σ, M). If the OPA performs the computation $\langle sb, q_i, [a, q_j]\gamma \rangle \vdash^* \langle b, q_k, \gamma \rangle$, then $^a[s]^b$ is necessarily a chain over (Σ, M), and there exists a support like the one above with $s = s_0 c_1 \ldots c_\ell s_\ell$ and $q_{\ell+1} = q_k$.

The *OP Max-Automaton* over Σ, M is $\mathcal{A}(\Sigma, M) = (\Sigma, M, \{q\}, \{q\}, \{q\}, \delta_{max})$ where $\delta_{max}(q, q) = q$, and $\delta_{max}(q, c) = q$, $\forall c \in \Sigma$. Each chain has a support in $\mathcal{A}(\Sigma, M)$. Since there is a chain $^{\#}[s]^{\#}$ for any string s compatible with M, a string is accepted by $\mathcal{A}(\Sigma, M)$ iff it is compatible with M. If M is complete, each string is accepted by $\mathcal{A}(\Sigma, M)$, which defines the universal language Σ^* by assigning to any string the unique structure compatible with M.

In conclusion, given an OP alphabet, the OPM M assigns a unique structure to any compatible string in Σ^*; unlike VPLs, such a structure is not visible in the string, and must be built by means of a non-trivial parsing algorithm. An OPA defined on the OP alphabet selects an appropriate subset within the "universe" of strings compatible with M. For a more complete description of the OPL family and of its relations with other CFL we refer the reader to [23].

Operator Precedence ω-Languages. All definitions regarding OPLs are extended to infinite words in the usual way. Given an alphabet (Σ, M), an ω-word $w \in \Sigma^\omega$ is compatible with M if every prefix of w is compatible with M. OP ω-words are not terminated by $\#$. An ω-word may contain never-ending chains of the form $c_0 \lessdot c_1 \doteq c_2 \doteq \cdots$, where the $\lessdot$ relation between c_0 and c_1 is never closed by a $\gtrdot$. Such chains are called *open chains* and may be simple or composed. A composed open chain may contain both open and closed chains.

We define the class of automata accepting the whole class of ω-OPLs by augmenting Definition 1 with Büchi acceptance condition [22]. Hence, the name Operator Precedence Büchi Automata (OPBA). The semantics of configurations, moves and infinite runs are defined as for finite OPA. For the acceptance condition, let ρ be a run on an ω-word w. Define $\mathrm{Inf}(\rho) = \{q \in Q \mid$ there exist infinitely many positions i s.t. $\langle \beta_i, q, x_i \rangle \in \rho\}$ as the set of states that occur infinitely often in ρ. ρ is successful iff there exists a state $q_f \in F$ such that $q_f \in \mathrm{Inf}(\rho)$. An OPBA $\mathcal{A}$ accepts $w \in \Sigma^\omega$ iff there is a successful run of $\mathcal{A}$ on w. The ω-language recognized by $\mathcal{A}$ is $L(\mathcal{A}) = \{w \in \Sigma^\omega \mid \mathcal{A}$ accepts $w\}$. Unlike OPA, OPBA do not require the stack to be empty for word acceptance: when reading an open chain, the stack symbol pushed when the first character of the body of its underlying simple chain is read remains into the stack forever; it is at most updated by shift moves.

The most important closure properties of OPLs are preserved by ωOPLs.

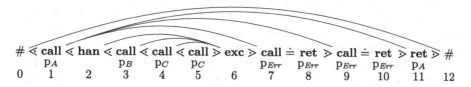

Fig. 2. w'_{ex} as an OP word, with edges showing the χ relation. Normal atomic propositions are below those in $M_{\mathbf{call}}$: p_l means a **call** or a **ret** is related to procedure p_l.

3   Background: Precedence Oriented Temporal Logic

Here we only describe a fragment of POTL, as not all of its operators are needed for our case study. For the full syntax, see [11]. Given a finite set of atomic propositions AP, $a \in AP$, and $t \in \{d, u\}$, the syntax of POTL follows:

$$\varphi ::= a \mid \neg\varphi \mid \varphi \vee \varphi \mid \bigcirc^t \varphi \mid \ominus^t \varphi \mid \chi_F^t \varphi \mid \chi_P^t \varphi \mid \varphi \,\mathcal{U}_\chi^t\, \varphi \mid \varphi \,\mathcal{S}_\chi^t\, \varphi.$$

The semantics of POTL is based on the *word structure*—also called *OP word* for short—(U, M_{AP}, P), where $U = \{0, 1, \ldots, n, n+1\}$ is a set of word positions; $P: U \to \mathcal{P}(AP)$ is a function associating each position with the set of atomic propositions holding in it, with $P(0) = P(n+1) = \{\#\}$. M_{AP} is only defined on a subset of AP, and exactly one of such labels may hold in each position. Given $i, j \in U$ and a PR π, we write $i \pi j$ to say that $a \in P(i)$, $b \in P(j)$ and $a \pi b$.

We define the chain relation $\chi \subseteq U \times U$ so that $\chi(i, j)$ holds between two positions i, j iff $i < j - 1$, and i and j are resp. the left and right contexts of the same chain. For composed chains, χ may not be one-to-one, but also one-to-many or many-to-one.

The truth of POTL formulas is defined w.r.t. a single word position. Let w be an OP word, and $a \in AP$. Then, for any position $i \in U$ of w, we have $(w, i) \models a$ if $a \in P(i)$. Operators such as $\vee$ and $\neg$ have the usual semantics from propositional logic.

The *downward* next and back operators $\bigcirc^d$ and $\ominus^d$ are true only if the next (resp. current) position is at a lower or equal ST level than the current (resp. preceding) one; replace 'lower' with 'higher' for the *upward* versions $\bigcirc^u$ and $\ominus^u$. Formally, $(w, i) \models \bigcirc^d \varphi$ iff $(w, i + 1) \models \varphi$ and $i \lessdot (i + 1)$ or $i \doteq (i + 1)$, and $(w, i) \models \ominus^d \varphi$ iff $(w, i - 1) \models \varphi$, and $(i - 1) \lessdot i$ or $(i - 1) \doteq i$. Substitute $\gtrdot$ for $\lessdot$ to obtain the semantics for $\bigcirc^u$ and $\ominus^u$. E.g., we can write $\bigcirc^d \textbf{call}$ to say that the next position is an inner call (holds in pos. 2, 3, 4 of Fig. 2), $\ominus^d \textbf{call}$ to say that the previous position is a **call**, and the current is the first of the body of a function (pos. 2, 4, 5), or the **ret** of an empty one (pos. 8, 10).

The *chain* next and back operators χ_F^t and χ_P^t, $t \in \{d, u\}$, evaluate their argument resp. on future and past positions in the chain relation with the current one. The *downward* (resp. *upward*) variant only considers chains whose right context goes down (resp. up) in the ST. Formally, $(w, i) \models \chi_F^d \varphi$ iff there exists $j > i$ such that $\chi(i, j)$, $i \lessdot j$ or $i \doteq j$, and $(w, j) \models \varphi$. $(w, i) \models \chi_P^d \varphi$ iff there exists $j < i$ such that $\chi(j, i)$, $j \lessdot i$ or $j \doteq i$, and $(w, j) \models \varphi$. Replace $\lessdot$ with $\gtrdot$ for the upward versions. In Fig. 2, $\chi_F^u \textbf{exc}$ is true in **call** positions whose procedure is terminated by an exception thrown by an inner procedure (e.g. pos. 3 and 4). $\chi_P^u \textbf{call}$ is true in **exc** statements that terminate at least one procedure other than the one raising it, such as the one in pos. 6. Note that these examples are not meant to be exhaustive: e.g., $\chi_P^u \textbf{call}$ holds also in position 11, and so on.

The *summary* until $\psi \mathcal{U}_\chi^t \theta$ (resp. since $\psi \mathcal{S}_\chi^t \theta$) operator is obtained by inductively applying the $\bigcirc^t$ and χ_F^t (resp. $\ominus^t$ and χ_P^t) operators. It holds in a position in which either θ holds, or ψ holds together with $\bigcirc^t(\psi \mathcal{U}_\chi^t \theta)$ (resp. $\ominus^t(\psi \mathcal{S}_\chi^t \theta)$) or $\chi_F^t(\psi \mathcal{U}_\chi^t \theta)$ (resp. $\chi_P^t(\psi \mathcal{S}_\chi^t \theta)$). It is an until operator on paths that can move not only between consecutive positions, but also between contexts of a chain, skipping its body. With $M_{\textbf{call}}$, this means skipping function bodies. The downward variants can move between positions at the same level in the ST (i.e., in the same simple chain body), or down in the nested chain structure. The upward ones remain at the same level, or move to higher levels of the ST.

E.g., $\top \mathcal{U}_\chi^u \textbf{exc}$ is true in positions contained in the frame of a function terminated by an exception. It is true in pos. 3 of Fig. 2 because of path 3-6, and false in pos. 1, because no path can enter the chain whose contexts are pos. 1 and 11. Formula $\top \mathcal{U}_\chi^d \textbf{exc}$ is true in call positions whose function frame contains **exc**s, such as the one in pos. 1 (with path 1-2-6). $\textbf{call} \mathcal{U}_\chi^d (\textbf{ret} \wedge p_{Err})$ holds in pos. 1 because of path 1-7-8 and 1-9-10, $(\textbf{call} \vee \textbf{exc})\, \mathcal{S}_\chi^u \, p_B$ in pos. 7 because of path 3-6-7, and $(\textbf{call} \vee \textbf{exc})\, \mathcal{U}_\chi^u \, \textbf{ret}$ in 3 because of path 3-6-7-8.

We additionally employ $\top$, $\wedge$, $\implies$ and $\iff$ with the usual semantics form propositional logic. We also use the operators $\Diamond$ and $\Box$ from LTL. They can be expressed in POTL as $\Box\psi := \neg(\top \, \mathcal{U}_\chi^u \, (\top \, \mathcal{U}_\chi^d \, \neg\psi))$ and $\Diamond\psi := \neg\Box\neg\psi$.

4 Model Checking OPA

We model-check POTL through the automata-theoretic procedure introduced in [11]. For any formula φ, we build an OPA (or OPBA) $\mathcal{A}_\varphi$ that only accepts models of φ. Then, given an OPA $\mathcal{A}$ to be checked, we check the product automaton $\mathcal{A}_\varphi \otimes \mathcal{A}$ for emptiness. The product automaton can be computed on-the-fly in a way similar to finite-state automata [22].

To cope with the state-space explosion problem, we propose an *on-the-fly* depth-first explicit-state exploration of the search space. We generate OPA states just before they are visited, and avoid wasting memory and time by generating unreachable states. Other tools [5,19] showed the benefits of this approach, especially when combined with the *early-termination* property, i.e. returning immediately when a counterexample is found. This has no benefits if no accepting state is ever reached, and the entire search space needs to be visited. On the other hand, it speeds up considerably cases when there is a counterexample.

Reachability. OPA are equipped with a stack, which must be considered when exploring the search space. Given an OP alphabet (Σ, M), let $\mathcal{A} = (\Sigma, M, Q, I, F, \delta)$ be an OPA, and $\Gamma = \Sigma \times Q \times \{\bot\}$ be the set of stack symbols.

Definition 3. *A semi-configuration of $\mathcal{A}$ is an element of $\mathcal{C} = Q \times \Gamma$.*

Definition 4. *The reachability relation is defined as $\mathcal{R}_{reach} \subseteq \mathcal{C} \times \mathcal{C} \times \Sigma$ so that, for any $p, q \in Q$, look-ahead $a \in \Sigma$, and $g_0, g_1 \in \Gamma$, we have*

$$\mathcal{R}_{reach}(p, g_0, q, g_1, a) \; iff \; \langle xay, \, p, \, g_0\rangle \vdash^* \langle ay, \, q, \, g_1\gamma\rangle,$$

for some $x, y \in \Sigma^*$, $\gamma \in \Gamma^*$.

To determine the (non) emptiness of $L(\mathcal{A})$, we must establish whether there exist some $q_i \in I$, $q_f \in F$ such that $(q_i, \bot, q_f, \bot, \#) \in \mathcal{R}_{reach}$.

Algorithm 1 solves the reachability problem for OPA by adapting a DFS to the use of summaries, similarly to [5]. It consists of an on-the-fly, early-terminating exploration to check if a given set $Q_R \times \Gamma_R$ of target semiconfigurations is reachable in an OPA $\mathcal{A}$. Function REACH receives as its arguments a state $q \in Q$, a stack symbol $g \in \Gamma$, a character $c \in \Sigma$, and a look-ahead $\ell \in \Sigma \cup \{*\}$. If $\ell = *$, then the look-ahead may be any character in Σ. The algorithm searches the transition graph and stops when it reaches a semiconfiguration $(q, g) \in Q_R \times \Gamma_R$. To solve the emptiness problem for OPA, we pose

$Q_R = F$ and $\Gamma_R = \{\bot\}$, and call REACH$(q, \bot, \#, *)$ for each $q \in I$. Each call to REACH has worst-case time complexity $O(|\delta||\delta_{push}|^2|\Sigma|)$ and space complexity $O(|\delta||\delta_{push}||\Sigma|)$. Note that the above bounds are reached only if the whole OPA is visited, i.e. when $L(\mathcal{A})$ is empty. Also, if Σ contains sets of atomic propositions, we consider only those on which the OPM is defined. E.g., with $M_{\mathbf{call}}$ we use only elements of $\Sigma_{\mathbf{call}}$ as look-aheads, and $|\Sigma_{\mathbf{call}}|$ is a small constant.

Summary Transitions. Suppose we are in a semiconfiguration (q_l, g) which can be followed by a push transition (q_l, b, r). This transition is the beginning of a chain support (let it be σ) that starts with symbol b. If we apply the reachability algorithm recursively, we may meet the push transition (q_l, b, r) again, which would lead us to the beginning of σ. To avoid a never-ending computation, we cannot follow it. At the same time, a semiconfiguration $s_p = (q_p, g_p)$ may be reachable such that q_p has a pop transition (q_p, q_l, q_r) which completes σ. s_p may not have been visited yet, due to the depth-first nature of the search, although it would allow us to continue the visit without getting stuck. We need to find a way to "suspend" the search and resume it later.

As a solution, we use a global variable (called *SupportStarts*) where we store semiconfigurations corresponding to the beginning of a chain support σ. While visiting σ, the algorithm matches all saved semiconfigurations for σ trying to perform a pop transition, thus completing σ and resuming the suspended explorations.

To establish if a saved semiconfiguration (q_l^{cand}, g^{cand}) is valid for σ, it must make sure that $smb(g^{cand})$ yields precedence to the first symbol read by σ (b in our example). This symbol is carried by parameter c in the REACH algorithm. Likewise, parameter l is used to restrict the set of possible characters to read after a pop transition only to those with which the input part of the stack symbol before popping is in a $\gtrdot$ relation.

This solution allows us to suspend the search safely when we encounter the beginning of a support in an already-visited semiconfiguration: if a way to go beyond exists, it will be explored. Therefore, we introduce *summary* transitions, which connect the first state of a chain support (q_l in our example) to the corresponding last state (q_r).

The algorithm also stores in *SupportEnds* a semiconfiguration whenever it exits a chain support. Thus, when it finds in a semiconfiguration the beginning of a support that has already been visited, it uses this pre-computed information to jump to the corresponding pop move directly.

Fair-Cycle Detection. We propose an adaptation of the reachability algorithm to the *fair-cycle detection* problem. Given an OPBA $\mathcal{A}_\varphi^\omega = \langle \mathcal{P}(AP), M_{AP}, Q_\omega, I, F, \delta \rangle$, algorithm FAIR-CYCLE-DETECT models the search space as a graph where vertices are semiconfigurations and edges are OPBA transitions, and looks for *fair* cycles, i.e. loops containing a state $q_\omega \in F$. To preserve the early-termination and on-the-fly properties, we follow an online approach: we represent and update Strongly Connected Components (SCCs) using

Algorithm 1. OPA semi-configuration reachability

```
1:  (Σ, M_Σ, Q, I, F, (δ_push, δ_shift, δ_pop)) := A
2:  V := SupportStarts := SupportEnds := ∅
3:  function REACH(q, g, c, ℓ)
4:      if (q, g, ℓ) ∈ V ∨ (q, g, *) ∈ V then return false
5:      V := V ∪ (q, g, ℓ)
6:      if q ∈ Q_R ∧ g ∈ Γ_R then return true
7:      a := smb(g)
8:      for all (q, b, p) ∈ δ_push s.t. a ⋖ b ∧ (b = ℓ ∨ ℓ = *) do
9:          SupportStarts := SupportStarts ∪ {(q, g, c)}
10:         if REACH(p, [b, q], b, *) then return true
11:     for all (s, q, c', ℓ') ∈ SupportEnds s.t. a ≐ c' do
12:         if REACH(s, g, c, ℓ') then return true
13:     if g ≠ ⊥ then
14:         [a, r] := g
15:         for all (q, b, p) ∈ δ_shift s.t. a ≐ b ∧ (b = ℓ ∨ ℓ = *) do
16:             if REACH(p, [b, r], c, *) then return true
17:         for all (q, r, p) ∈ δ_pop, b ∈ Σ ∪ {#} s.t. a ⋗ b ∧ (b = ℓ ∨ ℓ = *) do
18:             SupportEnds := SupportEnds ∪ {(p, r, c, b)}
19:             for all (r, g', c') ∈ SupportStarts s.t. smb(g') ⋖ c do
20:                 if REACH(p, g', c', b) then return true
21:     return false
```

an incremental algorithm while the REACH procedure discovers new portions of the graph. The algorithm we chose is a path-based depth-first search due to H. Gabow [16]. This algorithm finds SCCs and updates them dynamically in time linear on the number of graph nodes. It allows us to stop the search as soon as a non-trivial fair SCC is found. Otherwise, at the end it outputs the SCCs graph. It represents SCCs with simple auxiliary data structures such as stacks and arrays (hence the name *list-based* used in [16]) without contracting nodes in the actual graph. For performance reasons, we slightly modify our implementation to perform contractions.

Combining the REACH and GABOW routines into FAIR-CYCLE-DETECT is a crucial issue. A summary edge (corresponding to a summary transition) is added to the graph when we encounter a pop transition at the end of a chain support. Thus, the edge may be in a completely different part of the graph with respect to the current node. If followed, it breaks the depth-first property, which is required by the Gabow algorithm. Instead of restarting it for every pop transition, our solution is to save all the summary edges and process them later. FAIR-CYCLE-DETECT is then divided into two phases:

- a **search phase** when we discover new edges, following OPBA transitions, starting from the current initial semiconfigurations. If we find a summary edge, we do not feed it to the GABOW routine, but store it in the set *Summ*.
- a **collapse phase** when we add to the graph the summary edges in *Summ*, and run only the dynamic GABOW routine on it.

At the end of the collapse phase, we resume the exploration from semiconfigurations corresponding to the discovered summary transitions in *Summ*. If the set *Summ* is empty at the end of a search phase, there is no reachable fair cycle, and the algorithm terminates.

5   Modeling Procedural Programs

We use a simple procedural programming language with exceptions called MiniProc, which only admits Boolean variables. Its syntax is shown in Fig. 3.

```
PROGRAM = [DECLS] FUNCTION [FUNCTION ...]
DECLS = var IDENTIFIER [, IDENTIFIER ...] ;
FUNCTION = IDENTIFIER () { STMT; [STMT; ...] }
STMT = IDENTIFIER := BEXPR
     | while (BEXPR) { [STMT; ...] }
     | if (BEXPR) { [STMT; ...] } else { [STMT; ...] }
     | try { [STMT; ...] } catch { [STMT; ...] }
     | IDENTIFIER()
     | throw
BEXPR = BEXPR && BDISJ | BDISJ
BDISJ = BDISJ || BTERM | BTERM
BTERM = !BTERM | (BEXPR) | IDENTIFIER | true | false
```

```
program:
var foo;
pa() {
  foo = true;
  try { pb(); }
  catch { pc(); }
}
pb() {
  if (foo) { throw; }
  else {}
}
pc() { }
```

Fig. 3. MiniProc syntax (left) and a MiniProc program (right). Non-terminals are uppercase, and keywords lowercase. Parts in square brackets are optional, and ellipses mean that the enclosing group can be repeated zero or more times. An IDENTIFIER is any sequence of letters, numbers, or characters '.', ':' and '_', starting with a letter or an underscore.

A program starts with a variable declaration, which must include all variables used in the program. Then, a sequence of functions are defined, the first one being the entry-point to the program. Function bodies consist of semicolon-separated statements. Assignments, while loops and ifs have the usual semantics. The try-catch statement executes the catch block whenever an exception is thrown by any statement in the try block (or any function it calls). Exceptions are thrown by the throw statement, and they are not typed (i.e., there is no way to distinguish different kinds of exceptions). Functions can be called by prepending their name to the () token (they do not admit arguments, as all variables are global). Since all variables are Boolean, expressions can be composed with the logical and (&&), or (||) and negation (!) operators.

OPA and OPBA semantically equivalent to a MiniProc program can be generated automatically, both based on OPM M_{call}. We illustrate their construction through examples. First, an *extended* OPA is generated, in which every state corresponds to some program state, and transitions can be labeled with Boolean expression guards that must be true for them to be performed, or variable assignments. Figure 4 shows the extended OPA from the code in Fig. 3. The stack semantics of the two models coincide: a symbol is pushed for every function call, and popped after the corresponding return (or exception). Handlers are

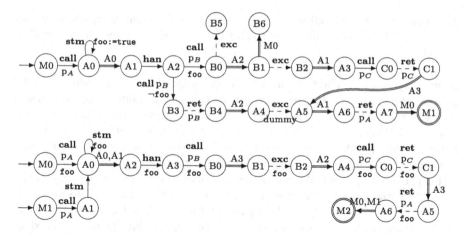

Fig. 4. Extended OPA (top) and OPA (bottom) generated from the code of Fig. 3.

paired to the exception they catch by a shift move updating the same symbol; a dummy exception is placed after the try body to uninstall the handler. The model-checking procedures of Sect. 4 do not take guards into account, so the extended OPA must be transformed into a normal one. This is done by enumerating all possible Boolean variable assignments for each state, leaving only those that are actually reachable. The resulting OPA for our example is in Fig. 4.

The last part of the OPA generation leads to a worst-case model size exponential in the number of variables. However, it performs well in most practical cases, since only feasible states are generated.

6 Experiments

We show how to use POMC to verify programs with exceptions with some experiments on real code for a well-known recursive algorithm, Quicksort. The properties we want to verify on an implementation of this algorithm are:

termination: the program always terminates for any input array.
correctness: any input array is correctly sorted at the end of the program.

We begin with two C programs packaged with the first version of the MOPED model checker [12,14,21]. Then, we move to a refinement which is targeted specifically to POMC. We call it *semi-safe* Java Quicksort, because of how it handles possible NullPointerExceptions. This experiment cannot be conducted on MOPED or tools such as VERA [5] or BEBOP [8], since their models require a matching single return statement for every function call. On the other hand, exceptions pop an indefinite amount of function frames on the stack until they meet a handler. With such formalisms, the automaton would be forced to read as many input symbols as the amount of popped function frames, thus consuming a portion of code from the catch block. In the following, the comparison of the three examples will allow the reader to grasp the greater expressive power of POMC. The experimental results and their execution times are reported in Table 1.

Buggy C QuickSort. The first one, called *Buggy Quicksort*, and contained in file quicksort_error.pds, has been proven to run into a infinite loop for certain values of the input array, violating the termination property. When modeling it with MiniProc, we consider an array of 2 values for performance reasons: a[left] and a[right]. We abstract away from the actual content of the array and replace all comparisons with non-deterministic choices, to get a smaller and better performing model. We use Boolean variables to represent the inequalities $(<, =, >)$ between local integer variables in the program. Then, we use the fair-cycle detection module of POMC to detect the mentioned never-ending loop. The problem can be expressed in terms of checking whether the main procedure always reaches the ret statement ($\chi_F^u(\text{ret} \wedge \text{main})$, experiment **B.2**). With this formula, we force the first position (the one reading call main) to be in the χ relation with the one reading the corresponding ret main. Anyway, call is in the $\doteq$ or $>$ (since we are imposing the upward variant) precedence relation only with ret and exc (see Fig. 1), and no exception is thrown in this model, so exc cannot be encountered. Therefore, we could simply use the formula $\chi_F^u \top$. However, the latter would be less clear. Moreover, the same reasoning does not hold for the third experiment: it contains exceptions. Therefore, we opt for the former. As expected, POMC returns False. Note that we can verify the termination property also with a simple LTL formula (**B.1**). Since termination is not guaranteed, it's meaningless to investigate the correctness for this implementation.

Correct C Quicksort. The implementation of file quicksort_correct.pds is known to satisfy both the termination and correctness properties. When modeling it with MiniProc, again by considering an array of 2 values, we introduce two boolean variables to indicate the relation between a[left] and a[right] explicitly. They are aleftGTaright and aleftEQaright, which respectively mean a[left] > a[right] and a[left] = a[right]. a[left] < a[right] is indicated by the expression !aleftGTaright && !aleftEQright.

First, we check for termination with the same formulas as in Buggy Quicksort (experiments **C.1** and **C.2**). Coherently with the early-termination property, the execution time is much greater in this case because the formulas hold. Then, we prove the correctness of the implementation. The algorithm is supposed to sort the array in ascending order, so we verify that !aleftGTaright holds at the end of the execution. There are two ways to state this. With LTL, we impose that sooner or later !aleftGTaright will hold forever (**C.3**). With POTL, we impose that the first position (the one which reads call main) is in the χ relation with a position where !aleftGTaright holds, using the upward variant of the operator. As introduced in the previous example, this position is necessarily the one reading the **return** statement. Therefore, experiments **C.4** and **C.6** equally verify the correctness of this implementation and both imply also the termination property. Inserting **ret** main is superfluous. Finally, **C.5** is meant to verify both correctness and termination together, but with a simple LTL formula.

```
main() {                                    qs() {
    // list may contain null elements          . . .                    accessValues() {
    try {                                       accessValues();            if (*) {
        qs();                                   . . .                        throw;
    } catch (){                              }                            } else {}
        parseList();                         parseList() {                }
        // null elements removed                hasParsed = true;
        qs();                                }
    }
}
```

Fig. 5. A portion of the semi-safe Java Quicksort model in MiniProc.

Semi-safe Java Quicksort. We consider the case of a Java implementation where the elements of the Array are of a non-primitive type. Since Java does not enforce *void-* (or *null-*) *safety* [24], accessing array elements may lead to a NullPointerException at runtime. A *semi-safe* solution is to:

- First, call the Quicksort procedure inside a try-catch construct, to handle potential exceptions.
- When the first null element is encountered and an exception is raised, parse the array in the catch body to remove all null elements.
- Last, call again the Quicksort procedure inside the catch body. This is potentially unsafe because the call is not contained in a try-catch construct. Thus, if accessing an element raised an exception, there would be no matching catch to handle it, and the **main** function would terminate abnormally. However, we know that it should not happen because of the previous processing of the array, hence the name *semi-safe*. Overall termination and correctness are not guaranteed *a priori*. They depend on the correctness of the parsing function which ensures void safety, thus preventing the throwing of non handled exceptions.

We model the entire procedure as a MiniProc program, by still considering a two-elements array. A sketch is reported in Fig. 5. We hide the Quicksort implementation with dots to highlight the exception-handling constructs. Note how the program strictly resembles real Java code. We treat the parsing function as a black box: we only use the Boolean variable hasParsed to indicate that the array has been processed to remove null elements. We introduce function accessValues to represent data access.

Firstly, we note that checking general termination (**S.1** and **S.2**) and correctness (**S.3** and **S.4**) returns False in all cases. As a remark, since exceptions are involved, here **ret** main is required in the formula of experiment **S.2**. Likewise, $\chi_F^u(\neg\text{aleftGTaright})$ (S.4) does not imply the termination of the **main** procedure anymore. With the use of the upward variant it imposes that at the end of program, no matter how it terminates, the array is correctly sorted.

Secondly, we examine the program-handling of the potential null-pointer exceptions. POTL can easily express properties related to exception handling [23]. E.g., the shortcut

$$CallThr(\psi) := \bigcirc^u(\mathbf{exc} \wedge \psi) \vee \chi_F^u(\mathbf{exc} \wedge \psi),$$

evaluated in a **call**, states that the procedure currently started is terminated by an **exc** in which ψ holds. So, $\square(\mathbf{call} \wedge \rho \wedge CallThr(\top) \implies CallThr(\theta))$ means that if precondition ρ holds when a procedure is called, postcondition θ must hold if that procedure is terminated by an exception. In object-oriented programming languages, if $\rho \equiv \theta$ is a class invariant asserting that a class instance's state is valid, this formula expresses *weak (or basic) exception safety* [1], and *strong exception safety* if ρ and θ express particular states of the class instance. Alternatively, postconditions may regard the type of exception which has occurred. The *no-throw guarantee* can be stated with $\square(\mathbf{call} \wedge p_A \implies \neg CallThr(\top))$, meaning procedure p_A is never interrupted by an exception. To begin with, we verify whether procedures **main** and **qs** satisfy the *no-throw guarantee* with experiments **S.5** and **S.6**: the result is False. Therefore, we inquire the conditions that lead to the potentially raised exceptions. The formula $\square(\mathbf{call} \wedge \mathrm{main} \wedge CallThr(\top) \implies CallThr(\mathrm{hasParsed}))$ specifies an exception-safety property meaning that, whenever a call to the function **main** is terminated by an exception, the array list has been parsed to ensure void safety. The property can be slightly modified into experiment **S.7**, which is verified. A second exception-safety property (**S.8**) verifies whether, in the case the **main** procedure is interrupted by an exception, correctness holds after the interruption. Unfortunately, the result is False.

However, the *stack inspection* property of experiment **S.9** holds. It means that every time the program accesses array values, either: i) there is a handler on the stack to handle a potential exception, or ii) we have already processed the array to remove null elements, thus guaranteeing void safety.

Lastly, we prove the *conditional* termination of this implementation (**S.10** and **S.11**), meaning that either the program terminates or an exception is raised after the parsing function has been called, indicating a bug in the parsing function itself. Likewise, we prove the *conditional* correctness (**S.12** and **S.13**), i.e. that either the array is correctly sorted at the end of the execution or an exception is raised after the parsing function has been called. Formula **S.14** verifies both conditional termination and correctness together.

6.1 Discussion

A limitation of the Case Study at hand is represented by the fact that all experiments deal with Quicksort implementations on arrays of only 2 cells. Indeed, it would be interesting to analyze how the tool's performances scale to bigger models. This is hindered by our tool's current lack of automatic abstraction and modeling techniques for real-world programs. For the time being, the only feasible approach is to model by hand all the possible execution traces, which becomes intractable for large arrays. We leave this task to future work. However, the preliminary works on arrays of 3 cells confirms our theoretical results that the latency is dominated by the formula (and especially formula size), and not by the model under verification.

Table 1. Results of verification of the Buggy Quicksort model (2259 OPBA states) (formulas **B.1** and **B.2**), the Correct Quicksort model (83980 OPBA states) (experiments from **C.1** to **C.6**), and the Semi Safe Correct Quicksort model (188456 OPBA states) (formulas from **S.1** to **S.14**). The experiments have been run on a server with a 2.0 GHz AMD CPU and 500 GB of RAM.

#	Formula	Time (s)	Result
B.1	$\Diamond(\mathbf{ret} \wedge \mathbf{main})$	0.067	False
B.2	$\chi_F^u(\mathbf{ret} \wedge \mathbf{main})$	1.011	False
C.1	$\Diamond(\mathbf{ret} \wedge \mathbf{main})$	36.3	True
C.2	$\chi_F^u(\mathbf{ret} \wedge \mathbf{main})$	101.8	True
C.3	$\Diamond(\Box \neg \mathrm{aleftGTaright})$	66.3	True
C.4	$\chi_F^u(\neg \mathrm{aleftGTaright})$	123.2	True
C.5	$\Diamond(\mathbf{ret} \wedge \mathbf{main} \wedge \neg \mathrm{aleftGTaright})$	49.0	True
C.6	$\chi_F^u(\mathbf{ret} \wedge \mathbf{main} \wedge \neg \mathrm{aleftGTaright})$	222.8	True
S.1	$\Diamond(\mathbf{ret} \wedge \mathbf{main})$	284.4	False
S.2	$\chi_F^u(\mathbf{ret} \wedge \mathbf{main})$	289.0	False
S.3	$\Diamond(\Box \neg \mathrm{aleftGTaright})$	279.5	False
S.4	$\chi_F^u(\neg \mathrm{aleftGTaright})$	276.5	False
S.5	$\Box((\mathbf{call} \wedge \mathbf{main}) \implies \neg(\bigcirc^u \mathbf{exc} \vee \chi_F^u \mathbf{exc}))$	245.9	False
S.6	$\Box((\mathbf{call} \wedge \mathrm{qs}) \implies \neg(\bigcirc^u \mathbf{exc} \vee \chi_F^u \mathbf{exc}))$	246.9	False
S.7	$(\bigcirc^u \mathbf{exc} \vee \chi_F^u \mathbf{exc}) \implies (\bigcirc^u \mathbf{exc} \wedge \mathrm{hasParsed}) \vee (\chi_F^u \mathbf{exc} \wedge \mathrm{hasParsed})$	19617.0	True
S.8	$(\bigcirc^u \mathbf{exc} \vee \chi_F^u \mathbf{exc}) \implies (\bigcirc^u \mathbf{exc} \wedge \neg \mathrm{aleftGTaright}) \vee (\chi_F^u \mathbf{exc} \wedge \neg \mathrm{aleftGTaright})$	387.2	False
S.9	$\Box((\mathbf{call} \wedge \mathrm{accessValues}) \implies \mathrm{hasParsed} \vee (\top\, S_\chi^d\, \mathbf{han}))$	446.2	True
S.10	$(\Diamond(\mathbf{ret} \wedge \mathbf{main})) \vee (\chi_F^u(\mathbf{exc} \wedge \mathrm{hasParsed}))$	1124.0	True
S.11	$(\chi_F^u(\mathbf{ret} \wedge \mathbf{main})) \vee (\chi_F^u(\mathbf{exc} \wedge \mathrm{hasParsed}))$	12809.0	True
S.12	$(\Diamond(\Box \neg \mathrm{aleftGTaright})) \vee (\chi_F^u(\mathbf{exc} \wedge \mathrm{hasParsed}))$	1615.0	True
S.13	$(\chi_F^u(\neg \mathrm{aleftGTaright})) \vee (\chi_F^u(\mathbf{exc} \wedge \mathrm{hasParsed}))$	12736.0	True
S.14	$(\Diamond(\mathbf{ret} \wedge \mathbf{main} \wedge \neg \mathrm{aleftGTaright})) \vee \chi_F^u(\mathbf{exc} \wedge \mathrm{hasParsed})$	2247.0	True

7   Conclusions

We presented efficient algorithms for reachability and fair-cycle detection for OPA and OPBA. We implemented them in the POMC tool, together with a user-friendly DSL (MiniProc) which allows to model procedural code with exceptions. We reported on a case study on the Quicksort algorithm to show the suitability of POMC for the verification of programs with exceptions. As future work, we plan to investigate the possibility of using POMC to verify properties on real-world programming languages through suitable automated abstractions, such as iterative abstraction refinement techniques. As discussed in Sect. 6.1, these techniques could address the quest for investigating the tool's performance scaling.

References

1. Abrahams, D.: Exception-safety in generic components. In: Jazayeri, M., Loos, R.G.K., Musser, D.R. (eds.) Generic Programming. LNCS, vol. 1766, pp. 69–79. Springer, Heidelberg (2000). https://doi.org/10.1007/3-540-39953-4_6

2. Alur, R., Arenas, M., Barceló, P., Etessami, K., Immerman, N., Libkin, L.: First-order and temporal logics for nested words. LMCS, vol. 4, no. 4 (2008). https://doi.org/10.2168/LMCS-4(4:11)2008

3. Alur, R., Benedikt, M., Etessami, K., Godefroid, P., Reps, T., Yannakakis, M.: Analysis of recursive state machines. ACM Trans. Program. Lang. Syst. **27**(4), 786–818 (2005). https://doi.org/10.1145/1075382.1075387

4. Alur, R., Bouajjani, A., Esparza, J.: Model checking procedural programs. In: Handbook of Model Checking, pp. 541–572. Springer, Cham (2018). https://doi.org/10.1007/978-3-319-10575-8_17

5. Alur, R., Chaudhuri, S., Etessami, K., Madhusudan, P.: On-the-fly reachability and cycle detection for recursive state machines. In: Halbwachs, N., Zuck, L.D. (eds.) TACAS 2005. LNCS, vol. 3440, pp. 61–76. Springer, Heidelberg (2005). https://doi.org/10.1007/978-3-540-31980-1_5

6. Alur, R., Etessami, K., Madhusudan, P.: A temporal logic of nested calls and returns. In: Jensen, K., Podelski, A. (eds.) TACAS 2004. LNCS, vol. 2988, pp. 467–481. Springer, Heidelberg (2004). https://doi.org/10.1007/978-3-540-24730-2_35

7. Alur, R., Madhusudan, P.: Visibly pushdown languages. In: ACM STOC (2004)

8. Ball, T., Rajamani, S.K.: Bebop: a symbolic model checker for Boolean programs. In: Havelund, K., Penix, J., Visser, W. (eds.) SPIN 2000. LNCS, vol. 1885, pp. 113–130. Springer, Heidelberg (2000). https://doi.org/10.1007/10722468_7

9. Ball, T., Rajamani, S.K.: The SLAM toolkit. In: Berry, G., Comon, H., Finkel, A. (eds.) CAV 2001. LNCS, vol. 2102, pp. 260–264. Springer, Heidelberg (2001). https://doi.org/10.1007/3-540-44585-4_25

10. Chiari, M., Mandrioli, D., Pradella, M.: Operator precedence temporal logic and model checking. Theor. Comput. Sci. **848**, 47–81 (2020). https://doi.org/10.1016/j.tcs.2020.08.034

11. Chiari, M., Mandrioli, D., Pradella, M.: Model-checking structured context-free languages. In: Silva, A., Leino, K.R.M. (eds.) CAV 2021. LNCS, vol. 12760, pp. 387–410. Springer, Cham (2021). https://doi.org/10.1007/978-3-030-81688-9_18

12. Esparza, J., Hansel, D., Rossmanith, P., Schwoon, S.: Efficient algorithms for model checking pushdown systems. In: Emerson, E.A., Sistla, A.P. (eds.) CAV 2000. LNCS, vol. 1855, pp. 232–247. Springer, Heidelberg (2000). https://doi.org/10.1007/10722167_20

13. Esparza, J., Kučera, A., Schwoon, S.: Model checking LTL with regular valuations for pushdown systems. Inf. Comput. **186**(2), 355–376 (2003). https://doi.org/10.1016/S0890-5401(03)00139-1

14. Esparza, J., Schwoon, S.: A BDD-based model checker for recursive programs. In: Berry, G., Comon, H., Finkel, A. (eds.) CAV 2001. LNCS, vol. 2102, pp. 324–336. Springer, Heidelberg (2001). https://doi.org/10.1007/3-540-44585-4_30

15. Floyd, R.W.: Syntactic analysis and operator precedence. JACM **10**(3), 316–333 (1963). https://doi.org/10.1145/321172.321179

16. Gabow, H.N.: Path-based depth-first search for strong and biconnected components. Inf. Process. Lett. **74**(3), 107–114 (2000). https://doi.org/10.1016/S0020-0190(00)00051-X

17. Grune, D., Jacobs, C.J.H.: Parsing Techniques: Monographs in Computer Science. Springer, New York (2008). https://doi.org/10.1007/978-0-387-68954-8
18. Harrison, M.A.: Introduction to Formal Language Theory. Addison Wesley, Boston (1978)
19. Holzmann, G.: The model checker SPIN. IEEE Trans. Softw. Eng. **23**(5), 279–295 (1997). https://doi.org/10.1109/32.588521
20. Jensen, T., Le Metayer, D., Thorn, T.: Verification of control flow based security properties. In: Proceedings of the 1999 IEEE Symposium on Security and Privacy, pp. 89–103 (1999). https://doi.org/10.1109/SECPRI.1999.766902
21. Kiefer, S., Schwoon, S., Suwimonteerabuth, D.: Moped. http://www2.informatik.uni-stuttgart.de/fmi/szs/tools/moped/
22. Lonati, V., Mandrioli, D., Panella, F., Pradella, M.: Operator precedence languages: their automata-theoretic and logic characterization. SIAM J. Comput. **44**(4), 1026–1088 (2015). https://doi.org/10.1137/140978818
23. Mandrioli, D., Pradella, M.: Generalizing input-driven languages: theoretical and practical benefits. Comput. Sci. Rev. **27**, 61–87 (2018). https://doi.org/10.1016/j.cosrev.2017.12.001
24. Meyer, B.: Attached types and their application to three open problems of object-oriented programming. In: Black, A.P. (ed.) ECOOP 2005. LNCS, vol. 3586, pp. 1–32. Springer, Heidelberg (2005). https://doi.org/10.1007/11531142_1

Counterexample Classification

Cole Vick[1], Eunsuk Kang[2($\boxtimes$)], and Stavros Tripakis[1($\boxtimes$)]

[1] Northeastern University, Boston, USA
{vick.c,stavros}@northeastern.edu
[2] Carnegie Mellon University, Pittsburgh, USA
eskang@cmu.edu

Abstract. In model checking, when a given model fails to satisfy the desired specification, a typical model checker provides a *counterexample* that illustrates how the violation occurs. In general, there exist many diverse counterexamples that exhibit distinct violating behaviors, which the user may wish to examine before deciding how to repair the model. Unfortunately, obtaining this information is challenging in existing model checkers since (1) the number of counterexamples may be too large to enumerate one by one, and (2) many of these counterexamples are redundant, in that they describe the same type of violating behavior. In this paper, we propose a technique called *counterexample classification*. The goal of classification is to partition the space of all counterexamples into a finite set of *counterexample classes*, each of which describes a distinct type of violating behavior for the given specification. These classes are then presented as a summary of possible violating behaviors in the system, freeing the user from manually having to inspect or analyze numerous counterexamples to extract the same information. We have implemented a prototype of our technique on top of an existing formal modeling and verification tool, the Alloy Analyzer, and evaluated the effectiveness of the technique on case studies involving the well-known Needham-Schroeder protocol with promising results.

1 Introduction

In formal verification, *counterexamples* are an invaluable aid for debugging a system model for possible defects. Typically, a counterexample is constructed by a verification tool as a *trace* (i.e., a sequence of states or events) that demonstrates how the system violates a desired property. The user of the tool would then inspect the counterexample for the underlying cause behind the violation and fix the model accordingly.

In practice, there are a number of challenges that the user may encounter while using counterexamples to debug and repair a model. First, a counterexample may contain details that are irrelevant to the root cause of a violation, requiring considerable effort by the user to manually analyze and extract the violating behavior. Second, the user may wish to investigate multiple different

This work has been supported by the National Science Foundation under NSF SaTC award CNS-1801546.

R. Calinescu and C. S. Păsăreanu (Eds.): SEFM 2021, LNCS 13085, pp. 312–331, 2021.
https://doi.org/10.1007/978-3-030-92124-8_18

types of counterexamples before deciding how to repair the model; this is, however, a challenging task because (1) the number of counterexamples may be too large to enumerate one by one, and (2) many of these counterexamples may be *redundant* in that they describe the same type of violating behavior.

This paper proposes a technique called *counterexample classification* as an approach to overcome these challenges. The key intuition behind this approach is that although a typical model contains a very large (or possibly infinite) set of counterexamples, (1) many of these can be considered "similar", in that they share a common, violating behavior and (2) this similarity can be captured as a specific relationship between states that is shared by these traces. Based on this insight, our technique automatically partitions the set of counterexamples into a finite number of *classes*, each of which is associated with a *constraint* that characterizes one particular type of violation. These constraints are then presented to the user, along with representative counterexamples, as distinct descriptions of possible defects in the system, freeing them from manually sorting through numerous counterexamples to extract the same information.

We have built a prototype implementation of our classification technique on top of an existing formal modeling and verification tool, the Alloy Analyzer [8]. Our tool accepts a formal model, a specification (that the model currently violates), and a set of *predicates* that describe relationships between states in the model. From these, the tool produces (if one exists) a set of classes that accounts for all of the violating behavior in the model. As a case study, we have successfully applied our technique to two variants of the Needham-Schroeder protocol [12], and were able to classify hundreds of thousands of counterexamples into only a handful of classes that represent known attacks to the protocol.

Our main contributions may be summarized as follows: a formal definition of the Counterexample Classification Problem (Sect. 3), a solution to the Counterexample Classification Problem (Sect. 4), and a case study on a well-established distributed protocol, Needham-Schroeder (Sect. 5), that demonstrates the efficacy of our solution.

1.1 Running Example

To motivate our technique, we introduce the following example. Alice and Bob are sending Messages to each other. Eve is able to view these messages as they are being sent. The content of a message can be either Plaintext or Encrypted. Eve is always able to read Plaintext messages, but needs Key_{AB}, Alice and Bob's shared key, to read Encrypted messages. Eve acquires Key_{AB} by seeing an Encrypted message, modelling Eve "breaking" the encryption of what should be a one-time key. A Message may be flagged as Secret, meaning that its content should not be read by Eve.

We model this example as a transition system, shown in Fig. 1. The transition system has four states, represented by two state variables, *EveKey* of type $Key = \{\emptyset, Key_{AB}\}$, and *EveSeenSecret* of type Boolean ($\top$ for true and $\bot$ for false). The initial state is $(\emptyset, \bot)$ meaning that Eve does not know the key and has not read any secret.

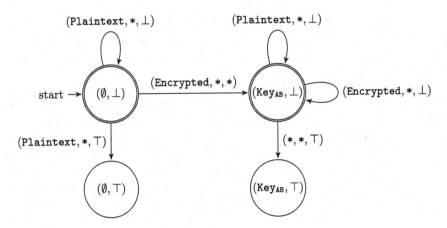

Fig. 1. Transition system of the running example.

Transitions between states are labeled by `Messages`. A `Message` is a tuple of the form $(type, sender, secret)$, where $type \in \{\texttt{Encrypted}, \texttt{Plaintext}\}$ denotes whether the message is encrypted or not (if encrypted, a message is encrypted by $\texttt{Key}_{\texttt{AB}}$), $sender \in \{\texttt{Alice}, \texttt{Bob}\}$ denotes the sender of the message, and $secret$ is a Boolean denoting whether the message is secret or not. For example, the transition $(\emptyset, \perp) \xrightarrow{(\texttt{Plaintext,Alice,T})} (\emptyset, \top)$ means that `Alice` sends a `Plaintext` (unencrypted) `Secret` message.[1] * indicates that the corresponding field can take any value within its type, i.e., there are multiple such transitions, one for each possible value.

We would like this system to satisfy the property that `Eve` never reads a `Message` that is flagged as `Secret`. This can be expressed as the temporal logic (LTL) formula

$$\Phi = \mathbf{G}(EveSeenSecret = \perp)$$

which states that $EveSeenSecret = \perp$ holds at every reachable state of the system, i.e., it is an *invariant*. As we can see, this is not the case for the model in Fig. 1. The top two double bordered states are the *good* states.

Note that this system has infinitely many *counterexample traces*, as self-loop transitions can be taken arbitrarily many times.

Take for instance the counterexample traces listed below:

$$\rho_1^1 = (\emptyset, \perp) \xrightarrow{(\texttt{Plaintext,Alice,T})} (\emptyset, \top)$$

$$\rho_1^2 = (\emptyset, \perp) \xrightarrow{(\texttt{Plaintext,Alice,}\perp)} (\emptyset, \perp) \xrightarrow{(\texttt{Plaintext,Alice,T})} (\emptyset, \top)$$

$$\rho_1^3 = (\emptyset, \perp) \xrightarrow{(\texttt{Plaintext,Bob,}\perp)} (\emptyset, \perp) \xrightarrow{(\texttt{Plaintext,Bob,T})} (\emptyset, \top)$$

$$\rho_1^4 = (\emptyset, \perp) \xrightarrow{(\texttt{Plaintext,Alice,}\perp)} (\emptyset, \perp) \xrightarrow{(\texttt{Plaintext,Bob,T})} (\emptyset, \top)$$

---

[1] The traces in this section have labels, i.e. `Messages`, on their transitions. We do this to make it clear how messages are sent and how different messages affect the state. Our formal definition will not include labels as they may be encoded directly into the state.

In ρ_1^1, Alice sends a Plaintext Secret message. Eve is be able to read it, as it is unencrypted, which leads to a violation of the property. In ρ_1^2, Alice first sends a Plaintext but non-secret message and then sends a Plaintext Secret message. In ρ_1^3, Bob first sends a Plaintext but non-secret message and then he sends a Plaintext Secret message. In ρ_1^4, Alice sends a Plaintext but non-secret message and then Bob sends a Plaintext Secret message.

These violating traces share important behavior: the fact that either Alice or Bob sends a Plaintext Secret message. Noticing this, we would like to group these traces together in the same *counterexample class*.

Now consider the counterexample traces listed below:

$$\rho_2^1 = (\emptyset, \bot) \xrightarrow{\text{(Encrypted,Alice,}\bot)} (\text{Key}_{\text{AB}}, \bot) \xrightarrow{\text{(Encrypted,Bob,}\top)} (\text{Key}_{\text{AB}}, \top)$$

$$\rho_2^2 = (\emptyset, \bot) \xrightarrow{\text{(Encrypted,Bob,}\bot)} (\text{Key}_{\text{AB}}, \bot) \xrightarrow{\text{(Encrypted,Alice,}\top)} (\text{Key}_{\text{AB}}, \top)$$

$$\rho_2^3 = (\emptyset, \bot) \xrightarrow{\text{(Encrypted,Alice,}\top)} (\text{Key}_{\text{AB}}, \bot) \xrightarrow{\text{(Encrypted,Alice,}\top)} (\text{Key}_{\text{AB}}, \top)$$

$$\rho_2^4 = (\emptyset, \bot) \xrightarrow{\text{(Encrypted,Bob,}\top)} (\text{Key}_{\text{AB}}, \bot) \xrightarrow{\text{(Encrypted,Alice,}\top)} (\text{Key}_{\text{AB}}, \top)$$

These traces exhibit a different way in which the property can be violated than the traces shown previously. Now, the violation happens when Alice or Bob send an Encrypted Secret message after an Encrypted message has already been sent, i.e. after Eve has broken the encryption. A description of this new class would be: Eve receives an Encrypted message before receiving an Encrypted Secret message.

The method and tool presented in this paper generate such counterexample classes automatically. Our tool does not output class descriptions in English but represents classes syntactically as *trace constraints*. A trace constraint is evaluated over a given trace ρ. If ρ satisfies the trace constraint then we say that ρ falls into the class that the trace constraint represents. The trace constraints that represent the two classes discussed above are:

$$TC_{Plaintext}[\rho] \equiv \exists i \in [0..len(\rho)] : \rho.type@i = \text{Plaintext} \land \rho.secret@i = \top$$
$$TC_{Encrypted}[\rho] \equiv \exists i, j \in [0..len(\rho)] : i < j \land \rho.EveKey@i = \text{Key}_{\text{AB}} \land$$
$$\rho.type@j = \text{Encrypted} \land \rho.secret@j = \top$$

where $len(\rho)$ denotes the length of trace ρ and the variables i and j represent indices to particular positions of states and transitions in ρ. The initial state is indexed at position s_0 and the first transition is indexed at position l_0 and leads to state s_1 thus following the general pattern: $s_0 \xrightarrow{l_0} s_1 \xrightarrow{l_1} s_2 \cdots$.

2   Background

Definition 1 (Symbolic transition system). *A* symbolic transition system *is a tuple* (X, I, T) *where:*

- X *is a finite set of* typed state variables. *Each variable* $x \in X$ *has a type, denoted* type(x). *A type is a set of values.*

- *The* initial state predicate I *is a predicate (i.e., Boolean expression) over* X.
- *The* transition relation predicate T *is a predicate over* $X \cup X'$, *where* X' *denotes the set of* primed *(next state) variables obtained from* X. *For example, if* $X = \{x, y, z\}$ *then* $X' = \{x', y', z'\}$. *Implicitly, every primed variable has the same type as the original variable:* $\forall x \in X : \mathsf{type}(x') = \mathsf{type}(x)$.

We let U denote the universe of all values. A *state* s over a set of state variables X is an assignment of a value (of the appropriate type) to each variable in X, i.e., s is a (total) function $s : X \to U$, such that $\forall x \in X : s(x) \in \mathsf{type}(x)$. A state s satisfies a predicate I over X, denoted $s \models I$, if when we replace all variables in I by their values as defined by s, I evaluates to true. For example, suppose $X = \{x, y, z\}$ where x and y are integer variables, and z is a Boolean variable. Let I be the predicate $x < y \wedge z$. Consider two states, $s_1 = (x = 3, y = 4, z = \top)$ and $s_2 = (x = 3, y = 1, z = \top)$. Then, $s_1 \models I$ but $s_2 \not\models I$.

Similarly, a pair of states (s, s') satisfies a predicate T over $X \cup X'$ if when we replace all variables from X in T by their values as defined by s, and all variables from X' in T by their values as defined by s', T evaluates to true. For example, suppose $X = \{x\}$ where x is an integer variable. Let T be the predicate $x' = x + 1$. Consider three states, $s_0 = (x = 0)$, $s_1 = (x = 1)$, and $s_2 = (x = 2)$. Then $(s_0, s_1) \models T$ and $(s_1, s_2) \models T$, but $(s_0, s_2) \not\models T$.

Definition 2 (Transition system defined from a symbolic transition system). *A symbolic transition system* (X, I, T) *defines a* transition system (S, S_0, R), *where:*

- *The set of* states S *is the set of all assignments over* X.
- *The set of* initial states S_0 *is the set:* $S_0 = \{s \in S \mid s \models I\}$.
- *The* transition relation R *is the set:* $R = \{(s, s') \in S \times S \mid (s, s') \models T\}$.

That is, the set of initial states is the set of all states satisfying I, and the transition relation R is the set of all pairs of states satisfying T. A pair $(s, s') \in R$ is also called a *transition*, and is sometimes denoted $s \to s'$.

Definition 3 (Trace). *A* trace ρ *over a set of state variables* X *is a finite sequence of states over* X: $\rho = s_0, ..., s_k$. *The length of* ρ *is* k, *and is denoted by* $\mathsf{len}(\rho)$; *note that* k *may equal* 0, *in which case the trace is empty. The set of states of* ρ *is* $\{s_0, ..., s_k\}$ *and is denoted* $\mathsf{States}(\rho)$.

Definition 4 (Property). *A* property Φ *over a set of state variables* X *is a set of traces over* X.

Definition 5 (Traces for an STS). *Let* $\mathsf{STS} = (X, I, T)$ *be a symbolic transition system and let* (S, S_0, R) *be the transition system of* STS. *The set of traces generated by* STS, *denoted* $\mathsf{Traces}(\mathsf{STS})$, *is the set of all traces* $\rho = s_0, s_1, ..., s_k$ *over* X *such that:*

- $s_0 \in S_0$. *That is,* ρ *starts at an initial state of* STS.
- $\forall i \in \{0, ..., k - 1\} : (s_i, s_{i+1}) \in R$. *That is, every pair of successive states in* ρ *is linked by a transition in* STS.

Definition 6 (Property satisfaction and counterexamples). *Let* STS $=$ (X, I, T) *be a symbolic transition system and let Φ be a property over X. We say that* STS *satisfies Φ, written* STS $\models \Phi$, *iff* Traces(STS) $\subseteq \Phi$. *If* STS $\not\models \Phi$, *then a* counterexample *is any trace $\rho \in$ Traces(STS) $\setminus \Phi$, i.e., any trace of* STS *which violates (does not belong in) Φ.*

3 Counterexample Classification

3.1 Classes and Classifications

Consider a set of traces P. A *class of* P is any non-empty subset of P. A *classification of* P is a partition of P into (not necessarily disjoint) classes.

Definition 7 (Classification). *Consider a set of traces P. A* classification *of P is a finite set C of classes of P such that $\bigcup_{c \in C} c = P$.*

Given a set of counterexample traces P, and a classification C of P, a *canonical counterexample* is a counterexample trace that belongs in exactly one class of C. A canonical counterexample thus represents the violating behavior of a particular class as it only appears in that particular class.

Definition 8 (Canonical Counterexample). *Given a set of counterexamples traces P and a classification C of P, a* canonical counterexample *ρ is any counterexample in P such that: $\forall c_1, c_2 \in C : (\rho \in c_1 \land \rho \in c_2) \rightarrow c_1 = c_2$. We denote by $c(\rho)$ the unique class in C that ρ belongs to.*

A classification is *redundant* if it contains classes that have no canonical counterexample:

Definition 9 (Redundant Classification). *A* classification C *of a set of counterexamples P is* redundant *if there exists a class $c \in C$ such that c does not contain a canonical counterexample.*

Example 1. Suppose $P = \{\rho_1, \rho_2, \rho_3, \rho_4, \rho_5\}$ and $C = \{c_1, c_2, c_3\}$ with $c_1 = \{\rho_1, \rho_2, \rho_3\}, c_2 = \{\rho_3, \rho_4, \rho_5\}, c_3 = \{\rho_1, \rho_4\}$. Note that C is a valid classification of P as $c_1 \cup c_2 \cup c_3 = P$. C is a redundant classification, because although c_1 has a canonical counterexample ρ_2, and c_2 has canonical counterexample ρ_4, c_3 has no canonical counterexample.

Often, we would like for a classification to guarantee that each class has a canonical counterexample, i.e., to be *non-redundant*. In general, we can transform every redundant classification into a non-redundant classification. First, we state the following two lemmas[2]:

Lemma 1. *A classification C of a set of counterexamples P is redundant iff there exist distinct classes $c, c_1, ..., c_n \in C$ such that $c \subseteq \bigcup_{i=1,...,n} c_i$.*

---

[2] Proofs for the following Lemmas and Theorems have been removed due to page restrictions. The full paper, with proofs, is available here https://arxiv.org/abs/2108.00885.

Lemma 2. *Let $C = \{c_1, ..., c_n\}$ be a classification of a set of counterexamples P. C is redundant iff there exists $i \in \{1, ..., n\}$ such that $c_i \subseteq \bigcup_{j \neq i} c_j$.*

Based on Lemma 2, we can construct an algorithm to transform any classification into a non-redundant classification.

3.2   The Counterexample Classification Problem

In Sect. 3.1, we defined the concepts of classes and classifications *semantically*. But in order to define the counterexample classification problem that we solve in this paper, we need a *syntactic* representation of classes. We define such a representation in this section, by means of *trace constraints*. A trace constraint is a special kind of predicate that evaluates over traces. A trace constraint is similar to predicates such as the I (initial state) predicate of a symbolic transition system, with two key differences: (1) a trace constraint is only conjunctive, and (2) a trace constraint can refer to state variables at certain positions in the trace and impose logical conditions over those positions. For example, if $X = \{x, y\}$ is the set of state variables, then here are some examples of trace constraints:

- $TC1[\rho] \equiv \exists i \in [0..len(\rho)] : x@i = y@i$: this trace constraint says that there is a position i in the trace such that the value of x at that position is the same as the value of y.
- $TC2[\rho] \equiv \exists i, j \in [0..len(\rho)] : i < j \wedge x@i > x@j$: this says that there are two positions i and j in the trace such that i is earlier than j and the value of x decreases from i to j.

We call formulas such as $x@i = y@i$ or $x@i > x@j$, which operate on indexed state variables, *atomic facts*. We call formulas such as $i < j$, which operate on position variables, *atomic position facts*. Then, a trace constraint is a conjunction of atomic facts and atomic position facts, together with an existential quantification of all position variables within the range of the length of the trace.

Atomic facts and atomic position facts are defined over a set of *user-defined predicates*. Some predicates will be standard, such as *equality* ($=$) for integers and *less-than* ($<$) for positions, while other predicates may be domain-specific. In addition to variables, we allow predicates to refer to constants. For example, $i \leq 10$ says that the position i must be at most 10, and $x@2 = 13$ says that the value of x at position 2 must be 13.

For example, recall the `Message` type from the running example. The user might want to define a predicate that checks whether two messages have the same sender. Then, the user can define the predicate $SendersEqual$ which is parameterized over two variables of type `Message` and defined as:

$$SendersEqual[m_1, m_2] \equiv m_1.sender = m_2.sender$$

This predicate may be then instantiated as:

$$SendersEqual[message@1, message@5]$$

This checks whether the `Message` at position 1 has the same sender as the `Message` at position 5.

Definition 10 (Trace Constraint). *A trace constraint over a set of state variables X and a set V of user-defined predicates is a formula of the form*

$$TC[\rho] \equiv \exists i_1, ..., i_k \in [0..len(\rho)] : \xi_0 \wedge \xi_1 \wedge \cdots \wedge \xi_n$$

where:

- $i_1, ..., i_k$ *are non-negative integer variables denoting positions in the trace t. We allow k to be 0, in which case the trace constraint has no position variables.*
- *Each ξ_j, for $j = 0, ..., n$, is either an atomic fact over state variables X and position variables $i_1, ..., i_k$ or an atomic position fact over position variables $i_1, ..., i_k$ using predicates in V.*

Given a trace constraint w, and a trace ρ, we can evaluate w on ρ in the expected way. For example, the trace $(x = 0) \longrightarrow (x = 0)$ over state variable x, satisfies the trace constraint $TC_1[\rho] \equiv \exists i_0, i_1 \in [0..len(\rho)] : i_0 < i_1 \wedge x@0 = x@1$ but does not satisfy the trace constraint $TC_2[\rho] \equiv \exists i_0, i_1 \in [0..len(\rho)] : i_0 < i_1 \wedge x@0 > x@1$. We write $\rho \models w$ if trace ρ satisfies trace constraint w. We also say that w *characterizes* ρ when $\rho \models w$. We denote by $c(w)$ the set of all traces satisfying constraint w.

Let W be a set of trace constraints. Then, let $C(W) = \{c(w) \mid w \in W\}$; i.e., $C(W)$ is the set of all sets of traces that are characterized by some trace constraint in W.

Consider a symbolic transition system STS and a property Φ that is violated by STS, i.e., STS $\not\models \Phi$. The problem that we are concerned with in this paper is to find a classification of all traces of STS that violate Φ, such that this classification is represented by a set of trace constraints defined over V. We call this problem the *counterexample classification problem* (CCP):

Definition 11 (Counterexample Classification Problem). *Given symbolic transition system* STS $= (X, I, T)$, *property Φ such that* STS $\not\models \Phi$, *and user-defined predicates V, find, if there exists, a set of trace constraints W such that: (1) each $w \in W$ is a trace constraint over X and V; and (2) $C(W)$ is a classification of P, where P is the set of all traces of* STS *that violate Φ.*

Lemma 3. *Let W be a solution to the CCP. Then, every trace constraint $w \in W$ is a sufficient condition for a violation, i.e., $\forall w \in W : c(w) \cap \Phi = \emptyset$.*

3.3 Solvability

The CCP is formulated as to find a set of trace constraints W *if one exists* (Definition 11). Indeed, while a semantic classification always exists (e.g., a trivial one is the one containing just one class, the set of all counterexamples P), a *syntactic classification* in the form of W might not always exist. Whether or not one exists depends on the set of user-defined predicates V.

Lemma 4. *If the set of counterexample traces P is finite, and V includes equality $=$, then CCP always has a solution.*

Lemma 4 shows that in the presence of equality =, and provided that the set of counterexamples is finite, CCP always has a solution. But in the absence of =, CCP may not have a solution.

For example, consider an STS with $X = \{a\}$ where a is an integer variable that can be non-deterministically incremented by 1, decremented by 1, or held constant at each step. Let the initial state be $a = 1$. Let the property Φ be $\mathbf{G}(a = 1)$, i.e., we require that a is always 1, which is clearly violated by this system.

Suppose that V only contains the predicate $lessThanOne[x]$, which returns true if and only if the given integer x is strictly less than 1. Then, we claim that CCP has no solution. Indeed, note that the set of counterexample traces includes all traces where at some point either $a < 1$ or $a > 1$. But the given V is unable to generate an atomic fact where a is greater than 1 (notice that negation is not allowed in trace constraints). Therefore we cannot classify all counterexample traces, and in particular not those where $a > 1$.

Now suppose that we change V to $\{lessThanOne, greaterThanOne\}$, with the obvious meanings. Then the following two trace constraints constitute a solution to CCP:

$$TC_1[\rho] \equiv \exists i \in [0..len(\rho)] : lessThanOne[x@i]$$
$$TC_2[\rho] \equiv \exists i \in [0..len(\rho)] : greaterThanOne[x@i]$$

3.4 Uniqueness of Solutions

The discussion in Sect. 3.3 shows that CCP may or may not have a solution, depending on the set V of predicates allowed in the trace constraints. In this section we show that even for a fixed V, CCP does not necessarily have a unique solution.

Consider the example given just above, in Subsect. 3.3. If we set V to $\{lessThanOne, greaterThanOne, \neq\}$, where $\neq$ is the not-equals predicate, the problem now admits at least two solutions. W_1 is still a solution, while the second solution $W_2 = \{TC_3\}$ uses only the $\neq$ predicate to characterize the violating behavior. The trace constraint TC_3 is defined as:

$$TC_3[\rho] \equiv \exists i \in [0..len(\rho)] : x@i \neq 1$$

4   Classification Method

In this section, we present a method for solving the CCP introduced in Sect. 3.2. We present an overview of our proposed classification algorithm (Sect. 4.1), describe optimizations to ensure the generation of a non-redundant classification with minimal classes (Sect. 4.2), and finally present a solution to the Running example (Sect. 4.3).

Input : An STS, a specification Φ, and a set of predicates V
Output: A set of trace constraints W
1 **Func** classify(STS, Φ, V):
2     $W = \emptyset$
3   **while** verify(STS $\wedge$ block(W), Φ) $==$ Violated **do**
4   ρ = counterexample(STS $\wedge$ block(W), Φ)
5   Γ = facts(ρ, V)
6   **if** $\Gamma = \emptyset$ **then**
7   **return** *"V cannot sufficiently characterize the violation in ρ"*
8   w = traceConstraint(Γ, ρ)
9   **if** verify(STS $\wedge$ w, $\neg\Phi$) $==$ Violated **then**
10   **return** *"V cannot sufficiently characterize the violation in ρ"*
11   w = minimizeTC(STS, w, Φ)
12         $W = W \cup w$
13   W = removeRedundant(STS, W, Φ)
14   **return** W

Algorithm 1: The counterexample classification algorithm.

4.1 Algorithm Overview

Given an STS, a property Φ, and a set of user-defined predicates V, the goal is to find a set of trace constraints W such that $C(W)$ is a solution to the CCP (Definition 11 in Sect. 3.2). We assume, without loss of generality, that V is non-empty. Indeed, an empty V implies that the only possible trace constraint is the empty trace constraint, which characterizes the set of all traces. This situation can be modelled by adding to V a trivial predicate that always returns $\top$ (true), thus having a non-empty V. To guarantee termination, we assume that the set of counterexamples $P = \text{Traces}(\text{STS}) \setminus \Phi$ is finite. To avoid the trivial solution where all traces are violating, we also assume that $\text{Traces}(\text{STS}) \cap \Phi \neq \emptyset$.

The pseudocode for the classification algorithm is shown in Algorithm 1. Procedure classify relies on the existence of a *verifier* that is capable of checking STS against Φ and generating a counterexample trace, if it exists. In particular, classify uses the following verifier functions:

- verify(STS $\wedge$ φ, Φ): Returns OK if STS satisfies Φ under the additional constraint φ, i.e., if $\text{Traces}(\text{STS} \wedge \varphi) \subseteq \Phi$; else, returns Violated. The constraint φ is typically a trace constraint. We provide examples of φ later in this section.
- counterexample(STS $\wedge$ φ, Φ): If verify(STS $\wedge$ φ, Φ) $==$ Violated, returns a trace ρ of STS such that $\rho \models \varphi$ and $\rho \not\models \Phi$; else, returns an empty output.

The algorithm begins by checking whether STS violates Φ (line 3) and if so, returning a counterexample that demonstrates how a violation can occur (line 4). The additional argument to the verifier, block(W), is used to prevent the verifier from re-generating a counterexample that belongs to any previously generated classes; we will describe this in more detail later in this section.

Next, given a particular counterexample ρ, the helper function facts generates the set Γ of all atomic facts and atomic position facts that hold over ρ, by instantiating the predicates V over the states in ρ (line 5). Then, based on Γ, traceConstraint builds a trace constraint that characterizes ρ. In particular, this procedure transforms Γ into a syntactically valid trace constraint w, by (1) introducing a sequence of existential quantifiers over all positional variables in ρ and (2) taking the conjunction of all facts in Γ (line 8).

In the next step, the verifier is used once again to ensure that the trace constraint w sufficiently captures the violating behavior in ρ (line 9). This is done by checking that every trace of STS that satisfies w (i.e., it shares the same characteristics of ρ as described by Γ) results in a violation of Φ. If not, it implies that w is not strong enough to guarantee a violation; i.e., V does not contain enough predicates to fully characterize ρ. In this case, a solution to the CCP cannot be produced and the algorithm terminates with an error (line 10).

If w guarantees a violation, it is added to the set of classes that will eventually form a solution classification to the CCP (line 12). The process from lines 4 to 12 is then repeated until it exhausts the set of all counterexample classes for STS and Φ.

To prevent the verifier from returning the same type of counterexample as ρ, classify passes block(W) as an additional constraint to verify, where:

$$\text{block}(W) \equiv \neg(\bigvee_{i=1}^{|W|} w_i)$$

In other words, by including block(W) as an additional constraint, the verifier ensures that it only explores traces that do not belong to any of the classes in W. Note that if W is empty (as in the first iteration of the loop), block(W) returns *true* (i.e., $\top$).

Once the verifier is no longer able to find any counterexample, the algorithm terminates by returning W as the solution classification (line 14).

Provided there is a finite number of counterexamples and a non-empty set of accepting traces, Algorithm 1 terminates because at least one counterexample is classified at each iteration of the while loop. The following theorems establish the correctness of the algorithm.

Theorem 1. *Any W returned by* classify *is a valid solution to the CCP.*

Theorem 2. *If* classify *returns no solution (lines 7 or 10 of Algorithm 1), then CCP has no solution for the given V.*

Example 2. Recall the example from Sect. 3.3. To make P finite, we assume that the length of counterexample traces is exactly 2. Then, $P = \{(a = 1) \xrightarrow{--} (a = 0), (a = 1) \xrightarrow{++} (a = 2)\}$. Let the set of user-defined predicates be $V = \{lessThanOne, greaterThanOne\}$.

Suppose that the verifier returns $\rho = (a = 1) \xrightarrow{--} (a = 0)$ as the first counterexample (line 4). Next, facts evaluates the predicates in V over the state variable a at position 0 and 1 (line 5), producing Γ that contains one fact: $\{lessThanOne[a@1]\}$. Then, the trace constraint w constructed based on Γ is:

$$TC_1[\rho] \equiv \exists i_1 \in [0..len(\rho)] : lessThanOne[a@i_1]$$

It can be shown that any trace of STS that satisfies TC_1 is a violation of Φ; thus, this newly created constraint $w \equiv TC_1$ is added to the set W.

In our example, there is one more counterexample; namely, $\rho = (a = 1) \xrightarrow{++} (a = 2)$, which can be used to construct the following additional trace constraint:

$$TC_2[\rho] = \exists i_1 \in [0..len(\rho)] : greaterThanOne[a@i_1]$$

Once TC_2 is added to W, there are no more remaining counterexamples, and the algorithm terminates by returning $W = \{TC_1, TC_2\}$.

4.2   Optimizations

Minimizing Trace Constraints. A trace constraint w generated on line 6 in Algorithm 1 may be a sufficient characterization of ρ, but it may also contain facts that are *irrelevant* to the violation. To be more precise, we consider a fact $f \in \Gamma$ to be irrelevant if trace constraint w that is constructed from $\Gamma' \equiv \Gamma - f$ is still sufficient to imply a violation.

Let us revisit Example 2. Suppose that we add to the set V of user-defined predicates an additional predicate $<$ over position variables. Then, for the counterexample $\rho = (a = 1) \xrightarrow{--} (a = 0)$, facts returns $\Gamma = \{lessThanOne[a@1], 1 < 2\}$ where 1 and 2 are positions in ρ. Then, the trace constraint generated by traceConstraint will be:

$$TC_3[\rho] = \exists i_1, i_2 \in [0..len(\rho)] : lessThanOne[a@i_2] \wedge i_1 < i_2$$

Although TC_3 is sufficient to imply a violation, it is less general than the previously generated TC_1 in the absence of predicate $<$ (see Example 2). Indeed, the constraint $i_1 < i_2$ in TC_3 forces the condition $a < 1$ to occur only at positions $i_2 > 0$, whereas in TC_1 the same condition can also occur at position $i_1 = 0$. Furthermore, this additional constraint can be safely removed from TC_3 while still guaranteeing a violation. Thus, constraint $i_1 < i_2$ is an irrelevant fact.

Our algorithm performs an additional *minimization* step to remove all such irrelevant facts from w. This additional procedure provides two benefits: (1) it reduces the amount of information that the user needs to examine to understand the classes and (2) each minimized class is a generalization of the original class and covers an equal or larger set of traces that share the common characteristics, thus also reducing the number of classes in the final classification.

As shown in Algorithm 2, minimizeTC relies on the ability of certain verifiers (such as the ones based on SAT [8] or SMT solvers [4]) to produce a *minimal core* for the unsatisfiability of a formula [15]. In particular, minCore(STS, w, $\neg\Phi$) computes a minimal subset of conjuncts in the symbolic representation of STS and w that are sufficient to ensure that $\neg\Phi$ holds (line 6). The facts (γ) that are common to this core and Γ represent the minimal subset of facts about ρ that are sufficient to imply a violation; a new trace constraint is then constructed based on this subset and returned as the output of minimizeTC (line 7).

Note that if verify on line 4 returns Violated (i.e., $\neg\Phi$ does not always hold under constraint w), this implies that the set of facts in Γ is not sufficient

Input : An STS, a trace constraint w, and a specification Φ
Output: A minimized trace constraint

1 **Func** minimizeTC(STS, w, Φ):
2   if verify(STS $\wedge w$), $\neg\Phi$) $==$ OK **then**
3        $\gamma = \Gamma \cap$ minCore(STS, $w, \neg\Phi$)
4   **return** traceConstraint(γ, ρ)
5   **else**
6   **return** *"Γ does not sufficiently characterize the violation in ρ"*

Algorithm 2: minimizeTC, which removes from trace constraint w all facts that are irrelevant to the violation depicted by ρ.

to imply a violation of Φ. However, if minimizeTC is invoked from line 9 in Algorithm 1, this side of the conditional branch should never be reachable.

Non-Redundancy. Although non-redundancy of classification W is not necessary for a valid solution to the CCP, it is a desirable property as it reduces the number of classes that the user needs to inspect. Thus, the main algorithm classify also performs a redundancy check at its end (line 11, Algorithm 1) to ensure the non-redundancy of any solution that it produces.

Input : an STS, a set of trace constraints W, and a specification Φ
Output: a set of trace constraints W'

1 **func** removeRedundant(STS, W, Φ):
2     $W' = \emptyset$
3   **for** $w \in W$ **do**
4   **if** verify(STS $\wedge$ block($W \setminus \{w\}$), Φ) $==$ Violated **then**
5           $W' = W' \cup w$
6   **return** W'

Algorithm 3: removeRedundant checks whether any $w \in W$ is redundant and if it is, removes it.

Function removeRedundant, shown in Algorithm 3, ensures that no trace constraint $w \in W$ is covered by any other trace constraints in W. Note that when the while loop in Algorithm 1 is exited, verify(STS $\wedge$ block(W), Φ) returns OK since W classifies all counterexamples in P. This means that all traces of STS which do not belong in any of the classes in W satisfy Φ. To find redundant trace constraints, we iterate over each $w \in W$ and check whether STS still satisfies Φ with w removed from W (line 4, Algorithm 3). If this is the case, then w is redundant, since $W \setminus \{w\}$ already covers P. Otherwise, w must characterize some $\rho \in P$ that the other trace constraints do not, and thus w is added to the non-redundant set W', which is returned at the end.

For example, recall the predicates $V = \{\neq, lessThanOne, greaterThanOne\}$ from Sect. 3.4. Suppose that classify finds two trace constraints in this order[3]:

$$TC_1[\rho] \equiv \exists i \in [0..len(\rho)] : lessThanOne[a@i]$$
$$TC_2[\rho] \equiv \exists i \in [0..len(\rho)] : a@i \neq 1$$

---

[3] Note that a newly created trace constraint is never redundant.

Notice that TC_2 classifies all counterexamples that TC_1 classifies. Thus, TC_1 is redundant and is not added to the final solution $W' = \{TC_2\}$.

4.3   Solution to the Running Example

Consider the running example presented in Sect. 1.1. For this example, Algorithm 1 outputs the trace constraints $TC_{Encrypted}$ and $TC_{Plaintext}$ in Sect. 1.1 given the set of predicates $V = \{=, <\}$. Equality $=$ operates over Messages and Booleans while $<$ operates on position variables.

Atomic position facts are generated just like atomic facts. Recall the following counterexample trace that is characterized by $TC_{Encrypted}$:

$$\rho = (\emptyset, \bot) \xrightarrow{(\text{Encrypted,Alice},\bot)} (\text{Key}_{AB}, \bot) \xrightarrow{(\text{Encrypted,Alice},\top)} (\text{Key}_{AB}, \top)$$

In the facts procedure, the $<$ predicate would generate two facts, $\{i_1 < i_2, i_2 < i_3\}$. These facts impose an ordering on any satisfying counterexample and capture the timing of the violation.

5   Implementation and Case Studies

5.1   Implementation

We have built a prototype implementation of the classify algorithm (Algorithm 1) on top of the Alloy Analyzer [8], a formal modeling and verification tool. In particular, Alloy uses an off-the-shelf SAT solver to perform bounded model checking (BMC), which is used for the verify procedure in the algorithm. As we demonstrate in this section, our prototype is capable of characterizing a large set of counterexamples (hundreds of thousands) with only a handful of generated classes. These generated classes are provided to the user in the form of trace constraints, along with representative counterexamples from each class.

Even though our current implementation uses Alloy and BMC, our technique does not depend on the use of BMC or any particular verification engine and could be implemented using other tools, provided they are capable of generating counterexample traces. Our current implementation does rely on the SAT solver being able to compute minimal unsatisfiable cores (which are used for minimizing the trace constraints).

5.2   Case Studies: Needham-Schroeder

As a case study, we applied our prototype to the well-known Needham-Schroeder protocol (NSP) [12], which has been known to be vulnerable to certain types of attacks [11]. We show how our classification methods can be used to classify the large number of counterexamples in a formal model of NSP into a small number of classes that correspond to these types of attacks.

The purpose of NSP is to allow two parties to communicate privately over an insecure network. NSP has two variants that look to accomplish this goal in different ways. The first variant is the Needham-Schroeder Symmetric protocol, from now on referred to as Symmetric, and the second variant is the Needham-Schroeder Public-Key protocol, from now on referred to as Public-Key. The two variants exhibit different violating behaviors, which allowed us to test our classification technique on the two separate variants, while not having to write two drastically different models.

Formal Modeling. We constructed Alloy models of both the Symmetric and Public-Key variants. Together, both variants total approximately 700 lines of Alloy code. These models serve as the input to our tool along with a specification Φ and a set of predicates V[4].

In both variants there are 4 Processes: Alice, Bob, Eve, and a central Server. The attacker, Eve, can read all of the Messages exchanged between the Processes. The setup is similar to the running example that has been discussed throughout the paper. Both variants must satisfy the following specification.

Specification (Φ). We consider only one property across both variants of NSP: the secret Key K_{AB} shared between Alice and Bob is not leaked to Eve. We express this property as the following LTL formula:

$$\Phi = \mathbf{G}(K_{AB} \notin Eve.knows)$$

where $p.knows$ denotes the state variable of a protocol participant representing the set of Keys that the participant p has access to.

Symmetric. In the Symmetric variant, Alice notifies the Server that she would like to communicate with Bob. The Server then generates a communication key, Key_{AB}, for Alice and Bob and sends it to Alice. This message is encrypted with Bob's secret key. Alice forwards this message to Bob so that he will be able to decrypt the message with his secret key and learn the shared key. Bob then sends a random nonce to Alice that is encrypted with their shared key. Alice verifies that she knows the shared key by sending back Bob's nonce decremented by 1 (Fig. 2).

Public-Key. In the Public-Key variant, Alice notifies the Server that she would like to communicate with Bob. The Server sends Alice a signed message with Bob's public key. Alice sends Bob a message including a nonce that is encrypted with Bob's public key. Bob receives this message and asks the Server for Alice's public key. The Server sends Bob Alice's public key. Bob now sends Alice's nonce back to Alice along with a new nonce encrypted with Alice's public key. Alice confirms that she has her private key by responding to Bob with his nonce encrypted with his public key.

Predicates. In the experiments described below, we used the following sets of predicates (V): Generic = $\{=, <\}$, consisting of only equality and one ordering predicate; V_1 = Generic $\cup$ {replay}; and V_2 = Generic $\cup$ {manInTheMiddle}. V_1

---

[4] The Alloy models and code for our tool can be found at https://github.com/cvick32/ CounterexampleClassificiation.

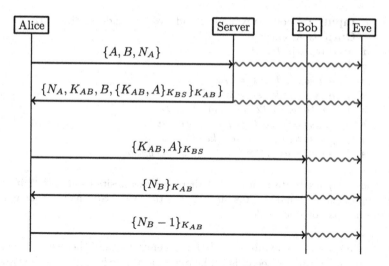

Fig. 2. A communication diagram of the Needham-Schroeder Symmetric protocol. A and B are identifiers for Alice and Bob respectively. There are three keys: K_{AB}, the shared key between Alice and Bob, K_{AS} and K_{BS} which are each Alice and Bob's server key. Alice and Bob also make use of a nonce, N_A and N_B respectively. Each arrow reprepresents a Message. $\{...\}_K$ denotes a Message encrypted by key K, and therefore requiring K to be read successfully. The snaking red lines represent Eve having access to all Messages that are sent over the network. (Color figure online)

and V_2 include all generic predicates plus some specialized predicates that characterize particular behavior in a model. The replay predicate, shown in Fig. 3, captures counterexamples where Eve sends the same message that was sent earlier by another process. The manInTheMiddle predicate captures counterexamples where Eve passes Alice and Bob's messages between them with no direct communication between Alice and Bob.

Predicates like replay and manInTheMiddle could be part of a library of predicates that any user could search and use. For example, replay can be used to check other communication protocols for replay attacks, provided that they follow a similar message-passing structure. Note that no information concerning the particularities of the Needham-Schroeder protocol is used in the definition of replay, meaning that this predicate can be used in a generic way. The same holds for manInTheMiddle.

Results. Our tool was able to produce classifications for both the Symmetric and Public-Key variants of NSP, as explained below. We were able to count up to 270,000 counterexamples (using the counterexample enumeration feature in Alloy) for both NSP variants until our program ran out of memory. The results are shown in Table 1.

Alloy employs bounded model checking for its verification engine; the *bound* column in Table 1 shows the upper bound used for the number of steps in traces explored by BMC. The V column shows the predicate set used in each experiment.

> **Input** : A counterexample ρ and two time indexes $t1$ and $t2$
> **Output:** A boolean
> 1 **pred** replay$[\rho, t1, t2]$:
> 2 $t1 < t2 \wedge$
> 3 $\rho.msg.sender.t1 \neq$ Eve $\wedge$
> 4 $\rho.msg.sender.t2 =$ Eve $\wedge$
> 5 $\rho.msg.nonce.t2 = \rho.msg.nonce.t1 \wedge$
> 6 $\rho.msg.process.t2 = \rho.msg.process.t1 \wedge$
> 7 $\rho.msg.key.t2 = \rho.msg.key.t1 \wedge$
> 8 $\rho.msg.encryption.t2 = \rho.msg.encryption.t1 \wedge$

Fig. 3. The replay predicate returns $\top$ if there are two positions $t1$ and $t2$ in ρ such that $t1$ occurs before $t2$ and the Message at $t1$ is the exact same as the Message at $t2$ except that Eve is now the sender.

The next column shows the number of classes generated and the last two columns show the execution time in seconds[5]. The execution time is split into the time our tool spent calling Alloy to find counterexamples and all other computations on the right. We found it instructive to show that the program was spending much of its time generating counterexamples in Alloy, while all other computations remained relatively constant for each respective experiment. Note that executions using V_2 take much longer than other executions. Most of this time is spent in generating the facts for manInTheMiddle as that particular predicate ranges over a number of time steps and all time steps in a counterexample must be checked. We also note that when using the Generic predicate set no redundant classes were found.

Table 1. Results on the Symmetric (left) and Public-Key (right) NSP variants. All times are recorded in seconds. All experiments were evaluated on a 2.5 GHz Quad-Core Intel i7 CPU with 16 GB of RAM.

bound	V	# classes	Alloy time	Total time
10	Generic	2	1.92	7.56
	V_1	3	4.29	10.23
25	Generic	2	9.37	16.24
	V_1	3	37.26	43.55
50	Generic	2	61.48	70.41
	V_1	3	220.49	226.37
75	Generic	2	254.38	267.96
	V_1	3	897.19	903.44
100	Generic	2	653.62	674.66
	V_1	3	1949.65	1955.133

bound	V	# classes	Alloy time	Total time
10	Generic	2	2.96	12.46
	V_2	3	6.01	100.61
25	Generic	2	12.96	24.04
	V_2	3	30.64	125.70
50	Generic	2	91.67	97.78
	V_2	3	157.62	251.89
75	Generic	2	321.95	349.21
	V_2	3	525.53	615.85
100	Generic	2	850.52	893.71
	V_2	3	1301.83	1396.92

Symmetric. This NSP variant is vulnerable to a replay attack. This attack has been addressed in implementations like Kerberos, although the attack was not found until 3 years after the initial publication of the protocol [5].

Using the Generic predicate set, our tool generated 2 non-redundant classes. These classes characterize counterexamples where either Alice or Bob

---

[5] Times were measured using the Java built-in System.nanoTime().

unknowingly establishes communication with Eve, who then manages to extract the secret key from this interaction. For example, the trace constraint $TC_{Generic}$ shown below represents one of these two classes and characterizes counterexamples where Alice sends a message and at a later state, Eve manages to learn the secret key:

$$TC_{Generic}[\rho] \equiv \exists i_1, i_2 \in [0..len(\rho)] : \rho.msg.sender@i_1 = \text{Alice} \wedge$$
$$\rho.\text{Eve}.knows@i_2 = \{\text{Key}_{\text{AB}}\} \wedge i_1 < i_2$$

Although this constraint is a valid characterization of counterexamples (in that it is sufficient to guarantee a violation of Φ), it is rather an abstract one, in that it does not describe the intermediate steps that Eve carries out in order to extract the secret key.

To generate more specialized classes, the user can provide additional predicates beside the generic ones. Using V_1 as the predicate set, our tool generated 3 classes: the two classes previously found with Generic, plus a third class represented by the trace constraint TC_{Replay} shown below:

$$TC_{Replay}[\rho] \equiv \exists i_1, i_2 \in [0..len(\rho)] : \text{replay}[\rho, i_1, i_2] \wedge i_1 < i_2 \wedge$$
$$\rho.msg.encryption@i_2 = \rho.msg.encryption@i_1 \wedge$$
$$\rho.msg.key@i_2 = \rho.msg.key@i_1$$

Our tool guarantees that we begin our classification with counterexamples that satisfy whichever predicate we choose, in this case replay. This is helpful as it constrains our classification to only those counterexamples which satisfy replay, allowing us to classify a subset of the total set of counterexamples. The constraint TC_{Replay} describes the type of violation where Eve carries out a replay attack, where she re-sends the message that was previously sent at step i_1 again at step i_2 with the identical message content. Note that although TC_{Replay} is a redundant class with respect to the other two classes generated using the generic predicates, it serves additional utility in that it provides more specific information about what Eve does in order to cause a security violation. The user of our tool (e.g., a protocol designer) could then use the information in these constraints to improve the protocol and prevent these types of violations.

Public-Key. This NSP variant is vulnerable to a man-in-the-middle attack [11]. Eve is able to forward messages between Alice and Bob and trick them into thinking they are communicating directly.

Similarly to the Symmetric variant, we were able to classify counterexamples that demonstrated the man-in-the-middle attack. The classes found in the Public-Key experiment reflected what we found in the Symmetric variant, i.e. 2 classes that show a general violating pattern with Generic and then 3 classes where 1 class demonstrates the known violation, using predicate set V_2. Our tool showed that the Public-Key variant is not vulnerable to replay attacks.

In summary, our classification method (1) significantly reduces the amount of information that the user needs to inspect to understand the different types of violations, by collapsing the large number of counterexamples ($\geq$ 270,000 for the case study) into a small number of classes and (2) enables the user to inspect these different violating behaviors in a high-level representation (i.e., trace constraints) that can encode domain-specific information (e.g., replay attacks).

6   Related Work

It is well known that predicates can be used to abstract needless detail in certain problem domains [3,9]. This is the first time, to our knowledge, that predicates have been used for counterexample classification.

Our work can be considered a kind of automated debugging technique [16] in the context of model checking. There have been a number of prior works into locating the relevant parts of counterexample that explain or even *cause* a violation [1,2,7]. While our work does not deal with an explicit notion of causality, the generated trace constraints are sufficient to imply a violation of the property. The major difference between these works and ours is that they focus on *explaining* one or more given counterexamples, while our objective to *classify* the set of all counterexamples into distinct classes. Our work is also related and complementary to [10], which focuses on generating short counterexamples. We take a different approach by focusing on generating minimal trace constraints, each of which characterize a *set* of counterexamples.

The approach in [6] has the similar goal of generating a *diverse* set of counterexamples. This work relies on a notion of diversity that depends on general properties about the structure of the given state machine (e.g., counterexamples that have different initial distinct and final states). In comparison, our notion of diversity is *domain-specific*, in that it is capable of classifying traces based on domain-specific predicates that can be provided by the user. In this sense, these are two complementary approaches and could potentially be combined into a single model debugging tool.

7   Conclusion and Future Work

In this paper, we have proposed *counterexample classification* as a novel approach for debugging counterexamples generated by a model checker. The key idea behind our approach is to classify the set of all counterexamples to a given model and a property into *trace constraints*, each of which describes a particular type of violation. Our work leverages the notion of *predicates* to distinguish between different types of violations; we have also demonstrated how these predicates can capture violations that are common within a domain (e.g., attacks on security protocols) and can facilitate the reuse of domain knowledge for debugging.

For future work, we plan to explore methods based on machine learning (such as clustering (e.g., [14]) to automatically extract predicates from a given set of counterexample traces. Another interesting direction is to explore how our classification method could be used to improve counterexample-guided approaches to program synthesis (such as CEGIS [13]), by reducing the number of counterexamples that need to be explored by the synthesis engine.

References

1. Ball, T., Naik, M., Rajamani, S.K.: From symptom to cause: localizing errors in counterexample traces. In: Proceedings of the 30th ACM SIGPLAN-SIGACT Symposium on Principles of Programming Languages, POPL 2003, pp. 97–105. Association for Computing Machinery, New York, January 2003
2. Beer, I., Ben-David, S., Chockler, H., Orni, A., Trefler, R.: Explaining counterexamples using causality. In: Bouajjani, A., Maler, O. (eds.) CAV 2009. LNCS, vol. 5643, pp. 94–108. Springer, Heidelberg (2009). https://doi.org/10.1007/978-3-642-02658-4_11
3. Cousot, P., Cousot, R.: Abstract interpretation: a unified lattice model for static analysis of programs by construction or approximation of fixpoints. In: Proceedings of the 4th ACM SIGACT-SIGPLAN Symposium on Principles of Programming Languages, POPL 1977, pp. 238–252. Association for Computing Machinery, New York, January 1977
4. de Moura, L., Bjørner, N.: Z3: an efficient SMT solver. In: Ramakrishnan, C.R., Rehof, J. (eds.) TACAS 2008. LNCS, vol. 4963, pp. 337–340. Springer, Heidelberg (2008). https://doi.org/10.1007/978-3-540-78800-3_24
5. Denning, D.E., Sacco, G.M.: Timestamps in key distribution protocols. Commun. ACM **24**(8), 533–536 (1981)
6. Dominguez, A., Day, A.: Generating multiple diverse counterexamples for an EFSM (2013)
7. Groce, A., Visser, W.: What Went Wrong: Explaining Counterexamples. In: Ball, T., Rajamani, S.K. (eds.) SPIN 2003. LNCS, vol. 2648, pp. 121–136. Springer, Heidelberg (2003). https://doi.org/10.1007/3-540-44829-2_8
8. Jackson, D.: Alloy: a lightweight object modelling notation. ACM Trans. Softw. Eng. Methodol. (TOSEM) **11**(2), 256–290. ACM, New York (2002)
9. Jhala, R., Podelski, A., Rybalchenko, A.: Predicate abstraction for program verification. In: Handbook of Model Checking, pp. 447–491. Springer, Cham (2018). https://doi.org/10.1007/978-3-319-10575-8_15
10. Kashyap, S., Garg, V.K.: Producing short counterexamples using "Crucial Events". In: Gupta, A., Malik, S. (eds.) CAV 2008. LNCS, vol. 5123, pp. 491–503. Springer, Heidelberg (2008). https://doi.org/10.1007/978-3-540-70545-1_47
11. Lowe, G.: An attack on the Needham-Schroeder public-key authentication protocol. Inf. Process. Lett. **56**(3), 131–133 (1995)
12. Needham, R.M., Schroeder, M.D.: Using encryption for authentication in large networks of computers. Commun. ACM **21**(12), 993–999 (1978)
13. Solar-Lezama, A., Tancau, L., Bodik, R., Saraswat, V., Seshia, S.: Combinatorial sketching for finite programs, p. 12 (2006)
14. Song, M., Günther, C.W., van der Aalst, W.M.P.: Trace clustering in process mining. In: Ardagna, D., Mecella, M., Yang, J. (eds.) BPM 2008. LNBIP, vol. 17, pp. 109–120. Springer, Heidelberg (2009). https://doi.org/10.1007/978-3-642-00328-8_11
15. Torlak, E., Chang, F.S.-H., Jackson, D.: Finding minimal unsatisfiable cores of declarative specifications. In: Cuellar, J., Maibaum, T., Sere, K. (eds.) FM 2008. LNCS, vol. 5014, pp. 326–341. Springer, Heidelberg (2008). https://doi.org/10.1007/978-3-540-68237-0_23
16. Zeller, A.: The Debugging Book. CISPA Helmholtz Center for Information Security, 2021. Accessed 12 Mar 2021

Be Lazy and Don't Care: Faster CTL Model Checking for Recursive State Machines

Clemens Dubslaff[1]([✉])[iD], Patrick Wienhöft[1]([✉]), and Ansgar Fehnker[2]

[1] Technische Universität Dresden, Dresden, Germany
{clemens.dubslaff,patrick.wienhoeft}@tu-dresden.de
[2] University of Twente, Enschede, The Netherlands
ansgar.fehnker@utwente.nl

Abstract. *Recursive state machines (RSMs)* are state-based models for procedural programs with wide-ranging applications in program verification and interprocedural analysis. Model-checking algorithms for RSMs and related formalisms and various temporal logic specifications have been intensively studied in the literature.

In this paper, we devise a new model-checking algorithm for RSMs and requirements in *computation tree logic (CTL)* that exploits the compositional structure of RSMs by ternary model checking in combination with a lazy evaluation scheme. Specifically, a procedural component is only analyzed in those cases in which it might influence the satisfaction of the CTL requirement. We evaluate our prototypical implementation on randomized scalability benchmarks and on an interprocedural data-flow analysis of JAVA programs, showing both practical applicability and significant speedups in comparison to state-of-the-art model-checking tools for procedural programs.

1 Introduction

Model checking [4,12] is a well-established technique for verifying that a system model meets a given requirement. System models are most commonly given as *Kripke structures*, i.e., directed graphs over states whose edges model the operational behavior of the system with labels over a set of atomic propositions specifying properties of states. Over these labels, requirements are usually formalized in a temporal logic such as *computation tree logic (CTL,* [11]).

In this paper, we revisit the model-checking problem for *recursive state machines (RSMs)* models and CTL requirements [1]. RSMs provide a standard model for the operational behavior of programs with recursive procedure calls. They closely follow the compositional structure of the procedural program by modeling procedures by separate Kripke structures (called *components*) that are

The authors are supported by the DFG through the Cluster of Excellence EXC 2050/1 (CeTI, project ID 390696704, as part of Germany's Excellence Strategy) and the TRR 248 (see https://perspicuous-computing.science, project ID 389792660).

R. Calinescu and C. S. Păsăreanu (Eds.): SEFM 2021, LNCS 13085, pp. 332–350, 2021.
https://doi.org/10.1007/978-3-030-92124-8_19

connected through *call* and *return* nodes. Due to the infinite-state semantics of RSMs, the standard CTL model-checking algorithm for finite Kripke structures [4,11] is not directly applicable [1]. Fortunately, the satisfaction of a given CTL formula in a component of an RSM solely depends on the satisfaction of subformulas in return nodes of the component, so-called *contexts* [9, 3]. Intuitively, contexts model the environmental influence on the component, i.e., how the satisfaction of the formula depends on the calling component. Exhaustively generating all contexts that could arise during program execution and applying the standard CTL model-checking algorithm for finite Kripke structures on components directly leads to an algorithm to model check RSMs against CTL formulas [1]. This algorithm runs in exponential time in the size of the RSM due to possibly exponentially many contexts that have to be considered for each component. Since the model-checking problem for RSMs and CTL formulas is EXPTIME-complete [5], this algorithm cannot be improved in the worst case. Nevertheless, there is plenty of room for heuristic optimizations that might show runtime improvements in practice.

This paper devises a new method to reduce the number of subformulas and contexts evaluated during the model-checking decision procedure, following a lazy rather than an exhaustive deduction scheme. The main idea behind our *lazy approach* is to use *ternary model checking* and successively refine the global satisfaction relation by step-wise evaluating new contexts that could contribute to deciding the overall model-checking problem [14]. While our lazy approach might also have to consider all subformulas and contexts in the worst case, this is usually not the case in practice, as we show in this paper.

We implemented a ternary variant of the exhaustive approach by Alur et al. [1] and our new lazy approach in a tool called RSMCHECK[1]. To the best of our knowledge, RSMCHECK is the first model checker specifically dedicated to RSMs, while existing state-of-the-art model checkers for procedural programs such as PDSOLVER [15] and PUMOC [20] rely on pushdown systems. RSMs and pushdown systems can be linearly transformed to each other while preserving their Kripke structure semantics (see, e.g., [6]). However, RSMs have the advantage of directly reflecting the compositional structure of a procedural program and providing an intuitive visual representation. To this end, choosing RSMs as model for procedural programs can ease the interpretation of counterexamples and witnesses generated by model checking and hence facilitate debugging during program development steps.

We conduct three experimental studies for RSMCHECK, addressing scalability, comparison to existing model-checking tools, and application to real-world examples in terms of an interprocedural data-flow analysis on JAVA programs. In these studies we show that our lazy approach is effective, evaluates less contexts than in the exhaustive case, and leads to significant speedups up to one order of magnitude compared to the exhaustive approach. Applied on their own benchmark suites, PDSOLVER and PUMOC show timeouts or exceed memory

---

[1] The tool along with data to reproduce our experimental studies can be downloaded at https://github.com/PattuX/RSMCheck.

constraints on several instances [20]. We demonstrate that our lazy approach manages to verify all instances and outperforms PDSOLVER and PuMoC by being up to two orders of magnitude faster.

Outline. After settling notations and basic definitions required to formally state the CTL model-checking problem for RSMs in Sect. 2, we first extend the exhaustive model-checking approach by Alur et al. [1] to the ternary setting in Sect. 3. The lazy approach is detailed in Sect. 4 and evaluated in Sect. 5. We close the paper with further related work and future work in Sect. 6.

2 Preliminaries

For a set X we denote by $\wp(X)$ the power set of X and by X^*, X^+, and X^ω the sets of finite, finite non-empty, and infinite sequences of elements in X, respectively. Given a sequence $\pi = x_1, x_2, \ldots$, we denote by $\pi[i] = x_i$ the ith element of π. A *(ternary) interpretation* over X is a function $\partial \colon X \to \{\mathsf{tt}, \mathsf{ff}, \mathsf{??}\}$ where tt stands for "true", ff for "false", and $\mathsf{??}$ for "unknown". We denote by $\Delta(X)$ the set of all interpretations over X. An interpretation $\partial \in \Delta(X)$ is a *refinement* of $\partial' \in \Delta(X)$ if for all $x \in X$ we have $\partial'(x) = \mathsf{tt}$ implies $\partial(x) = \mathsf{tt}$, and $\partial'(x) = \mathsf{ff}$ implies $\partial(x) = \mathsf{ff}$.

A *Kripke structure* (see, e.g., [4]) is a tuple $\mathcal{K} = (S, \longrightarrow, AP, L)$ where S is a set of states, $\longrightarrow \subseteq S \times S$ is a transition relation, AP is a finite set of atomic propositions, and $L \colon S \to \wp(AP)$ is a labeling function that labels states with atomic propositions. To ease notations, we write $s \longrightarrow s'$ for $(s, s') \in \longrightarrow$. A *path* in $\mathcal{K}$ is a sequence $s_1, s_2, \ldots \in S^\omega$ where for each $i \in \mathbb{N}$ we have $s_i \longrightarrow s_{i+1}$. The set of all paths starting in a state $s \in S$ is denoted by $\Pi(s)$.

2.1 Computation Tree Logic

To reason about Kripke structures we specify system requirements in *computation tree logic* (CTL, [11]). A CTL formula over AP is defined by the grammar

$$\Phi \ = \ \mathsf{tt} \mid a \mid \neg\Phi \mid \Phi \vee \Phi \mid \exists\mathsf{X}\Phi \mid \exists\mathsf{G}\Phi \mid \exists\Phi\,\mathsf{U}\,\Phi$$

where a ranges over AP. Further standard operators, e.g., $\wedge$, F, and $\forall$, can be derived through standard transformations such as DeMorgan's rule [4]. We denote by $Subf(\Phi)$ and $Subf_\exists(\Phi)$ the set of subformulas and existential quantified subformulas of Φ, respectively. Given a Kripke structure $\mathcal{K} = (S, \longrightarrow, AP, L)$ we define the satisfaction relation $\models$ for CTL formulas over AP recursively by

$$
\begin{aligned}
&s \models \mathsf{tt} && s \models \Phi_1 \vee \Phi_2 \text{ iff } s \models \Phi_1 \text{ or } s \models \Phi_2 \\
&s \models a && \text{iff } a \in L(s) \quad s \models \exists\mathsf{X}\Phi \quad \text{iff } \exists\pi \in \Pi(s).\pi[2] \models \Phi \\
&s \models \neg\Phi \text{ iff } s \not\models \Phi && s \models \exists\mathsf{G}\Phi \quad \text{iff } \exists\pi \in \Pi(s).\forall i \in \mathbb{N}.\pi[i] \models \Phi \\
&s \models \exists\Phi_1\,\mathsf{U}\,\Phi_2 \text{ iff } \exists\pi \in \Pi(s), j \in \mathbb{N}.\forall i < j.\pi[i] \models \Phi_1 \wedge \pi[j] \models \Phi_2
\end{aligned}
$$

An interpretation ∂ over $S \times Subf(\Phi)$ is *consistent* with $\mathcal{K}$ if for all $s \in S$ and $\phi \in Subf(\Phi)$ we have $\partial(s, \phi) = \mathsf{tt}$ implies $s \models \phi$ and $\partial(s, \phi) = \mathsf{ff}$ implies $s \not\models \phi$.

2.2   Recursive State Machines

A labeled *recursive state machine* (RSM, [1]) over a set of atomic propositions AP is a tuple $\underline{\mathcal{A}} = (\mathcal{A}_1, \ldots, \mathcal{A}_k)$ comprising *components*

$$\mathcal{A}_i = (N_i, B_i, Y_i, En_i, Ex_i, \longrightarrow_i, I_i, AP, L_i)$$

for $i = 1, \ldots, k$ where

- N_i is a set of nodes for which $N_i \cap N_j = \varnothing$ for all $j = 1, \ldots, k$, $i \neq j$,
- B_i is a set of boxes for which $B_i \cap B_j = \varnothing$ for all $j = 1, \ldots, k$, $i \neq j$,
- $Y_i \colon B_i \to \{1, \ldots, k\}$ is a mapping assigning a component index to every box,
- $En_i, Ex_i \subseteq N_i$ with $En_i \cap Ex_i = \varnothing$, are sets of *entry* and *exit* nodes, respectively,
- $\longrightarrow_i \subseteq (N_i \backslash Ex_i) \cup Return_i \times (N_i \backslash En_i) \cup Call_i$ is a transition relation, and
- $L_i \colon N_i \cup Call_i \cup Return_i \to \wp(AP)$ is a node labeling function for which $L_i((b, n)) = L_{Y(b)}(n)$ for all $(b, n) \in Call_i \cup Return_i$.

Here, $Call_i = \bigcup_{b \in B_i} Call_b$ where $Call_b = \{(b, en) \mid en \in En_{Y(b)}\}$ denotes the set of *call nodes* of a box b and $Return_i = \bigcup_{b \in B_i} Return_b$ where $Return_b = \{(b, ex) \mid ex \in Ex_{Y(b)}\}$ denotes the set of *return nodes* of a box b. We assume that all nodes except exit nodes are not final, i.e., for all $i \in \{1, \ldots, k\}$ and $n \in (N_i \backslash Ex_i) \cup Return_i$ there is $n' \in (N_i \backslash En_i) \cup Call_i$ such that $n \longrightarrow_i n'$. Note that we allow for direct transitions from return to call nodes. By omitting component indices, we denote the union of all corresponding entities in the RSM, e.g., we write N for $\bigcup_{i=1}^{k} N_i$, B for $\bigcup_{i=1}^{k} B_i$, and $\longrightarrow$ for $\bigcup_{i=1}^{k} \longrightarrow_i$. The semantics of a component $\mathcal{A}_i$ is defined as Kripke structure $[\![\mathcal{A}_i]\!] = (N_i \cup Call_i \cup Return_i, \longrightarrow_i, AP, L_i)$. The semantics of $\underline{\mathcal{A}}$ is a Kripke structure

$$[\![\underline{\mathcal{A}}]\!] = (B^* \times (N \cup Call \cup Return), \Longrightarrow, AP, L)$$

where L labels each state as the corresponding node, i.e., $L((\sigma, n)) = L_i(n)$ for all $\sigma \in B^*$ and $n \in N_i \cup Call_i \cup Return_i$, and $\Longrightarrow$ is the smallest transition relation that obeys the following rules:

$$(\text{loc}) \frac{\sigma \in B^* \quad n \longrightarrow n'}{(\sigma, n) \Longrightarrow (\sigma, n')} \qquad (\text{call}) \frac{\sigma b \in B^+ \quad (b, en) \in Call_b \quad en \longrightarrow n}{(\sigma, (b, en)) \Longrightarrow (\sigma b, n)}$$

$$(\text{loop}) \frac{ex \in Ex}{(\varepsilon, ex) \Longrightarrow (\varepsilon, ex)} \qquad (\text{return}) \frac{\sigma b \in B^+ \quad (b, ex) \in Return_b \quad (b, ex) \longrightarrow n}{(\sigma b, ex) \Longrightarrow (\sigma, n)}$$

Intuitively, a state (σ, n) of the Kripke structure $[\![\underline{\mathcal{A}}]\!]$ comprises a *call stack* σ and a local node n of some component of $\underline{\mathcal{A}}$. Rule (loc) represents an internal transition of a component, (loop) implements that the execution stays in the exit nodes when leaving the outermost component, and (call) and (return) formalize entering and leaving a box, respectively. For a CTL formula Φ, we write $\underline{\mathcal{A}} \models \Phi$ if for all $n \in En_1$ we have $(\varepsilon, n) \models \Phi$ in $[\![\underline{\mathcal{A}}]\!]$ [9,10]. The *model-checking problem* we consider here in this paper asks whether $\underline{\mathcal{A}} \models \Phi$ for a given RSM $\underline{\mathcal{A}}$ and CTL formula Φ, both over AP.

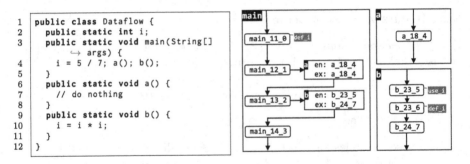

```
1    public class Dataflow {
2        public static int i;
3        public static void main(String[]
                ↪ args) {
4            i = 5 / 7; a(); b();
5        }
6        public static void a() {
7            // do nothing
8        }
9        public static void b() {
10           i = i * i;
11       }
12   }
```

Fig. 1. JAVA Dataflow example from [15] and its generated control-flow RSM.

Example. Figure 1 depicts a JAVA program (left) and an automatically generated RSM model (right). Nodes in the RSM stand for control-flow locations with names encoding references back to the abstract syntax tree of the source code. Furthermore, nodes are labeled with use_i and def_i, which indicate whether the variable i is read or written, respectively. Model checking on RSMs with such use-def annotations can be used for an interprocedural data-flow analysis. For instance, the requirement that whenever the variable i is defined, it is eventually used, can be expressed by the CTL formula $\forall \mathsf{G}(\mathsf{def}_i \to \exists \mathsf{F}(\mathsf{use}_i))$. Our Dataflow example does not meet this requirement: after squaring i in Line 10, the new value of i is not used in later program execution steps. In the RSM of Fig. 1, this is witnessed by the only existing execution that starts in the initial node main_11_0, reaches the def_i-labeled node b_23_6 after calling b(), and finally continues with b_24_7 and main_14_3 that are both not labeled with use_i.

3   Ternary RSM Model Checking

This section provides the foundations for our exhaustive and lazy model-checking algorithms. For this, we closely follow the approach of [1] and adapt their algorithm for model checking single-exit RSMs against CTL* requirements towards a ternary model-checking algorithm of multi-exit RSMs against CTL. Multi-exit RSMs, i.e., RSMs where components might have more than one exit node, are especially relevant for modeling real-world procedural programs. In fact, except the Dataflow example from Fig. 1, all examples we consider in our experimental studies of Sect. 5 require multi-exit RSMs for their analysis. Meanwhile, CTL as a subclass of CTL* is still expressive enough to specify lots of relevant properties, e.g., use-def properties for interprocedural static analysis.

The support of ternary CTL model checking follows the ideas by [7] and replaces the role of refinement operations on satisfaction sets as employed in [1]. To ensure compositional RSM model checking, we discuss two kinds of deductions: first, how ternary interpretations are refined locally on each component, and second, how ternary refinements are globally propagated.

Algorithm 1: CONTEXTUALIZE($\underline{\mathcal{A}}, \Phi, \underline{\partial}, b$)

input : an RSM $\underline{\mathcal{A}} = (\mathcal{A}_1, \ldots, \mathcal{A}_k)$, a CTL formula Φ, a vector $\underline{\partial} = (\partial_1, \ldots, \partial_k)$
of ternary interpretations ∂_j for $\mathcal{A}_j$, and a box $b \in B_i$

output: a modified RSM $\underline{\mathcal{A}}'$ with a Φ-contextualized interpretation $\underline{\partial}'$

1   $\gamma_b := \{(ex, \phi, \eta) \mid \phi \in Subf(\Phi), (b, ex) \in Return_b, \partial_i((b, ex), \phi) = \eta\}$

2   **if** *there is j where $\gamma_b \subseteq \partial_j$* **then**

3 | $\underline{\mathcal{A}}' := \underline{\mathcal{A}}$

4 | $Y_i'(b) := j$

5   **else**

6 | $\mathcal{A}_{k+1} := \mathcal{A}_{Y_i(b)}$

7 | $\underline{\mathcal{A}}' := (\mathcal{A}_1, \ldots, \mathcal{A}_k, \mathcal{A}_{k+1})$

8 | $\partial_{k+1} := \partial_{Y_i(b)}$

9 | **forall** $(s, \phi, \eta) \in \gamma_b$ **do** $\partial_{k+1}(s, \phi) := \gamma_b(s, \phi)$

10 | $\underline{\partial}' := (\partial_1, \ldots, \partial_k, \partial_{k+1})$

11 | $Y_i'(b) := k + 1$

12 **return** $\underline{\mathcal{A}}', \underline{\partial}'$

3.1 Local Deduction

To locally refine ternary interpretations on RSM components, we use a function LOCALDEDUCE($\mathcal{K}, \Phi, \partial$) that maps a finite Kripke structure $\mathcal{K} = (S, \longrightarrow, AP, L)$, a CTL formula Φ over AP, and an interpretation $\partial \colon S \times Subf(\Phi) \to \{\text{tt}, \text{ff}, ??\}$ that is consistent with $\mathcal{K}$ to an interpretation $\partial' \colon S \times Subf(\Phi) \to \{\text{tt}, \text{ff}, ??\}$ refining ∂. In essence, LOCALDEDUCE implements one step of the CTL model-checking algorithm by [7] where interpretations on subformulas are refined in a bottom-up fashion as in classical CTL model checking [11] but on ternary interpretations instead of binary ones. To achieve ternary deduction, an optimistic and a pessimistic run of the classical CTL deduction step is performed on binary interpretations of subformulas. In the optimistic run all subformulas that are "unknown" are assumed to hold, while in the pessimistic run they are assumed to not hold. Then, all subformulas that do not hold after the optimistic run do surely not hold in the ternary setting and likewise, all subformulas that do hold after the pessimistic run surely hold.

3.2 Contextualization of Components

A slight difference of our LOCALDEDUCE method compared to a single deduction step by [7] is that we explicitly give an arbitrary consistent partial interpretation ∂ as input parameter, while the algorithm by [7] assumes a maximally refined consistent partial interpretation over all subformulas. To this end, we can include assumptions on the satisfaction of subformulas in the deduction process such as knowledge on the environment the system is executed in. In the setting of RSMs, the environment of a component is constituted by their calling components. Specifically, following the notion of *contexts* [3,9], the environmental influence on a component can be fully captured by a given satisfaction relation on existential

---

Algorithm 2: GLOBALDEDUCE($\underline{\mathcal{A}}, \Phi, \underline{\partial}$)

> **input** : an RSM $\underline{\mathcal{A}} = (\mathcal{A}_1, \ldots, \mathcal{A}_k)$, a CTL formula Φ, and a vector
> $\underline{\partial} = (\partial_1, \ldots, \partial_k)$ of ternary interpretations ∂_j for $\mathcal{A}_j$
> **output:** refined interpretations $\underline{\partial}'$ of $\underline{\partial}$

1 $\underline{\partial}' := \underline{\partial}$
2 **repeat**
3      $\underline{\hat{\partial}} := \underline{\partial}'$
4   **forall** $i \in \{1, \ldots, k\}$ **do**
5   **forall** $(b, en) \in Call_i$ **do**
6           $\partial_i'((b, en), \Phi) := \partial'_{Y_i(b)}(en, \Phi)$
7         $\partial_i' := $ LOCALDEDUCE($[\![\mathcal{A}_i]\!], \Phi, \partial_i'$)
8 **until** $\underline{\hat{\partial}} = \underline{\partial}'$
9 **return** $\underline{\partial}'$

---

formulas in exit nodes of the components.[2] For an RSM $\underline{\mathcal{A}}$ and a CTL formula Φ both over a set of atomic propositions AP as formalized in Sect. 2, a Φ-*context* of a component $\mathcal{A}_i$ in $\underline{\mathcal{A}}$ is formalized as an interpretation $\gamma_i \in \Delta(Ex_i \times Subf_\exists(\Phi))$ over the component's exit nodes and existential subformulas of Φ.

To reason about components in a modular way, we have to keep track of the contexts and deduction results under these contexts for their reuse. This is achieved by the function CONTEXTUALIZE, described in Algorithm 1, which maps $\underline{\mathcal{A}}$, a tuple $\underline{\partial} = (\partial_1, \ldots, \partial_k)$ of local interpretations for components $\mathcal{A}_1, \ldots, \mathcal{A}_k$ of $\underline{\mathcal{A}}$, and a target box $b \in B_i$ to a possibly modified RSM $\underline{\mathcal{A}}'$ with a Φ-contextualized interpretation $\underline{\partial}'$. Our algorithm for CONTEXTUALIZE checks whether we already considered the component assigned to b w.r.t. the context induced from b's return nodes. If this is the case, we (re)assign b to the found contextualized component. Otherwise a copy[3] $\mathcal{A}_{k+1}$ of the component $\mathcal{A}_{Y_i(b)}$ with the new context is generated (i.e., the number of components of the RSM increases from k to $k + 1$) and the box b is reassigned to the fresh component $\mathcal{A}_{k+1}$ by updating function Y_i (see Sect. 2.2).

3.3 Global Deduction

To propagate information from inside a component to a calling component, we use a function GLOBALDEDUCE, described in Algorithm 2, that maps an RSM $\underline{\mathcal{A}}$, a target CTL formula Φ, and a tuple $\underline{\partial} = (\partial_1, \ldots, \partial_k)$ of local interpretations to refined interpretations $\underline{\partial}' = (\partial_1', \ldots, \partial_k')$. Our algorithm for GLOBALDEDUCE starts with $\underline{\partial}' = \underline{\partial}$ and performs the following two steps until a fixed point is reached for the local interpretations, i.e., $\underline{\partial}'$ does not change anymore: First, a

---

[2] Since the standard CTL model-checking deduction follows a backward-search approach, the contextual information contained in the exit nodes of the component propagates towards the entry nodes of the component during a local deduction step.

[3] This is done due to better understandability of the approach. For practical implementations, one might only copy and modify interpretations on the components.

Algorithm 3: EXHAUSTIVECHECK($\underline{\mathcal{B}}, \Phi$)

---

input : an RSM $\underline{\mathcal{B}} = (\mathcal{B}_1, \ldots, \mathcal{B}_\ell)$ and a CTL formula Φ, both over AP
output: tt if $\underline{\mathcal{B}} \models \Phi$ and ff if $\underline{\mathcal{B}} \not\models \Phi$

1 $\underline{\mathcal{A}}, \underline{\partial} := $ INITIALIZE($\underline{\mathcal{B}}, \Phi$)
2 $F := \varnothing$
3 **while** $F \neq Subf(\Phi)$ **do**
4   Pick $\phi \in Subf(\Phi)$ with $Subf(\phi) \setminus F = \{\phi\}$
5     $F := F \cup \{\phi\}$
6   **repeat**
7   **forall** $b \in B$ **do** $\underline{\mathcal{A}}, \underline{\partial} := $ CONTEXTUALIZE($\underline{\mathcal{A}}, \phi, \underline{\partial}, b$)
8         $\underline{\partial} := $ GLOBALDEDUCE($\underline{\mathcal{A}}, \phi, \underline{\partial}$)
9   **until** $\underline{\partial}$ *did not change*
10   **forall** $i \in \{1, \ldots, k\}$, $n \in N_i$ with $\partial_i(n, \phi) = $?? **do**
11   **if** $\phi = \exists G\psi$ **then** $\partial_i(n, \phi) := $ tt
12   **if** $\phi = \exists \psi_1 \cup \psi_2$ **then** $\partial_i(n, \phi) := $ ff
13 **if** *there is* $en \in En_1$ *with* $\partial_1(en, \Phi) = $ ff **then return** ff
14 **else return** tt

---

local deduction step LOCALDEDUCE($\mathcal{A}_i, \Phi, \partial_i$) is performed for each component $\mathcal{A}_i$ and their current interpretations ∂_i. Second, we copy the refined interpretations on the entry nodes of each component $\mathcal{A}_i$ to their corresponding call nodes in the calling component. This refinement in the call nodes may cause new possible local deductions in the calling components, leading to further refinements in their entry nodes. As such, we alternate between these two steps until we reach a fixed point.

3.4   Exhaustive Approach to RSM Model Checking

Piecing together the algorithms sketched so far, we define a compositional algorithm for model checking RSMs against CTL formulas. That is, the algorithm runs locally on the components of the RSM and propagates their satisfaction relations towards a global satisfaction relation. The procedure follows ideas from [1] where satisfaction of CTL subformulas is evaluated in a bottom-up fashion, determining the truth value of minimal subformulas in all nodes before proceeding to larger subformulas. During the evaluation, contextualized components are created whenever there is not enough information present to fully determine the truth values for subformulas in all nodes of calling components. Algorithm 3 shows the decision procedure EXHAUSTIVECHECK($\underline{\mathcal{A}}, \Phi$) that decides for an RSM $\underline{\mathcal{A}}$ and a CTL formula Φ whether $\underline{\mathcal{A}} \models \Phi$ or not. The algorithm starts with an initialization of the local ternary interpretations of the components of $\underline{\mathcal{A}}$ (function INITIALIZE, see in Line 1). Specifically, INITIALIZE sets all local interpretations to evaluate to ?? and then performs a local deduction for $\mathcal{A}_1$ to determine basic truth assignments in the exit nodes of $\mathcal{A}_1$ following rule (loop) in the definition of RSM semantics. After initialization, EXHAUSTIVECHECK iterates over all subformulas of Φ in a bottom-up fashion as within classical CTL model checking. For each formula we alternate between contextualizing components assigned to boxes by CONTEXTUALIZE and a global deduction by GLOBALDEDUCE, refining local interpretations of components and determining new contexts towards a propagation from calling components to called ones. This is done until we reach a fixed point, i.e., local interpretations are not refined any further by GLOBALDEDUCE.

Global Dependency Cycle Resolution.
The reached fixed point does not solely ensure that all truth values for the considered subformula are determined in all nodes, i.e., some local interpretations may still map to ??. This can happen when the context of a box depends on the evaluation of the boxes' entry nodes. To illustrate this situation, let us consider an example RSM $\underline{\mathcal{A}} = (\mathcal{A}_1, \mathcal{A}_2)$ over $AP = \{\circ, \ominus, \bullet\}$ depicted in Fig. 2: The truth value of $\Phi = \exists X \exists G \circ$ in n_1 depends on the truth value of $\phi = \exists G \circ$ in the return node (b, n_7), providing the context of $\mathcal{A}_2$ in its exit node n_7. However, we cannot deduce

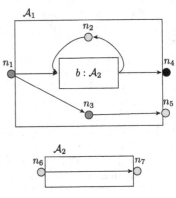

Fig. 2. Example RSM

this truth value locally in $\mathcal{A}_1$ as it depends on whether ϕ holds in the call node (b, n_6) or not. Intuitively, we thus have a cycle of dependencies connected through several components that hinders further refinement via CONTEXTUALIZE and GLOBALDEDUCE. We resolve such situations by the following reasoning: Since there is a dependency cycle that hindered refinement, all nodes on this cycle have to satisfy $\circ$. Thus, this cycle can serve as a witness of ϕ to hold and we refine all local interpretations for ϕ and nodes on the cycle towards tt. A similar argumentation can be applied when ϕ is an until formula but with refining all ??-nodes towards ff. For instance, $\ominus$ is not reachable from (b, n_6), such that $\phi = \exists \circ U \bullet$ cannot hold on the dependency cycle illustrated above. Note that our efficient resolution of global dependency cycles relies on ternary deduction, since cycles of ??-nodes directly provide information about undeducibility of truth values. While our algorithm is based on [1], their algorithm uses binary refinements and thus cannot exploit such a resolution. However, their algorithm also includes mechanisms to reason about satisfaction of formulas expressed in linear temporal logic (LTL), which is used to cover the cycle resolution step.

Exhaustive RSM Model Checking. Taking global dependency cycle resolution into account and with proof techniques from [7, 1], we obtain correctness of our exhaustive model-checking algorithm EXHAUSTIVECHECK:

Theorem 1. EXHAUSTIVECHECK($\underline{\mathcal{A}}, \Phi$) *terminates for any RSM $\underline{\mathcal{A}}$ and CTL formula Φ over a common set of atomic propositions and returns* tt *iff* $\underline{\mathcal{A}} \models \Phi$.

Proof sketch. We show termination and soundness of each of the subroutines INITIALIZE, LOCALDEDUCE, GLOBALDEDUCE and CONTEXTUALIZE, and then lift the results to the full algorithm for EXHAUSTIVECHECK. First, observe that

INITIALIZE can be seen of a special case of a CONTEXTUALIZE where the context is given by the rule (loop) in the definition of $[\![A]\!]$.

The termination of LOCALDEDUCE directly follows from [7]. Termination of CONTEXTUALIZE is straight forward (see Algorithm 1). For GLOBALDEDUCE the important observation is that it strictly refines an interpretation until a fixed point is reached, which is done in finitely many steps as the set of nodes N and subformulas $Subf(\Phi)$ are finite. Since the number of contextualizations of each box is bounded by $3^{|Ex| \cdot |Subf_\exists(\Phi)|}$, the calls of CONTEXTUALIZE in Line 7 can only add finitely many contextualized components to $\mathcal{A}$. Further, GLOBALDEDUCE is idempotent and ∂ does not change if $\mathcal{A}$ did not change. Thus, each iteration of the main loop from Line 3 to Line 12 is guaranteed to terminate. Lastly, it is clear that the main loop is executed exactly once for each $\phi \in Subf(\Phi)$ and thus the algorithm terminates.

For soundness, we show that at each execution point of the algorithm the computed partial interpretation ∂ is sound, i.e.,

$$\partial(s, \phi) = \mathsf{tt} \implies \forall \sigma \in B^* : (\sigma, s) \models \phi$$

and

$$\partial(s, \phi) = \mathsf{ff} \implies \forall \sigma \in B^* : (\sigma, s) \not\models \phi.$$

Soundness of LOCALDEDUCE follows immediately from [7]. For GLOBALDEDUCE and CONTEXTUALIZE the statement follows from using the definition of the underlying Kripke structure $[\![\mathcal{A}]\!]$ of $\mathcal{A}$ and the soundness of LOCALDEDUCE. The main effort in the proof is to show that the assertions following Line 10 are correct. The arguments here follow the same ideas as outlined in the last section about global dependency cycle resolution.   □

4   Lazy RSM Model Checking

The model-checking algorithm presented in Sect. 3 mainly combined existing techniques for model-checking RSMs and CTL formulas [11, 9, 7, 3]. In this section, we devise a new algorithm that uses elements of the former but aims towards reducing the number of deduction steps involved. This is achieved by exploiting the structure of the target CTL formula and the compositional structure of the RSM towards lazy evaluation of subformulas and components, respectively.

4.1   Lazy Contextualization

Exhaustive RSM model checking determines satisfaction of subformulas $\phi \in Subf(\Phi)$ in all nodes of the RSM $\mathcal{A}$ by evaluating the satisfaction relation within components w.r.t. all possible contexts. The possibly exponentially many contexts that have to be considered with this approach is the main reason for CTL model checking over RSMs to be EXPTIME-complete [5]. Reducing the number of contexts considered during the deduction process thus provides a potential to speed up the model checking of RSMs.

Ternary Formula Evaluation. The main idea towards reducing the number of contexts to be evaluated is to leave satisfaction of subformulas ϕ of Φ unspecified in case they do not have any influence on the satisfaction of Φ. For instance, let us consider the RSM of Fig. 2 and $\Phi = \exists X \bullet \vee \exists X (\exists \circ \, U \, \bullet)$. Then, satisfaction of Φ can be determined by solely regarding $\phi = \exists X \bullet$ in n_1 and not reasoning about either disjunct in other nodes, which would be necessarily done in the bottom-up approach. Further, evaluating ϕ in n_1 does not require any contextualization of box b since n_3 is labeled by $\bullet$ and thus, in component $\mathcal{A}_1$ we can already locally deduce ϕ to hold in n_1 and thus $n_1 \models \Phi$, directly leading to $\underline{\mathcal{A}} \models \Phi$. In this example, we reduced the number of contexts to be evaluated as we did not evaluate any context for component $\mathcal{A}_2$.

Lazy Expansion. To determine those contexts that have to be evaluated to solve the model-checking problem, we combine the ternary formula evaluation with a heuristic that determines those contexts that might be the reason for underspecified satisfaction of subformulas and impact satisfaction of Φ in the RSM. We provide such a heuristic by the function GETNEXTEXPANSION, specified by Algorithm 4. Depending on a node n where it is unknown whether the target formula Φ holds or not, this function selects a box for which a contextualization step in combination with a global deduction (see Sect. 3.3) could determine the truth value of Φ in n. GETNEXTEXPANSION is defined in a recursive manner, traversing Φ in a top-down fashion to reason on *why* Φ is unknown in n and to find a box b where adding a subformula to its context might refine the interpretation of Φ in n. By lazily contextualizing heuristically selected boxes rather than contextualizing all boxes as in the case of the exhaustive approach, we can potentially save contextualization steps.

Algorithm 4 considers several cases during recursion, from which we exemplify the most significant ones. First, those properties that could be locally resolved are considered. For instance, Line 2 deals with Φ being a disjunction where it is known that at least one disjunct must be unknown since otherwise Φ would be determined in n. Then, a disjunct ϕ_i is chosen nondeterministically and GETNEXTEXPANSION is recursively called, determining which contextualization could resolve whether ϕ_i holds in n. The cases of entering and leaving a box b are considered in Line 5 and Line 6, respectively. Notably, if n is an exit node, we consider the satisfaction of Φ in the calling component, i.e., in its return node. If Φ is already known, we found a box where contextualizing yields additional information and thus return that box as our base case in Line 8. Otherwise, we continue our search. For existential path properties, let us exemplify the case where $\Phi = \exists \phi \, U \, \psi$ (see Line 10). Here, we determine the next recursive call arguments following the well-known CTL expansion law $\Phi = \psi \vee (\phi \wedge \exists X(\phi \, U \, \psi))$. First, we consider the local cases where ψ or ϕ are unknown in n, asking for a box to contextualize by invoking GETNEXTEXPANSION on ψ and ϕ, respectively. Otherwise, the reason for Φ being unknown in n cannot be locally given and we continue in a successor node of n where Φ is still unknown.

Algorithm 4: GETNEXTEXPANSION($\underline{\mathcal{A}}, n, \Phi, \underline{\partial}, \sigma$)

---

input : RSM $\underline{\mathcal{A}} = (\mathcal{A}_1, \ldots, \mathcal{A}_k)$, node $n \in N_i$, formula Φ, a vector
$\underline{\partial} = (\partial_1, \ldots, \partial_k)$ of interpretations ∂_j for $\mathcal{A}_j$, and a call stack $\sigma \in B^+$
output: a box b to contextualize

1   // ... other local case $\Phi = \neg\phi$ ...
2   **if** $\Phi = \phi_1 \vee \ldots \vee \phi_\ell$ **then**
3   choose $j \in \{1, \ldots, \ell\}$ with $\partial_i(n, \phi_j) = $??
4   **return** GETNEXTEXPANSION($\underline{\mathcal{A}}, n, \phi_j, \underline{\partial}, \sigma$)
5   **if** $n = (b, en) \in Call_i$ **then return** GETNEXTEXPANSION($\underline{\mathcal{A}}, en, \Phi, \underline{\partial}, \sigma b$)
6   **if** $n \in Ex_i$ and there are $\rho \in B^*$ and $b \in B$ with $\rho b = \sigma$ **then**
7   **if** $\partial_{Y_i(b)}((b, n), \Phi) = $?? **then return**
      GETNEXTEXPANSION($\underline{\mathcal{A}}, (b, n), \Phi, \underline{\partial}, \rho$)
8   **return** b // base case
9   // ... other existential cases $\Phi = \exists G\phi$ and $\Phi = \exists X\phi$ ...
10 **if** $\Phi = \exists \phi \cup \psi$ **then**
11   **if** $\partial_i(n, \psi) = $?? **then return** GETNEXTEXPANSION($\underline{\mathcal{A}}, n, \psi, \underline{\partial}, \sigma$)
12   **if** $\partial_i(n, \phi) = $?? **then return** GETNEXTEXPANSION($\underline{\mathcal{A}}, n, \phi, \underline{\partial}, \sigma$)
13   choose n' with $n \longrightarrow_i n'$ and $\partial_i(n', \Phi) = $??
14   **return** GETNEXTEXPANSION($\underline{\mathcal{A}}, n', \Phi, \underline{\partial}, \sigma$)

Global Dependency Cycle Resolution. Similar as in the case of exhaustive RSM model checking (see Sect. 3.4), global dependency cycles are an issue also within GETNEXTEXPANSION. When implementing GETNEXTEXPANSION exactly as described in Algorithm 4, the algorithm is not ensured to terminate: If an exit node's context depends on itself, we recursively call GETNEXTEXPANSION infinitely often, not reaching the base case in Line 8. An example where this happens is in the RSM Fig. 2 when checking against the formula $\Phi = \forall X \exists \bigcirc \cup \bullet$ where GETNEXTEXPANSION would be called with (b, n_6) and $\phi = \exists \bigcirc \cup \bullet$. In the following steps, GETNEXTEXPANSION would be invoked with ϕ on n_6, n_7, (b, n_7), n_2, and finally (b, n_6) again. To resolve such cycles, we first keep track of the node-formula pairs for which GETNEXTEXPANSION has been already invoked. If a cycle is detected by trying to invoke GETNEXTEXPANSION with the same parameters, we backtrack until we can make a different choice in a disjunction- or exists-case, possibly leading to a box to be contextualized. This backtracking procedure is only successful if there is such a box not involved in any dependency cycle. For instance, in the example above such a box does not exist. However, in such a case, similar reasoning as done for global dependency cycle resolution in Sect. 3.4 can be applied to refine interpretations in nodes of a global dependency cycle.

4.2 Lazy Approach to RSM Model Checking

The idea of lazy contextualization of boxes in an RSM can be incorporated into the exhaustive RSM model-checking approach EXHAUSTIVECHECK presented in Algorithm 3. This leads to a method LAZYCHECK presented in Algorithm 5.

Algorithm 5: LAZYCHECK($\underline{\mathcal{B}}, \Phi$)

---

input : RSM $\underline{\mathcal{B}} = (\mathcal{B}_1, \ldots, \mathcal{B}_k)$ and CTL formula Φ, both over AP
output: tt if $\underline{\mathcal{A}} \models \Phi$ and ff if $\underline{\mathcal{A}} \not\models \Phi$

1 $\underline{\mathcal{A}}, \underline{\partial} :=$ INITIALIZE($\underline{\mathcal{B}}, \Phi$)
2 $F := \varnothing$
3 **while** $F \neq Subf(\Phi)$ **do**
4 $\quad$ Pick $\phi \in Subf(\Phi)$ with $Subf(\phi) \setminus F = \{\phi\}$
5 $\quad$ $F := F \cup \{\phi\}$
6 $\quad$ $\underline{\partial} :=$ GLOBALDEDUCE($\underline{\mathcal{A}}, \phi, \underline{\partial}$)
7 **if** *there is en $\in En_1$ with $\partial_1(en, \Phi) =$ ff* **then return** ff
8 **while** *there is en $\in En_1$ with $\partial_1(en, \Phi) =$??* **do**
9 $\quad$ $b =$ GETNEXTEXPANSION($\underline{\mathcal{A}}, en, \Phi, \underline{\partial}, \varepsilon$)
10 $\quad$ CONTEXTUALIZE($\underline{\mathcal{A}}, \Phi, \underline{\partial}, b$)
11 $\quad$ **while** $F \neq Subf(\Phi)$ **do**
12 $\quad\quad$ Pick $\phi \in Subf(\Phi)$ with $Subf(\phi) \setminus F = \{\phi\}$
13 $\quad\quad$ $\underline{\partial} :=$ GLOBALDEDUCE($\underline{\mathcal{A}}, \phi, \underline{\partial}$)
14 $\quad$ **if** *there is en $\in En_1$ with $\partial_1(en, \Phi) =$ ff* **then return** ff
15 **return** tt

While EXHAUSTIVECHECK surely contextualizes all boxes with contexts encountered during global deduction GLOBALDEDUCE, Algorithm 5 uses GETNEXTEXPANSION to contextualize only those boxes that might contribute to deciding whether the target formula Φ holds in the outermost component of the RSM. In essence, Algorithm 5 follows the same reasoning principles as EXHAUSTIVECHECK given in Algorithm 3 by employing functions INITIALIZE, GLOBALDEDUCE, and CONTEXTUALIZE. The main difference is that due to the lazy evaluation of subformulas, the satisfaction of subformulas is not a priori known before invoking a global deduction GLOBALDEDUCE (see Line 13). However, due to our ternary reasoning implemented in LOCALDEDUCE and the progress in contextualizing boxes through GETNEXTEXPANSION in combination with the global dependency cycle resolution described in Sect. 4.1, we obtain correctness and soundness of our new model-checking algorithm for RSMs.

Theorem 2. LAZYCHECK($\underline{\mathcal{A}}, \Phi$) *terminates for any RSM $\underline{\mathcal{A}}$ and CTL formula Φ over a common set of atomic propositions and returns* tt *iff* $\underline{\mathcal{A}} \models \Phi$.

Proof sketch. The termination and soundness arguments are analogous to the arguments in the proof of Theorem 1 but require an additional step to prove that GETNEXTEXPANSION terminates and is sound. This is achieved by careful analysis of the implementation of the cycle resolution described in the last section about global dependency cycle resolution. Termination of the full algorithm LAZYCHECK then follows from the strict refinements also within adding new contexts, for which there are only finitely many. Soundness follows by the soundness of all subroutines as LAZYCHECK does not directly modify $\underline{\partial}$. $\qquad\square$

Note that in the worst case, all boxes have to be contextualized to determine whether the RSM $\mathcal{A}$ satisfies a CTL formula Φ. In this case, our algorithm is also an exhaustive algorithm with a slight polynomial-time overhead of the reasoning steps involved in GETNEXTEXPANSION. However, the termination condition might be satisfied after fewer contextualizations as we have seen in our example of Fig. 2, resulting in strictly less computation steps than EXHAUSTIVECHECK and illustrating the potential of our lazy model-checking approach.

5   Implementation and Evaluation

We implemented both the exhaustive and the lazy approach presented in this paper in a prototypical tool RSMCHECK. Written in PYTHON3, it is supported by almost all common operating systems. RSMs are specified by a dedicated JSON format, to which our tool also provides a translation from pushdown systems for model checkers PDSOLVER [15] or PuMoC [20] that follows the standard translation method (see, e.g., [6]).

Research Questions. To demonstrate applicability of our tool and investigate properties of the algorithms presented in this paper, we conducted several experimental studies driven by the following research questions:

(RQ1) Is our lazy approach effective, i.e., generates significantly less contexts and is faster compared to the exhaustive approach?

(RQ2) How do analysis times of our approaches implemented in RSMCHECK compare to state-of-the-art procedural model checkers?

(RQ3) Can real-world procedural programs be verified with our approaches?

Experimental Setup. All our experiments were carried out using PYPY 7.3.3 on an Intel i9-10900K machine running Ubuntu 21.04, with a timeout threshold of 30 min and a memory limit of 4 GB of RAM.

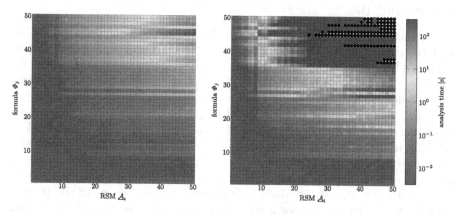

Fig. 3. Analysis times for the scalability experiment in seconds (logarithmic scale, lazy on the left, exhaustive on the right, • marks stand for memouts)

5.1 Scalability Experiment

First, we conducted a scalability experiment to compare the exhaustive and lazy approach. We randomly generated 2500 RSM/CTL-formula pairs $(\underline{\mathcal{A}}_i, \Phi_j)$ of increasing sizes and formula lengths: For $i, j \in \{1, \dots, 50\}$ the RSM $\underline{\mathcal{A}}_i$ contains i components, each having $\lfloor i/3 \rfloor$ boxes and $3i$ nodes with connectivity of 20%, while the formula Φ_j has a quantifier depth of $\lfloor j/9 \rfloor$. Figure 3 shows the analysis times in seconds for our lazy (left) and exhaustive (right) approach. We observe that the more compositional structure and the bigger the requirement formulas, the more the lazy approach pays off compared to the exhaustive approach, both in memory consumption and analysis speed. In 5% of the cases, the exhaustive approach ran into memouts and in all other cases the lazy approach is on average eight times faster than the exhaustive one. For (RQ1) we conclude that lazy contextualization is an effective method that allows for faster RSM model checking.

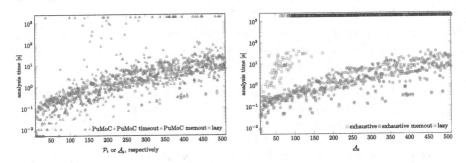

Fig. 4. Analysis times for 500 PuMoC examples in seconds (logarithmic scale)

5.2 PuMoC Benchmark Set

Our second experimental study compares RSMCHECK to the procedural CTL model checker PuMoC on its benchmark set [20]. The benchmark set of PuMoC comprises 500 randomly generated pushdown systems $\mathcal{P}_i$ and CTL formulas Φ_i, numbered as in [20] with $i \in \{10, \dots, 509\}$. Here, the sizes of the pushdown systems increase with increasing i. To enable RSM model checking, we translated each $\mathcal{P}_i$ to an RSM $\underline{\mathcal{A}}_i$ in the input format of RSMCHECK. The resulting RSMs have only one component and thus, our lazy approach is expected to not fully use its potential. However, while PuMoC runs into time- or memouts in 28 examples, the lazy approach successfully completes each experiment in less than 40 s. Most of the analysis times are in the same range (see Fig. 4 on the left) even though PuMoC is implemented in C, while RSMCHECK is implemented in PYTHON, known for broad applicability but comparably weak performance. Regarding (RQ2), we can conclude that RSMCHECK is competitive with the state-of-the-art model checker PuMoC even on single-component

RSMs. Figure 4 on the right shows a comparison of the lazy approach to the exhaustive one, applied on the 500 PuMoC examples. The exhaustive approach is always slower than the lazy approach and runs into memouts in 69% of the cases. This also supports our positive answer to (RQ1) drawn in the last section.

5.3   Interprocedural Static Analysis for JAVA Programs

Our last experimental study considers an interprocedural analysis for real-world systems, borrowed from the benchmark set of [15]. These benchmarks comprise pushdown systems modeling the control-flow of JAVA programs with use-def annotations for all variables of the program, allowing for a data-flow analysis of the program. We first used our implementation to translate programs and the annotated requirement from the input formalism of PDSOLVER to the input formalisms of PuMoC and RSMCHECK. The requirement formalizes that whenever the selected variable is defined, it is eventually used (see the Dataflow example in the preliminaries). Table 1 shows characteristics of our analysis. First, the lazy and even the exhaustive approach are significantly faster than PDSOLVER and PuMoC. Thus, contributing to (RQ2) and (RQ3), RSMCHECK can be faster than state-of-the-art procedural model checkers also on real-world models. This can be explained by the compositional structure of RSMs and their generation of contexts: Even the exhaustive approach generates only those contexts that arise during deduction steps in exit nodes. These studies also support that our lazy approach is effective (cf. (RQ1)): Column k of Table 1 indicates the number of components of the RSM for the JAVA program, while #ctx indicates the number of generated contexts during analysis. We can observe that the lazy approach effectively avoids context generation, having a direct impact on the analyzed state spaces and timings. Further, we observe speedups of up to two orders of magnitude compared to the exhaustive approach.

Table 1. Analysis statistics for JAVA interprocedural analysis (time in seconds)

JAVA program	Result	PDSOLVER time	PuMoC time	k	Exhaustive		Lazy	
					#ctx	time	#ctx	time
Dataflow (Fig. 1)	ff	<0.01	0.02	3	6	<0.01	1	<0.01
avroraCFG	tt	>1 800	>1 800	3 169	4 372	133.41	2	7.46
avroraDisassemble	tt	806.66	>1 800	2 085	4 628	233.18	1	3.19
avroraELF	tt	26.68	71.28	248	614	4.79	1	0.29
avroraMedTest	tt	12.48	37.09	238	264	1.28	4	0.43
avroraReg	tt	8.73	16.12	173	477	1.69	2	0.32
dom2pdf	tt	80.46	1 345.56	615	2 002	17.88	1	0.76
fop2pdf	tt	61.68	>1 800	607	2 029	27.65	6	1.19

6   Conclusion and Discussion

We presented a novel technique to model check RSMs against CTL requirements, combining ternary reasoning with lazy contextualization of components. While of heuristic nature, our experimental studies showed significant speedups compared to existing methods in both scalability benchmarks and in an interprocedural data-flow analysis on real-world systems. Our tool RSMCHECK is, to the best of our knowledge, the first tool that implements the RSM model-checking approach by Alur et al. [1] for verifying CTL formulas.

Counterexamples and Witnesses. One major advantage of model-checking approaches is the generation of counterexamples or witnesses for refuting or fulfilling the analyzed requirement, respectively. Also in RSMCHECK we implemented a witness-generation method that traverses the nodes of the RSM according to computed interpretations similarly as GETNEXTEXPANSION does to find a path responsible for requirement satisfaction. The main difference to the standard witness-generation methods in Kripke structures is that not only nodes are tracked but also call stacks and contexts. Counterexamples for universally quantified requirements are obtained by our witness-generation method applied on the complement existential requirement.

Expansion Heuristics. Central in our lazy approach is the nondeterministic algorithm GETNEXTEXPANSION, which determines the next context to be considered. This algorithm leaves some freedom in how the nondeterminism is resolved, for which plenty of heuristics are reasonable. We implemented two methods, a random selection of subformulas and a deterministic selection that chooses the left-most unknown subformula for further recursive calls, e.g., in the disjunctive case in Line 2 of Algorithm 4. The latter is set as default to enable developers to control the verification process by including domain knowledge, e.g., by placing most influential subformulas upfront to further exploit lazy context evaluation. In our experimental studies, choosing either heuristic did not significantly change runtimes, which is explainable since the CTL requirements were either randomly generated or a comparably simple use-def formula.

Related Work. The most commonly used state-based formalisms for procedural programs are pushdown systems (PDSs) and RSMs, for which there are linear-time transformations that lead to bisimilar Kripke structure semantics [2]. While PDSs take a more theoretical perspective, essentially encoding pushdown automata, RSMs directly reflect the programs procedural structure. Model checkers for procedural programs have been first-and-foremost implemented for PDSs, ranging from PUMOC [20] for CTL requirements and PDSOLVER [15] for requirements specified in the CTL-subsuming μ-calculus, to the LTL model checker MOPED [19] also integrated into PUMOC. The latter relies on a symbolic engine that uses *binary decision diagrams (BDDs)* [8], shown to be beneficial for LTL model checking on large-scale procedural programs [19]. On-demand or lazy approaches for interprocedural analysis have been considered, e.g., to determine evaluation points for a priori narrowed scopes [16], or to analyze the interplay between classes and objects in JAVASCRIPT programs [17]. Contrary, our approach focuses on lazy verification on state-based models.

Further Work. In next development steps, we plan to also include the support for CTL* requirements, using well-known automata-theoretic constructions for LTL model checking (see, e.g., [1,4]). Further, we plan to extend RSMCHECK with a BDD-based model-checking engine to investigate the impact of our lazy algorithms also in the symbolic setting. Remind that our experiments showed that explicit lazy model checking is already efficient on large real-world systems where state-of-the-art (symbolic) procedural model checkers were not able to complete the verification process. Many extensions for PDSs have been presented in the literature, which could also serve as bases for extending our work on lazy RSM model checking. For instance, *weighted RSMs* (see, e.g., [18]) equip RSMs with labels from a semi-ring, similarly as *probabilistic RSMs* equip transitions with probabilities (see, e.g., [6,13]).

References

1. Alur, R., Benedikt, M., Etessami, K., Godefroid, P., Reps, T., Yannakakis, M.: Analysis of recursive state machines. ACM Trans. Program. Lang. Syst. **27**(4), 786–818 (2005)
2. Alur, R., Bouajjani, A., Esparza, J.: Model checking procedural programs. In: Handbook of Model Checking, pp. 541–572. Springer, Cham (2018). https://doi.org/10.1007/978-3-319-10575-8_17
3. Alur, R., Yannakakis, M.: Model checking of hierarchical state machines. ACM Trans. Program. Lang. Syst. **23**(3), 273–303 (2001)
4. Baier, C., Katoen, J.P.: Principles of Model Checking. The MIT Press, Cambridge (2008)
5. Bouajjani, A., Esparza, J., Maler, O.: Reachability analysis of pushdown automata: application to model-checking. In: Mazurkiewicz, A., Winkowski, J. (eds.) CONCUR 1997. LNCS, vol. 1243, pp. 135–150. Springer, Heidelberg (1997). https://doi.org/10.1007/3-540-63141-0_10
6. Brázdil, T.: Verification of Probabilistic Recursive Sequential Programs. Ph.D. thesis, Masaryk University Brno (2007)
7. Bruns, G., Godefroid, P.: Model checking partial state spaces with 3-valued temporal logics. In: Halbwachs, N., Peled, D. (eds.) CAV 1999. LNCS, vol. 1633, pp. 274–287. Springer, Heidelberg (1999). https://doi.org/10.1007/3-540-48683-6_25
8. Bryant, R.E.: Graph-Based Algorithms for Boolean Function Manipulation. IEEE Trans. Comput. **35**, 677–691 (1986). https://doi.org/10.1109/TC.1986.1676819
9. Burkart, O., Steffen, B.: Model checking for context-free processes. In: Cleaveland, W.R. (ed.) CONCUR 1992. LNCS, vol. 630, pp. 123–137. Springer, Heidelberg (1992). https://doi.org/10.1007/BFb0084787
10. Burkart, O., Steffen, B.: Model checking the full modal mu-calculus for infinite sequential processes. Theor. Comput. Sci. **221**(1–2), 251–270 (1999)
11. Clarke, E.M., Emerson, E.A.: Design and synthesis of synchronization skeletons using branching time temporal logic. In: Kozen, D. (ed.) Logic of Programs 1981. LNCS, vol. 131, pp. 52–71. Springer, Heidelberg (1982). https://doi.org/10.1007/BFb0025774

12. Clarke, E.M., Grumberg, O., Peled, D.A.: Model Checking. The MIT Press, Cambridge (2000)
13. Etessami, K., Yannakakis, M.: Recursive Markov chains, stochastic grammars, and monotone systems of nonlinear equations. J. ACM **56**(1), 1–66 (2009)
14. Fehnker, A., Dubslaff, C.: Inter-procedural analysis of computer programs. US Patent 8,296,735 (2012)
15. Hague, M., Ong, C.H.: A saturation method for the modal μ-calculus over pushdown systems. Inf. Comput. **209**(5), 799–821 (2011)
16. Horwitz, S., Reps, T., Sagiv, M.: Demand interprocedural dataflow analysis. In: Proceedings of SIGSOFT 1995, pp. 104–115. ACM (1995)
17. Jensen, S.H., Møller, A., Thiemann, P.: Interprocedural analysis with lazy propagation. In: Cousot, R., Martel, M. (eds.) SAS 2010. LNCS, vol. 6337, pp. 320–339. Springer, Heidelberg (2010). https://doi.org/10.1007/978-3-642-15769-1_20
18. Reps, T.W., Schwoon, S., Jha, S., Melski, D.: Weighted pushdown systems and their application to interprocedural dataflow analysis. Sci. Comput. Program. **58**(1–2), 206–263 (2005)
19. Schwoon, S.: Model checking pushdown systems. Ph.D. thesis, Technical University Munich, Germany (2002)
20. Song, F., Touili, T.: PuMoC: a CTL model-checker for sequential programs. In: Proceedings of ASE 2012, pp. 346–349. ACM (2012)

Fairness, Assumptions, and Guarantees for Extended Bounded Response LTL+P Synthesis

Alessandro Cimatti[1], Luca Geatti[1,2(✉)], Nicola Gigante[3], Angelo Montanari[2], and Stefano Tonetta[1]

[1] Fondazione Bruno Kessler, Trento, Italy
{cimatti,lgeatti,tonettas}@fbk.eu
[2] University of Udine, Udine, Italy
{luca.geatti,angelo.montanari}@uniud.it
[3] Free University of Bozen-Bolzano, Bolzano, Italy
nicola.gigante@unibz.it

Abstract. Realizability and reactive synthesis from temporal logics are fundamental problems in the formal verification field. The complexity of the Linear-time Temporal Logic with Past (LTL+P) case led to the definition of fragments with lower complexities and simpler algorithms. Recently, the logic of Extended Bounded Response LTL+P (LTL$_{EBR}$+P) has been introduced. It allows one to express any safety language definable in LTL and it is provided with an efficient, fully-symbolic algorithm for reactive synthesis.

In this paper, we extend LTL$_{EBR}$+P with fairness conditions, assumptions, and guarantees. The resulting logic, called GR-EBR, preserves the main strength of LTL$_{EBR}$+P, that is, efficient realizability, and makes it possible to specify properties beyond safety. We study the problem of reactive synthesis for GR-EBR and devise a fully-symbolic algorithm that reduces it to a number of safety subproblems. To ensure soundness and completeness, we propose a general framework for safety reductions in the context of realizability of (fragments of) LTL+P. The experimental evaluation shows the feasibility of the approach.

1 Introduction

One of the most important problems in formal methods and requirement analysis is establishing whether a specification over a set of controllable and uncontrollable actions is *implementable* (or *realizable*), that is, whether there exists a controller that chooses the value of the controllable actions and satisfies the

N. Gigante acknowledges the Free University of Bozen-Bolzano, Faculty of Computer Science RTD project TOTA (*Temporal Ontologies and Tableaux Algorithms*). The work was partially supported by the Italian GNCS project *CATHARSIS* (L. Geatti, N. Gigante and A. Montanari).

R. Calinescu and C. S. Păsăreanu (Eds.): SEFM 2021, LNCS 13085, pp. 351–371, 2021.
https://doi.org/10.1007/978-3-030-92124-8_20

specification, no matter what the values of uncontrollable actions are. This problem has been formalized in the literature under the name of *realizability* [3]. The very close problem of *reactive synthesis* aims at synthesizing such a controller, whenever the specification is realizable. Usually, these problems are modelled as two-player games between Environment, who tries to violate the specification, and Controller, who tries to fulfill it. Realizability is known to have a very high worst-case complexity. In particular, it has a non-elementary lower bound for S1S specifications [2], and it is 2EXPTIME-complete for LTL specifications [22,23].

In order to apply realizability and reactive synthesis in real-world scenarios, research has focused on the identification of fragments of logics like S1S and LTL, with a limited expressive power, for which realizability can be solved efficiently.

A well-known example is *Generalized Reactivity(1)* logic (GR(1), for short) [1]. In this fragment, a specification is syntactically partitioned into *assumptions* about the environment and *guarantees* for the controller. Both of them are either Boolean formulas (α) or safety formulas ($G\alpha$) or conjunctions of recurrence formulas ($\bigwedge_{i=1}^{n} GF\alpha_i$). The dichotomy between *assumptions* and *guarantees* reflects the way a system engineer usually formalizes system's requirements, which is summarized by the following sentence: *"the controller has to behave in conformance to the guarantees, under the given assumptions on the environment".*

On a different direction, other approaches focused on safety fragments of LTL [4,25]. In particular, *Extended Bounded Response LTL* (LTL$_{EBR}$+P, for short) is a safety fragment of LTL+P that allows for a fully symbolic compilation of formulas into deterministic automata. Such a feature contributes to a great improvement in solving time for the synthesis problem. Moreover, LTL$_{EBR}$+P has a well-established expressiveness: LTL$_{EBR}$+P can define exactly the set of safety languages definable in LTL.

Contributions. The main contributions of this paper are the following ones. First, we introduce GR-EBR, an extension of LTL$_{EBR}$+P that admits: (i) fairness conditions, in particular, conjunctions of *recurrence formulas*, that is, $\bigwedge_i GF\alpha_i$, forcing each formula α_i to be true infinitely often; (ii) assumptions/guarantees in the form of an LTL$_{EBR}$+P formula augmented with fairness conditions. In addition to be able to express any LTL$_{EBR}$+P formula, and, consequently, any safety property definable in LTL, GR-EBR allows also for the definition of properties beyond the safety fragment, like, for instance, $G(p) \rightarrow G(q)$.

Second, we devise a novel framework for deriving *complete* safety reductions in the context of realizability of (fragments of) LTL. A notable feature of the framework is that it provides a link to safety reductions for the model checking problem and proves that if a reduction is complete for model checking, then it is also complete for realizability. On one hand, this allows one to reason on Kripke structures instead of on strategies, which is simpler; on the other hand, it enables the use of some reductions already exploited in model checking for realizability, provided that they conform to the framework.

Third, the proposed framework is used to derive a *complete* safety reduction for the realizability problem of GR-EBR. A crucial property of the algorithm is that the realizability check of each safety sub-problem is performed in a *fully symbolic* way, thus retaining the distinctive feature of $LTL_{EBR}+P$.

Last but not least, we provide an implementation of the algorithm as a prototype tool called GRACE (*GR-ebr reAlizability ChEcker*). The experimental evaluation shows good performance against tools for full LTL+P synthesis.

Related Work. GR(1) has been introduced in [1,21]. It is known that GR(1) is a good candidate for writing specifications of real-world scenarios, with a relatively low complexity: the realizability problem can be solved with at most a quadratic number of symbolic steps in the size of the specification [1]. On the other hand, GR(1) presents some restrictions that limit its use as a specification language: (i) safety assumptions/guarantees are either Boolean formulas or formulas of the form $G\alpha$, where the only temporal operator admitted in α is the *next* operator X; (ii) assumptions are syntactically constrained to be formulas *controlled* by Environment, in the sense that the variables inside the *next* operators of the safety part of the assumptions must be *uncontrollable*. In GR-EBR we relax that syntactical restrictions of GR(1): for example, the safety assumptions and guarantees can be any arbitrary $LTL_{EBR}+P$ formula, like, for instance, $G(r \rightarrow F^{[0,10]}g)$. For this reason, GR-EBR can be considered an extension not only of $LTL_{EBR}+P$, but also of GR(1). On the semantic side, the comparison is more problematic. On the one hand, all (standard) realizability problems for GR(1) specifications are definable in LTL+P [1] and also in GR-EBR. On the other hand, we do not known whether GR-EBR is able to express more properties than GR(1). Our conjecture is that this is the case. Take for instance the bounded-response property $G(r \rightarrow F^{[0,k]}g)$: it is easily expressible in GR-EBR, but we see no way it could be definable in GR(1) without introducing additional variables (that would maintain realizability but not language equivalence).

Bounded synthesis [9,13] belongs to the class of *Safraless techniques* [17], and it consists in bounding the number of times Controller is forced to visit a rejecting state of a Universal co-Büchi automaton (UCW, for short) for the initial formula. This corresponds to a safety automaton, which can be either (i) made deterministic by a suitable generalization of the classical subset construction [7,11], or (ii) encoded into a constraint system [9,13] (*e.g.,* SAT- or SMT-based) which bounds also the *size* of a candidate controller (this also allows one to tackle undecidable problems, for instance in the case of distributed or parametric synthesis). Both choices work for the whole class of UCW, and thus for full LTL. A significant drawback of such an approach is that the UCW, which can be exponentially larger than the initial specification, is explicitly represented. Moreover, in the first case, the algorithm for the determinization turns out to be quite complex, since each state of the resulting automaton is actually a *function*. This can also result into a very large state space, that can be tackled by exploiting either *antichains* [11] or BDDs [7]. In contrast, as we will see, we define a reduction tailored to GR-EBR formulas that allows us to exploit the $LTL_{EBR}+P$ transformations introduced in [4] for a *fully symbolic* mapping of the initial formula directly into a sequence of symbolic safety automata. In particular, we never build any explicit-state automaton and we avoid the subsequent use of determinization algorithms.

Organization. The rest of the paper is organized as follows. In Sect. 2, we introduce the notation and provide the basic definitions. In Sect. 3, we define the logic GR-EBR and give an example of GR-EBR specification. The framework for deriving complete reductions is presented in Sect. 4. In Sect. 5 we describe the algorithm for the realizability of GR-EBR specifications. The outcomes of the experimental evaluation are reported in Sect. 6. Finally, in Sect. 7, we point out some interesting future research directions.

2 Preliminaries

2.1 Temporal Logics

Linear Temporal Logic with Past (LTL+P) is a modal logic interpreted over infinite state sequences. Let Σ be a set of propositions. LTL+P formulas are inductively defined as follows:

$$\phi := p \mid \neg\phi \mid \phi_1 \vee \phi_2 \mid \mathsf{X}\phi \mid \phi_1 \; \mathsf{U} \; \phi_2 \mid \mathsf{Y}\phi \mid \phi_1 \; \mathsf{S} \; \phi_2$$

where $p \in \Sigma$. Temporal operators can be subdivided into the *future operators*, *next* (X) and *until* (U), and *past operators*, *yesterday* (Y) and *since* (S). We define the following common abbreviations (where $\top$ stands for any tautology such as $p \vee \neg p$): (i) *release*: $\phi_1 \; \mathsf{R} \; \phi_2 \equiv \neg(\neg\phi_1 \; \mathsf{U} \; \neg\phi_2)$; (ii) *eventually*: $\mathsf{F}\phi_1 \equiv \top \; \mathsf{U} \; \phi_1$; (iii) *globally*: $\mathsf{G}\phi_1 \equiv \neg\mathsf{F}\neg\phi_1$; (iv) *once*: $\mathsf{O}\phi_1 \equiv \top \; \mathsf{S} \; \phi_1$; (v) *historically*: $\mathsf{H}\phi_1 \equiv \neg\mathsf{O}\neg\phi_1$. LTL+P formulas are interpreted over infinite state sequences (or ω-words) $\pi \in (2^\Sigma)^\omega$. We call *language* a set of ω-words. We write $\pi \models \phi$ to denote the fact that the state sequence π is a *model* (or *satisfies*) the formula ϕ. We refer to [4] for the semantics of the LTL+P operators. With $|\phi|$, we refer to the *size* of the formula ϕ, defined as the number of symbols in it. We define the *language* of ϕ, written $\mathcal{L}(\phi)$, as the set of all and only the models of ϕ.

An important class of languages is the class of safety properties, that express the fact that "something bad never happens". Formally, we define a *safety property* (or *safety language*) as a language for which it holds that, for any ω-word that does not belong to language, there exists a finite prefix of it such that all its continuations do not belong to the language as well. A formula ϕ is called a *safety formula* if $\mathcal{L}(\phi)$ is a safety language. Recently, Cimatti *et al.* [4] introduced a subset of LTL+P, called *Extended Bounded Response* LTL+P, which expresses exactly the safety properties that can be defined in LTL+P [5], and gave a symbolic procedure to turn formulas of this fragment into symbolic automata.

Definition 1 (The logic LTL$_{\text{EBR}}$+P[4]). *Let* $a, b \in \mathbb{N}$. *An* LTL$_{\text{EBR}}$+P *formula* χ *is inductively defined as follows:*

$$\eta := p \mid \neg\eta \mid \eta_1 \vee \eta_2 \mid \mathsf{Y}\eta \mid \eta_1 \mathsf{S} \eta_2 \qquad\qquad \textit{Pure Past Layer}$$

$$\psi := \eta \mid \neg\psi \mid \psi_1 \vee \psi_2 \mid \mathsf{X}\psi \mid \psi_1 \mathsf{U}^{[a,b]}\psi_2 \qquad \textit{Bounded Future Layer}$$

$$\phi := \psi \mid \phi_1 \wedge \phi_2 \mid \mathsf{X}\phi \mid \mathsf{G}\phi \mid \psi \mathsf{R} \phi \qquad\qquad \textit{Future Layer}$$

$$\chi := \phi \mid \chi_1 \vee \chi_2 \mid \chi_1 \wedge \chi_2 \qquad\qquad\qquad \textit{Boolean Layer}$$

We define the *bounded until* operator $\psi_1 \mathsf{U}^{[a,b]}\psi_2$ as a *shortcut* of the formula $\bigvee_{i=a}^{b}(\mathsf{X}^i\psi_2 \wedge \bigwedge_{j=0}^{i-1}\mathsf{X}^j\psi_1)$, where $\mathsf{X}^i\phi := \mathsf{X}_{(1)}\ldots\mathsf{X}_{(i)}\phi$. We define LTL$_\mathsf{P}$ (the *pure past fragment of LTL+P*) as the set of all the formulas belonging to the *Pure Past Layer* of Definition 1, respectively. With some abuse of notation, we will denote with the symbol of the logic (*e.g.,* LTL+P or LTL$_{\text{EBR}}$+P) also the *set* of all the formulas of the respective logic.

2.2 Automata

Temporal logic has a strong relation with automata on infinite words [24]. Since in the following we will work only with symbolic representations, we give here the definition of symbolic automata. It is well-known that the symbolic representation can be exponentially more succinct than the explicit-state one.

Definition 2 (Symbolic Automaton on Infinite Words). *A symbolic automaton on infinite words over the alphabet* Σ *is a tuple* $\mathcal{A} = (V, I, T, \alpha)$, *such that (i)* $V = X \cup \Sigma$, *where* X *is a set of* state variables *and* Σ *is a set of* input variables, *(ii)* $I(X)$ *and* $T(X, \Sigma, X')$, *with* $X' = \{x' \mid x \in X\}$, *are Boolean formulas which define the set of initial states and the transition relation, respectively, and (iii)* $\alpha(X)$ *is an LTL+P formula over the variables in* X *which defines the accepting condition.*

Definition 3 (Languages of Symbolic Automata). *An* ω-*word (or simply a word)* $\sigma = \langle\sigma_0, \sigma_1, \ldots\rangle$ *is an infinite sequence of letters in* Σ. *A run* $\tau = \langle\tau_0, \tau_1, \ldots\rangle$ *is an infinite sequence of* states *(i.e.,evaluations of the variables in* X*) that are in relation with respect to* T *(i.e.,such that any two consecutive evaluations satisfy the formula* T*). A run* τ *is induced by the word* σ *iff* $\tau_0 \models I$ *and* $(\tau_i, \sigma_i, \tau_{i+1}) \models T$, *for all* $i \geq 0$. *We say that* $\mathcal{A}$ *is* deterministic *iff there exists exactly one trace induced by* σ, *for each* $\sigma \in \Sigma^\omega$. *A word* σ *is accepted by* $\mathcal{A}$ *iff there exists an accepting run induced by* σ *in* $\mathcal{A}$. *The language of* $\mathcal{A}$, *denoted with* $\mathcal{L}(\mathcal{A})$, *is the set of all and only the words accepted by* $\mathcal{A}$.

We will refer to three important classes of accepting conditions: (i) *safety*: $\alpha(X) := \mathsf{G}\beta$; (ii) *Reactivity(1)*: $\alpha(X) := \mathsf{GF}\beta \rightarrow \mathsf{GF}\beta'$; (iii) *Generalized Reactivity(1)*: $\alpha(X) := \bigwedge_{i=1}^{m} \mathsf{GF}\beta_i \rightarrow \bigwedge_{j=1}^{n} \mathsf{GF}\beta_j'$; where each $\beta, \beta', \beta_i, \beta_j' \in$ LTL$_\mathsf{P}$.

2.3   Model Checking, Realizability, and Synthesis

A Kripke structure is a tuple $M = (\Sigma, Q, I, T, L)$ where: (i) Σ is the input alphabet, (ii) Q is the (finite) set of states, (iii) $I \subseteq Q$ is the set of initial states, (iv) $T \subseteq Q \times Q$ is a *complete* transition relation, and (v) $L : Q \to 2^\Sigma$ is the labeling function that assigns to each state the set of atoms in Σ that are true in that state. We denote with $|M|$ the number of states in M, i.e., $|Q|$. Given a path $\pi := \langle q_0, q_1, \dots \rangle$ in M, we denote with $L(\pi)$ the sequence $\langle L(q_0), L(q_1), \dots \rangle$. The path π is called *initialized* iff $q_0 \in I$. The model checking problem takes as input a Kripke structure and a temporal formula, and asks to find whether all the initialized traces of the former satisfy the latter.

Definition 4 (The model checking problem). *Given a Kripke structure M and a linear temporal formula ϕ, the model checking problem is the problem of finding whether all the initialized traces π of M are such that $L(\pi) \models \phi$, written $M \models \mathsf{A}\phi$ (where A is the "for all paths" operator of CTL).*

Realizability and reactive synthesis are in some sense more ambitious problems than model checking, since they aim to find whether a given temporal formula ϕ over two sets $\mathcal{U}$ and $\mathcal{C}$ of uncontrollable and controllable variables, respectively, is implementable and, if this is the case, to synthesize a possible *implementation*. Usually, realizability is modeled as a two-player game between Environment, who tries to violate the specification and Controller, who tries to fulfill it. In this setting, an implementation of the specification is represented by a *strategy*.

Definition 5 (Strategies and Languages of Strategies). *Let $\mathcal{U}$ and $\mathcal{C}$ be two disjoint sets of* input *(or uncontrollable) and* output *(or controllable) variables, respectively. A strategy g is a function $g : (2^\mathcal{U})^+ \to 2^\mathcal{C}$. We define the* language *of the strategy g, denoted as $\mathcal{L}(g)$, as the set of all and only the sequences $\langle (\mathsf{U}_0 \cup \mathsf{C}_0), (\mathsf{U}_1 \cup \mathsf{C}_1), \dots \rangle$ such that $\mathsf{U}_i \in 2^\mathcal{U}$ and $\mathsf{C}_i = g(\langle \mathsf{U}_0, \dots, \mathsf{U}_i \rangle)$, for all $i \geq 0$.*

Definition 6 (Realizability and Synthesis for LTL). *Let ϕ be a temporal formula over the alphabet $\Sigma = \mathcal{U} \cup \mathcal{C}$, where $\mathcal{U}$ is the set of input variables, $\mathcal{C}$ the set of output variables, and $\mathcal{U} \cap \mathcal{C} = \varnothing$. We say that ϕ is realizable if and only if there exists a strategy $g : (2^\mathcal{U})^+ \to 2^\mathcal{C}$ such that $\mathcal{L}(g) \subseteq \mathcal{L}(\phi)$. If ϕ is realizable, the synthesis problem is the problem of computing such a strategy.*

The strategies which we are mainly interested in are the ones that can be represented finitely. In the literature, there are two main (and equivalent) representations for finite strategies, that is, *Mealy machines* and *Moore machines*. In this paper, we are mainly interested in the first ones.

Definition 7 (Mealy Machine). *A Mealy machine is a tuple $M = (\Sigma_\mathcal{U}, \Sigma_\mathcal{C}, Q, q_0, \delta)$ such that: (i) $\Sigma_\mathcal{U}$ and $\Sigma_\mathcal{C}$ are the input and output alphabets, respectively; (ii) Q is the (finite) set of states and q_0 is the initial state; (iii) $\delta : Q \times \Sigma_\mathcal{U} \to \Sigma_\mathcal{C} \times Q$ is the total transition function. We say that an infinite* *word* $\sigma = \langle \sigma_0, \sigma_1, \dots \rangle \in (\Sigma_{\mathcal{U}} \cup \Sigma_{\mathcal{C}})^\omega$ *is accepted by* M *iff there exists a* trace $\langle (q_0, \sigma_0), (q_1, \sigma_1), \dots \rangle (Q \times (\Sigma_{\mathcal{U}} \cup \Sigma_{\mathcal{C}}))^\omega$ *such that* $\delta(q_i, \sigma_i \cap \Sigma_{\mathcal{U}}) = (\sigma_i \cap \Sigma_{\mathcal{C}}, q^{i+1})$, *for all* $i \geq 0$. *We define the language of* M, *written as* $\mathcal{L}(M)$, *as the set of all the infinite words accepted by* M.

A fundamental feature is the *small model property* for realizability of LTL+P [11,17,22], which ensures that each realizable LTL+P formula has at least a finitely representable strategy.

Proposition 1 (Small model property of LTL+P [22]). *Let* ϕ *be an LTL+P formula and* $n = |\phi|$. *If* ϕ *is realizable by a strategy* g, *then there exists a Mealy machine* M_g *such that (i)* M_g *has at most* $2^{2^{c \cdot n}}$ *states, for some constant* $c \in \mathbb{N}$, *and (ii)* $\mathcal{L}(M_g) \subseteq \mathcal{L}(\phi)$.

3   LTL_EBR+P with Fairness, Assumptions, and Guarantees

In this section, we extend LTL_EBR+P (see Definition 1) with fairness conditions (i.e., of type $GF\alpha$), assumptions and guarantees (that correspond to the antecedent and the consequent of a logical implication). The syntax of the resulting logic, called GR-EBR, is the following.

Definition 8 (The logic GR-EBR). *The GR-EBR logic comprises all and only those formulas that can be written in the following form:*

$$(\psi_{ebr}^1 \wedge \bigwedge_{i=1}^{m} GF\alpha_i) \rightarrow (\psi_{ebr}^2 \wedge \bigwedge_{j=1}^{n} GF\beta_j)$$

where $m, n \in \mathbb{N}$, $\psi_{ebr}^1, \psi_{ebr}^2 \in$ LTL_EBR+P *and* $\alpha_i, \beta_j \in$ LTL_p, *for each* $i, j \in \mathbb{N}$.

3.1   Expressiveness of GR-EBR

Each LTL_EBR+P formula ϕ is a GR-EBR formula as well. In fact, $\phi \equiv (\top \wedge \top) \rightarrow (\phi \wedge \top) \in$ GR-EBR. It follows that any safety language definable in LTL+P is definable in GR-EBR as well. In addition, GR-EBR is *strictly* more expressive than LTL_EBR+P, since the former can express also non-safety properties, like $G(p) \rightarrow G(q)$.

Consider the temporal hierarchy defined by Manna and Pnueli in [19]. The Reactivity class is defined as the set of all and only those languages definable by formulas of type $\bigwedge_i (GF\alpha_i \rightarrow GF\beta_i)$ where each α_i and each β_i are pure-past LTL+P formulas. It is known that LTL+P is expressively equivalent to the Reactivity class. Moreover, if we fix the number of conjuncts of the formula above to be N, that the resulting class (called Reactivity(N)) strictly contains Reactivity(N-1) and is strictly contained in Reactivity(N+1). Compared to this classification, we have that GR-EBR is at least as expressive as the Reactivity(1) class, since each formula of type $GF(\alpha) \rightarrow GF(\beta)$ belongs to GR-EBR. However, the exact expressiveness of GR-EBR is still unknown.

On a more practical side, we found that some benchmarks of SYNTCOMP [15], like *simple_arbiter_N* (for each $N \in \{2, 4, 6, 8, 10, 12\}$) and also *escalator_bidirectional*, can be translated in GR-EBR with minor rewritings.

3.2 An Example

We take the example proposed in [4] and we extend it with fairness, assumptions and guarantees. Suppose that we want to synthesize an arbiter that, given a request from client i (for some $i \in \{1, \dots, n\}$) in the environment, assigns the grant to the corresponding client, in such a way to guarantee the following properties: (1) *bounded response*: the grant is assigned at most k time units, for some $k > n$, after the request is issued; (2) *mutual exclusion*: the arbiter can assign a grant at most to one client at a time. The conjunction of the previous two requirements form the guarantees for the controller. The assumptions for the environment are the following: (1) initially, there are no requests; (2) if a request is issued at time i, then it cannot be issued until time $i + k$; (3) there are infinitely many requests from each client.

In order to write a specification of the arbiter, we can model the requests for the n clients with the (uncontrollable) variables $r_1, \dots, r_n$. Similarly, the grant corresponding to the request r_i can be modeled with the (controllable) variable g_i, for each $i \in \{1, \dots, n\}$. The assumption for the environment corresponds to the LTL$_{\mathsf{EBR}}$+P formula ϕ_e defined as follows:

$$\bigwedge_{i=1}^{n} \neg r_i \;\wedge\; \bigwedge_{i=1}^{n} \mathsf{G}(r_i \to \mathsf{G}^{[1,k]} \neg r_i) \;\wedge\; \bigwedge_{i=1}^{n} \mathsf{GF} r_i$$

The guarantees for the controller correspond to the LTL$_{\mathsf{EBR}}$+P formula ϕ_c defined as follows:

$$\bigwedge_{i=1}^{n} \mathsf{G}(r_i \to F^{[0,k]} g_i) \;\wedge\; \mathsf{G}(\bigwedge_{1 \leq i < j \leq n} \neg(g_i \wedge g_j))$$

The overall specification is $\phi_e \to \phi_c$ and syntactically belongs to GR-EBR.

Our goal is to solve the realizability problem for GR-EBR specifications by reducing it to realizability subproblems for safety specifications. The reduction to safety, which we will give in Sect. 5, generates a safety formula for each integer k, in such a way to guarantee the following important properties: (i) *soundness*, ensuring that the realizability of the kth subproblem implies the realizability of the starting formula, and (ii) *completeness*, establishing the existence of an upper bound μ such that the unrealizability of all the kth subproblems with $k \leq \mu$ implies the unrealizability of the starting formula. In the next section we will give a general framework for (sound and) complete reductions. From it, in Sect. 5, we will derive one for GR-EBR specifications, showing also how the realizability of each safety subproblems can be solved symbolically.

4 A Framework of Safety Reductions for LTL+P Realizability

The central question of this section is: *how can we obtain a complete safety reduction for the realizability problem of specifications written in (fragments of) LTL?* In the following, we propose a framework to answer it.

The core and the main novelty of our framework is a link with safety reductions for model checking: in order to design a complete reduction for the realizability problem, one can prove that it is complete for the model checking problem and then use our framework to derive completeness for realizability. On one hand, this allows to prove completeness at the level of model checking, which is simpler than proving completeness for realizability. On the other hand, this opens the possibility of using existing safety reductions already devised for model checking for realizability as well. We start by defining what is a safety reduction in the context of our framework.

Definition 9 (Safety reduction). *Let $S \subseteq$ LTL be a fragment of LTL. A safety reduction for S is a function $[\![\cdot]\!]$ such that, for each formula $\phi \in S$ over the alphabet Σ, it holds that $[\![\phi]\!] = \{\phi_k\}_{k \in \mathbb{N}}$, where ϕ_k is a safety formula over the alphabet Σ such that $\phi_k \to \phi$, for any $k \in \mathbb{N}$. With $[\![\phi]\!]^k$, we will denote the formula ϕ_k of the set above.*

Link Between Realizability and Model Checking. The rationale behind the link between realizability and model checking is the following one: since we can easily view Mealy machines as (a particular type of) Kripke structures and viceversa, and since by Proposition 1 we can restrict realizability to the search of finite strategies representable by Mealy machines, the realizability problem of the LTL+P formula ϕ can be reduced to checking if there exists a Mealy machine M_g such that $M_g' \models A\phi$, where M_g' is the Kripke structure *corresponding to* M_g.

The Kripke structure M_g' *corresponding to* the Mealy machine $M_g = (2^{\mathcal{U}}, 2^{\mathcal{C}}, Q, q_0, \delta)$ is defined as $M_g' = (2^{\mathcal{U} \cup \mathcal{C}}, Q', I', T', L')$ where:

1. $Q' = Q \times \{q_U \mid U \in 2^{\mathcal{U}}\} \times \{q_C \mid C \in 2^{\mathcal{C}}\}$;
2. $I' = \{(q_0, q_U, q_C) \in Q' \mid \delta(q_0, U) = (C, q')$ for any $U \in 2^{\mathcal{U}}, C \in 2^{\mathcal{C}}$ and $q' \in Q\}$,
3. $T' = \{((q, q_U, q_C), (q', q_{U'}, q_{C'})) \mid \delta(q, U) = (C, q')$ for any $U, U' \in 2^{\mathcal{U}}, C, C' \in 2^{\mathcal{C}}$, and $q, q' \in Q'\}$ and
4. $L'((q, q_U, q_C)) = U \cup C$.

The Kripke structure M_g' is such that each trace of M_g' corresponds to a word of M_g, and viceversa.

In proving the completeness theorem, we will abstract from the concrete safety reduction and give the conditions for a general safety reduction $[\![\cdot]\!]$ (as defined in Definition 9) to be complete. These conditions are formalized in Definition 10.

Definition 10 (Sound and Complete safety reduction). *Let $S \subseteq$ LTL be a fragment of LTL, ϕ a formula in S, and $[\![\cdot]\!]$ a safety reduction for S. We say that $[\![\cdot]\!]$ is μ-complete, for a given function $\mu : \mathbb{N} \to \mathbb{N}$ if and only if, for all $\phi \in S$ and for all Kripke structures M:*

$$M \models A\phi \quad \Leftrightarrow \quad \exists k \leq \mu(|M|) . M \models A[\![\phi]\!]^k$$

We can finally state the main theorem of our framework, which uses Definition 10 and Proposition 1 in order to establish that if a safety reduction is complete for the model checking problem, then it is complete for the realizability problem as well.

Theorem 1 (Soundness and Completeness for LTL+P Realizability).
Let $S \subseteq$ LTL be a fragment of LTL, $\phi \in S$ a formula over the input alphabet $\mathcal{U}$ and output alphabet $\mathcal{C}$ (with $n = |\phi|$) and $[\![\cdot]\!]$ a μ-complete safety reduction for S, for a given function μ. It holds that:

$$\phi \text{ is realizable} \quad \Leftrightarrow \quad \exists k \leq \mu(2^{|\mathcal{U}|} \cdot 2^{|\mathcal{C}|} \cdot 2^{2^{c \cdot n}}).[\![\phi]\!]^k \text{ is realizable}$$

Proof. We first prove the *soundness*, which corresponds to the right-to-left direction. Suppose there exist a $k \leq \mu(2^{|\mathcal{U}|} \cdot 2^{|\mathcal{C}|} \cdot 2^{2^{c \cdot n}})$ such that $[\![\phi]\!]^k$ is realizable. Then, there exists a strategy $g : (2^{\mathcal{U}})^+ \to 2^{\mathcal{C}}$ such that $\mathcal{L}(g) \subseteq \mathcal{L}([\![\phi]\!]^k)$. By Proposition 1, there exists a Mealy machine $M_g = (2^{\mathcal{U}}, 2^{\mathcal{C}}, Q, q_0, \delta)$ with input alphabet $2^{\mathcal{U}}$ and output alphabet $2^{\mathcal{C}}$ such that $\mathcal{L}(M_g) \subseteq \mathcal{L}([\![\phi]\!]^k)$. Starting from M_g, let $M_g' = (2^{\mathcal{U} \cup \mathcal{C}}, Q', I', T', L')$ be the *corresponding* Kripke structure. The Kripke structure M_g' is such that each trace of M_g' corresponds to a word of M_g, and viceversa. Therefore all the traces π of M_g' are such that $L'(\pi) \models [\![\phi]\!]^k$, that is $M_g' \models \mathsf{A}[\![\phi]\!]^k$. Since by hypothesis $[\![\cdot]\!]$ is a μ-complete safety reduction, by Definition 10, it holds that $M_g' \models \mathsf{A}\phi$. This means that also $\mathcal{L}(M_g) \subseteq \mathcal{L}(\phi)$. Since M_g is a Mealy machine, this implies that ϕ is realizable.

We now prove *completeness*, which corresponds to the left-to-right direction. Suppose that ϕ is realizable. Since $\phi \in S$ and since $S \subseteq$ LTL, ϕ is an LTL formula as well. Therefore, by Proposition 1, there exists a Mealy machine M_g with input alphabet $2^{\mathcal{U}}$ and output alphabet $2^{\mathcal{C}}$ such that $\mathcal{L}(M_g) \subseteq \mathcal{L}(\phi)$ with at most $2^{2^{c \cdot n}}$ states, for some constant $c \in \mathbb{N}$. From M_g, we build an equivalent Kripke structure M_g' with input alphabet $\Sigma' = 2^{\mathcal{U} \cup \mathcal{C}}$, as described above for the soundness proof. It holds that $M_g' \models \mathsf{A}\phi$. Since by hypothesis $[\![\cdot]\!]$ is a μ-complete safety reduction for S, and since $|Q'| = 2^{|\mathcal{U}|} \cdot 2^{|\mathcal{C}|} \cdot |Q|$ (where Q and Q' are the set of states of M_g and M_g', respectively), by Definition 10, there exists a $k \leq \mu(2^{|\mathcal{U}|} \cdot 2^{|\mathcal{C}|} \cdot 2^{2^{c \cdot n}})$ such that $M_g' \models \mathsf{A}[\![\phi]\!]^k$. This means that also $\mathcal{L}(M_g) \subseteq \mathcal{L}([\![\phi]\!]^k)$. Since M_g is a Mealy machine, this means that there exists a $k \leq \mu(2^{|\mathcal{U}|} \cdot 2^{|\mathcal{C}|} \cdot 2^{2^{c \cdot n}})$ such that $[\![\phi]\!]^k$ is realizable. $\square$

Novelty and Usage. As already mentioned before, a distinguished and important feature of our framework is that it provides a link with safety reductions for the *model checking problem*. This opens the possibility to use model checking safety reductions for the realizability problem as well, provided that the reduction fulfills the requirements in Definition 10. In the next sections, we will define a *concrete* safety reduction for GR-EBR specifications that is *complete* with respect to Definition 10, and we will use it for introducing a novel algorithm for GR-EBR realizability. Using Theorem 1, we will derive a corollary for the completeness of our algorithm.

In Practice. The upper bound for the value of $\mu(\cdot)$ (after which we can answer *unrealizable*) is doubly exponential in the size of the initial formula and therefore, in practice, it is prohibitively large. It follows that usually the *completeness* of a safety reduction can be exploited in practice only for making sure that, starting from a *realizable* specification, we will eventually find a $k \in \mathbb{N}$ such that the kth subproblem is realizable. Therefore, like K-Liveness for model checking [6], we can use our algorithm in parallel with another one that checks for the unrealizability of the specification. The first that terminates stops the other and, thus, the entire procedure. We remark that we cannot check the unrealizability of ϕ by solving the dualized game (i.e.,looking for a Moore-type strategy of Environment) for $\neg\phi$, because GR-EBR and LTL$_{\text{EBR}}$+P are *not* closed under complementation.

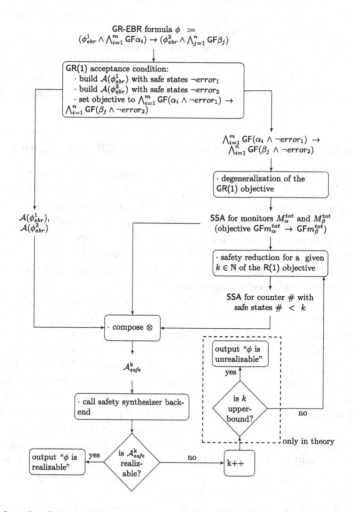

Fig. 1. Low-level view of the procedure for the realizability of GR-EBR formulas.

5   A Safety Reduction for GR-EBR

In this section, we describe the algorithm for solving realizability of GR-EBR specifications. It consists in three steps. Firstly, we build the product between the two symbolic and safety automata for the safety parts of both assumptions and guarantees. This product automaton has a GR(1) accepting condition. The second step consists in a so-called *degeneralization*, that, by using deterministic monitors, turns the GR(1) accepting condition into a Reactivity(1) (R(1), for short) condition. The third and last step, that is the core of the procedure, reduces the realizability problem over the above automaton to a *sequence* of safety synthesis problems, that is, realizability problems over safety (and symbolic) automata $\mathcal{A}_{safe}^k$, one for each index $k \in \mathbb{N}$. By introducing a *concrete* safety reduction $\llbracket \cdot \rrbracket_{ebr}$ for GR-EBR, and by proving that it is *complete* with respect to Definition 10, we prove the completeness of the entire procedure. The structure of the full procedure is depicted in Fig. 1.

Finally, note that, as for now, there is no incrementality between an iteration and the next one, because of the lack of incremental safety synthesizers. The only point that we save between one iteration and the next one is the construction of the two symbolic safety automata, which is performed only once during the procedure.

5.1   Construction of the Automaton with a GR(1) Condition

In this part, we describe the first step of the algorithm. Starting from a GR-EBR formula $\phi := (\phi_{ebr}^1 \wedge \bigwedge_{i=1}^m \mathsf{GF}\alpha_i) \rightarrow (\phi_{ebr}^2 \wedge \bigwedge_{j=1}^n \mathsf{GF}\beta_j)$, the objective is to obtain an automaton $\mathcal{A}$ such that: (i) it has a GR(1) accepting condition, and (ii) it recognizes the same language of ϕ, i.e., $\mathcal{L}(\phi) = \mathcal{L}(\mathcal{A})$. In order to do that, we first build the two symbolic safety automata for the safety parts of both the assumptions and the guarantees, that is for ϕ_{ebr}^1 and ϕ_{ebr}^2. Since by definition both are $\mathsf{LTL}_{\mathsf{EBR}}+\mathsf{P}$ formulas, we use the transformation described in [4], to which the reader is referred for more details.

From now on, let $\mathcal{A}(\phi_{ebr}^1)$ and $\mathcal{A}(\phi_{ebr}^2)$ be the automata for ϕ_{ebr}^1 and ϕ_{ebr}^2, respectively. Let $\mathcal{A}_{\phi_{ebr}}$ be the product automaton $\mathcal{A}(\phi_{ebr}^1) \times \mathcal{A}(\phi_{ebr}^2)$. The question is how to set the acceptance condition of $\mathcal{A}_{\phi_{ebr}}$ such that the conditions (i) and (ii) of above are fulfilled. We answer this question by examining how the automata $\mathcal{A}(\phi_{ebr}^1)$ and $\mathcal{A}(\phi_{ebr}^2)$ are made internally. Take for example the formula $\mathsf{G}p$ (for some atomic proposition $p \in \Sigma$). The safety automaton corresponding to this formula comprises an *error bit* as one of its state variables, let us call it error, which is initially set to be false. The transition function for error is deterministic and updates error to true if $\neg p$ holds in the current state, or keeps its value otherwise. The set of safe states comprises all and only those states in which error is false. In a symbolic setting, this is expressed by the formula $\mathsf{G}\neg\mathsf{error}$. In this way, p is forced to hold constantly in all (and only) the words accepted by the automaton.

A crucial property of each error bit is *monotonicity*: once error is set to true, it can never be set to false again. Formally, given a trace τ of the automaton, it holds that, if there exists $i \geq 0$ such that $\tau(i) \models$ error, then $\tau(j) \models$ error, for all $j \geq i$. Monotonicity of the error bits allows us to express an accepting condition of type $G\neg$error in terms of $GF\neg$error, by maintaining the equivalence.

Lemma 1 (Monotonicity of Error Bits). *Each error bit is monotone.*

Proof. Consider a trace τ of an automaton with an accepting condition of the type $G\neg$error. If $\tau \models G\neg$error then of course $\tau \models GF\neg$error. Suppose now that $\tau \models GF\neg$error. If by contradiction we suppose that $\tau \not\models G\neg$error, we have that there exists an $i \geq 0$ such that $\tau(i) \models$ error. By the monotonicity property, this would mean that also $\tau(j) \models$ error, for all $j \geq i$, that is $\tau \models FG$error, but this a contradiction with out hypothesis. Therefore, we proved that changing the acceptance condition of an automaton from a $G\neg$error to $GF\neg$error maintains the equivalence.   □

Let error_1 and error_2 be the error bits of $\mathcal{A}(\phi^1_{ebr})$ and $\mathcal{A}(\phi^2_{ebr})$, respectively. Let $\mathcal{A}^{\wedge\rightarrow\wedge}_{ebr}$ be the automaton obtained from $\mathcal{A}_{\phi_{ebr}}$ by replacing its acceptance condition with the following GR(1) condition:

$$(GF\neg\text{error}_1 \wedge \bigwedge_{i=1}^{m} GF\alpha_i) \rightarrow (GF\neg\text{error}_2 \wedge \bigwedge_{j=1}^{n} GF\beta_j) \tag{1}$$

The intuition is that error_1 and error_2 keep track of the *safety* parts of ϕ, that is ϕ^1_{ebr} and ϕ^2_{ebr}. The following lemma proves the equivalence between ϕ and $\mathcal{A}^{\wedge\rightarrow\wedge}_{ebr}$.

Lemma 2. *Let ϕ be an GR-EBR formula. It holds that $\mathcal{L}(\phi) = \mathcal{L}(\mathcal{A}^{\wedge\rightarrow\wedge}_{ebr})$.*

Proof. Let $\phi \in$ GR-EBR. ϕ is of the following form:

$$(\phi^1_{ebr} \rightarrow \bigwedge_{i=1}^{m} GF\alpha_i) \rightarrow (\phi^2_{ebr} \rightarrow \bigwedge_{j=1}^{n} GF\beta_j)$$

By the theorems proved in [4], it holds that $\mathcal{L}(\phi^1_{ebr}) = \mathcal{L}(\mathcal{A}(\phi^1_{ebr}))$ and $\mathcal{L}(\phi^2_{ebr}) = \mathcal{L}(\mathcal{A}(\phi^2_{ebr}))$.

Consider first the left-to-right direction. Let $\sigma \in \mathcal{L}(\phi)$. We prove that $\sigma \in \mathcal{L}(\mathcal{A}^{\wedge\rightarrow\wedge}_{ebr})$. Each $\sigma \in \mathcal{L}(\phi)$ is such that: a. either $\sigma \models \neg\phi^1_{ebr} \vee \neg(\bigwedge_{i=1}^{m} GF\alpha_i)$, b. or $\sigma \models \phi^2_{ebr} \wedge \bigwedge_{j=1}^{n} GF\beta_j$ Recall that $\mathcal{A}^{\wedge\rightarrow\wedge}_{ebr}$ is defines as the product automaton $\mathcal{A}(\phi^1_{ebr}) \times \mathcal{A}(\phi^2_{ebr})$ with the acceptance condition α defined as $(GF\neg\text{error}_1 \wedge \bigwedge_{i=1}^{m} GF\alpha_i) \rightarrow (GF\neg\text{error}_1 \wedge \bigwedge_{j=1}^{n} GF\beta_j)$.

Consider case a. If $\sigma \models \neg\phi^1_{ebr} \vee \neg(\bigwedge_{i=1}^{m} GF\alpha_i)$, then *the* trace induced by σ in $\mathcal{A}^{\wedge\rightarrow\wedge}_{ebr}$ is such that at least one of the following two cases hold:

a.1. either $\exists i \geq 0$ such that $\tau(i) \models \text{error}_1$, that is $\tau \models F(\text{error}_1)$. In this case, we exploit *monotonicity* of error_1. Since $\tau \models F(\text{error}_1)$, it also holds that $\tau \models FG(\text{error}_1)$, that is $\tau \not\models GF(\neg\text{error}_1)$. As a consequence, $\tau \models \alpha$, where α is the acceptance condition of $\mathcal{A}^{\wedge\rightarrow\wedge}_{ebr}$, and thus $\sigma \in \mathcal{L}(\mathcal{A}^{\wedge\rightarrow\wedge}_{ebr})$.

a.2. or $\tau \models \neg \bigwedge_{i=1}^{m} \mathsf{GF}\alpha_i$. In this case, of course, $\tau \models \alpha$ (that is, τ satisfies the acceptance condition of $\mathcal{A}_{\text{ebr}}^{\wedge \to \wedge}$), and thus $\sigma \in \mathcal{L}(\mathcal{A}_{\text{ebr}}^{\wedge \to \wedge})$.

Consider now the case b. If $\sigma \models \phi_{ebr}^2 \wedge \bigwedge_{j=1}^{n} \mathsf{GF}\beta_j$, then $\sigma \models \phi_{ebr}^2$ and $\sigma \models \bigwedge_{j=1}^{n} \mathsf{GF}\beta_j$. Therefore, *the* trace induced by σ in $\mathcal{A}_{\text{ebr}}^{\wedge \to \wedge}$ is such that $\tau \models \mathsf{G}(\neg \mathbf{error}_2) \wedge \bigwedge_{j=1}^{n} \mathsf{GF}\beta_j$, that implies that $\tau \models \mathsf{GF}(\neg \mathbf{error}_2) \wedge \bigwedge_{j=1}^{n} \mathsf{GF}\beta_j$. Therefore, $\tau \models \alpha$, and thus $\sigma \in \mathcal{L}(\mathcal{A}_{\text{ebr}}^{\wedge \to \wedge})$. The opposite direction can be proved similarly.   □

5.2 Degeneralization

The objective of this part is to transform the GR(1) accepting condition of the automaton $\mathcal{A}_{\text{ebr}}^{\wedge \to \wedge}$, that is of the form $\bigwedge_{i=1}^{m} \mathsf{GF}\alpha_i \to \bigwedge_{j=1}^{n} \mathsf{GF}\beta_j$, into a condition of the form $\mathsf{GF}\alpha \to \mathsf{GF}\beta$ (also called *Reactivity(1)* objective, R(1), for short). In this context, we will use the term *monitor* as a synonym of *deterministic automaton*. In order to accomplish the task, for each α_i (resp. for each β_i), we define a monitor M_{α_i} (resp. M_{β_i}) that is set to *true* when α_i (resp. β_i) has been read and is reset to *false* when all the α_i (resp. β_i) have been read. For this last condition, we define the monitors M_α^{tot} and M_β^{tot}.

Let M_{α_i} and M_α^{tot} be the symbolic safety automata such that their input alphabet is 2^Σ (where Σ is the alphabet of the starting GR-EBR formula), their set of *state variables* are $\{m_{\alpha_i}\}$ and $\{m_\alpha^{tot}\}$, respectively, all their reachable states are safe states, and their transition relations are the following:

```
init(m_αᵢ)  := 0                    init(m_α^tot)   := 0
next(m_αᵢ)  := case                 next(m_α^tot)   := case
    αᵢ      :  1                        m_α₁ ∧ ⋯ ∧ m_αₘ : 1
    m_α^tot :  0                        default          : 0
    default :  m_αᵢ                  esac
esac
```

We define M_{β_i} and M_β^{tot} as M_{α_i} and M_α^{tot}, respectively, but with α_i substituted with β_i and α substituted with β. Let $\mathcal{A}_{degen}$ be the product between all the M_{α_i}, M_{β_i}, M_α^{tot} and M_β^{tot}. Let $\mathcal{A}_{degen}^{\mathsf{GF} \to \mathsf{GF}}$ be the automaton obtained from $\mathcal{A}_{degen}$ by replacing its accepting condition with the Reactivity(1) condition $\mathsf{GF}m_\alpha^{tot} \to \mathsf{GF}m_\beta^{tot}$. We can prove the following lemma, which states that this step of the algorithm maintains the equivalence.

Lemma 3. $\mathcal{L}(\mathcal{A}_{\text{ebr}}^{\wedge \to \wedge}) = \mathcal{L}(\mathcal{A}_{\phi_{\text{ebr}}} \times \mathcal{A}_{degen}^{\mathsf{GF} \to \mathsf{GF}})$.

Proof. We prove separately the two directions. Consider first the right-to-left direction. Let σ be an infinite word of $\mathcal{L}(\mathcal{A}_{\phi_{\text{ebr}}} \times \mathcal{A}_{degen}^{\mathsf{GF} \to \mathsf{GF}})$. Then σ is a word in $\mathcal{L}(\mathcal{A}_{\phi_{\text{ebr}}})$. Moreover, σ is a word in $\mathcal{L}(\mathcal{A}_{degen}^{\mathsf{GF} \to \mathsf{GF}})$ and thus there exists a run τ induced by σ such that $\tau \models \mathsf{GF}m_\alpha^{tot} \to \mathsf{GF}m_\beta^{tot}$, that is, $\tau \models \mathsf{FG}\neg m_\alpha^{tot} \vee \mathsf{GF}m_\beta^{tot}$. We divide in cases:

- if $\tau \models \mathsf{FG}\neg m_\alpha^{tot}$, then by the semantics of the temporal operators F and G, there exists an $i \geq 0$ such that for all $j \geq i$, $\tau_j \models \neg m_\alpha^{tot}$. By construction of the monitors m_α^{tot}, this means that there exists an $i \geq 0$ such that for all $j \geq i$, $\tau_j \models \bigvee_{k=1}^m \neg m_{\alpha_k}$. This implies that, there exists a $k \in [1, m]$ and an $i \geq 0$ such that for all $j \geq i$, such that $\tau_j \models \neg m_{\alpha_k}$. Indeed, suppose by contradiction that it is not so: then for all $k \in [1, m]$, there exists infinitely many positions $i \geq 0$ such that $\tau_i \models m_{\alpha_k}$. This would mean that the monitor M_α^{tot} is set to *true* infinitely many times, that is $\mathsf{GF}m_\alpha^{tot}$, but this is a contradiction with our hypothesis. Therefore, it holds that $\tau \models \bigvee_{k=1}^m \mathsf{FG}\neg m_{\alpha_k}$, and thus also that $\tau \models \bigwedge_{i=1}^m \mathsf{GF}\alpha_i \to \bigwedge_{j=1}^n \mathsf{GF}\beta_j$. Overall, since τ is induced by σ, we have that σ is a word of $\mathcal{L}(\mathcal{A}_{\phi_{ebr}})$ that induces a run τ such that $\tau \models \bigwedge_{i=1}^m \mathsf{GF}\alpha_i \to \bigwedge_{j=1}^n \mathsf{GF}\beta_j$, that is $\sigma \in \mathcal{L}(\mathcal{A}_{ebr}^{\wedge\to\wedge})$.

- If otherwise $\tau \models \mathsf{GF}m_\beta^{tot}$, then there exists infinitely many positions $i \geq 0$ such that $\tau_i \models m_\beta^{tot}$. Moreover, it holds that for all $i_1 \geq 0$ and for all $i_2 \geq i_1$, if $\tau_{i_1} \models m_\beta^{tot}$ and $\tau_{i_2} \models m_\beta^{tot}$, then, for all $1 \leq k \leq n$, there exists a $i_1 \leq j \leq i_2$ such that $\tau_j \models m_{b_k}$. Putting together these two points, we have that for all $1 \leq k \leq n$, there exists infinitely many $i \geq 0$ such that $\tau_i \models m_{b_k}$. That is, $\tau \models \bigwedge_{k=1}^n \mathsf{GF}m_{b_k}$. By definition of the monitors M_{β_i} and since τ is induced by σ, we have that σ is a word in $\mathcal{L}(\mathcal{A}_{\phi_{ebr}})$ that induces a run τ such that $\tau \models \bigwedge_{i=1}^m \mathsf{GF}\alpha_i \to \bigwedge_{j=1}^n \mathsf{GF}\beta_j$. That is, $\sigma \in \mathcal{L}(\mathcal{A}_{ebr}^{\wedge\to\wedge})$.

The proof the left-to-right direction is specular, and therefore is omitted from the presentation.   □

5.3   Reduction to Safety for Reactivity(1) Objectives

In this part, we describe a *complete* safety reduction (see Definition 10) tailored for Reactivity(1) objectives. We will apply this reduction on the automaton $\mathcal{A}_{degen}^{\mathsf{GF}\to\mathsf{GF}}$ obtained from the previous step. The intuition is to use a *counter* to count and limit the number of positions, after a position in which m_β^{tot} holds, in which $m_\alpha^{tot} \wedge \neg m_\beta^{tot}$ holds. We define the counter as follows.

Definition 11 (Counter for the Reactivity(1) objective). *Let $\mathcal{A}_{\#_{\alpha,\beta}^{\to}}^k$ be the symbolic and deterministic safety automaton whose set of safe states is represented by the formula $\mathsf{G}(\#_{\alpha,\beta}^{\to} < k)$ and whose transition relation is the following:*

$init\,(\#_{\alpha,\beta}^{\to})$	$:=$	0
$next\,(\#_{\alpha,\beta}^{\to})$	$:=$	$case$
m_β^{tot}	$:$	0
m_α^{tot}	$:$	$\#_{\alpha,\beta}^{\to} + 1$
$default$	$:$	$\#_{\alpha,\beta}^{\to}$
$esac$		

We define $\mathcal{A}_{safe}^k := \mathcal{A}_{\phi_{ebr}} \times \mathcal{A}_{degen} \times \mathcal{A}_{\#_{\alpha,\beta}^{\to}}^k$, and we set the accepting condition of $\mathcal{A}_{safe}^k$ to be the one of $\mathcal{A}_{\#_{\alpha,\beta}^{\to}}^k$, i.e., $\mathsf{G}(\#_{\alpha,\beta}^{\to} \leq \#_{\alpha,\beta}^{\to} < k)$. The automaton $\mathcal{A}_{safe}^k$ is a symbolic and deterministic safety automaton, and therefore it can be used as an arena for a safety game. In practice, we check the realizability of $\mathcal{A}_{safe}^k$ by means of a tool for safety synthesis. We start with $k = 0$, and we check the realizabilty of $\mathcal{A}^k_{safe}$: if Controller has a strategy, than we stop, otherwise we increment k and we repeat the cycle.

In order to prove that this step is sound and complete, we use the framework described in Sect. 4. We call $[\![\cdot]\!]_{ebr}$ the safety reduction described in this part. Since the framework works with formulas rather than with automata, for all $\phi \in$ GR-EBR, we define $[\![\phi]\!]^k_{ebr}$ to be any *safety formula* such that $\mathcal{L}([\![\phi]\!]^k_{ebr}) = \mathcal{L}(\mathcal{A}^k_{safe})$. From now, with $\mathsf{id} : \mathbb{N} \to \mathbb{N}$ we denote the *identity* function.

Theorem 2. $[\![\cdot]\!]_{ebr}$ *is a* id-*complete safety reduction for GR-EBR.*

Proof. We have to prove that, for all $\phi \in$ GR-EBR, for all Kripke structures M and for all $k \in \mathbb{N}$, it holds that:

$$M \models \mathsf{A}\,\phi \quad \Leftrightarrow \quad \exists k \leq \mathsf{id}(|M|).M \models \mathsf{A}[\![\phi]\!]^k_{ebr}$$

We prove separately the two directions. Consider first the *soundness* which corresponds to the right-to-left direction. Suppose that $M \models \mathsf{A}[\![\phi]\!]^k_{ebr}$. It holds that, for each initialized trace π of M, $L(\pi) \models [\![\phi]\!]^k_{ebr}$, where $L(\cdot)$ is the labeling function of M. Let π be an initialized trace of M. By definition of $[\![\cdot]\!]_{ebr}$, it holds that, there exists a run τ induced by $L(\pi)$ such that: (i) τ is accepting in $\mathcal{A}_{\phi_{ebr}} \times \mathcal{A}_{degen}$, and (ii) τ is accepting in $\mathcal{A}^k_{\#_{\alpha,\beta}^{\rightarrow}}$. From the second point, we have that:

- either, $\#_{\alpha,\beta}^{\rightarrow}$ make infinitely many *resets*. This means that there exists infinitely many positions in τ in which m^{tot}_α holds and, after at most k occurrences of m^{tot}_β, there is a m^{tot}_β. Therefore, in particular, there exists infinitely many positions in which m^{tot}_β holds, that is $\tau \models \mathsf{GF}m^{tot}_\beta$.
- or the counter $\#_{\alpha,\beta}^{\rightarrow}$ stops to increment because, because it does not read any m^{tot}_α. This means that there exists *finitely* many positions in which m^{tot}_α holds, that is $\tau \models \mathsf{FG}\neg m^{tot}_\alpha$.

Therefore, it holds that $\tau \models \mathsf{FG}\neg m^{tot}_\alpha \vee \mathsf{GF}m^{tot}_\beta$, that is $\tau \models \mathsf{GF}m^{tot}_\alpha \to \mathsf{GF}m^{tot}_\beta$. Finally, we have that τ is an accepting run of $\mathcal{A}_{\phi_{ebr}} \times \mathcal{A}_{degen}$ such that $\tau \models \mathsf{GF}m^{tot}_\alpha \to \mathsf{GF}m^{tot}_\beta$. Since by hypothesis $L(\pi)$ is induced by τ, by definition of $\mathcal{A}^{\mathsf{GF}\to\mathsf{GF}}_{degen}$, we have that $L(\pi) \in \mathcal{L}(\mathcal{A}_{\phi_{ebr}} \times \mathcal{A}^{\mathsf{GF}\to\mathsf{GF}}_{degen})$. By concatenating Lemma 2 and Lemma 3, we have that $L(\pi) \in \mathcal{L}(\phi)$, and therefore $\pi \models \phi$. It follows that $M \models \mathsf{A}\,\phi$.

We now prove *completeness*, which corresponds to the left-to-right direction. Suppose that $M \models \mathsf{A}\phi$, where $\phi \in$ GR-EBR. We prove this case by contradiction. Suppose therefore that for all $k \leq \mathsf{id}(|M|)$, $M \not\models \mathsf{A}[\![\phi]\!]^k_{ebr}$. This means that there exists an initialized trace π in M such that $L(\pi) \notin \mathcal{L}([\![\phi]\!]^k_{ebr})$, for all $k \leq \mathsf{id}(|M|)$. By definition of $[\![\cdot]\!]_{ebr}$, for $k = \mathsf{id}(|M|)$, we have that *for all* runs τ induced by $L(\pi)$ in $\mathcal{A}_{\phi_{ebr}} \times \mathcal{A}_{degen} \times \mathcal{A}^k_{\#_{\alpha,\beta}^{\rightarrow}}$, it holds that $\tau \not\models \mathsf{G}(\#_{\alpha,\beta}^{\rightarrow} \leq k)$. Let τ be one of these runs. There exists a position i in τ such that $\tau_i \models (\#_{\alpha,\beta}^{\rightarrow} = v)$, for some $v > k$. By definition of the counter $\#_{\alpha,\beta}^{\rightarrow}$, the run τ is such that:

$$\exists 0 < h_1 < h_2 < \cdots < h_v \,.\, (\quad \tau_{h_1} \models m^{tot}_\alpha \wedge \tau_{h_2} \models m^{tot}_\alpha \wedge \ldots \tau_{h_v} \models m^{tot}_\alpha \wedge$$
$$\forall h_1 \leq h \leq h_v.(\tau_j \models \neg m^{tot}_\beta))$$

Recall that τ is a run induced by $L(\pi)$. Since $v > k$, $k = \mathsf{id}(|M|)$ and M is a *finite-state* Kripke structure, the positions $h_1 \ldots h_v$ in π (attention: *not* in τ) cannot be all different. That is, there exists at least two indexes $s, e \in \mathbb{N}$ such that: (i) $1 \leq s < e \leq v$, (ii) $\pi_{h_s} = \pi_{h_e}$, and (iii) $\pi_{h_s} \models m_\alpha^{tot}$. Starting from π, we can build a *looping trace* π' that agrees with π in the prefix $\pi_{[0,h_e]}$ and then loops on the interval $\pi_{[h_s,h_e]}$. It holds that π' is an initialized trace of M and it induces a run τ' such that $\tau' \models \mathsf{GF}m_\alpha^{tot} \wedge \mathsf{FG}\neg m_\beta^{tot}$, that is $\tau' \not\models \mathsf{GF}m_\alpha^{tot} \rightarrow \mathsf{GF}m_\beta^{tot}$. Nevertheless, since $M \models \mathsf{A}\,\phi$, by Lemma 2 and Lemma 3, we have that $L(\pi') \in \mathcal{L}(\mathcal{A}_{\phi_{ebr}} \times \mathcal{A}_{degen}^{\mathsf{GF}\rightarrow\mathsf{GF}})$, and therefore this is a contradiction. This means that it has to hold that $L(\pi) \in \mathcal{L}(\llbracket\phi\rrbracket_{ebr}^k)$, that is $\pi \models \llbracket\phi\rrbracket_{ebr}^k$ for all the initialized traces π of M, and thus there exists a $k \leq \mathsf{id}(|M|)$ such that $M \models \mathsf{A}\llbracket\phi\rrbracket_{ebr}^k$. $\quad\square$

With Theorem 1, we derive the following corollary that proves the completeness of our procedure.

Corollary 1. *For any formula $\phi \in$ GR-EBR, it holds that: ϕ is realizable iff $\exists k \leq \mathsf{id}(2^{|\mathcal{U}|} \cdot 2^{|\mathcal{C}|} \cdot 2^{2^{c \cdot n}})$ such that $\llbracket\phi\rrbracket_{ebr}^k$ is realizable.*

6   Experimental Evaluation

We implemented the algorithm described in Sect. 5 and summarized in Fig. 1 in a prototype tool called GRACE (which stands for *GR-ebr reAlizability ChEcker*)[1]. We chose SAFETYSYNTH [14] as a BDD-based backend for solving each safety game.

As competitor tools, we chose BoSy [9,10,12] and STRIX [18,20]. BoSy implements the Bounded Synthesis approach (see the paragraph on the related works in Sect. 1), while STRIX is based on parity games and is the winner of SYNTCOMP 2018, 2019 and 2020. We set a timeout of 180 s. The experiments have been run on a 16-cores machine with a 2696.6 MHz AMD core with 62 GB of RAM.

We remark that a comparison with GR(1) synthesis tools is nontrivial. The majority of the tools for GR(1) only support the realizability of the *strict* implication (see for example [8]), not the standard one (which is our case). Therefore, although the latter can be reduced to the former [1], a non-trivial practical effort is required to write an algorithm for this translation.

We considered benchmarks of two types: (i) artificial, and (ii) derived from the SYNTCOMP [14] benchmarks'set. Regarding the artifical benchmarks, we partitioned them in four categories, each containing 30 benchmarks scalable in their dimension N, for a total of 120 formulas. The categories are the following ones:

1. $\mathsf{G}(u_0 \rightarrow \mathsf{X}(u_1 \rightarrow \mathsf{X}(u_2 \rightarrow \cdots \rightarrow \mathsf{X}(u_N)\ldots))) \rightarrow \mathsf{G}(\bigwedge_{i=1}^{N}(u_i \leftrightarrow \mathsf{X}c_i))$
2. $(\mathsf{G}(u_0 \rightarrow \mathsf{X}(u_1 \rightarrow \mathsf{X}(u_2 \rightarrow \cdots \rightarrow \mathsf{X}(u_N)\ldots))) \wedge \mathsf{X}^N\mathsf{G}u_N \wedge \mathsf{GF}u_N) \rightarrow$
   $(\bigwedge_{i=1}^{N}(u_i \leftrightarrow \mathsf{X}^Nc_i) \wedge \mathsf{GF}c_N)$

---

[1] https://es-static.fbk.eu/tools/grace/.

3. $(G(u_0) \wedge XG(u_1) \wedge \cdots \wedge X^N G(u_N) \wedge \bigwedge_{i=1}^N GFu_i) \rightarrow (\bigwedge_{i=1}^N G(u_i \leftrightarrow c_i) \wedge \bigwedge_{i=1}^N GFc_i)$
4. $(\neg u_0 \wedge G^{[0,N]}\neg u_0 \wedge X^{N+1}Gu_0) \rightarrow (\bigwedge_{i=1}^N G(u_0 \leftrightarrow Xc_i) \wedge \bigwedge_{i=1}^N GF(c_i \wedge u_0))$

The variables starting with u are uncontrollable, while those starting with c are controllables. All the benchmarks are realizable, and were specifically crafted to elicit potential criticalities of GRACE. In particular, the benchmarks in the fourth category have been specifically designed in order to force the minimum k of the termination of GRACE to increase with their dimension.

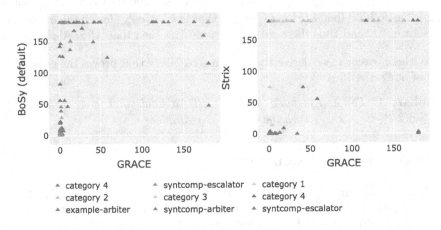

Fig. 2. GRACE compared to BoSy (on the left) and to STRIX (on the right)

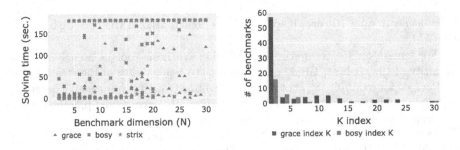

Fig. 3. On the left, the size of the benchmarks compared to solving time. On the right, GRACE vs BoSy on number of safety sub-problems.

Regarding the benchmarks derived from the SYNTCOMP benchmarks'set, we included (i) *simple_arbiter_N* (for each $N \in \{2,4,6,8,10,12\}$), *escalator_bidirectional*, which belong to the SYNTCOMP benchmarks' set, and (ii) our example for an arbiter (Sect. 3.2), with $N \in \{1,\ldots,15\}$.

Figure 2 show the comparison between the tools on all the benchmarks of both types. All times are in seconds. From Fig. 2 (left), it is clear the exponential blowup in solving time in which BoSy occurs. The blowup involves formulas of both types, and of all four categories (of artificial benchmarks). For example, (i) on category 4, the solving times of BoSy on $N = 13, 14$ are 19.4 and 136.3 s, respectively, and the corresponding automata have 27 and 31 states, respectively. (ii) on `simple_arbiter_N`, BoSy takes 45.714 s for $N = 8$, and reaches the timeout for $N = 10$. Figure 3 (left), which compares the dimension of the benchmarks (X axis) with the solving time of GRACE, BoSy and STRIX (Y axis), clearly shows this trend. A more precise study of the complexity of BoSy shows that the majority of the time spent by it is due to the construction of the UCWcorresponding to the input formula, which is the task of the tools LTL3BA and SPOT. On the contrary, it is clear from Fig. 2 (left) that GRACE avoids this bad behavior, most likely due to the fact that the explicit state UCWis never built. Similar considerations can be made for the tool STRIX (see Fig. 2, right), except for the category `example-arbiter`, in which the solving times of STRIX are consistently better than the ones of GRACE. A careful study revealed that all these benchmarks are transformed to the equi-realizable formula `true` by the preprocessor of OWL [16] (a tool for ω-automata manipulation), which STRIX is based on.

The plot in Fig. 3 (right) shows, for each index k ranging from 1 to 31 (these correspond to the columns), on how many benchmarks (of both types) GRACE or BoSy terminate with index k (this corresponds to the height of a column). The benchmarks in category 4 and the ones of `simple_arbiter_N` force GRACE to terminate with increasing values of k. The plot in Fig. 3 points out that BoSy does not incur in this growth, except for one benchmark. Nevertheless, the solving times of GRACE are still better than the ones of BoSy. This witnesses the fact that each safety sub-problem generated by GRACE is very simple to solve.

7 Conclusions

In this paper, we introduced the logic of GR-EBR, an extension of LTL$_{EBR}$+P [4] adding fairness conditions and assumes-guarantees formulas, and studied its realizability problem. We aim at extending the work done in three directions: (i) as far as we know, there are no safety synthesizer (like SAFETYSYNTH) that are able to exploit *incrementality*; since in our context, the only part of the automaton that changes between one iteration and the next one is the counter, some work may be saved; (ii) since GR(1) is a very efficient fragment, it is important to investigate whether there is a compilation from GR-EBR to GR(1); (iii) last but not least, we aim at giving a semantic characterization of GR-EBR, and at exploiting the proposed framework for more expressive logics, such as full LTL.

References

1. Bloem, R., Jobstmann, B., Piterman, N., Pnueli, A., Saar, Y.: Synthesis of reactive (1) designs. J. Comput. Syst. Sci. **78**(3), 911–938 (2012)
2. Buchi, J.R., Landweber, L.H.: Solving sequential conditions by finite-state strategies. In: Mac Lane, S., Siefkes, D. (eds.) The Collected Works of J. Richard Büchi, pp. 525–541. Springer, New York (1990). https://doi.org/10.1007/978-1-4613-8928-6_29
3. Church, A.: Logic, arithmetic, and automata. In: Proceedings of the International Congress of Mathematicians, vol. 1962, pp. 23–35 (1962)
4. Cimatti, A., Geatti, L., Gigante, N., Montanari, A., Tonetta, S.: Reactive synthesis from extended bounded response LTL specifications. In: 2020 Formal Methods in Computer Aided Design (FMCAD), pp. 83–92. IEEE (2020)
5. Cimatti, A., Geatti, L., Gigante, N., Montanari, A., Tonetta, S.: Expressiveness of extended bounded response LTL. arXiv preprint arXiv:2109.08319 (2021)
6. Claessen, K., Sörensson, N.: A liveness checking algorithm that counts. In: 2012 Formal Methods in Computer-Aided Design (FMCAD), pp. 52–59. IEEE (2012)
7. Ehlers, R.: Symbolic bounded synthesis. In: Touili, T., Cook, B., Jackson, P. (eds.) CAV 2010. LNCS, vol. 6174, pp. 365–379. Springer, Heidelberg (2010). https://doi.org/10.1007/978-3-642-14295-6_33
8. Ehlers, R., Raman, V.: Slugs: extensible GR(1) synthesis. In: Chaudhuri, S., Farzan, A. (eds.) CAV 2016. LNCS, vol. 9780, pp. 333–339. Springer, Cham (2016). https://doi.org/10.1007/978-3-319-41540-6_18
9. Faymonville, P., Finkbeiner, B., Rabe, M.N., Tentrup, L.: Encodings of bounded synthesis. In: Legay, A., Margaria, T. (eds.) TACAS 2017. LNCS, vol. 10205, pp. 354–370. Springer, Heidelberg (2017). https://doi.org/10.1007/978-3-662-54577-5_20
10. Faymonville, P., Finkbeiner, B., Tentrup, L.: BoSy: an experimentation framework for bounded synthesis. In: Majumdar, R., Kunčak, V. (eds.) CAV 2017. LNCS, vol. 10427, pp. 325–332. Springer, Cham (2017). https://doi.org/10.1007/978-3-319-63390-9_17
11. Filiot, E., Jin, N., Raskin, J.-F.: An antichain algorithm for LTL realizability. In: Bouajjani, A., Maler, O. (eds.) CAV 2009. LNCS, vol. 5643, pp. 263–277. Springer, Heidelberg (2009). https://doi.org/10.1007/978-3-642-02658-4_22
12. Finkbeiner, B., Hahn, C., Lukert, P., Stenger, M., Tentrup, L.: Synthesizing reactive systems from hyperproperties. In: Chockler, H., Weissenbacher, G. (eds.) CAV 2018. LNCS, vol. 10981, pp. 289–306. Springer, Cham (2018). https://doi.org/10.1007/978-3-319-96145-3_16
13. Finkbeiner, B., Schewe, S.: Bounded synthesis. Int. J. Softw. Tools Technol. Transfer **15**(5–6), 519–539 (2013)
14. Jacobs, S., Bloem, R.: The 5th reactive synthesis competition (SYNTCOMP 2018)
15. Jacobs, S., Bloem, R., Brenguier, R., Ehlers, R., Hell, T., Könighofer, R., Pérez, G.A., Raskin, J.F., Ryzhyk, L., Sankur, O., et al.: The first reactive synthesis competition (SYNTCOMP 2014). Int. J. Softw. Tools Technol. Transfer **19**(3), 367–390 (2017)
16. Křetínský, J., Meggendorfer, T., Sickert, S.: Owl: a library for ω-words, automata, and LTL. In: Lahiri, S.K., Wang, C. (eds.) ATVA 2018. LNCS, vol. 11138, pp. 543–550. Springer, Cham (2018). https://doi.org/10.1007/978-3-030-01090-4_34
17. Kupferman, O., Vardi, M.Y.: Safraless decision procedures. In: 46th Annual Symposium on Foundations of Computer Science (FOCS), pp. 531–540. IEEE (2005)

18. Luttenberger, M., Meyer, P.J., Sickert, S.: Practical synthesis of reactive systems from LTL specifications via parity games. Acta Informatica **57**(1), 3–36 (2020)
19. Manna, Z., Pnueli, A.: A hierarchy of temporal properties (invited paper, 1989). In: Proceedings of the 9th Annual ACM Symposium on Principles of Distributed Computing, pp. 377–410 (1990)
20. Meyer, P.J., Sickert, S., Luttenberger, M.: Strix: explicit reactive synthesis strikes back! In: Chockler, H., Weissenbacher, G. (eds.) CAV 2018. LNCS, vol. 10981, pp. 578–586. Springer, Cham (2018). https://doi.org/10.1007/978-3-319-96145-3_31
21. Piterman, N., Pnueli, A., Sa'ar, Y.: Synthesis of reactive(1) designs. In: Emerson, E.A., Namjoshi, K.S. (eds.) VMCAI 2006. LNCS, vol. 3855, pp. 364–380. Springer, Heidelberg (2005). https://doi.org/10.1007/11609773_24
22. Pnueli, A., Rosner, R.: On the synthesis of an asynchronous reactive module. In: Ausiello, G., Dezani-Ciancaglini, M., Della Rocca, S.R. (eds.) ICALP 1989. LNCS, vol. 372, pp. 652–671. Springer, Heidelberg (1989). https://doi.org/10.1007/BFb0035790
23. Rosner, R.: Modular synthesis of reactive systems. Ph.D. thesis, Weizmann Institute of Science (1992)
24. Vardi, M.Y., Wolper, P.: Reasoning about infinite computations. Inf. Comput. **115**(1), 1–37 (1994)
25. Zhu, S., Tabajara, L.M., Li, J., Pu, G., Vardi, M.Y.: A symbolic approach to safety LTL synthesis. In: HVC 2017. LNCS, vol. 10629, pp. 147–162. Springer, Cham (2017). https://doi.org/10.1007/978-3-319-70389-3_10

TACoS: A Tool for MTL Controller Synthesis

Till Hofmann[1]([✉]) [ID] and Stefan Schupp[2] [ID]

[1] Knowledge-Based Systems Group, RWTH Aachen University, Aachen, Germany
hofmann@kbsg.rwth-aachen.de
[2] Cyber-Physical Systems Group, TU Wien, Vienna, Austria
stefan.schupp@tuwien.ac.at

Abstract. We introduce TACoS, a tool for synthesizing controllers satisfying MTL specifications of undesired behavior with timing constraints. Our contribution extends an existing theoretical approach towards practical applications. The most notable features include: Online labeling to terminate early if a solution has been found, heuristic search to expand the most promising nodes first, search graph pruning to reduce the problem size by pruning irrelevant parts of the search graph, and reusing previously explored search nodes to further reduce the search graph. Finally, multi-threading support allows to make use of modern CPUs with many parallel threads. TACoS comes with a C++ library with minimal external dependencies and simple-to-use API. We evaluate our approach on a number of scenarios and investigate how each of the enhancements improves the performance.

The tool is publicly available at https://github.com/morxa/tacos.

Keywords: Controller synthesis · Metric temporal logic

1 Introduction

Controller synthesis is the problem of determining a controller for a given system to ensure the behavior of the composed system follows a certain specification. The problem has been researched extensively for different kinds of systems and different kinds of specifications (e.g., [4,7,9]). It has also seen interest in the AI community (e.g., [8]) and in robotics (e.g., [12,13,15]). One particular synthesis problem is *controller synthesis for MTL specifications* [7], where the system is modeled as timed automaton (TA) and the specification of undesired behavior is given as a metric temporal logic (MTL) formula. The problem has shown to be decidable for finite words and fixed resources [7]. While several applications are based on metric temporal constraints (e.g., [17,20,22]), to the best of our knowledge, no general implementation of such a synthesis approach exists.

Supported by DFG RTG 2236 *UnRAVeL* and DFG grant GL-747/23-1 *ConTrAkt*.

R. Calinescu and C. S. Păsăreanu (Eds.): SEFM 2021, LNCS 13085, pp. 372–379, 2021.
https://doi.org/10.1007/978-3-030-92124-8_21

Related Work Controller synthesis for timed systems has been researched extensively, in different settings. Tools such as ACACIA+ [6] and UNBEAST [10] synthesize controllers for LTL specifications, which does not allow time constraints.
SYNTHKRO and FLYSYNTH [1] synthesize controllers that remain in or reach a
given set of states of a timed automaton. UPPAAL-TIGA [5] and SYNTHIA [19]
control timed automata against a TCTL specification to accomplish reachability
or safety. UPPAAL-TIGA has also been extended to models with partial observ-
ability [11], using pre-defined controller templates. CASAAL [16] synthesizes a
controller for $MTL_{0,\infty}$ specifications. $MTL_{0,\infty}$ is a subset of MTL, where every
bounded until operator may only use an upper or a lower time-bound (not both).

In this work, we present TACoS, a *TA Controller Synthesis* tool for MTL
specifications, based on theoretical decidability results from [7]. In Sect. 2, we
summarize the MTL synthesis problem, before we describe our tool in more
detail in Sect. 3. In Sect. 4, we evaluate TACoS on benchmarks from several
scenarios, before we conclude in Sect. 5.

2   The MTL Synthesis Problem

Timed automata (TA) [2] are a widely used model for representing real-timed and
hybrid systems. Their properties are often described with MTL [14], a temporal
logic that extends linear temporal logic (LTL) with metric time on the *Until*
modality. One commonly used semantics for MTL is a *pointwise semantics*, in
which formulas are interpreted over timed words. A timed word ρ over a finite set
of atomic propositions AP is a finite or infinite sequence $\rho = (\sigma_0, \tau_0)(\sigma_1, \tau_1)\ldots$
where $\sigma_i \in AP$ and $\tau_i \in \mathbb{R}_+$ such that the sequence (τ_i) is monotonically non-
decreasing and non-Zeno. We use $|\rho|$ to denote the number of elements in ρ.
For a set AP of atomic propositions, the formulas of MTL are built from $\phi ::=$
$a \mid \neg\phi \mid \phi \wedge \phi \mid \phi\,\mathbf{U}_I\,\phi$ (where $a \in AP$). We use the short-hand notations
$\phi\,\widetilde{\mathbf{U}}_I\,\psi := \neg(\neg\phi\,\mathbf{U}_I\,\neg\psi)$ *(dual until)*, $\mathbf{F}_I\phi := (\top\,\mathbf{U}_I\,\phi)$ *(finally)* and $\mathbf{G}_I\phi :=$
$\neg\mathbf{F}_I\neg\phi$ *(globally)*. Given a timed word $\rho = (\sigma_0, \tau_0)(\sigma_1, \tau_1)\ldots$ over alphabet AP
and an MTL formula ϕ, $\rho, i \models \phi$ is defined as usual for the boolean operators,
and with the following rule for $\mathbf{U}_I$: $\rho, i \models \phi_1\,\mathbf{U}_I\,\phi_2$ iff there exists j such that
(1) $i < j < |\rho|$, (2) $\rho, j \models \phi_2$, (3) $\tau_j - \tau_i \in I$, (4) and $\rho, k \models \phi_1$ for all k with
$i < k < j$. We also write $\rho \models \phi$ for $\rho, 0 \models \phi$ and we define the language of ϕ as
$L(\phi) = \{\rho \mid \rho \models \phi\}$.

MTL Control Problem. The goal is to synthesize a controller $\mathcal{C}$ that *controls* a
plant $\mathcal{P}$ against a specification of undesired behaviors Φ such that all resulting
traces in the composition of $\mathcal{P}$ and $\mathcal{C}$ satisfy the specification Φ without blocking
the plant $\mathcal{P}$. In this context, *control* means that $\mathcal{C}$ has control over some actions,
while the environment controls the remaining actions. The synthesis problem on
finite words and finite resources (i.e., fixed number of clocks and fixed constants)
is decidable [7]. We refer to [7] for the formal definition.

3   Approach

Based on [7], our tool works as follows: First, it translates the specification into an alternating timed automaton (ATA) [18]. Next, it recursively constructs a tree over regionalized configurations of the synchronous product of the plant TA $\mathcal{A}$ and the specification ATA $\mathcal{B}$. Intuitively, each node n in the search tree contains a single regionalized configuration $n_{\mathcal{A}}$ of $\mathcal{A}$ and a set $n_{\mathcal{B}}$ of possible configurations of $\mathcal{B}$, which represents parts of the specification that have not been satisfied yet. Each newly discovered node in the search tree is *expanded* by computing all (regionalized) time and jump successors $n'_{\mathcal{A}}$ of $n_{\mathcal{A}}$ and the respective $N'_{\mathcal{B}}$ for all symbols. Nodes in which the $\mathcal{A}$ configuration is in a final location and Φ has fully been satisfied ($\mathcal{B}$ is accepting) are labeled as *bad*, as they represent cases in which the plant is in a final state and the specification has been violated. After building the search tree, the tree is traversed and labeled bottom-up (*good, bad*) based on the labels of the leaf nodes. A controller exists if the root node is labeled *good*.

TACoS aims to provide a practicable tool to synthesize TA controllers against an MTL specification, with a focus on performance and usability. We summarize the most notable features in the following.

Parallelization. To make use of multi-threading, the node expansion is parallelized. Pending nodes are stored in a globally accessible queue and worker threads take nodes from the queue, expand those and push resulting successors into the queue for further processing.

Incremental Labeling. Instead of first constructing a complete search tree and then labeling the tree bottom-up, it is also possible to partially label the tree during expansion. Nodes are labelled recursively until either the root node has been labeled or not enough information is available to label a node. This approach allows to label the root node without constructing the complete search tree.

Pruning. With incremental labeling, a node's label may be determined during search. With pruning, whenever a node's label is determined, all of its unlabeled successors are marked as *canceled*, which prevents them from being expanded later on. The combination of incremental labeling and pruning allows to effectively skip large parts of the search graph during construction.

Node Reusing. When constructing the search tree as described, many nodes are created multiple times. This may occur whenever certain states of the system are reachable via different execution paths of the plant. Duplicate nodes consequently agree on their subtrees, i.e., the work of exploring these subtrees will be done several times. To overcome this, we identify duplicate nodes during the search. Instead of re-creating the sub-tree, we reuse the existing node instead and add the corresponding edges. This changes the underlying data structure from a search tree to a *search graph*, affecting all other improvements as well.

Search Heuristics. Incremental labeling and search-graph pruning heavily depend on the order in which nodes are expanded. We provide several heuristics which determine the order of nodes in the queue: breadth-first-search (**bfs**) and depth-first-search (**dfs**) work as expected. A heuristics based on timing (**time**) prioritizes the node with the shortest accumulated time (global time). The heuristic **cw** prefers nodes with configurations where more parts of the specification (of undesired behavior) are not yet satisfied. The heuristic **env** prefers environment actions over controller actions, based on the intuition that the controller should only act if necessary (and let the plant run otherwise). The composite heuristic **comp** is a weighted sum of other heuristics. In the following, we have used $\texttt{comp} = 16 \cdot \texttt{cw} + 4 \cdot \texttt{env} + 1 \cdot \texttt{time}$. Finally, the tool also provides a **random** heuristic, which is mainly helpful for comparison and testing.

Action- and Location-Based Specification. The approach in [7] suggests a method designed for *action-based* specifications in which labels on transitions (the *actions*) are used. However, *location-based* specifications, which specify the desired or undesired behavior in terms of properties on locations, sometimes allow a more intuitive specification. Our tool supports both types of specifications.

Utility. To ease debugging, we provide several utility functions such as plotting of the input automata, the resulting controller, or the search graph. TACoS reads text input and is shipped with a C++ library with simple API to create input programmatically. The synthesis result can be stored in a human-readable or binary format. TACoS can also be run in an interactive mode after search, which allows to debug the controller synthesis step-by-step with visual support.

4   Evaluation

We evaluated our system on several scenarios and ran each scenario in each configuration five times. All experiments were conducted on an AMD Ryzen 7 3700X with 16 parallel threads and 32 GB memory. We measured the number of locations in the input problem, the number of nodes in the search graph, the number of explored nodes in the search graph, and the number of locations in the resulting controller. We used three scenarios:

Example 1 (Railroad). This is a variant of the train-gate controller [3]. A train approaches a crossing, the controller needs to open and close the gate such that the train can pass. The problem is modeled as product of two TAs. The train performs the uncontrollable actions *get_near, enter, leave, travel* in sequence, i.e., approaches and passes through the gate section. The gate may perform the controllable actions *start_close, start_open, finish_close, finish_open* to change its state. The composed system is safe if the gate is closed when the train enters and opens after the train leaves the crossing. Thus, the bad behavior is defined by

$$enter \; \widetilde{\mathbf{U}} \; \neg finish\_close \lor start\_open \; \widetilde{\mathbf{U}} \; \neg leave \lor travel \; \widetilde{\mathbf{U}} \; \neg finish\_open$$

We have parameterized the problem by the number of crossings and the distances before each crossing, where `Railroad(4,8)` is the problem with two crossings and a distance of 4 and 8 time units before the first and second crossing.

Table 1. A comparison of the heuristics implemented in TACoS for an instance of the railroad example. We compare the used heuristics (heu), the resulting running time (wall) and CPU time (CPU) in seconds, the size of the search tree (nodes) and the number of explored nodes (expl) in thousands of nodes as well as the number of locations in the resulting controller (ctrl). Standard deviations are given in brackets, e.g., 1.1(2) means 1.1 ± 0.2.

Scenario	size	heu	wall (s)	CPU (s)	nodes (k)	expl (k)	ctrl
Railroad(2,2)	144	bfs	5.39(9)	5.38(9)	1.832(2)	0.78(2)	53(7)
		dfs	1.1(4)	1.1(4)	1.2(2)	0.8(1)	79(29)
		cw	0.8(3)	0.8(3)	1.0(2)	0.60(9)	71(8)
		env	1.1(3)	1.1(3)	1.1(2)	0.33(8)	46(3)
		time	6.56(9)	6.55(9)	1.799(8)	0.309(7)	52(10)
		rand	1.3(5)	1.3(5)	1.3(2)	0.27(6)	71(20)
		comp	0.4(3)	0.4(3)	0.6(3)	0.4(2)	32(10)

Example 2 (Robot). A robot transports goods between stations (based on [22]). It has a camera that needs to be enabled 1 s before the robot performs a *pick* or a *put* action. As the camera may overheat, it must not run continuously for longer than 4 s. The camera is controllable with the actions *on* and *off*, the robot's actions *pick*, *put*, and *move* are not controllable. The robot takes exactly 3 s to move between the stations. The specification of undesired behavior is given as:

$$\neg on\ \mathbf{U}\ pick \vee \mathbf{F}(off \wedge (\neg on\ \mathbf{U}\ pick)) \vee \mathbf{F}(on\ \mathbf{U}_{[0,1]}\ pick)$$
$$\vee \neg on\ \mathbf{U}\ put \vee \mathbf{F}(off \wedge (\neg on\ \mathbf{U}\ put)) \vee \mathbf{F}(on\ \mathbf{U}_{[0,1]}\ put)$$

Example 3 (Conveyor Belt). A conveyor belt moves luggage in an airport (based on [21]). If a piece of luggage gets stuck, the belt must stop, which allows the luggage to be removed. The conveyor must not immediately continue but instead wait for at least 2 s. Also, the conveyor should not stop without reason. The controllable actions are *move* and *stop*, while the uncontrollable actions are *release*, *resume*, and *stuck*. The undesired behavior is specified as follows:

$$\mathbf{F}(release \wedge \mathbf{F}_{[0,2]}move) \vee (\neg stuck)\ \mathbf{U}\ stop \vee \mathbf{F}(stop \wedge (\neg stuck)\ \mathbf{U}\ stop)$$

Results We first compare the different heuristics in Table 1. We can see that using heuristics is generally helpful and improves both the running time and the resulting search size and controller size when compared to `bfs`. Interestingly, the heuristic `time` does not perform well and is actually worse than `bfs`, `dfs`, and even `random`. Also, `dfs` performs surprisingly well compared to the other

Table 2. A comparison of single- and multi-threading (with 16 threads). We compare the used heuristics (heu), whether multi-threading is used (multi), the resulting running time (wall) and CPU time (CPU) in seconds, the size of the search tree (nodes) and the number of explored nodes (expl) in thousands of nodes as well as the number of locations in the resulting controller (ctrl). Standard deviations are given in brackets, e.g., 24(3) means 24 ± 3.

Scenario	heu	multi	wall (s)	CPU (s)	nodes (k)	expl (k)	ctrl
Railroad(2,2)	comp	n	0.4(3)	0.4(3)	0.6(3)	0.4(2)	32(10)
	comp	y	0.12(4)	1.0(4)	0.9(2)	0.6(2)	60(27)
Robot	comp	n	0.0289(2)	0.0289(2)	0.0182(1)	0.0067(9)	30(7)
	comp	y	0.0134(3)	0.066(1)	0.040(4)	0.0065(8)	34.4(5)
Conveyor	comp	n	0.044(7)	0.044(7)	0.045(2)	0.035(5)	150(33)
	comp	y	0.037(2)	0.057(2)	0.046(1)	0.037(2)	166(5)

Table 3. The *railroad* problem scaled to different travel times and number of crossings, using the comp heuristic and multi-threading. We provide the size of the timed automaton (size), the resulting running time (wall) and CPU time (CPU) in seconds, the size of the search tree (nodes) and the number of explored nodes (expl) in thousands of nodes as well as the number of locations in the resulting controller (ctrl). Standard deviations are given in brackets, e.g., 0.14(5) means 0.14 ± 0.05.

Scenario	size	wall (s)	CPU (s)	nodes (k)	expl (k)	ctrl
Railroad(2,2)	144	0.12(1)	1.0(1)	0.93(7)	0.58(5)	43(5)
Railroad(2,4)	144	0.42(4)	4.1(8)	2.26(7)	1.4(2)	49(9)
Railroad(2,8)	144	2.0(7)	21(10)	5.8(7)	3.1(8)	47(10)
Railroad(4,4)	144	1.14(7)	15(1)	3.24(1)	2.238(8)	48(2)
Railroad(4,8)	144	6(1)	91(19)	8.3(6)	5.1(5)	64(19)
Railroad(8,8)	144	28(9)	431(151)	11.1(3)	7.5(1)	45(10)
Railroad(1,1,1)	832	4(1)	38(14)	13(4)	6(1)	74(82)
Railroad(2,1,1)	832	1877(287)	29 858(4582)	45(3)	33(2)	101(31)
Railroad(2,2,2)	832	3654(1243)	58 228(19820)	49(13)	37(7)	103(45)

heuristics, at least in this scenario. With some margin, the composite heuristic comp performs best. Second, we evaluate multi-threaded search, running times are shown in Table 2. We can see that multi-threading reduces the running time, but increases CPU time and often has a negative impact on search size and controller size, most likely as additional nodes with a worse heuristic value are expanded as well when computing with multiple threads. Finally, Table 3 shows the performance on the scaled railroad problem. We can see that TACoS is able to find a controller even for large input problems, although the running time increases significantly. Further results are available on the tool webpage[1].

---

[1] https://github.com/morxa/tacos.

5   Conclusion

We have presented TACoS, to our knowledge the first tool for TA controller synthesis against MTL specifications. TACoS comes with a number of features aiming to provide both good performance and usability. We have evaluated the tool in three settings, which showed that it is capable of synthesizing controllers with reasonable performance. To further improve its performance, investigating more sophisticated heuristics would be a promising next step. Also, in future work, we want to investigate the applicability of the presented approach for control program synthesis and its performance on real robotic systems.

References

1. Altisen, K., Tripakis, S.: Tools for controller synthesis of timed systems. In: RT-TOOLS (2002)
2. Alur, R., Dill, D.: A theory of timed automata. TCS **126**(2) (1994). https://doi.org/10.1016/0304-3975(94)90010-8
3. Alur, R., Henzinger, T., Vardi, M.: Parametric real-time reasoning. In: STOC (1993)
4. Asarin, E., Maler, O., Pnueli, A., Sifakis, J.: Controller synthesis for timed automata. IFAC **31**(18) (1998). https://doi.org/10.1016/S1474-6670(17)42032-5
5. Behrmann, G., Cougnard, A., David, A., Fleury, E., Larsen, K.G., Lime, D.: UPPAAL-Tiga: time for playing games! In: Damm, W., Hermanns, H. (eds.) CAV 2007. LNCS, vol. 4590, pp. 121–125. Springer, Heidelberg (2007). https://doi.org/10.1007/978-3-540-73368-3_14
6. Bohy, A., Bruyère, V., Filiot, E., Jin, N., Raskin, J.-F.: Acacia+, a tool for LTL synthesis. In: Madhusudan, P., Seshia, S.A. (eds.) CAV 2012. LNCS, vol. 7358, pp. 652–657. Springer, Heidelberg (2012). https://doi.org/10.1007/978-3-642-31424-7_45
7. Bouyer, P., Bozzelli, L., Chevalier, F.: Controller synthesis for MTL specifications. In: Baier, C., Hermanns, H. (eds.) CONCUR 2006. LNCS, vol. 4137, pp. 450–464. Springer, Heidelberg (2006). https://doi.org/10.1007/11817949_30
8. De Giacomo, G., Vardi, M.: Synthesis for LTL and LDL on finite traces. In: IJCAI (2015)
9. D'souza, D., Madhusudan, P.: Timed control synthesis for external specifications. In: Alt, H., Ferreira, A. (eds.) STACS 2002. LNCS, vol. 2285, pp. 571–582. Springer, Heidelberg (2002). https://doi.org/10.1007/3-540-45841-7_47
10. Ehlers, R.: Unbeast: symbolic bounded synthesis. In: Abdulla, P.A., Leino, K.R.M. (eds.) TACAS 2011. LNCS, vol. 6605, pp. 272–275. Springer, Heidelberg (2011). https://doi.org/10.1007/978-3-642-19835-9_25
11. Finkbeiner, B., Peter, H.-J.: Template-based controller synthesis for timed systems. In: Flanagan, C., König, B. (eds.) TACAS 2012. LNCS, vol. 7214, pp. 392–406. Springer, Heidelberg (2012). https://doi.org/10.1007/978-3-642-28756-5_27
12. He, K., Lahijanian, M., Kavraki, L., Vardi, M.: Reactive synthesis for finite tasks under resource constraints. In: IROS (2017). https://doi.org/10.1109/IROS.2017.8206426
13. Hofmann, T., Lakemeyer, G.: Controller synthesis for Golog programs over finite domains with metric temporal constraints. arXiv:2102.09837 (2021)

14. Koymans, R.: Specifying real-time properties with metric temporal logic. Real-Time Syst. **2**(4), 255–299 (1990). https://doi.org/10.1007/BF01995674
15. Kress-Gazit, H., Fainekos, G., Pappas, G.: Temporal-logic-based reactive mission and motion planning. IEEE Trans. Robot. **25**(6), 1370–1381 (2009). https://doi.org/10.1109/TRO.2009.2030225
16. Li, G., Jensen, P.G., Larsen, K.G., Legay, A., Poulsen, D.B.: Practical controller synthesis for MTL0,∞. In: SPIN (2017). https://doi.org/10.1145/3092282.3092303
17. Nikou, A., Tumova, J., Dimarogonas, D.: Cooperative task planning of multi-agent systems under timed temporal specifications. In: ACC (2016). https://doi.org/10.1109/ACC.2016.7526793
18. Ouaknine, J., Worrell, J.: On the decidability of metric temporal logic. In: LICS (2005). https://doi.org/10.1109/LICS.2005.33
19. Peter, H.-J., Ehlers, R., Mattmüller, R.: Synthia: verification and synthesis for timed automata. In: Gopalakrishnan, G., Qadeer, S. (eds.) CAV 2011. LNCS, vol. 6806, pp. 649–655. Springer, Heidelberg (2011). https://doi.org/10.1007/978-3-642-22110-1_52
20. Saha, S., Julius, A.: An MILP approach for real-time optimal controller synthesis with metric temporal logic specifications. In: ACC (2016). https://doi.org/10.1109/ACC.2016.7525063
21. van Hulst, A.C., Reniers, M.A., Fokkink, W.J.: Maximally permissive controlled system synthesis for non-determinism and modal logic. Discrete Event Dyn. Syst. **27**(1), 109–142 (2016). https://doi.org/10.1007/s10626-016-0231-8
22. Viehmann, T., Hofmann, T., Lakemeyer, G.: Transforming robotic plans with timed automata to solve temporal platform constraints. In: IJCAI (2021). https://doi.org/10.24963/ijcai.2021/287

Emerging Domains

Lightweight Nontermination Inference with CHCs

Bishoksan Kafle[1]([✉]) [ID], Graeme Gange[2] [ID], Peter Schachte[3] [ID],
Harald Søndergaard[3] [ID], and Peter J. Stuckey[2] [ID]

[1] IMDEA Software Institute, Madrid, Spain
[2] Faculty of IT, Monash University, Melbourne, Australia
[3] Computing and Information Systems, The University of Melbourne,
Melbourne, Australia

Abstract. Non-termination is an unwanted program property (considered a bug) for some software systems, and a safety property for other systems. In either case, automated discovery of preconditions for non-termination is of interest. We introduce NTHORN, a fast lightweight non-termination analyser, able to deduce non-trivial sufficient conditions for non-termination. Using Constrained Horn Clauses (CHCs) as a vehicle, we show how established techniques for CHC program transformation and abstract interpretation can be exploited for the purpose of non-termination analysis. NTHORN is comparable in power to the state-of-the-art non-termination analysis tools, as measured on standard competition benchmark suites (consisting of integer manipulating programs), while typically solving problems an order of magnitude faster.

1 Introduction

Inference of preconditions for Non-Termination (NT) is of interest in program analysis, debugging and verification. For some systems, the possibility of non-termination is a bug. For other systems, premature termination is unwanted, so that non-termination becomes a safety property.

Non-termination is an archetypal undecidable problem. Assume P ranges over the set of programs expressible in some Turing complete language, and S ranges over (non-empty) sets of inputs to P. Then the problem of whether P fails to terminate on every $s \in S$ is undecidable, and not semi-decidable. This is true even when S is restricted to being a *finite* non-empty set. Moreover, a proof that P *terminates* on every element of some set S tells us nothing about P's behaviour on (subsets of) S's complement, and in particular it tells us nothing about non-termination. Obviously, absence of a proof of termination is no proof of the absence of termination.

Inferring sufficient conditions for NT is not always possible even for non-terminating programs. For instance, if the variable i ranges over $\mathbb{Z}$, the program `while(i ≥ 0) i = nondet()` can be shown non-terminating by choosing always a *non-negative* value for i (*demonic non-determinism*), but no condition on the

© Springer Nature Switzerland AG 2021
R. Calinescu and C. S. Păsăreanu (Eds.): SEFM 2021, LNCS 13085, pp. 383–402, 2021.
https://doi.org/10.1007/978-3-030-92124-8_22

```
int main(int a, int b) {
    if (b ≥ 100) b = b − 100;
    else b = 100 − b;
    if (b ≠ 0)
    //reachability query
    while (a ≥ 1)
        a = 2a + b; b = b − 1;
        assume(a ≥ 1);
    //reachability query
    return 0;
}
```

c_1. $\text{init}(a, b) \leftarrow true$.
c_2. $\text{if}(a, b − 100) \leftarrow b \geq 100, \text{init}(a, b)$.
c_3. $\text{if}(a, 100 − b) \leftarrow b \leq 99, \text{init}(a, b)$.
c_4. $\text{wh}(a, b) \leftarrow b \neq 0, \text{if}(a, b)$.
c_8. $\text{en} \leftarrow b \neq 0, \text{if}(a, b)$.
c_5. $\text{wh}(a', b − 1) \leftarrow a \geq 1, a' = 2a + b,$
                    $a' \geq 1, \text{wh}(a, b)$.
c_6. $\text{ret} \leftarrow a \leq 0, \text{wh}(a, b)$.
c_9. $\text{ex} \leftarrow a \leq 0, \text{wh}(a, b)$.
c_7. $\text{ret} \leftarrow b = 0, \text{if}(a, b)$.

Fig. 1. Original program (left) and CHC encoding of its reachable states (right)

input i (apart from the trivial *false*) is sufficient to ensure non-termination. Namely, the *loop* iteration does not depend on the initial value of i, only on non-deterministic assignments within the loop.

A central tool for proving non-termination is the notion of *recurrence set* [24], a set of runtime states from which flow of control cannot escape. The non-termination problem is complementary to proving termination; but while a safety violation can be witnessed by a finite trace, a failure to terminate has no such witness. Instead, a witness to non-termination is a path from an initial state to a recurrence set. So we are interested in finding some conditions on the initial state that ensure that such a path occurs.

Although finding preconditions for non-termination is a fundamental problem, it has received far less attention than other termination and non-termination problems (the work of Le et al. [32] is a notable exception). Our approach to the problem is inspired by Chen et al. [10] who reduce the problem to proving safety using a sequence of *reachability queries*. Let *bad states* be those that exit the program (or loop) under consideration, and *good states* those that get stuck in it. Then the problem is to infer preconditions that ensure all executions stay within *good states*. We achieve this in two steps: (i) compute a *necessary* precondition from the *bad states*, whose complement is a potential candidate for non-termination and (ii) refine the candidate with a *sufficient* precondition from the states that enter the program (loop). Our method is potentially applicable to large code bases, as it rests on relatively cheap program analysis and transformation. To our knowledge, the combination of necessary and sufficient precondition reasoning has not previously been applied to the task.

Before we present the approach formally, let us consider the example in Fig. 1 (left), a modified version of a program studied by Le et al. [32]. Assume the variables range over the full set $\mathbb{Z}$ of integers. Then the program fails to terminate if the input satisfies $(b > 100 \land a \geq 1) \lor (b < 100 \land a \geq 1)$ (equivalently $b \neq 100 \land a \geq 1$). This is because a and b are always positive when entering the loop, and the loop condition $a \geq 1$ is always maintained, as a increases at a higher rate than b decreases. Automatic derivation of these preconditions is challenging for at least three reasons:

(i) The desired result is a disjunction of linear constraints—so we need the ability to express disjunctive information.
(ii) Abstract interpretation working forward or backward from the goal such as $(a \leq 0)$ derives *top* as invariant for the loop. That is, without a more sophisticated approach, we lose critical information about a and b.
(iii) We use over- and under-approximations to obtain sound and precise results, since the precondition must ensure that all traces enter the loop but none exit. While the first part (*all traces enter the loop*) requires under-approximation, the second part (*none exit*) can be achieved by negating an over-approximation that exits the loop.

We address Challenge (i) via partial evaluation or control flow refinement, creating a finite number of versions of each predicate—this is essential for deriving disjunctive invariants.

Challenge (ii) is addressed via forward and backward abstract interpretation, together with constraint specialisation. Challenge (iii) is addressed by refining over-approximations with under-approximations (Sect. 4).

While our approach is inspired by the ideas behind HIPTNT+ [32], it rests entirely on simpler methods from transformation-based program analysis of Constrained Horn Clauses: control flow refinement via *partial evaluation* [17], *constraint specialisation* [27], and *clause splitting* [19]. We make these contributions:

- We reduce the problem of precondition inference for non-termination to precondition inference for safety using a sequence of *reachability queries* inspired by the work of Chen et al. [10], which reduces proving non-termination to proving safety.
- We present an enhanced modular algorithm that combines under- and over-approximation techniques based on abstract interpretation and program transformation to derive sound and precise preconditions. It includes a novel mechanism of deriving a more general precondition through iterative refinement, which comes with refined termination criteria (Sect. 4).
- Our method uniformly handles non-linear clauses (arising from modelling function calls, recursion, and nested loops) over linear integer arithmetic.
- A proof of concept is implemented in the tool NTHORN, and we present experiments which show that our prototype implementation is competitive with state-of-the-art tools for automated proof of non-termination (Sect. 5).

2 CHCs, Recurrence Sets and Preconditions

We represent a program as a set of Constrained Horn clauses (CHCs). This is convenient for representing imperative programs and properties such as *reachability queries* in a uniform way. Analysis of the program and its properties is then done by analysing the corresponding CHCs. The translation of imperative programs to CHCs is standard [16,23,25,36] so we omit the details. From here on, by 'program' we mean a program's CHC encoding, unless otherwise stated.

Constrained Horn Clauses (CHCs). An *atom* is a formula $p(\mathbf{x})$ with p a predicate symbol and $\mathbf{x}$ a tuple of arguments. A CHC is a first-order formula written $p_0(\mathbf{x}_0) \leftarrow \varphi, p_1(\mathbf{x}_1), \ldots, p_k(\mathbf{x}_k)$, with φ a finite conjunction of quantifier-free *constraints* on variables $\mathbf{x}_i$ wrt. some constraint theory $\mathbb{T}$, and $p_i(\mathbf{x}_i)$ are atoms. A clause $p_0(\mathbf{x}_0) \leftarrow \varphi_1 \vee \varphi_2, \beta$ with a disjunctive constraint is rewritten as $p_0(\mathbf{x}_0) \leftarrow \varphi_1, \beta$ and $p_0(\mathbf{x}_0) \leftarrow \varphi_2, \beta$. A *constrained fact* is a clause of the form $p_0(\mathbf{x}_0) \leftarrow \varphi$, where φ is a constraint. A clause is *linear* if $k \leq 1$, otherwise *non-linear*. A *program* is linear if all of its clauses are linear.

Given a clause set P, we assign a unique identifier to each clause in P. Further, we assume the theory $\mathbb{T}$ is equipped with a decision procedure and a projection operator, and that it is closed under negation. The notation $\varphi|_V$ represents the constraint formula φ projected onto variable set V. $\varphi \models_{\mathbb{T}} \psi$ (or equivalently $\models_{\mathbb{T}} \varphi \Rightarrow \psi$) says that φ entails ψ over $\mathbb{T}$. We write $P \vdash_{\mathbb{T}} A$ when an atom A is derivable from program P wrt. an axiomatisation of $\mathbb{T}$. We omit the subscript $\mathbb{T}$ when it is clear from the context.

CHC Encoding. Figure 1 (right) shows the CHC representation of the example, encoding the reachable states. The clause c_1 specifies the *initial states* of the program via the predicate *init* which is always reachable. Similarly, c_2 and c_3 encode the reachability of the second *if* condition via the predicate *if*. Clauses c_4 and c_5 encode the reachability of the *while* loop via the predicate *wh*. Clause c_4 states that the loop is reachable if *if* is reachable, while c_5 states that the loop is (re-)reachable from the end of its own body (recursive case). Clauses c_6 and c_7 encode the return from the program. Clause c_6 states that the program terminates if $\mathbf{a} < 0$ upon loop exit, while clause c_7 states that the program terminates when $\mathbf{b} = 0$ and the control does not satisfy the condition of the second *if*. The coloured clauses are not part of the program, but are added to aid the analysis. We employ two *special predicates* en and ex which respectively encode the states entering the loop and exiting the loop or the program. Note that multiple clauses for these predicates are possible given multiple loop entries/exits.

Definition 1 (Initial clauses and nodes). Let P be a program with a distinguished predicate p^I which we call the *initial predicate*. The *constrained facts* of the form $p^I(\mathbf{x}) \leftarrow \theta$ are the *initial clauses* of P. We extend the term "initial predicate" and use the symbol p^I to refer also to renamed versions of the initial predicate that arise during clause transformations.

For the program in Fig. 1, init is the initial predicate and $\mathrm{init}(\mathbf{a}, \mathbf{b}) \leftarrow true$ is the initial clause. We shall assume integer programs, that is, all variables take integer values. Let $\mathrm{val} : V \rightarrow \mathbb{Z}$ map variables to their values. We overload val to also map a tuple of variables to the tuple of their values.

A set of CHCs defines a *transition system*, defined as follows (in the following we shall freely interchange these concepts):

Definition 2 (Transition system). A transition system of a linear program P is a tuple $\mathcal{T} = (S, R, I)$, where

- $S = Pd \times 2^{\mathbb{Z}^{|V|}}$ is the set of states where Pd is the set of predicates of P (including *false*) and V is a finite set of program variables.
- $R \subseteq S \times S$ is a transition relation. There is a transition from $(p, \mathtt{val}(\mathbf{x}))$ to $(p', \mathtt{val}(\mathbf{x}'))$ labelled by c if there is a clause $p'(\mathbf{x}') \leftarrow \varphi \wedge p(\mathbf{x}) \in P$ with identifier c and if $\mathtt{val}(\mathbf{x}) \models \varphi$ then $\mathtt{val}(\mathbf{x}') \models \varphi$.
- $I \subseteq S$ is a set of initial states.

Non-termination and Recurrence Set. A transition system $\mathcal{T} = (S, R, I)$ is non-terminating iff there is an infinite sequence $s_0, s_1, s_2 \ldots$, of states, with $s_0 \in I$ and $(s_i, s_{i+1}) \in R$. Non-termination of a relation R is witnessed by the existence of an *(open) recurrence set* [24]: a non-empty set $\mathcal{G}$ of states such that (i) $\mathcal{G}$ contains an initial state and (ii) each $s \in \mathcal{G}$ has a successor in $\mathcal{G}$. A program is non-terminating iff its transition system contains a recurrence set [24].

Chen et al. [10] extend the notion to *closed recurrence set* which facilitates automation using established techniques like abstract interpretation or model checking. A *closed recurrence set* is an open recurrence set $\mathcal{G}$ with the additional property that, for each $s \in \mathcal{G}$, all of its successors are in $\mathcal{G}$. Our method relies on closed recurrence sets to automate the reasoning.

Preconditions. Given a transition system $\mathcal{T} = (S, R, I)$, we define functions $\mathsf{pre} : 2^S \to 2^S$, $\mathsf{post} : 2^S \to 2^S$ and $\widetilde{\mathsf{pre}} : 2^S \to 2^S$ as follows.

- $\mathsf{post}(S') = \{s' \in S \mid \exists s \in S' : (s, s') \in R\}$ returns the set of states having at least one of their predecessors in the set $S' \subseteq S$;
- $\mathsf{pre}(S') = \{s \in S \mid \exists s' \in S' : (s, s') \in R\}$ returns the set of states having at least one of their successors in the set $S' \subseteq S$;
- $\widetilde{\mathsf{pre}}(S') = \{s \in S \mid \forall s' \in S : (s, s') \in R \Rightarrow s' \in S'\}$ returns the set of states having all of their successors in the set $S' \subseteq S$.

With these functions, we can now state precondition inference problems.

Invariants. Given a transition system $\mathcal{T} = (S, R, I)$ and a set of initial states $S' \subseteq S$, the *invariant inference problem* consists of inferring the set of reachable states from S' as $\mathsf{inv}(\mathcal{T}, S') = \mathsf{lfp} \, \lambda X. \, S' \cup \mathsf{post}(X)$.

Necessary Preconditions. Given a transition system $\mathcal{T} = (S, R, I)$ and a *goal* set $S' \subseteq S$ of states, the *necessary precondition inference problem* consists of inferring the set of *initial states* as $\mathsf{nec\_pre}(\mathcal{T}, S') = \mathsf{lfp} \, \lambda X. \, S' \cup \mathsf{pre}(X)$, which guarantees that some of its executions will stay in S'.

Sufficient Preconditions. Given a transition system $\mathcal{T} = (S, R, I)$ and a *goal* set $S' \subseteq S$ of states, the *sufficient precondition inference problem* consists of inferring the set of *initial states* as $\mathsf{suf\_pre}(\mathcal{T}, S') = \mathsf{gfp} \, \lambda X. \, S' \cap \widetilde{\mathsf{pre}}(X)$, which guarantees that all of its executions will stay in S'.

Note that the functions inv, $\mathsf{nec\_pre}$ and $\mathsf{suf\_pre}$ are not computable in general. Therefore, approximations of these functions are computed instead, which provide "one-sided" guarantees. The state-of-the-art techniques for computing $\mathsf{nec\_pre}$ use over-approximations based on abstract interpretation [12] and are given in [2,3,13,30,37], while that for computing suf_pre use backward under-approximation or negation of some necessary preconditions [28,34,35,37]. In addition, these techniques can profitably be combined with CHC transformations such as [15,17,21,27] to enhance the precision of these analyses.

Example 1. Our approach derives preconditions as follows. First $\lambda_{en} = b \neq 100$ and $\lambda_{ex} = (b \geq 101 \wedge a \leq 0) \vee (b \leq 99 \wedge a \leq 0) \equiv a \leq 0 \wedge b \neq 100$ are found as necessary preconditions for the reachability of en and ex, resp. Now $\lambda = \lambda_{en} \wedge \neg\lambda_{ex} \equiv a \geq 1 \wedge b \neq 100$ represents the initial states that might reach the loop entry but not the loop exit. We consider λ a candidate for sufficient precondition, using that to strengthen the initial clause to $init(a,b) \leftarrow a \geq 1 \wedge b \neq 100$. Then using backward under-approximation [34] from the goal en, we derive $a \geq 1 \wedge b \neq 100$ as a sufficient precondition for the reachability of en—which happens to be the optimal precondition for non-termination in this case. If we just used under-approximations without strengthening the initial clauses, we would obtained only $a \geq 1 \wedge b > 100$ or $a \geq 1 \wedge b < 100$, and not both. □

3   CHC Transformations and Their Roles in Non-termination Analysis

We now summarise common CHC transformations that we use, such as partial evaluation, constraint specialisation and clauses splitting. We highlight their role in non-termination analysis. They are *goal preserving* transformations (or *specialisations*): given a program P and a goal A, the transformation of P wrt. to the goal A yields another program P' such that $P \vdash_T A$ *iff* $P' \vdash_T A$. In our setting, the goals are en and ex. Informally, we produce a specialised version of P that preserves the derivations of en and ex, but not necessarily other goals.

1. Partial Evaluation (PE). PE of a set P of CHCs wrt. goal A produces a specialised version of P preserving only those derivations that are relevant for deriving A. It produces a polyvariant specialisation, which is essential for deriving disjunctive information. The partial evaluation algorithm utilised here is an instantiation of the algorithm given in [20], which is parameterised by an "unfolding rule" unfold$_P$ and an abstraction operation abstract$_\Psi$.

The unfolding rule unfold$_P$ takes a set S of constrained facts and "partially evaluates" each element of S, using the following unfolding rule. For each $(p(\mathbf{x}) \leftarrow \theta) \in S$, first construct the set of clauses $p(\mathbf{x}) \leftarrow \psi', \beta'$ where $p(\mathbf{x}) \leftarrow \psi, \beta$ is a clause in P, and ψ', β' is obtained by unfolding $\psi \wedge \theta, \beta$ by selecting atoms so long as they are deterministic (atoms defined by a single clause) and is not a call to a recursive predicate, and ψ' is satisfiable in $\mathbb{T}$. unfold$_P$ returns the set of constrained facts $q(\mathbf{y}) \leftarrow \psi'|_{\mathbf{y}}$ where $q(\mathbf{y})$ is an atom in β'.

Given an initial set S_0, the closure of the unfold$_P$ operation can be obtained as lfp $\lambda S. S_0 \cup$ unfold$_P(S)$. It is not computable in general; so instead we compute a set cfacts(S_0) = lfp $\lambda S. S_0 \cup$ abstract$_\Psi$(unfold$_P(S)$), where the abstraction

```
init_1(a, b) ← b ≥ 101.
init_2(a, b) ← b ≤ 99.
if_2(a, b) ← b ≥ 1, init_1(a, b + 100).
if_2(a, b) ← b ≥ 1, init_2(a, 100 − b).
wh_3(a, b) ← b ≥ 1, a ≤ 0, if_2(a, b).
ex ← a ≤ 0, wh_3(a, b).
wh_3(a, b) ← b ≤ −1, a ≤ 0, if_1(a, b).
```

```
init_1(a, b) ← a ≤ 0, b ≥ 101.
init_2(a, b) ← a ≤ 0, b ≤ 99.
if_2(a, b) ← a ≤ 0, b ≥ 1,
              init_1(a, b + 100).
if_2(a, b) ← a ≤ 0, b ≥ 1,
              init_2(a, 100 − b).
wh_3(a, b) ← a ≤ 0, b ≥ 1, if_2(a, b).
ex ← a ≤ 0, b ≥ 1, wh_3(a, b).
```

Fig. 2. PE of Fig. 1 wrt. ex (left) and its CS version (right) with inferred constraints underlined. The last clause on LHS is eliminated since its body is strengthened to *false*.

operation abstract$_\Psi$ performs property-based abstraction [23] wrt. a finite set of properties Ψ. A set of clauses is then generated by applying unfold$_P$ to each cfacts(S_0) and renaming the predicates in the resulting clauses according to the different versions produced by abstract$_\Psi$. We refer to [21] for more details.

2. Constraint Specialisation (CS). A CS of P wrt. goal A and set Ψ of properties [27] is a transformation in which each clause $(p(\mathbf{x}) \leftarrow \varphi, \beta) \in P$ is replaced by $p(\mathbf{x}) \leftarrow \varphi, \underline{\psi}, \beta$ (the difference from the original underlined), where $(p(\mathbf{x}) \leftarrow \psi) \in \Psi$, such that the resulting set of clauses preserves the derivation of A. As a result, all paths that are irrelevant for deriving A can be eliminated.

Example 2 (Continued from Example 1). The program in Fig. 2 (left) is obtained by PE of Fig. 1 wrt. ex. Observe that the recursive clause wh is effectively eliminated, as it cannot contribute to a derivation of ex. The constraint in the initial clauses $b \geq 101 \vee b \leq 99 \equiv b \neq 100$ is a necessary precondition for the reachability of ex. This is further strengthened to $(a \leq 0 \wedge b \geq 101) \vee (a \leq 0 \wedge b \leq 99) \equiv a \leq 0 \wedge b \neq 100$ with constraint specialisation wrt. ex to Fig. 2 (left), which propagates $a \leq 0$ from the goal ex and $b \geq 101 \vee b \leq 99$ from the constrained facts to other clauses, resulting in the program on the right. Similarly, we obtain $b \neq 100$ as a necessary precondition for the reachability of en. □

3. Clause Splitting. Given a clause $(p(\mathbf{x}) \leftarrow \varphi, \beta) \in P$ and a set Ψ of properties, clause splitting replaces the clause by $p(\mathbf{x}) \leftarrow \varphi, \underline{\psi}, \beta$ and $p(\mathbf{x}) \leftarrow \varphi, \underline{\neg\psi}, \beta$, producing P' (new constraints are underlined), where $(p(\mathbf{x}) \leftarrow \psi) \in \Psi$. This embodies case splits, allowing case-based reasoning. Fioravanti et al. [19] use a related technique for splitting clauses to achieve deterministic programs. Unlike the previous transformations, it is goal independent, that is, for all atoms A of P, $P \vdash_T A$ iff $P' \vdash_T A$.

Common to these transformations is the set Ψ of properties, which determine the quality of the resulting clauses. Soundness of CS also depends on the choice of Ψ. Though the above program transformation techniques are generic for CHCs and are taken from the literature, application or program specific choices of Ψ that we describe next make them surprisingly effective in practice. In addition

$$\left\{\begin{array}{l} \mathsf{p(a,b)} \leftarrow \mathsf{a = b}. \ \mathsf{p(a,b)} \leftarrow \mathsf{a > 0}. \\ \mathsf{p(a,b)} \leftarrow \mathsf{a > b}. \\ \mathsf{p(a,b)} \leftarrow \mathsf{b > a}. \end{array}\right\}$$

$$\overline{\begin{array}{l} \mathsf{ex} \leftarrow \mathsf{b > a}, \mathsf{p_1(a,b)}. \\ \mathsf{p_1(a,b)} \leftarrow \mathit{false}. \end{array}}$$

$$\left\{\begin{array}{l} \mathsf{p(a,b)} \leftarrow \mathsf{a = b}. \\ \mathsf{p(a,b)} \leftarrow \mathsf{a > b}. \end{array}\right\}$$

$$\overline{\begin{array}{l} \mathsf{p(a,b)} \leftarrow \mathsf{a = b}. \\ \mathsf{p(a+b,b)} \leftarrow \mathsf{a > 0}, \mathsf{p(a,b)}. \\ \mathsf{ex} \leftarrow \mathsf{a < b}, \mathsf{p(a,b)}. \end{array}}$$

Fig. 4. PE of Fig. 3 wrt. **ex**; respective Ψs are shown in upper part

to this, our contribution is to put these transformation together and apply them for inferring preconditions for NT, which has not been considered before.

We now discuss the specific choices we make for each of the transformations and illustrate the differences with other choices using the synthetic but representative example shown in Fig. 3.

$$\begin{array}{l} c_1. \ \mathsf{p(a,b)} \leftarrow \mathsf{a = b}. \\ c_2. \ \mathsf{p(a+b,b)} \leftarrow \mathsf{a > 0}, \mathsf{p(a,b)}. \\ c_3. \ \mathsf{ex} \leftarrow \mathsf{a < b}, \mathsf{p(a,b)}. \end{array}$$

Fig. 3. Synthetic example

For PE. The set Ψ contains the following constrained facts, generated from each clause $p(\mathbf{x}) \leftarrow \varphi, p_1(\mathbf{x_1}), \ldots, p_n(\mathbf{x_n}) \in P$.

- $p(\mathbf{x}) \leftarrow \varphi|_{\mathbf{x}}$ and for each $z \in \mathbf{x}$, $p(\mathbf{x}) \leftarrow \varphi|_{\{z\}}$
- for $1 \leq i \leq n$, $p_i(\mathbf{x_i}) \leftarrow \varphi|_{\mathbf{x_i}}$ and for each $z \in \mathbf{x_i}$, $p_i(\mathbf{x_i}) \leftarrow \varphi|_{\{z\}}$.

The effect of property-based abstraction using this choice for Ψ is to create a finite number (at most $2^{|\Psi|}$) of versions of a predicate for different call contexts and answer constraints. This choice of Ψ, *obtained syntactically from the program*, has been found to provide a good balance of speed and precision.

Example 3. Figure 4 shows PE programs for the program P in Fig. 3 wrt. **ex** with two different choices of the set of properties Ψ. Ψ in Fig. 4 (left) are computed as described above, while on the right are computed as follows: $\Psi = \bigcup_{(p(\mathbf{x}) \leftarrow \varphi, B) \in P} \{p(\mathbf{x}) \leftarrow \varphi|_{\mathbf{x}}\}$. The purpose here is to show that the choice of Ψ is important in getting a right specialisation. The program on the left is an empty program since there is a vacuous base case ($p_1(\mathsf{a,b}) \leftarrow \mathit{false}$), while the program on the right is identical to the original (no specialisation was performed). □

For CS. The properties Ψ have to be invariants for the program to produce sound transformation. They can be obtained e.g., via forward (from the constrained facts) or backward (from the goal) abstract interpretation or their combination [3]. In our case, they are obtained from forward abstract interpretation of the query-answer transformed program [27]. Ψ thus obtained *analysing the program* produces sound transformation, which is also found to be precise.

Example 4. Forward analysis of the program in Fig. 3 yields $\mathsf{p(a,b)} \leftarrow \mathsf{a \geq b}$ as invariant for $\mathsf{p(a,b)}$. This is because (i) if c_2 is not taken then we have

$a = b$ from c_1 and obviously $a \geq b$ holds, (ii) if c_2 is taken then $a > 0$ is maintained since a is incremented by b in each iteration and we initially had $a = b$. Since b is not modified in c_2, $a \geq b$ holds. We now use $\Psi = \{p(a, b) \leftarrow a \geq b\}$ to specialise the program in Fig. 3 wrt. ex, obtaining the clauses c_1, $p(b + c, b) \leftarrow a > 0, a \geq b, p(c, b)$ and $ex \leftarrow a < b, a \geq b, p(a, b)$. Note that the last clause is trivially satisfied. Instead of applying forward or backward analysis in isolation, applying forward-backward analysis will immediately detect that $p(a, b) \leftarrow false$, and the subsequent specialisation using the result yields an empty program.   □

For Clause Splitting. We describe some heuristics specific to *(non-)termination analysis*, requiring separation of terminating and non-terminating computations. The targets are recursive clauses (loops) $p(\mathbf{x}') \leftarrow \varphi, p(\mathbf{x})$. (i) Given a loop, a *potential ranking function* for the loop is an expression $e(\mathbf{x})$ over variables $\mathbf{x}$ which is *non-negative* (bounded from below) but not necessarily *decreasing* from $p(\mathbf{x})$ to $p(\mathbf{x}')$. In this case, we choose the property $\{p(\mathbf{x}) \leftarrow e(\mathbf{x}) > e(\mathbf{x}')\}$ (see Example 5). (ii) The property $\{p(\mathbf{x}) \leftarrow x \geq 0 \mid x \in \mathbf{x}, \models_{\mathbb{T}} \varphi \wedge x \geq 0\}$ is useful when we have non-deterministic branches or assignments; but care needs to be taken to control the blow-up of clauses.

Example 5. Taking $p(a, b) \leftarrow a = b$ to be the initial clause of the program in Fig. 3, the program does not terminate; e.g., for input $a = 1, b = 1$. Below we apply clause splitting which reveals which clause causes non-termination. The expression a is a potential ranking function for the loop, as it is non-negative and not necessarily decreasing. We derive $\Psi = \{p(a, b) \leftarrow a + b < a\}$. Now splitting c_2 with Ψ yields c_{2a}: $p(a + b, b) \leftarrow a > 0, \underline{b \leq 0}, p(a, b)$ and c_{2b}: $p(a + b, b) \leftarrow a > 0, \underline{b \geq 0}, p(a, b)$ (the new constraints are underlined). Such a splitting guarantees that every infinite run of the program must use c_{2b} as suffix. This information can be exploited by (non-)termination analysers.   □

4   An Algorithm for Conditional Non-termination

We now present an algorithm for inferring sufficient preconditions for non-termination. The main method is Algorithm 1. As a program can only get stuck in loops or recursive code, and the translation to CHCs replaces loops with recursion, the analysis focuses on the recursive strongly connected components (SCCs) in the CHC dependency graph. As the first step, we compute the SCCs of the input set P of CHCs. Each component is a set of (non-constraint) predicates, which is either non-recursive or a set of (possibly mutually) recursive predicates. The algorithm for computing SCCs returns the components in topologically sorted order $S_1, \ldots, S_n$, such that for each S_i, no predicate in S_i depends on any predicate in S_j where $j > i$. Then it annotates the program with appropriate *reachability queries* and computes a sufficient precondition for each annotated program using Algorithm 2 in a modular way. These preconditions are combined disjunctively to yield the overall result. The function annotate_program(P, C) inserts two sets of clauses to P given an SCC C as follows.

$$\{\text{en} \leftarrow \varphi|_{\text{vars}(\beta)}, \beta \mid (H \leftarrow \varphi, \beta) \in P, \text{pred}(H) \in C, \forall a \ (a \in \text{pred}(\beta) \Rightarrow a \notin C)\}$$
$$\cup \{\text{ex} \leftarrow \varphi|_{\text{vars}(\beta)}, \beta \mid (H \leftarrow \varphi, \beta) \in P, \text{pred}(H) \notin C, \forall a \ (a \in \text{pred}(\beta) \Rightarrow a \in C)\}$$

where $\text{pred}(H)$ is the predicate symbols of H and $\text{pred}(\beta)$ is the set of predicate symbols in β. The special clauses for **en** encode the reachability of C in P while the clauses for **ex** encode the exit condition of C in P. We explore all SCCs with the aim of obtaining a more general precondition but for proving non-termination it suffices to find a *non-trivial* precondition for an SCC.

Example 6. For the program in Fig. 1, there is a single SCC, namely the one containing the predicate {wh}. The clauses c_8 and c_9 respectively encode the reachability of the entry and exit of this SCC.   □

Algorithm 2 takes as input and annotated program P (with clauses for **en** and **ex**); it returns a sufficient precondition for non-termination (a linear constraint over $\mathbb{T}$ in DNF). Recall that we derive preconditions in two steps: (i) compute a necessary precondition from the *bad states*, encoded by the predicate **ex**, whose complement is a potential candidate for non-termination and (ii) refine the candidate with a sufficient precondition from the states that enter the loop, encoded by the predicate **en**. Let us first focus on step (i), the generation of necessary preconditions, using backward over-approximating analysis. Since these conditions need to be negated to derive candidates, their precision is important. It is well known that program specialisations, possibly applied iteratively [28] can enhance (refine) precision of such analysis. A disadvantage of this is the blind refinement of states possibly exiting the loop without knowing its frontier with the states entering it. This misses opportunities to avoid redundant computation as well as to guide the refinement process at an early stage. We therefore choose to maintain two over-approximations, namely of the states entering the loop (λ_{en}) *and* of the states exiting it (λ_{ex}). We iteratively refine these (See Algorithm 2). This enables the use of over-approximating analyses which are more developed than their under-approximating counterparts. Further, step (ii) is only applied to strengthen the candidate $\lambda = \lambda_{\text{en}} \wedge \neg\lambda_{\text{ex}}$ to a sufficient condition. This is achieved by applying under-approximating analysis to replace_init(P, λ) instead of the original P, so as to retain refined initial condition λ derived from the analysis of step (i).

Definition 3 (replace_init(P, λ))). Let P be a program and λ a constraint over $\mathbb{T}$. The function replace_init returns clauses of P by replacing the initial clauses $\{(p^I(\mathbf{x}) \leftarrow \theta_i) \mid 1 \leq i \leq \overline{k}\}$ by $\{(p^I(\mathbf{x}) \leftarrow \lambda)\}$.

Algorithm 2. The variable σ_{nt} accumulates the result and is initialised to *false*. φ_{old} keeps track of the *initial states* that could reach both **en** and **ex**; it is initialised to *true* (*line 3*). The following operations are carried out within the *while* loop. The formulae λ_{en} and λ_{ex} (*line 5 and 6*) represent the set of initial states that can reach **en** and **ex**, resp., and are computed using the method nec_pre. The algorithm returns when (i) no initial state can reach **en** ($\lambda_{en} \equiv$ *false*) (*line 8*), or (ii) the initial states satisfying $\varphi_{new} = \lambda_{en} \wedge \lambda_{ex}$ that can reach

---

Algorithm 1. Inferring sufficient precondition for non-termination of a program

1: **Input**: A program P
2: **Output**: Sufficient precondition σ_{nt} for non-termination of P.
3: **Initialisation**: $\sigma_{nt} \leftarrow \textit{false}$;
4: $S_1, \ldots, S_n \leftarrow$ topologically sorted SCCs of P
5: **for** $i = 1 \ldots n$ **do**
6:      **if** (recursive S_i) **then**
7:          $P_{an} \leftarrow$ annotate_program(P, S_i);
8:          $\sigma_{nt} \leftarrow \sigma_{nt} \vee$ precond_scc(P_{an}) ▷ Algorithm 2
9: **return** σ_{nt}

Algorithm 2. precond_scc: Inferring sufficient precondition wrt. a SCC

1: **Input**: Program P annotated with clauses for **en** and **ex**
2: **Output**: Sufficient precondition σ_{nt} for NT.
3: **Initialisation**: $\sigma_{nt} \leftarrow \textit{false}$; $\varphi_{old} \leftarrow \textit{true}$;
4: **while** true **do**
5:      $\lambda_{en} \leftarrow$ nec_pre(P, en);
6:      $\lambda_{ex} \leftarrow$ nec_pre(P, ex);
7:      **if** $\lambda_{en} \equiv \textit{false}$ **then**   ▷ no state reaches **en**
8:          **return** σ_{nt}
9:      $\varphi_{new} \leftarrow \lambda_{en} \wedge \lambda_{ex}$;   ▷ states that *may* both reach **en** and **ex**
10:      $\lambda \leftarrow \lambda_{en} \wedge \neg\lambda_{ex}$;   ▷ states that *may* reach **en** but not **ex**
11:      $P_1 \leftarrow$ replace_init(P, λ);   ▷ Definition 3
12:      $\sigma_{en} \leftarrow$ suf_pre(P_1, en);   ▷ strengthen λ to sufficient condition
13:      $\sigma_{nt} \leftarrow \sigma_{nt} \vee \sigma_{en}$;
14:      **if** $\varphi_{new} \equiv \textit{false}$ or $\varphi_{old} \models_{\mathbb{T}} \varphi_{new}$ **then**
15:          ▷ λ_{en} may not reach **ex**, or states reaching both **en** and **ex** don't shrink.
16:          **return** σ_{nt}
17:      $\varphi_{old} \leftarrow \varphi_{new}$;
18:      $P \leftarrow$ constrain_init(P, φ_{new}) ▷ refine P, Definition 4

---

both **en** and **ex** amount to *false*, or the set of initial states does not shrink further from its previous value φ_{old} (*line 14*). The set of states captured by φ_{new} is an over-approximation. The algorithm aims to reduce the slack as much as possible, to be able to separate terminating traces from non-terminating ones. To this end it (i) constructs a revised program from P focusing only on the shared region and (ii) shrinks either of the regions $(\lambda_{en}, \lambda_{ex})$ via iterative specialisations. We construct the revised program as follows.

Definition 4 (constrain_init(P, φ)). Let P be a program and φ a constraint over $\mathbb{T}$. constrain_init returns the clauses of P by replacing the initial clause set $\{(p^I(\mathbf{x}) \leftarrow \theta_i) \mid 1 \leq i \leq k\}$ by the set $\{(p^I(\mathbf{x}) \leftarrow \varphi \wedge \theta_i) \mid 1 \leq i \leq k\}$.

Proposition 1. constrain_init(P, φ) is an under-approximation of P.

Proof (Sketch). $P_1 = $ constrain_init(P, φ) contains exactly the same clauses as P, except for the *initial clauses*, which are possibly constrained. Hence for all atoms A, if $P_1 \vdash_\mathbb{T} A$ then $P \vdash_\mathbb{T} A$. That is, P_1 is an under-approximation of P.

Since non-termination is preserved by under-approximation [10], we need to ensure that the precondition does as well. This is in fact the case given that these program only differ in their initial clauses. Thus, any initial state that definitely reaches **en** and stays in the loop of P_1 also does the same in P. Before formally stating this property, let us first define (in terms of CHCs) what it means for a program P to have φ as a sufficient precondition for NT.

Definition 5 (Sufficient precondition for CHCs). Let P be a program annotated with appropriate *reachability queries* (for **en** and **ex**) as described above and φ a constraint over $\mathbb{T}$. Let $P_1 = $ replace_init(P, φ). Then we say φ is a sufficient precondition for NT of P if $\varphi \rightarrow (P_1 \vdash_\mathbb{T}$ **en** $\wedge\ P_1 \not\vdash_\mathbb{T}$ **ex**).

Proposition 2 (Lifting sufficient conditions). If φ is a sufficient precondition for non-termination of constrain_init(P, σ) (for some σ) then it is also a sufficient precondition of P.

Proof (Sketch). Let $P_1 = $ constrain_init(P, σ). Since P_1 and P have identical clauses except for the *initial clauses*, replace_init(P_1, φ) and replace_init(P, φ) yield identical clauses. So φ is also a sufficient precondition of P (Definition 5). □

Note the initial states satisfying the formula $(\lambda_{en} \wedge \neg\lambda_{ex})$ may reach **en** but definitely not **ex**, so they are seen as potential candidates for non-termination. The candidates are then strengthened to sufficient preconditions (σ_{en}) using the method suf_pre (*line 12*). If $\sigma_{en} \equiv$ *false*, then either all traces of P_1 (*line 11*) are terminating or suf_pre loses precision. Observe that we use replace_init(P, λ) (computed from P and λ using Definition 3) where $\lambda = \lambda_{en} \wedge \neg\lambda_{ex}$ instead of P to limit our attention to those initial states that can reach **en**. If no termination criterion is satisfied, the algorithm repeats (*line 18*) with constrain_init(P, φ_{new}) (Definition 4) since the states that satisfy φ_{new} are the ones whose termination status is unknown so far. Note that the construction of constrain_init(P, φ_{new}) requires φ_{new} to be converted to DNF, which may blow up the number of resulting *initial clauses*, but in our experiments we have not observed that.

Soundness and Termination of the Algorithms. We now study some properties, including soundness and termination of the Algorithms 1 and 2.

All the components used in Algorithm 2 terminate, but the algorithm itself may not, owing to the fact that φ_{new} can be decreased indefinitely (the algorithm keeps refining). This is typical of algorithms for *undecidable* problems such as non-termination. So we want to ensure a weaker property, that is, of *progress*. Progress is made, in the sense that each iteration explores a strictly smaller set of initial states whose termination status are not yet known. We state this formally:

Proposition 3 (Progress and Termination of Algorithm 2). Algorithm 2 either terminates or progresses.

Proof (Sketch). By induction on the number of iteration of the *while* loop.

Progress. Let φ_{old} and φ_{new} be formulas characterising the set of initial states yet to be proven non-terminating at each successive iteration respectively. Note that the algorithm iterates only if $\varphi_{new} \models \varphi_{old}$ and $\varphi_{old} \not\models \varphi_{new}$, that is, if φ_{new} is strictly smaller than φ_{old}, in the set view.

Termination. Note that each individual operation in the loop, including nec_pre, which is computed using abstract interpretation and program transformations, terminate. The only condition under which the algorithm diverges is when φ_{new} is *strictly smaller* than φ_{old}; in this case the algorithm progresses. □

Observe that each iteration of Algorithm 2 computes a valid precondition for non-termination of P even when under-approximations are used (Proposition 2). The disjunctive combination of such preconditions is also a valid precondition for non-termination of P. Again, we state this as a proposition.

Proposition 4 (Composing Preconditions). Let $\varPhi$ be a set of formulas such that each $\varphi \in \varPhi$ is a sufficient precondition for non-termination of P. Then so is $\bigvee \varPhi$.

Proof (Sketch). $\bigvee \varPhi$ satisfies the condition of Definition 5. □

Proposition 5 (Soundness of Algorithm 2). Let P be a program. If Algorithm 2 returns σ for P, then σ is a sufficient precondition for non-termination of P.

Proof (sketch). This follows from Proposition 2 and 4, with Definition 5: At each iteration the algorithm computes a formula that satisfies the condition of Definition 5 (the formula is a sufficient precondition). Proposition 2 allows us to lift any such formula computed for constrain_init(P, φ) (for some φ) to P itself, and Proposition 4 allows us to disjunctively combine such formulas to a valid precondition for P. □

The program shown here does not terminate when $x \neq 0$. On input $x > 0$ it gets stuck in the first loop, on $x < 0$ in the second. Generally, a program P with n loops may get stuck in loops $l_1, \ldots, l_n$, resp., on input satisfying formulas $\varphi_1, \ldots, \varphi_n$. If each such φ_i is a sufficient precondition for non-termination of P, then so is $\bigvee_{i=1}^{n} \varphi_i$. Taken together, Proposition 4 and 5 ensure the correctness of Algorithm 1:

```
foo(int x){
   while(x > 0)
     x = x + 1
   while(x < 0)
     x = x - 1
}
```

Theorem 1 (Soundness of Algorithm 1). Let P be a program. If Algorithm 1 returns σ for P, then σ is a sufficient precondition for non-termination of P.

Corollary 1. If $\varphi \not\equiv false$ is a precondition for non-termination of a program P, then P is non-terminating.

Proof (Sketch). $\varphi \not\equiv false$ implies there is at least an input (satisfying φ) to P on which it does not terminate.   □

If Algorithm 1 returns *false* for P, then P's non-termination status is *unknown*.

5   Implementation and Experiments

Implementation. We implemented Algorithm 1 as a prototype tool, NtHorn, available from https://github.com/bishoksan/NtHorn.git. It is written in Ciao Prolog [8] and uses PPL [1] and Yices 2.2 [18] for constraint manipulation. While refinement of candidate preconditions to the sufficient ones can be done with a tool such as [34], currently the implementation uses a simpler approach, namely, the reachability of the respective *loop* entry from each candidate—using the *safety prover* Rahft [29]. This gives a proof of non-termination as well as some conditions on the initial states and is used in the experiments. NtHorn handles integer programs only (the classical setting for (non-)termination work [10]), but our techniques apply beyond integer arithmetic.

We rely on abstract interpretation and CHC transformations for inferring sound and precise *necessary preconditions*. In particular, our implementation performs forward and backward constraint propagation using the constraints derived from polyhedral abstraction [14] obtaining a specialised version of the program [27]. To enhance the precision of the analysis further, we apply a sequence of program transformations including control-flow refinement using partial evaluation [21], *clause splitting*, strengthening of initial clauses, and we iteratively refine necessary preconditions for entering and exiting a loop.

Experimental Setting. We evaluated the approach on benchmarks from the C_Integer category of TermComp'20 [38]. The benchmark suite consists of 335 programs with nondeterminism: 111 non-terminating, 223 terminating, and one (Collatz) for which termination is unknown. Evaluation was done on 111 *non-terminating* programs, ignoring the terminating ones, as NtHorn can only prove non-termination. These are typical loop programs (simple or nested) with branches. Some of these loops have non-deterministic conditions while others contain non-deterministic assignments. We used small-step encoding to translate them to CHCs, obtaining only linear clauses. We run several configurations of NtHorn, namely NtHorn(X) where X can be partial evaluation pe, constraint specialisation cs, clause splitting csp, or some combination. Then we compare against state-of-the-art (non)-termination tools that participated in this category: AProVE [22], iRankFinder [5], UltimateAutomizer [26] and Very-Max [31]. We used TermComp'20 versions of these tools. We add HipTNT+ [32] (http://loris-7.ddns.comp.nus.edu.sg/~project/hiptnt/plus/), as it shares with NtHorn's the ability to infer preconditions. We run several configurations of NtHorn to study the impact of different CHC transformations. Since we could not run iRankFinder due to some front-end issues, we took the evaluation results from StarExec [38].

Table 1. Experimental results on the TermComp'20 (`C_Integer`) suite.

Tool	Proved NT	Gave up	Avg. time (s)
APROVE	100	11	12.72
IRANKFINDER	93	18	27.00
ULTIMATEAUTOMIZER	83	28	10.94
VERYMAX	102	9	14.48
HIPTNT+	94	17	2.34
NTHORN(cs)	58	53	0.48
NTHORN(cs·pe)	94	17	0.62
NTHORN(cs·pe·csp)	98	13	0.86

Experiments were performed on a MacBook Pro, 2.7 GHz Intel Core i5 processor, 16 GB memory, running OS X 10.11.6. Timeout was 300 s (the competition standard) per instance. The results are shown in Table 1. The three last columns show, in order, the number of programs proved non-terminating, the number given up within 300 s or timeout, and the average time taken by all instances including the "gave up" instances. Among the tools, NTHORN and HIPTNT+ are the only tools capable of deriving a precondition. It would be interesting to compare the generality of the preconditions inferred by our tools. But we could not do so due to the difference in our (non-standard) output formats. So with these experiments, we seek to answer the following questions:

Q1. Will the proposed method allow us to derive non-termination preconditions (or prove non-termination) in practice?
Q2. How does it compare to state-of-the-art tools for proving non-termination?
Q3. What role do the CHC transformations play?

Results. The results show different profiles wrt. to solved instances and performance for the tools. APROVE (resp. VERYMAX), the category winner in 2020 (resp. 2019), solves two (resp. four) instances more than NTHORN, while the rest solve less. This shows a remarkable effectiveness of our particular combination of mostly off-the-shelf techniques. The configuration NTHORN(cs) solves only 58 instances, while NTHORN(cs·pe) solves 94. The best result is achieved with NTHORN(cs·pe·csp). We find that each component transformation has a positive impact. Not only can we solve more problems (at the cost of solving time), we also generate more general preconditions. The combination cs·pe·csp has been chosen based on experiments, but its effectiveness aligns with our intuition. Namely, csp derives new domain specific constraints that pe can take advantage of during polyvariant specialisation, and cs, which is based on abstract interpretation, greatly benefits from the resulting specialised form.

As for speed, NTHORN(cs·pe·csp) (from here on "NTHORN") is an order of magnitude faster than the alternatives, solving each case in less than a second, while giving up on 13 cases. The median time was 1 s, while the instance such as NO_04 with 5-level of nesting and Lcm resp. took 135 and 58 s and a few other took slightly more than a second. We believe the speed is due to abstract interpretation (which in this context is relatively efficient), together with the lightweight program transformation. Also, unlike other tools, NTHORN focuses on proving just non-termination. Among the 13 cases, NTHORN fails to handle LogMult and DoubleNeg because they involve non-linear operations. They are proved non-terminating only by IRANKFINDER. The cases Narrowing and NarrowKonv are shown non-terminating only by NTHORN, VERYMAX and HIPTNT+, while ChenFlurMukhopadhyay-SAS2012-Ex2.11 only by NTHORN and HIPTNT+. NTHORN could not generate preconditions for 4 programs. These programs contain non-deterministic assignments that affect loop conditions; it might be possible that sufficient preconditions do not exist for them, though they can be shown terminating, as discussed in Sect. 1.

In summary, the results answer Q1–Q3 positively. NTHORN can be used to derive preconditions for NT and is comparable in power to the leading non-termination analysis tools, when applied to integer programs. Notably, NTHORN solves problems several orders of magnitude faster than the state-of-the-art analyzers and CHC transformations play an important role in this.

A new non-termination prover, REVTERM [9] was published recently and has not been part of our tool comparison. Like NTHORN, it does not prove termination. The experimental evaluation [9] suggests that its precision (for non-termination) is on a par with that of VERYMAX, but obtained 2–3 times faster. Comparison data from the paper [9] are in agreement with what we have found, for both precision and performance (they use a timeout of 60 s, rather than 300, so the average running times reported are somewhat shorter.)

6 Related Work

There is a rich body of work on proving non-termination, e.g., [2,7,10,11,24, 31,32,39]. Most of these provers either provide a *stem* (a sequential part from entry to loop) and the *loop*, or some precondition from which there exists a non-terminating run as a witness to non-termination. But for some applications like web-servers, a sufficient precondition (under which no trace is finite) is more useful. To our knowledge, prior to NTHORN, HIPTNT+ [32] was the only tool able to infer sufficient conditions for non-termination. Le et al. [32] propose a specification logic and Hoare-style reasoning to infer sufficient preconditions for both termination and non-termination of programs and, unlike ours, can handle programs manipulating pointers. We infer preconditions for non-termination only, relying on reduction to precondition inference for safety. But our approach is considerably simpler, as we combine existing techniques, refined iteratively.

Many non-termination provers [22,24,26,39] search exhaustively for candidate *lassos* (simple while loops without branches), and attempt to prove non-termination by deriving a recurrence set using constraint solving [22,24,39] or automata based approaches [26]. An orthogonal approach [33] considers *lassos* with linear arithmetic and represents infinite runs as geometric series.

We exploit the notion of closed recurrence set [10] as it is useful not only for automation using a safety prover, but also for proving non-termination of non-deterministic programs and programs involving aperiodic non-termination. The method of Chen et al. [10] inserts appropriate reachability queries and uses a safety prover to eliminate terminating paths iteratively until it finds a program under-approximation and a closed recurrence set in it. The method is likely to diverge as there can be infinitely many terminating paths. Hence we use abstract interpretation to derive initial conditions that lead to the terminating paths. We negate the conditions to bar those paths. Similar to our approach, the method [31] (implemented in VeryMax [6]) searches for witnesses to non-termination in the form of quasi-invariants (sets of states that do not exit the loop once entered) whose reachability from initial states is checked using a safety prover. Where VeryMax infers such invariants using Max-SMT solving, we do it using abstract interpretation.

Chatterjee et al. [9] rely on syntactic program reversal (applicable only to *while* programs; corresponding to linear CHCs) to derive backward polynomial conjunctive invariants using off-the-shelf tools and prove NT. Our method is more generally applicable to programs with procedures and can also infer pre-conditions as disjunction of linear constraints. Unlike our method, theirs provides *relative completeness guarantees*, that is, it is guaranteed to find the proof of NT under certain conditions. Bakhirkin [2], as we do, uses forward and backward abstract interpretation to find potential recurrence sets whose reachability implies non-termination. The approach can be applied to heap manipulating programs but is limited to simple *while* program. Ben-Amram et al. [4] derive a recurrence set from a failed attempt to prove termination of *multi-phase* loops, while our approach is direct and only proves non-termination.

While the above methods target programs with linear arithmetic, Cook et al. [11] prove non-termination of programs with non-linear arithmetic and heap-based operations. The key is the notion of *live abstraction*, an abstraction heuristic that ensures that any abstract trace corresponding to a terminating concrete trace is also terminating. In other words, it does not introduce any non-termination and is a sound abstraction heuristic for non-termination. This allows over-approximating non-linear assignments and heap-based commands with non-deterministic linear assignments.

7 Concluding Remarks

We have presented a new approach to preconditions for non-termination. The problem is reduced to inference of preconditions for safety, via insertion of "reachability queries" in program loops. The reduction enables us to use existing tools and techniques for safety preconditions. A prototype implementation is competitive with the state-of-the-art tools for automated proof of non-termination.

NTHORN can only infer preconditions for non-termination and is limited to programs manipulating linear integer arithmetic, whose applicability is determined by the underlying tool for inferring preconditions for safety. In future, we plan to complement it with termination analysis as done in other tools and also extend to programs that manipulate structured data, a la Cook et al. [11].

Acknowledgements. We thank the three anonymous reviewers for their careful reading of an earlier version of the paper, and their constructive suggestions for how to improve it. Bishoksan Kafle has been partially funded by the Spanish Ministry of Research, Science and Innovation, grant MICINN PID2019-108528RB-C21 *ProCode* and Madrid P2018/TCS-4339 *BLOQUES-CM*.

References

1. Bagnara, R., Hill, P.M., Zaffanella, E.: The Parma Polyhedra Library. Sci. Comput. Program. **72**(1–2), 3–21 (2008). https://doi.org/10.1016/j.scico.2007.08.001
2. Bakhirkin, A.: Recurrent sets for non-termination and safety of programs. Ph.D. thesis, University of Leicester (2016)
3. Bakhirkin, A., Monniaux, D.: Combining forward and backward abstract interpretation of Horn clauses. In: Ranzato, F. (ed.) SAS 2017. LNCS, vol. 10422, pp. 23–45. Springer, Cham (2017). https://doi.org/10.1007/978-3-319-66706-5_2
4. Ben-Amram, A.M., Doménech, J.J., Genaim, S.: Multiphase-linear ranking functions and their relation to recurrent sets. In: Chang, B.-Y.E. (ed.) SAS 2019. LNCS, vol. 11822, pp. 459–480. Springer, Cham (2019). https://doi.org/10.1007/978-3-030-32304-2_22
5. Ben-Amram, A.M., Genaim, S.: Ranking functions for linear-constraint loops. J. ACM **61**(4), 26:1–26:55 (2014). https://doi.org/10.1145/2629488
6. Borralleras, C., Brockschmidt, M., Larraz, D., Oliveras, A., Rodríguez-Carbonell, E., Rubio, A.: Proving termination through conditional termination. In: Legay, A., Margaria, T. (eds.) TACAS 2017. LNCS, vol. 10205, pp. 99–117. Springer, Heidelberg (2017). https://doi.org/10.1007/978-3-662-54577-5_6
7. Brockschmidt, M., Ströder, T., Otto, C., Giesl, J.: Automated detection of non-termination and NullPointerExceptions for Java Bytecode. In: Beckert, B., Damiani, F., Gurov, D. (eds.) FoVeOOS 2011. LNCS, vol. 7421, pp. 123–141. Springer, Heidelberg (2012). https://doi.org/10.1007/978-3-642-31762-0_9
8. Bueno, F., Cabeza, D., Carro, M., Hermenegildo, M., López-García, P., Puebla, G.: The Ciao Prolog system: reference manual. Technical Report CLIP 3/97.1, UPM (1997). http://www.clip.dia.fi.upm.es/
9. Chatterjee, K., Goharshady, E.K., Novotný, P., Žikelić, Ð.: Proving non-termination by program reversal. In: Proceedings of PLDI 2021, pp. 1033–1048. ACM (2021)
10. Chen, H.-Y., Cook, B., Fuhs, C., Nimkar, K., O'Hearn, P.: Proving nontermination via safety. In: Ábrahám, E., Havelund, K. (eds.) TACAS 2014. LNCS, vol. 8413, pp. 156–171. Springer, Heidelberg (2014). https://doi.org/10.1007/978-3-642-54862-8_11
11. Cook, B., Fuhs, C., Nimkar, K., O'Hearn, P.W.: Disproving termination with over-approximation. In: Proceedings of FMCAD 2014, pp. 67–74. IEEE (2014). https://doi.org/10.1109/FMCAD.2014.6987597
12. Cousot, P., Cousot, R.: Abstract interpretation: a unified lattice model for static analysis of programs by construction or approximation of fixpoints. In: Proceedings of POPL 1977, pp. 238–252. ACM (1977). https://doi.org/10.1007/978-3-642-35873-9_10

13. Cousot, P., Cousot, R., Fähndrich, M., Logozzo, F.: Automatic inference of necessary preconditions. In: Giacobazzi, R., Berdine, J., Mastroeni, I. (eds.) VMCAI 2013. LNCS, vol. 7737, pp. 128–148. Springer, Heidelberg (2013). https://doi.org/10.1007/978-3-642-35873-9_10

14. Cousot, P., Halbwachs, N.: Automatic discovery of linear restraints among variables of a program. In: Proceedings of POPL 1978, pp 84–96. ACM (1978). https://doi.org/10.1145/512760.512770

15. De Angelis, E., Fioravanti, F., Pettorossi, A., Proietti, M.: Program verification via iterated specialization. Sci. Comput. Program. **95**, 149–175 (2014). https://doi.org/10.1016/j.scico.2014.05.017

16. De Angelis, E., Fioravanti, F., Pettorossi, A., Proietti, M.: Semantics-based generation of verification conditions via program specialization. Sci. Comput. Program. **147**, 78–108 (2017). https://doi.org/10.1016/j.scico.2016.11.002

17. Doménech, J.J., Gallagher, J.P., Genaim, S.: Control-flow refinement by partial evaluation, and its application to termination and cost analysis. Theory Pract. Log. Program. **19**(5–6), 990–1005 (2019). https://doi.org/10.1017/S1471068419000310

18. Dutertre, B.: Yices 2.2. In: Biere, A., Bloem, R. (eds.) Computer-Aided Verification, volume 8559 of LNCS, pp. 737–744. Springer, Cham (2014). https://doi.org/10.1007/978-3-319-41528-4

19. Fioravanti, F., Pettorossi, A., Proietti, M.: Specialization with clause splitting for deriving deterministic constraint logic programs. In: Proceedings of IEEE Conference Systems, Man and Cybernetics. IEEE Press (2002). https://doi.org/10.1109/ICSMC.2002.1167971

20. Gallagher, J.P.: Tutorial on specialisation of logic programs. In: PEPM'93: Proceedings of 1993 ACM SIGPLAN Symposium on Partial Evaluation and Semantics-Based Program Manipulation, pp. 88–98. ACM (1993). https://doi.org/10.1145/154630.154640

21. Gallagher, J.P.: Polyvariant program specialisation with property-based abstraction. In: Lisitsa, A., Nemytykh, A.P. (eds.) Proceedings of Seventh International Workshop on Verification and Program Transformation, volume 299 of EPTCS, pp. 34–48 (2019). https://doi.org/10.4204/EPTCS.299.6

22. Giesl, J., et al.: Proving termination of programs automatically with AProVE. In: Demri, S., Kapur, D., Weidenbach, C. (eds.) IJCAR 2014. LNCS (LNAI), vol. 8562, pp. 184–191. Springer, Cham (2014). https://doi.org/10.1007/978-3-319-08587-6_13

23. Grebenshchikov, S., Lopes, N.P., Popeea, C., Rybalchenko, A.: Synthesizing software verifiers from proof rules. In: Vitek, J., Lin, H., Tip, F. (eds.) Proceedings of PLDI 2012, pp. 405–416. ACM (2012). https://doi.org/10.1145/2254064.2254112

24. Gupta, A., Henzinger, T.A., Majumdar, R., Rybalchenko, A., Xu, R.: Proving nontermination. In: Proceedings of 35th ACM Symposium on Principles of Programming Languages, pp. 147–158. ACM (2008). https://doi.org/10.1145/1328438.1328459

25. Gurfinkel, A., Kahsai, T., Komuravelli, A., Navas, J.A.: The SeaHorn verification framework. In: Kroening, D., Păsăreanu, C.S. (eds.) CAV 2015. LNCS, vol. 9206, pp. 343–361. Springer, Cham (2015). https://doi.org/10.1007/978-3-319-21690-4_20

26. Heizmann, M., Hoenicke, J., Podelski, A.: Termination analysis by learning terminating programs. In: Biere, A., Bloem, R. (eds.) CAV 2014. LNCS, vol. 8559, pp. 797–813. Springer, Cham (2014). https://doi.org/10.1007/978-3-319-08867-9_53

27. Kafle, B., Gallagher, J.P.: Constraint specialisation in Horn clause verification. Sci. Comput. Program. **137**, 125–140 (2017). https://doi.org/10.1016/j.scico.2017.01.002

28. Kafle, B., Gallagher, J.P., Gange, G., Schachte, P., Søndergaard, H., Stuckey, P.J.: An iterative approach to precondition inference using constrained Horn clauses. Theory Pract. Log. Program. **18**, 553–570 (2018). https://doi.org/10.1017/S1471068418000091

29. Kafle, B., Gallagher, J.P., Morales, J.F.: RAHFT: a tool for verifying Horn clauses using abstract interpretation and finite tree automata. In: Chaudhuri, S., Farzan, A. (eds.) CAV 2016. LNCS, vol. 9779, pp. 261–268. Springer, Cham (2016). https://doi.org/10.1007/978-3-319-41528-4_14

30. Kafle, B., Gange, G., Schachte, P., Søndergaard, H., Stuckey, P.J.: Transformation-enabled precondition inference. Theory Pract. Log. Program. **21**(6) (2021)

31. Larraz, D., Nimkar, K., Oliveras, A., Rodríguez-Carbonell, E., Rubio, A.: Proving non-termination using max-SMT. In: Biere, A., Bloem, R. (eds.) CAV 2014. LNCS, vol. 8559, pp. 779–796. Springer, Cham (2014). https://doi.org/10.1007/978-3-319-08867-9_52

32. Le, T.C., Qin, S., Chin, W.-N.: Termination and non-termination specification inference. In: Grove, D., Blackburn, S.M. (eds.) Proceedings of PLDI 2015, pp. 489–498. ACM (2015). https://doi.org/10.1145/2737924.2737993

33. Leike, J., Heizmann, M.: Geometric nontermination arguments. In: Beyer, D., Huisman, M. (eds.) TACAS 2018. LNCS, vol. 10806, pp. 266–283. Springer, Cham (2018). https://doi.org/10.1007/978-3-319-89963-3_16

34. Miné, A.: Inferring sufficient conditions with backward polyhedral under-approximations. Electron. Notes Theor. Comp. Sci. **287**, 89–100 (2012). https://doi.org/10.1016/j.entcs.2012.09.009

35. Moy, Y.: Sufficient preconditions for modular assertion checking. In: Logozzo, F., Peled, D.A., Zuck, L.D. (eds.) VMCAI 2008. LNCS, vol. 4905, pp. 188–202. Springer, Heidelberg (2008). https://doi.org/10.1007/978-3-540-78163-9_18

36. Peralta, J.C., Gallagher, J.P., Sağlam, H.: Analysis of imperative programs through analysis of constraint logic programs. In: Levi, G. (ed.) SAS 1998. LNCS, vol. 1503, pp. 246–261. Springer, Heidelberg (1998). https://doi.org/10.1007/3-540-49727-7_15

37. Seghir, M.N., Schrammel, P.: Necessary and sufficient preconditions via eager abstraction. In: Garrigue, J. (ed.) APLAS 2014. LNCS, vol. 8858, pp. 236–254. Springer, Cham (2014). https://doi.org/10.1007/978-3-319-12736-1_13

38. Termination competition 2020: C Integer. https://termcomp.github.io/Y2020/job_41519.html. Accessed 1 June 2021

39. Velroyen, H., Rümmer, P.: Non-termination checking for imperative programs. In: Beckert, B., Hähnle, R. (eds.) TAP 2008. LNCS, vol. 4966, pp. 154–170. Springer, Heidelberg (2008). https://doi.org/10.1007/978-3-540-79124-9_11

A Denotational Semantics of Solidity in Isabelle/HOL

Diego Marmsoler and Achim D. Brucker(✉)

University of Exeter, Exeter, UK
{d.marmsoler,a.brucker}@exeter.ac.uk

Abstract. Smart contracts are programs, usually automating legal agreements such as financial transactions. Thus, bugs in smart contracts can lead to large financial losses. For example, an incorrectly initialized contract was the root cause of the Parity Wallet bug that made USD 280mil worth of Ether inaccessible. Ether is the cryptocurrency of the Ethereum blockchain that uses Solidity for expressing smart contracts.

In this paper, we address this problem by presenting an executable denotational semantics for Solidity in the interactive theorem prover Isabelle/HOL. This formal semantics builds the foundation of an interactive program verification environment for Solidity programs and allows for inspecting Solidity programs by (symbolic) execution. We combine the latter with grammar-based fuzzing to ensure that our formal semantics complies to the Solidity implementation on the Ethereum Blockchain. Finally, we demonstrate the formal verification of Solidity programs by two examples: constant folding and memory optimization.

Keywords: Solidity · Denotational semantics · Isabelle/HOL · Gas optimization

1 Introduction

An increasing number of businesses are adopting blockchain-based solutions. Notably, the market value of Bitcoin, most likely the first and most well-known blockchain-based cryptocurrency, passed USD 1 trillion in February 2021 [1]. While Bitcoin might be the most well-known application of a blockchain, it lacks features that applications outside of cryptocurrencies require and that make blockchain solutions attractive to businesses.

The Ethereum blockchain [40] is a feature-rich distributed computing platform that provides not only a cryptocurrency, called *Ether*: Ethereum also provides an immutable distributed data structure (the *blockchain*) on which distributed programs, called *smart contracts*, can be executed. Essentially, smart contracts are programs, usually automating legal agreements, e.g., financial transactions. To support such applications, Ethereum provides a dedicated account data structure on its blockchain that smart contracts can modify, i.e., transferring Ether between accounts. Thus, bugs in smart contracts can

© Springer Nature Switzerland AG 2021
R. Calinescu and C. S. Păsăreanu (Eds.): SEFM 2021, LNCS 13085, pp. 403–422, 2021.
https://doi.org/10.1007/978-3-030-92124-8_23

lead to large financial losses. For example, an incorrectly initialized contract was the root cause of the Parity Wallet bug that froze USD 280mil worth of Ether [32]. This risk of bugs being costly is already a big motivation for using formal verification techniques. The fact that smart contracts are deployed on the blockchain immutably, i.e., they cannot be updated or removed easily, makes it even more important to "get smart contracts right", before they are deployed on a blockchain for the very first time.

For implementing smart contracts, Ethereum provides *Solidity* [30], a Turing-complete, statically typed programming language that has been designed to look familiar to people knowing Java, C, or JavaScript. The following shows a simple (artificial) function of a smart contract in Solidity for withdrawing Ether:

```
1  function wd(uint256 n, address payable r) public returns(bool) {
2      if (n < address(this).balance) {
3          r.transfer(n);
4          return true;
5      }
6      return false;
7  }
```

The type system provides, e.g., numerous integer types of different sizes (e.g., uint256) and the Solidity programs can make use of different types of stores for data (e.g., storage and memory). While Solidity is designed to be a Turing-complete language, the gas model ensures termination. The reason for this is that executing Solidity operations costs *gas*, a tradeable commodity on the Ethereum blockchain. Gas does cost Ether and hence, programmers of smart contracts have an incentive to write highly optimized contracts whose execution consumes as little gas as possible. For example, the size of the integer types used can impact the amount of gas required for executing a contract. Similarly, different type of stores induce different gas costs. Thus, the authors of Solidity contracts try to optimize the costs of executing a contract. This desire for highly optimized contracts can conflict with the desire to write correct and secure contracts.

We address the problem of developing smart contracts in Solidity that are correct: we present an executable denotational semantics for Solidity in the interactive theorem prover Isabelle/HOL [28]. Our contributions are four-fold:

1. A formal semantics of (a subset of) Solidity as conservative embedding into Isabelle/HOL. We follow the LCF-approach [15] and do not use any axiomatic definitions and, hence, our semantics is consistent "by construction".
2. A grammar-based fuzzing framework that can automatically validate our formal semantics against the Ethereum blockchain. Thus, we can provide strong evidence that our formal semantics complies to the official implementation.
3. We use our formal semantics for building an integrated verification and symbolic execution environment for Solidity programs on top of Isabelle/HOL. For this, we developed domain-specific automated proof methods.
4. We showcase our verification approach by formally analyzing two optimization strategies from which we derive rules that can be used to optimize the gas consumption of Solidity programs while preserving their semantics.

Our approach combines an expressive logic, i.e., higher-order logic (HOL) within an interactive theorem prover with a testing framework allowing us to validate the formalization against the actual implementation. This combination enables us to quickly analyze the impact of changes to the semantics while ensuring formal consistency and compliance to the implementation. The ability to quickly assess changes in Solidity is important, as Solidity is a fast evolving language. The Solidity manual [30], e.g., states: "When deploying contracts, you should use the latest released version of Solidity. This is because breaking changes as well as new features and bug fixes are introduced regularly."

2 Semantics

In the following, we describe our denotational semantics for a subset of Solidity v0.5.16 [30].[1] The complete semantics is formalized in Isabelle/HOL [28]. The formalization consists of 1500 lines of Isabelle code.

Our subset supports the following features of Solidity:

- *Fixed-size integer types* of various lengths and corresponding arithmetic with support for overflows.
- *Domain-specific primitives*, such as money transfer or balance queries.
- *Different types of stores*, such as storage, memory, and stack.
- *Complex data types*, such as hash-maps and arrays.
- *Assignments with different semantics*, depending on the location of the involved data types.
- An extendable *gas model*.

Our formalization is based on higher-order logic using inductive datatypes [7]. To this end, we use **bold** font for types and *italics* for type constructors.

2.1 Value Types

Solidity supports four different basic data types, called *value types*:

$$\textbf{Types} \quad ::= \quad \textit{TBool} \mid \textit{TAddr} \mid \textit{TSInt} \ \textbf{Nat} \mid \textit{TUInt} \ \textbf{Nat}$$

TBool denotes boolean values and *TAddr* denotes addresses. Solidity also supports signed and unsigned integers from 8 to 256 bits in steps of 8. Thus, *TSInt b* and *TUInt b* denote signed and unsigned integers of 2^b bit size.

In Solidity, raw data is encoded in hexadecimal format, however, to simplify the computation of locations for reference types (as discussed in more detail in Sect. 2.2), we use strings to model raw data in our model. Thus, type **Valuetype** is actually just a synonym for type string and it is used to represent the data of value types in the store. In addition, we shall write $\lfloor v \rfloor$ and $\lceil v \rceil$ to convert the value v of a basic data type to and from a string representation, respectively.

Converting an integer to a corresponding bit representation can result in an overflow which needs to be considered. Thus, we define two functions *createSInt*

---

[1] This is the currently supported default version of the Truffle test framework.

and *createUInt* to convert an arbitrary number to a corresponding signed or unsigned integer representation of a certain size:

$$createSInt \colon \mathbf{Nat} \times \mathbf{Int} \to \mathbf{Valuetype}$$

$$createSInt(b, v) = \begin{cases} \lfloor ((v + 2^{b-1}) \bmod 2^b) - 2^{b-1} \rfloor & \text{if } v \geq 0 \\ \lfloor 2^{b-1} - ((2^{b-1} - v - 1) \bmod 2^b) - 1 \rfloor & \text{if } v < 0 \end{cases}$$

where $x \bmod y$ denotes the non-negative remainder when dividing x by y. The definition of *createUInt* is similar.

Essentially, the functions can be used to create a representation of a given number which fits into a certain bit size. For example, $createSInt(8, 200) = $ "-56" whereas $createUInt(8, 200) = $ "200".

We can then define functions to lift basic arithmetic and boolean operations to corresponding operations over signed and unsigned integers of various sizes. The operation *add*, for example, can be defined by the following equations using usual pattern-matching notation:

$$add \colon \mathbf{Types} \times \mathbf{Types} \times \mathbf{Valuetype} \times \mathbf{Valuetype} \to (\mathbf{Valuetype} \times \mathbf{Types})_{\bot}$$

$$add\,(TUInt(b_l), TUInt(b_r), v_l, v_r) = createU\,(max(b_l, b_r), \lceil v_l \rceil + \lceil v_r \rceil)$$

$$add\,(TSInt(b_l), TSInt(b_r), v_l, v_r) = createS\,(max(b_l, b_r), \lceil v_l \rceil + \lceil v_r \rceil)$$

$$add\,(TUInt(b_l), TSInt(b_r), v_l, v_r) = \begin{cases} createS\,(b_r, \lceil v_l \rceil + \lceil v_r \rceil) & \text{if } b_l < b_r \\ \bot & \text{if } b_l \geq b_r \end{cases}$$

$$add\,(TSInt(b_l), TUInt(b_r), v_l, v_r) = \begin{cases} createS\,(b_l, \lceil v_l \rceil + \lceil v_r \rceil) & \text{if } b_r < b_l \\ \bot & \text{if } b_r \geq b_l \end{cases}$$

where $createU(b, v) = (createUInt(b, v), TUInt(b))$, and

$\qquad createS(b, v) = (createSInt(b, v), TSInt(b))$.

According to the current specification of Solidity, adding two integers of the same type is always possible but results in a new integer of the size of the larger one. Adding integers of different type is only possible if the size of the signed integer is strictly greater than the one of the unsigned one, in which case the result is always a signed integer with the size of the signed one. Moreover, the result of adding two numbers might not fit into the corresponding result type in which case an overflow occurs.

Consider, e.g., the following two additions of an unsigned with a signed integer:

$$add(TUInt(8), TSInt(16), \text{"200"}, \text{"32600"}) = (\text{"} - 32736\text{"}, TSInt(16))$$

$$add(TUInt(16), TSInt(16), \text{"100"}, \text{"32700"}) = \bot$$

In the first case, $32600 + 200$ does not fit into the resulting 16-bit signed integer (which can only store numbers up to 32767) and thus we get an overflow. In the second case, we try to add two incompatible types which results in an error. Similar definitions can be provided for the remaining arithmetic and logical operators.

2.2 Stores and Reference Types

In Solidity, storage cells are addressed by hexadecimal numbers. Again, however, we use strings to model them to simplify computation of locations for reference types. Thus, type **Loc** denotes the type of strings and is used to represent storage locations. We can then model a general store for values of type v as a parametric data type:

$$\textbf{Store } v \quad ::= \quad (\textbf{Loc} \rightarrow v) \times \textbf{Nat}$$

It consists of a mapping to assign values to locations and in addition it holds a pointer to the next free location. We can then define function $access(l, s)$ to access the value at location l in store s and function $updateStore(l, v, s)$ to store value v at location l of store s. The definition of these functions is standard and thus not discussed further. However, the way Solidity computes storage locations for reference types is a bit special and thus worth a closer look. To this end, assume that a storage cell loc contains a reference type, such as a mapping. Then, the storage cell which contains the value of the entry for key k is computed by $keccak256$ ("k" + loc), where $keccak256$ denotes the Keccak hash function [8] and + denotes string concatenation.

The main objective of this approach is to obtain a unique storage cell for every element. The purpose of using the hash value is to deal with a limited amount of storage cells which are available in practice. In theory, collisions are possible when using a hash function, however, in practice, such collisions are very unlikely to happen and thus they may be neglected. Thus, in our model, the location of the storage cell which holds the value of an element ix of a reference type which is stored at location loc is obtained by concatenating ix with loc separated by a dot:

$$h(loc, \; ix) = ix + \text{"."} + loc$$

Types of Storage. Solidity has three different stores: stack, memory, and storage. The *stack* stores the values for variables which can either be concrete values (for value type variables) or pointers to either memory or storage (for reference type variables). Thus, a stack can be modelled as a store which can keep three different types of values:

$$\textbf{Stackvalue} ::= \textit{Value } \textbf{Valuetype} \mid \textit{Memptr } \textbf{Loc} \mid \textit{Stoptr } \textbf{Loc}$$
$$\textbf{Stack} \quad ::= \textbf{Store Stackvalue}$$

Solidity supports two additional stores *memory* and *storage* for storing the value of *reference types*. While memory supports only arrays, storage also supports mappings:

$$\textbf{MTypes} ::= \textit{MTValue } \textbf{Types} \mid \textit{MTArray } \textbf{Nat MTypes}$$
$$\textbf{STypes} ::= \textit{STValue } \textbf{Types} \mid \textit{STArray } \textbf{Nat STypes} \mid \textit{STMap } \textbf{Types STypes}$$

The internal organization of the two stores differs fundamentally: While memory uses pointer structures to organize the values of reference types, storage values are accessed directly by computing the corresponding location. Thus we model memory as a store which can keep two different types of values:

$$\text{\textbf{Memoryvalue}} ::= \textit{Value } \text{\textbf{Valuetype}} \mid \textit{Pointer } \text{\textbf{Loc}}$$
$$\text{\textbf{Memory}} ::= \text{\textbf{Store Memoryvalue}}$$

Storage, on the other hand is modeled as a simple store of value types:

$$\text{\textbf{Storage}} ::= \text{\textbf{Store Valuetype}}$$

Storage access is non-strict, which means that access to an undefined storage cell returns a default value. To this end, we first define a function $ival$: **Types** → **Valuetype** which returns a default value for each value type. Now, we can define a corresponding access function for storage:

$$accessStorage: \text{\textbf{Types}} \times \text{\textbf{Loc}} \times \text{\textbf{Storage}} \rightarrow \text{\textbf{Valuetype}}$$

$$accessStorage(t, loc, sto) = \begin{cases} v, & \text{if } v \neq \bot \\ ival(t), & \text{if } v = \bot \end{cases} \quad \text{where } v = access(loc, sto)$$

Copying of Reference Types. Often, we need to copy values from one type of store to another, i.e., we need different types of copy functions. To specify them, we use a higher-order function

$$iter : (\text{\textbf{Int}} \rightarrow a \rightarrow a) \rightarrow a \rightarrow \text{\textbf{Int}} \rightarrow a$$

such that $iter(f, x, v)$ executes function f on value v and the passes the outcome on to another execution of f until f was executed x times.

In the following we use $iter$ to define the function to copy from storage to memory:

$$cp_m^s: \text{\textbf{Loc}} \times \text{\textbf{Loc}} \times \text{\textbf{Int}} \times \text{\textbf{STypes}} \times \text{\textbf{Storage}} \times \text{\textbf{Memory}} \rightarrow \text{\textbf{Memory}}_\bot$$
$$cp_m^s(l_s, l_m, i, t, s, m) = iter(\lambda i', m'.\ cprec_m^s(h(l_s, \lfloor i' \rfloor), h(l_m, \lfloor i' \rfloor), t, s, m'), m, i)$$

where

$$cprec_m^s(l_s, l_m, STArray(i, t), s, m)$$
$$= iter\ (\lambda i', m'.\ cprec_m^s(h(l_s, \lfloor i' \rfloor), h(l_m, \lfloor i' \rfloor), t, s, m''), m'', i)$$
$$\text{where } m'' = updateStore(l_m, Pointer(l_m), m) \tag{1}$$
$$cprec_m^s(l_s, l_m, STValue(t), s, m) = updateStore(l_m, Value(v), m)$$
$$\text{where } v = accessStorage(t, l_s, s) \tag{2}$$
$$cprec_m^s(l_s, l_m, STMap(t, t'), s, m) = \bot \tag{3}$$

In Solidity, value types are just copied between stores which is reflected by Eq. (2). For reference types, however, the situation is different. Mappings can only be kept in storage and not in memory which is why a mapping is never copied from storage to memory, and we just return $\bot$ for this case (Eq. (3)).

Arrays, on the other hand, can be kept in both: storage and memory. As mentioned above, however, the way of storing them differs depending on the type of store: in storage, we just calculate the location of the elements of an array whereas in memory arrays are stored using a pointer structure. Thus, when copying arrays from storage to memory we need to create the corresponding pointer structure as shown by Eq. 1.

Our model contains similar functions to copy from memory to storage or storage to storage. Copying from memory to memory is not required since memory operations do not copy the data structure but rather just the pointer as discussed in more detail in Sect. 2.4). It also contains similar functions to copy from memory to storage or storage to storage. Copying from memory to memory is not required since memory operations do not copy the data structure but rather just the pointer (see Sect. 2.4).

State. Accounts are associated with an address in hexadecimal format. We model **Address** as strings and accounts as mappings from addresses to their balance:

$$\textbf{Accounts} ::= \ \textbf{Address} \rightarrow \textbf{Valuetype}$$

A state of a Solidity program consists of the balances of the accounts as well as the state of the different stores:

$$\textbf{State} ::= \ \textbf{Accounts} \times \textbf{Stack} \times \textbf{Memory} \times \textbf{Storage}$$

In the following we shall use $sck(s)$, $mem(s)$, $sto(s)$, $acc(s)$ to access the stack, memory, storage, and account of a state s. Moreover, we use $upSck(k,s)$, $upMem(m,s)$, $upSto(t,s)$, and $upAcc(a,s)$ to change stack, memory, storage, or account, of a state s to k, m, t, or a, respectively.

2.3 Expressions

Our subset of Solidity supports basic arithmetic and boolean expressions over signed and unsigned integers of various bit sizes:

$$\textbf{B} ::= 8 \mid 16 \mid \ldots \mid 256$$
$$\textbf{L} ::= \textit{Id } \textbf{S} \mid \textit{Ref } \textbf{S } [\textbf{E}]$$
$$\textbf{E} ::= \textit{Address } \textbf{S} \mid \textit{Balance } \textbf{S} \mid L \textbf{ L} \mid \textit{SInt } \textbf{B Int} \mid \textit{UInt } \textbf{B Int} \mid \textit{True} \mid \textit{False}$$
$$\mid \textbf{E} == \textbf{E} \mid \textbf{E} + \textbf{E} \mid \textbf{E} - \textbf{E} \mid \textbf{E} < \textbf{E} \mid \neg \textbf{E} \mid \textbf{E} \wedge \textbf{E} \mid \textbf{E} \vee \textbf{E}$$

where **S** denotes the type of strings, **Int** the type of integer symbols, and $[a]$ a list of elements of type a.

Environment. Expressions are always interpreted w.r.t. an environment which assigns types and values to variables. To this end, we introduce a new type **Identifier** (a synonym of type string) for variable names. Variables in Solidity can either be storage references or stack references which can again be pointers to either storage or memory. In addition, the environment also contains the address of the currently executing contract:

$$\textbf{Type} ::= \textit{Value } \textbf{Types} \mid \textit{Memory } \textbf{MTypes} \mid \textit{Storage } \textbf{STypes}$$
$$\textbf{Denvalue} ::= \textit{Stackloc } \textbf{Loc} \mid \textit{Storeloc } \textbf{Loc}$$
$$\textbf{Environment} ::= \textbf{Address} \times (\textbf{Identifier} \rightarrow \textbf{Type} \times \textbf{Denvalue})$$

Lookup Functions. To access the value of a reference type we define a function which looks up the corresponding value in memory:

$$\mathcal{M} \colon [\textbf{E}] \rightarrow \textbf{MTypes} \rightarrow \textbf{Loc} \rightarrow \textbf{Environment} \rightarrow \textbf{State} \rightarrow \textbf{Loc} \times \textbf{MTypes}_\perp$$

$$\mathcal{M}[\![x]\!]t \; l \; e \; s = \begin{cases} (h(l,v), t') & \text{if } lookup(x,t,e,s,t',v) \\ \perp & \text{otherwise} \end{cases}$$

$$\mathcal{M}[\![x\#xs]\!]t \; l \; e \; s = \begin{cases} \mathcal{M}[\![xs]\!]t' \; l' \; e \; s & \text{if } lookup(x,t,e,s,t',v) \\ & \wedge \; access(h(l,v), mem(s)) = Pointer(l') \\ \perp & \text{otherwise} \end{cases}$$

where $lookup(x,t,e,s,t',v) \iff \exists lg, t'' \colon t = MTArray(lg, t')$
$$\wedge \; \mathcal{E}[\![x]\!]e \; s = (Value(v), Value(t''))$$
$$\wedge \; less(t'', TUInt(256), v, \lfloor lg \rfloor) = (\textit{``True''}, TBool)$$

Since memory uses pointer structures, we need to access the memory in every iteration to look up the next location.

Let us assume that $t = MTArray(5, MTArray(6, MTValue(TBool)))$, and the memory of state s is $[\textit{``3.2''} \mapsto Pointer(\textit{``5''}), \textit{``4.5''} \mapsto Value(\textit{``True''})]$. Then,

$$\mathcal{M}[\![[UInt(8,3)]]\!]t \; \textit{``2''} \; e \; s = (\textit{``3.2''}, MTArray(6, MTValue(TBool))) \quad (4)$$
$$\mathcal{M}[\![[UInt(8,3), SInt(8,4)]]\!]t \; \textit{``2''} \; e \; s = (\textit{``4.5''}, MTValue(TBool)) \quad (5)$$
$$\mathcal{M}[\![[UInt(8,5)]]\!]t \; \textit{``2''} \; e \; s = \perp \quad (6)$$
$$\mathcal{M}[\![[UInt(8,2)]]\!]t \; \textit{``2''} \; e \; s = \perp \quad (7)$$

A similar function to $\mathcal{M}$ is defined to look up storage values with two notable differences:

- Since storage does not support pointer structures, we do not access the store while iterating through the list of selectors. Thus, the function always returns a storage location as long as we access indices within the range of the array (Eq. (7), for example would return a valid storage location).
- Since storage also supports mappings, the function can be used to look up also the value for mapping variables.

Using these functions we can then define two additional functions to look up the value or location of a variable:

$$\mathcal{R} \colon \textbf{L} \rightarrow \textbf{Environment} \rightarrow \textbf{State} \rightarrow \textbf{Stackvalue} \times \textbf{Type}_\perp$$
$$\mathcal{L} \colon \textbf{L} \rightarrow \textbf{Environment} \rightarrow \textbf{State} \rightarrow \textbf{LType} \times \textbf{Type}_\perp$$

with $\textbf{LType} ::= \textit{Stackloc } \textbf{Loc} \mid \textit{Memloc } \textbf{Loc} \mid \textit{Storeloc } \textbf{Loc}$

The definition of these functions is straightforward using the lookup functions discussed before and not discussed further here.

Semantics of Expressions. Finally we can define the semantic function for expressions.

$$\mathcal{E} : \mathbf{E} \to \mathbf{Environment} \to \mathbf{State} \to \mathbf{Stackvalue} \times \mathbf{Type}_{\perp}$$

The definition of the function mainly follows traditional denotational semantics definitions [34, 35] with the exception that we use the operators introduced in Sect. 2.1 to manipulate integers:

$$\mathcal{E}[\![SInt(b,n)]\!]e \ s = (Value(createSInt(b,n)), Value(TSInt(b)))$$

$$\mathcal{E}[\![x_1 + x_2]\!]e \ s = \begin{cases} (Value(v), Value(t)) & \text{if } \mathcal{E}[\![x_1]\!]e \ s = (Value(v_1), Value(t_1)) \\ & \wedge \ \mathcal{E}[\![x_2]\!]e \ s = (Value(v_2), Value(t_2)) \\ & \wedge \ add(t_1, t_2, v_1, v_2) = (v, t) \\ \perp & \text{otherwise} \end{cases}$$

2.4   Statements

So far, our subset of Solidity supports variable declarations with optional initialisation and basic programming language statements:

$$\mathbf{D} ::= \mathbf{S} \times \mathbf{Type} \times \mathbf{E}_{\perp}$$
$$\mathbf{C} ::= Skip \mid \mathbf{L} = \mathbf{E} \mid \mathbf{C} \ ; \ \mathbf{C} \mid Ite \ \mathbf{E} \ \mathbf{C} \ \mathbf{C} \mid While \ \mathbf{E} \ \mathbf{C} \mid Transfer \ \mathbf{S} \ \mathbf{E} \mid$$
$$Block \ \mathbf{D} \ \mathbf{C}$$

We can then define a semantic function for statements:

$$\mathcal{C} : \ \mathbf{C} \to \mathbf{Environment} \to \mathbf{State} \to \mathbf{Nat} \to (\mathbf{State} \times \mathbf{Nat})_{\perp}$$

The definition of it is mostly standard denotational semantics with some exceptions discussed in the following.

Gas. One interesting aspect of Solidity is that execution of statements is subject to fees, i.e., the execution consumes gas: if all gas is consumed, the execution terminates with an exception. Consequently, Solidity programs always terminate. The actual gas fees are computed on the level of the Ethereum byte code [39] and, moreover, are frequently updated. Thus, our Solidity formalization does not provide a built-in gas model trying to faithfully represent the actual gas model on the level of Ethereum bytecode: we only assume the existence of a generic cost function $costs : \mathbf{C} \times \mathbf{Environment} \times \mathbf{State} \to \mathbf{N}$ which provides the gas costs for executing a given statement. A separate gas function for expressions can be defined and used with the cost function for statements. Moreover, in our subset of Solidity, the while statement is the only program statement that does not terminate in all states. Therefore, we require:

$$0 < costs(While(ex, s), e, s') \tag{8}$$

This requirement is not a limitation, as the actual costs for any execution of a while loop will be positive [39, Appendix G]. While our cost model can, in principle, be used for proving upper or lower bounds for the gas consumption of a given contract, the usefulness of such a statement depends on how faithful the user-provided cost functions model the actual costs which may also depend on compiler optimizations.

We can now verify a general statement about the semantics, namely that it always terminates. Note that we model error states (e.g., failing transfers) using an explicit error type. This is a standard construction to model partial functions in HOL, which requires that all functions are total from a "logical perspective."

Theorem 1. $\mathcal{C}[\![c]\!]$ *e s g is always defined.*

Proof. The proof is a simple inductive argument over c using Eq. (8). □

Indeed, Isabelle automatically proves it for us and provides us with corresponding proof methods to support reasoning over $\mathcal{C}$.

Semantics of Assignments. Another particularity of Solidity is that the semantics of an assignment depends on the type of store to which the involved variables refer. Let us consider, for example, the case in which the right-hand side of an assignment evaluates to a value stored in memory:

$\mathcal{C}[\![v=x]\!]e\ s\ g$

$$= \begin{cases} (1a) & \textit{if } ex(g,x,e,s,p,i,t) \wedge \mathcal{L}[\![v]\!] \ s=(Stackloc(l),Memory(t')) \\ (2a) & \textit{if } ex(g,x,e,s,p,i,t) \wedge \mathcal{L}[\![v]\!] \ s=(Stackloc(l),Storage(t')) \\ & \wedge\ access(l,sck(s))=Stoptr(p') \wedge cp_s^m(p,p',i,t,mem(s),sto(s))=o \\ (3a) & \textit{if } ex(g,x,e,s,p,i,t) \wedge \mathcal{L}[\![v]\!] \ s=(Storeloc(l),t') \\ & \wedge\ cp_s^m(p,l,i,t,mem(s),sto(s))=o \\ (4a) & \textit{if } ex(g,x,e,s,p,i,t) \wedge \mathcal{L}[\![v]\!] \ s=(Memloc(l),t') \\ & \dots \end{cases}$$

where $ex(g,x,e,s,p,i,t) \Longleftrightarrow costs(v=x,e,s)<g$

$$\wedge\ \mathcal{E}[\![x]\!] \ s=(Memptr(p),Memory(MTArray(i,t)))$$

$$(1a)=(upSck(updateStore(l,Memptr(p),sck(s)),s),costs(v=x,e,s))$$

$$(2a,3a)=(upSto(o,s),costs(v=x,e,s))$$

$$(4a)=(upMem(updateStore(l,Pointer(p),mem(s)),s),costs(v=x,e,s))$$

In this case, the semantics of the assignment changes, depending on the $\mathcal{L}$-value of the left-hand side: If it is a pointer to memory (cases (1) and (4)), we just assign the pointer but if it is a reference to storage (cases (2) and (3)), we copy the whole structure to memory using the copy functions discussed in Sect. 2.2.

Transferring Money. Another aspect which sets Solidity apart from traditional programming languages is its support for features to transfer funds from one account to another. To this end, every contract is associated with an account and Solidity supports a command which can be used to transfer funds from it to another account:

$$\mathcal{C}[\![\mathit{Transfer}\ a\ x]\!]e\ s\ g = \begin{cases} (1b) & \textit{if}\ \mathit{costs}(\mathit{Transfer}(a,x),e,s) < g \\ & \wedge\ \mathcal{E}[\![x]\!]e\ s = (\mathit{Value}(v), \mathit{Value}(t)) \\ & \wedge\ \mathit{transfer}(\mathit{address}(e),a,t,v,\mathit{acc}(s)) = ac \\ \dots \end{cases}$$

where $(1b) = (upAcc(ac, s), costs(\mathit{Transfer}(a,x),e,s))$

$$\mathit{transfer}(s,d,t,v,ac) = \begin{cases} addB(d,t,v,ac') & \text{if}\ subB(s,t,v,ac) = ac' \\ \bot & \text{otherwise} \end{cases}$$

Here, $address(e)$ denotes the address of the contract's account, and $addB(a,t,v,ac)$ and $subB(a,t,v,ac)$ are functions to increase and decrease the balance of an address a of accounts ac by a certain amount v. Note that both functions use the corresponding add and sub functions for signed and unsigned integers discussed in Sect. 2.1. Moreover, $subB$ may also fail if an account has not enough funds in which case it evaluates to $\bot$.

3   Compliance to the Official Solidity Implementation

For ensuring that our formal semantics is a faithful representation of the official Solidity implementation, we provide a test framework that supports comparing the result of evaluating a Solidity program in our formal semantics to its execution on the Ethereum blockchain.

We use Isabelle's code generator to automatically generate a Solidity evaluator from our formal semantics. In our current implementation, we use Haskell as target platform for the code generator. Moreover, we need to provide a concrete cost function for computing the gas consumption (recall Sect. 2.4). In Isabelle, we can achieve this by instantiating a so-called locale [5] with a trivial implementation satisfying Eq. (8).

We then generate Solidity programs using a grammar-based fuzzer and compare the results of executing those programs on both the reference implementation of Solidity and our evaluator. The test framework is fully automated. Figure 1 shows the main steps of our test framework that we discuss in the following in more detail.

- **Generate Random Solidity Code.** The test framework generates a random Solidity program from a given grammar, using the grammar-based fuzzer Grammarinator [21]. To avoid the generation of programs which do not compile, the grammar needs to be strict to only accept programs which are type-correct. The grammar is given in the format used by ANTLR4 [31].

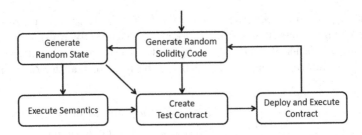

Fig. 1. Fuzzy testing Solidity smart contracts.

- **Generate Random State.** For each generated Solidity program, our testing framework generates a set of random input states. To this end, the script analyses the generated program and extracts the variables which occur in it. Based on the type of the variable, the script then generates random values for each variable.
- **Execute Semantics.** Before we can compute the output state with our semantics, we first need to transform the generated Solidity program to the abstract syntax which is accepted by the semantics. Finally, the abstract syntax of the program and the generated input state can be passed to the executable semantics, i.e., the evaluator automatically generated by Isabelle, to compute a corresponding output state.
- **Create Test Contract.** The generated Solidity program, together with the generated input state and the computed output state, is used to create a test contract for the Truffle testing framework [11]. Listing 1.1 shows parts of a generated contract, consisting of a single function which contains the generated Solidity program. The extracted storage variables are declared as contract variables whereas the extracted memory/stack variables are declared locally. Then, the variables are initialized according to the generated input state whereas the computed output state is used to create corresponding assertions for the Truffle framework.
- **Deploy and Execute Contracts.** Finally, the script deploys the test contract to a local instance of the Ganache blockchain [10] and executes the test using Truffle [11]. It then parses the output of the test, reports in a log file and starts a new iteration.

3.1   Results

To test our semantics, we run the framework for several days which resulted in more than 10000 successful tests. To cross-validate the effectiveness of the testing framework we also collected coverage information for the semantics using the Hpc tool [14]. The results are summarized in Fig. 2: Out of 123 definitions, 121 were executed during the tests. In addition, 186 alternatives (out of 524) and 1592 expressions (out of 2394) were executed. Hpc also generates detailed coverage reports for every module. When inspecting these reports it turns out that the low number of covered alternatives is mainly because of missing executions of error cases (e.g. ill-typed programs). This is because the test framework only generates well-formed Solidity programs and thus the error cases are not executed.

```
1  contract TestContract0 {
2      uint8 v_u8_s8;
3      mapping(uint16 => uint8) v_m_u16_u8_9;          ⎫ Extracted
4      bool[1][2] a_b_12_s5;                           ⎬ storage variables
5      ...                                             ⎭
6      function test() public {
7          uint104 v_u104_m2;                          ⎫ Extracted
8          uint104[1][1] memory a_u104_11_m2;          ⎬ memory/stack variables
9          ...                                         ⎭
10         v_u104_m2=146227093555696759631786653339646; ⎫ Generated
11         v_m_u16_u8_9[59381]=79;                       ⎬ input state
12         ...                                           ⎭
13         int8 counter1=int8(0);                         ⎫
14         while((v_m_u224_s240_1[uint224(444)]==          ⎪
15             (v_u216_s1-v_u104_m2)) && counter1<int8(10)){⎪
16             0xf7218C33533a3F22e3296F8b1DC0074B399355Eb  ⎬ Generated
17                 .transfer(v_m_u16_u8_9[uint16(0)]);      ⎪ program
18             counter1=counter1+int8(1);                   ⎪
19         }                                               ⎪
20         ...                                             ⎭
21         Assert.equal(v_m_u16_u8_9[59381]==79, true);    ⎫
22         Assert.equal(a_u104_11_m2[0][0]==                ⎪
23             8130097819054169632795960896007, true);      ⎪
24         Assert.equal(                                     ⎬ Computed
25             0xf7218C33533a3F22e3296F8b1DC0074B399355Eb    ⎪ result state
26             .balance==100000000000000000000, true);       ⎪
27         ...                                              ⎭
28     }
29 }
```

Listing 1.1. Example test contract generated by our testing framework.

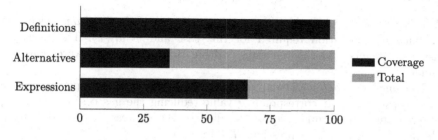

Fig. 2. Overall test coverage of semantics.

4   Verified Constant Folding

Constant folding is a common type of program optimization technique in which
constant sub-expressions are replaced by their value. For example, the expression
$SInt(16, 250) + UInt(8, 500)$ can be replaced with the expression $SInt(16, 494)$
in every program without affecting its outcome.

When it comes to smart contracts, constant folding is a good candidate for
gas optimization. For example, according to the Remix IDE [29], computing the
original expression costs 20 gas whereas computing the optimized version costs
only 8 gas which leads to a saving of 12 gas just for this simple expression.

We can define a function for constant folding of Solidity expressions as follows:

$$update: \mathbf{E} \rightarrow \mathbf{E}$$

$$update(SInt(b,v)) = \begin{cases} SInt\left(b,((v+2^{b-1}) \bmod 2^b)-2^{b-1}\right) & if\ v \geq 0 \\ SInt\left(b,2^{b-1}-((2^{b-1}-v-1) \bmod 2^b)-1\right) & if\ v < 0 \end{cases}$$

$$update(x_1+x_2) = \begin{cases} (1c) & if\ \exists b_1,v_1,b_2,v_2.\ sint(x_1,b_1,v_1,x_2,b_2,v_2) \wedge v_1+v_2 \geq 0 \\ (2c) & if\ \exists b_1,v_1,b_2,v_2.\ sint(x_1,b_1,v_1,x_2,b_2,v_2) \wedge v_1+v_2 < 0 \\ (3c) & if\ \exists b_2 < b_1,v_1,v_2.\ uint(x_1,b_1,v_1,x_2,b_2,v_2) \wedge v_1+v_2 \geq 0 \\ (4c) & if\ \exists b_2 < b_1,v_1,v_2.\ uint(x_1,b_1,v_1,x_2,b_2,v_2) \wedge v_1+v_2 < 0 \\ \dots \end{cases}$$

with

$$sint(x_1,b_1,v_1,x_2,b_2,v_2) \Longleftrightarrow update(x_1)=SInt(b_1,v_1) \wedge update(x_2)=SInt(b_2,v_2)$$

$$uint(x_1,b_1,v_1,x_2,b_2,v_2) \Longleftrightarrow update(x_1)=SInt(b_1,v_1) \wedge update(x_2)=UInt(b_2,v_2)$$

$$(1c)=SInt\left(max(b_1,b_2),\left((2^{max(b_1,b_2)-1}+v) \bmod 2^{max(b_1,b_2)}\right)-2^{max(b_1,b_2)-1}\right)$$

$$(2c)$$
$$=SInt\left(max(b_1,b_2),2^{max(b_1,b_2)-1}-\left((2^{max(b_1,b_2)-1}-v-1) \bmod 2^{max(b_1,b_2)}\right)-1\right)$$

$$(3c)=SInt\left(b_1,((v+2^{b_1-1}) \bmod 2^{b_1})-2^{b_1-1}\right)$$

$$(4c)=SInt\left(b_1,2^{b_1-1}-((2^{b_1-1}-v-1) \bmod 2^{b_1})-1\right)$$

where for every case $(1c)$–$(4c)$, variables b_1,v_1,b_2,v_2 denote the *unique* elements
satisfying the condition required for this case and $v=v_1+v_2$. The cases for
unsigned integers and the remaining arithmetic and boolean expressions are
similar.

The function *update* can be applied to a Solidity program to replace constant
expressions with their corresponding value reducing the gas cost of executing
the program. For example, *update* applied to the expression $SInt(16, 250) +$
$UInt(8, 500)$ returns the expression $SInt(16, 494)$.

Having a formal semantics of Solidity expressions in Isabelle allows us to
mechanically verify the correctness of our *update* function, i.e., we proved in
Isabelle/Isar [38] that it does not modify the semantics of an expression:

Theorem 2. $\mathcal{E}[\![x]\!]e\ s = \mathcal{E}[\![update(x)]\!]e\ s$

5   Memory Optimization

In the following, we describe a failed verification attempt to demonstrate the type of problems which can be detected with our approach.

In Solidity, access to storage variables is far more expensive than access to memory variables. Thus, instead of directly working on a storage variable, a common pattern is to first copy its content to memory, manipulate the corresponding memory variable, and finally copy the results back to storage. We can capture this pattern in another optimizer program which automatically replaces storage variables with corresponding memory variables. To this end, we first create three functions to update identifiers in $\mathcal{L}$-values, expressions, and statements, respectively. The corresponding function for $\mathcal{L}$-values, for example, looks as follows:

$$lupdate : \mathbf{S} \times \mathbf{S} \times \mathbf{L} \to \mathbf{L}$$

$$lupdate(j, j', Id(i)) = \begin{cases} Id(j') & \text{if } i = j \\ Id(i) & \text{if } i \neq j \end{cases}$$

$$lupdate(j, j', Ref(i, xs)) = \begin{cases} Ref(j', map(eupdate(j, j'), xs)) & \text{if } i = j \\ Ref(i, map(eupdate(j, j'), xs)) & \text{if } i \neq j \end{cases}$$

where map is a higher-order function which executes another function over a sequence of values. The functions for expressions and statements are straightforward and thus not discussed further.

We can now define a function which implements the pattern discussed above:

$$optimize : \mathbf{S} \times \mathbf{S} \times \mathbf{MTypes} \times \mathbf{C} \to \mathbf{C}$$
$$optimize(v_s, v_m, MTValue(t), s) = Block((v_m, Value(t), L(Id(v_s))), up(v_s, v_m, s))$$
$$optimize(v_s, v_m, MTArray(i, t), s) =$$
$$Block((v_m, Memory(MTArray(i, t)), L(Id(v_s))), up(v_s, v_m, s))$$
where $up(v_s, v_m, s) = supdate(v_s, v_m, s) ; Id(v_s) = L(Id(v_m))$

As an example, consider the following contract:

```
1  contract MyContract {
2    bool[1] sa;
3
4    function myFunction() public {
5      bool[1] memory ma = [false];
6      sa = ma;
7      sa[uint8(0)] = true;
8    }
9  }
```

```
bool[1] memory x = sa;
{
  x = ma;
  x[0] = true;
  sa = x;
}
```

Applying function *optimize* on it would replace the lines 6 and 7 with the program shown in the connected box. Again, it is important to ensure that *optimize* does not modify the semantics of programs and again we can formulate a corresponding correctness criterion in Isabelle.

To formulate the correctness statement, we first need to add two additional functions:

- Function $fresh(i, c)$ checks if an identifier i is not present in a statement c so far.
- Function $convert(t)$ converts a memory type to a corresponding storage type.

We can now define correctness of the optimizer program as follows:

$$fresh(v_m, c) \land v_m \neq v_s \land accessEnv(v_s, e) = (Storage(convert(t_m)), v)$$
$$\implies C[\![c]\!]e\ s = C[\![optimize(v_m, v_s, t_m, c)]\!]e\ s$$

where $accessEnv(v, e)$ is used to obtain the type and value of a variable v in an environment e.

This time, when trying to verify the statement in Isabelle, it turns out that the statement does not hold in general. In particular, the substitution of reference type variables is critical. Consider, for example, again contract MyContract above. In the original program, line 6 copies the complete content of memory array ma to storage array sa. In line 7, the program then updates the value of the storage array without modifying ma. Indeed, given a definition of a corresponding environment env and state st, we can easily verify the following lemma in Isabelle:

Lemma 1. $C[\![P]\!]e\ s = s' \land access(``0.1", mem(s')) = MValue(``False")$

where P is the program consisting of lines 6 and 7 of contract MyContract and "0.1" is the location of the first element of array ma in memory.

On the other hand, the modified version of the program behaves as follows: First, it copies the complete content of storage array sa to the newly created memory array x. Now, however, since x is also a memory array, the semantics of the assignment $x = ma$ is different from the one in line 6 of the original program. Instead of copying again the content of the array, this time, the assignment just copies a pointer to the content of array ma to x. Therefore, the next line $x[0] = \text{true}$ does not only change the value of $x[0]$, but in addition it also changes the value of $ma[0]$. Thus, while the value of array sa after execution is the same for both programs, the optimized program has the additional side effect of changing also the content of array ma. Indeed, we can easily show the following lemma in Isabelle:

Lemma 2. $C[\![optimize(sa, x, MTArray(1, MTValue(TBool)), P)]\!]e\ s = s'$
$\land access(``0.1", mem(s')) = (MValue(``True"))$

6   Related Work

Early work on formalizing Ethereum smart contracts has focused on the Ethereum Virtual Machine (EVM) [40]. One of the first examples in this area is the work of Hirai [20], which provides a formalization of the EVM in Lem [27]. Later on, Hildebrandt et al. provide an alternative formalization using the $\mathbb{K}$-framework [33] called KEVM [19]. Around the same time, Grischenko et al. [16] provide a formalization of the EVM in F* [36] and Amani et al. one for the interactive theorem prover Isabelle/HOL [4]. All the work in this area describes the formalization of the Ethereum Virtual Machine to support the verification of contracts at the byte-code level. With our work we focus on the higher level language Solidity which allows more abstract reasoning.

More recently, also work on formalizing and analyzing smart contracts in Solidity emerged: Bhargavan et al. [9], for example, describe an approach to map a Solidity contract to F* where it can then be verified. In addition, Mavridou et al. [26], provide an approach based on FSolidM [25], in which a Solidity smart contract is modeled as a state machine to support model checking of common security properties. TinySol [6] and Featherweight Solidity[12], on the other hand, are two calculi formalizing some core features of Solidity. Crosara et al. [13] describe an operational semantics for a subset of Solidity. Moreover, Ahrendt and Bubel describe SolidiKeY [3], a formalization of a subset of Solidity in the KeY tool [2] to verify data integrity for smart contracts. In addition, Zakrzewski [42] describes a big-step semantics of a small subset of Solidity and Yang and Lei [41] describe a formalization of a subset of Solidity in Coq [37].

While all these works provide important insights into the formal foundation of Solidity, most of them are not executable and therefore difficult to evaluate. On the other hand, we considered it important to have an executable semantics that can be evaluated against the reference implementation. We share this desire with Hajdu and Jovanovic [17,18], which provide a formalization of Solidity in terms of a simple SMT-based intermediate language which they evaluate on a set of manually developed tests. In addition, Jiao et al. [22,23], provide a formalization of Solidity in $\mathbb{K}$ with a rigorous evaluation using the Solidity compiler test set. Our work differs from the above works mainly in two main aspects:

1. We provide the first implementation of a semantics for Solidity for the interactive theorem prover Isabelle/HOL.
2. Our approach comes with an integrated fuzzy-testing framework which allows to automatically test the semantics against the reference implementation every time the semantics is updated.

7   Conclusion

We presented a formal semantics of Solidity, as a conservative extension of Isabelle/HOL. Our work includes a test framework for automatically validating that our semantics describes the behavior of the actual Solidity implementation faithfully. As a first step of showing the usefulness of our semantics, we demonstrated the formal analysis of two different optimizations of Solidity programs that potentially help to make smart contracts more "gas efficient".

In our current work, we focused on the core of the Solidity language and the more exotic features such as its memory model and the numerous types of integers. We plan to extend the formalization with support for missing language features such as function calls. And we also plan to improve and extend the verification framework, e.g., by providing support for the keywords require and assert, and a verified verification condition generator. Moreover, we started already to increase the level of proof automation by developing domain specific tactics.

Availability. Our formalisation, the test framework, and the evaluation results are available under BSD license (SPDX-License-Identifier: BSD-2-Clause) [24].

Acknowledgement. We would like to thank Tobias Nikpkow for useful discussions about the compliance testing. Moreover, we would like to thank Silvio Degenhardt and Nick Papavasileiou for their support with implementing the semantics.

References

1. The Bitcon market capitalisation. https://coinmarketcap.com/currencies/bitcoin/. Accessed 4 May 2021
2. Ahrendt, W., Beckert, B., Bubel, R., Hähnle, R., Schmitt, P.H., Ulbrich, M.: Deductive Software Verification-The KeY Book, vol. 10001. Springer, Cham (2016). https://doi.org/10.1007/978-3-319-49812-6
3. Ahrendt, W., Bubel, R.: Functional verification of smart contracts via strong data integrity. In: Margaria, T., Steffen, B. (eds.) ISoLA 2020. LNCS, vol. 12478, pp. 9–24. Springer, Cham (2020). https://doi.org/10.1007/978-3-030-61467-6_2
4. Amani, S., Bégel, M., Bortin, M., Staples, M.: Towards verifying Ethereum smart contract bytecode in Isabelle/HOL. In: CPP, CPP 2018, pp. 66–77. ACM (2018). https://doi.org/10.1145/3167084
5. Ballarin, C.: Interpretation of locales in Isabelle: theories and proof contexts. In: Borwein, J.M., Farmer, W.M. (eds.) MKM 2006. LNCS (LNAI), vol. 4108, pp. 31–43. Springer, Heidelberg (2006). https://doi.org/10.1007/11812289_4
6. Bartoletti, M., Galletta, L., Murgia, M.: A minimal core calculus for Solidity contracts. In: Pérez-Solà, C., Navarro-Arribas, G., Biryukov, A., Garcia-Alfaro, J. (eds.) DPM/CBT -2019. LNCS, vol. 11737, pp. 233–243. Springer, Cham (2019). https://doi.org/10.1007/978-3-030-31500-9_15
7. Berghofer, S., Wenzel, M.: Inductive datatypes in HOL — lessons learned in formal-logic engineering. In: Bertot, Y., Dowek, G., Théry, L., Hirschowitz, A., Paulin, C. (eds.) TPHOLs 1999. LNCS, vol. 1690, pp. 19–36. Springer, Heidelberg (1999). https://doi.org/10.1007/3-540-48256-3_3
8. Bertoni, G., Daemen, J., Peeters, M., Van Assche, G.: Keccak. In: Johansson, T., Nguyen, P.Q. (eds.) EUROCRYPT 2013. LNCS, vol. 7881, pp. 313–314. Springer, Heidelberg (2013). https://doi.org/10.1007/978-3-642-38348-9_19
9. Bhargavan, K., et al.: Formal verification of smart contracts: short paper. In: Programming Languages and Analysis for Security, pp. 91–96. PLAS, ACM (2016). https://doi.org/10.1145/2993600.2993611
10. ConsenSys Software Inc.: Ganache. https://www.trufflesuite.com/docs/ganache/. Accessed 1 May 2021
11. ConsenSys Software Inc.: Truffle. https://www.trufflesuite.com/truffle. Accessed 1 May 2021

12. Crafa, S., Di Pirro, M., Zucca, E.: Is Solidity solid enough? In: Bracciali, A., Clark, J., Pintore, F., Rønne, P.B., Sala, M. (eds.) FC 2019. LNCS, vol. 11599, pp. 138–153. Springer, Cham (2020). https://doi.org/10.1007/978-3-030-43725-1_11

13. Crosara, M., Centurino, G., Arceri, V.: Towards an operational semantics for Solidity. In: van Rooyen, J., Buro, S., Campion, M., Pasqua, M. (eds.) VALID, pp. 1–6. IARIA, November 2019

14. Gill, A., Runciman, C.: Haskell program coverage. In: Haskell Workshop, Haskell 2007, pp. 1–12. ACM (2007). https://doi.org/10.1145/1291201.1291203

15. Gordon, M.: From LCF to HOL: a short history. In: Plotkin, G., Stirling, C., Tofte, M. (eds.) Proof, Language, and Interaction: Essays in Honour of Robin Milner, pp. 169–185 (2000)

16. Grishchenko, I., Maffei, M., Schneidewind, C.: A semantic framework for the security analysis of Ethereum smart contracts. In: Bauer, L., Küsters, R. (eds.) POST 2018. LNCS, vol. 10804, pp. 243–269. Springer, Cham (2018). https://doi.org/10.1007/978-3-319-89722-6_10

17. Hajdu, Á., Jovanović, D.: SOLC-VERIFY: a modular verifier for Solidity smart contracts. In: Chakraborty, S., Navas, J.A. (eds.) VSTTE 2019. LNCS, vol. 12031, pp. 161–179. Springer, Cham (2020). https://doi.org/10.1007/978-3-030-41600-3_11

18. Hajdu, Á., Jovanović, D.: SMT-friendly formalization of the Solidity memory model. In: ESOP 2020. LNCS, vol. 12075, pp. 224–250. Springer, Cham (2020). https://doi.org/10.1007/978-3-030-44914-8_9

19. Hildenbrandt, E.: KEVM: a complete formal semantics of the Ethereum virtual machine. In: CSF, pp. 204–217 (2018). https://doi.org/10.1109/CSF.2018.00022

20. Hirai, Y.: Defining the Ethereum virtual machine for interactive theorem provers. In: Brenner, M., et al. (eds.) FC 2017. LNCS, vol. 10323, pp. 520–535. Springer, Cham (2017). https://doi.org/10.1007/978-3-319-70278-0_33

21. Hodován, R., Kiss, A., Gyimóthy, T.: Grammarinator: a grammar-based open source Fuzzer. In: Automating TEST Case Design, A-TEST 2018, pp. 45–48. ACM (2018). https://doi.org/10.1145/3278186.3278193

22. Jiao, J., Kan, S., Lin, S.W., Sanan, D., Liu, Y., Sun, J.: Semantic understanding of smart contracts: executable operational semantics of Solidity. In: SP, pp. 1695–1712. IEEE (2020)

23. Jiao, J., Lin, S.-W., Sun, J.: A generalized formal semantic framework for smart contracts. In: FASE 2020. LNCS, vol. 12076, pp. 75–96. Springer, Cham (2020). https://doi.org/10.1007/978-3-030-45234-6_4

24. Marmsoler, D., Brucker, A.D.: A denotational semantics of Solidity in Isabelle/HOL: Implementation and test data (2021). https://doi.org/10.5281/zenodo.5573225

25. Mavridou, A., Laszka, A.: Tool demonstration: FSolidM for designing secure Ethereum smart contracts. In: Bauer, L., Küsters, R. (eds.) POST 2018. LNCS, vol. 10804, pp. 270–277. Springer, Cham (2018). https://doi.org/10.1007/978-3-319-89722-6_11

26. Mavridou, A., Laszka, A., Stachtiari, E., Dubey, A.: VeriSolid: correct-by-design smart contracts for Ethereum. In: Goldberg, I., Moore, T. (eds.) FC 2019. LNCS, vol. 11598, pp. 446–465. Springer, Cham (2019). https://doi.org/10.1007/978-3-030-32101-7_27

27. Mulligan, D.P., Owens, S., Gray, K.E., Ridge, T., Sewell, P.: Lem: reusable engineering of real-world semantics. SIGPLAN Not. **49**(9), 175–188 (2014). https://doi.org/10.1145/2692915.2628143

28. Nipkow, T., Paulson, L.C., Wenzel, M.: Isabelle/HOL – A Proof Assistant for Higher-Order Logic, LNCS, vol. 2283. Springer, Heidelberg (2002). https://doi.org/10.1007/3-540-45949-9
29. Online: Remix - Solidity IDE. https://remix-ide.readthedocs.io/en/latest. Accessed 1 May 2021
30. Online: Solidity documentation. https://docs.soliditylang.org/en/v0.5.16/. Accessed 1 May 2021
31. Parr, T.: ANTLR (another tool for language recognition). https://www.antlr.org/index.html. Accessed 1 May 2021
32. Perez, D., Livshits, B.: Smart contract vulnerabilities: vulnerable does not imply exploited. In: USENIX Security. USENIX Association, August 2021
33. Roşu, G., Şerbănută, T.F.: An overview of the K semantic framework. J. Logic Algebraic Program. **79**(6), 397–434 (2010). https://doi.org/10.1016/j.jlap.2010.03.012
34. Scott, D.: Outline of a mathematical theory of computation. Oxford University Computing Laboratory, Programming Research Group Oxford (1970)
35. Scott, D., Strachey, C.: Toward a mathematical semantics for computer languages, vol. 1. Oxford University Computing Laboratory, Programming Research Group Oxford (1971)
36. Swamy, N., et al.: Dependent types and multi-monadic effects in F*. In: Symposium on Principles of Programming Languages, POPL 2016, pp. 256–270. ACM (2016). https://doi.org/10.1145/2837614.2837655
37. The Coq development team: The Coq proof assistant reference manual. LogiCal Project, version 8.0 (2004)
38. Wenzel, M.: Isabelle/Isar - a generic framework for human-readable proof documents. From Insight to Proof - Festschrift in Honour of Andrzej Trybulec **10**(23), 277–298 (2007)
39. Wood, G.: Ethereum: a secure decentralised generalised transaction ledger (version 2021-04-21). Technical report (2014)
40. Wood, G., et al.: Ethereum: a secure decentralised generalised transaction ledger. Ethereum project yellow paper **151**(2014), 1–32 (2014)
41. Yang, Z., Lei, H.: Lolisa: formal syntax and semantics for a subset of the Solidity programming language in mathematical tool Coq. Math. Probl. Eng. **2020**, 6191537 (2020)
42. Zakrzewski, J.: Towards verification of Ethereum smart contracts: a formalization of core of Solidity. In: Piskac, R., Rümmer, P. (eds.) VSTTE 2018. LNCS, vol. 11294, pp. 229–247. Springer, Cham (2018). https://doi.org/10.1007/978-3-030-03592-1_13

Configuration Space Exploration for Digital Printing Systems

Jasper Denkers[1]([✉])[ID], Marvin Brunner[2], Louis van Gool[2], and Eelco Visser[1][ID]

[1] Delft University of Technology, Delft, The Netherlands
{j.denkers,e.visser}@tudelft.nl
[2] Canon Production Printing B.V., Venlo, The Netherlands
{marvin.brunner,louis.vangool}@cpp.canon

Abstract. Within the printing industry, much of the variety in printed applications comes from the variety in finishing. Finishing comprises the processing of sheets of paper after being printed, e.g. to form books. The configuration space of finishers, i.e. all possible configurations given the available features and hardware capabilities, are large. Current control software minimally assists operators in finding useful configurations. Using a classical modelling and integration approach to support a variety of configuration spaces is suboptimal with respect to operatability, development time, and maintenance burden.

In this paper, we explore the use of a modeling language for finishers to realize optimizing decision making over configuration parameters in a systematic way and to reduce development time by generating control software from models.

We present CSX, a domain-specific language for high-level declarative specification of finishers that supports specification of the configuration parameters and the automated exploration of the configuration space of finishers. The language serves as an interface to constraint solving, i.e., we use low-level SMT constraint solving to find configurations for high-level specifications. We present a denotational semantics that expresses a translation of CSX specifications to SMT constraints. We describe the implementation of the CSX compiler and the CSX programming environment (IDE), which supports well-formedness checking, inhabitance checking, and interactive configuration space exploration. We evaluate CSX by modelling two realistic finishers. Benchmarks show that CSX has practical performance (<1s) for several scenarios of configuration space exploration.

1 Introduction

Digital printing systems are flexible manufacturing systems, i.e. manufacturing systems that are capable of adjusting their abilities to manufacture different types and quantities of products, without expensive hardware changes. The variety in printing applications stems from both printing (printing on sheets of paper) and finishing (processing collections of printed sheets, e.g. to form a

© The Author(s) 2021
R. Calinescu and C. S. Păsăreanu (Eds.): SEFM 2021, LNCS 13085, pp. 423–442, 2021.
https://doi.org/10.1007/978-3-030-92124-8_24

book). The *configuration space* for a digital printing system consists of all possible configurations given the system's features and hardware constraints. For producing a booklet of a particular size, a printed stack of sheets can be stitched, it can be folded, and it can be trimmed. Optionally, the sheets can be rotated in an intermediate production step such that a single trimming component can be used for trimming in multiple dimensions. The decisions made for these manufacturing parameters influence important factors such as productivity (production time increases when sheets are rotated) or efficiency (paper is wasted when input sheets are trimmed).

Ideally, control software assists operators in exploring the configuration space. For example, given some available paper and the intent to produce a booklet, the software should automatically derive a viable manufacturing configuration. Such a configuration e.g. comprises the orientation of the input sheets, the number of stitches, and the amount of side and face trimming needed to get the desired end result. In addition, an optimization objective can be relevant while finding a configuration, e.g. minimizing paper waste. The control software and user interfaces of state of the art digital printing systems do not support such automated configuration space exploration. Instead, operators have to provide configurations for finishers manually. A configuration can be simulated; by "executing" the finishing process in software, finishing viability can be checked without wasting resources. Still, it remains a cognitively intensive task for operators to find a valid or optimal configuration.

Finishers are produced by many vendors and integrating them with printers is non-trivial. Such integration involves connecting the control software of the printer and finishers and driving embedded software components. Using a classical modeling and integration approach to support the variety of finishing is suboptimal with respect to development time and maintenance burden. Issues with such a classical approach are the long code-build-test cycle and the large amount of finisher vendors and models that must be supported for many years. The translation of the mechanical specifications into control software code gives rise to additional complexity.

Our objective is to obtain an effective, efficient, and scalable method for modeling finishers and obtaining control software for finishers that support automated configuration space exploration. In this work, we investigate how linguistic abstraction can help to model the configuration space of digital printing systems, and how we can automatically derive environments for configuration space exploration from such specifications.

The global characteristics of finishers make the use of constraint (SMT) solving a natural fit for realizing environments for configuration space exploration. For example, trimming the paper along a certain dimension might impose a specific orientation or transformation in an earlier production step. A constraint-based approach considers its specifications as global and will take into account interdependent system-level constraints when finding solutions, i.e., configurations. A constraint-based model of a finisher contains a representation of the input materials at intermediate locations in the system. However, for modelling domain objects such as sheets and stacks, abstraction mechanisms such as classes are not naturally available in SMT modelling. An SMT model of a finisher requires low-level encoding of the properties of the materials at all locations. Therefore, expressing finishers in SMT by hand is tedious, error prone, and is not in terms of domain concepts. Additionally, an SMT model of a finisher is complex to understand and difficult to maintain.

In this paper, we present CSX, a domain-specific language for the high-level declarative specification of finishers. The language supports specification of input materials, configuration parameters, output products, and finishing constraints in terms of domain concepts. The CSX IDE supports the development and checking of specifications and the automated derivation of an environment for configuration space exploration by operators of the finishers.

CSX provides a domain-specific interface to SMT solving by abstracting and structuring over low-level properties. We translate specifications to the SMT domain and use existing solvers to find solutions at the level of properties and finishing parameters. A solution in the SMT domain corresponds to a valid configuration. Unsatisfiability at the SMT level indicates an empty configuration space, i.e., no finishing possibilities. By mapping SMT solutions back to the specification level, we can interpret CSX specifications in multiple modes: checking whether a configuration is valid, finding an (optimal) configuration, and validating specifications. By caching invocations of the solver in the IDE, response times are improved which leads to an interactive editing experience.

The approach of specifying a finisher with CSX and deriving control software has similarities with the approach of simulation in control software. Both approaches take representations of the products being produced at intermediate locations in the devices. However, while simulation involves an operational and sequential application of transformations on objects, a constraint-based approach considers the devices globally. CSX improves over simulation in the sense that it derives environments that can search for (optimal) configurations in an automated way, taking system-global interdependencies into account.

We evaluated the design and implementation of CSX by modelling two finishers: a perfect binder and a booklet maker. In the process of modelling these devices, we have experimented with various encodings. For both cases, we benchmark the configuration space exploration performance for several scenarios.

Contributions. To summarize, the contributions of this paper are the following:

- We have developed CSX, a declarative language for the specification of finishers at the conceptual level of the domain. We interpret CSX specifications for several modes of configuration space exploration: checking whether configurations are valid, finding optimal configurations under objectives, and interactively validating specifications.
- We define a denotational semantics of CSX in terms of SMT constraints that serves as an interface to solvers that can be used to find models in order to check inhabitance of a specification and to explore the configuration space of the specified finisher.

- We realize a programming environment for CSX that integrates an SMT solver as back-end and that presents solutions in terms of the specification.
- We evaluate CSX by specifying two types of finishers: a perfect binder and a booklet maker. For these cases, we benchmark the performance for a configuration space exploration scenario with and without optimization.

2   Finishers in the Digital Printing Domain

In this section, we discuss the domain of digital printing systems with finishers. Complete printing systems for e.g. producing books include, in addition to printing itself, finishing capabilities. Finishing comprises the processing of printed sheets of paper into end products. For example, a stack of printed sheets could be stapled, folded, and trimmed to result into a booklet; stapling, folding, and trimming are finishing operations. Finishing devices need to be integrated with the printing system for realizing an integrated end-to-end experience for the print system end-users (i.e. operators in print shops).

The turnaround time of integrating finishers with printers is high because of multiple challenging aspects. First, finishers are often produced by external vendors and communication is mostly documentation based and thus requires interpretation, reviews, implementation, and testing. Second, obtaining good system behavior requires mechanical, electrical and software interfaces to be matched well between the printer and finisher. Third, total aspects such as reliability are the result of all the mentioned interfaces to be well designed. Considerable testing time is needed to confirm reliability.

Creating control software that is user-friendly for operators is difficult and requires a lot of manual programming. This is because of the high variability and many configuration parameters in print and finishing systems. A typical print and finishing system has more than 200 accessible parameters for the operator, that are also interdependent. Because the whole production process is a sequence of production steps, choices that you have to make in the beginning influence the steps later on. From the product line perspective, the control software supports tens of different finisher types, that each of them can have more than 100 commercial variations. For all variations, the parameters that are accessible for operators can vary.

Ideally, operators can use the combination of a printer with finishers as an end-to-end solution instead of having to configure each device separately. Additionally, optimization capabilities are also useful when considering the system as a whole. For example, an operator would like to produce booklets with the available resources and while minimizing paper waste or while optimizing productivity. If the different configuration possibilities impose a tradeoff between e.g. resource consumption and productivity, an operator should be able to make a motivated choice with ease, i.e., without thinking about and manually trying out many combinations of configuration parameters.

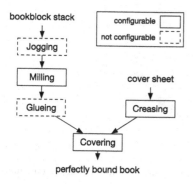

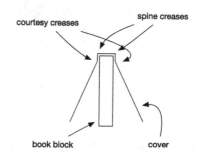

Fig. 1. Schematic view of the perfect binding book producing process. Only milling, creasing, and covering are configurable and therefore impact the configuration space. Jogging and glueing are automatically configured by the device itself.

Fig. 2. A perfectly bound book viewed from the top. Spine creases result into a sharper fold, reduce wrinkles, and improve the fit of the cover around the bookblock. Courtesy creases ease opening the front and back part of the cover. Glue in the spine holds the bookblock sheets and cover together.

2.1   Perfect Binding

As an example, we discuss a *perfect binder*: a finisher that produces books by binding a stack of sheets with glue and by covering the bookblock in a cover sheet. A perfect binder typically has two inputs: one for the stack of sheets that form the book block and one for the cover sheets. Figure 1 shows the perfect binding process. Figure 2 depicts the components of a perfectly bound book, viewed from above.

After collecting a stack of sheets, jogging makes sure the stack of sheets becomes aligned in a corner of the spine. Then, a clamp grasps the bookblock under pressure. Next, a few millimeters of paper are milled along the spine edge to prepare the spine for application of glue. Milling makes the paper along the spine rough, improving adherence of the glue. Then, the spine travels through a bath of heated glue.

Separately, cover sheets are prepared before being bound around the bookblock. The preparation consists of creasing, i.e., applying pressure on the paper to ease folding of the paper later. Two creases are applied at the location of the cover that end up along the edges of the spine of the book. These creases improve the fit of the cover along the spine of the book block, supporting a tight fold around the spine. Additionally, two courtesy creases are applied on the cover. Courtesy creases are applied on the front and back of the resulting book to support the folding of the cover sheet. Note that courtesy creases are applied at the opposite side as the spine creases, as they are used for folds in opposite directions.

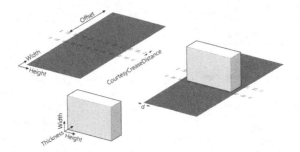

Fig. 3. Components of a perfectly bound book (cover and bookblock) and the dimensions as how we use them in the CSX specification.

After preparing the bookblock and cover, the covering occurs. The bookblock with glue is positioned in the center of the cover sheet. The cover sheet is folded around the bookblock and fixed with a clamp. After a delay for the glue to solidify, the book is released. In practice, the resulting book could be processed further in a cutting machine to trim along the edges of the book and cover to result into a nice book.

Perfect binders are flexible in the books they can produce, e.g. in terms of sheet size or book thickness. Not all flexible manufacturing steps have impact on the configuration space. For example, jogging and glueing occur automatically and are configured by the device itself based on measurements. Other settings such as the milling depth and positioning of the bookblock on the cover are of interest to the operator and therefore do impact the configuration space; e.g. more milling might increase the overall production time.

3   CSX

The key idea of CSX is that we model objects such as sheets and stacks and that we specify symbolic values, i.e. instances, for these objects at several intermediate steps in the finishing process. By adding constraints and indicating configuration parameters, a specification defines the configuration space of a device. In CSX we also describe *jobs*, i.e., (partial) descriptions of the production process in terms of the production objects and parameters. We achieve configuration space exploration by synthesizing configurations from a configuration space for a given job.

CSX is declarative: a specification in the language describes behavior and configuration spaces of finishers. A CSX specification does not describe algorithms to compute configurations. Specifications include relations between objects at locations in the systems. We use the language to model devices as sequences of components that perform actions. Components instantiate generic, reusable actions. Actions establish a relationship between snapshots of objects in the finishers and thus, transitively, devices define a relation between all snapshots of the products being produced. Parameters in actions represent a dimension of

```
type Sheet {
  width: int, [width > 0],
  height: int, [height > 0]
}
type Stack {
  width: int, [width > 0],
  height: int, [height > 0],
  thickness: int, [thickness > 0],
  volume = width * height * thickness
}
type PerfectBoundBook {
  book: Stack,
  frontCover: Sheet, backCover: Sheet
}
```

```
type CreasedSheet {
  sheet: Sheet,
  spineFront: Crease,
  spineBack: Crease,
  courtesyFront: Crease,
  courtesyBack: Crease
}

type Crease {
  // Offset:
  off: int, [off ≥ 0],
  // Direction: 0 = down, 1 = up
  dir: int, [dir == 0 or dir == 1]
}
```

Fig. 4. The specification of types for the example perfect binder in CSX. Dimensions are in 0.1mm.

```
action ToMill(in: Stack, out: Stack) {
  parameter millingDepth: int
  [millingDepth ≥ 0] [out.width == in.width - millingDepth]
  [out.height == in.height] [out.thickness == in.thickness]
}
action ToCrease(in: Sheet, out: CreasedSheet) {
  [out.sheet.width == in.width] [out.sheet.height == in.height]
  [out.spineFront.dir == 0] [out.spineBack.dir == 0]
  [out.courtesyFront.dir == 1] [out.courtesyBack.dir == 1]
  // Ensure a minimum distance between creases
  parameter minDist: int [minDist > 0] [out.courtesyFront.off ≥ minDist]
  [out.spineFront.off ≥ out.courtesyFront.off + minDist]
  [out.spineBack.off ≥ out.spineFront.off + minDist]
  [out.courtesyBack.off ≥ out.spineBack.off + minDist]
  [out.courtesyBack.off ≤ in.width - minDist]
}
action ToCover(cover: CreasedSheet, book: Stack, out: PerfectBoundBook) {
  parameter d: int [0 ≤ d and d ≤ cover.sheet.height - book.height]
  [out.book.width == book.width] [out.book.height == book.height]
  [out.book.thickness == book.thickness]
  [out.frontCover.width * 2 == cover.sheet.width - book.thickness]
  [out.frontCover.height == cover.sheet.height]
  [out.backCover.width * 2 == cover.sheet.width - book.thickness]
  [out.backCover.height == cover.sheet.height]
  [cover.spineFront.off * 2 == cover.sheet.width - book.thickness]
  [cover.spineBack.off * 2 == cover.sheet.width + book.thickness]
  parameter courtesyCreaseDist: int
  [cover.courtesyFront.off * 2 ==
    cover.sheet.width - book.thickness - courtesyCreaseDist * 2]
  [cover.courtesyBack.off  * 2 ==
    cover.sheet.width + book.thickness + courtesyCreaseDist * 2]
}
```

Fig. 5. The specification of actions for the example perfect binder in CSX. See Fig. 3 for the dimensions used in this specification.

```
device ExamplePerfectBinder {
 location bookIn : Stack location coverIn : Sheet
 [1000 ≤ bookIn.height and bookIn.height ≤ 3000]
 [2000 ≤ bookIn.width and bookIn.width ≤ 5000]
 component toMill = ToMill(bookIn, milledBook) {
  [millingDepth ≤ 30] // Max 3mm of milling
  [bookIn.thickness < 170] // Max 17mm book thickness
 }
 location milledBook : Stack
 component toCrease = ToCrease(coverIn, creasedCover) {
  [minDist ≥ 50] // At least 5 mm between creases
 }
 location creasedCover : CreasedSheet
 component toCover = ToCover(creasedCover, milledBook, out) {}
 location out : PerfectBoundBook
}
```

Fig. 6. The specification of the example perfect binder device in CSX.

configuration that is of interest to operators of the devices. Constraints restrict instances of types and restrict the behavior of actions and devices, reducing the configuration space. We will now introduce the language concepts in more detail based on a specification for an example perfect binder such as described in Sect. 2.

Defined *types* are records of properties that model objects at locations in a device. In Fig. 4, we define several types for the example perfect binder. Dimensions (widths, heights, lengths, distances) are modelled with integers with a precision of 0.1mm, such that an integer value of 10 stands for a length of 1mm. Types contain *defining properties* that are of a primitive type (boolean or integer) or of a defined type such that types can be nested. The nesting of types may not contain a cycle. Types optionally contain *constraints* and *derived properties*. Constraints restrict the inhabitants of a type. In Fig. 4, the constraints (between square brackets) e.g. restrict sheets to have positive non-zero width and height. Derived properties are shorthands for expressions over other properties. Defining properties are required to instantiate a type. Derived properties are not required to instantiate a type and their values can be derived from other properties. A derived property expression may refer to the type's properties and to other derived properties, but derived properties may not contain cyclic references. In Fig. 4, Stack has a derived property volume which is defined in terms of defining properties.

Actions define a relation between locations. In Fig. 5, we define several actions for the example perfect binder. The body of an action definition contains parameters and constraints that indicate the relations between its parameters.

Devices are sequences of *components* connected through *locations*. Components instantiate actions and can restrict or specify behavior further by adding constraints. Thus, action behavior is defined separately from specific instantiations in components. Therefore, actions are generic and potentially reusable between different device specifications. Limitations of a particular instance of an action in a device can be specified by adding constraints to the component. In Fig. 6 we define a perfect binder device by instantiating several actions in components and by connecting them through the locations.

3.1   Configurations and Jobs

A configuration for a device is a value assignment to all locations and parameters. A valid configuration is a configuration that conforms to the constraints of the types of the locations, the actions, the components, and the device itself. In practice, an operator is only interested in the values for the input and output locations, and not in the intermediate locations.

A job is an expression of intent for which a configuration needs to be found. Whereas configurations are a complete specification of locations and parameters, we could see jobs as a partial configuration. For example, a job could define the input and the output of the finisher. The remaining parts of the configuration, i.e. the finishing parameters, need to be derived in order to instruct the finisher to realize the intent of the job. Different usage scenarios of a device lead to different jobs and approaches to configuration.

3.2   Exploration and Validation

The CSX language supports configuration space exploration, which includes leveraging exploration at the specification level for validation. Given the specification of a device, the language supports describing scenarios for testing devices by asserting expectations on configuration spaces.

The following test scenario validates that the correct cover dimensions are chosen for a particular input bookblock and desired output perfectly bound book:

```
scenario device ExamplePerfectBinder
  config bookIn = Stack(2125,2970,50)
  config out = PerfectBoundBook(Stack(2100,2970,50), Sheet(2100,2970), Sheet(2100,2970)) {
    [coverIn.width == 2100 + 2100 + 50]
    [coverIn.height == 2970]
    [toMill.millingDepth == 25]
}
```

The body of the scenario contains expectations (between square brackets) on its configuration space. In particular, it validates the cover dimensions that must be chosen. Since the configuration space could contain multiple configurations, expectations should only validate common properties of the configuration space and not on individual configurations.

Scenarios can optionally specify an objective. *Objectives* indicate a dimension for optimization of a property of the system, typically expressed using derived properties. Potentially relevant objectives are e.g. maximizing throughput, minimizing energy consumption, or minimizing resource waste. Alternatively, scenarios with optimization can characterize the device. For example, based on the following scenario a scenario can be found for the largest book that the perfect binder can produce:

```
scenario device ExamplePerfectBinder
         maximize out.book.volume
```

4   Denotational Semantics

Because of the declarative characteristic of CSX, a translation to SMT constraints is natural. In this section, we define the denotational semantics of CSX that expresses a translation of CSX specifications to SMT constraints. Figure 7 contains the denotational semantics of CSX with the denotation expressed in MiniZinc [9,13] definitions. Because we use MiniZinc in the implementation of CSX (Sect. 5), we also use it as syntax for the denotation. The MiniZinc grammar can be found online[1].

The intuition behind the translation is that the properties of locations and the parameters of components are mapped to constraint variables. Additionally, all CSX-defined constraints translate to corresponding constraints in MiniZinc. The translation is from the perspective of a device, making use of type and actions definitions of the CSX specification of which the device is part.

The translation starts with the DEVICE rule, generating MiniZinc definitions for members of the device: locations, components, and device-level constraints. The translation is defined under the context of a namespace N, starting with the empty namespace. The naming scheme for constraint variables follow their corresponding hierarchical position in the CSX specification. Since the translation is for a single device, we do not have to prefix the namespace with the device name.

A location translates into variables for its properties and into constraints to restrict its inhabitants (LOCATION). Locations are always of a user-defined type. Each property of the type translates to variables. If the property is of primitive type, the translation is a variable of this primitive type (DEFPROP-PRIMTYPE)). If the property is of a user-defined type, the translation is the translation of its nested properties in the namespace of the property (DEFPROP-DEFTYPE).

The COMP rule defines the translation for a component, i.e. an action instantiation. The action's parameters translate into variables in the namespace of the component (PARAM). Both the action and the component can define constraints (E_i^A and E_i^C, respectively). These constraints are mapped to corresponding MiniZinc constraints. Since the action's constraints are defined on the action's location parameters, and the action gets instantiated with specific location arguments, renaming is required. The translation defines R: a mapping from the location's parameter names to the component's location argument names. We only use the renaming for translating references to locations from constraints defined in the action definition.

---

[1] https://www.minizinc.org/doc-2.5.5/en/spec.html?highlight=grammar#spec-grammar.

$[\![S']\!]_{S,N,R} = M$ Specification part S' of S translates to M in namespace N with location renaming R

$N = [x_1, x_2, \ldots, x_n]$ Namespace N consisting of parts x_1 to x_n

$R = \{\ldots, L_i \rightarrow L'_i, \ldots\}$ Renaming of location names L_i to L'_i

$name([x_1, x_2, \ldots, x_n]) = x_1\_x_2\_\ldots\_x_n$ Identifier for namespace $[x_1, x_2, \ldots, x_n]$

Locations L, components C, constraints E, defining properties P, types T, action parameters PM.

Devices $[\![\texttt{device } d \texttt{ \{ } L_1 \ldots L_n, C_1 \ldots C_m, E_1 \ldots E_q, \ldots \texttt{ \}}]\!]_{S,[],\emptyset} =$

$$\bigcup_{i=1}^{n}[\![L_i]\!]_{S,[],\emptyset} \cup \bigcup_{i=1}^{m}[\![C_i]\!]_{S,[],\emptyset} \cup \bigcup_{i=1}^{q}[\![E_i]\!]_{S,[],\emptyset} \quad \text{(Device)}$$

Locations $\dfrac{\texttt{type } T \texttt{ \{ } P_1{:}T_1 \ldots P_n{:}T_n, E_1 \ldots E_m, \ldots \texttt{ \}} \in S}{[\![\texttt{location } L : T]\!]_{S,[],\emptyset} = \bigcup_{i=1}^{n}[\![P_i{:}T_i]\!]_{S,[L],\emptyset} \cup \bigcup_{i=1}^{m}[\![E_m]\!]_{S,[L],\emptyset}}$ (Location)

$\dfrac{T \in \{\texttt{int}, \texttt{bool}\}}{[\![P{:}T]\!]_{S,N,\emptyset} = \texttt{var } T : name(N \mathbin{+\!\!+} [P]) \texttt{ ;}}$ (DefProp-PrimType)

$\dfrac{\texttt{type } T \texttt{ \{ } P_1{:}T_1 \ldots P_n{:}T_n, E_1 \ldots E_m, \ldots \texttt{ \}} \in S}{[\![P{:}T]\!]_{S,N,\emptyset} = \bigcup_{i=1}^{n}[\![P_n{:}T_n]\!]_{S,N \mathbin{+\!\!+} [P],\emptyset} \cup \bigcup_{i=1}^{m}[\![E_m]\!]_{S,N \mathbin{+\!\!+} [P],\emptyset}}$ (DefProp-DefType)

Components $\texttt{action } A(L_1{:}T_1^L \ldots L_n{:}T_n^L) \cdot$
$\{\texttt{parameter } PM_1 : T_1^P \ldots \texttt{parameter } PM_m : T_m^P, E_1^A \ldots E_q^A, \ldots\} \in S$

$\dfrac{R = \{L_1 \rightarrow L'_1, \ldots, L_n \rightarrow L'_r\}}{[\![\texttt{component } C = A \texttt{ (} L'_1 \ldots L'_r \texttt{) } \{ E_1^C \ldots E_s^C \}]\!]_{S,[],\emptyset} =}$ (Comp)

$$\bigcup_{i=1}^{m}[\![\texttt{parameter } PM_m : T_m^P]\!]_{S,[C],\emptyset} \cup \bigcup_{i=1}^{q}[\![E_i^A]\!]_{S,[C],R} \cup \bigcup_{i=1}^{s}[\![E_s^C]\!]_{S,[C],\emptyset}$$

$\dfrac{T \in \{\texttt{int}, \texttt{bool}\}}{[\![\texttt{parameter } PM{:}T]\!]_{S,N,\emptyset} = \texttt{var } T{:}name(N \mathbin{+\!\!+} [PM]) \texttt{ ;}}$ (Param)

Constraints & References $[\![\texttt{ [} e \texttt{] }]\!]_{S,N,R} = \texttt{constraint } [\![e]\!]_{S,N,R};$ (Constraint)

$\dfrac{x \text{ is a defining property or parameter}}{[\![x]\!]_{S,N,R} = name(N \mathbin{+\!\!+} [x])}$ (DefProp-Ref/Param-Ref)

$\dfrac{x \text{ is a location} \quad x \rightarrow x' \notin R}{[\![x]\!]_{S,N,R} = name(N \mathbin{+\!\!+} [x])}$ (Location-Ref)

$\dfrac{x \text{ is a location} \quad x \rightarrow x' \in R}{[\![x]\!]_{S,N,R} = name(N \mathbin{+\!\!+} [x'])}$ (ActionLocation-Ref)

$\dfrac{x \text{ is a derived property with body } e}{[\![x]\!]_{S,N,R} = [\![e]\!]_{S,N,R}}$ (DerProp-Ref)

$[\![e.x]\!]_{S,N,R} = [\![e]\!]_{S,N,R} + \_x$ (Proj)

Fig. 7. Denotational semantics of CSX, expressed in MiniZinc. We have omitted the rules for literals and arithmetic for brevity; they map one-to-one. $\mathbin{+\!\!+}$ is namespace concatenation. $+$ is identifier concatenation.

The expressions that are used to define constraints, except references and projection, map mostly one-to-one to their MiniZinc counterparts. For references and projection, we consider several cases. A reference to property or parameter (DEFPROP-REF/PARAM-REF) translates to a name for x in the context. For example, a reference of x in namespace $[a, b]$ will result in the denotation into a reference to name a_b_x. For projection (PROJ), we recursively translate the base expressions into a name and concatenate the projected name.

For a location reference, we consider two cases. Location references from outside actions translate similarly as regular references (LOCATION-REF). Location references within actions refer to location parameters, while the actions are instantiated with location arguments from a device. Therefore, for such location references, we replace the location parameter name by the argument name for which it is instantiated (ACTIONLOCATION-REF).

Types, actions, and devices can have derived properties. These only translate into constraints if they are referenced, i.e. by replacing the reference with the body of the derived property and by propagating the namespace and location renaming (DERPROP-REF). For the definition of derived properties, no translation takes place. The definition of derived properties are ignored by ... in the specification.

Solutions found for the MiniZinc denotations are related to valid configurations for CSX specifications, and we can translate such solutions back to CSX Specifications. The correspondence between location properties and component parameters in CSX and MiniZinc is defined by the naming scheme used in the denotation, and mapping them back is thus straightforward.

5   Implementation

In this section we describe how we obtain a usable integrated development environment (IDE) for CSX by integrating an implementation of the language with configuration space exploration and interactive validation. The IDE contains components for parsing, syntax highlighting, code completion, name binding and type checking, and interactive reporting of static semantics violations. The CSX validation constructs are interpreted interactively and invalid assertions are marked on the specification.

We have implemented the CSX language using Spoofax [7], a language workbench [5] that provides infrastructure for designing, implementing, and deploying DSLs by means of declarative specification of language aspects using meta-DSLs. We define the syntax of CSX in SDF3 [11], a meta-language for multi-purpose syntax definition. From the CSX syntax definition, SDF3 automatically derives a parser, pretty printer, syntax highlighting, and syntactic code completion. The parser yields abstract syntax trees (ASTs) on which we first apply desugaring. Desugaring e.g. involves propagating the properties of a scenario to the tests within that scenario. The desugared ASTs are input to the static analysis and further transformations. We specify desugaring and other transformations using the Stratego [2] meta-language. Based on the language specification, Spoofax automatically generates an IDE for the language.

We define the CSX static semantics in NaBL2 [1,10]. NaBL2 is a meta-language for specifying static semantics for languages from which name binding and type checking is automatically derived. Static semantic violations are reported interactively in the IDE. For CSX, this could be invalid composition of components in a device or incorrect type checking of constraint expressions. Interactive reporting of errors assists users of the language during specification writing.

In addition to the automated derivation of name binding and type checking, we implement analysis for other well-formedness conditions. If well-formedness checking succeeds, the result is a desugared AST that is annotated with name binding and typing information. The name binding information is used to check non-cyclic references of defining properties and derived properties, i.e., by following references of properties and checking whether those do not contain cycles.

To realize configuration space exploration, we implement a translation of CSX specifications to SMT constraints for which we can use existing solving techniques. In particular, we translate CSX to the MiniZinc constraint modelling language [9,13]. MiniZinc is solver-independent, which enables us to use multiple solvers as a backend for CSX. In particular, we use solvers with the theories of linear arithmetic and optimization modulo theories.

We implement the translation from CSX to MiniZinc as an AST-to-AST transformation using Stratego. In addition to the syntax definition of CSX, we have also defined the syntax of MiniZinc in Spoofax with SDF3[2]. The syntax definitions of both languages generate an AST schema on which we define the Stratego transformation. After transforming a parsed CSX AST to a MiniZinc AST, the MiniZinc pretty printer generates concrete MiniZinc syntax from the AST.

The translation uses information from name binding and type analysis. This is necessary for references and projection expressions. By using name binding and typing information, the distinction between references to properties, parameters, locations, and action locations can be made to generate the correct reference on the MiniZinc level.

We integrate solving of constraint models by calling MiniZinc from Stratego through integration with Java. Stratego provides an API for integrating transformations with custom Java code. We implement such a custom transformation and use a Java program to call the MiniZinc command-line interface. The Java program is called with as input the generated MiniZinc model. The Java program parses the textual solving result that is returned by MiniZinc and returns it as a list of variable binding. In the Stratego code, for the interpretation of configurations, we evaluate expressions and lookup values for references by following the same naming schema as in the translation semantics. After replacing the referenced properties and parameters by their values on the constraint level, the evaluation of expressions remains regular expression evaluation. As a result, we have a configuration space exploration pipeline from interpreting specifications

---

[2] https://github.com/metaborgcube/metaborg-minizinc.

using constraint solving with the solution mapped back to the specification level as a configuration.

The configuration space exploration pipeline serves two purposes in the IDE: test evaluation and inhabitance checking. For test evaluation, the configuration space of the device that is selected in the scenario is translated to MiniZinc and passed as an input to the pipeline. Additional constraints are added to reduce the configuration space, e.g. to configure the input or output location values, or parameters as specified in the scenario. If the scenario contains an objective, the objective is also mapped to MiniZinc and provided as input to the pipeline. The configuration that is returned by the pipeline is used to evaluate test expectations. This evaluation is done by a basic interpreter that evaluates expressions which should result into true. The expressions can contain references to parameters and location properties, and based on the name binding information the references are mapped to the corresponding value from the configuration. For failed test expectations we report an error which is marked with red underlining on the original specification using origin tracking [4].

The evaluation of tests and reporting of results is triggered in the IDE on file changes, resulting into an interactive experience. Additionally, the experience is improved by providing information while hovering over references to locations, properties, and parameters in test expectations. The same interpretation approach as for test expectations is used to evaluate the expression being hovered over and the value is presented in a popup, giving the user insight in the configuration that is found.

Similar to the treatment of scenarios, inhabitance checks are triggered on file changes. The pipeline is triggered for each type, action, and device using the translations semantics. For inhabitance checking of a type, we translate a random instance of that type to SMT. For an action, we instantiate it with instances for all its parameters. Instead of finding a configuration for it, for inhabitance checking we only check satisfiability on the constraint level. If the pipeline concludes in satisfiability, we report an error on the corresponding construct to indicate that the construct is not inhabited.

To prevent unnecessary checking of inhabitance and evaluation of tests, we use simple caching of analysis results with ASTs of the subjects as the caching key. If a type definition AST has not changed, it does not have to be checked again for inhabitance. If a scenario has not changed, it does not have to be evaluated again.

While we have described the realization of a programming environment for CSX specifications, the eventual goal of CSX is to deploy control software to finishers. Figure 8 gives an overview of how configuration space exploration with CSX would with fit in a realistic setting. The configuration space exploration component would be integrated with a software component, implemented using a general-purpose language, that provides a UI and that instructs low-level embedded software components.

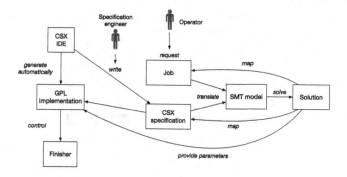

Fig. 8. An architecture for applying CSX in control software. GPL stands for general purpose programming language, such as C# or Java.

6   Evaluation

We evaluate CSX by modelling two realistic cases, a perfect binder and a booklet maker, and by benchmarking the configuration space exploration for a scenario with and without optimization. The perfect binder case corresponds to the example of Sect. 3. In the scenario without optimization, CSX derives the required input cover given an input bookblock and a desired output. In the scenario with optimization, CSX finds a configuration for the smallest size book the finisher can produce. The bookletmaker case concerns a finisher that performs rotating, stitching, folding, and trimming in order to produce a booklet from a stack of sheets. In the scenario without optimization, CSX finds the action parameters given an input and output. In the scenario with optimization, CSX finds a configuration that minimizes paper waste given only the desired output. Both specifications are based on realistic cases present at Canon Production Printing B.V.

By writing scenarios in the language, we can interactively validate the specification within the IDE. Initially loading a specification can take a few seconds: a specification typically consists of multiple type definitions, action definitions, a device definition, and several scenarios. For the type, action, and device definitions, inhabitance checking is triggered, which for each check leads to an invocation of the SMT solver. Additionally, for each scenario the solver is invoked. The caching of invocations of the solver decreases response times after a change, making the IDE usable in an interactive way. For example, inhabitance for a type will not be re-checked if only a test scenario changes.

We set up a benchmark which makes use of Spoofax core, i.e. the core of Spoofax which enables integration of language components with Java, such that we can only execute the relevant part of the pipeline in the benchmark. For benchmarking, we use the JMH framework[3]. We executed the benchmarks on a server with two 32-core processors with a base frequency of 2.3 GHz and 256

---

[3] https://openjdk.java.net/projects/code-tools/jmh/.

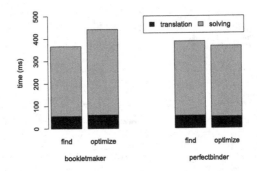

Fig. 9. The benchmarking results on a perfect binder and a booklet maker for a scenario of finding a configuration and for finding an optimal configuration.

GB RAM, running Ubuntu 20.04, using OpenJDK version 1.8.0_275-b01. From experimentation it appeared that the ORTools solver[4] had best performance, and therefore we use this solver in the benchmarks. We use MiniZinc version 2.5.5 and ORTools version 9.0. We measure 10 iterations and average the result. In the benchmarks, we separately measure the translation time and solving time. We leave out parsing, name binding and type checking time, as they are minimal compared to translation and solving time.

Figure 9 shows the benchmarking results. For each scenario, solving time is in the order of 100's ms. We consider sub-second performance as practical and therefore conclude that CSX's performance for the two cases we consider has practical performance for finding (optimal) configurations.

For specifying these devices in CSX, we have chosen a model of objects (sheets, stacks) with a certain level of detail. The bookletmaker and perfect binding cases translated in the SMT level into 32 and 29 variables and 56 and 58 constraints, respectively. Although we achieve useful configuration space exploration for these scenarios, it could be that in practice more detail has to be added to the model, which could also influence solving performance. By deploying CSX at Canon Production Printing B.V., we aim to further evaluate whether CSX is adequate in modeling and integrating the full product line of finishers available and evaluate its usability for domain experts.

7   Related Work

We discuss related work that uses constraint solving in the backend of high-level specification or domain-specific languages for realizing static analyses, validation, verification, consistency checking or synthesis.

Keshishzadeh et al. use SMT solving for validation of domain-specific properties to achieve fault detection early in the software development cycle. In particular, they develop a DSL with industrial application in a case on collision prevention for medical imaging equipment [8]. The approach includes delta

---

[4] https://developers.google.com/optimization.

debugging, i.e., an approach to trace causes of property violations and report them back to the specification in a systematic way. The work is related to CSX because it also uses SMT solving in the backend of a domain-specific language.

Voelter et al. use SMT solving with the Z3 solver for advanced error checking and verification in the KernelF language [16], a reusable functional language for the development of DSLs. Voelter et al. apply SMT solving successfully in a DSL on a case study for the domain of payroll calculations [17], i.e. for statically checking completeness and overlap of domain-specific switch-like expressions. Similarly to CSX, in this work SMT solving is used in the backed of a domain-specific language for realizing static analyses. While the application of SMT was successful in the domain-specific case, the authors report difficulties in applying SMT solving generically in KernelF. The authors plan to develop a successor to KernelF that is realized with SMT solving completely.

Constraint solving in feature models solves a different problem than CSX. Feature models describe systems as compatible compositions of features or software components; finding/checking feature compositions occurs "statically" from which a software artifact can be derived. CSX specifications express physical properties of finishers; finding configurations occurs "dynamically" (at run time) to find instances of the manufacturing process. This goes all the way down to the "semantic" level, e.g. by using sheet dimensions and the location of fold edges instead of only an abstract feature that enumerates the kinds of folds a device can do. Feature modelling is useful in the finishing context e.g. to derive which devices are necessary for a production route for booklets. In CSX, we assume the production route is known.

Relational model finders are related to CSX in the sense that they map high-level specifications to constraints and map solutions back to the specification level. Alloy [6] is a specification language that applies finite model finding to check formal specifications of software. Alloy is backed by KodKod [15], a relational model finder for problems expressed using first order logic, relational algebra, and transitive closures. In contrast to CSX, KodKod does not offer support for reasoning over data nor for optimization objectives. In CSX, the nature of specifications is not relational: manufacturing paths are fixed and we consider snapshots of the product being manufactured at different steps in the process.

AlleAlle [12] adds support for first-class data attributes and optimization to relational model finding. Similar to KodKod, Stoel et al. consider AlleAlle as an intermediate language. AlleAlle and CSX are related in the sense that both approaches take the data of problems into account and use SMT solving for model finding. While AlleAlle is an intermediate language generally targeting relational problems, CSX is a more domain-specific language in which relations are not a first class concept. Similar to CSX, for AlleAlle it is unclear yet how to map reasons for unsatisfiability that are found in the constraint level back to the specification level.

Rosette [14] is a solver-aided programming language that supports verification, debugging, and synthesis. Rosette extends the Racket language with support for symbolic values that stand for e.g. an arbitrary integer value. Such values translate to a constraint variable in the runtime. Rosette realizes verification and synthesis in the runtime by integrating its symbolic virtual machine with SMT solvers. Whereas in Rosette selected variables are replaced by symbolic values, in CSX all variables in the specification translate to constraint variables. Rosette is a general language tailored to program verification and synthesis whereas CSX is focused on a particular domain, i.e. manufacturing systems, although we have only experimented with CSX in the digital printing domain.

Muli [3] is a constraint-logic object oriented language that integrates constraint solving with object oriented programming in the Java programming language. Muli extends Java's syntax with the `free` keyword for indicating symbolic values that translate to constraint variables in the runtime. Fragments of programs that are considered as search regions are executed non-deterministically, searching for concrete values for the constraint variables. The Muli runtime is based on a symbolic Java virtual machine that integrates constraint solvers. Muli only supports primitive types as constraint variables. Support for arrays and objects as constraint variables is listed as future work. CSX does support search on non-primitive types such as user-defined record types. Similar to how support for arrays is desired for Muli, support for lists is desired for CSX, but that is future work. Muli differs from CSX in the sense that Muli preserves the Java syntax and, by doing so, serves as a general purpose programming language, whereas CSX introduces a new domain-specific language. In contrast to Muli, CSX supports optimization.

8   Conclusions

We have presented CSX, a language and method for high-level declarative specification of finishers and their configuration spaces. We have developed a translation of CSX to SMT constraints which enables us to use constraint solving to find (optimal) configurations for finishers. We have presented an implementation of the CSX programming environment, including support for well-formedness checking, inhabitance checking, and interactive configuration space exploration. Our benchmarks show that, on two realistic cases, CSX has practical subsecond performance in finding configurations for scenarios with and without optimization.

Future work. Our focus has been on finding a domain abstraction for configuration space exploration applied in the digital printing domain for finishers. While we have designed the language in collaboration with control software engineers, we plan to further evaluate CSX by deploying it at Canon Production Printing B.V. By doing so, we can further evaluate the adequacy of CSX in covering the full product line of finishers. Additionally, we plan to evaluate the language in terms of usability for control software engineers and in terms of validatability by mechanical engineers.

To improve the usability of the environments for configuration space exploration for operators, it would be useful to characterize the reduced configuration spaces for given jobs. In particular, when multi-objective optimization is relevant for objectives such as maximizing throughput and minimizing waste, it would be useful if CSX could indicate the tradeoff between these objectives.

Acknowledgment. We thank the reviewers for their feedback. This research was partially supported by a grant from the Top Consortia for Knowledge and Innovation (TKIs) of the Dutch Ministry of Economic Affairs and by Canon Production Printing. We thank Bas Hermus for providing a 3D drawing of perfect binding. This work is related to the European patent application EP3855304 A1 which is published on 28 July 2021.

References

1. van Antwerpen, H., Néron, P., Tolmach, A.P., Visser, E., Wachsmuth, G.: A constraint language for static semantic analysis based on scope graphs. In: Erwig, M., Rompf, T. (eds.) Proceedings of the 2016 ACM SIGPLAN Workshop on Partial Evaluation and Program Manipulation, PEPM 2016, St. Petersburg, FL, USA, 20–22 January 2016, pp. 49–60. ACM (2016). https://doi.org/10.1145/2847538.2847543
2. Bravenboer, M., Kalleberg, K.T., Vermaas, R., Visser, E.: Stratego/XT 01.7. A language and toolset for program transformation. Sci. Comput. Program. **72**(1–2), 52–70 (2008). https://doi.org/10.1016/j.scico.2007.11.003
3. Dageförde, J.C., Kuchen, H.: A compiler and virtual machine for constraint-logic object-oriented programming with muli. J. Comput. Lang. **53**, 63–78 (2019). https://doi.org/10.1016/j.cola.2019.05.001
4. van Deursen, A., Klint, P., Tip, F.: Origin tracking. J. Symb. Comput. **15**(5/6), 523–545 (1993)
5. Erdweg, S., et al.: Evaluating and comparing language workbenches: existing results and benchmarks for the future. Comput. Lang. Syst. Struct. **44**, 24–47 (2015). https://doi.org/10.1016/j.cl.2015.08.007
6. Jackson, D.: Alloy: a lightweight object modelling notation. ACM Trans. Softw. Eng. Methodol. **11**(2), 256–290 (2002). https://doi.org/10.1145/505145.505149
7. Kats, L.C.L., Visser, E.: The Spoofax language workbench: rules for declarative specification of languages and IDEs. In: Cook, W.R., Clarke, S., Rinard, M.C. (eds.) Proceedings of the 25th Annual ACM SIGPLAN Conference on Object-Oriented Programming, Systems, Languages, and Applications, OOPSLA 2010, pp. 444–463. ACM, Reno/Tahoe (2010). https://doi.org/10.1145/1869459.1869497
8. Keshishzadeh, S., Mooij, A.J., Mousavi, M.R.: Early fault detection in DSLs using SMT solving and automated debugging. In: Hierons, R.M., Merayo, M.G., Bravetti, M. (eds.) SEFM 2013. LNCS, vol. 8137, pp. 182–196. Springer, Heidelberg (2013). https://doi.org/10.1007/978-3-642-40561-7_13
9. Nethercote, N., Stuckey, P.J., Becket, R., Brand, S., Duck, G.J., Tack, G.: MiniZinc: towards a standard CP modelling language. In: Bessière, C. (ed.) CP 2007. LNCS, vol. 4741, pp. 529–543. Springer, Heidelberg (2007). https://doi.org/10.1007/978-3-540-74970-7_38
10. Neron, P., Tolmach, A., Visser, E., Wachsmuth, G.: A theory of name resolution. In: Vitek, J. (ed.) ESOP 2015. LNCS, vol. 9032, pp. 205–231. Springer, Heidelberg (2015). https://doi.org/10.1007/978-3-662-46669-8_9
11. de Souza Amorim, L.E., Visser, E.: Multi-purpose syntax definition with SDF3. In: de Boer, F., Cerone, A. (eds.) SEFM 2020. LNCS, vol. 12310, pp. 1–23. Springer, Cham (2020). https://doi.org/10.1007/978-3-030-58768-0_1

12. Stoel, J., van der Storm, T., Vinju, J.J.: AlleAlle: bounded relational model finding with unbounded data. In: Masuhara, H., 0001, T.P. (eds.) Proceedings of the 2019 ACM SIGPLAN International Symposium on New Ideas, New Paradigms, and Reflections on Programming and Software, Onward! 2019, Athens, Greece, 23–24 October 2019, pp. 46–61. ACM (2019). https://doi.org/10.1145/3359591.3359726

13. Stuckey, P.J., Feydy, T., Schutt, A., Tack, G., Fischer, J.: The MiniZinc challenge 2008–2013. AI Mag. **35**(2), 55–60 (2014)

14. Torlak, E., Bodík, R.: Growing solver-aided languages with rosette. In: Hosking, A.L., Eugster, P.T., Hirschfeld, R. (eds.) ACM Symposium on New Ideas in Programming and Reflections on Software, Onward! 2013, part of SPLASH 2013, Indianapolis, IN, USA, 26–31 October 2013, pp. 135–152. ACM (2013). https://doi.org/10.1145/2509578.2509586

15. Torlak, E., Jackson, D.: Kodkod: a relational model finder. In: Grumberg, O., Huth, M. (eds.) TACAS 2007. LNCS, vol. 4424, pp. 632–647. Springer, Heidelberg (2007). https://doi.org/10.1007/978-3-540-71209-1_49

16. Voelter, M.: The design, evolution, and use of KernelF. In: Rensink, A., Sánchez Cuadrado, J. (eds.) ICMT 2018. LNCS, vol. 10888, pp. 3–55. Springer, Cham (2018). https://doi.org/10.1007/978-3-319-93317-7_1

17. Voelter, M., Koščejev, S., Riedel, M., Deitsch, A., Hinkelmann, A.: A domain-specific language for payroll calculations: an experience report from DATEV. In: Domain-Specific Languages in Practice, pp. 93–130. Springer, Cham (2021). https://doi.org/10.1007/978-3-030-73758-0_4

Bit-Precise Verification of Discontinuity Errors Under Fixed-Point Arithmetic

Stella Simić[1]([⊠]) [iD], Omar Inverso[2] [iD], and Mirco Tribastone[1] [iD]

[1] IMT School for Advanced Studies, Lucca, Italy
stella.simic@imtlucca.it
[2] Gran Sasso Science Institute, L'Aquila, Italy

Abstract. Non-integer arithmetic is prone to numerical errors due to the finite representation of numbers. These errors propagate, possibly non-linearly, throughout the variables of a program and can affect its control flow, altering reachability, and thus safety. We consider the problem of rigorous bit-precise numerical accuracy certification of programs in the presence of control structures and operations under fixed-point arithmetic over (non-deterministic) variables of arbitrary, mixed precision. By applying program transformation, we reduce the problem of assessing whether a given error bound can be exceeded in the initial program to a reachability problem in a bit-vector program. We implement our technique as a pre-processing module that integrates seamlessly with an existing mature BMC-based verification workflow. We present an experimental evaluation of our error certification technique on a set of arithmetic routines commonly used in the industry.

Keywords: Fixed-point arithmetic · Control-flow · Numerical error · Program transformation · Discontinuity error · Bounded model checking

1 Introduction

Safety checking can be particularly troublesome for various software components of common use nowadays in a variety of applications. Numerically-intensive routines, for instance, are typically characterised by nondeterminism (stemming from physical sensor readings or values computed by large external modules) and complex data dependencies (as in control loops) which complicate the state space and can lead to subtle unexpected behaviour.

Non-integer arithmetic represents an additional element of complexity for automated analysis, as one has to take into account the *numerical inaccuracy* arising from the finite representation of numbers. Such inaccuracy not only propagates among the variables of a routine, but can affect the control flow, altering

Partially supported by MIUR projects PRIN 2017TWRCNB SEDUCE (Designing Spatially Distributed Cyber-Physical Systems under Uncertainty) and PRIN 2017FTXR7S IT-MATTERS (Methods and Tools for Trustworthy Smart Systems).

R. Calinescu and C. S. Păsăreanu (Eds.): SEFM 2021, LNCS 13085, pp. 443–460, 2021.
https://doi.org/10.1007/978-3-030-92124-8_25

reachability, and therefore *safety*. In such circumstances, the program is said to be affected by a *discontinuity error* [11].

Fixed-point arithmetic [2,36] allows to run a variety of algorithms on inexpensive hardware as it maps relatively straightforwardly to integer arithmetics. As such, it is an appropriate choice for many embedded applications. In some real-time systems, in order to meet strict requirements on energy consumption and latency, numerical routines such as neural networks are often quantised into fixed-point implementations on top of bit-wise integer arithmetic [16].

Clearly, fixed-point programs are particularly exposed to numerical inaccuracy and discontinuity errors, because the programmer can allocate more or less bits to represent the fractional or integer part of a variable. Automatically analysing discontinuity errors can be particularly desirable to assess the numerical robustness of existing arithmetic routines, but also to work out an appropriate tradeoff between speed and accuracy when synthesising fixed-point code from pseudocode algorithms developed under more idealised arithmetics.

The ISO/IEC has been proposing language extensions for the C programming language to support the fixed-point data-type [2], which have already been implemented in the GNU compiler collection. However, there is very little work concerning the estimation of numerical errors under fixed-point arithmetic and it is either limited to straight-line code [17,24,30], or it cannot guarantee tight bounds on the errors [11]. Indeed, the majority of existing formal verification methods for non-integer arithmetics concerns floating-point arithmetics and is based on over-approximation [11,18,34].

In this paper, we propose a bit-precise verification flow to certify exact error bounds for programs over mixed-precision fixed-point arithmetic in the presence of discontinuity errors. We apply program transformation to reduce the problem of assessing whether a given error bound can be exceeded in the initial program to a reachability problem in a bit-vector program. In particular, we transform the initial fixed-point program into a modified one which preserves all its feasible behaviours and at the same time keeps track (via auxiliary variables and statements injected appropriately) of the errors arising from control-flow diversions. Under this transformation, for all branching points defined by a condition containing a fixed-point variable, whose value may be prone to errors, we compare the finite-precision control flow with the ideal mathematical one that would have been executed in absence of numerical errors.

As this requires the computation of the mathematical values of program variables, we build on top of our existing control flow-insensitive technique [30] that encodes a fixed-point program as a bit-vector program, such that the problem of finding a numerical error bound for the former reduces to simple reachability queries on the latter. Our approach is novel in that no other existing approach is able to issue exact certificates of numerical discontinuity errors.

We implement our approach as a pre-processing module that integrates seamlessly with a mature bounded model checking-based verification flow. We experiment with our prototype analyser on a set of fixed-point implementations of numerical routines commonly used in the industry, including a neural network, different interpolation methods [15], and a jet-engine controller [11]. The experiments show that our error certification technique can be successfully used to identify divergence between the ideal and finite-precision control flow and to precisely compute the overall numerical errors on output variables.

The rest of the paper is organized as follows. In Sect. 2 we briefly introduce fixed-point arithmetic and numerical errors. In Sect. 3 we derive the expressions for numerical error propagation arising from diverging control flows. Section 4 illustrates the details of the proposed program transformation. In Sect. 5 we report our experimental evaluation. We overview related work and discuss conclusions and further developments in Sects. 6 and 7.

2   Preliminaries

2.1   Fixed-Point Arithmetic

Fixed-point arithmetic [36] is a finite-precision approximation for computations over the rational numbers. It is based on standard integer arithmetic in that it relies on integer representation and computing architecture, while implicitly applying a scaling factor to interpret the values stored in variables. We indicate with $\mathbf{x}_{(p.q)} = \langle x_{p-1}, \ldots, x_0.x_{-1}, \ldots, x_{-q} \rangle$ a fixed-point variable whose integral and fractional parts are represented using p and q binary digits, respectively, and indicate with $(p.q)$ the fixed-point format of $\mathbf{x}$. Since the position of the radix point is not part of the representation, the storage size for a fixed-point variable is $p + q$, plus a sign bit x_p in case of signed arithmetic.

Assuming the customary two's complement representation is used, the value of a signed fixed-point variable $\mathbf{x}_{(p.q)}$ is interpreted as

$$\mathbf{x}_{(p.q)} = \left(-x_p \cdot 2^{p+q} + \sum_{i=-q}^{p-1} x_i \cdot 2^{i+q} \right) \cdot 2^{-q} \tag{1}$$

Notice that the expression in brackets represents the integer underlying $\mathbf{x}$, i.e. the integer encoded by the bit-sequence of $\mathbf{x}$, to which the scaling factor 2^{-q} is applied. It follows that the range of values that are representable in the format $(p.q)$ is $[-2^p, 2^p - 2^{-q}] \cap 2^{-q} \cdot \mathbb{Z}$, i.e. all rational values in the range $[-2^p, 2^p - 2^{-q}]$ with a step of 2^{-q}, called the resolution of the format.

Operations on fixed-point variables are carried out by relying on integer operations and applying appropriate scaling factors to the results. For example, the sum/difference of two variables in the same format, $\mathbf{x}_{(p.q)}$ and $\mathbf{y}_{(p.q)}$, is obtained by adding/subtracting the underlying integers and applying a scaling factor of 2^{-q}. Since the extremal result of this operation may be as negative as -2^{p+1} or as positive as $2^{p+1} - 2^{-q+1}$, the necessary format to correctly store the result needs $p+2$ integral bits, i.e. $\mathbf{z}_{(p+1.q)} = \mathbf{x}_{(p.q)} \pm \mathbf{y}_{(p.q)}$. The product of two variables $\mathbf{x}_{(p.q)}$ and $\mathbf{y}_{(p'.q')}$ is obtained by multiplying the underlying integers and applying a scaling factor of $2^{-(q+q')}$ to the result. It follows from the representation ranges of the operands that the format to correctly represent all possible values of the product requires an integral part of $p + p' + 2$ bits, while the fractional part may be as small as $2^{-(q+q')}$, i.e. $z_{(p+p'+1.q+q')} = x_{(p.q)} \times y_{(p'.q')}$.

The format for the result of a fixed-point division, when such result is representable (i.e. not periodic), may be deduced similarly. Other arithmetic operations on fixed-point variables are right and left arithmetic bit-shifts, which do not currently follow any specific semantics. They are performed as in integer arithmetic, by shifting the entire bit-sequence of the operand, but the formats for their results may be user-defined. Indeed, based on the purpose of the bit-shift, the scaling factor for the result may vary. Bit-shifts may be used either for a re-scaling of the operand or to get rid of redundant bits. Possible semantics for fixed-point bit-shifts, as well as for divisions are given in [23, 30, 36].

2.2 Numerical Errors

Numerical inaccuracies arise when the format of a variable is not sufficient to correctly store the desired value. For instance, overflow may occur when trying to use a variable to store a value that is outside of its representation range. In these cases the stored value can be very different than the intended one. It may be either the maximum representable value, if saturation arithmetic is used, or the wrapped value, in case of modular arithmetic.

An insufficient fractional precision may be another source of error. An example is shown in Listing 1, in which the value of $y_{(3.2)}$ is non-deterministic, i.e. it symbolises any possible value taken by y, provided it can be stored in the given precision. If we consider a run of this program in which $y_{(3.2)}$ is assigned to the value 0.25_{10} (in decimal notation), the correct result of multiplying $x_{(3.2)}$ and $y_{(3.2)}$, namely 0.125_{10}, would require 3 fractional bits of precision, such as (3.3). Hence, having to store the result in $z_{(3.2)}$ forces the least significant bit to be dropped and the obtained result is 0.0_{10}. This constitutes a quantization error equal to $0.125_{(10)}$, i.e. the difference between the intended mathematical value and the computed one.

The exact mathematical error $\bar{z}$ incurred by an imprecise operation on a program variable z may be expressed as $\bar{z} = \tilde{z} - z$, where $\tilde{z}$ indicates the correct mathematical value z should ideally hold. This last value would be obtained if all the operations leading to the computation of z were carried out in infinite precision. Notice that, if $\tilde{z}$ is periodic (for example a periodic quotient) and thus not representable in any fixed-point format, consequently $\bar{z}$ is not representable either. In [30], we presented an error estimation technique that leverages the error expression introduced above and explicitly derives the expressions for $\bar{z}$ or a sound over-approximation thereof, in case of periodic quotients, for each arithmetic statement of the input program. To track the error propagation throughout the entire program, each original program statement is transformed by a re-write function $[\![\cdot]\!]$ into a set of statements that compute the error incurred by the single operation, in terms of the operands and of the errors of the operands. To make sure that no additional errors are introduced by this computation, the formats for all newly introduced variables are guaranteed to be sufficiently large and the operands are correctly aligned when necessary. The quantization mode for

```
1  fixedpoint x(3.2), y(3.2), z(3.2), w(3.2);
2  x(3.2) = 0.5;                               // +000.10, 000010
3  y(3.2) = * ;                        // assume +0.25, +000.01, 000001
4  z(3.2) = x(3.2) * y(3.2);                //+0.0, +000.00, 000000
5  if z(3.2) <= 0 then {           // will have an error of 0.001 on z
6       w(3.2) = z(3.2)           // entering this branch due to error on z
7  } else {
8       w(3.2) = z(3.2) * 4      // should have entered this branch instead
9  }
```

Listing 1. A fixed-point program with numerical errors.

$[\cdot]$ is truncation, which corresponds to rounding towards $-\infty$ when using two's complement representation.

Consider again the error on z in line 4 of Listing 1. This numerical inaccuracy will now propagate to the rest of the computation, affecting other operations where z may appear as an operand. With particularly complex dependency relationships between variables, keeping the overall numerical inaccuracy under control would not be easy, more so in the presence of non-determinism or uncertainty on the variables. In this paper, we consider a more subtle case, i.e., when the numerical inaccuracy alters the control flow.

The additional trouble here is that, due to the numerical error on z, the program enters the first branch erroneously. w is assigned to the current, incorrect, value of z and one might be tempted to conclude that the error on z should propagate to w unchanged. However, the value that should be stored in w at the end of the program, had all the computations been carried out correctly, is $0.125_{10} \cdot 4_{10} = 0.5_{10}$. The total error on w is therefore not simply due to the incorrect operand in the assignment in line 6, but is incurred by a wrong assignment altogether. In this case, we say that w is affected by a *discontinuity error* [11].

2.3 Fixed-Point Programs

In the rest of the paper we consider the C-like syntax for programs shown in Fig. 1, extended with an extra datatype `fixedpoint` for fixed-point variables. Here, var is a fixed-point variable $x_{(p.q)}$ of arbitrary precision, k is an integer constant, $\diamond \in \{+, -, \times\}$ are the arithmetic operations and $\circ \in \{\gg, \ll\}$ are arithmetic bit-shifts, whose semantics is defined in [30]. The program can also contain standard C-like elements such as scalars or arrays. We include verification-oriented primitives for symbolic initialisation (var = *), assumptions (`assume(condition)`) and assertion checking (`assert(condition)`) to express safety properties of interest, in form of predicates over the variables.

Note that, in safety-critical software, loops are required to have a statically determinable upper bound on the number of iterations and recursion is not permitted (see coding standards and guidelines, for example MISRA-C [1], ISO-26262 [4], DO-178C [3] and NASA/JPL [22]). We therefore assume that the program has already been fully unfolded, hence we avoid explicitly including a construct for loops in our syntax. In programs which do contain loops our error analysis technique can be used for bounded reachability checks. As our goal is exact error certification, we do not consider division here, as this operation may produce non-representable errors (see Sect. 2.2). It is also worth to notice that the fixed-point arithmetic considered here generalises the ISO/IEC fixed-point standard proposal [2] in that it allows arbitrary, mixed precisions for variables.

$$\texttt{stmt} ::= \texttt{fixedpoint var} \mid \texttt{expr} \mid \texttt{assert(condition)} \mid \texttt{assume(condition)} \mid$$
$$\texttt{if } (v \le 0) \texttt{ stmt else stmt} \mid \texttt{stmt ; stmt}$$
$$\texttt{expr} ::= \texttt{var} = * \mid \texttt{var} = v \mid \texttt{var} = v \diamond v \mid \texttt{var} = v \circ k$$
$$v ::= k \mid \texttt{var}$$

Fig. 1. Syntax of fixed-point input programs.

3 Propagation of Discontinuity Errors

3.1 Motivating Example

A concrete example of a discontinuity error can be seen in Listing 2, which shows an implementation of a simple feedforward neural network (NN) with a positive linear activation function. Constants I, H, and O denote the number of input, hidden, and output neurons, respectively. The input vector represents the network inputs, iw and lw are the weights between the input and hidden layer and the hidden and output layer, respectively. b1, b2, are the biases of the hidden and output layers, hout are the outputs of the hidden layer and output are the outputs of the network. We consider the case of an NN that is previously trained on expensive hardware and deployed as a component of a cheap embedded application using fixed-point arithmetic. In this case, the input is non-deterministic, while iw, lw, b1 and b2 are fixed.

Although this simple routine might look just fine at a first glance, it is prone to discontinuity errors. Specifically, the activation function controlled by the guarded statement within the first loop may behave differently depending on the numerical error introduced on hout. Accordingly, the output of the network may be more or less altered, which in the NN context may lead to a misclassification error. The verification of finite-precision implementations of NNs and, in particular, their robustness to adversarial attacks, is gaining increasing attention [16,26,37]. We use the routine above as a motivating example and consider an instantiation of it as a case study to evaluate our discontinuity error identification technique in Sect. 5.

```
input[I] = *; output[O];
w[H][I] = ..; lw[O][H] = ..; b1[H] = ..; b2[O] = ..; hout[H];

for (h=0; h<H; h++) {
    hout[h] = b1[h];

    for (i=0; i<I; i++)
        hout[h] = hout[h] + iw[h][i] * input[i];

    if (hout[h] < 0) hout[h] = 0;
}

for (o=0; o<O; o++) {
    output[o] = b2[o];

    for (h=0; h<H; h++)
        output[o] = output[o] + lw[o][h] * hout[h];
}
```

Listing 2. Implementation of a simple feedforward neural network.

3.2 Computing the Discontinuity Error

Let x be a variable in the condition (guard) of an if-then-else statement:

$$s := \text{if } (x \leq 0) \text{ stmt}' \text{ else stmt}''. \tag{2}$$

For simplicity we only consider guards of the form $var \leq 0$ as the other cases may be reduced to this. Based on the value of x, the program may enter either the "then" or the "else" branch, executing either stmt' or stmt''. Besides errors due to the arithmetic operations appearing in the body of the two branches, an additional error may be entailed by choosing the wrong branch altogether, due to an inaccuracy on the value of x. In such cases the total error on a program variable will be due not only to the finite nature of operations leading to its computation, but also due to the incorrect sequence of operations. Here we derive the mathematical expressions for such discontinuity errors.

Let v be a program variable affected by either stmt' or stmt'', i.e. a variable whose value is updated in at least one of the branches of s. As introduced in Sect. 2, the error in computing v can be expressed, in general, as the difference between its ideal mathematical value and its computed value. The mathematical value would be the result if all operations leading to the computation of v were computed correctly, in infinite precision, on error-free operands. In particular, correctly computing v implies computing the correct sequence of operations.

Given an "if-then-else" statement, we first need to define the set of program variables that may be affected by such a wrong branching choice. Given a fixed-point program in the syntax of Fig. 1, let V be the set of program variables and let S be the set of program statements. Consider the function $W \colon S \to V$ defined recursively as follows:

$$
\begin{aligned}
W(\texttt{fixedpoint v}) &= \emptyset \\
W(\texttt{v = v}') &= \{\texttt{v}\} \\
W(\texttt{v = v}' \diamond \texttt{v}'') &= \{\texttt{v}\} \\
W(\texttt{v = v}' \circ \texttt{k}) &= \{\texttt{v}\} \\
W(\texttt{if (x} \leq \texttt{0) stmt}' \texttt{ else stmt}'') &= W(\texttt{stmt}') \cup W(\texttt{stmt}'') \\
W(\texttt{stmt}'; \texttt{ stmt}'') &= W(\texttt{stmt}') \cup W(\texttt{stmt}'')
\end{aligned}
\tag{3}
$$

$W(\texttt{stmt})$ computes the set of variables whose values are affected by the execution of stmt. Let $S' \subset S$ denote the subset of "if-then-else" statements. Given $\texttt{s} \in S'$, i.e. $\texttt{s}$ as in Eq. 2, we define the three functions $T, E, I \colon S' \to V$ as follows, using the previously defined function W:

$$
\begin{aligned}
T(\texttt{s}) &= W(\texttt{s}) \setminus W(\texttt{stmt}'') \\
E(\texttt{s}) &= W(\texttt{s}) \setminus W(\texttt{stmt}') \\
I(\texttt{s}) &= W(\texttt{stmt}') \cap W(\texttt{stmt}'')
\end{aligned}
\tag{4}
$$

In particular, $T(\texttt{s})$ computes the set of variables modified only by the "then" branch of the ITE statement, i.e. by $\texttt{stmt}'$. Similarly, $E(\texttt{s})$ computes the set of variables modified only by the "else" branch, namely by $\texttt{stmt}''$. $I(\texttt{s})$ computes the set of variables modified by both branches.

Consider a program variable $\texttt{v} \in W(\texttt{s})$, where $\texttt{s}$ is again the control structure from Eq. 2 and consider the case in which the chosen branch may differ from the correct one due to a numerical error in the variable of the guard. Let $\texttt{v}$ indicate the value of the variable prior to entering the $\texttt{s}$ statement and let us indicate with $\texttt{v}_\texttt{f}$ the updated value of $\texttt{v}$ computed in the branch chosen by the finite-precision computation. We want to compute the error on $\texttt{v}$ entailed by this computation by using the identity $\overline{v_f} = \widetilde{v}_c - \texttt{v}_\texttt{f}$, where $\widetilde{v}_c$ is the correct mathematical value $\texttt{v}$ should hold at the end of $\texttt{s}$.

Let $\texttt{v}_\texttt{c}$ now indicate the value that would be computed in finite precision in the correct branch. $\widetilde{v}_c$ corresponds to the mathematical value that $\texttt{v}$ would hold if the correct branch were computed mathematically, in infinite precision. Then $\overline{v_c} = \widetilde{v}_c - \texttt{v}_\texttt{c}$ is the error in computing $\texttt{v}_\texttt{c}$. We can express the total error on $\texttt{v}$ entailed by the $\texttt{s}$ statement as follows:

$$
\overline{v_f} = \widetilde{v}_c - \texttt{v}_\texttt{f} = (\widetilde{v}_c - \texttt{v}_\texttt{c}) + (\texttt{v}_\texttt{c} - \texttt{v}_\texttt{f}) = \overline{v_c} + (\texttt{v}_\texttt{c} - \texttt{v}_\texttt{f}).
\tag{5}
$$

This last expression shows that the error of $\texttt{v}$ can be viewed as the sum of two components. The first term represents the numerical error incurred by the finite-precision computation of $\texttt{v}$ in the correct branch, i.e. the difference between the infinite-precision and finite-precision computations of the correct sequence of operations. The second term is the difference between the value that would be computed in finite-precision in the correct branch and the value that is actually computed in finite-precision in the incorrect branch.

Notice that we limited the use of the typewriter font for the original program variable $\texttt{v}$, for its updated value $\texttt{v}_\texttt{f}$ and for the newly introduced variable $\texttt{v}_\texttt{c}$ that represents a value that is computable by the program. We used the italic font for the variable that represents the mathematical value of a program variable and for its error. This is to distinguish between values that are certainly representable in a fixed-point format and those whose values may not be representable.

However, we argue that even these latter two variables, $\widetilde{v_c}$ and $\overline{v_c}$ are representable in an adequately chosen fixed-point format for programs in the considered syntax. This claim can be easily proved by structural induction on the set of program statements. In particular, it is based on the observation that no arithmetic operation or program statement in the syntax of Fig. 1 produces periodic, non-representable results, as there are no divisions. Hence, both the ideal results and their errors are representable in finite precision. We do not include the proof here due to lack of space. From now on we use the typewriter font for all the above variables.

Let $\mathtt{x} \leq 0$ be the guard of the statement from Eq. 2. Let $\tilde{x}$ be the mathematical value of $\mathtt{x}$. To compute the incurred error for a variable affected by $\mathtt{s}$, we need to compute the expression in Eq. 5. To this end we need to double the two original branches by considering four possible cases:

1. $\mathtt{x} \leq 0 \wedge \tilde{x} \leq 0$. The two control-flows agree, entering the "then" branch, and the error incurred by $\mathtt{s}$ is due only to the errors produced by the arithmetic operations in the body of the "then" branch and only concerns variables $\mathtt{v} \in W(\mathtt{stmt}')$; Indeed, in this case $\mathtt{v_f} = \mathtt{v_c} = \mathtt{v_{then}}$ and thus the expression in Eq. 5 becomes $\overline{\mathtt{v_f}} = \overline{\mathtt{v_{then}}}$.

2. $\mathtt{x} > 0 \wedge \tilde{x} > 0$. Both the inexact and the mathematical control-flows choose the "else" branch, and the error incurred by $\mathtt{s}$ is due only to the errors produced by the operations in the body of the "else" branch, concerning only variables $\mathtt{v} \in W(\mathtt{stmt}'')$. We have that $\mathtt{v_f} = \mathtt{v_c} = \mathtt{v_{else}}$ and the expression for the error is now $\overline{\mathtt{v_f}} = \overline{\mathtt{v_{else}}}$.

3. $\mathtt{x} \leq 0 \wedge \tilde{x} > 0$. The "then" branch is executed instead of the "else" branch, producing a discontinuity error, affecting variables in both branches, i.e. $\mathtt{v} \in W(\mathtt{stmt})$. In particular:

   a) If $\mathtt{v} \in I(\mathtt{s})$, then it is modified in the incorrectly chosen "then" branch, but should have been modified in the "else" branch, possibly by a different sequence of operations. In this case $\mathtt{v_c} = \mathtt{v_{else}}$ while $\mathtt{v_f} = \mathtt{v_{then}}$ and the error expression is $\overline{\mathtt{v_f}} = \widetilde{\mathtt{v_{else}}} - \mathtt{v_{then}}$.

   b) If $\mathtt{v} \in T(\mathtt{s})$, then it is modified in the incorrectly chosen "then" branch, but wouldn't have been modified at all in the correct "else" branch. In this case $\mathtt{v_c} = \mathtt{v}$ and $\mathtt{v_f} = \mathtt{v_{then}}$ and the error expression is $\overline{\mathtt{v_f}} = \tilde{v} - \mathtt{v_{then}}$.

   c) If $\mathtt{v} \in E(\mathtt{s})$, then it is not modified in the incorrectly chosen "then" branch, but would have been modified in the correct "else" branch. In this case $\mathtt{v_c} = \mathtt{v_{else}}$ and $\mathtt{v_f} = \mathtt{v}$ and the error expression is $\overline{\mathtt{v_f}} = \widetilde{\mathtt{v_{else}}} - \mathtt{v}$.

4. $\mathtt{x} > 0 \wedge \tilde{x} \leq 0$. The "else" branch is executed instead of the "then" branch, producing a discontinuity error, affecting all variables $\mathtt{v} \in W(\mathtt{stmt})$:

   a) If $\mathtt{v} \in I(\mathtt{s})$, then $\mathtt{v_f} = \mathtt{v_{else}}$, $\mathtt{v_c} = \mathtt{v_{then}}$ and $\overline{\mathtt{v_f}} = \widetilde{\mathtt{v_{then}}} - \mathtt{v_{else}}$.

   b) If $\mathtt{v} \in E(\mathtt{s})$, then $\mathtt{v_c} = \mathtt{v}$, $\mathtt{v_f} = \mathtt{v_{else}}$ and $\overline{\mathtt{v_f}} = \tilde{v} - \mathtt{v_{else}}$

   c) If $\mathtt{v} \in T(\mathtt{s})$, then $\mathtt{v_c} = \mathtt{v_{then}}$, $\mathtt{v_f} = \mathtt{v}$ and $\overline{\mathtt{v_f}} = \widetilde{\mathtt{v_{then}}} - \mathtt{v}$.

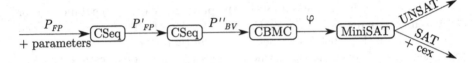

Fig. 2. Analysis flow for programs over fixed-point arithmetic.

4   Program Analysis

4.1   Verification Workflow

Given a fixed-point program P_{FP} with non-deterministic inputs and control structures, and given an error bound 2^{-h}, we wish to know whether any execution of P_{FP} can lead to errors that exceed 2^{-h} for any variable of interest and in any location of the program. We encode this as an assertion-based verification problem, whose complete workflow is shown in Fig. 2. For simplicity, we assume overflow has already been checked (for overflow checking see [30]).

The first module, implemented in CSeq [13], transforms the input program P_{FP} into a modified one P'_{FP}, by rewriting the control structures to compute the discontinuity errors and introduces assertions to test them against the error bound. The program transformation is based on the error expressions derived in Sect. 3.2 and the encoding is shown in Sect. 4.2. This module functions as a pre-processing phase to the rest of the toolchain, based on [30]. P'_{FP} can now be transformed into an equivalent bit-vector program P''_{BV}, by introducing additional statements to compute and propagate the numerical errors in a discontinuity-insensitive manner, generating a propositional formula φ using CBMC [9]. The formula, solved by MiniSAT [12], produces a counterexample in case of satisfiability, i.e. reachable assertion failure in P''_{BV}, or it certifies that the errors never exceed the established bound if it is not satisfiable.

The input parameters of our workflow are: e_i, e_f, and eb. The first two are the integer and fractional precision used for the newly introduced variables that compute the errors, i.e. $\bar{x}_{(e_i.e_f)}$. In our prototype tool these values are guessed to be large enough not to store their designated values. eb is such that $eb = e_f - h$, where 2^{-h} is the error bound. Notice that checking whether $\bar{x}_{(e_i.e_f)}$ does not exceed 2^{-h} is equivalent to checking whether all but its last e_b bits are zero. We check this using a right shift by eb positions on $\bar{x}_{(e_i.e_f)}$. By construction, P''_{BV} will contain a reachable assertion failure if and only if (i) P_{FP} can exceed the given error bound on a variable of interest, or (ii) (e_i, e_f) is not a sufficient precision for an accurate error analysis. In this case, we adjust $(e_i.e_f)$ (and, consequently, eb) and re-encode.

4.2   Program Transformation

Here we describe the encoding of an if-then-else statement into a modified one. We will denote with $\mathbf{x}'$ a temporary variable that does not belong to the initial program, but is introduced during the encoding. The purpose of such variables is to store the result of an operation without overflow or numerical error, thus they will always be given sufficient precision. A variable $\tilde{\bar{\mathtt{x}}}$ will be used to represent the error that arises from the computation of $\mathtt{x}$. All other variables introduced by the encoding will be denoted by letters of the alphabet not appearing in P_{FP}.

The error variables introduced by the encoding are themselves fixed-point variables, but their manipulation is more involved. If we were to treat error variables as we do program variables, by keeping track of the errors arising from their computation, we would incur a recursive definition and have to compute errors of higher degree. Hence, we denote with $\oplus$ two functions that compute sums/differences of error components and internally check that the result is not subject to additional errors.

$$
\left[\!\left[\begin{array}{l}
\mathtt{if}\ (\mathtt{x}_{(x_i.x_f)} \leq 0)\ \{ \\
\quad \mathtt{stmt}'; \\
\};\ \mathtt{else}\ \{ \\
\quad \mathtt{stmt}'';\ \}
\end{array}\right]\!\right]
\longrightarrow
\begin{array}{l}
\mathtt{fixedpoint}\ \tilde{\bar{\mathtt{x}}}_{(e_i.e_f)}, \mathtt{x}'_{(e_i.e_f)}; \\
\mathtt{x}'_{(e_i.e_f)} = \mathtt{x}_{(x_i.x_f)} \ll \mathtt{e_f} - \mathtt{x_f}; \\
\tilde{\bar{\mathtt{x}}}_{(e_i.e_f)} = \mathtt{x}'_{(e_i.e_f)} \oplus \bar{\mathtt{x}}_{(e_i.e_f)}; \\
\\
\mathtt{if}\ \mathtt{x}_{(x_i.x_f)} \leq 0 \wedge \tilde{\bar{\mathtt{x}}}_{(e_i.e_f)} \leq 0 \\
\quad [\![\mathtt{stmt}';]\!] \\
\\
\mathtt{else\ if}\ \mathtt{x}_{(x_i.x_f)} > 0 \wedge \tilde{\bar{\mathtt{x}}}_{(e_i.e_f)} > 0 \\
\quad [\![\mathtt{stmt}'';]\!] \\
\\
\mathtt{else\ if}\ \mathtt{x}_{(x_i.x_f)} \leq 0 \wedge \tilde{\bar{\mathtt{x}}}_{(e_i.e_f)} > 0 \\
\quad \mathtt{fixedpoint\ vthen}_{(v_i.v_f)},\ \mathtt{vthen}'_{(e_i.e_f)}\ \forall \mathtt{v} \in W(\mathtt{stmt}'); \\
\quad \mathtt{vthen}_{(v_i.v_f)} = \mathtt{v}_{(v_i.v_f)}\ \forall \mathtt{v} \in W(\mathtt{stmt}'); \\
\quad \mathtt{stmt}'[\mathtt{vthen/v},\ \forall \mathtt{v} \in W(\mathtt{stmt}')]; \\
\quad \mathtt{vthen}'_{(e_i.e_f)} = \mathtt{vthen}_{(v_i.v_f)} \ll \mathtt{e_f} - \mathtt{v_f};\ \ \forall \mathtt{v} \in W(\mathtt{stmt}'); \\
\quad [\![\mathtt{fixedpoint\ velse}_{(v_i.v_f)}\ \forall \mathtt{v} \in W(\mathtt{stmt}'');]\!] \\
\quad [\![\mathtt{velse}_{(v_i.v_f)} = \mathtt{v}_{(v_i.v_f)}\ \forall \mathtt{v} \in W(\mathtt{stmt}'');]\!] \\
\quad [\![\mathtt{stmt}''[\mathtt{velse/v},\ \forall \mathtt{v} \in W(\mathtt{stmt}'')];]\!] \\
\quad \mathtt{fixedpoint\ velse}'_{(e_i.e_f)},\ \widetilde{\mathtt{velse}}_{(e_i.e_f)}\ \forall \mathtt{v} \in W(\mathtt{stmt}''); \\
\quad \mathtt{velse}'_{(e_i.e_f)} = \mathtt{velse}_{(v_i.v_f)} \ll \mathtt{e_f} - \mathtt{v_f}\ \forall \mathtt{v} \in W(\mathtt{stmt}''); \\
\quad \widetilde{\mathtt{velse}}_{(e_i.e_f)} = \mathtt{velse}'_{(e_i.e_f)} \oplus \overline{\mathtt{velse}}_{(e_i.e_f)}\ \forall \mathtt{v} \in W(\mathtt{stmt}''); \\
\quad \mathtt{fixedpoint}\ \mathtt{v}'_{(e_i.e_f)}\ \forall \mathtt{v} \in W(\mathtt{s}) \setminus \{\mathtt{x}\}; \\
\quad \mathtt{v}'_{(e_i.e_f)} = \mathtt{v}_{(v_i.v_f)} \ll \mathtt{e_f} - \mathtt{v_f}\ \forall \mathtt{v} \in W(\mathtt{s}) \setminus \{\mathtt{x}\}; \\
\quad \mathtt{fixedpoint}\ \tilde{\bar{\mathtt{v}}}_{(e_i.e_f)}\ \forall \mathtt{v} \in T(\mathtt{s}) \setminus \{\mathtt{x}\}; \\
\quad \tilde{\bar{\mathtt{v}}}_{(e_i.e_f)} = \mathtt{v}'_{(e_i.e_f)} \oplus \bar{\mathtt{v}}_{(e_i.e_f)}\ \forall \mathtt{v} \in T(\mathtt{s}) \setminus \{\mathtt{x}\}; \\
\quad \bar{\mathtt{v}}_{(e_i.e_f)} = \tilde{\bar{\mathtt{v}}}_{(e_i.e_f)} \ominus \mathtt{vthen}'_{(e_i.e_f)}\ \forall \mathtt{v} \in T(\mathtt{s}); \\
\quad \bar{\mathtt{v}}_{(e_i.e_f)} = \widetilde{\mathtt{velse}}_{(e_i.e_f)} \ominus \mathtt{vthen}'_{(e_i.e_f)}\ \forall \mathtt{v} \in I(\mathtt{s}); \\
\quad \bar{\mathtt{v}}_{(e_i.e_f)} = \widetilde{\mathtt{velse}}_{(e_i.e_f)} \ominus \mathtt{v}'_{(e_i.e_f)}\ \forall \mathtt{v} \in E(\mathtt{s}); \\
\quad \mathtt{fixedpoint}\ \mathtt{s}_{(e_i.e_f)}\ \forall \mathtt{v} \in W(\mathtt{s}); \\
\quad \mathtt{s}_{(e_i.e_f)} = \mathtt{abs}(\bar{\mathtt{v}}_{(e_i.e_f)})\ \forall \mathtt{v} \in W(\mathtt{s}); \\
\quad \mathtt{assert}((\mathtt{s}_{(\mathtt{e_i.e_f})} \gg \mathtt{eb}) == 0)\ \forall \mathtt{v} \in W(\mathtt{s}); \\
\quad \mathtt{v}_{(v_i.v_f)} = \mathtt{vthen}_{(v_i.v_f)}\ \forall \mathtt{v} \in W(\mathtt{stmt}'); \\
\\
\mathtt{else\ if}\ \mathtt{x}_{(x_i.x_f)} > 0 \wedge \tilde{\bar{\mathtt{x}}}_{(e_i.e_f)} \leq 0 \\
\quad \textit{symmetric to previous case};
\end{array}
$$

Fig. 3. Transformation of the conditional statement.

Figure 3 defines the effect of our transformation function $[\![\cdot]\!]$ applied to an "if-then-else" statement s as in Eq. 2. Notice that we require the precision for error variables $(e_f.e_i)$ to be at least equal to the precision of any variable $v \in W(s) \cup \{x\}$, otherwise the values of e_i and e_f have to be incremented. The transformation generates 5 blocks of statements. In the first block we compute the mathematical value of x, i.e. $\tilde{x}$. We then use $\tilde{x}$ in the next 4 blocks of statements to compare its sign to that of x. The following four blocks correspond to the four cases described in Sect. 3.2.

Case 1: Block 2 checks if both x and $\tilde{x}$ are ≤ 0, i.e. if both the inexact and the exact computation would enter the "then" branch in the original if-then-else statement. If so, the error is computed simply as the error due to the body of the "then" branch, applying the $[\![\cdot]\!]$ function to the body of the "then" branch.

Case 2: Block 3 is analogous; if the signs of both test variables are positive the error will be due only to the computation of the "else" block itself.

Case 3: Block 4 considers the situation in which $x \leq 0$ but $\tilde{x} > 0$. In particular, it translates the effect of the program choosing the "then" branch when the ideal computation would choose the "else" branch.

First, for all the variables that are affected by the "then" branch, i.e. $\forall v \in W(\mathtt{stmt}')$, we introduce a set of four statements whose effect is to store the values computed by the "then" branch in new variables $\mathtt{vthen}'$, without altering the current values of v, since we will need the latter to simulate what an ideal computation would do if it chose the "else" branch.

Now, for all the variables that would be affected by the "else" block, i.e. $\forall v \in W(\mathtt{stmt}'')$, we introduce a set of six statements whose effect is to simulate the computation of the "else" block, coupled with the error propagation it would entail, without actually updating the values for the variables that would have been affected. To this end we use the $[\![\cdot]\!]$ function applied to the statements of the "else" branch. The mathematical values that would be obtained for v in the infinite-precision computation of $\mathtt{stmt}''$ is now stored in $\mathtt{ve\tilde{l}se}$.

The next two statements have the effect of storing the value of v in a variable of greater format, v', $\forall v \in W(s) \setminus \{x\}$. Then, the next two statements compute $\forall v \in T(s) \setminus \{x\}$ the mathematical value that v should have held prior to entering s. This value is now stored in $\tilde{v}$. These last four statements are not needed for x, since we have already computed x' and $\tilde{x}$ in the first block.

Now we have all the ingredients to compute the errors due to the diverging control-flow. $\forall v \in T(s)$ we compute $\bar{v}$ as the difference of $\tilde{v}$ and $\mathtt{vthen}'$, corresponding to case 3.b). $\forall v \in I(s)$, we compute $\bar{v}$ as the difference of $\mathtt{ve\tilde{l}se}$ and $\mathtt{vthen}'$, corresponding to case 3.a). $\forall v \in E(s)$ $\bar{v}$ is computed as the difference of $\mathtt{ve\tilde{l}se}$ and v', corresponding to case 3.c). In the following set of three statements, we check whether the absolute value of the error for the affected variables exceeds the given error bound. Finally, for all variables affected by the "then" branch, we assign their updated values, currently stored in $\mathtt{vthen}$, to v.

Case 4: Symmetric to case 3 and considers $x > 0$ and $\tilde{x} \leq 0$.

5 Experimental Evaluation

We evaluated our approach on a set of routines of common use in the industry: `cav10` [15], loosely based on non-linear interpolation methods, `cosine` [15], a third order polynomial interpolation of the cosine function, `jet−engine` [11], a piece-wise polynomial approximation of a jet-engine controller, and `neural−net`, a fixed-point implementation of the NN of Listing 2 with $H = 13, I = 1, O = 1$. For each routine, we considered 5 different configurations, i.e. 5 different custom precisions for the program variables. We considered the input variables to be non-deterministic in a given input range and to be subject to initial errors to reflect the fact that they may vary at run time, representing sensor readings or output values of other numerical routines, making their values prone to errors. We set the formats for non-deterministic variables to a unique custom precision for each routine, according to their allowed range of values.

We evaluated the numerical precision of the four routines in their various configurations by computing the errors on output variables in function of the initial errors on input variables. Figure 4 shows the experimental results for the four considered benchmarks. We include the absolute errors certified with our control-flow sensitive approach (colored bars) and compare them to the errors obtained by using only the control flow-insensitive part of the verification flow (striped bars). The latter are always less or equal to the former, as is expected.

For `cav10`, we considered formats (7.8), (7.12), (7.16), (7.20), (7.24) for program variables and (7.8) for non-deterministic variables. The routine consists of three arithmetic operations followed by an if-then-else statement, with one operation per branch, for a total of 5 arithmetic statements. Figure 4.a) shows how the upper bounds on the absolute error for the output variable are equal for all five program configurations, regardless of the initial error. However, not taking into account the discontinuity error yields strictly lower output errors and a clear pattern emerges showing that incrementing the initial error while lowering the precision for program variables produces greater output errors.

For `cosine` we set the formats to (23.24), (23.28), (23.32), (23.36), (23.40) and (11.8) for the non-deterministic inputs. To simplify the implementation of our error estimation technique we flattened the original code consisting in a nested if-then-else statement into four separate statements, each containing 2 to 8 operations, for a total of 18 operations. `jet−engine` contains 27 operations: a subtraction followed by an if-then-else statement with 13 operations per branch. We set the formats to (7.8), (7.12), (7.16), (7.20), (7.24) and (7.4) for the input variables. Both benchmarks present the same pattern for numerical errors (Fig. 4.b) and c)): by incrementing the initial error and decreasing the precision of variables, the output error grows. An exception can be observed for `cosine`, in which the output error oscillates; for the format (23.36), the output error for an initial error of 2^{-8} is smaller than the output error for an initial error

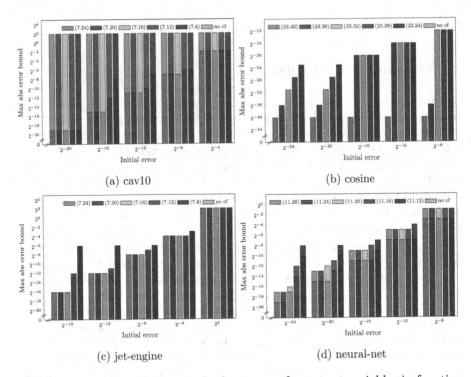

Fig. 4. Benchmarks: maximum absolute errors for output variables in function of initial errors on the inputs.

of 2^{-12}. For both case studies, the control-flow sensitive error bounds coincide with the control-flow insensitive ones. This may be interpreted as an indicator of continuity of the two piece-wise polynomial interpolations.

For the `neural−net` routine we set the formats to (11.12), (11.16), (11.20), (11.24), (11.28) and (3.12) for the input variables. The case study contains 28 operations and a conditional statement with an assignment in one branch. Figure 4.d) shows how both the discontinuity-sensitive and insensitive errors grow as the variable precision decreases and the initial errors increase, and the former is always strictly greater than the latter, indicating that this numerical routine presents a clear discontinuity.

We performed the analyses on a standard consumer laptop, generally taking a couple of seconds and up to a minute for satisfiable instances, both for the control flow-sensitive and insensitive approach. Unsatisfiable instances generally took under a minute and up to a maximum of 28 min. for the discontinuity-sensitive approach in the `cosine` case, which constitutes the largest case study in terms of state-space (2^{20} possible assignments).

6   Related Work

Bit-precise analyses of safety properties in finite-precision arithmetic have been proposed in [7,14] for floating-point arithmetic and [6,19] for fixed-point arithmetic, but do not compute numerical error bounds. [30] extends [19] and gives tight error bounds for fixed-point implementations of numerical routines, but is limited to straight-line code. We have implemented our method on top of [30] to account for exact, bit-precise discontinuity error propagation.

Other work tackling sound discontinuity error estimation in finite-precision arithmetic relies on abstraction-based techniques [32], which produce sound but often pessimistic error bounds. In particular, fixed-point arithmetic is supported in [10,11], which combine exact SMT solving over reals with approximate and sound affine and interval arithmetic. Floating-point error is estimated in [18,34] in an abstract interpretation framework. For straight-line code in fixed-point arithmetic a technique based on interval analysis is proposed in [24].

A number of automated tools exist for soundly estimating numerical errors for finite precision arithmetic in the presence of control structures. Rosa [11] supports both fixed and floating-point arithmetic, while the floating-point specific tool PRECiSA [34,35] uses program transformation to detect unstable tests. Fluctuat [17,18] supports floating-point error estimation in the presence of control structures, while for fixed-point implementations it issues a warning in the presence of unstable tests. FPTaylor [31] uses global optimization to emit error certificates of floating-point errors, but does not handle conditionals directly.

Generation of robust model predictive control implementations in which numerical errors do not exceed a given error bound is proposed in [29]. Stability and safety analysis in the context of control system implementations in also studied in [5,25]. All the above approaches support fixed-point arithmetic. Robustness, i.e. the property of producing small variations on outputs for small variations on inputs, while not explicitly concerned with computing numerical errors, is addressed in [8,21] and in [28,33] for control software.

7   Conclusion and Future Directions

We have presented a bit-precise verification flow to certify the magnitude of numerical errors in programs with conditionals and fixed-point arithmetic in mixed-precision and possibly non-deterministic values. The key element of our approach is a technique that transforms a conditional of a given program into a modified one which preserves the control flow, but also collects information on the propagation of errors due to a wrong branching choice. The program transformation is implemented as a pre-processing technique and seamlessly integrated into an existing discontinuity-insensitive verification workflow, allowing to exactly certify the overall error on a given program variable. The modularity allows overflow and general safety checks to be performed as well.

Our approach is novel, in that it is currently the only one to exactly certify discontinuity errors in fixed-point implementations of numerical routines. In particular, all error expressions are exact and introduce no over-approximations. To the best of our knowledge, all existing approaches for error estimation in finite-precision computations rely on over-approximations of variable values.

As a result of the introduction of additional variables and statements, our program transformation clearly generates overhead in terms of program size. We plan on testing the current workflow on instances of larger size to assess scalability in terms of running times and memory usage. SAT-based verification techniques are indeed known to be resource intensive. However, the recent advances in solvers and their potential for parallelization [20] make them a powerful tool for complex software verification problems.

The bit-vector program generated by our encoding on its own provides a bit-precise representation of the propagated numerical error, but the program itself can be analysed by any verification tool that supports bit-vectors of mixed, arbitrary sizes. In particular, we plan on testing different bounded model checkers, coupled with different SAT solvers, as well as SMT-solvers for the theory of bit-vectors for a word-level approach. While the bit-precise BMC approach is well suited for analysing the sources of numerical errors, abstraction-based tools can provide guarantees on larger error bounds by using over-approximation. To test abstraction-based approaches, we are considering developing (via Crab [27]) an abstract interpreter for bit-vector programs that would allow over-approximated error bound analysis with different abstract domains.

References

1. MISRA-C:2004 — Guidelines for the use of the C language in critical systems. Technical report, MIRA Ltd. (2004)
2. Programming languages — C — Extensions to support embedded processors. ISO/IEC Technical Report 18037:2008. EEE, New York (2008)
3. DO-178C/ED-12C, Software considerations in airborne systems and equipment certification. Technical report, RTCA/EUROCAE (2011)
4. ISO 26262 Road Vehicles - Functional Safety. Technical report. ISO, Geneva, Switzerland (2011)
5. Abate, A., et al.: Automated formal synthesis of digital controllers for state-space physical plants. In: Majumdar, R., Kunčak, V. (eds.) CAV 2017. LNCS, vol. 10426, pp. 462–482. Springer, Cham (2017). https://doi.org/10.1007/978-3-319-63387-9_23
6. Bessa, I., Abreu, R.B., Filho, J.E.C., Cordeiro, L.C.: SMT-based bounded model checking of fixed-point digital controllers. In: IECON, pp. 295–301. IEEE (2014)
7. Brillout, A., Kroening, D., Wahl, T.: Mixed abstractions for floating-point arithmetic. In: FMCAD, pp. 69–76. IEEE (2009)
8. Chaudhuri, S., Gulwani, S., Lublinerman, R.: Continuity and robustness of programs. Commun. ACM 55(8), 107–115 (2012)
9. Clarke, E., Kroening, D., Lerda, F.: A tool for checking ANSI-C programs. In: Jensen, K., Podelski, A. (eds.) TACAS 2004. LNCS, vol. 2988, pp. 168–176. Springer, Heidelberg (2004). https://doi.org/10.1007/978-3-540-24730-2_15
10. Darulova, E., Kuncak, V.: Sound compilation of reals. In: POPL, pp. 235–248. ACM (2014)

11. Darulova, E., Kuncak, V.: Towards a compiler for reals. ACM Trans. Program. Lang. Syst. **39**(2), 8:1–8:28 (2017)
12. Eén, N., Sörensson, N.: An extensible SAT-solver. In: Giunchiglia, E., Tacchella, A. (eds.) SAT 2003. LNCS, vol. 2919, pp. 502–518. Springer, Heidelberg (2004). https://doi.org/10.1007/978-3-540-24605-3_37
13. Fischer, B., Inverso, O., Parlato, G.: CSeq: a concurrency pre-processor for sequential C verification tools. In: ASE, pp. 710–713. IEEE (2013)
14. Gadelha, M.R., Cordeiro, L.C., Nicole, D.A.: An efficient floating-point bit-blasting API for verifying C programs. In: Christakis, M., Polikarpova, N., Duggirala, P.S., Schrammel, P. (eds.) NSV/VSTTE -2020. LNCS, vol. 12549, pp. 178–195. Springer, Cham (2020). https://doi.org/10.1007/978-3-030-63618-0_11
15. Ghorbal, K., Goubault, E., Putot, S.: A logical product approach to zonotope intersection. In: Touili, T., Cook, B., Jackson, P. (eds.) CAV 2010. LNCS, vol. 6174, pp. 212–226. Springer, Heidelberg (2010). https://doi.org/10.1007/978-3-642-14295-6_22
16. Giacobbe, M., Henzinger, T.A., Lechner, M.: How many bits does it take to quantize your neural network? In: TACAS 2020. LNCS, vol. 12079, pp. 79–97. Springer, Cham (2020). https://doi.org/10.1007/978-3-030-45237-7_5
17. Goubault, E., Putot, S.: Static analysis of finite precision computations. In: Jhala, R., Schmidt, D. (eds.) VMCAI 2011. LNCS, vol. 6538, pp. 232–247. Springer, Heidelberg (2011). https://doi.org/10.1007/978-3-642-18275-4_17
18. Goubault, E., Putot, S.: Robustness analysis of finite precision implementations. In: Shan, C. (ed.) APLAS 2013. LNCS, vol. 8301, pp. 50–57. Springer, Cham (2013). https://doi.org/10.1007/978-3-319-03542-0_4
19. Inverso, O., Bemporad, A., Tribastone, M.: Sat-based synthesis of spoofing attacks in cyber-physical control systems. In: ICCPS, pp. 1–9. IEEE/ACM (2018)
20. Inverso, O., Trubiani, C.: Parallel and distributed bounded model checking of multi-threaded programs. In: PPoPP, pp. 202–216. ACM (2020)
21. Ivancic, F., Ganai, M.K., Sankaranarayanan, S., Gupta, A.: Numerical stability analysis of floating-point computations using software model checking. In: MEMOCODE, pp. 49–58. IEEE (2010)
22. Jet Propulsion Laboratory, C.I.o.T.: JPL Institutional Coding Standard for the C Programming Language. Standard (2009)
23. Martel, M., Najahi, A., Revy, G.: Toward the synthesis of fixed-point code for matrix inversion based on Cholesky decomposition. In: DASIP, pp. 1–8. IEEE (2014)
24. Martel, M., Najahi, A., Revy, G.: Trade-offs of certified fixed-point code synthesis for linear algebra basic blocks. J. Syst. Archit. **76**, 133–148 (2017)
25. Martinez, A.A., Majumdar, R., Saha, I., Tabuada, P.: Automatic verification of control system implementations. In: EMSOFT, pp. 9–18. ACM (2010)
26. Narodytska, N., Kasiviswanathan, S.P., Ryzhyk, L., Sagiv, M., Walsh, T.: Verifying properties of binarized deep neural networks. In: AAAI, pp. 6615–6624. AAAI Press (2018)
27. Navas, J.A., Schachte, P., Søndergaard, H., Stuckey, P.J.: Signedness-agnostic program analysis: precise integer bounds for low-level code. In: Jhala, R., Igarashi, A. (eds.) APLAS 2012. LNCS, vol. 7705, pp. 115–130. Springer, Heidelberg (2012). https://doi.org/10.1007/978-3-642-35182-2_9
28. Park, J., Pajic, M., Sokolsky, O., Lee, I.: Automatic verification of finite precision implementations of linear controllers. In: Legay, A., Margaria, T. (eds.) TACAS 2017. LNCS, vol. 10205, pp. 153–169. Springer, Heidelberg (2017). https://doi.org/10.1007/978-3-662-54577-5_9

29. Salamati, M., Salvia, R., Darulova, E., Soudjani, S., Majumdar, R.: Memory-efficient mixed-precision implementations for robust explicit model predictive control. ACM Trans. Embed. Comput. Syst. **18**(5s), 100:1–100:19 (2019)

30. Simić, S., Bemporad, A., Inverso, O., Tribastone, M.: Tight error analysis in fixed-point arithmetic. In: Dongol, B., Troubitsyna, E. (eds.) IFM 2020. LNCS, vol. 12546, pp. 318–336. Springer, Cham (2020). https://doi.org/10.1007/978-3-030-63461-2_17

31. Solovyev, A., Baranowski, M.S., Briggs, I., Jacobsen, C., Rakamarić, Z., Gopalakrishnan, G.: Rigorous estimation of floating-point round-off errors with symbolic Taylor expansions. ACM Trans. Program. Lang. Syst. **41**(1), 2:1–2:39 (2019)

32. Stol, J., De Figueiredo, L.H.: Self-validated numerical methods and applications. In: Monograph for 21st Brazilian Mathematics Colloquium, IMPA. Citeseer (1997)

33. Tabuada, P., Balkan, A., Caliskan, S.Y., Shoukry, Y., Majumdar, R.: Input-output robustness for discrete systems. In: EMSOFT, pp. 217–226. ACM (2012)

34. Titolo, L., Feliú, M.A., Moscato, M., Muñoz, C.A.: An abstract interpretation framework for the round-off error analysis of floating-point programs. In: VMCAI 2018. LNCS, vol. 10747, pp. 516–537. Springer, Cham (2018). https://doi.org/10.1007/978-3-319-73721-8_24

35. Titolo, L., Moscato, M., Feliu, M.A., Muñoz, C.A.: Automatic generation of guard-stable floating-point code. In: Dongol, B., Troubitsyna, E. (eds.) IFM 2020. LNCS, vol. 12546, pp. 141–159. Springer, Cham (2020). https://doi.org/10.1007/978-3-030-63461-2_8

36. Yates, R.: Fixed-point arithmetic: an introduction. Digital Signal Labs (2009)

37. Zhao, Y., Shumailov, I., Mullins, R.D., Anderson, R.: To compress or not to compress: understanding the interactions between adversarial attacks and neural network compression. In: MLSys. mlsys.org (2019)

Machine Learning and Cyber-Physical Systems

`OSIP`: Tightened Bound Propagation for the Verification of ReLU Neural Networks

Vahid Hashemi[1], Panagiotis Kouvaros[2(✉)], and Alessio Lomuscio[2]

[1] Audi AG, Ingolstadt, Germany
[2] Imperial College London, London, UK
p.kouvaros@imperial.ac.uk

Abstract. Abstraction-based methods for the verification of ReLU-based neural networks suffer from rapid degradation in their effectiveness as the neural network's depth increases. We propose `OSIP`, an abstraction method based on symbolic interval propagation in which the choice of the ReLU relaxation at each node is determined via optimisation. We present an implementation of `OSIP` on top of `Venus`, a publicly available toolkit for complete verification of neural networks. In the experiments reported, `OSIP` calculated bounds that were tighter than the state-of-the-art on ReLU networks from the first competition for neural network verification. As a case study we apply the method for the verification of VGG16, a deep, high-dimensional, 300,000 node-strong model used for object classification in autonomous vehicles against local robustness properties. We demonstrate that `OSIP` could verify the correctness of the model against perturbations that are larger than what can be analysed with the present state-of-the-art.

1 Introduction

Methods based on machine-learning (ML) are increasingly being deployed in AI-based, safety-critical applications, including autonomous vehicles. Rather than being directly programmed by software engineers, these modules often take the form of neural networks (NN) synthesised directly from data. A notable example of these are the class of ML-based object detectors and classifiers presently used in autonomous vehicles. These are typically deep (i.e., multi-layered) networks often comprising hundreds of thousands of neurons that can automatically detect and classify objects of interest in an image, whether these are vehicles, humans, fixed and moving obstacles, etc. While the performance of neural classifiers is high, their error rates are often in the region of 1–2%, hence still too high to be deployed safely on their own. It is also known that neural models are particularly fragile against out of sample data, i.e., while the nominal performance may be high on data with the same statistical distribution of the training set, this may not be the case with out-of-distribution inputs. To mitigate these problems the area of verification of neural networks has grown to propose methods to verify the correctness of classifiers.

© Springer Nature Switzerland AG 2021
R. Calinescu and C. S. Păsăreanu (Eds.): SEFM 2021, LNCS 13085, pp. 463–480, 2021.
https://doi.org/10.1007/978-3-030-92124-8_26

Due to their importance in applications, particular emphasis to date has been devoted to methods addressing the verification of feed-forward (i.e., non-recurrent) neural networks based on Rectified-Linear Units (ReLU). A key specification that is analysed in this context is *local robustness*. Simply stated, local robustness refers to whether or not the network alters its output in the presence of small changes to the input. This can be useful to analyse the network's stability in the presence of input noise, or its susceptibility to adversarial attacks [12].

Related work. Methods in formal verification of ReLU-based neural networks can be partitioned into *complete*, or exact, and *incomplete*, or approximate. Complete methods [2, 4, 6, 9, 11, 13, 17–19, 21, 21, 22, 29, 31, 32] can theoretically solve a verification query, such as local robustness, both with a positive and a negative answer. However, they also suffer from scalability issues and may not be able to resolve queries when the network or the perturbation range is large.

In contrast with this, incomplete methods [3, 7, 8, 10, 23, 24, 26, 28, 33, 34, 36, 37, 37] rely on various abstraction methods to overapproximate the computation of a neural network. Because of this overapproximation, incomplete methods can only certify that a network is compliant against a specification, but not that it is not. While leading incomplete approaches can solve some verification problems that cannot be established via complete approaches, they still fall short of being capable of addressing large models of industrial sizes. This is because the abstraction methods are often too coarse thereby inhibiting the evaluation of significant perturbations on the input. This is particularly evident in *symbolic interval propagation* (SIP)-based methods [26, 28, 33–35, 37] whereby the ReLU function is linearly approximated and the bounds for the nodes are computed via backward passes of variable substitutions through the network. Whilst this often achieves state-of-the-art scalability, it trades off precision by inducing coarser overapproximations as compared to other methods.

Contribution. In this paper we aim to make a contribution in this direction. We propose an incomplete, SIP-based method that improves the precision. Differently from related methods, where the relaxation for a ReLU node is heuristically chosen to induce the minimum local, i.e., at neuron-level, overapproximation area [26, 37] or the minimum local maximum error [32], our method jointly determines via optimisation the relaxations to be conducted for all the nodes in a layer, thereby accounting for intra-layer dependencies to improve precision. Additionally, it provides a simple, yet effective treatment for max-pooling layers towards further improving precision. This enables solving verification queries that could not previously be determined by the state-of-the-art. We experimentally evaluate the method proposed by benchmarking on the ReLU networks from the first competition for neural network verification. Additionally we report the results obtained when analysing VGG16, an image classifier consisting of over 300,000 nodes. The results show that our method produces tighter bounds and is able to solve verification queries that cannot be solved by present methods.

The rest of the paper is organised as follows. In Sect. 2 we fix the notation and present key concepts used throughout the paper. Section 3 reports OSIP, the SIP method here developed. Section 4 reports details of the resulting implementation and reports experimental results against ReLU networks from the first competition for neural network verification and VGG16. We conclude in Sect. 5.

2 Preliminaries

Feed-Forward Neural Networks. A *feed-forward neural network* (FFNN) is a vector-valued function $f\colon \mathbb{R}^{s_0} \to \mathbb{R}^{s_L}$ that composes a sequence of $L \geq 1$ layers $f_1\colon \mathbb{R}^{s_0} \to \mathbb{R}^{s_1}, \ldots, f_L\colon \mathbb{R}^{s_{L-1}} \to \mathbb{R}^{s_L}$. Each layer f_i, $i \in \{1, \ldots, L-1\}$, is said to be a *hidden layer*; the last layer f_L of the network is said to be the *output layer*. Each element of each layer f_i is said to be a *neuron*, or a *node*. We use $n_{i,q}$ to refer to the q-th node of layer i. Each layer f_i, $i \in \{1, \ldots, L\}$, implements one of the following functions for input x_{i-1}:

1. an affine transformation $f_i(x_{i-1}) = W^{(i)}x_{i-1} + b_i$, for a weight matrix $W^{(i)} \in \mathbb{R}^{n_i \times n_{i-1}}$ and a bias vector $b \in \mathbb{R}^{n_i}$.
2. a ReLU activation function $f_i(x_{i-1}) = \max(x_{i-1}, 0)$, where the maximum function is applied element-wise.
3. a max-pool function which collapses rectangular neighbourhoods of its input into the maximal value within each neighbourhood.

Note that for ease of presentation we separate affine transformations from the ReLU activation function, where we consider each as a different layer, as opposed to their standard treatment whereby their composition defines a layer. Also, we hereafter assume that the bias vector for all the layers is the zero vector. There is no technical difficulty to extend the discussion to non-zero bias vectors.

Verification Problem. Given a FFNN, the verification problem is to answer positively or negatively as to whether the output of the network for every input within a linearly definable set of inputs[1] is contained within a linearly definable set of outputs. Formally, we have:

Definition 1. *Verification problem. Given a FFNN f, a linearly definable set of inputs $\mathcal{X} \subset \mathbb{R}^{s_0}$ and a linearly definable set of outputs $\mathcal{Y} \subset \mathbb{R}^{s_L}$, the verification problem is to establish whether*

$$\forall x \in \mathcal{X}\colon f(x) \in \mathcal{Y}.$$

One of the most well-studied instantiations of the verification problem is the *local adversarial robustness* problem. The problem concerns answering whether all images within a norm-ball of a given input image are classified equivalently by the network f [1,2,8,15,17,31]. Formally, the local adversarial robustness problem is derived from the verification problem by setting

$$\mathcal{X} = \{x' \mid x - \epsilon \leq x' \leq x + \epsilon\}$$
$$\mathcal{Y} = \{y \mid \forall i \neq c\colon f(x')_i < f(x')_c\},$$

---

[1] A linearly definable set is a set that can be expressed as a finite set of affine constraints over real-valued variables.

Algorithm 1. Verification via over-approximation.

1: **procedure** VERIFY($f, \mathcal{X}, \mathcal{Y}$)
2:     **Input:** network f, set of inputs $\mathcal{X}$, set of outputs $\mathcal{Y}$
3:     **Output: yes/unknown**
4:     compute $\hat{\mathcal{R}}$ such that $\hat{\mathcal{R}} \supseteq \{f(x) \mid x \in \mathcal{X}\}$
5:     **if** $\hat{\mathcal{R}} \subseteq \mathcal{Y}$ **then**
6:         **return yes**
7:     **else**
8:         **return unknown**

---

for a given image x with class label c and perturbation radius $\epsilon \geq 0$. In this paper, we focus on verification problems whereby the set of inputs $\mathcal{X}$ is defined by a lower and an upper bound for each element of the input x_0 to the network, i.e., $\mathcal{X} = \{x_0 \mid l_i \leq x_{0,i} \leq u_i\}$, where $l_i, u_i \in \mathbb{R}$.

3   OSIP: Tightened Bound Propagation

In this section we present OSIP (*optimised* SIP), a novel tight symbolic interval propagation method for the verification of feed-forward neural networks.

Given a network and lower and upper bounds of its inputs, OSIP estimates lower and upper bounds of the network's output nodes. OSIP can then potentially use these bounds to determine the satisfaction of the verification property in question. OSIP is incomplete in that the bounds may be overestimated to such a degree that solving the verification problem is not possible.

The key novel element of OSIP consists in a novel treatment of the ReLU function whereby the linear approximation of the function is selected via optimisation. As it will be clear in the next section, this results in a method that in experiments calculates the tightest overestimation when compared to leading methods. The size of the approximation is essential in incomplete methods. Intuitively, the smaller the uncertainty, the more likely it is that a verification query can be solved.

Overview. OSIP is an instance of verification algorithms operating by overapproximating the network computation (see Algorithm 1 for a high level description of this class of algorithms). The method computes an overapproximation $\hat{\mathcal{R}}$ of the reachable output set $\mathcal{R} = \{f(x) \mid x \in \mathcal{X}\}$ for a given network f and set of inputs $\mathcal{X}$ concerning a verification problem $\forall x \in \mathcal{X}: f(x) \in \mathcal{Y}$. This over-approximation is obtained from a layer-by-layer application of the layers' functions to the input set $\mathcal{X}$, where the ReLU function is linearly relaxed.

Depending of the tightness of the overapproximation, Algorithm 1 may or may not be able to solve the verification problem. In particular, if $\hat{\mathcal{R}} \subseteq \mathcal{Y}$, then the algorithm outputs yes, i.e., the verification property is satisfied. For

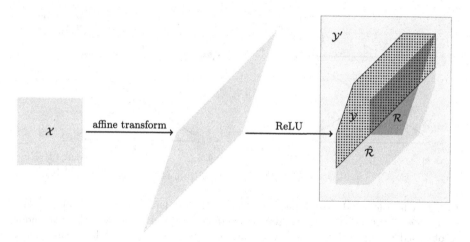

Fig. 1. Over-approximation of a network's bounds. The network has a two-dimensional input and two layers: an affine transformation layer and a ReLU layer. The verification problem $\forall x \in \mathcal{X} : f(x) \in \mathcal{Y}'$ is satisfied whereas the verification problem $\forall x \in \mathcal{X} : f(x) \in \mathcal{Y}$ cannot be solved.

instance, if analysing a local adversarial problem and $\hat{\mathcal{R}} \subseteq \mathcal{Y}$, then all images whose network output is within $\hat{\mathcal{R}}$ are classified equally to the image given as input to the problem. Since these images form a superset of the set $\mathcal{X}$ of images within the norm-ball of the image in question, the verification problem is satisfied.

Otherwise, if $\hat{\mathcal{R}} \not\subseteq \mathcal{Y}$, then Algorithm 1 outputs `unknown`, i.e., the verification problem cannot be solved. For instance, if analysing a local adversarial problem and $\hat{\mathcal{R}} \not\subseteq \mathcal{Y}$, then any image whose network output is within $\hat{\mathcal{R}} \setminus \mathcal{Y}$, i.e., any image that potentially falsifies the verification problem, may or may not lie within the norm-ball of the image in question; consequently, it cannot be used to falsify the verification problem. Figure 1 gives a graphical illustration of these two possible outcomes of Algorithm 1.

Detailed Description. In line with previous symbolic interval propagation methods [26,31,32,37], OSIP analyses a given network in a layer-by-layer fashion, where for each node $n_{i,j}$, it constructs the following:

- a (symbolic) linear constraint $\beta_{i,j}^{\geq}$ of its lower bound, built from variables expressing the inputs to the node,
- a similarly defined linear constraint $\beta_{i,j}^{\leq}$ of its upper bound;
- a concrete (i.e., numeric) lower bound $l_{i,j}$,
- a concrete upper bound $u_{i,j}$.

This results in the derivation of concrete lower and upper bounds for the output nodes of the network, which can potentially be used to determine the satisfaction of the verification problem as per Algorithm 1.

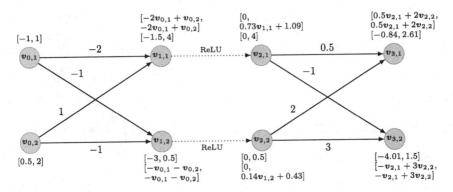

Fig. 2. A feed-forward neural network. The inputs are depicted in green colour. Concrete ranges next to a node indicate the concrete lower and upper bounds of the node as obtained via OSIP. Symbolic ranges next to a node indicate the lower and upper bound constraints of the node as obtained via OSIP.

Following the presentation from [26] we now describe the computation of the constraints and bounds for each of the types of layers constituting the networks considered in this paper. The novel elements of OSIP consist in the treatment of the ReLU and max-pool layers. In the following we use symbolic variables $v_{i,j}$ for the value of each node $n_{i,j}$; we use these variables to build the bound constraints. To exemplify each computation we use the network from Fig. 2. We begin with the constraints and bounds of the input to the network. We then propagate these through the network to derive the constraints and bounds of the output of the network.

Input. The constraints and bounds for the input to the network are instantiated from the bounds of the input prescribed by the verification problem:

$$\beta^{\geq}_{0,j} = l_j; \quad \beta^{\leq}_{0,j} = u_j; \quad l_{0,j} = l_j; \quad u_{0,j} = u_j.$$

Affine Transformation Layer. Given the vector $v_i = \begin{bmatrix} v_{i,1}, v_{i,2}, \ldots, v_{i,s_i} \end{bmatrix}^T$ of layer i's variables, the lower and upper bound constraints of an affine transformation layer f_{i+1} are defined by:

$$\beta^{\geq}_{i+1,j} = \beta^{\leq}_{i+1,j} = W^{(i+1)}_{j,:} v_i.$$

In other words, the lower and upper bound constraints for affine transformation layers are identical and instantiated to the network function for the node in question.

Example 1. Consider the network from Fig. 2. Given the vector of input variables $\begin{bmatrix} v_{0,1} & v_{0,2} \end{bmatrix}^T$, the lower and upper bound constraints of node $n_{1,1}$ are

$$\beta^{\geq}_{1,1} = \beta^{\leq}_{1,1} = W^{(1)}_{1,:} \begin{bmatrix} v_{0,1} & v_{0,2} \end{bmatrix}^T = \begin{bmatrix} -2 & 1 \end{bmatrix} \begin{bmatrix} v_{0,1} & v_{0,2} \end{bmatrix}^T = -2v_{0,1} + v_{0,2}.$$

The concrete bounds of the layer are obtained by replacing the variables in the nodes' constraints with their associated lower or upper bound constraints, depending on the signs of the variables. In particular, to compute the lower bound (upper bound, respectively) of a node, we replace the variables within its lower bound constraint (upper bound constraint, respectively) with the lower bound constraints (upper bound constraints, respectively) of the nodes of the previous layer if the sign of the variables is positive; otherwise, if it is negative, then we use the upper bound constraints (lower bound constraints, respectively) of said nodes. We continue by replacing the newly introduced variables with their corresponding constraints, and so on, until the constraints depend only on the input variables whereby we can compute the concrete bounds.

Formally, the derivation of the concrete bounds is defined as follows. We begin by replacing the $v_{i,j}$ variables in $\beta_{i+1}^{\geq}$ and $\beta_{i+1}^{\leq}$ with their corresponding bound constraints:

$$\beta_{i+1,j}^{\geq} = \left(W_{j,:}^{(i+1)-} \beta_i^{\leq} + W_{j,:}^{(i+1)+} \beta_i^{\geq} \right) v_{i-1},$$

$$\beta_{i+1,j}^{\leq} = \left(W_{j,:}^{(i+1)-} \beta_i^{\geq} + W_{j,:}^{(i+1)+} \beta_i^{\leq} \right) v_{i-1},$$

where:

- $W^{(i+1)-}$ and $W^{(i+1)+}$ are obtained from $\min(W^{(i+1)}, 0)$ and $\max(W^{(i+1)}, 0)$ with the element-wise application of the min and max functions;
- $W_{j,:}^{(i+1)x} \beta_i^y$, $x \in \{-, +\}$, $y \in \{\leq, \geq\}$, denotes (with slight abuse of notation) the multiplication of $W_{j,:}^{(i+1)x}$ with the matrix of the coefficients of the constraints β_i^y over v_{i-1}.

We then repeat this back-substitution step until all layers have been processed and the upper and lower bounds for the node in question are instantiated by numerical values.

Example 2. Consider the network from Fig. 2. We execute the computation of the concrete lower and upper bounds of node $n_{3,1}$ whose lower and upper bound constraints are

$$\beta_{3,1}^{\geq} = 0.5 \cdot v_{2,1} + 2 \cdot v_{2,2} \leq v_{3,1} \leq 0.5 \cdot v_{2,1} + 2 \cdot v_{2,2} = \beta_{3,1}^{\leq}.$$

We begin by replacing the variables $v_{2,1}$, $v_{2,2}$ in $\beta_{3,1}^{\geq}$ with the lower bound constraints of nodes $n_{2,1}$, $n_{2,2}$ and by replacing said variables in $\beta_{3,1}^{\leq}$ with the upper bound constraints of said nodes:

$$0 \leq v_{3,1} \leq 0.37 \cdot v_{1,1} + 0.28 \cdot v_{1,2} + 1.41.$$

Next, we perform similar replacements to the newly introduces variables:

$$0 \leq v_{3,1} \leq -1.02 \cdot v_{0,1} + 0.09 \cdot v_{0,2} + 1.41$$

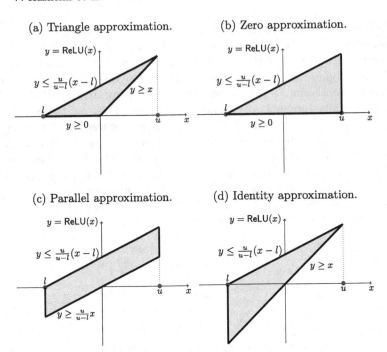

(a) Triangle approximation.   (b) Zero approximation.

(c) Parallel approximation.   (d) Identity approximation.

Fig. 3. Convex approximations of the ReLU function $\mathsf{ReLU}(x) = \max(x, 0)$.

From above, the concrete lower bound of $v_{3,1}$ equals 0. To obtain its concrete upper bound, we replace $v_{0,1}$ with the lower bound of its associated input and $v_{0,2}$ with the upper bound of its associated input. This gives $0 \leq v_{3,1} \leq 2.61$.

Remark 1. Observe that the concrete bounds for a node can alternatively be directly computed by replacing the variables in the bound constraints of the node with the concrete bounds of the nodes associated with the variables. While this is more efficient than the back-substituting the variables, it is known to lead to looser bounds [24].

ReLU layer. The derivation of the bound constraints for a ReLU node requires a convex approximation of the ReLU function $\mathsf{ReLU}(x) = \max(x, 0)$. The optimal convex approximation of the function is the triangle approximation [9]. The approximation bounds the function from above with $\mathsf{ReLU}(x) \leq \frac{u}{u-l}(x - l)$, where l and u are the lower and upper bounds of x, and from below with $\mathsf{ReLU}(x) \geq 0$, $\mathsf{ReLU}(x) \geq x$ (Fig. 3a). Though optimal, the approximation is problematic in that it uses two lower bound constraints, thereby leading to an exponential blow-up of the number of constraints required for the overall analysis [26]. To circumvent this, the ReLU function is instead typically bounded from below with $\mathsf{ReLU}(x) \geq \lambda x$, $\lambda \in [0, 1]$. Commonly used approximations are the *parallel approximation* with $\lambda = \frac{u}{u-l}$ (Fig. 3c) [31,33], the *zero approximation* with $\lambda = 0$ (Fig. 3b) [26,37] and the *identity approximation* with $\lambda = 1$

(Fig. 3d) [26,37]. State-of-the-art methods select a node's approximation either on the basis of the minimum maximum distance from the ReLU function [32] (i.e., always select the parallel approximation) or in terms of the smallest over-approximation area induced [26,37] (i.e., the select the identity approximation if $|l| < u$, otherwise the zero approximation). However, as we experimentally show in the next section, since these heuristic rules operate at a local, neuron level and do not account for intra-layer neuron dependencies, their comparative performance (in terms of the tightness of the derived output bounds) varies with different verification problems.

Differently from these works, we now propose a method that efficiently determines the ReLU approximation for each node via optimisation. The key idea is to jointly optimise the approximation slopes of a layer to bring about the tightest bounds in the subsequent layer. By jointly optimising the slopes we account for the nodes' intra-layer dependencies and the influence thereof in the bounds of the subsequent layer. As we experimentally show in the next section, this results in a method that consistently outperforms the leading methods.

We focus on optimising the slopes to maximise the concrete lower bounds of layer $i+1$; the case of minimising the upper bounds is analogous. We begin with setting

$$\beta^{\geq}_{i+1,j} = \lambda^{\geq}_{i+1,j} v_{i,j}, \quad \beta^{\leq}_{i+1,j} = \frac{u_{i,j}}{u_{i,j} - l_{i,j}}(v_{i,j} - l_{i,j}),$$

where $\lambda^{\geq}_{i+1,j}$ is an optimisation variable for the slope of node $n_{i+1,j}$ and $v_{i,j}$ is the variable representing the input to said node. Now, recall that the bound constraints $\beta^{\geq}_{i+2}, \beta^{\leq}_{i+2}$ of the subsequent layer are constraints over the variables associated with the nodes at layer $i+1$. By performing a single back-substitution step we obtain the constraints $W^{(i+2)-}\beta^{\leq}_{i+1} + W^{(i+2)+}\beta^{\geq}_{i+1}$ which are over the variables associated with the nodes at layer i. These constraints can be used to compute the concrete lower bounds of layer $i + 2$ by concretising their variables as follows: $l_{i+2} = K^+ l_i + K^- u_i$, where $K = W^{(i+2)-}\beta^{\leq}_{i+1} + W^{(i+2)+}\beta^{\geq}_{i+1}$. Our aim is to derive the approximations which maximise the sum of these bounds. Formally, our aim is to solve the following optimisation problem:

$$\begin{aligned}
\max_{\lambda^{\geq}_{i+1}} \quad & \sum_j K^+_{j,:} l_{i,j} + K^-_{j,:} u_{i,j} \\
\text{subject to} \quad & K = W^{(i+2)-}\beta^{\leq}_{i+1} + W^{(i+2)+}\beta^{\geq}_{i+1}, \\
& \beta^{\geq}_{i+1,j} = \lambda^{\geq}_{i+1,j} v_{i,j}, \quad \beta^{\leq}_{i+1,j} = \frac{u_{i,j}}{u_{i,j} - l_{i,j}}(v_{i,j} - l_{i,j}), \\
& \lambda^{\geq}_{i+1,j} \in [0, 1].
\end{aligned} \tag{1}$$

The solution to this optimisation problem determines the slopes to be used in the lower bound constraints $\beta^{\geq}_{i+1} = \lambda^{\geq}_i v_i$ when computing the concrete lower bound of a node in a subsequent layer using back-substitution. The analogous optimisation problem (which minimises the bounds in the subsequent layer) determines the slopes $\lambda^{\leq}_i$ to be used when computing the upper bound of a node in a subsequent layer.

This concludes the derivation of the bound constrains for a ReLU node. The concrete bounds of each ReLU node $n_{i,j}$ are

$$l_{i+1,j} = \min(\lambda^{\geq}_{i+1,j} \cdot l_{i,j}, \lambda^{\leq}_{i+1,j} \cdot l_{i,j}), \quad u_{i+1,j} = u_{i,j}.$$

Remark 2. Note that the optimisation problem 1 is non-convex and therefore hard to solve for large layers. Still, as we experimentally show in the next section, instead of jointly optimising the slopes of layer $i+1$ to tighten all concrete bounds in layer $i+2$, it is sufficient to consider the bounds of only a small number of nodes to efficiently and consistently (i.e., for all the networks and radii considered in our experiments) outperform the state-of-the-art. We hereafter refer to this number of nodes as the *number of optimised nodes parameter*. The selection of the nodes to be considered in the optimisation problem is carried out on the basis of the looseness of the nodes' bounds: the nodes having the looser bounds are the ones to be selected. The bounds are computed by concretising the nodes' bound constraints with the concrete bounds from layer $i+1$, i.e., $W^{(i+2)-}u_{i+1}+W^{(i+2)+}l_{i+1}$ for the lower bounds and $W^{(i+2)+}u_{i+1}+W^{(i+2)-}l_{i+1}$ for the upper bounds (note that as the bounds l_{i+1} depend on the approximation slopes of layer $i+1$, which have not been determined yet, we here use the slopes from the smallest overapproximation area heuristic).

Example 3. Consider the network from Fig. 2. We execute the computation of the upper and lower bound constraints of node $n_{2,1}$. The concrete lower and upper bounds of the input $v_{1,1}$ to the node are -1.5 and 4, respectively. We therefore have that the upper bound constraint equals

$$\beta^{\leq}_{2,1} = \frac{4}{4-(-1.5)}(v_{1,1}-(-1.5)) = 0.73v_{1,1}+1.09.$$

We compute two lower bound constraints for the node: one constraint to be used in the back-substitution process for the computation of a concrete lower bound of a node in a subsequent layer; the other to be used for the computation of a concrete upper bound. Consider the former constraint. The constraint has the form $\beta^{\geq}_{2,1} = \lambda^{\geq}_{2,1} \cdot v_{1,1}$. To determine $\lambda^{\geq}_{2,1}$, we maximise the sum of the lower concrete bounds of nodes $n_{3,1}$ and $n_{3,2}$:

$$\max_{\lambda^{\geq}_{2,1},\lambda^{\geq}_{2,2}} l_{3,1} + l_{3,2}$$
$$= \max_{\lambda^{\geq}_{2,1},\lambda^{\geq}_{2,2}} 0.5 \cdot v_{2,1} + 2 \cdot v_{2,2} - v_{2,1} + 3 \cdot v_{2,2}$$
$$= \max_{\lambda^{\geq}_{2,1},\lambda^{\geq}_{2,2}} 0.5 \cdot \lambda^{\geq}_{2,1} \cdot v_{1,1} + 2 \cdot \lambda^{\geq}_{2,2} \cdot v_{1,2} - 0.73 \cdot v_{1,1} - 1.09 + 3 \cdot \lambda^{\geq}_{2,2} \cdot v_{1,2}$$
$$= \max_{\lambda^{\geq}_{2,1},\lambda^{\geq}_{2,2}} -0.75\lambda^{\geq}_{2,1} - 15\lambda^{\geq}_{2,2} - 4.01.$$

Since $0 \leq \lambda^{\geq}_{2,1} \leq 1$, $0 \leq \lambda^{\geq}_{2,2} \leq 1$, it follows that $\lambda^{\geq}_{2,1} = 0$. Analogously we can determine the slope $\lambda^{\leq}_{2,1}$ of the constraint $\beta^{\geq}_{2,1} = \lambda^{\leq}_{2,1} \cdot v_{1,1}$ associated with the computation of concrete upper bounds by minimising the sum of the upper concrete bounds of nodes $n_{3,1}$ and $n_{3,2}$: $\lambda_{2,1}^{\leq} = 0$.

Max-pool Layers. We provide a novel treatment of max-pool layers (in the context of SIP) as follows. To derive the bound constraints of a max-pool node, we express the max-pool function as a sequence of affine transformations and ReLU layers, whose constraints can be computed as above. We begin with expressing the multivariate maximum function as a composition of maximum functions of two variables:

$$\max(v_1, v_2, \dots, v_{n-1}, v_n) = \max(\dots \max(\max(\max(v_1, v_2), v_3), v_4) \dots, v_n)$$

Then we use that $max(v_1, v_2) = max(v_1 - v_2, 0) + v_2$ to obtain

$$
\begin{aligned}
&\max(v_1, v_2, \dots, v_{n-1}, v_n) \\
&= \max(\dots \max(\max(\max(v_1 - v_2, 0) + v_2 - v_3, 0) + v_3 - v_4, 0) + v_4 \\
&\quad \dots - v_n, 0) + v_n \\
&= \mathsf{ReLU}(\dots \mathsf{ReLU}(\mathsf{ReLU}(\mathsf{ReLU}(v_1 - v_2) + v_2 - v_3) + v_3 - v_4) + v_4 \dots - v_n) + v_n,
\end{aligned}
$$

which is a sequence of affine and ReLU transformations.

Note that this symbolic treatment of max-pools differs from [26], where the upper bound constraints are *concretised* to equal the concrete upper bounds, thereby potentially leading to bigger overapproximations. Also note that our symbolic treatment comes at the cost of computing bound constraints for the affine transformation and ReLU layers that compose the max-pool one.

Summary. Having concluded the description of the various approximations, Algorithm 2 summarises the overall algorithm that computes $\mathcal{R}$ from Algorithm 1. Algorithm 2 and Algorithm 1 can therefore be combined to solve a verification query.

4   Implementation and Evaluation

In this section we evaluate OSIP, the verification procedure introduced in the previous section, and present comparisons with different approximations of the ReLU function and with Eran [26], a state-of-the-art SIP-based tool. OSIP is implemented in Python 3.7 on top of Venus, a MILP-based, complete tool with several optimisations including dependency analysis [4,19]. The experiments were carried out on an Intel Core i9-10920X (12 cores) equipped with 128GB RAM, running Linux kernel 5.4.

Comparison with Different ReLU Aapproximations. We compare OSIP with the zero [26,37], identity [26,37] and parallel [31,33] approximations. We also compare OSIP with the *Min_Area* [26,37] heuristic which selects the approximation with the smallest over-approximation area for each ReLU node. The comparisons are drawn with respect to the tightness of the bounds of the output nodes, which is a key aspect to (i) determine the ability of a method to

---

Algorithm 2. OSIP

1: **procedure** APPROXIMATION OF OUTPUT BOUNDS(f, l, u)
2:     **Input:** network f, vectors of input lower and upper bounds l and u
3:     **Output:** vectors of output lower and upper bounds
4:     $f' \leftarrow$ replace each max-pool in f as a composition of affine and ReLU transformations
5:     $\beta_0^{\geq,l}, \beta_0^{\geq,u} \leftarrow l, \; l_0 \leftarrow l$
6:     $\beta_0^{\leq} \leftarrow u, \; u_0 \leftarrow u$
7:     **for** each layer f_i' in f' **do**
8:         **if** f_i' is an affine transformation layer **then**
9:             $\beta_i^{\geq,l}, \beta_i^{\geq,u} \leftarrow W^{(i)} v_{i-1}, \; \beta_i^{\leq} \leftarrow W^{(i)} v_{i-1}$
10:            $l_i \leftarrow W^{(i)}, \; u_i \leftarrow W^{(i)}$
11:            **for** $j \leftarrow i$ to 1 **do**
12:                $l_i \leftarrow l_i^- \beta_{i-1}^{\leq} + l_i^+ \beta_{i-1}^{\geq,l}, \; u_i \leftarrow u_i^- \beta_{i-1}^{\geq,u} + u_i^+ \beta_{i-1}^{\leq}$
13:        **else if** f_i' is a ReLU layer **then**
14:            **for** each neuron j in the layer **do**
15:                $\beta_{i,j}^{\leq} \leftarrow \frac{u_{i,j}}{u_{i,j} - l_{i,j}} (v_{i,j} - l_{i,j})$
16:                $\lambda_{i,j}^{\geq} \leftarrow$ solution to optimisation problem 1
17:                $\lambda_{i,j}^{\leq} \leftarrow$ solution to the analogous minimisation problem of 1
18:                $\beta_{i,j}^{\geq,l} \leftarrow \lambda_{i,j}^{\geq} \cdot v_{i,j} \; \beta_{i,j}^{\geq,u} \leftarrow \lambda_{i,j}^{\leq} \cdot v_{i,j}$
19:                $u_{i,j} \leftarrow u_{i-1,j}$
20:                $l_{i,j} \leftarrow \min(\lambda_{i,j}^{\geq} \cdot l_{i-1,j}, \lambda_{i,j}^{\leq} \cdot l_{i-1,j})$
                return l_L, u_L

---

resolve a verification query (as discussed in Sect. 3) and (ii) formulate strong mixed integer linear programming encodings towards improved scalability in complete verification [29]. We consider the following benchmarks for fully connected ReLU FFNNs from the first competition for neural network verification (VNN-COMP) [30]:

- *ACASXU* [16] is a collection of 45 ReLU FFNNs which were developed as part of an airborne collision avoidance system to advise horizontal steering decisions for unmanned aircraft. Each network has 5 inputs, 300 ReLU nodes arranged in 6 layers with 50 neurons each, and 5 outputs. We verify the networks against the safety specifications from [17]. These include four properties that are checked on all of the 45 networks and 6 properties that are checked on a single network. Overall this results in a total of 186 verification problems.
- *MNIST* [20] is a dataset comprising images of hand-written digits 0–9, each formatted as a $28 \times 28 \times 1$-pixel grayscale image.
  We use three fully connected ReLU FFNNs trained on the dataset: FC2, FC4 and FC6. The networks comprise 2, 4 and 6 layers, respectively. Each layer of each of the networks has 256 ReLU nodes. We verify the networks against the local adversarial robustness property w.r.t 25 correctly classified images and perturbation radii of 0.02 and 0.05. This results in a total of 150 verification problems.

We additionally use two convolutional networks: CONV1 and CONV3. The architecture of the networks includes two layers. The first layer has 32 filters of size 5×5, a padding of 2 and strides of 2. The second layer has 64 filters of size of 4×4, a padding of 2 and strides of 1. CONV3 has the same architecture with CONV1 but for 128 filters in the second layer. We verify the networks against the local adversarial robustness property w.r.t 100 correctly classified images. We use a perturbation radius of 0.1 for CONV1 and 0.3 for CONV3.

OSIP was run with the number of optimised nodes parameter set to 4 for all fully connected networks and to 200 for all convolutional networks.

Table 1 reports the experimental results obtained. We observe that the zero and Min_Area approximations always outperform the identity and parallel approximations. However, the comparative performance of the zero and Min_Area approximations varies with the networks and perturbation radii. For instance, the zero approximation outperforms the Min_Area one on FC2 for the 0.05 radius, whereas the Min_Area approximation outperforms the zero one on the same network for the 0.02 radius. In contrast, OSIP consistently outperforms all of the approximations on all of the networks and radii, often exhibiting less than half of the bound interval of either the zero or the Min_Area approximation.

We additionally observe that OSIP is more effective for fully connected networks than it is for convolutional ones. We conjecture that this is because the nodes in a convolutional layer are only connected to a small subset of nodes in the previous layer thereby exhibiting less sensitivity to intra-layer dependencies between the nodes.

Lastly we note that OSIP needs only small values for the number of optimised nodes parameter to outperform all of the approximations. Indeed, as we can observe from Fig. 4, which shows the average bound interval of the output nodes computed by OSIP on FC6 as a function of the parameter, said interval initially decreases rapidly before having a more gradual decrement with larger values of the parameter.

Comparison on VGG16. We now proceed to evaluate OSIP on a variant of the VGG16 model [25] that forms a key component of the Multi-View 3D Detector (MV3D) [5], a high-accuracy 3D object detection network for autonomous driving. The model we produced was trained on the GTSRB dataset [27].

The model comprises the sequence of layers $c(32, 3, 3)$, $c(32, 3, 3)$, $p(2, 2)$, $c(64, 3, 3)$, $c(64, 3, 3)$, $p(2, 2)$, $c(128, 3, 3)$, $c(128, 3, 3)$, $c(128, 3, 3)$, $p(2, 2)$, $c(128, 3, 3)$, $c(128, 3, 3)$, $c(128, 3, 3)$, 43, where $c(\alpha, \beta, \gamma)$ denotes a convolutional layer with output channel α, kernel width β and kernel height γ (padding and strides equal 1 for all convolutional layers), $p(\alpha, \beta)$ denotes a pooling layer with pooling width α and pooling height β, and 43 denotes a fully connected layer of 43 nodes. In total the network has 290304 ReLUs. We chose to run this experiment to evaluate the performance of OSIP on large perception systems that are closer in size to industrial applications.

Table 1. Experimental results comparing the ReLU approximations from Sect. 3. The *ver* columns report the number of images that were verified, the *time* column reports the average times, and the *range* column reports the average range of the bounds of the output nodes. Highlighted cells denote the approximation that generated the tightest bounds. The zero, identity, parallel and Min_Area approximations have equal average times.

Model	Radius	OSIP			Zero			Identity		Parallel		Min Area	
		ver	time	range	ver	time	range	ver	range	ver	range	ver	range
FC2	0.02	15	12.24	0.21	13	0.06	0.44	1	15.18	13	0.58	14	0.29
	0.05	0	15.89	2.98	0	0.05	3.33	0	52.30	0	12.53	0	6.61
FC4	0.02	21	10.4	0.32	17	0.10	0.81	3	1.15K	17	4.31	21	0.99
	0.05	0	24.76	182.3	0	0.10	310.6	0	20K	0	16.6K	0	251.87
FC6	0.02	17	14.89	159.71	8	0.15	243.53	0	245K	15	1.5K	18	161.21
	0.05	0	29.96	13.2K	0	0.15	13.2K	0	4.29e6	0	19.3K	0	14.7K
Conv1	0.1	88	11.76	10.83	72	5.27	16.05	16	32.60	81	13.80	89	11.62
Conv3	0.3	5	16.65	13.66	0	7.43	28.12	0	62.10	0	40.89	4	14.15
ACASXU	-	3	0.69	899.73	3	0.00	1.02K	0	38K	2	4.6K	10	1.9K

We verified the local robustness of the VGG16 for perturbation radiuses of 0.001, 0.0015, and 0.002 against 10 correctly classified images from the GTSRB dataset. We compare OSIP with Eran [26], a tool for the verification of feed-forward neural networks whose DeepPoly domain (which is SIP with the Min_Area approximation) presents the state-of-the art in bound propagation-based methods. We refer to [30] for more tools and details.

OSIP was run with the number of optimised nodes parameter set to 200. Eran was run using the DeepPoly domain. Each verification problem was run with a timeout of two days. Table 2 reports the experimental results obtained. We observe that OSIP provides tighter bounds than Eran, ranging from three times tighter bounds for the smallest perturbation radius to progressively tighter bounds for the larger perturbation radiuses. As previously discussed, this directly impacts the number of verification queries that each tool is able to solve. Both tools were able to resolve some of the queries for the smallest perturbation radius (with OSIP resolving 9 of them and Eran 5 of them). In our experiments only OSIP was able to resolve some of the queries (5 of them) for the intermediate radius; none of the tools was able to resolve any query for the largest perturbation radius. As far as we are aware these are the first documented successful verification results for large and complex perception systems such as VGG16 and for perturbation radiuses of 10^{-3}. We note that additional experiments on the *refinepoly* domain of Eran, which is DeepPoly enhanced with optimisation-based bound tightening methods, were not concluded after the timeout of two days. Also, experiments with NNV [14], a set-based verification tool for neural networks, were not concluded because of memory errors.

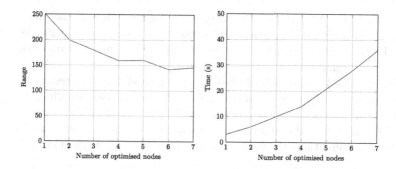

Fig. 4. Average bound interval of the output nodes and average runtime of OSIP as a function of the number of optimised nodes for the FC6 network and the 0.02 perturbation radius.

Table 2. Experimental results obtained on VGG16. The *ver* columns report the number of images that were verified, the *time* column reports the average times, and the *range* column reports the average range of the bounds of the output nodes.

Radius	OSIP			Eran (Deeppoly)		
	ver (#)	time (s)	range	ver (#)	time (s)	range
0.0010	9	66811	0.0179	5	9605	0.0460
0.0015	7	66889	0.0623	0	9718	0.4921
0.0020	0	66642	0.2915	0	10040	18.5823

The bound tightness exhibited by OSIP comes at the cost of the tool being slower (approximately 6.5 times) than Eran. This is mainly to be attributed to the handling of the max-pooling layers where additional layers are introduced to the analysis chain of OSIP.

5   Conclusions

In this paper we analysed the problem of obtaining tight bounds for the verification of feed-forward neural networks. As we observed, present state-of-the-art incomplete tools may often be unable to determine the result of a verification query for large and deep models, such as those in object classifiers, due to the compounding errors in the bound estimations.

We presented OSIP, a novel verification method based on symbolic interval propagation. OSIP provides tighter approximations than the present SoA approximations of a single univariate ReLU function in most commonly accepted benchmarks. This is obtained by determining the choice of the ReLU approximation at each node via optimisation.

We additionally benchmarked OSIP against Eran, a state-of-the-art symbolic interval propagation tool. To assess their performance in a setting close to industrial applications we carried out experiments on a variant VGG16, the largest component of the MV3D object detector and classifier for autonomous vehicles. This is a convolutional neural network consisting of approximately 300,000 ReLU nodes. In our benchmarks OSIP obtained bounds that were at times two orders of magnitude smaller than Eran.

Tighter bounds are directly linked to an increased ability to reduce the number of unknowns in the verification queries. This was confirmed in our experiments in which we documented cases in which OSIP was the only method capable of solving the verification query. In summary, to the best of our knowledge, at present OSIP constitutes the most performing tool for the verification of VGG16.

Acknowledgements. The authors acknowledge support from the Audi Verifiable AI project and by BMWi under the KARLI project (grant 19A21031C).

References

1. Anderson, R., Huchette, J., Ma, W., Tjandraatmadja, C., Vielma, J.P.: Strong mixed-integer programming formulations for trained neural networks. Math. Progr. **183**(1), 3–39 (2020). https://doi.org/10.1007/s10107-020-01474-5
2. Bastani, O., Ioannou, Y., Lampropoulos, L., Vytiniotis, D., Nori, A.V., Criminisi, A.: Measuring neural net robustness with constraints. In: Proceedings of the 30th International Conference on Neural Information Processing Systems (NIPS16), pp. 2613–2621 (2016)
3. Battern, B., Kouvaros, P., Lomuscio, A., Zheng, Y.: Efficient neural network verification via layer-based semidefinite relaxations and linear cuts. In: International Joint Conference on Artificial Intelligence (IJCAI21), pp. 2184–2190. ijcai.org (2021)
4. Botoeva, E., Kouvaros, P., Kronqvist, J., Lomuscio, A., Misener, R.: Efficient verification of neural networks via dependency analysis. In: Proceedings of the 34th AAAI Conference on Artificial Intelligence (AAAI20). AAAI Press (2020)
5. Chen, X., Ma, H., Wan, J., Li, B., Xia, T.: Multi-view 3D object detection network for autonomous driving. In: Proceedings of the IEEE Conference on Computer Vision and Pattern Recognition, pp. 1907–1915 (2017)
6. Cheng, C.-H., Nührenberg, G., Ruess, H.: Maximum resilience of artificial neural networks. In: D'Souza, D., Narayan Kumar, K. (eds.) ATVA 2017. LNCS, vol. 10482, pp. 251–268. Springer, Cham (2017). https://doi.org/10.1007/978-3-319-68167-2_18
7. Dathathri, S., et al.: Enabling certification of verification-agnostic networks via memory-efficient semidefinite programming. In: NeurIPS20 (2020)
8. Dvijotham, K., Stanforth, R., Gowal, S., Mann, T., Kohli, P.: A dual approach to scalable verification of deep networks. In: UAI. vol. 1, p. 2 (2018)
9. Ehlers, R.: In: D'Souza, D., Narayan Kumar, K. (eds.) ATVA 2017. LNCS, vol. 10482, pp. 269–286. Springer, Cham (2017). https://doi.org/10.1007/978-3-319-68167-2_19
10. Fazlyab, M., Morari, M., Pappas, G.J.: Safety verification and robustness analysis of neural networks via quadratic constraints and semidefinite programming (2019). arXiv preprint arXiv:1903.01287
11. Fischetti, M., Jo, J.: Deep neural networks and mixed integer linear optimization. Constraints **23**(3), 296–309 (2018). https://doi.org/10.1007/s10601-018-9285-6

12. Goodfellow, I., Shlens, J., Szegedy, C.: Explaining and harnessing adversarial examples (2014). arXiv preprint arXiv:1412.6572
13. Henriksen, P., Lomuscio, A.: DEEPSPLIT: an efficient splitting method for neural network verification via indirect effect analysis. In: Proceedings of the 30th International Joint Conference on Artificial Intelligence (IJCAI21), pp. 2549–2555. ijcai.org (2021)
14. Tran, H.-D., et al.: NNV: the neural network verification tool for deep neural networks and learning-enabled cyber-physical systems. In: Lahiri, S.K., Wang, C. (eds.) CAV 2020. LNCS, vol. 12224, pp. 3–17. Springer, Cham (2020). https://doi.org/10.1007/978-3-030-53288-8_1
15. Huang, X., Kwiatkowska, M., Wang, S., Wu, M.: Safety verification of deep neural networks. In: Majumdar, R., Kunčak, V. (eds.) CAV 2017. LNCS, vol. 10426, pp. 3–29. Springer, Cham (2017). https://doi.org/10.1007/978-3-319-63387-9_1
16. Julian, K., Lopez, J., Brush, J., Owen, M., Kochenderfer, M.: Policy compression for aircraft collision avoidance systems. In: DASC16, pp. 1–10 (2016)
17. Katz, G., Barrett, C., Dill, D.L., Julian, K., Kochenderfer, M.J.: Reluplex: an efficient SMT solver for verifying deep neural networks. In: Majumdar, R., Kunčak, V. (eds.) CAV 2017. LNCS, vol. 10426, pp. 97–117. Springer, Cham (2017). https://doi.org/10.1007/978-3-319-63387-9_5
18. Katz, G., et al.: The marabou framework for verification and analysis of deep neural networks. In: Proceedings of the 31st International Conference on Computer Aided Verification (CAV19), pp. 443–452 (2019)
19. Kouvaros, P., Lomuscio, A.: Towards scalable complete verification of relu neural networks via dependency-based branching. In: International Joint Conference on Artificial Intelligence (IJCAI21), pp. 2643–2650. ijcai.org (2021)
20. LeCun, Y., Cortes, C., Burges, C.J.: The MNIST database of handwritten digits (1998)
21. Lomuscio, A., Maganti, L.: An approach to reachability analysis for feed-forward relu neural networks. CoRR abs/1706.07351 (2017)
22. Henriksen, P., Lomuscio, A.: Efficient neural network verification via adaptive refinement and adversarial search. In: ECAI20 (2020)
23. Raghunathan, A., Steinhardt, J., Liang, P.: Semidefinite relaxations for certifying robustness to adversarial examples. In: Advances in Neural Information Processing Systems 31, pp. 10877–10887. Curran Associates, Inc. (2018)
24. Salman, H., Yang, G., Zhang, H., Hsieh, C., Zhang, P.: A convex relaxation barrier to tight robustness verification of neural networks. In: Advances in Neural Information Processing Systems 32, pp. 9835–9846. Curran Associates, Inc. (2019)
25. Simonyan, K., Zisserman, A.: Very deep convolutional networks for large-scale image recognition (2014). arXiv preprint arXiv:1409.1556
26. Singh, G., Gehr, T., Püschel, M., Vechev, P.: An abstract domain for certifying neural networks. In: Proceedings of the ACM on Programming Languages 3(POPL), 41 (2019)
27. Stallkamp, J., Schlipsing, M., Salmen, J., Igel, C.: The german traffic sign recognition benchmark: a multi-class classification competition. In: The 2011 International Joint Conference on Neural Networks, pp. 1453–1460. IEEE (2011)
28. Tjandraatmadja, C., Anderson, R., Huchette, J., Ma, W., Patel, K., Vielma, J.: The convex relaxation barrier, revisited: tightened single-neuron relaxations for neural network verification. In: NeurIPS20 (2020)
29. Tjeng, V., Xiao, K.Y., Tedrake, R.: Evaluating robustness of neural networks with mixed integer programming. In: Proceedings of the 7th International Conference on Learning Representations (ICLR19) (2019)

30. VNN-COMP: Vefication of neural networks competition (2020). https://sites. google.com/view/vnn20/vnncomp
31. Wang, S., Pei, K., Whitehouse, J., Yang, J., Jana, S.: Efficient formal safety analysis of neural networks. In: Proceedings of the 31st Annual Conference on Neural Information Processing Systems 2018 (NeurIPS18), pp. 6369–6379 (2018)
32. Wang, S., Pei, K., Whitehouse, J., Yang, J., Jana, S.: Formal security analysis of neural networks using symbolic intervals. In: Proceedings of the 27th USENIX Security Symposium, (USENIX18), pp. 1599–1614 (2018)
33. Weng, T., et al.: Towards fast computation of certified robustness for relu networks (2018). arXiv preprint arXiv:1804.09699
34. Wong, E., Kolter, J.: Provable defenses against adversarial examples via the convex outer adversarial polytope (2017). arXiv preprint arXiv:1711.00851
35. Wong, E., Schmidt, F., Metzen, J., Kolter, J.: Scaling provable adversarial defenses. In: Proceedings of the 32nd Conference on Neural Information Processing Systems (NeurIPS18) (2018)
36. Xiang, W., Tran, H., Johnson, T.: Output reachable set estimation and verification for multilayer neural networks. IEEE Trans. Neural Netw. Learn. Syst. **29**(11), 5777–5783 (2018)
37. Zhang, H., Weng, T., Chen, P., Hsieh, C., Daniel, L.: Efficient neural network robustness certification with general activation functions. In: Proceedings of the 31st Annual Conference on Neural Information Processing Systems 2018 (NeurIPS2018), pp. 4944–4953. Curran Associates, Inc. (2018)

Active Model Learning of Stochastic Reactive Systems

Martin Tappler[1,2] (iD), Edi Muškardin[1,2(✉)] (iD), Bernhard K. Aichernig[2] (iD),
and Ingo Pill[1] (iD)

[1] Silicon Austria Labs, TU Graz - SAL DES Lab, Graz, Austria
edi.muskardin@silicon-austria.com
[2] Institute of Software Technology, Graz University of Technology, Graz, Austria

Abstract. Black-box systems are inherently hard to verify. Many verification techniques, like model checking, require formal models as a basis. However, such models often do not exist, or they might be outdated. Active automata learning helps to address this issue by offering to automatically infer formal models from system interactions. Hence, automata learning has been receiving much attention in the verification community in recent years. This led to various efficiency improvements, paving the way towards industrial applications. Most research, however, has been focusing on deterministic systems. Here, we present an approach to efficiently learn models of stochastic reactive systems. Our approach adapts L^*-based learning for Markov decision processes, which we improve and extend to stochastic Mealy machines. Our evaluation demonstrates that we can reduce learning costs by a factor of up to 8.7 in comparison to previous work.

Keywords: Active automata learning · Model mining · Probabilistic verification · Stochastic mealy machines · Markov decision processes

1 Introduction

Via active automata learning, where we learn a formal automaton for a black-box reactive system, we can enable the exploitation of formal techniques and tools like model checkers for systems where this would otherwise be impossible. Consequently, this has been a very active research area since the inception of the field with Angluin's L^* algorithm [4] for learning deterministic finite automata (DFAs). Corresponding extensions that have paved the way to applying the concept in an industrial context range from general algorithmic improvements [16,24] over domain-specific optimizations [15] to learning other automata variants, like Mealy machines [20,25] or timed automata [1].

Learning automata in settings with uncertainty has received less attention, though. So, we presented in previous work [26,27] a first L^*-based learning algorithm that allows to learn Markov decision processes (MDPs) of stochastic systems. In this paper, we evolve over our previous work via the following contributions: We (1) present L^*_{SMM}, an L^*-based approach for learning stochastic

© Springer Nature Switzerland AG 2021
R. Calinescu and C. S. Păsăreanu (Eds.): SEFM 2021, LNCS 13085, pp. 481–500, 2021.
https://doi.org/10.1007/978-3-030-92124-8_27

Mealy machines (SMMs) along with algorithmic improvements that also apply to learning MDPs, and (2) report on a thorough experimental evaluation with implementations in our open-source library AALPY [21]. As we will show, learning SMMs optimizes the learning process (i.e., the required number of interactions with a system under learning (SUL)). An automatic translation from SMMs to MDPs enables the use of probabilistic model-checkers like PRISM[17] or STORM[9]. Thus, L^*_{SMM} can be used for learning-based verification of black-box systems.

Structure. In Sect. 2, we recapitulate preliminaries like L^*-based automata learning. We present our approach to active learning of SMMs in detail in Sect. 3, followed by a corresponding evaluation and comparison to learning MDPs in Sect. 4. After a discussion of related work in Sect. 5, we will conclude with a summary of our findings and an outlook on future work in Sect. 6.

2   Preliminaries

In this section, we will introduce our notation as well as background knowledge.

A discrete probability distribution μ over a countable set X is a function $\mu : X \to [0,1]$ such that $\sum_{x \in X} \mu(x) = 1$, where we refer with $Dist(X)$ to the set of all probability distributions over X. To ease probability estimations from sampled data, we focus on rational probabilities only, i.e., $\mu(x)$ takes only rational values. Furthermore, we support partial functions μ by assuming $\mu(x) = 0$ if μ is undefined for some x. The set $supp(\mu) = \{x \in X \mid \mu(x) > 0\}$ is referred to as the support of μ. We use $A(e) \in \mathbb{N}_0$ to denote the multiplicity of e in some multiset A.

For a finite set X, let $u, v, w \in X^*$ be finite sequences over X: $u = v \cdot w$ is the concatenation of v and w, where v is a prefix of u, and w is a suffix. The length of u is denoted $|u|$, ϵ denotes the empty sequence, and we lift $x \in X$ to be a sequence of length one. For $A, B \subseteq X^*$, $A \cdot B$ is the set of all concatenations of sequence pairs in A and B. $A \subseteq X^*$ is prefix/suffix-closed if A contains all prefixes/suffixes of all $s \in A$.

We consider reactive systems M that produce exactly one output $o \in O$ at a time in response to an input $i \in I$ for in- and output alphabets I and O. Thus an interaction with M, coined a *trace*, is a finite sequence $t \in (I \cdot O)^*$, and a single interaction step consists of an input-output pair in $I \cdot O$. For convenience, we adopt the notions of prefix, suffix, and length for traces, referring to input-output pairs as atomic elements then. That is, $|t|$ gives the number of input-output pairs in t and the trace set $\{\epsilon, a \cdot b, a \cdot b \cdot c \cdot d\}$ for $a, c \in I$ and $b, d \in O$ is prefix-closed.

In addition to traces $t \in \mathcal{TR} = (I \cdot O)^*$, we consider *test sequences* from $\mathcal{TS} = (I \cdot O)^* \cdot I$, which test a system's response to an input i following a trace t. We also consider continuation sequences $\mathcal{CS} = I \cdot (O \cdot I)^*$, which extend traces to test sequences $\mathcal{TR} \cdot \mathcal{CS} = \mathcal{TS}$. Analogously to traces, we extend the notions of prefix and suffix by considering input-output pairs and trailing/leading inputs in these types of sequences. For example, $C = \{i_2 \cdot o_2 \cdot i_1, i_1\} \subseteq \mathcal{CS}$ is suffix-closed.

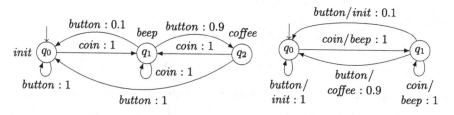

Fig. 1. An MDP model (left) and an SMM model (right) of a faulty coffee machine

We learn SMMs and transform them into labeled MDPs. This has the advantage that learning SMMs is more efficient as we will show in our experiments, while the transformation enables model-based analyses with probabilistic model-checkers [9,17] that use MDPs as input format. Analogously to Mealy and Moore machines, SMMs and MDPs differ in the way outputs are produced. An SMM produces an output considering its current state and an input, whereas the output of an MDP depends only on the current state. Like in a non-stochastic setting, SMMs are potentially smaller as illustrated in Fig. 1 for a brief example.

On the left of Fig. 1, we show an MDP modeling a faulty coffee machine, and a corresponding SMM on the right (see Definitions 1, 2). Both models are observationally equivalent, except for the initial output produced by the MDP. For both we have inputs and probabilities as edge labels, s.t. the probabilities follow after a colon. In the MDP, the outputs are defined by the labels on the states, whereas for the SMM they are part of the edge label—separated from the input via a slash. The described coffee machine works such that it sounds a *beep* with probability one upon receiving a *coin*. When a *button* is pressed, a *coffee* is issued with a probability of 0.9, or we have *init* with the complementary probability of 0.1.

Definition 1 (Markov Decision Processes). *A labeled MDP is a tuple* $\mathcal{M} = \langle Q, I, O, q_0, \Delta, L \rangle$ *where* Q *is a finite set of states,* $q_0 \in Q$ *is the initial state,* I *and* O *are finite sets of input and output symbols,* $\Delta : Q \times I \to Dist(Q)$ *is the probabilistic transition function, and* $L : Q \to O$ *is the labeling function.*

Definition 2 (Stochastic Mealy Machines). *An SMM is a tuple* $\mathcal{M} = \langle Q, I, O, q_0, \delta \rangle$ *where* $Q, q_0, I,$ *and* O *are defined as for MDPs and* $\delta : Q \times I \to Dist(Q \times O)$ *is the probabilistic transition function.*

We use $q \xrightarrow{i \cdot o} q'$ to denote $\delta(q, i)(q', o) > 0$ and extend this notation to traces t in $(I \cdot O)^*$ by $q \xrightarrow{\epsilon} q$ and $q \xrightarrow{i \cdot o \cdot t} q'$ if $\exists q'' : q \xrightarrow{i \cdot o} q'' \wedge q'' \xrightarrow{t} q'$. As is common in automata learning and testing, we consider input-enabled systems, such that δ and Δ are total and are thus defined for all $q \in Q$ and $i \in I$. Furthermore, we consider *deterministic* MDPs and SMMs, such that for every trace t, there is exactly one path producing t. More formally, we require for all $q \in Q, i \in I$ that

- $\forall q', q'' \in supp(\Delta(q, i))$: if $L(q') = L(q'')$ then $q' = q''$ (MDPs) and
- $\forall (q', o'), (q'', o'') \in supp(\delta(q, i))$: if $o' = o''$ then $q' = q''$ (SMMs).

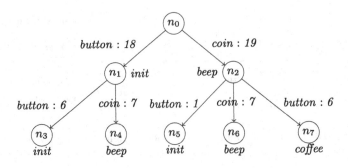

Fig. 2. An IFOPT for the faulty coffee machine

Consequently, while an input may cause different outputs, an input-output pair cannot lead to different states. Non-determinism results only from the environment's choice of inputs. Under these conditions, we can define an SMM output function λ by $\lambda(q, i) \in Dist(O)$ and $\lambda(q, i) = \{o \mapsto p \mid (q', o) \mapsto p \in \delta(q, i)\}$.

These requirements enable a transformation from SMMs to MDPs similar to the one from deterministic Mealy to Moore machines. That is, we basically have to create an MDP state for every pair of (1) an SMM state s and (2) an output of one of s's incoming transitions. After creating another state with a new special label as initial state, we transfer the transitions from the SMM.

We use input-output prefix trees (IOPTs) as compact representations of a set of traces. An IOPT is a tree with edges labeled by inputs and nodes labeled by outputs. Similar trees are, for instance, used in passive automata learning [5,13]. Figure 2 shows an IFOPT for the faulty coffee machine. The figure shows that we actually use IOPTs with input frequencies (IFOPTs) where each edge is labeled with an input symbol and a frequency value in the natural numbers. For example, the frequency of *button* in node n_2 is 7 (combined frequency from the edges labeled *button*), denoted by $freqLabel(n_2, button) = 7$. We use frequencies to define how often an input should occur in relation to other inputs. We discuss this in more detail in Sect. 3.4.

Angluin presented her L^* algorithm and introduced the minimally adequate teacher (MAT) framework in her seminal paper on active automata learning [4]. With L^* we can learn DFAs accepting regular languages and L^* has been serving as the basis for several adaptations and variations to learn further automata types, such as Mealy machines [25], timed automata [12], and MDPs [26].

L^*-based algorithms in the MAT framework learn automata capturing some (regular) language L by querying a teacher for information. Generally, learners use two types of queries: (1) *membership queries* for asking whether a word $u \in X^*$ is in L and (2) *equivalence queries* to check whether a hypothesized automaton accepts exactly L. Most L^*-based algorithms share furthermore a similar structure and concept of how to derive hypotheses from queried data. In principle, L^* operates in rounds, such that it issues multiple membership queries in a round to gain information about L. Once the learner has sufficient information to create a hypothesis automaton (for the original L^* this is a DFA), it finishes the round by issuing an equivalence query. The teacher may now respond with *yes* for signaling that the automaton a.k.a. hypothesis accepts L, so that the learning process concludes. However, the teacher may respond also with a counterexample, i.e., a word c in the symmetric difference between L and the automaton's language. Thus, when receiving a counterexample c, the learner integrates c into its knowledge and continues via starting the next round. L^* stores information in observation tables and creates hypotheses from these tables. In the next section, we adapt this concept to stochastic Mealy machines.

3   Queries-Based Learning of SMMs via Sampling

In this section, we present L^*_{SMM}, an algorithm for learning SMMs. For this purpose, we extend, adapt, and improve our L^*-based algorithm for MDPs [26,27]. First, we define the setting and basics for learning SMMs, such as semantics. Next, we introduce the queries that are used in the interaction between learner and teacher. After that, we discuss learning itself and present implementation details on selected aspects, such as queries and stopping. We conclude the section with a complexity analysis and a discussion of convergence.

3.1   Basics

Let us assume that $\mathcal{M} = \langle Q, I, O, q_0, \delta \rangle$ is an SMM underlying the black-box SUL, representing the knowledge we would like to learn. A learner initially only knows the available inputs and outputs, but we use the SUL behavior to formalize learning. Thus, let us define input-output semantics $[\![\mathcal{M}]\!]$ that maps traces followed by an input to the output distribution produced by the input. Formally, $[\![\mathcal{M}]\!] : (I \cdot O)^* \cdot I \to Dist(O) \cup \{\bot\}$ with $[\![\mathcal{M}]\!](t \cdot i) = \lambda(q, i)$ if there is a $q \in Q$ such that $q_0 \xrightarrow{t} q$ and $[\![\mathcal{M}]\!](t \cdot i) = \bot$ otherwise. We will query a teacher that samples SUL traces to gain information about $[\![\mathcal{M}]\!]$. For sampling, the teacher performs inputs on the SUL and observes outputs produced by the SUL, which are distributed according to $[\![\mathcal{M}]\!]$. In this way, the teacher collects multisets of SUL traces. In the following, we define trace equivalence, as an adaptation of the Nerode relation for regular languages [22], and equivalence of SMMs.

Definition 3 (Trace Equivalence). *Two traces $t, t' \in (I \cdot O)^*$ are equivalent if for all continuation sequences $cs \in I \cdot (O \cdot I)^*$:*

$$[\![\mathcal{M}]\!](t \cdot cs) = [\![\mathcal{M}]\!](t' \cdot cs).$$

Definition 4 (SMM Equivalence). *Let $\mathcal{M}_1$ and $\mathcal{M}_2$ be two SMMs over the same input and output alphabets. $\mathcal{M}_1$ and $\mathcal{M}_2$ are equivalent iff for all test sequences*

$$ts \in (I \cdot O)^* \cdot I : [\![\mathcal{M}_1]\!](ts) = [\![\mathcal{M}_2]\!](ts).$$

Two traces are equivalent if they produce the same output distributions in response to the last input of every continuation sequence. Likewise, two SMMs are equivalent if they produce the same output distributions for all test sequences.

Since we sample traces with outputs distributed according to SUL semantics $[\![\mathcal{M}]\!]$, we cannot determine exact equivalence of output distributions as required by Definition 3. We instead perform statistical tests for difference between sampled output frequencies. More concretely, we check difference based on Hoeffding bounds [14], like other stochastic automata learning algorithms [5,26].

To formalize the problem of approximating equivalence checking between sampled frequencies, let tc_1 and tc_2 be two sequences in $(I \cdot O)^* \cdot I$ and let $\mathcal{T}$ be a multiset of traces collected from the SUL $\mathcal{M}$. We define the frequency function as $\mathbf{freq}_{\mathcal{T}}(tc) = o \mapsto \mathcal{T}(tc \cdot o)$ for $o \in O$, extend the notion of support $supp()$ to frequencies, and introduce $Freq(O)$ for $O \to \mathbb{N}_0$, the set of all output frequency functions. Our goal is to approximate $[\![\mathcal{M}]\!](tc_1) \neq [\![\mathcal{M}]\!](tc_2)$ by testing whether $f_1 = \mathbf{freq}_{\mathcal{T}}(tc_1)$ and $f_2 = \mathbf{freq}_{\mathcal{T}}(tc_2)$ have been sampled from different distributions. We say that the frequencies f_1 and f_2 are compatible, denoted $f_1 \approx f_2$, if they are not different. Let $n_i = \sum_{o \in O} f_i(o)$. In the special case that $n_1 = 0$ or $n_2 = 0$, we define $f_1 \approx f_2$ to hold, since then we do not have sufficient information to detect a difference. For $n_1 > 0$ and $n_2 > 0$, the *Hoeffding check* w.r.t. α defining the significance level is: Frequencies f_1 and f_2 are different if

$$\exists o \in O : \left| \frac{f_1(o)}{n_1} - \frac{f_2(o)}{n_2} \right| > \sqrt{\frac{1}{2} \ln \frac{2}{\alpha}} \left(\frac{1}{\sqrt{n_1}} + \frac{1}{\sqrt{n_2}} \right). \tag{1}$$

(correct with probability $\geq (1 - \alpha)^2$ [5])

3.2   Queries

The learner and teacher interact with each other via two types of queries: (1) *tree queries* and (2) *equivalence queries*. The teacher samples traces for both query types, but with different goals. Tree queries attempt to gain more accurate information about the SUL, whereas equivalence queries attempt to falsify a hypothesis SMM – as proving equivalence is not possible in a black-box setting, we target falsification.

Tree query (tq): Let FT be an IFOPT, a tree query $\mathbf{tq}(FT)$ returns a multiset of traces from $(I \cdot O)^*$, where inputs are chosen according to FT and outputs are sampled according to the SUL semantics $[\![\mathcal{M}]\!]$.

Equivalence query (eq): Let $\mathcal{H}$ be a hypothesis SMM, an equivalence query $\mathbf{eq}(\mathcal{H})$ returns a pair $(r, \mathcal{T}_{\text{cex}})$ where r is the query result in $\{yes\} \cup (I \cdot O)^* \cdot I$ and $\mathcal{T}_{\text{cex}}$ is a multiset of traces sampled for the query.

For a tree query $\mathbf{tq}$, the learner creates an IFOPT FT and asks the teacher to sample paths from FT, while selecting inputs i with a probability proportional to the frequency value of i in FT. The result of a $\mathbf{tq}$ is a multiset of sampled SUL traces. For an equivalence query, the learner forms a hypothesis SMM $\mathcal{H}$ and asks if $\mathcal{H}$ is equivalent to the SUL $\mathcal{M}$. The teacher responds either with yes or with a counterexample to equivalence in $(I \cdot O)^* \cdot I$. Additionally, the teacher returns a multiset of traces that have been sampled to perform the query.

3.3   Learner

Data Structures. The learner uses two main data structures, a multiset T of sampled traces and an observation table, a triple $\langle S, E, T \rangle$. Based on $\mathbf{freq}_T(tc)$, the output frequencies observed so far, S, E, and T are defined by:

- $S \subseteq (I \cdot O)^*$ is a prefix-closed set of traces,
- $E \subseteq I \cdot (O \cdot I)^*$ with $I \subseteq E$ is a suffix-closed set of continuations, and
- $T : (S \cup Lt(S)) \cdot E \rightarrow Freq(O)$ with $Lt(S) = \{s \cdot i \cdot o \mid s \in S, i \in I, o \in O : \mathbf{freq}_T(s \cdot i)(o) > 0\}$ and $T(s \cdot e) = \mathbf{freq}_T(s \cdot e)$ stores output frequencies.

An observation table can be represented as a two-dimensional table with rows labeled by *short* traces in S and by *long* traces in $Lt(S)$, columns labeled by continuation sequences in E, and with cell content given by T. Table 1 shows an observation table from a learning run of L^*_{SMM} on the coffee machine shown in Fig. 1. As is commonly done in L^*-based learning, we create hypotheses as follows. We partition S based on the row content given by functions $row(s) : E \rightarrow Freq(O)$ with $row(s)(e) = T(s \cdot e)$ and create a state for every block in the partition. We further create transitions for input-output pairs $i \cdot o$ between blocks b and b' by determining the block b containing an $s \in S$ and the block b' containing its input-output extension $s \cdot i \cdot o$, if it exists. The long traces $Lt(S)$ ensure that traces can be created for all observed input-output pairs. To partition S, we extend the notion of frequency compatibility to rows. We say that two rows labeled by traces s and s' are compatible if all their cells are compatible, i.e., $\forall e \in E : row(s)(e) \approx row(s')(e)$. We also say that the traces s and s' are compatible. In Table 1, the first, third, fourth, and fifth row are compatible. Hence, they would be in the same block of a partition of S and correspond to the same state in the hypothesis derived from Table 1.

In partitioning, we face the difficulty that compatibility is not an equivalence relation, as transitivity does not hold in general. A row may be compatible to multiple other rows that are not necessarily pairwise compatible. To tackle this challenge, we create compatibility classes $cg(r)$ that partition S, like in our previous work [26]. Each compatibility class $cg(r) \subseteq S$ has a unique representative r in the set of representatives $R \subseteq S$ and every trace t in $cg(r)$ is compatible to r. The function $rep(t) = r$ returns the unique representative r for short and long traces t. We create compatibility classes by iteratively selecting a new representative r from the unpartitioned part of S and greedily adding other unpartitioned traces to $cg(r)$. The selection of a new representative r is based on how often r was observed during sampling, which ensures that $\epsilon \in R$ can be used as initial hypothesis state. For further details, we refer to [26].

Hypothesis Generation. To create a hypothesis from an observation table $\langle S, E, T \rangle$, the table must be closed and consistent. Adapting the standard notion of closedness and consistency [4,26], we say that an observation table is *closed* if for all $l \in Lt(S)$ there is an $r \in R$ such that r and l are compatible. Closedness ensures that we can create transitions for all inputs in all states.

Table 1. Observation table for the faulty coffee machine shown in Fig. 1.

		button	coin
S	ϵ	$\{init: 247\}$	$\{beep: 414\}$
	$coin \cdot beep$	$\{coffee: 147, init: 16\}$	$\{beep: 134\}$
$Lt(S)$	$button \cdot init$	$\{init: 69\}$	$\{beep: 82\}$
	$coin \cdot beep \cdot button \cdot coffee$	$\{init: 64\}$	$\{beep: 53\}$
	$coin \cdot beep \cdot button \cdot init$	$\{init: 9\}$	$\{beep: 6\}$
	$coin \cdot beep \cdot coin \cdot beep$	$\{coffee: 65, init: 7\}$	$\{beep: 61\}$

An observation table is *consistent* if for all pairs of compatible short traces $s, s' \in S$ and all input-output pairs $i \cdot o \in I \cdot O$: either (1) $s \cdot i \cdot o$ and $s' \cdot i \cdot o$ are compatible or (2) $T(s \cdot i)(o) = 0$ or $T(s' \cdot i)(o) = 0$. Consistency requires that the extensions of compatible traces are also compatible. Put differently, if s leads to the same hypothesis state as s', then its extension $s \cdot i \cdot o$ should lead to the same state as $s' \cdot i \cdot o$. This corresponds to the determinism requirement of SMMs.

When an observation table is not closed, there is an $l \in Lt(S)$ such that there is no compatible $r \in R$. We can make an observation table closed by adding such an l violating closedness to the set of short traces S and recalculating the set R. When an observation table is not consistent, there exists a pair of compatible traces s, s', an input-output pair $i \cdot o$, and a column sequence e such that $s \cdot i \cdot o \cdot e \not\approx s' \cdot i \cdot o \cdot e$. In such a case, we add $i \cdot o \cdot e$ to E. The iterated application of these updates – adding traces to S and sequences to E – eventually establishes closedness and consistency. We refer to this operation as `MakeClosedAndConsistent`. In contrast to deterministic learning, this does not require resampling as compatibility is defined for any amount of samples.

Given a closed and consistent observation table $\langle S, E, T \rangle$ with representatives R, we derive a hypothesis SMM $hyp(S, E, T) = \langle Q_h, I, O \cup \{undef\}, q_{0h}, \delta_h \rangle$ via:

- $Q_h = R \cup \{q_{undef}\}$ and $q_{0h} = \epsilon$
- For $q \in R$ and $i \in I$, if $\sum_{o \in O} T(q \cdot i)(o) = 0$:
    $\delta_h(q, i)((q_{undef}, undef)) = 1$
    Otherwise:
    $\delta_h(q, i) = \mu$ where for $o \in O$ if $T(q \cdot i)(o) > 0$:
    $q' = rep(q \cdot i \cdot o)$ and $\mu((q', o)) = \frac{T(q \cdot i)(o)}{\sum_{o' \in O} T(q \cdot i)(o')}$
- If q_{undef} is reachable, then for $i \in I$:
    $\delta_h(q_{undef}, i)((q_{undef}, undef)) = 1$

We create a state for every representative with $\epsilon \in R$ being the initial state. Transitions from $q \in R$ lead to the representatives of the input-output extensions $q \cdot i \cdot o$, where transition probabilities are estimated from T. If we have no observations for an input, we create transitions to a sink state q_{undef}.

Learning Algorithm. Algorithm 1 implements the stochastic L^* algorithm for SMMs, adapting L^* for MDPs [26]. In Line 1, we initialize the learning data structures. The main loop starts with a tree query in lines 5 and 6. After

Algorithm 1. The main algorithm implementing L^*_{SMM}

Input: input alphabet I, teacher capable of answering **tq** and **eq**
Output: final learned model $\mathcal{H}$
1: $S \leftarrow \{\epsilon\}, E \leftarrow I, T \leftarrow \{\}, \mathcal{T} \leftarrow \{\epsilon\}$ ▷ initialize observation table and samples $\mathcal{T}$
2: $round \leftarrow 0$
3: **repeat**
4: │ $round \leftarrow round + 1$
5: │ $FTree \leftarrow$ CREATEIFOPT($\langle S, E, T \rangle$)
6: │ $\mathcal{T} \leftarrow \mathcal{T} \uplus \mathbf{tq}(FTree)$
7: │ **for all** $s \in S \cup Lt(S), e \in E$ **do**
8: │ │ $T(s \cdot e) \leftarrow \mathbf{freq}_{\mathcal{T}}(s \cdot e)$ ▷ update observation table
9: │ **while** $\langle S, E, T \rangle$ not closed or not consistent **do**
10: │ │ $\langle S, E, T \rangle \leftarrow$ MAKECLOSEDANDCONSISTENT($\langle S, E, T \rangle$)
11: │ $\mathcal{H} \leftarrow$ hyp(S, E, T) ▷ create hypothesis
12: │ $\langle S, E, T \rangle \leftarrow$ TRIM($\langle S, E, T \rangle, \mathcal{H}$) ▷ remove cells not needed
13: │ $(r, \mathcal{T}_{cex}) \leftarrow \mathbf{eq}(\mathcal{H})$ ▷ Check hypothesis $\mathcal{H}$ against SUL $\mathcal{M}$
14: │ $\mathcal{T} \leftarrow \mathcal{T} \uplus \mathcal{T}_{cex}$
15: │ **if** $r \neq yes$ **then** ▷ we found a counterexample
16: │ │ $\langle S, E, T \rangle \leftarrow$ PROCESSCEX($r, \langle S, E, T \rangle$)
17: **until** STOP($\langle S, E, T \rangle, \mathcal{H}, round$)
18: **return** $\mathcal{H}$ ▷ output final hypothesis

updating the learner's data structures, we make the observation table closed and consistent (Line 10) and form a hypothesis $\mathcal{H}$ (Line 11). Given $\mathcal{H}$, we remove table rows and columns that are not needed for hypothesis generation. Line 12 basically removes rows that carry the same information as other rows and cells that do not distinguish rows. For more details, we refer to our previous work [26].

In Line 13, we perform an equivalence query. If it returns a counterexample r, we process it by updating the observation table with information derived from r. L^*-based learning [4,25] commonly stops once an equivalence query returns *yes*, but we continue learning until the stopping criterion in Line 17 is fulfilled. The reason is that in stochastic learning, we may not be able to find a counterexample given an inaccurate hypothesis that could be improved by additional tree queries. Therefore, we employ a stopping criterion that takes hypothesis generation into account. Once we stop, we return the final hypothesis.

3.4 Implementation

We implemented Algorithm 1 in AALPY, an open-source automata-learning library.[1] AALPY supports learning of both MDPs and SMMs, which we compare empirically in Sect. 4. In the following, we discuss selected aspects of the implementation with a focus on improvements over the original algorithm for MDPs [26], for example, stopping and resampling by the tree query.

---
[1] An interactive example illustrating learning is available at https://github.com/DES-Lab/AALpy/blob/master/notebooks/MDP_and_SMM_Example.ipynb.

SUL Interface. The teacher assumes an application-specific SUL interface comprising two operations **step** and **reset**. They facilitate sampling, where at each point, the SUL is in a current state q_c. The **reset** operation resets q_c to q_0. The **step** operation takes an input i as parameter, executes it on the SUL, and returns the SUL output. More concretely, it samples a state-output pair (q, o) according to the distribution $\delta(q, i)$ of the SUL, sets $q_c = q$, and returns o.

Equivalence Queries and Counterexample Processing. The teacher performs two steps in equivalence queries. The first step is checking compatibility between already sampled traces (multiset $\mathcal{T}$ in Algorithm 1) and the hypothesis. The second, optional step samples new traces to reveal a counterexample to equivalence between hypothesis and SUL. Sampling happens only when the compatibility check does not reveal a counterexample. This ensures that we use existing samples as efficiently as possible and when there is no counterexample in $\mathcal{T}$ we try to find new counterexamples via sampling. The implementation of these steps follows our previous work [26]. We check compatibility between $\mathcal{T}$ and the hypothesis using Eq. 1 and we apply random testing for sampling. To ensure that every counterexample can be detected, every input and every trace length has a non-zero probability to be selected during testing.

A counterexample c returned from an equivalence query indicates that the observation table shall be extended in a way to ensure that upcoming hypotheses are correct w.r.t. c. Since hypotheses in active automata learning [4,26] are generally the smallest models consistent with the queried information, the goal of counterexample processing is to reveal new states. There are various ways to process counterexamples in L^*-based learning. Our implementation provides two counterexample processing strategies that are commonly applied in deterministic learning.

- *Angluin-style:* Angluin adds all prefixes of a counterexample to S [4].
- *Longest-prefix:* The *longest-prefix* strategy by Shahbaz and Groz [25] splits c into a prefix p and a suffix e, where p is the longest prefix that is already in S. It then adds e to E. We generally use *longest-prefix* in Sect. 4.

Alternative strategies based on the extraction of so-called distinguishing suffixes are very efficient in deterministic learning [3,16], but we found them to be inefficient in stochastic learning. This is due to the usually low amount of statistical information on counterexample suffixes. Such strategies would require repeated sampling of representative traces from R concatenated with counterexample suffixes until a distinguishing suffix can be found via Eq. 1. In contrast, the other two techniques rely on sampling performed in subsequent learning rounds.

Tree Queries. Membership queries in L^* provide information about newly added sequences in the observation table. Tree queries have an analogous purpose. They gather more information on sequences that are in the observation table. While deterministic learning requires a single query (sample) for every

---

Algorithm 2. *Tree* query

Input: IFOPT *FTree*, SUL with **reset** and **step**
Output: a sampled trace t

1: $node \leftarrow root(FTree),\ t \leftarrow \epsilon$ ▷ initialize
2: **reset**()   ▷ reset SUL
3: **loop**
4:     $freqSum \leftarrow \sum_{i \in I} freqLabel(node, i)$ ▷ sum frequencies in IFOPT
5:     $inputDist \leftarrow \left\{ i \mapsto p \mid i \in I, p = \frac{freqLabel(node,i)}{freqSum} \right\}$
6:     $in \leftarrow$ CHOOSE$(I, inputDist)$ ▷ choose input
7:     $out \leftarrow$ **step**(in) ▷ execute SUL and observe output
8:     $t \leftarrow t \cdot in \cdot out$ ▷ extend traces
9:     **if** $\nexists n \in nodes(FTree) : node \xrightarrow{in/out} n$ **then**   ▷ did we leave the tree?
10:       **return** *trace*
11:     $node \leftarrow n$ with $node \xrightarrow{in/out} n$ ▷ walk down one tree level

---

sequence, uncertainties affect stochastic learning. We address this issue by sampling traces with the goal of reducing uncertainties.

Uncertainties in stochastic L^* mainly arise from the difference tests and the derived compatibility relation. As discussed in the context of hypothesis generation, this relation is not necessarily an equivalence relation for finite sample sizes. The resulting uncertainties directly affect hypothesis generation, as a trace in $S \cup Lt(S)$ may be compatible to multiple other traces that are not pairwise compatible. Hence, the target state of a transition may be ambiguous. In particular, a trace may be compatible to multiple compatibility class representatives. We devise a sampling strategy with the goal of reducing this form of ambiguity, in order to learn the correct model structure. We start from the viewpoint of the learner and then present the teacher's tree query implementation.

Learner. Given an observation table $\langle S, E, T \rangle$ and $se \in (S \cup Lt(S)) \cdot E$, we assign an uncertainty value *uncert(se)* to *se* as follows. Let s be the longest prefix trace of *se* s.t. $s \in S \cup Lt(S)$ and let the number of compatible representatives be

$$cr(s) = |\{r \in R \mid r \approx s\}| \text{ in } uncert(se) = \max(2 \cdot (cr(s) - 1), 1).$$

The rationale behind *uncert(se)* is that every trace should be compatible to at most one representative. Since we are only interested in compatibility of rows, we consider the longest trace that labels a row and is a prefix of *se*. The uncertainty grows with the number of compatible representatives cr, where the multiplication by two puts more weight on this number. We further subtract one, as every trace is compatible to at least one representative in a closed observation table. Finally, we ensure *uncert(se)* is at least one for two reasons. We may spuriously conclude that $cr = 1$. Furthermore, we account for the estimation of transition probabilities as another source of uncertainty affecting hypothesis generation in general. Thus, every trace should have a non-zero probability to be sampled.

Now, we can define the function `createIFOPT` in Line 5 of Algorithm 1.

1. *Trace creation.* Extend the sequences in $(S \cup Lt(S)) \cdot E$ to traces by adding a special output $leaf \notin O$ at the end of every sequence, let $Tr = \{s \cdot e \cdot leaf \mid s \in S \cup Lt(S), e \in E\}$.
2. *IOPT creation.* Create an IOPT $Tree$ from the traces in Tr.
3. *IFOPT initialization.* Create an IFOPT $FTree$ from $Tree$ by initializing every input frequency with zero.
4. *Adding frequencies.* For each $se \in (S \cup Lt(S)) \cdot E$: add $uncert(se)$ to the frequency of every input on the path from the root node to the last edge reached by se.

The frequency label for a given edge ed in $FTree$ is the sum of uncertainty values $uncert(se)$, for sequences se traversing ed when starting from the root. Aside from the IFOPT $FTree$, the implementation of tree queries takes another parameter n_{tree} that defines the number of traces to be sampled by the teacher. We determine n_{tree} proportional to the uncertainty and observation table size via

$$n_{tree} = \left\lfloor \frac{\sum_{se \in (S \cup Lt(S)) \cdot E} uncert(se)}{2} \right\rfloor. \tag{2}$$

Roughly speaking, we take one sample for every unambiguous cell in the table and additional samples for ambiguity.

Teacher. The teacher performs tree queries by sampling n_{tree} traces corresponding to directed random walks on the IFOPT $FTree$ created by the learner. Algorithm 2 implements this form of sampling. It starts with an initialization in lines 1 and 2. The sample loop starts with the selection of an input in in lines 4 to 6, where the selection probability of in is proportional to the frequency assigned to in. Here, we use CHOOSE(I, d) to sample an input in I according to a probability distribution d. Next, we execute in on the SUL and extend the sampled trace t with in and the SUL output. When there is no path in the IFOPT corresponding to t, we return t. This is guaranteed to happen when reaching a leaf, as leaves are labeled with a symbol not in the output alphabet.

Stopping. Similarly to tree queries, stopping takes ambiguity into account. We stop, when ambiguity decreases. For stopping, we quantify ambiguity or rather the absence thereof as the number of row traces that have a single compatible representative. This number *unambiguity* is given by:

$$unambiguity = \frac{|\{s \in S \cup Lt(S) \mid cr(s) = 1\}|}{|S \cup Lt(S)|}$$

We also used this value to decide stopping to learn MDPs [26]. Previously, we stopped learning once *unambiguity* was greater than a fixed threshold. However, we concluded from experiments that a fixed threshold is not an ideal choice for

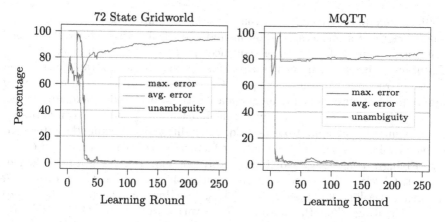

Fig. 3. Relation between number of unambiguous rows and hypothesis accuracy.

SMM learning concerning efficiency. In these experiments, we measured hypothesis accuracy in relation to the value of *unambiguity* during the course of learning. For this purpose, we quantified accuracy as the average error made in model-checking computations, as compared to model checking performed on the true model of the SUL. We observed a general trend that the hypothesis accuracy converges at the same time when *unambiguity* converges to a plateau.

Figure 3 shows plots of the *unambiguity* value, the maximum error in various model-checking computations, and the corresponding average error on two examples that we discuss in more detail in Sect. 4. The x-axis displays the number of learning rounds. We can see that upon reaching an *unambiguity* value of approximately 0.8, the maximum and average error are close to zero and stay close to zero. At this point, further learning and sampling costs resources, but does not contribute to model's accuracy. For this reason, we stop learning when we detect that *unambiguity* reaches a plateau, i.e., the difference between several consecutive *unambiguity* values is below a small positive ϵ.

In common with previous work [26], we do not stop when q_{undef} is reachable in the hypothesis. This state is reachable, when there is a state-action pair for which there is no information at all. Additionally, it is possible to specify a minimum number of rounds and a maximum of rounds. The early stopping criterion can also be disabled in favor of a fixed threshold.

3.5   Analysis of L^*_{SMM}

Complexity. In the following, we will analyze the complexity of individual operations performed by L^*_{SMM}, such as queries. For this purpose, let m be the length of the longest sampled trace, let n be the number of sampled steps, and let k be the number of different sampled traces. In the worst case, k grows linearly in n. For simplicity, we consider the set of sampled traces to be prefix-closed, because whenever we observe a trace, we basically observe all its prefixes as well.

494   M. Tappler et al.

Since we add only traces to S that have been sampled at least once, we can bound length of sequences in S by m and the cardinality of S by k. We can analogously bound the length of sequences in E and the cardinality of E, as E contains suffixes of sampled traces. Making an observation table closed and consistent requires time in $O(k^3 \cdot |O|)$. Checking consistency requires iterating over all pairs of rows and checking compatibility for each cell. There are at most k^2 row pairs and at most k columns (cells in each rows) and each compatibility check requires $|O|$ computations (see Eq. 1). Additionally checking the extensions of compatible rows only adds a constant factor. Hence, the runtime is in $O(k^3 \cdot |O|)$. Fixing a consistency violation, simply amounts to adding a new element to a set. Checking closedness requires compatibility checks between every pair consisting of a long and a short row. Thus, closedness checks are in $O(k^3 \cdot |O|)$ as well. Creating a hypothesis from an observation table is in $O(k \cdot |I| \cdot |O|)$. We need to potentially create a transition for every input-output pair from every state. There are $|I| \cdot |O|$ such pairs and there are at most k states.

The IFOPT creation for tree queries takes time in $O(k \cdot m)$, as every unique trace of length at most m is added at most once. The value n_{tree} of traces sampled during a tree query (see Eq. 2) is at most k^2, but generally much lower. Hence, a tree query performs at most $k^2 \cdot m$ sampling steps.

Equivalence queries consist of two steps, checking compatibility and sampling traces to actively check for equivalence between hypothesis and SUL. The amount of sampling can be adjusted freely according to sampling budget and accuracy requirement. The compatibility check between sampled information and hypothesis requires runtime in $O(k \cdot m \cdot |O|)$. For every sampled trace t we determine a hypothesis state and its representative trace r, which has a length of at most m. For t and r, we perform a compatibility check, which takes time linear in the number of outputs. This analysis matches our experience in that making observation tables closed and consistent takes the most time. While the analysis of sampling steps performed by tree queries provides a conservative upper bound, we observe that tree queries perform thorough sampling leading to accurate models.

We use a heuristic to decide stopping, which prevents stating a complexity bound on entire runs of L^*_{SMM}.

Convergence. Under mild, common assumptions on equivalence queries (every trace must have a non-zero probability to be sampled), the learned model converges in the limit, i.e., with stopping disabled, to a minimal SMM equivalent to the SUL. A proof of convergence is not possible due to space limitations, but can be adapted from [26]. In the next section, we empirically analyze the accuracy of models learned from finitely many traces.

4   Evaluation

To evaluate our method, we performed a benchmarking study. The study considered five different stochastic systems also used in previous work [2, 26]. More

Table 2. Comparison of MDP and SMM learning.

	Learning time (s)			# Traces		
	MDP	SMM	Improvement	MDP	SMM	Improvement
First grid	8.61	5.67	51.85%	68736	44954	52.9%
Second grid	40.92	29.85	37.09%	199789	113690	75.73%
Slot machine	60.65	306.4	−80.21%	456243	622285	−26.86%
MQTT	8.59	6.97	23.24%	68964	39904	72.82%
TCP	21.94	13.4	63.73%	98333	54514	80.38%

concretely, we simulated known models of stochastic reactive systems through a **reset** and a **step** operation, thus treating them as black boxes. After learning models from the simulations, we measured the accuracy of the learned models. As a measure of accuracy, we use the absolute difference between probabilities computed by model checking properties on a learned model and the corresponding known true model. In the following, we report this form of error averaged over several properties for each system.

Systems used as a basis for learning are: a 35-state and a 72-state *Grid-world* [26], the *slot-machine* previously also used in [18,19], parts of the *MQTT* protocol encoded as a 61-state MDP, and parts of the *TCP* protocol encoded as a 151-state MDP. For the first three systems, we used model-checking properties also used in previous work [26] to enable a direct comparison. We derived the *MQTT* model and the *TCP* model from learned deterministic models [11,28] by injecting stochastic faults (see also [2]). The properties corresponding to them check for bounded reachability of the faults with varying bounds. Throughout the remainder of this section, we will reason about the benchmark model's underlying structure and how it affects learning performance.

All experiments have been performed with our implementation in the open-source library AALPY v1.0.0 running on a Dell Lattitude 5410 with an Intel Core i7-10610U processor, 8 GB of RAM running Windows 10 and using Python 3.9. We configure the Hoeffding-bound-based difference check with a constant $\alpha = 0.05$ and we limit the number of traces sampled during equivalence queries by $n_{cextraces} = 150$. In comparison to previous work [26], we reduced the number of configurable parameters, while achieving robust learning performance. Due to the stochastic nature of the experiments, we repeated every experiment, consisting of learning and model checking, 20 times and report average results.

Comparing MDP and SMM Learning. To compare the performance of MDP and SMM learning, we measured the learning time and the number of traces sampled by the teacher. While total learning time can be used to evaluate the feasibility of our approach in simulated environments, it is important to note that in real-world non-simulated environments, sampling of traces, i.e., the interaction with the SUL, is the most time-consuming aspect of active automata

Table 3. Results for learning models of the 72-state Gridworld.

	True	MDP	SMM	Error MDP	Error SMM	Improvement
# Traces	–	199789	113690	–	–	75.73%
# Steps	–	1363233	762338	–	–	78.82%
$\mathbb{P}_{max}(F^{\leq 14}(goal))$	0.9348	0.931	0.94	0.0038	0.0052	−26.92%
$\mathbb{P}_{max}(F^{\leq 12}(goal))$	0.6712	0.6943	0.681	0.0231	0.0098	135.71%
$\mathbb{P}_{max}(\neg M\ U^{\leq 18}(goal))$	0.9743	0.9721	0.973	0.0022	0.0013	69.23%
$\mathbb{P}_{max}(\neg S\ U^{\leq 20}(goal))$	0.1424	0.2138	0.1482	0.0714	0.0058	1131.03%

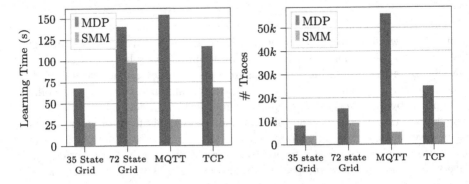

Fig. 4. Learning time in seconds (left) and number of traces (right) needed to reach at most 2% error for all properties.

learning. Table 2 summarizes the results of our benchmarking study. We see that for all examples but *slot machine* SMMs are the preferred formalism.

Table 3 shows detailed results of learning MDPs and SMMs of the 72-state *Gridworld*. In this example, learning SMMs reduces the state space by about 75%, as the SUL can be modeled by a 42-state SMM. This size difference accounts for the better and faster learning of SMMs compared to MDPs. Note that on average both learned the underlying model accurately, with the maximum average error for MDP learning being 7.1% and 0.9% for SMM learning.

Convergence. To evaluate learning speed, we disabled stopping and checked how long it takes for the learned hypothesis to reach a certain accuracy. For this purpose, we learned until creating a hypothesis with a model-checking error of at most 2% for all properties defined for the respective example. Figure 4 summarizes the results of these experiments. Notice in Fig. 3 that the error stays close to zero after a certain number of rounds. Hence, these experiments serve to estimate how long it takes to converge to an accurate model.

All examples but *slot-machine* show noticeable improvements in both learning time and more importantly required traces when comparing MDP and SMM learning. The largest improvements between MDP and SMM learning are noticeable for *MQTT* and *TCP*. In those examples, models can be more compactly encoded as SMMs than as MDPs. On the other hand, the structure of the *slot-machine* favors MDP learning. Learning a *slot-machine* MDP, required 25% fewer traces than learning an SMM. The exact results are not shown in the figure, since they are substantially larger, thus they would distort the graph. The good performance of MDP learning results from the fact that the minimal slot-machine MDP is only slightly larger than the minimal SMM and that many MDP states can be distinguished solely based on their output label without statistical tests. In general, when the output alphabet size is large, then MDP learning may be more efficient. In the extreme case, where every state is labeled with a unique output, the model structure is already given and learning amounts to estimating transition probabilities.

Comparison with Related Work. To put the improvements presented in this paper in context, we will compare results found in Table 2 to results found in [26]. For this purpose, we show the improvements that the new approach brings compared to the original version of L^*_{MDP} [26] and IoAlergia [18,19]. L^*_{MDP} required 391,530 traces to accurately learn the 35-state *Gridworld*, whereas IoAlergia failed to learn the accurate representation of the model from 387,746 traces. Our approach needs only 44,954 (8.7 times less than L^*_{MDP}) traces to learn the SMM representation of the 35-state *Gridworld* accurately. For the 72-state *Gridworld*, SMM learning managed to learn a more accurate model than L^*_{MDP}, while requiring only 113,690 traces, about 4.5 less than the 515,950 traces sampled by L^*_{MDP}. Suppose that sampling of a trace takes 20 ms; our approach would need 37.9 min compared to the 172 min needed by L^*_{MDP}. As previously discussed, MDP learning is faster for the *slot machine* example but produces less accurate results. SMMs learning approach with our new implementation required on average 622,285, whereas L^*_{MDP} required 2.5 times more (1,567,487) traces to learn a comparably accurate model.

5   Related Work

In the following, we discuss approaches to learn stochastic and non-deterministic models, focusing on models controllable by inputs.

Two early, notable approaches for identifying stochastic regular languages are Alergia [5] and rlips [6]. They implement passive learning, meaning that they learn from a given sample of traces. Alergia has been extended to MDPs by Mao et al. [18,19] and dubbed IoAlergia. Like IoAlergia, we compute transition probabilities based on observed output frequencies. Active extensions of IoAlergia can be found in [8] and [2], where the latter targets learning-based verification w.r.t reachability objectives. Casacuberta and Vidal proposed the GIATI algorithm [7], a passive approach for inferring stochastic transducers from a training corpus of source-target pairs of sentences.

Our work builds upon [26], an active approach to learning of MDPs. As discussed in the previous sections, we substantially improve the approach for learning MDPs itself and adapt it to learning SMMs. Our approach shares similarities with active learning of observable non-deterministic finite state machines (ONFSMs) [10]. While [10] requires all possible outputs to be observed after executing a query to build observation tables, we do not make this assumption by relying on statistical tests. Another L^*-based learning approach for ONFSMs has been proposed by Pferscher and Aichernig [23], which is specifically well-suited to learning non-deterministic behavior resulting from abstraction. The state q_{undef} that indicates the need for further sampling was inspired by active learning of non-deterministic labeled transition systems [29].

6   Conclusion

We presented L^*_{SMM}, an L^*-based algorithm for active learning of models of stochastic reactive systems. By improving previous work [26] and adapting it from learning MDPs to SMMs, we learn models more efficiently while achieving accurate results. The experimental evaluation of our implementation available in AALPY [21] shows a significant reduction in the number of required system interactions. Since interactions with the system are typically the time-consuming aspect of applications of automata learning, this number is the most important efficiency metric. In particular, we reduced the required number of system traces, i.e., sequences of interactions, by up to 8.7 times, as compared to MDP learning. Through these improvements, we hope to enable industrial applications of stochastic active automata learning. As future work, we plan to combine the stochastic L^* algorithm with learning-based verification techniques, such as [2], and apply it in case studies with stochastic reactive systems, such as communication protocols over a lossy channel. Another promising direction for future research is the combination with other machine-learning techniques, such as reinforcement learning.

Acknowledgments. This work has been supported by the "University SAL Labs" initiative of Silicon Austria Labs (SAL) and its Austrian partner universities for applied fundamental research for electronic based systems.

References

1. Aichernig, B.K., Pferscher, A., Tappler, M.: From passive to active: learning timed automata efficiently. In: Lee, R., Jha, S., Mavridou, A., Giannakopoulou, D. (eds.) NFM 2020. LNCS, vol. 12229, pp. 1–19. Springer, Cham (2020). https://doi.org/10.1007/978-3-030-55754-6_1
2. Aichernig, B.K., Tappler, M.: Probabilistic black-box reachability checking (extended version). Formal Methods Syst. Des. **54**(3), 416–448 (2019). https://doi.org/10.1007/s10703-019-00333-0
3. Aichernig, B.K., Tappler, M., Wallner, F.: Benchmarking combinations of learning and testing algorithms for active automata learning. In: Ahrendt, W., Wehrheim, H. (eds.) TAP 2020. LNCS, vol. 12165, pp. 3–22. Springer, Cham (2020). https://doi.org/10.1007/978-3-030-50995-8_1

4. Angluin, D.: Learning regular sets from queries and counterexamples. Inf. Comput. **75**(2), 87–106 (1987)

5. Carrasco, R.C., Oncina, J.: Learning stochastic regular grammars by means of a state merging method. In: Carrasco, R.C., Oncina, J. (eds.) ICGI 1994. LNCS, vol. 862, pp. 139–152. Springer, Heidelberg (1994). https://doi.org/10.1007/3-540-58473-0_144

6. Carrasco, R.C., Oncina, J.: Learning deterministic regular grammars from stochastic samples in polynomial time. RAIRO: Theor. Inform. Appl. (RAIRO: ITA) **33**(1), 1–20 (1999)

7. Casacuberta, F., Vidal, E.: Machine translation with inferred stochastic finite-state transducers. Comput. Linguist. **30**(2), 205–225 (2004)

8. Chen, Y., Nielsen, T.D.: Active learning of Markov decision processes for system verification. In: 11th International Conference on Machine Learning and Applications, ICMLA, Boca Raton, FL, USA, 12–15 December 2012, vol. 2, pp. 289–294. IEEE (2012)

9. Dehnert, C., Junges, S., Katoen, J.-P., Volk, M.: A STORM is coming: a modern probabilistic model checker. In: Majumdar, R., Kunčak, V. (eds.) CAV 2017. LNCS, vol. 10427, pp. 592–600. Springer, Cham (2017). https://doi.org/10.1007/978-3-319-63390-9_31

10. El-Fakih, K., Groz, R., Irfan, M.N., Shahbaz, M.: Learning finite state models of observable nondeterministic systems in a testing context. In: ICTSS 2010, pp. 97–102 (2010)

11. Fiterău-Broştean, P., Janssen, R., Vaandrager, F.: Combining model learning and model checking to analyze TCP implementations. In: Chaudhuri, S., Farzan, A. (eds.) CAV 2016. LNCS, vol. 9780, pp. 454–471. Springer, Cham (2016). https://doi.org/10.1007/978-3-319-41540-6_25

12. Grinchtein, O., Jonsson, B., Leucker, M.: Learning of event-recording automata. Theor. Comput. Sci. **411**(47), 4029–4054 (2010)

13. de la Higuera, C.: Grammatical Inference: Learning Automata and Grammars. Cambridge University Press, New York (2010)

14. Hoeffding, W.: Probability inequalities for sums of bounded random variables. J. Am. Stat. Assoc. **58**(301), 13–30 (1963)

15. Hungar, H., Niese, O., Steffen, B.: Domain-specific optimization in automata learning. In: Hunt, W.A., Somenzi, F. (eds.) CAV 2003. LNCS, vol. 2725, pp. 315–327. Springer, Heidelberg (2003). https://doi.org/10.1007/978-3-540-45069-6_31

16. Isberner, M., Howar, F., Steffen, B.: The TTT algorithm: a redundancy-free approach to active automata learning. In: Bonakdarpour, B., Smolka, S.A. (eds.) RV 2014. LNCS, vol. 8734, pp. 307–322. Springer, Cham (2014). https://doi.org/10.1007/978-3-319-11164-3_26

17. Kwiatkowska, M., Norman, G., Parker, D.: PRISM 4.0: verification of probabilistic real-time systems. In: Gopalakrishnan, G., Qadeer, S. (eds.) CAV 2011. LNCS, vol. 6806, pp. 585–591. Springer, Heidelberg (2011). https://doi.org/10.1007/978-3-642-22110-1_47

18. Mao, H., Chen, Y., Jaeger, M., Nielsen, T.D., Larsen, K.G., Nielsen, B.: Learning Markov decision processes for model checking. In: Proceedings of the Quantities in Formal Methods, QFM 2012. EPTCS, Paris, France, 28 August 2012, vol. 103, pp. 49–63 (2012)

19. Mao, H., Chen, Y., Jaeger, M., Nielsen, T.D., Larsen, K.G., Nielsen, B.: Learning deterministic probabilistic automata from a model checking perspective. Mach. Learn. **105**(2), 255–299 (2016). https://doi.org/10.1007/s10994-016-5565-9

20. Margaria, T., Niese, O., Raffelt, H., Steffen, B.: Efficient test-based model generation for legacy reactive systems. In: 2004 Ninth IEEE International High-Level Design Validation and Test Workshop, Sonoma Valley, CA, USA, 10–12 November 2004, pp. 95–100. IEEE Computer Society (2004)
21. Muškardin, E., Aichernig, B.K., Pill, I., Pferscher, A., Tappler, M.: AALpy: an active automata learning library. In: Hou, Z., Ganesh, V. (eds.) ATVA 2021. LNCS, vol. 12971, pp. 67–73. Springer, Cham (2021). https://doi.org/10.1007/978-3-030-88885-5_5 https://github.com/DES-Lab/AALpy
22. Nerode, A.: Linear automaton transformations. Proc. Am. Math. Soc. 9(4), 541–544 (1958)
23. Pferscher, A., Aichernig, B.K.: Learning abstracted non-deterministic finite state machines. In: Casola, V., De Benedictis, A., Rak, M. (eds.) ICTSS 2020. LNCS, vol. 12543, pp. 52–69. Springer, Cham (2020). https://doi.org/10.1007/978-3-030-64881-7_4
24. Rivest, R.L., Schapire, R.E.: Inference of finite automata using homing sequences. Inf. Comput. 103(2), 299–347 (1993)
25. Shahbaz, M., Groz, R.: Inferring mealy machines. In: Cavalcanti, A., Dams, D.R. (eds.) FM 2009. LNCS, vol. 5850, pp. 207–222. Springer, Heidelberg (2009). https://doi.org/10.1007/978-3-642-05089-3_14
26. Tappler, M., Aichernig, B.K., Bacci, G., Eichlseder, M., Larsen, K.G.: L^*-based learning of Markov decision processes (extended version). Formal Aspects Comput. 33(4), 575–615 (2021). https://doi.org/10.1007/s00165-021-00536-5
27. Tappler, M., Aichernig, B.K., Bacci, G., Eichlseder, M., Larsen, K.G.: L^*-based learning of Markov decision processes. In: ter Beek, M.H., McIver, A., Oliveira, J.N. (eds.) FM 2019. LNCS, vol. 11800, pp. 651–669. Springer, Cham (2019). https://doi.org/10.1007/978-3-030-30942-8_38
28. Tappler, M., Aichernig, B.K., Bloem, R.: Model-based testing IoT communication via active automata learning. In: 2017 IEEE International Conference on Software Testing, Verification and Validation, ICST 2017, Tokyo, Japan, 13–17 March 2017, pp. 276–287. IEEE Computer Society (2017)
29. Volpato, M., Tretmans, J.: Approximate active learning of nondeterministic input output transition systems. ECEASST 72 (2015)

Mixed-Neighborhood, Multi-speed Cellular Automata for Safety-Aware Pedestrian Prediction

Sebastian vom Dorff[1,2(✉)], Chih-Hong Cheng[1], Hasan Esen[1], and Martin Fränzle[2]

[1] Corporate R&D Department of DENSO Automotive Deutschland GmbH, Freisinger Street 21–23, 85386 Eching, Germany
{s.vomdorff,c.cheng,h.esen}@eu.denso.com
[2] Department of Computing Science, Carl von Ossietzky University, 26111 Oldenburg, Germany
fraenzle@informatik.uni-oldenburg.de

Abstract. Predicting pedestrian movement in unregulated traffic areas, such as parking grounds, marks a complex challenge in safety for automated vehicles. Without the ability to make certifiable predictions and judgments about safe interactions with other traffic agents in a real-time capable and economical fashion, the goal of self-driving vehicles cannot be reached. We propose a computationally efficient model for pedestrian behavior prediction on a short finite time horizon to ensure safety in automated driving. The model is based on a cellular automaton, working on an occupancy grid map and assumes a physical pedestrian capability constraint. It is enriched by a variable update rate with a mixed neighborhood, overcoming the limitations of vanilla cellular automata and coming closer to the results of state-of-the-art algorithms, while keeping the benefits of its straightforward parallelizability. The approach is evaluated on synthetic benchmarks outlining the general performance parameters as well as in an implementation on potential real-world situations.

1 Introduction

It is indisputable that safety is a crucial factor in the successful realization of automated driving. In practice, reflecting the safety mindset inside engineering requires that components designed towards performance (e.g., neural networks) carefully interact with components whose design is driven by safety.

For prediction of pedestrians, although their motion speed is relatively slow, safety issues arise since these agents can change their speed and direction quickly or may suddenly appear from occluded areas. In that safety-aware design context we require the created algorithm to *simultaneously exhibit* the following characteristics:

- **(Safe, but not overly conservative)** the algorithm should demonstrate *reasonably conservative* safe behavior such as handling potentially hidden agents,

© Springer Nature Switzerland AG 2021
R. Calinescu and C. S. Păsăreanu (Eds.): SEFM 2021, LNCS 13085, pp. 501–520, 2021.
https://doi.org/10.1007/978-3-030-92124-8_28

- **(Certifiable)** implementing the algorithm in software should be compatible with existing automotive safety norms such as ISO-26262, and finally,
- **(Economical)** the *computational efficiency* of the algorithm shall make the overall approach economically feasible to be deployed in multiple hardware platforms.

In this paper, we propose an improved algorithm to predict pedestrian behavior by revisiting the idea of *cellular automata (CA)* [8]. CA are discrete computational models for mimicking the evolution of cells. Yet by seizing on the above-mentioned practical safety-aware design criteria, despite the algorithm being easily certifiable due to its automata-theoretic nature, we find that a vanilla CA algorithm fails to deliver the promises of precision and versatility. This is due to (a) existing results using CA lead to an *overly-conservative* extrapolation behavior due to the static update rate and the coarse "neighborhood" definition [33], while (b) the algorithm is *incapable of simulating directionally guided movements*.

The innovation of this paper is thus based on a novel algorithmic improvement on CA models:

1. We improve the precision of prediction by relaxing the standard definition where each agent moves with the same speed.
2. We introduce variable propagation shapes, thereby improving the precision and have the capability to represent guided behavior of pedestrians.

For evaluation, we have implemented the algorithm and tested it on synthetic and realistic scenarios. We show the impact on computation time of different parameters and compare it to a simple, straightforward cell-infection algorithm. While maintaining better precision, the performance is significantly faster. The complexity analysis demonstrates that the algorithm can achieve an execution time reduction when executed on a multi-processor platform, paving the way for an economic realization of accurate prediction.

2   Related Work

Several works regarding pedestrian prediction emerged especially during the last years in the verge of automated driving. These works model pedestrians on different levels, starting from physical models, over maneuver-based prediction, until interaction-aware approaches [6,23]. Earlier works focused on mathematical models, describing kinetic behavior as seen in [16] are still an object of research today [27]. Furthermore, a probability-based factor to predict the pedestrians' movement has been introduced e.g. in [7,19]. In more recent works, set-based approaches have been investigated [21] yet fall short in areas where no given traffic rules or clear paths, such as sidewalks, exist. The same problem applies to context-based methodologies, as typical guidance patterns do hardly exist in parking areas [26]. Other approaches focus on the posture of single pedestrians, assuming their most likely trajectory [15,19,20]. Besides partially relying on the before-mentioned contextual information, these models tend to create heavy computation loads when significant numbers of pedestrians must be predicted at a time. Especially in recent research, the utilization of machine learning is used to create estimations of pedestrians' actions, such as in [1,31,32,38]. Nevertheless, the assumption of constant speed behavior of pedestrians outperforms several neural network based approaches as elaborated in [35]. Furthermore, neural network based approaches are difficult to validate and verify on their safety. Provably safe methodologies have been introduced earlier [24] yet struggle with providing reasonable predictions around occluded areas and their computation time grows with the number of pedestrians in the vicinity. Motivated by the challenge of limitations of perception in general [9,29], as well as by dealing with occlusions in particular [17,22], the question of ensuring safety under such circumstances has been tackled from various fields, for example by probabilistic methods [5]. Performance limitations of prediction models have been addressed in [2], giving an estimation of state-of-the-art capabilities.

Cellular automata have been used and discussed for decades regarding their specific attributes, characterization, and efficient implementation [10,13,14]. Traffic-specific works have focused on crowd simulation [3,18] or lane-bound highway [25] and walkway scenarios [4]. In [34] the interaction between pedestrians and transportation robots in factories has been focused. All these approaches have in common to take advantage of simulating large amounts of space-interdependent agents with simple rule sets as pointed out in [36] but relying on coarse definitions of the movement patterns. In contrast, [33] proposes a fine-grid solution significantly improving the accuracy at the cost of simulation speed. Dynamic partitioning of the grid to model complex processes have been suggested in [37] yet tend to become unintuitive when considering the heterogeneous behavior of the cells. Recent works on path planning utilizing CA, as in [28,30], nourish the idea of establishing the principles of this methodology in monitoring systems.

3   Preliminaries

In this section, we first give a brief formulation of cellular automata, and subsequently, concretize the formulation to be used for pedestrian prediction.

3.1   Cellular Automaton (CA)

A (finite) cellular automaton $\mathcal{C}$ is a tuple $(\mathcal{L}, d, \mathcal{S}, c_0, \mathcal{N}, f)$, where $\mathcal{L} = \{0, \ldots, \kappa\}$ is a finite set of positive integers ranging from 0 to κ and $d \in \mathbb{N}$ is the dimension. We call $\vec{n} \in \mathcal{L}^d$ a *cell*. $\mathcal{S} = S_1 \times S_2 \times \ldots \times S_n$ is called *state set vector* with each set S_i ($i \in 1, \ldots, n$) being finite. We call each $s = (s_1, \ldots, s_n)$, where $\forall i \in \{1, \ldots, n\} : s_i \in S_i$, a *state*. c_0 is the initial configuration. $\mathcal{N} : \mathcal{L}^d \to (\mathcal{L}^d \cup \{\bot\})^m$ is a function which maps a cell $\vec{n}$ to a list of cells called *neighborhood*. The token $\bot$ is used when the neighbor is undefined; this happens in the case of a cell being in the boundary e.g., $\vec{n} = (0,0)$ in the 2-dimensional case. Lastly, $f : \mathcal{S}^m \to \mathcal{S}$ is a function updating a state (of a cell) based on the states of its m neighboring cells.

A *configuration* of a CA is $c = (s_{(0,\ldots,0)}, \ldots, s_{(\kappa,\ldots,\kappa)})$, where every cell $\vec{n}$ is assigned with state $s_{\vec{n}}$ in the state set vector. The semantics of a CA is based on synchronous update where states of all cells are updated simultaneously using a function f. Starting from the initial configuration c_0, perform *transition* as follows:

1. Apply the neighborhood function on each cell $\vec{n}$ to derive its neighboring m cells $(\vec{n}_0, \ldots, \vec{n}_m)$.
2. For the neighboring cell $\vec{n}_i$ where $i \in \{0, \ldots, m\}$, let $s(\vec{n}_i)$ be the corresponding state.
3. For cell $\vec{n}$ in step 1, based on $f(s_1, \ldots, s_m)$ of the neighboring m cells, apply f to update the state. All cells perform synchronous update.

3.2   Cellular Automaton for Pedestrian Prediction

To use CA for pedestrian prediction, we consider the following CA, where $d = 2$, and S for each cell equals (S_{access}, S_{vel}), where $S_{access} = \{0,1\}$, defining if a cell can be potentially accessed by pedestrians or is blocked, and $S_{vel} = (S_N, S_{NW}, S_W, S_{SE}, S_S, S_{SE}, S_E, S_{NE})$ where each $S_i = \{0, 0.1, 0.2, \ldots, v_c - 0.1, v_c\}, i \in \{N, NW, \ldots, E, NE\}$, corresponding to the assumed speed of a pedestrian in a cell. v_c is the so-called speed of light (SoL) [13], the maximum attainable propagation speed in the CA. We index the states of the state vector S_{vel} as $(s_0, s_1, s_2, \ldots, s_7)$. We use the same notation structure to index cells around the currently observed cell, i.e. $\vec{n_0}$ refers to the cell north of the currently focused cell. Thus, the speed into a certain direction of a neighboring cell is queried as $s_i(\vec{n_k}$ with $i, k \in \{0, 1, \ldots, 7\}$. For example, $s_0(\vec{n_2}$ refers to the speed towards the north (0) of the cell that is located west (2) of the currently focused cell. In case we assume the cells to feature the same speed in all directions, the index i is omitted, e.g. $s(\vec{n_4}$ delivers the universal speed in all directions of the cell south from the currently focused cell. Note that in the definition of CA, time is abstracted as discrete transitions. To map the logical time to physical time, we made the following requirements:

- Each transition $c \mapsto c'$ occurs at discrete time steps $t + \Delta t$.
- The physical time is considered in a frame $0 \leq t \leq T$, with T being the time horizon. The steps of the cellular automaton map to physical time with $t_\alpha \in [t_0 = 0, t_1, t_2, \ldots, t_n = T]$ and $t_\alpha = \alpha \cdot \Delta t$.
- We further note that $c(t_\alpha) = c(t_\alpha + \epsilon)$, with $0 \leq \epsilon < \Delta t$ and $\epsilon \in \mathbb{R}$. $c'(t_\alpha)$ is the successor configuration of $c(t_\alpha)$ according to the transition function. I.e. the cellular automaton only changes its configuration instantaneously at discrete time points.

We match each cell to a square with an edge length of $l_{cell} = 0.5$ m and adjust κ accordingly to the size of the geographic region it represents. For the neighborhood, we use two different definitions in our work: First the von Neumann neighborhood, which is defined via the Manhattan distance

$$\mathcal{V}_r^2 = \{(x_i, y_i) : |x_i - x| + |y_i - y| \leq r_N\},$$

where (x, y) are the coordinates of $\vec{n}$, (x_i, y_i) are coordinates of the neighboring cell $\vec{n}_i$, and r_N is the range used to limit the distance. Second, we use a modified Moore neighborhood, which is regularly defined by the Chebyshev distance but excludes the cells from the von Neumann neighborhood in our case, defined as

$$\mathcal{M}_r^2 = \{(x_i, y_i) : |x_i - x| \leq r_N, |y_i - y| \leq r_N\} \setminus \mathcal{V}_r^2.$$

The used range r_N is set to 1 in this work. Following the above requirements, the SoL is calculated as

$$v_c = \frac{r_N \cdot l_{cell}}{\Delta t}.$$

3.3   Initialization of c_0

The initial configuration c_0 shall be attainted as follows:

- We use a map of our static surroundings, e.g. a parking garage. From there we generate an occupancy grid map (OGM), which is mapped to the size of $\mathcal{L}^d$. Cells that are not accessible, e.g. blocked by walls, shall be initialized with $s_{access} = 0$, all others with 1. As stated, these are static objects that are not supposed to change their state over the run-time of the algorithm. Other objects such as a shopping cart that is left alone in the parking space would also be considered as statics. The authors are aware that these corner cases have to be addressed in the future but choose to neglect them for the moment for the sake of simplicity. In the course of the paper it becomes clear that such special cases could also be addressed by the approach.
- With a proprietary tool we generate a 360-degree field-of-view (FOV) from our ego position in the map. Cells that are not blocked by the static environment but outside the FOV are initialized with $s_{i=0}^7 = v_{max}$, with v_{max}, the highest speed considered for a pedestrian. This measure makes sure that pedestrians outside the perceived areas cannot become an unconsidered hazard. The credo here is *"everything is unsafe as long as it is not judged to be safe"*. The paper will show that the implication of large numbers of potentially hidden pedestrians interfering with the vehicle's trajectory does not jeopardize the real-time capabilities of the approach.
- Lastly, pedestrians detected in the area are initialized with their speed and expected movement direction. The vectorial layout of S_{vel} is used as a representation of the cardinal points as shown in Fig. 1. For example, a pedestrian detected moving with 2 m/s to the south-east is initialized with $s_{4,5,6} = 2.0$. This of course relies on a perfect perception. While the algorithm can safely handle areas which are known to be unknown, it cannot mitigate risks when the perception inputs faulty data.

4   Transition Rule

The novelty in our approach lies within the transition rule f. In a vanilla CA, the transition occurs at a static rate. Therefore, all pedestrians are set to the

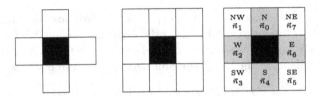

Fig. 1. From left to right: The von Neumann neighborhood, the *regular* Moore neighborhood, and our translation of the cardinal directions to the neighboring cell indices $\vec{n}_i$ and the directions in in the tuple of S_{vel}. For the right graphic, light grey cells depict the von Neumann neighborhood $\mathcal{V}_1^2$, white cells are members of the *modified* Moore neighborhood $\mathcal{M}_1^2$, the black cell is the current cell $\vec{n}$.

same speed. For example, the top row of Fig. 2 shows the propagation of a single cell with a Moore neighborhood with the $f : s' \leftarrow \max_{0 \leq i \leq 7} s(\vec{n}_i)$, assuming $(r_N = 1, l_{cell} = 1\,\text{m}, \Delta t = 0.125\,\text{s})$ and therefore $(v_c = 8\,\text{m/s})$.

- At $(t = 0\,\text{s})$ only the blue cell is occupied.
- Seen from the three adjacent cells, the blue cell lies within the neighborhood and therefore the adjacent cells get marked red. The red cells are changing their state according to f at $(t = 0.125\,\text{s})$ and now behave like the original blue cell.
- The same template is applied iteratively at **each** single time-step. At $(t = 0.500\,\text{s})$. All but the outer lines of cells are now occupied.

We introduce a methodology to realize a variable update rate, while keeping the time-steps constant in order to be capable of monitoring a given system with hard real-time requirements.

4.1   Variable Update-Rate

In order to simulate different pedestrian speeds in the presented use case, we add criteria to the transition rule. A cell is only updated iff the ratio of the SoL and the maximum cell-speed in the neighborhood is a multiple of the elapsed time divided by the minimum time-step:

$$f \iff \frac{t_\alpha}{\Delta t} \mod \frac{v_c}{s(\vec{n}_i)} = 0. \tag{1}$$

For example, a cell with half or quarter the SoL will only be updated in every second or fourth time-step. Figure 2 shows this behavior in the bottom row with two occupied cells with the speeds (2 m/s) and (4 m/s):

- The first iteration is analogous to the unconstrained CA.
- At $(t = 0.125\text{ s})$, none of the cells fulfills Eq. 1. Therefore, no propagation is observed.

- At ($t = 0.250$ s) the cells with the speed of (4 m/s) fulfill Eq. 1 and are therefore considered in f. Thus, their neighboring cells are marked red for changing the state.
- The iteration at ($t = 0.375$ s) is analogous to ($t = 0.125$ s) and thus not further depicted.
- At ($t = 0.500$ s) both speeds, (2 m/s) and (4 m/s) fulfill Eq. 1. Accordingly, all blue cells are considered by f and the neighboring cells shift their state, again indicated in red.

The ratio of the cell speed to the SoL is asymptotically reached since all cells propagate at $t = 0$, disregarding their speed. This makes sure not to under-approximate the movement of the pedestrian if it is not initially located at the center of a grid cell.

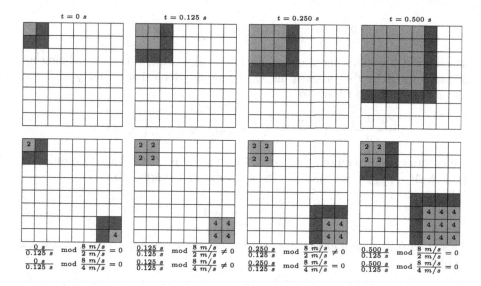

Fig. 2. Example showing the comparison between static update rate in the top and variable update rate in the bottom row, with $\Delta t = 0.125$ s.

Theorem 1. *An omnidirectionally moving pedestrian slower or equally fast as the SoL will always be covered by the propagation area of the CA with a Moore neighborhood.*

Proof. Let A_{Ped} be the set of coordinates $(x_i, y_i) \in \mathbb{R}^2$ with $i \in \{1, 2\}$ fulfilling the constraint

$$\sqrt{(x_2 - x_1)^2 + (y_2 - y_1)^2} \leq r = \frac{r_N \cdot l_{cell}}{\Delta t} \cdot t. \tag{2}$$

Let the point $(0,0)$ be the center of the first cell,

$$(x_1, y_1): \quad -\frac{l_{cell}}{2} \leq x_1 \leq \frac{l_{cell}}{2} \quad \wedge \quad -\frac{l_{cell}}{2} \leq y_1 \leq \frac{l_{cell}}{2} \tag{3}$$

defines all possible starting positions within the grid cell. Considering the symmetry of the problem, only the right part of the equation is used. Resolving Eq. 2 to x_1, y_1 and inserting Eq. 3 delivers

$$x_2 \leq \frac{r_N \cdot l_{cell}}{\Delta t} \cdot t + \frac{l_{cell}}{2} \quad \wedge \quad y_2 \leq \frac{r_N \cdot l_{cell}}{\Delta t} \cdot t + \frac{l_{cell}}{2}. \tag{4}$$

We call all pairs of (x_2, y_2) which fulfill Eq. 4 $\mathcal{A}_{Box}$. Therefore $\mathcal{A}_{Ped} \subseteq \mathcal{A}_{Box}$.

For the growth of the propagated area, we can simply add the cell lengths multiplied by r_N as

$$| x, y | \leq \frac{l_{cell}}{2} + l_{cell} \cdot r_N + \lfloor \frac{t}{\Delta t} \rfloor \cdot l_{cell} \cdot r_N, \tag{5}$$

which we will note as requirement for all $(x, y) \in \mathcal{A}_{Prop}$, the set defining all points covered by the propagating CA function. Replacing x and y with the inequation from Eq. 4 leads to

$$| \frac{r_N \cdot l_{cell}}{\Delta t} \cdot t + \frac{l_{cell}}{2} | \leq \frac{l_{cell}}{2} + l_{cell} \cdot r_N + \lfloor \frac{t}{\Delta t} \rfloor \cdot l_{cell} \cdot r_N,$$

representing the requirements for $\mathcal{A}_{Box} \subseteq \mathcal{A}_{Prop}$ to hold. Considering $\{l_{cell}, t, \Delta t, r_N\} \geq 0$, we can omit the absolutes and simplify to

$$\frac{t}{\Delta t} \leq \lfloor \frac{t}{\Delta t} \rfloor + 1.$$

This is trivially true and therefore shows the condition $\mathcal{A}_{Ped} \subseteq \mathcal{A}_{Box} \subseteq \mathcal{A}_{Prop}$ to hold.

Since the ratio of $\frac{v_c}{s(\vec{n}_i)}$ might be an odd value, a flooring function is put over it. The resulting discretization error E has an upper bound

$$|E| < \frac{s(\vec{n}_i)}{v_c} = 5.4\%,$$

assuming a pedestrian moves at $(2.7\,\text{m/s})$ and the SoL is valued at $(50\,\text{m/s})$.

4.2 Multiple Neighborhood Usage

A second mechanism to improve the precision of resembling our assumed pedestrian model is to use two different neighborhoods. Since $\mathcal{M}_1^2$ is an over- and $\mathcal{V}_1^2$ an under-approximation of an omnidirectional movement both neighborhoods shall be combined.

$\mathcal{V}_1^2$ shall be used as described above and apply the maximum value of $s(\vec{n}_i)$, therefore

$$f_v : s' \leftarrow \max s(\vec{n}), \ \vec{n} \in \mathcal{V}_1^2 \iff \frac{t_\alpha}{\Delta t} \mod \lfloor \frac{v_c}{s(\vec{n}_i)} \rfloor = 0, i \in \{0, 2, 4, 6\}.$$

In order to eliminate the under-approximation error, $\mathcal{M}_1^2$ will be used as shown in Fig. 1. The SoL will be multiplied by a factor β before checking the fulfillment of Eq. 1 to achieve a longer update interval, taking the diagonal position of the neighboring cells into account, thus

$$f_M : s' \leftarrow \max s(\vec{n}), \ \vec{n} \in \mathcal{M}_1^2 \iff \frac{t_\alpha}{\Delta t} \mod \lfloor \frac{v_c \cdot \beta}{s(\vec{n}_i)} \rfloor = 0, i \in \{1, 3, 5, 7\}.$$

The resulting pattern shows an octagonal shape, being much closer to a circular shape than using just one single neighborhood. To achieve the shape of a regular octagon as in Fig. 3a, the ratio of f_v and f_M has to be tuned. We therefore observe the following mechanisms,

$$D' \leftarrow D + 2 \cdot l_{cell} \equiv r'_{in} \leftarrow r_{in} + l_{cell},$$

when applying f_v and

$$a' \leftarrow a + 2 \cdot l_{cell},$$

when applying f_M respectively. Given that for a regular octagon $r_{in} = \frac{1+\sqrt{2}}{2} \cdot a$ has to hold, we can solve towards a and transfer the requirement to

$$r_{in} + l_{cell} = a + \frac{1+\sqrt{2}}{2} \cdot l_{cell},$$

which leads to the ratio

$$\frac{f_M}{f_v} \simeq \frac{2}{\frac{1+\sqrt{2}}{2}} \approx 1.657.$$

Concluding, f_M has to be applied with a factor of 1.657 on the execution time-points of T^v of f_v, which resembles β. This implies that f_M has to be sequentially executed after f_v. It might otherwise occur that f_M is virtually skipped when sharing the same execution time point as a multiple of T_v.

Theorem 2. *The resulting octagonal shape from combining f_v and f_M propagates at least as fast as a continuously, omnidirectionally moving pedestrian, as defined in Eq. 2.*

Proof. First, we notice that the inner radius of the regular octagon calculates as

$$r_{in} = (\frac{1+\sqrt{2}}{2}) \cdot a, \text{ with } a = \frac{D}{1+\sqrt{2}},$$

with a being the side length of the regular octagon and D being the diagonal length of the regular octagon as seen in Fig. 3a and D calculated as

$$D = 2 \cdot (\frac{l_{cell}}{2} + l_{cell} + \lfloor \frac{t}{\Delta t} \rfloor \cdot l_{cell}).$$

Resolving these equations leads to

$$r_{in} = (\frac{1+\sqrt{2}}{2}) \cdot a = (\frac{1+\sqrt{2}}{2}) \cdot \frac{D}{1+\sqrt{2}} = (\frac{1+\sqrt{2}}{2}) \cdot \frac{2 \cdot (\frac{l_{cell}}{2} + l_{cell} + \lfloor \frac{t}{\Delta t} \rfloor \cdot l_{cell})}{1+\sqrt{2}},$$

which resembles the right part of Eq. 5. From there, Theorem 1 can be applied consecutively.

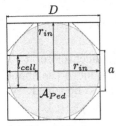

(a) The desired regular octagon shape.

(b) The achieved propagation shown for two pedestrians. The left one with 1 $meter/sec$ omnidirectionally and the right one with 2.7 $meters/sec$ limited to the directions $\{0, 6, 7\}$.

Fig. 3. The desired and achieved variable propagation patterns.

As a result, a notable refinement of the estimated movement pattern is achieved. While the von Neumann neighborhood bears the risk of underestimating the capabilities of a pedestrian and is therefore not safely applicable, the Moore neighborhood adds a considerable overhead to the approximated areas. The mixing of both neighborhoods leads to a reduction of

$$\frac{A_C - A_M}{A_M} = \frac{D^2 - 2 \cdot (\sqrt{2} - 1) \cdot D^2}{D^2} = -17.2\%,$$

where A_M is the area resulting of applying a Moore neighborhood and A_C the resulting area of the combined neighborhood approach respectively.

4.3   Cardinal Directions Vectorization

Just as when combining the two neighborhoods, each single cell of $\mathcal{M}_1^2$ can be seen as a unique item which can be considered or ignored during the cell update. To achieve this behavior, each cell encodes the desired propagation direction in its vector s_{vel}. When updating a cell, it has to be considered that the direction of the propagation reverses from the current point of view. E.g. if the current cell considers taking over the state of the cell south, it has to be checked that this cell inhabits a propagation direction to the north. Therefore, the transition rule is applied as

$$f : s'(\vec{n}) \leftarrow \max_{0 \leq i \leq 7} s_q(\vec{n}_i), s_q(\vec{n}),$$

with i being one of the cardinal directions and q being its opposing direction, i.e. $q = i + 4 \mod 8$.

4.4   Over-Propagation

A phenomenon of this approach that must be controlled is implicit over-propagation of $\mathcal{M}_1^2$. For example, we assume f_v is applied in each and f_M in every third time-step. Figure 4a shows the propagation from $t = 1 \rightarrow t = 2$, showing the typical von Neumann pattern. In the transition $t = 2 \rightarrow t = 3$ not only the blue cells switch their state as desired, but also the red cells as f_M does not consider that the black cells have just transited in the last time step. To avoid this behavior, cells in $\mathcal{M}_1^2$ are only considered if they have two orthogonal neighbors which have the same state as the destined transit state, i.e.

$$P : s(\vec{n}_i) = s(\vec{n}_{i-1}) = s(\vec{n}_{i+1}).$$

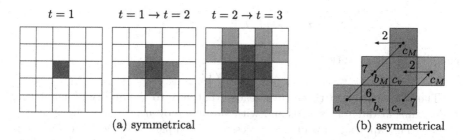

(a) symmetrical   (b) asymmetrical

Fig. 4. The two phenomena of over-propagation.

This phenomenon also occurs when the propagation is not omnidirectional. Anyhow, the requirement of having two orthogonal neighbors cannot be met if one of the neighboring cells has a non-propagating neighbor itself. For example, if a cell is only supposed to propagate into the directions 6 and 7. There will be only one orthogonal neighbor. The missing information of the second orthogonal cell needs to be reconstructed by knowledge of the direction vector and which cell is empty as shown in Fig. 4b, where the green box is intended to be propagated while the red one is not. Therefore, it must be determined which is the last orthogonal propagation direction before the outer diagonal propagation direction, in our example $i = 6$, neighboring the outer diagonal direction $i = 7$. To make this a little easier to follow, consider the example from Fig. 4b.

- In the beginning, only cell a is populated.
- In a second step, the cells b_v and b_M are populated. The problem already occurs here already but we will skip it at this point as another difficulty occurs in the following step.
- The propagation via the von Neumann neighborhood populates the blue cells c_v.
- The propagation via the Moore neighborhood is supposed to populate the green cell c_M. Unfortunately, the red cell also fulfills the requirement and becomes marked as c_M.
- There are now two differences to observe: The cell south of the two cells c_M are once populated and once empty. Considering the propagation direction 7 and the corresponding $q = 3$, the cell to the south equals the direction 4 or $q + 1$. This alone is not enough to determine which of cells is desired to be populated as the problem could occur in a symmetrical fashion with reversed signs.
- Additionally, we can observe that the cell at $q - 1 = 2$ is once populated and once empty. These two properties can be used to solve the problem of symmetry.

Consequently, the cell opposing the direction of the orthogonal neighbor from the currently focused cell c_M must be unequal to $s(\vec{n}_i)$ of the diagonal cell, in this case $i = 2$, which is expressed by

$$Q : s(\vec{n}_i) \neq s(\vec{n}_{i+p}), \quad p = \begin{cases} 1, & s_{q-1}(\vec{n}_i) = 0 \\ -1, & s_{q+1}(\vec{n}_i) = 0, \end{cases}$$

completing our condition

$$f_M \Rightarrow P \vee Q.$$

The combination of those rules leads eventually to the ability of simulating pedestrians at different speeds and with variable movement corridors as seen in Fig. 3b. This approach avoids the necessity of complex neighborhood functions and relies on a range of $r_N = 1$, mitigating the need to check whether a cell in the neighborhood is blocked by an inaccessible area to avoid transiting through walls. In contrast, a range of $r_N > 1$ would consider cells that might be physically departed from the populated cell. For example, a pedestrian standing right behind a thin wall, that could be a fire door, is not capable of moving directly into the cell on the other side the wall. When the neighborhood is chosen larger than $r_N = 1$ this cell would nevertheless be considered for propagation and requires an additional check to prevent a ghostly move through the wall.

5   Implementation

To demonstrate the functionality, we implemented the algorithm in Python with Numba and created two experiments. The first one is of synthetic nature and varies the simulation parameters to show the impact on the computation time. The second one features an infection algorithm to show the competitiveness of the CA against simpler algorithms.

Algorithm 1: The cellular automaton algorithm.

---

1 **foreach** $t_\alpha \in [0, T]$ **do**
> // Iterate over discrete time-steps
2   **foreach** $\vec{n} \in \mathcal{L}^d$ **do**
>   // Iterate over all cells
3   **if** $s_{access}(\vec{n}) \neq 0$ **then**
>   // Check if cell is accessible
4   **foreach** $\vec{n}_i \in \mathcal{V}_1^2$ **do**
>   // Iterate over all cells in von Neumann neighborhood
5              $q = (i + 4) \mod 8$;
>   // Determine opposing direction of current neighborhood cell
6   **if** $\frac{t_\alpha}{\Delta t} \lfloor mod \frac{SoL}{s_q(\vec{n}_i)} \rfloor = 0$ **then**
>   // Check if neighboring cell fulfills propagation requirement
7                 $s'^7_{i=0}(\vec{n}) \leftarrow \max_{0 \leq k \leq 7} s_k(\vec{n}_i), s_k(\vec{n})$;
>   // Select highest speed from current cell and neighboring cells and set as cell's speed for future configuration
8     $c \leftarrow c'$;
>   // Update configuration with new cell speeds
9   **foreach** $\vec{n} \in \mathcal{L}^d$ **do**
>   // Same process as in the loop before
10   **if** $s_{access}(\vec{n}) \neq 0$ **then**
11   **foreach** $\vec{n}_i \in \mathcal{M}_1^2$ **do**
12   **if** $\frac{t_\alpha}{\Delta t} \lfloor mod \frac{SoL*1.657}{s_q(\vec{n}_i)} \rfloor = 0$ **then**
13   **if** $P \vee Q$ **then**
>   // For the Moore neighborhood check if requirements P or Q are met before proceeding to avoid over-propagation
14                    $s'^7_{i=0}(\vec{n}) \leftarrow \max_{0 \leq k \leq 7} s_k(\vec{n}_i), s_k(\vec{n})$;
15     $c \leftarrow c'$;

Algorithm 1 shows the CA from 4 in pseudo-code. All experiments have been conducted on the same set-up, featuring Intel Core i7-6700k @ 8x 4.00 GHz, 32 GB RAM, Ubuntu 18.04 64-Bit, Python 3.6.9 64-Bit, Numpy 1.19.1, Numba 0.50.1. To keep the results comparable, only single-core performance has been tested.

5.1 Performance Implications of Environment Density

In the first experiment we created an empty map with $\kappa = 99$ and placed different amounts of pedestrians with random starting positions and speeds in the range of $0.1 \ldots 2.7$ m/s in the map. Furthermore, we varied whether the pedestrians move omnidirectionally or follow a random amount of the eight cardinal directions. The time horizon has been fixed at $T = 2$ s with a time-step width $\Delta t = 0.01$ s.

Table 1. Computation time in relation to the number of pedestrians simulated with different movement patterns. Average values of $N = 1000$ test runs.

Number of pedestrians	Computation time	
	Omnidirectional	Random directions
1	0.397 s	0.396 s
10	0.396 s	0.402 s
100	0.408 s	0.401 s

Table 1 shows how the CA does neither depend on the number of pedestrians nor their movement directions. Only small, negligible variations around the mean value of 0.4 s occur.

As a variation we simulated a single pedestrian with omnidirectional movement at a constant speed of 1 m/s and varied the time horizon and the time-step width as shown in Table 2. Since this directly influences the outer for-loop, it impacts the computation time of the CA. It grows linearly with the time-horizon and reciprocal to the time-step width, which trivially derives from the number of loop iterations calculated as $T/\Delta t$.

Table 2. Comparison of computation times of the cellular automaton depending on time-step width and time horizon. Average values of $N = 1000$ test runs.

Time horizon	Time-step width	Computation time
2 s	0.01 s	0.396 s
2 s	0.1 s	0.042 s
10 s	0.01 s	2.028 s
10 s	0.1 s	0.201 s

5.2 Performance Compared to Simple Cell-Growth Algorithm

In the second experiment we compared the CA to a simple infection algorithm on the same test platform. This algorithm draws a circle with the potential movement range within the current time step of the pedestrian at each occupied cell. All cells that are touched by this circle will get "infected". The implementation can be seen in Algorithm 2. Additionally, a list of all potential pedestrian positions at $t = 0$ is created to prevent scanning the whole grid at each time-step. For a reasonable testing set-up, the map of a real garage has been used as shown

---

Algorithm 2: The circular infection algorithm.

---

1   **for** $t \in \{0, \Delta t, ..., T - \Delta t, T\}$ **do**
     // Iterate over discrete time-steps until T
2   **for** $i, k \in \mathcal{L}^d$ **do**
       // Access each cell in grid
3   **if** $s_{vel}^{i,k} \neq 0$ **then**
         // Check if cell is populated
4          $r \leftarrow s_{vel}^{i,k} * t$;
         // Calculate movement radius based on speed and elapsed
           time
5          $r_{grid} \leftarrow \lceil r / l_{cell} \rceil$;
         // Discretize movement radius into grid cells
6   **for** $x \in [-r_{grid}, r_{grid}]$ **do**
           // Select all x-values within in movement radius
7            $y_{max} \leftarrow \lceil \sqrt{r_{grid}^2 - x^2} \rceil$;
           // Calculate maximum y value for each x
8            $rx \leftarrow i + x$;
9            $ry \leftarrow k + y_{max}$;
10   **for** $y \in [-ry, ry]$ **do**
             // Access all x,y pairs within movement radius
11   **if** $s_{access}^{x,y} \neq 0$ **then**
               // If cell is accessible, "infect" it in copy of
                 current grid with pedestrian speed
12                $s_{vel}'^{x,y} \leftarrow s_{vel}^{i,k}$;

---

in Fig. 5, simulated with $\kappa = 199$ and $\Delta t = 0.01$ s. Within this garage, a random position is selected and c_0 is initialized as described in 3.3.

In Fig. 5, an exemplary outcome is shown on the right side for the CA simulation with $T = 2$ s. Table 3 shows that the CA outperforms the infection

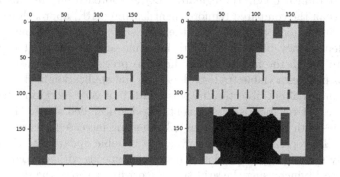

Fig. 5. The blue print of the parking garage. Accessible areas are marked in yellow, walls in green. The prediction of assumed pedestrians considering limited visibility. Only purple areas can be entered safely at $T = 2$ s. (Color figure online)

Table 3. Comparison of computation times between a cellular automaton and a basline cell-infection algorithm. Average values of $N = 1000$ test runs.

Time horizon	Cellular automaton, computation time	Infection algorithm, computation time
1 s	0.126 s	0.306 s
2 s	0.217 s	0.936 s
3 s	0.291 s	2.458 s

algorithm. Its computation time grows linearly $(O(n))$, while the infection algorithm's computation time grows with $O(n^2)$. Even though the OGM size quadrupled, the calculation times stay below the values from the first experiment. This can be explained with three mechanisms. First, the map is only partially accessible due to limited driving areas, reducing the amount of considered cells. Second, parts of the map become saturated, meaning that already occupied cells can be omitted in further iterations. Third, the computation time is also influenced by swapping the memory for each read and copy process. Even though the map size increases, it can be batch-copied, therefore does not linearly add up to the computation time.

6   Discussion

We have exhibited the properties of our novel approach. To begin with, it can be pointed out that the CA is ideal to comply with real-time requirement since its computation time does not vary with the amount of simulated entities in the area. This is crucial for the utilization as a safety critical monitor in automated vehicles. Furthermore, the CA supports creating assumptions about occluded areas, without implications on performance. Comparing state of the art approaches with similar aims, such as [2], the CA is about factor ten slower than the presented linear quadratic regulator (LQR) approach but also about factor ten faster than the compared reinforcement learning (RL) approach when using the same simulation parameters for the grid size, Δt, and T. The CA shows a linear dependency between computation time and precision. It can neglect precision to match the faster LQR or increase precision at the cost of slowing down. This enables a viable trade-off based on the application field, e.g. making coarse estimates about objects with noisy data in a very short time frame as a conservative, yet reliable risk assessment, also for occluded areas. This observation matches with the outcomes from [33], showing increased accuracy by using fine-grid OGM representations. However, our variable update rate CA manages to similarly refine the quantization of pedestrian speeds without comprising the performance by increasing the grid size. Algorithm 1 shows the dependence of the for-loops in lines 2 and 9 on the grid size. Since the approach is dealing with two-dimensional models, a quadratic growth of the computation time goes along with the increase of the grid resolution. Since both approaches rely on

CA a combination of both approaches is imaginable, with the strengths of both methodologies complementing each other. A very recent approach relying on neural networks focusing unordered pedestrians can be found in [31]. It shows a reliable accuracy for the motion prediction with about 0.46 m displacement for certain scenarios. Considering the results from [35] and the underlying cell size of 0.5 m for the CA, a comparable accuracy can be cautiously assumed. Unfortunately, also the performance can only be compared roughly since the scale of the considered map can only be matched by a rule of thumb. Nevertheless, when assuming a predicted area of about 20 m times 20 m - derived from the test scenario documentation - the computation time of 60 ms would be matched by the CA when considering the quadratic impact of the grid size.

The second experiment has shown that the approach of a CA can be superior over a simple algorithm when assuming realistic conditions. Even though its architecture is way more complex, the CA manages to keep the computational effort low, while featuring better estimates by avoiding ghosting through walls. This feature can be crucial in compressed traffic areas as it cancels out impossible paths in its prediction, maintaining safety without being overly conservative.

Considering alternative approaches to realize more complex movement patterns, the Margolus neighborhood [37] is a prominent candidate that comes to mind. Since every reversible CA using the Margolus neighborhood can be expressed by a classical CA with a bigger set of cell states, there is no immanent need to use this approach. In contrast, it would make the allocation of pedestrian speed to the cell's state less intuitive while risking to introduce ghosting effects by introducing larger neighborhoods.

While relying on single-core executions for the experiments, CA can heavily benefit from a multi-core implementation since all operations on the grid map can be parallelized when executing the rules for one neighborhood per time-step. Recall [11, 14] stating achievable speed-ups of one or two orders of magnitude if implemented properly. This shows the potential superiority of our approach to solve the described problems when exploiting its specific properties with parallel-computing hardware as it is commonly available.

Another benefit of the cellular automaton is the simplicity of the basic algorithm as seen in Algorithm 1. The overall complexity arises from the highly parallel execution of the same process. Hence, a checking of the basic code for correctness becomes easier to handle as there are only comparable few lines to validate. Furthermore, the principles of implementing a cellular automaton are well understood, thus minimizes the the likelihood of errors.

Meanwhile, a feasible realization of the presented algorithm has been shown in [12] for realistic scenarios. This includes the combination of the capabilities of the shown cellular automaton with a path planning algorithm in a parking garage scenario based on a real environment. The results have shown general practicality of the presented approach, especially for the case of occluded areas in garages.

7   Conclusion

We presented a novel approach for a mixed neighborhood, multi-speed pedestrian prediction based on CA, avoiding the restrictions of traditional CA. We pointed out the benefits of CA approaches in terms of safety, certifiability and economical feasible implementation. We have proven complete coverage of pedestrian movement within the boundaries implied by the pedestrian's assumed physical capabilities. We have shown different benchmarks, underlining the capabilities of our approach and the computational competitiveness compared to other methodologies. Our novel approach offers inherent parallelizability while maintaining a safe over-approximation. At the same time, we reduce the over-approximation to an acceptable, not overly conservative level. As an outlook, an implementation on suitable multi-core hardware can be aimed for. This should enable achieving low computation times and open the door to use it as an environment filter for critical cases. Furthermore, a classic model checking based on the CA can be performed, exploiting its deterministic behavior to ensure certifiable safety.

References

1. Bansal, M., Krizhevsky, A., Ogale, A.: ChauffeurNet: Learning to Drive by Imitating the Best and Synthesizing the Worst. arXiv preprint arXiv:1812.03079 (2018)
2. Batkovic, I., Zanon, M., Lubbe, N., Falcone, P.: A computationally efficient model for pedestrian motion prediction, pp. 374–379 (2018)
3. Blue, V.J., Embrechts, M.J., Adler, J.L.: Cellular automata modeling of pedestrian movements. In: ICSMC, vol. 3, pp. 2320–2323. IEEE (1997)
4. Blue, V.J., Adler, J.L.: Cellular automata microsimulation for modeling bi-directional pedestrian walkways. Transp. Res. Part B Methodol. **35**(3), 293–312 (2001)
5. Brechtel, S., Gindele, T., Dillmann, R.: Probabilistic decision-making under uncertainty for autonomous driving using continuous POMDPs. In: ITSC, pp. 392–399. IEEE (2014)
6. Camara, F., et al.: Pedestrian models for autonomous driving part II: high-level models of human behavior. IEEE Trans. Intell. Transp. Syst. **22**(9), 5453–5472 (2021)
7. Chai, Y., Sapp, B., Bansal, M., Anguelov, D.: Multipath: multiple probabilistic anchor trajectory hypotheses for behavior prediction. In: CoRL, pp. 86–99 (2020)
8. Chopard, B., Droz, M.: Cellular automata modeling of physical systems (1999)
9. Czarnecki, K., Salay, R.: Towards a framework to manage perceptual uncertainty for safe automated driving. In: Gallina, B., Skavhaug, A., Schoitsch, E., Bitsch, F. (eds.) SAFECOMP 2018. LNCS, vol. 11094, pp. 439–445. Springer, Cham (2018). https://doi.org/10.1007/978-3-319-99229-7_37
10. Das, A.K., Ganguly, A., Dasgupta, A., Bhawmik, S., Chaudhuri, P.P.: Efficient characterisation of cellular automata. IEE Proc. E - Comput. Digit. Tech. **137**(1), 81–87 (1990)
11. Dascalu, M.: Cellular Automata Hardware Implementations - an Overview. Rom. J. Inf. Sci. Technol. **19**(4), 360–368 (2016)
12. Dorff, S.V., Kneissl, M., Fränzle, M.: Safe, deterministic trajectory planning for unstructured and partially occluded environments. In: ITSC. IEEE (to appear September 2021)

13. Gardner, M.: Mathematical games. Sci. Am. **223**(4), 120–123 (1970)
14. Gibson, M.J., Keedwell, E.C., Savić, D.A.: An investigation of the efficient implementation of cellular automata on multi-core CPU and GPU hardware. J. Parallel Distrib. Comput. **77**, 11–25 (2015)
15. Goldhammer, M., Gerhard, M., Zernetsch, S., Doll, K., Brunsmann, U.: Early prediction of a pedestrian's trajectory at intersections. In: ITSC, pp. 237–242. IEEE (2013)
16. Helbing, D.: A mathematical model for the behavior of pedestrians. Behav.l Sci. **36**(4), 298–310 (1991)
17. Hoermann, S., Kunz, F., Nuss, D., Renter, S., Dietmayer, K.: Entering crossroads with blind corners. A safe strategy for autonomous vehicles. In: IV. IEEE, June 2017
18. Klüpfel, H.L.: A cellular automaton model for crowd movement and egress simulation. PhD Thesis (2012)
19. Kooij, J.F., Schneider, N., Gavrila, D.M.: Analysis of pedestrian dynamics from a vehicle perspective. In: IV, pp. 1445–1450. IEEE (2014)
20. Kooij, J.F.P., Flohr, F., Pool, E.A.I., Gavrila, D.M., Schneider, N.: Context-based path prediction for targets with switching dynamics. Int. J. Comput. Vis. **127**, 239–262 (2018)
21. Koschi, M., Pek, C., Beikirch, M., Althoff, M.: Set-based prediction of pedestrians in urban environments considering formalized traffic rules. In: ITSC, pp. 2704–2711. IEEE (2018)
22. Lee, M., Jo, K., Sunwoo, M.: Collision risk assessment for possible collision vehicle in occluded area based on precise map. In: ITSC, pp. 1–6. IEEE (2017)
23. Lefèvre, S., Vasquez, D., Laugier, C.: A survey on motion prediction and risk assessment for intelligent vehicles. ROBOMECH J. **1**(1), 1–14 (2014). https://doi.org/10.1186/s40648-014-0001-z
24. Liu, S.B., Roehm, H., Heinzemann, C., Lütkebohle, I., Oehlerking, J., Althoff, M.: Provably safe motion of mobile robots in human environments. In: IROS, pp. 1351–1357. IEEE (2017)
25. Nagel, K., Schreckenberg, M.: A cellular automaton model for freeway traffic. J. de Physique I **2**(12), 2221–2229 (1992)
26. Neogi, S., Hoy, M., Chaoqun, W., Dauwels, J.: Context based pedestrian intention prediction using factored latent dynamic conditional random fields. In: SSCI, pp. 1–8. IEEE
27. Nikolić, M.: Data-driven fundamental models for pedestrian movements. Technical report EPFL (2017)
28. Oliveira, G.M.B., et al.: A cellular automata-based path-planning for a cooperative and decentralized team of robots. In: CEC, pp. 739–746 (2019)
29. Orzechowski, P.F., Meyer, A., Lauer, M.: Tackling occlusions and limited sensor range with set-based safety verification. In: ITSC, pp. 1729–1736. IEEE (2018)
30. Pei, H., Lou, Y., Ye, F.: Robot path planning based on cellular automata with mixed neighborhoods. In: ISCID, pp. 114–117. IEEE (2018)
31. Radwan, N., Burgard, W., Valada, A.: Multimodal interaction-aware motion prediction for autonomous street crossing. Int. J. Robot. Res. **39**(13), 1567–1598 (2020)
32. Rehder, E., Wirth, F., Lauer, M., Stiller, C.: Pedestrian prediction by planning using deep neural networks. In: ICRA, pp. 5903–5908. IEEE (2018)
33. Sarmady, S., Haron, F., Talib, A.Z.: Simulation of pedestrian movements using fine grid cellular automata model. arXiv preprint arXiv:1406.3567 (2014)

34. Schaefer, L., Mackulak, G., Cochran, J., Cherilla, J.: Application of a general particle system model to movement of pedestrians and vehicles. In: WSC, vol. 2, pp. 1155–1160. IEEE (1998)
35. Schöller, C., Aravantinos, V., Lay, F., Knoll, A.: What the constant velocity model can teach us about pedestrian motion prediction. IEEE Robot. Autom. Lett. 5(2), 1696–1703 (2020)
36. Seitz, M.J.: Simulating pedestrian dynamics. Dissertation, Technische Universität München, München (2016)
37. Toffoli, T., Margolus, N.: Cellular Automata Machines: a New Environment for Modeling. MIT Press, Cambridge (1987)
38. Yi, S., Li, H., Wang, X.: Pedestrian behavior understanding and prediction with deep neural networks. In: Leibe, B., Matas, J., Sebe, N., Welling, M. (eds.) ECCV 2016, Part I. LNCS, vol. 9905, pp. 263–279. Springer, Cham (2016). https://doi.org/10.1007/978-3-319-46448-0_16

Author Index